Community care and the law

second edition

Luke Clements is a solicitor in private practice in Hereford and a recognised authority on community care law; he has been involved in many judicial review cases that have shaped the law in this field. He is also Senior Research Fellow at Cardiff Law School (University of Wales), a training consultant to many public and voluntary organisations, community care legal adviser to the Carers National Association and a member of the Law Society's Mental Health and Disability Committee. He is the author of *European Human Rights* (Sweet & Maxwell, 1999).

Luke Clements can be contacted by e-mail: clementslj@cf.ac.uk

The Legal Action Group is a national, independent charity which campaigns for equal access to justice for all members of society. Legal Action Group:
- provides support to the practice of lawyers and advisers
- inspires developments in that practice
- campaigns for improvements in the law and the administration of justice
- stimulates debate on how services should be delivered.

Community care and the law

SECOND EDITION

Luke Clements

Legal Action Group
2000

This edition published in Great Britain 2000
by LAG Education and Service Trust Ltd
242 Pentonville Road
London
N1 9UN

First edition printed 1996
Reprinted with revisions 1997

Legal Action Group
242 Pentonville Road
London
N1 9UN

British Library Cataloguing in Publication Data
A CIP catalogue record for this book is available from the British Library

ISBN 0 905099 94 x

Typeset by Regent Typesetting, London
Printed in Great Britain by Bell & Bain Ltd, Glasgow

For my mother,
for whom, as a nurse and a mother,
a wife, a widow and a lover of defenceless animals,
family and community care has not proved to be
an academic subject.

Preface

Community care law results from a hotchpotch of statutes, many of which originated as private members' bills (and all the better for it). Although there are a number of general rules which can be applied to the subject, the most important appears to be that for every general rule there is at least one exception.

As with the first edition, I have had great difficulty in deciding what to exclude. How can any text do justice to the subject and yet exclude detailed consideration of welfare benefits or special education or powers of attorney or the general law of incapacity? And so on. These subjects, however, are not covered in detail. I have tried to keep to the central community care statutes as listed in the National Health Service and Community Care Act 1990 s46. Welfare benefits are not covered for two reasons: the first is that they change so frequently and the second is that the Child Poverty Action Group and the Disability Alliance already publish comprehensive and indispensable annual guides. The same can also be said for the excellent *Education Law and Practice* published by the Legal Action Group. I cover, only briefly (at para 7.63 below), the huge and quite separate questions which are caused by the inadequate law on mental capacity; to deal with these in issue would have doubled the book's size.

I have tried to keep to a minimum the use of abbreviations, but have had to shorten reference to some statutes with excessively long titles, such as the Disabled Persons (Services, Consultation and Representation) Act 1986. The National Health Service is also referred to simply as the NHS.

I have referred throughout to the most important general policy guidance, *Community Care in the Next Decade and Beyond: Policy Guidance* (1990) as the Policy Guidance. In several chapters or sections a particular piece of practice guidance is important and in that section I have given it a shortened title, having of course explained what the shortened title refers to.

In writing this book I have received enormous assistance from countless kind and wise people. Many important concepts have been explained to me by social workers in particular, and my clients have taught me far more than (I hope) they will ever realise. Special thanks are due to:

Carol Ackroyd (formerly of Redbridge and Waltham Forest Health Authority), District Judge Gordon Ashton, Francine Bates of Contact-a-Family, Joanna Bunting Assistant Head of Legal Services, Leicester City Council, Russell Campbell of Shelter, Marion Chester of ACHC, Phil Fennell of Cardiff Law School, Jenny Hambidge of Powys, Penny Letts of the Law Society, Robert McLean of Flintshire, Janet Read of Warwick University, Adrian Rhead of Thorpes, Pauline Thompson of Age Concern England.

What is wrong in this text is entirely my own doing and I would welcome any critical feedback. The opportunity has been taken, before printing, to include reference to the Court of Appeal decision in *R v Richmond LBC ex p Watson* [2000] LGR 318 and the government's announcement on the funding of long-term care, *The NHS Plan: The Government's Response to the Royal Commission on Long-term Care*, July 2000. The law is otherwise stated as at April 2000.

Contents

Preface   vii
Table of cases   xiii
Table of statutes   xix
Table of statutory instruments   xxvii
Table of circulars and guidance   xxxi
Table of local government ombudsman complaints   xli
Table of European Conventions   xliii
List of diagrams   xliv
Abbreviations   xlv

Introduction   1

1   Social services statutes, regulations and guidance   11
Introduction   12
Statutory duties and powers   12
Regulations   16
Directions and guidance   17

2   The duty to plan and to inform   25
Introduction   26
The social services duty to plan   26
The duty to inform   33

3   The duty to assess and the provision of services   43
Introduction   45
The duty to assess: when does it arise?   48
The nature of an assessment   53
Screening assessments   54
The minimum criteria for an assessment   55
Timescale for assessments   57
Practice guidance   59
The meaning of 'need' under s47(1)(a)   65
Delegation of duty to assess   68
Assessment under s47(2)   69

The written record of the assessment   70
Community care assessments and disabled children   70
The service provision decision: what needs must be satisfied by the
    provision of services?   71
Eligibility criteria and the question of resources   72
The provision of services and the care plan   80
Reviews and reassessments   87
Provision of services without an assessment   88

4   Residential and nursing accommodation   89
Introduction   91
Accommodation under NAA 1948 s21   91
Ordinary residence   101
The nature of residential accommodation   108
Choice of accommodation   112
Inspection duties   115
NAA 1948 s47: local authority's removal powers   118
NAA 1948 s48: duty to protect property   119
Closure of residential and nursing homes   119
Health and safety issues   122
Residential accommodation services and the NHS overlap   124
Accommodation under MHA 1983 s117   125
Accommodation under NAA 1948 s29(4)(c)   125
Accommodation under Children Act 1989 s17   126

5   Domiciliary services   127
Introduction   130
Services under NAA 1948 s29   133
Services under Health Services and Public Health Act 1968 s45   144
Services under Chronically Sick and Disabled Persons Act 1970 s2
    148
Services under National Health Services Act 1977 Sch 8   167
Services under MHA 1983 s117   177
Mental Health (Patients in the Community) Act 1995   184
Direct payments   190

6   NHS responsibilities for community care services   201
Introduction   204
Health care and the NHS – historical overview   205
NHSA 1977   212
The medical/social divide   220
NHS primary health care responsibilities   225
NHS's continuing care responsibilities   230
Health authority payments to social services   255
Code of Practice on Openness in the NHS   260

NHS complaints 261
Health Service Ombudsman 268

7 **Carers, advocates and mental capacity** 271
Introduction 273
Carers 273
Advocates 293
Decision-making and mental capacity 296

8 **Charges for community care services** 305
Introduction 307
Accommodation charges 307
Charges for non-accommodation services 335

9 **Drug/alcohol and HIV/AIDS services** 355
Introduction 356
Assessment procedures 357
The provision and commissioning of services 361
Residential care and nursing home accommodation 362
Community care services 367
Drug and alcohol specific grant 368
People with HIV/AIDS 369

10 **Housing and community care** 371
Introduction 372
Collaboration in assessment and care planning 374
Housing homeless persons overlap 377
Disabled facilities grants 381

11 **Children Act 1989 duties to children in need** 393
Introduction 394
The assessment of children in need 395
Services for children in need 396
The transition into adulthood13 401
Charging for children's services 402

12 **Remedies** 405
Introduction 407
Local authority complaints procedures 408
Local government ombudsman procedures 428
Judicial review 432
Default procedures 445
European Convention on Human Rights 446

APPENDICES

A **Legislation: key provisions** 455

National Assistance Act 1948 ss21–29 455

Health Services and Public Health Act 1968 s45 463

Chronically Sick and Disabled Persons Act 1970 ss1 and 2
463

Local Authority Social Services Act 1970 ss6, 7 and 7A–E
464

National Health Service Act 1977 ss1–3, 21, Sch 8 paras 1–3
466

Mental Health Act 1983 s117 469

Health and Social Services and Social Security Adjudications
Act 1983 ss17, 21, 22, 24 and Sch 9, Pt II 470

Disabled Persons (Services, Consultation and Representation)
Act 1986 ss4, 8 and 16 473

Children Act 1989 s17 474

National Health Service and Community Care Act 1990 ss46
and 47 475

Carers (Recognition and Services) Act 1995 s1 477

Housing Grants, Construction and Regeneration Act 1996
ss23 and 24 478

B **Regulations and directions** 481

LAC(93)10 Appendix 1 481

LAC(93)10 Appendix 2 484

LAC(93)10 Appendix 3 485

Complaints Procedure Direction 1990 487

National Assistance Act 1948 (Choice of Accommodation)
Directions 1992 488

C **Precedents** 497

Community care assessment request 497

Access to information letter 498

Formal complaint letter 499

Table of cases

A v United Kingdom (1998) 27 EHRR 611   7.91
Airedale NHS Trust v Bland [1993] AC 789   7.84
Ashingdane v UK (1985) 7 EHRR 528   12.132
Associated Provincial Picture House v Wednesbury
    Corporation [1948] 1 KB 223   6.42, 12.93, 12.111
Avon CC v Hooper [1997] 1 All ER 532;
    (1998) 1 CCLR 366   8.83

Barclays Bank v Eustice [1995] 1 WLR 1238   8.47
Barrett v Enfield LBC (1999) Times 18 June, HL   5.101
Blackpool Corporation v Locker [1947] 1 KB 349   6.42

C (Adult: refusal of treatment), Re [1994] 1 WLR 290   7.84
C (Mental patient: contact), Re [1993] 1 FLR 940   7.84
Charnock v Liverpool Corporation [1968] 3 All ER 473   3.27
Chief Adjudication Officer v Quinn and Gibbon
    (1998) 1 CCLR 529, HL   4.7
Clunis v Camden and Islington Health Authority
    (1998) 1 CCLR 215, CA   5.101
Council of Civil Service Unions v Minister for the
    Civil Service [1985] AC 374, HL   12.95, 12.110
Croydon LBC v Moody (1999) 2 CCLR 92   3.98, 10.6

Dunkley v Evans [1981] 1 WLR 1522   1.14

Ellis v Chief Adjudication Officer [1998] 1 FLR 184   8.38

F (Mental patient: sterilisation), Re [1990] 2 AC 1, HL   2.29, 7.67, 12.97
Findlay, In re [1985] 1 AC 316   12.105

Gaskin v Liverpool CC [1980] 1 WLR 1549   2.29
Gaskin v UK (1989) 12 EHRR 36   2.29, 12.139
Gillick v West Norfolk Area Health Authority
    [1986] AC 112   1.24

H v UK (1987) 10 EHRR 95   12.137
Harris v Newcastle Health Authority [1989] 1 WLR 96   2.29
Harrison v Cornwall CC (1992) 90 LGR 81, CA   4.5
Hemns v Wheller [1948] 2 KB 61   12.101

Höfner & Elser v Macroton [1991] ECR I-1079,
   [1993] 4 CMLR 306   9.9

Johnson (Stanley) v UK (1997) *Times* 4 December   12.132

King v Henderson [1898] AC 720   1.14
Kruse v Johnson [1898] 2 QB 91   12.93

Laker Airways Ltd v Department of Trade [1967] QB 643   1.26

Marckx v Belgium (1979) 2 EHRR 330   12.142
Micahel Aerts v Belgium (1998) 29 EHRR 50   12.132
Midland Bank v Wyatt [1995] 1 FLR 697   8.47

North ex p Hasluck, Re [1895] 2 QB 264   3.27

Oritz v City of Westminster (1995) 27 HLR 364   10.15

P (GE) (and infant), Re [1965] Ch 568   4.31
P & D v UK [1996] EHRLR 526   12.137
Palser v Grinling [1948] AC 291   7.21
Patel v UK (the East Africans case) (1973) 3 EHRR 76
   Comm Rep: CM DH (77)2   12.129
Poucet v Assurances Generales de France
   (Cases C–159 & 160/91) [1993] ECR 637   9.9
Poyser and Mills' Arbitration, In re [1964] 2 QB 467   12.49

R v Avon CC ex p M (1999) 2 CCLR 185;
   [1994] 2 FLR 1006; [1994] 2 FCR 259, QBD
                                     3.47, 3.89, 4.60,
                                     12.29, 12.33, 12.48,
                                     12.101, 12.102
R v Barnet LBC ex p Foran (1999) 2 CCLR 329   11.15
R v Berkshire CC ex p P (1998) 1 CCLR 141   3.10, 3.17, 5.12, 5.27
R v Bexley LBC ex p B (2000) 3 CCLR 15   3.12, 5.47, 5.76,
                                     5.79, 8.118, 11.20,
                                     11.22, 12.82
R v Bexley LBC ex p Jones [1995] ELR 42   12.105
R v Birmingham CC ex p A [1997] 2 FLR 841   12.59
R v Birmingham CC ex p Taj Mohammed
   (1998) 1 CCLR 441   3.68, 10.29
R v Bournewood Community and Mental Health
   Trust ex p L [1998] 3 WLR 107; [1998] 3 All ER 289   12.133
R v Brent LBC ex p D (1998) 1 CCLR 234   4.18
R v Brent LBC ex p Gunning (1986) 84 LGR 168   4.78, 12.113
R v Brent LBC ex p Sawyers [1994] 1 FLR 203, CA   12.90
R v Bristol CC ex p Bailey and Bailey
   (1995) 27 HLR 307, QBD   12.15
R v Bristol CC ex p Penfold (1998) 1 CCLR 315   3.10, 3.14, 3.16,
                                       3.23, 3.68, 3.100,
                                      4.41, 4.42, 8.21,
                                      10.14

R v Bristol Corporation ex p Hendy [1974] 1 WLR 498   1.2
R v Calderdale DC ex p Houghton (1999)
    (unreported but *see* (1999) 2 CCLR 119)   8.91
R v Cambridge Health Authority ex p B
    [1995] 2 All ER 129, CA   6.35, 6.36, 12.128
R v Camden LBC ex p Gillan (1988) *Independent*
    13 October, DC   10.10
R v Chiltern DC ex p Roberts (1990) 23 HLR 387, DC   10.10
R v Commissioner for Local Administration
    ex p Eastleigh BC [1988] 3 All ER 151, CA   12.61
R v Commissioner for Local Administration ex p PH
    [1999] COD 382   12.71
R v Devon CC ex p Baker [1985] 1 All ER 73   12.119
R v Devon CC ex p Baker and Durham CC ex p Curtis
    [1995] 1 All ER 72, CA   4.78, 12.90, 12.112
R v Ealing District HA ex p Fox [1993] 3 All ER 170, QBD   1.8, 5.109, 5.134
R v Ealing LBC ex p Leaman (1984)
    Times 10 February, QBD   5.70, 12.104
R v Eastleigh BC ex p Betts [1983] 2 AC 613, HL   12.104
R v Foreign Secretary ex p World Development
    Movement [1995] 1 All ER 611, QBD   12.86
R v Further Education Funding Council and Bradford
    MBC ex p Parkinson (1996) *Times* 31 October   5.56
R v Gloucestershire CC ex p Barry [1996] 4 All ER 421;
    (1997) 1 CCLR 19, CA;
    Reversed [1997] AC 584; [1997] 2 All ER 1;
    (1997) 1 CCLR 40, HL   1.26, 3.51, 3.58,
    3.66, 3.68, 3.75, 3.78
R v Gloucestershire CC ex p Mahfood
    (1997) 1 CCLR 7; 94 LGR 593, DC   1.8, 3.65, 5.32, 5.48,
    5.53, 5.75, 12.82,
    12.86, 12.103
R v Gloucestershire CC ex p RADAR
    (1998) 1 CCLR 476; [1996] COD 253   3.11, 3.33, 3.51, 5.74,
    8.79, 12.86, 12.89
R v Hammersmith and Fulham LBC ex p Damoah
    (1999) 2 CCLR 18   11.14
R v Hammersmith and Fulham LBC ex p M
    (1997) 1 CCLR 69, QBD   4.5, 4.17, 4.19
R v Haringey LBC ex p Norton (1998) 1 CCLR 168   3.24, 5.52
R v Havering LBC ex p K (1997) *Times* 18 November   5.58
R v Hereford and Worcester CC ex p Chandler (1992)
    (unreported but see September 1992 *Legal Action* 15)   1.11, 5.53
R v Higher Education Funding Council ex p Institute
    of Dental Surgery [1994] 1 All ER 651, QBD   12.25
R v Hull University Visitors ex p Page
    [1993] AC 682, HL   12.98
R v Inner London Education Authority ex p Ali
    (1990) 2 Admin LR 822   1.6, 5.10, 5.79

R v Islington LBC ex p McMillan (1997) 1 CCLR 7   1.11, 3.79, 5.50
R v Islington LBC ex p Rixon (1998) 1 CCLR 119;
    (1996) *Times* 17 April   1.6, 1.8, 1.9, 1.26,
                                                         1.27, 1.29, 3.31, 3.60,
                                                         3.64, 3.80, 3.86,
                                                         5.10, 5.53, 5.55,
                                                         6.41, 12.47, 12.114
R v Kensington and Chelsea RLBC ex p Kujtim
    (1999) 2 CCLR 340   3.98, 4.23, 10.7
R v Kent CC ex p Bruce (1996) *Times* 8 February   12.90, 12.119
R v Kent CC ex p Salisbury and Pierre
    (2000) 3 CCLR 38, QBD   4.36, 5.43
R v Kingston and Richmond Health Authority
    ex p Paxman [1995] COD 410   4.69
R v Kirklees MBC ex p Daykin (1998) 1 CCLR 512   3.48, 3.96, 10.24,
                                                         10.26
R v Kirklees MBC ex p Good (1998) 1 CCLR 506   7.32, 10.24, 12.87,
                                                         12.120
R v Lambeth LBC ex p A1 and A2 (1998) 1 CCLR 336   3.79
R v Lambeth LBC ex p Caddell [1998] 1 FLR 235   4.34
R v Lambeth LBC ex p Sarhangi (1999) 2 CCLR 145   4.18
R v Lancashire CC ex p Ingham (1995) 5 July,
    QBD; CO/777 and 108/95 (unreported)   3.96
R v Lancashire CC ex p RADAR [1996] 4 All ER 421, CA   3.96
R v Lewisham LBC ex p Pinzon and Patino
    (1999) 2 CCLR 152   10.11
R v Liverpool CC ex p Winter (1997) (unreported
    but *see* (1997) 1 CCLR 5 and (1998) 1 CCLR 118)   3.81, 5.53
R v Local Commissioner for Administration for the
    North and East Area of England ex p Bradford MCC
    [1979] 2 All ER 881   12.61
R v Mental Health Review Tribunal ex p Hall
    [1999] 3 All ER 132; (1999) *Times* 20 May;
    (1999) 2 CCLR 361, CA   5.110, 5.114, 5.115,
                                                         5.129, 6.61
R v Mid Glamorgan CC ex p Miles (1993) (unreported
    but *see* January 1994 *Legal Action* 21)   3.49
R v Mid Glamorgan Family Health Services
    ex p Martin [1995] 1 WLR 110   2.29
R v Ministry of Defence ex p Smith [1996] QB 517   12.139
R v Monopolies Commission ex p S Yorks Ltd
    [1993] 1 WLR 23, HL   7.21
R v Newcastle upon Tyne Corporation (1889) 60 LT 963   1.2
R v Newham LBC ex p Gorenkin (1998) 1 CCLR 309   4.19
R v Newham LBC ex p Medical Foundation for the
    Care of Victims of Torture (1998) 1 CCLR 227   4.41
R v Newham LBC ex p Plastin (1998) 1 CCLR 304   4.17
R v North Derbyshire Health Authority
    ex p Fisher (1998) 1 CCLR 150   1.19, 6.37, 6.42, 6.74

R v North and East Devon HA ex p Coughlan
(1999) 2 CCLR 285; (1999) *Times* 20 July, CA — 4.77, 4.82, 5.30,
6.38, 6.51, 6.91,
6.96, 12.59, 12.110,
12.111, 12.139

R v North East Devon HA ex p Pow (1998) 1 CCLR 280 — 4.77, 6.37, 6.51

R v North West Lancashire HA ex p A
(1999) *Times* 24 August — 6.37, 12.105

R v North Yorkshire CC ex p Hargreaves
(1997) 1 CCLR 104 — 3.24, 3.40, 7.30,
12.49, 12.114

R v North Yorkshire CC ex p Hargreaves (No 2)
(1998) 1 CCLR 331 — 5.70

R v Northavon DC ex p Palmer (1995) 27 HLR 576, CA — 12.82

R v Northavon DC ex p Smith [1994] 3 All ER 313, HL — 10.10, 11.15

R v Parliamentary Commissioner ex p Bachin
(1999) EGCS 78 — 12.71

R v Portsmouth Hospitals NHS Trust ex p Glass
(1999) 2 FLR 905; (1999) 50 BMLR 269 — 7.85

R v Powys CC ex p Hambridge (1998) 1 CCLR 458 — 5.77, 8.117

R v Powys CC ex p Hambridge (No 2)
(2000) *Times* 16 March — 8.79, 8.93

R v Redbridge LBC ex p East Sussex CC
(1992) *Times* 31 December; [1993] COD 265, QBD — 4.32

R v Richmond LBC ex p McCarthy [1992] 2 AC 48 — 8.113

R v Richmond LBC ex p Watson (1999) 2 CCLR 402,
QBD; [2000] LGR 318, CA — 5.111, 5.121, 8.111

R v Secretary of State for Health ex p Hammersmith
and Fulham LBC, M and K (1997) 1 CCLR 96, QBD — 4.19

R v Secretary of State for Health ex p M and K
(1998) 1 CCLR 495, CA — 4.19

R v Secretary of State for Health ex p Pfizer Ltd
(1999) 2 CCLR 270 — 1.24, 6.43, 6.68

R v Secretary of State for the Environment
ex p Nottinghamshire CC [1986] AC 240, HL — 12.93

R v Secretary of State for the Environment
ex p Ward [1984] 1 WLR 849 — 5.10

R v Secretary of State for the Home Department
ex p Doody [1993] 3 WLR 154, HL — 12.115

R v Secretary of State for the Home Department
ex p Fire Brigades Union [1995] 2 All ER 244 — 3.18, 5.143

R. v Secretary of State for the Home Department
ex p Zakrocki (1998) 1 CCLR 374 — 7.6

R v Secretary of State for Social Services and Others
ex p Hincks [1980] 1 BMLR 93, CA — 6.38

R v Secretary of State for Transport ex p Cumbria CC
[1983] RTR 129, QBD — 12.49

R v Sefton MBC ex p Help the Aged (1997) 1 CCLR 57 — 3.68, 3.78, 4.8

R v Southwark LBC ex p Hong Cui (1999) 2 CCLR 86 — 4.17

R v Sutton LBC ex p Tucker (1998) 1 CCLR 251   3.74, 3.87, 3.88
R v Tower Hamlets LBC ex p Begum
    (1993) 25 HLR 319, HL   10.10
R v Tower Hamlets LBC ex p Bradford
    (1997) 1 CCLR 294   11.13, 11.14, 12.99
R v Waltham Forest LBC ex p Vale
    (1985) *Times* 25 February, QBD   4.31, 4.32, 4.36
R v Wandsworth LBC ex p Beckwith
    [1996] 1 WLR 60; [1996] 1 All ER 129, HL   4.44, 4.79
R v Warwickshire CC ex p Collymore [1995] ELR 217   12.105
R v Westminster CC and Others ex p M, P, A and X
    (1997) 1 CCLR 85, (1998) 30 HLR 10, CA   4.17, 12.120
R v Westminster CC ex p P (1998) 1 CCLR 486   12.87, 12.120
R v Wigan MBC ex p Tammadge (1998) 1 CCLR 581   3.72, 4.41, 10.14
R v Worthing BC ex p Birch (1985) 50 P&CR 53   1.24
Ripon, Re [1939] 2 KB 838   1.14
Robertson v Fife Council (2000) GWD 4-172   8.39
Roy v Kensington and Chelsea Family Practitioners
    Committee [1992] 1 AC 625, HL   12.82

S (Hospital patient: court's jurisdiction), Re
    [1995] 3 All ER 290   7.84, 12.97
Sagnata Investments v Norwich Corporation
    [1971] 2 QB 614, CA   12.101
Schuler-Zgraggen v Switzerland (1993) 16 EHRR 405   12.142
Secretary of State for Education and Science
    v Tameside MBC ex p Ellerton [1985] 1 WLR 749   12.89
Secretary of State for Trade and Industry v Langridge
    [1991] 3 All ER 591   12.114
Shah v Barnet LBC [1983] 1 All ER 226   4.29, 4.30
Smith v Secretary of State for Trade and Industry
    (1999) *Times* 15 October   12.59
Starrs v Procurator Fiscal (1999) *Times* 17 November   12.59
Steane v Chief Adjudication Officer
    (1998) 1 CCLR 538, HL   4.7, 8.21

T (A Minor), Re (1998) 1 CCLR 352   3.68

Westminster CC v Great Portland Estates PLC
    [1985] 1 AC 661   12.49
Winterwerp v Netherlands (1979) 2 EHRR 387   12.132

X v Bedfordshire CC; X v UK [1995] 2 AC 633   5.101
X & Y v Netherlands (1998) 8 EHRR 235   7.91
X (minors) v Bedfordshire CC [1995] 3 All ER 353, HL   12.82
X v UK (1981) 4 EHRR 188   12.132

Yule v South Lanarkshire Council (1998) 1 CCLR 571   8.34

Z v UK (1999) 10 September, Report of the ECHR   7.91

Table of statutes

Access to Files Act 1987
    2.21, 2.37
Access to Health Records Act 1990
    2.21, 2.37
Asylum and Immigration Act 1996
    4.17
Care Standards Act 2000
    4.45, 4.62
s112   8.99
Carers and Disabled Children Act
    2000   3.24, 5.143,
    7.10, 7.33, 7.34, 7.35, 7.37, 8.67,
    11.10
s1   7.38
s2   7.39, 7.41,
    7.42
s3   7.40, 7.44
s4   7.41
s5   5.142, 7.42
s6   7.43
s7   7.44
s8   7.45
Carers (Recognition and Services)
    Act 1995   I.27, 1.25, 3.9
    3.24, 5.41, 6.65, 7.10, 7.12–7.14,
    7.17, 7.21, 7.23, 7.24, 7.28, 7.38,
    7.48
s1   3.24, 7.11–
    7.14, 7.34
s1(1)   7.15, 7.28, 7.47
s1(2)   7.15, 7.28, 7.47
s1(2)(a)   5.79
s1(3)   7.13, 7.25
s1(4)   3.18, 7.29
s1(7)   7.34
Children Act 1989   I.16, I.28,
    1.25, 4.34, 4.36, 5.6, 5.46, 5.47,
    5.76, 5.78, 5.79, 5.139, 5.143,
    7.13, 7.31, 7.49, 7.54, 7.55, 8.2,
    8.3, 10.14, 11.5, 11.6, 11.10,
    11.11, 11.20–11.22, 11.25,
    11.30, 12.8, 12.9, 12.20, 12.59,
    12.116, 12.121
Pt III   5.6, 5.78, 5.94,
    7.36, 8.68,
    11.12–11.15,
    12.58, 12.99
s17   4.1, 4.34, 4.95,
    7.43, 7.44,
    7.51, 11.13
s17(1)   7.50, 11.1,
    11.10
s17(1)(b)   7.55
s17(3)   7.35, 7.56,
    11.11
s17(5)   11.11
s17(6)   5.94, 11.10,
    11.11
s17(10)   7.50, 11.2
s17(10(a)   3.61, 11.4
s17(10(b)   11.4
s17(11)   5.46, 7.47, 11.3
s17A   7.44
s17B   7.44
s20   10.18, 11.13,
    11.18
s20(4)   11.18
s24   4.34
s27   6.58, 6.59,
    10.10, 10.11,
    11.18
s29   8.86
s29(2)   11.27
s29(3)   11.27
s29(4)   11.28
s29(5)   11.28

Children Act 1989 *continued*
s47(3)	10.11
s84	12.116
s108(5)	5.78
Sch 2	11.11
Sch 2 Pt I	11.20
Sch 2 Pt I para 1	2.20
Sch 2 Pt I para 2	2.9, 11.5
Sch 2 Pt I para 3	11.7
Sch 2 Pt I para 6	11.11
Sch 2 Pt III	11.30
Sch 2 para 3	5.79
Sch 2 para 8	11.20
Sch 13 para 27	5.78

Children and Young Persons Act
1969   I.15

Chronically Sick and Disabled
Persons Act 1970
          I.17, 3.5, 4.36,
5.3, 5.4, 5.27, 5.39, 5.41, 5.42,
5.47, 5.65, 5.69, 8.118, 10.41,
11.7, 11.20, 11.22, 11.29
s1	5.39
s1(1)	2.10
s1(2)	2.18, 2.19
s2	I.17–I.20, I.22,

1.7–1.9, 3.3, 3.5, 3.33, 3.51,
3.65, 3.66, 3.68, 3.78, 3.96, 4.36,
5.6–5.8, 5.10, 5.20, 5.21, 5.32,
5.35, 5.39, 5.41–5.46, 5.48–5.50,
5.55, 5.66, 5.67, 5.73–5.80, 5.96,
5.97, 5.100, 5.116, 7.13, 7.32,
7.36, 8.68, 8.104, 8.108, 8.112,
8.117, 8.118, 9.23, 9.29, 10.40,
11.20, 11.22, 11.29, 12.2, 12.118
s2(1)	3.3, 3.4, 3.101,
	5.10, 5.42, 5.53,
	5.79, 12.82
s2(1)(a)	5.49, 5.50,
	5.75, 5.97,
	5.98, 12.104
s2(1)(b)	5.51
s2(1)(c)	5.26, 5.39,
	5.52–5.57
s2(1)(d)	5.57
s2(1)(e)	5.60, 5.63,
	5.64, 5.66,
	5.68, 10.3,
	10.40, 12.106

s2(1)(f)	5.27, 5.70, 5.97,
	7.36, 12.104
s2(1)(g)	5.39, 5.71
s2(1)(h)	5.72
s3	10.4
s4(a), (c)	3.3
s21	5.59
s28A	5.46, 5.78,
	11.20

Community Care (Direct Payments)
Act 1996   5.28, 5.139,
          5.140–5.143
s1	5.8, 5.143,
	7.42
s1(1)	5.142
s1(4)	5.143
s2	5.143

Community Care (Residential
Accommodation) Act 1998
          8.21
s1	4.9
s22	4.9

Competition Act 1998
s18	9.8

County Courts Act 1984
s3	10.5

Crime (Sentences) Act 1997
          5.106

Criminal Justice Act 1991
          9.5

Data Protection Act 1984   2.21
Data Protection Act 1998
          2.21–2.23,
          2.25, 2.28
Pt IV	2.37
s7(2)(a)	2.31
s7(4)	2.25, 2.35
s7(5)	2.36
s7(6)	2.35, 2.36
s7(8)	2.31
s8(2)	2.33
s8(3)	2.34
s14	2.32
s29	2.37
s30(1)	2.37
s68	2.22

Disability Discrimination Act 1995
          8.93, 10.17
s201	8.94

Disabled Persons (Employment)
   Act 1944 — 5.25
   s15(1) — 5.81
Disabled Persons (Services,
   Consultation and
   Representation) Act 1986 — 3.18, 5.41, 7.2, 7.12, 7.14, 11.7
   ss1–2 — 7.57
   s1 — 3.37
   s1(2) — 7.47
   s2 — 3.37
   s3 — 3.18
   s4 — I.22, 3.3–3.5, 3.33
   ss5, 6 — 11.24
   s8 — 3.3, 3.4, 7.10, 7.11
   s8(1) — 7.12
Education Act 1944 — I.1
   s8 — 1.6
   s41 — 5.55, 5.56
   s68 — 5.55
   s99 — 5.55
Education Act 1962 — 4.20
Education Act 1996
   Pt IV — 11.7, 11.19, 11.24
Employment and Training Act 1973 — 5.25
Employment Relations Act 1996
   s57A — 7.46
   s57A(1) — 7.46
   s57A(2) — 7.46
   s57A(3) — 7.46
Employment Relations Act 1999
   s8 — 7.46
   Sch 4 Pt II — 7.46
Enduring Powers of Attorney Act
   1985 — 7.73, 7.75
Family Law Reform Act 1969 — I.15
Family Law Reform Act 1987
   s1 — 8.63
Further and Higher Education Act
   1992
   s11 — 5.55
   Sch 2 — 5.56

Government of Wales Act 1998 — 1.14, 6.22, 6.26
Health Act 1999 — 6.10, 6.13, 6.17, 6.54, 6.140, 6.146
   s1 — 6.11
   ss2–12 — 6.17
   s12 — 6.49
   s23 — 6.147
   s27 — 6.49, 6.54
   s28(1) — 6.48
   ss29–31 — 6.139
   s29 — 6.140, 6.141
   s30 — 6.140, 6.142
   s31 — 6.143
   s31(5) — 6.144
Health Authorities Act 1995 — 6.9
Health Services and Public Health
   Act 1968 — 5.4, 5.97, 6.3, 6.5, 7.11
   s12 — 5.20
   s45 — I.19, I.21, 1.7, 1.18, 2.12, 4.20, 5.7, 5.8, 5.33–5.35, 5.37–5.40, 5.71, 5.89, 5.97
   s45(1) — 5.33, 5.97, 8.67
   s45(3) — 5.39
   s45(4)(a) — 5.38
   s45(4)(b) — 5.38
   s45(4A) — 5.40
Health and Safety at Work Act 1974 — 4.83
Health and Social Services and Social
   Security Adjudications Act 1983
   Pt III — 8.43
   s17 — 5.66–5.68, 5.74, 5.77, 5.143, 7.45, 8.58, 8.67, 8.81, 8.97, 8.99, 8.107, 10.40, 11.27, 12.57
   s17(1) — 8.73, 8.80, 8.81
   s17(2) — 8.108, 8.116
   s17(3) — 8.73, 8.80, 8.83, 8.97, 8.100
   s17(4) — 8.106
   s21 — 8.36, 8.44
   s21(1) — 8.43

HASSASSAA 1983 *continued*

s22	5.66, 8.26,
	8.48–8.50
s24	8.26, 8.48
Sch 9 Pt II para 1	5.97, 8.67
Housing Act 1985	2.12, 6.57,
	10.9
ss8 et seq	6.57
s8	10.4
s59(1)	10.16
s85	10.5
ss228 et seq	10.9
Housing Act 1988	
s9	10.5
Housing Act 1996	4.6, 4.16,
	10.10, 11.15
Pt VII	4.28, 10.10,
	10.15, 10.16
s175	10.15
s184	10.10
s189	3.13
s189(1)	10.16
s189(1)(c)	10.15, 10.17
s213(1)	6.145
Housing Grants, Construction and	
Regeneration Act 1996	
	5.65, 10.23
Pt I	5.63, 5.66,
	10.21
s19(5)	10.42
s23	5.67, 10.22,
	10.40, 12.106
s23(1)	10.29
s23(1)(k)	10.37
s23(2)	10.38
s24(3)	10.13
s24(3)(a)	10.25
s24(3)(b)	10.24
s24(4)	10.24
s34	10.46
s36	10.47
Housing (Homeless Persons) Act	
1977	I.9, I.16, 10.14
Human Fertilisation and Embryology	
Act 1990	
s30	2.37
Human Rights Act 1998	
	3.83, 4.72,
	4.82, 5.101,

	6.36, 6.53,
	12.59, 12.121
s3	12.123
s4	12.122, 12.124
s6	12.78, 12.125
s8	12.125
Immigration Act 1971	5.108
Immigration and Asylum Act 1999	
	4.20
Pt IV	4.16, 4.20
s95	4.2, 5.81
s95(3)	4.2, 4.20
s95(5)	4.2
s95(8)	4.2
s115	4.2, 5.81
s116	4.20
s117	4.20, 5.40,
	5.91
Sch 8 para 2	4.2, 5.81
Insolvency Act 1986	8.36, 8.45
s339	8.46, 8.47
s340	8.46
s341(2)	8.46
s341(3)	8.46
s423	8.46, 8.47
s435	8.46
Limitation Act 1980	
s9	8.106
Local Authorities (Goods and Services)	
Act 1970	6.145
Local Authority Social Services Act	
1970	1.1, 1.10, 1.12,
	6.3, 6.6, 12.59
s1	1.10
s6	1.11
s6(1)–(6)	1.10
s6(6)	1.11, 5.26
s7	1.15, 7.89
s7(1)	1.15, 1.20,
1.25–1.29, 3.27, 5.42, 7.16, 8.8,	
8.21, 8.54, 8.70, 12.114	
s7A	1.15, 1.31,
	2.14, 6.40
s7A(1)	1.17
ss7B–7E	1.12
s7B	12.5, 12.8,
	12.89
s7B(1)	12.8
s7B(2)	12.6

Local Authority Social Services Act
  1970 *continued*
  s7D   12.1, 12.90,
                         12.116, 12.117,
                         12.120
  s7E   5.136, 9.26
  s7E(b)   9.26
  Sch 1   7.14, 8.99,
                         12.116
Local Government Act 1929
                         6.4
Local Government Act 1972
                         6.3, 6.7
  s111   7.35, 8.48,
                         8.113
  s113   6.145
Local Government Act 1974
  Pt III   12.60, 12.83
  s25   12.60
  s26   12.60
  s26(4)   12.62
  s26(5)   12.63, 12.68
  s26(6)   12.71
  s29   12.72
  s30   12.72
Local Government Act 2000
  s2   6.49
Local Government and Housing Act
  1989   5.69
  s5   12.83
  s54   5.137
  s114(3)   5.66
  s114(4)   5.66
Local Government Finance Act 1988
  s88B(5)   4.19
Local Government Planning and
  Land Act 1980
  s194   1.10
Local Government (Scotland) Act 1975
  Pt II   12.83
London Regional Transport Act 1984
                         5.27
Magistrates' Courts Act 1980
  s58(1)   8.106
Mental Health Act 1983
                         I.16, I.20,
  1.10, 4.12, 5.4, 5.86, 5.96, 5.103,
  5.131, 5.143, 7.11, 7.64, 7.65,
  7.90, 8.2, 8.108, 8.109, 12.121

  Pt II   5.81, 5.102,
                         5.111, 6.129
  Pt III   5.81
  Pt VII   7.69
  s1   5.20
  s1(3)   9.23
  s2   5.104, 5.131
  s3   4.91, 5.104,
                         5.109, 5.111,
                         5.112, 5.122,
                         5.123
  s3(2)(a)   7.65
  s4   5.131
  s5   5.131
  ss7–9   8.112
  s7   7.80, 12.97
  s8   7.81
  s12   5.102
  s17   5.111
  s19   8.113, 8.115
  s25A   5.143
  s32   5.102
  s37   4.91, 5.102,
                         5.105, 5.109
  s45A   5.102, 5.106,
                         5.109
  s47   4.91, 5.102,
                         5.107–5.109,
                         5.122
  s48   4.91, 5.102,
                         5.108, 5.109
  s57   7.65
  s58   7.65
  s63   7.65
  s95   7.69
  s117   I.20, I.21, 1.7,
  1.8, 2.12, 4.1, 4.29, 4.36, 4.91,
  4.92, 5.7, 5.8, 5.20, 5.35, 5.92,
  5.100–5.103, 5.109, 5.111–5.114,
  5.116–5.118, 5.120–5.122, 5.124,
  5.125, 5.131, 5.134, 6.61, 8.2,
  8.3, 8.109–8.113, 8.115, 12.1
  s117(2)   5.101, 5.109,
                         5.115, 5.116,
                         6.60, 6.61
  s117(3)   5.113, 5.114
  s127   7.90
  s135   7.90
  s136   5.131

Mental Health (Patients in
  Community) Act 1995
                       5.103, 5.118,
                       5.126
s117   5.126–5.128
National Assistance Act 1948
                       I.1, I.18, 1.14,
  3.96, 4.12, 4.34–4.36, 5.10, 5.30,
  6.3, 6.5, 8.14, 8.59
Pt I   I.2, I.7
Pt II   I.8
Pt III   I.7, I.9, I.21,
  1.18, 2.13, 4.1, 4.55, 5.7, 5.8,
  5.74, 8.2–8.4, 8.58
s1   I.4
ss21–27   3.96
s21   I.2, I.9, I.10,
  I.11, I.14, 1.7, 3.14, 3.98, 4.1,
  4.2, 4.4, 4.7, 4.10, 4.12, 4.13,
  4.15–4.21, 4.40, 4.41, 4.44, 4.55,
  4.71, 4.75, 4.79, 4.91, 4.92, 4.94,
  5.6, 5.9, 5.12, 5.13, 5.26, 5.30,
  5.43, 5.89, 5.98, 5.100, 5.122,
  7.36, 8.21, 8.53, 8.112, 9.14,
  9.17, 9.28, 10.7, 10.14, 12.104,
  12.120
s21(a)   4.25
s21(1)   4.2
s21(1)(a)   4.2, 4.22, 4.26,
                   4.27, 10.14
s21(1)(aa)   4.2, 4.26, 4.27,
                   5.85, 5.94
s21(1)(b)   10.14
s21(1A)   4.2
s21(1A)A   4.16, 4.20
s21(1B)   4.2
s21(2A)   4.9
s21(3)   4.44
s21(7)(b)   6.5
s21(8)   5.30
s22   8.67
s22(1)   1.13, 8.5
s22(2)   4.56, 8.6, 8.9
s22(3)   8.7
s22(4)   8.7, 8.12, 8.13
s22(5)   1.13, 8.8
s22(5A)   7.36, 8.4, 8.60,
                   8.69
s22(6)   8.9

s24   4.28
s24(3)   4.33, 9.5
s24(3)(a), b)   9.5
s24(4)   4.26
s24(5)   4.33
s24(6)   4.33
s26   4.79, 8.5, 8.53,
                   8.67
s26(1)   4.44
s26(1C)   9.20
s26(1D)   9.20
s26(2)   4.56
s26(3A)   8.11
s26(4)   4.56
s26A   8.53, 8.54
s29   I.12, I.14, I.15,
  I.17, I.18, I.22, 1.7, 1.9, 2.5, 2.6,
  2.8–2.10, 2.18, 3.17, 3.44, 3.56,
  4.10, 4.13, 4.36, 5.3, 5.4, 5.6,
  5.8–5.10, 5.12–5.30, 5.32, 5.33,
  5.35, 5.38, 5.39, 5.42, 5.44–5.46,
  5.57, 5.59, 5.70, 5.73–5.78, 5.90,
  5.92, 5.96, 5.97, 5.143, 7.21,
  7.35, 8.67, 8.88, 8.116, 8.117,
  10.20, 11.3, 11.5
s29(1)   5.9, 5.12, 5.16,
                   5.27
s29(1)(a)   2.17
s29(1)(g)   2.4
s29(4)   4.1, 5.25–5.27
s29(4)(a)   5.285.28
s29(4)(b)   5.26
s29(4)(c)   4.93, 5.26
s29(4)(f)   5.26
s29(4)(g)   2.5, 5.26
s29(4A)   4.94, 5.26
s29(5)   5.27, 8.67
s29(6)   5.20, 5.23,
                   5.32, 5.75
s29(6)(a)   5.24, 5.28,
                   5.94, 5.140
s29(6)(b)   5.24, 5.26,
                   5.29–5.32,
                   5.96
s29(7)   5.12
s32   9.5
s32(3)   4.35, 4.36,
                   5.43, 5.113
s36(1)   12.116

National Assistance Act 1948
  continued
  s42 — 8.15, 8.63, 8.64
  s43 — 8.15
  s47 — 4.72, 4.73, 4.75, 7.90, 12.134–12.136
  s48 — 4.75
  s51 — I.6
National Assistance (Amendment)
  Act 1951 — 4.73, 12.135
National Health Service Act 1946 — I.1, 6.3, 6.5, 6.7
  s23 — 6.5
  s24 — 6.5
  s27 — 6.5
  Sch 4 Pt II — 6.5
National Health Service Act 1977 — 5.4, 5.20, 5.23, 5.24, 5.29, 5.30, 5.32, 5.38, 5.39, 5.50, 5.75, 5.81, 5.82, 5.90, 5.96, 5.98, 5.99, 6.7, 6.23, 6.57, 6.63, 6.64, 6.145, 7.36, 7.37, 8.58, 10.9
  Pt I — 6.23
  Pt II — 6.24
  ss1–5 — 5.81
  s1 — 1.5, 6.26, 6.35, 6.38
  s1(1) — 6.38
  s2 — 6.27, 6.31
  s2(b) — 6.41
  s3 — 6.28, 6.31, 6.38
  s3(1) — 5.30, 5.81, 6.29, 6.38
  s4 — 6.30
  s5 — 6.31
  s8 — 6.31
  s11 — 6.30
  s13 — 1.17, 1.31, 6.23, 6.31, 6.40, 6.42
  s17 — 6.14, 6.157
  s17A — 6.49
  s17B — 6.49
  s18(1) — 1.17
  s21 — I.21, 1.10, 2.12, 5.7, 5.8, 5.80, 5.81, 5.92

s21(1) — 5.81
ss22–28 — 5.81
s22 — 6.54, 6.55, 6.145
s26 — 6.145
s27 — 6.145
s28A — 6.140, 6.141, 6.146–6.148, 6.152, 8.107
s29 — 6.34, 6.62
s41 — 6.70
s128 — 4.12
s128(1) — 5.86
Sch 8 — I.10, I.19, I.21, 1.10, 1.18, 2.12, 4.20, 5.7, 5.8, 5.20, 5.24, 5.26, 5.35, 5.79–5.81, 5.91, 5.92, 5.96, 5.100, 6.64, 6.120, 8.58, 8.67, 9.29
Sch 8 paras 13 — 5.81
Sch 8 para 1 — 5.84, 5.93,
Sch 8 para 2 — 4.12, 5.84, 5.93, 7.36, 7.47, 9.23, 9.24, 12.104
Sch 8 para 2(1) — 7.35
Sch 8 para 2(2) — 5.28, 5.94, 5.95
Sch 8 para 2(2)(a) — 5.96, 5.140
Sch 8 para 2A — 5.91
Sch 8 para 2(4AA) — 5.96
Sch 8 para 3 — 3.56, 5.6, 5.39, 5.50, 5.79, 5.83, 5.87, 5.93, 5.97, 5.98, 7.35, 7.36, 7.47, 11.6, 11.22
Sch 8 para 3(3)(d) — 7.36
Sch 8 para 4A — 5.87
Sch 8 para 31 — 6.121
Sch 8 para 42 — 6.121
National Health Service and
  Community Care Act 1990 — I.10, I.23–I.25, I.27, 2.19, 3.18, 3.25, 5.92, 6.3, 6.8, 6.32, 6.145, 10.18
  Pt I — 6.32
  Pt II — 6.33
  Pt III — 5.7
  s4 — 6.32
  s5(1) — 6.32
  s42 — 5.92
  s43 — 8.53

NHS and Community Care Act 1990
  continued
  s46   I.21, I.22, 2.12,
                       3.56, 3.65, 5.7,
                       5.74, 5.79, 7.8,
                       7.47
  s46(1)   2.12
  s46(2)   2.13, 2.14
  s46(2)(a)   6.47
  s46(2)(d)   7.8
  s46(3)   4.91, 5.7, 7.8
  s47   I.22, 1.9, 2.19,
                       3.50, 5.79,
                       5.142, 7.38,
                       10.18, 11.6
  s47(1)   2.2, 3.8, 3.9,
      3.17, 3.31, 3.51, 3.56, 3.58, 3.99,
      5.79, 7.11, 7.28, 7.47, 11.6, 12.109
  s47(1)(a)   3.15, 3.43,
                       3.44, 3.46,
                       3.57–3.59,
                       3.99, 4.12,
                       6.57, 7.13
  s47(1)(b)   3.43, 3.46,
                       3.57–3.60,
                       3.62, 3.74,
                       3.84, 3.96,
                       3.99
  s47(2)   3.18, 3.33,
                       3.51, 5.74
  s47(3)   3.24, 3.44,
                       6.57, 10.5,
                       10.9
  s47(4)   3.18, 7.29
  s47(5)   3.7, 3.8, 3.84,
                       3.102, 4.39
  s 47(6)   3.8
  s48   4.66
  s50   12.5, 12.116
  Sch 2   6.32
  Sch 2 para 6(2)(a)   6.157
  Sch 9 para 18(4)   5.92
  Sch 10   4.12, 8.58
National Health Service (Primary
      Care) Act 1997   6.17, 6.25
  Pt I   6.25
National Health Service Reorgan-
      isation Act 1973 6.6

Powers of Attorney Act 1971
                       7.70
Powers of the Criminal Courts Act
      1973
  Sch 1A   9.5
Registered Homes Act 1984
                       4.5, 4.63, 6.92,
                       8.53, 8.57
  Pt I   4.46
  Pt II   4.50
  s1   4.45, 4.64
  s1(1)   9.13
  s1(4)   4.46, 4.63
  s1(5)   4.46
  s1(5)(j)   4.46
  s3   4.47
  s4   4.63
  s9   4.47
  s17   4.63
  s20(1)   4.5
  s21   4.49, 9.13
  s21(3)   4.50
  s22   4.50
  s22(2)   4.50
  s23   4.50, 4.68,
                       9.13
  s25(1)   4.51
  s25(1)(f)   4.51
  s25(3)   4.51
  s26(1C)   4.53
  s26(1D)   4.53
Registered Homes (Amendment) Act
      1991   4.63, 12.140
  s1   4.63, 12.141
Residential Homes Act 1980
  s8   8.67
Social Security Administration Act
      1992
  ss78(6), 105(3)   8.63
Social Security Contributions and
      Benefits Act 1992
  s73(14)   5.57, 8.89
Statutory Instruments Act 1946
                       1.14
Transport Act 1985   5.27
  s93(7)   5.27
Transport Act 2000
  ss123–129   5.27

Table of statutory instruments

Civil Procedure Rules	
r3.1	10.5
r3.2	10.5
Community Care (Direct Payments) Amendment Regulations	
2000 SI No 11	5.143
Community Care (Direct Payments) Regulations 1997 SI No 734	5.142
reg 2(1)	5.143
reg 2(1)(b)	5.143
reg 3	5.143
Community Health Council Regulations 1996 SI No 640	4.77, 6.51
reg 18	6.37
Data Protection (Miscellaneous Subject Access Exemptions)	
Order 2000 SI No 419	2.37
Data Protection (Subject Access Modification) (Health) Order	
2000 SI No 413	2.37
Data Protection (Subject Access Modification) (Social Work)	
Order 2000 SI No 415	2.37
Disability Facilities Grants and Home Repairs Assistance	
(Maximum Amounts) Order 1996 SI No 2888	10.19
Education (Special Educational Needs) Regulations 1984	
SI No 1047	11.24
Health Authorities (Membership and Procedure) Regulations	
1996 SI No 707	
regs 14, 15	6.14
Housing Renewal Grants Regulations 1996 SI No 2890	10.44
reg 10	10.45
Income Support (General) Regulations 1987 SI No 1967	8.8, 8.14
reg 51	8.32
reg 51(1)	8.32
Joint Consultative Committees Order 1985 SI No 305	6.147
Local Authority Social Services (Complaints Procedure)	
Order 1990 SI No 2244	12.5, 12.59
Manual Handling Operation Regulations 1992 SI No 2793	4.85
reg 4	4.85
Misuse of Drugs Regulations 1985 SI No 2006	
Sch 2	6.68
National Assembly for Wales (Transfer of Functions) Order	
1999 SI No 672	6.26

National Assistance (Assessment of Resources) Regulations 1992
    SI No 2977   1.13, 8.8
    reg 2   4.5
    reg 4   4.86
National Assistance (Assessment of Resources) (Amendment
    No 2) Regulations No 6 1995 SI No 3054   8.26
National Assistance (Sums for Personal Allowances) Regulations
    1996 SI No 391   8.7, 8.23
    Pt II   8.14
    Pt III   8.18
    reg 20   8.20
    reg 25   8.32, 8.44
    reg 25(1)   8.29
    reg 26   8.29, 8.35
    reg 27(2)   8.23
    Sch 4 paras 16, 18   8.22
National Assistance (Sums for Personal Requirements)
    Regulations 2000 SI No 798   8.12
National Health Service (Functions of Health Authorities)
    (Complaints) Regulations 1996 SI No 669   6.157
National Health Service (Functions of Health Authorities and
    Administration Arrangements) Regulations 1996
    SI No 708   4.50
    reg 3(1)   4.68
    Sch 1   6.31
National Health Service (General Medical Services) Amendment
    (No 2) Regulations 1999 SI No 1627   6.43, 6.62
National Health Service (General Medical Services) Regulations
    1992 SI No 635   6.34, 6.62
    reg 43   6.69
    Sch 2 para 12   6.63
    Sch 2 para 12(1)   1.24, 6.43
    Sch 2 para 16   6.66
    Sch 2 para 37(1)   6.71
    Sch 2 para 43   6.67
    Sch 2 para 43(3)   6.68
    Sch 2 para 44   6.67, 6.68
    Sch 9   6.71
    Sch 10   6.68
National Health Service (Pharmaceutical Services) Regulations
    1992 SI No 662
    reg 18   6.70
Nursing Homes and Mental Nursing Homes Regulations 1984
    SI No 1578
    reg 11   4.68
    reg 12   4.52
Representations Procedure (Children) Regulations 1991 SI No 894 12.59
    regs 5, 6   12.20,
                                              12.58

Residential Accommodation (Relevant Premises, Ordinary
    Residence and Exemptions) Regulations 1993 SI No 477   8.54
    reg 2(1)   8.57, 8.60
    reg 5   8.59
Residential Care Homes Regulations 1984 SI No 1345
    reg 10   4.48
    reg 17   12.56
    reg 18(1)   4.63
Rules of the Supreme Court
    Order 53   12.82
    Order 53 r3(7)   12.85
    Order 53 r7   12.1
Social Security (Amendments Consequential upon Introduction
    of Community Care) Regulations 1992 SI No 3147   8.52
Social Security (Attendance Allowance) (No 3) Regulations 1983
    SI No 1741
    reg 4(1)(c)   4.7
Social Security (Claims and Payments) Regulations 1987
    SI No 1968
    reg 33   7.77
Social Security (Hospital In-patients) Regulations 1975 SI No 555
    reg 16(2)   7.77

Transport Act 1985 (Extension of Eligibility for Travel
    Concessions) Order 1986   5.27

Table of circulars and guidance

Circulars

Department of Education Circulars
1/93   5.55

Department of Health Circulars
12/70 The Chronically Sick and
    Disabled Persons Act 1970
    para 5   2.11, 2.19
13/74
    para 11(ii)   5.26
19/71   1.18, 5.34
    para 3   5.34
    para 4   5.27, 5.38,
        5.39
    para 5(b)   5.39
    para 6(a)   5.39
    para 6(b)   5.39
    para 7   5.36, 5.39
    para 10   5.39
    para 11 onwards   5.39
HC(81)8   4.68
HC(84)21 Annex B   4.54
HC(86)5   4.68
HC(90)23   5.129, 5.134,
        10.17

**Department of the Environment
    Circulars**
10/90   5.64, 10.21
    para 15   12.106
10/92   10.12
    para 11   10.12
    para 16   10.12
    para 19   10.12
17/96   5.64, 5.67,
        5.69, 10.13,
        10.21

para 7.4.1   10.40
para 7.5.2   10.28
para 7.5.4   10.47
para 7.6.1   10.41
para 7.6.2   10.41
para 7.7.2   10.13
Annex 1   10.25, 10.27,
        10.40, 10.47
    para 2   10.4
    para 4   10.23
    paras 5–6   10.40
    paras 7–9   10.41
    para 11   10.42
    para 15   10.32
    para 17   10.31
    para 20   10.33
    para 21   10.34
    para 22   10.35
    para 24   10.36
    para 30   10.30
    paras 32–36   10.38
    para 45   10.46
    paras 47–49   10.25
    para 51   10.24
    para 52   10.24
Annex J2   10.44
    para 17   10.45
4/98   5.64, 10.22

Health Service Circulars
HSC(98)21   6.14
HSC(98)30   6.14
HSC(98)47   4.68
HSC(98)48 *The transfer of frail older
    NHS patients to other long-stay
    settings*   4.81, 4.82,
        6.52

Health Service Circulars *continued*

HSC(98)65	6.14
HSC(98)120	6.14
HSC(98)139	6.14
HSC(98)158	6.43
HSC(98)167. See also LAC(98)23.	
	6.50
HSC(98)171	6.14
HSC(98)176	6.41
HSC(98)190	6.14
HSC(98)228	6.14
HSC(98)230	6.14
HSC(98)198 *Commissioning in the new NHS: Commissioning Services 1999–2000*	
	6.12
HSC(99)38	5.136
HSC(99)48	6.14
HSC(99)50	5.137
HSC(99)115	6.43
HSC(99)116	6.25
HSC(99)167	6.14
HSC(99)193	6.173
HSC(99)207	6.14
L23	4.85, 4.86
WHC(95)7 (Welsh Assembly)	
	5.134, 6.81
WHC(95)38	6.130
WHC(95)40	5.128, 5.129,
	5.134
paras 10, 11, 14	5.129
WHC(96)11	5.128
WHC(96)21	1.25, 7.16
WHC(96)26	5.134
WHC(98)5	4.68
WOC 12/93	4.55
WOC 15/93	5.55
WOC 35/93	1.18, 4.3,
	5.11, 5.25,
	5.84, 5.93
WOC 47/93	4.55
WOC 47/95	6.130
WOC 16/95	6.81
WOC 16/96	1.25, 7.16
WOC 27/98	4.9

Local Authority Circulars

CRAG. See LAC(95)7.	
LAC 13/74	
para 11(i)	5.15, 5.17,
	5.19
LAC(77)13	6.92
LAC(84)15	4.54, 6.92
para 16	4.70
LAC(86)6	
paras 12–16	9.13
LAC(87)6	3.3, 7.12
para 6	7.32
paras 7–8	4.48
LAC(87)10	2.21
LAC(88)16	2.21
LAC(88)17	2.21
LAC(89)2	2.21
LAC(90)7	5.64, 5.66,
	10.21
para 14	5.64
paras 15–17	5.66
para 15	5.64
para 19	5.68
paras 36 onwards	10.25
para 58	5.66
LAC(91)6	2.13
LAC(92)12	9.2, 10.12,
	10.16
para 3	10.16
para 4	10.16
para 16	10.12
para 19	10.12
Annex para 2	9.2
LAC(92)15	6.137
LAC(92)17	6.137, 6.146,
	6.147, 6.151,
	6.152
para 4.7	6.159
para 4.8	6.160
para 4.11	6.161
para 4.12	6.162
paras 4.16–4.18	6.163
paras 4.22–4.24	6.164
paras 4.27 onwards	6.165
para 4.37	6.165
para 5.2	6.166, 6.167
para 5.7	6.167
para 5.10	6.167
para 5.14	6.168

Local Authority Circulars *continued*

LAC(92)17 *continued*

para 5.18	6.169
para 6.4	6.170
para 6.8	6.171
para 6.9	6.171
para 6.14	6.172
para 6.15	6.171
para 6.20	6.172
para 6.29	6.172
para 7.2	6.175
para 7.9	6.176
para 7.10	6.176
para 7.30	6.177
para 7.32	6.177
para 7.35	6.177
para 7.51	6.176
Annex A para 3	6.147
para 10	6.151
para 12	6.152
Annex B para 7	6.148
LAC(92)22	4.53
para 5	4.53, 9.20
LAC(92)24	6.89, 6.116,
	6.119
para 2	6.93
para 7	6.93
Annex A para 7	6.89
LAC(92)27	4.55, 6.126
para 4.1	4.56
para 4.3	4.57
para 7.2	4.55
para 7.4	4.57
para 7.6	4.57
para 7.7	4.57
para 10	4.60
para 11.9	4.61
para 11.13	4.56
para 13	4.59
para 17	4.61
LAC(93)2	1.30, 3.29,
	3.50, 4.38,
	9.3–9.5,
	9.15, 9.18
para 1	9.3
para 7	9.18
para 10	9.15
para 11	9.10, 9.15
para 12	9.4

paras 13–25	9.5
para 14	3.29, 3.50
paras 16–20	3.29
para 17	3.102
paras 21–22	3.102
para 25	3.50
paras 26–27	3.29, 4.38
para 27	3.50
LAC(93)4	2.13
LAC(93)6	1.25, 8.54
LAC(93)7	4.38, 4.32,
	4.35
Pt II	9.5
para 10	4.33
para 12	4.32
para 14	4.33
para 15	4.33
paras 16–17	4.28
para 16	4.37
LAC(93)10	1.12, 1.18,
	1.20, 4.48,
	5.26
para 2(1)(a)	4.26
para 2(1)(b)	4.39
para 2(3)	4.24
para 2(6)	4.25
para 4	4.79
para 6	5.92
App 1	4.3, 4.15,
	4.22, 4.37,
	5.97
App 1 para 2(3)	4.15, 4.37
App 1 para 2(5)	4.12
App 1 para 2(6)	4.15, 9.14,
	12.104
App 1 para 3	4.14, 4.28
App 1 para 4	4.48
App 2	5.11, 5.25
App 2 para 2 onwards	
	2.6
App 2 para 2(1)	2.17, 5.12
App 2 para 2(1)(a)	5.26
App 2 para 2(1)(b)	5.26, 5.31
App 2 para 2(1)(c)	5.26
App 2 para 2(1)(2)	2.5, 5.26
App 2 para 2(2)	2.4
App 2 para 2(3)	5.27
App 2 para 2(4)	4.93,
	5.26–5.28

Local Authority Circulars *continued*

LAC(93)10 *continued*

App 2 para 3	5.25, 5.39
App 2 para 4	5.25
App 3	5.84, 5.85, 5.93, 9.24
App 3 para 2	5.94
App 3 para 3(g)	5.86
App 3 para 3(1)(a)	5.97
App 3 para 3(1)(b)	5.97
App 3 para 3(2)	5.96
App 3 para 3(3)(a)	5.96
App 3 para 3(3)(b)	5.96
App 3 para 3(3)(e)	7.42
App 3 para 3(3)(g)	12.104
App 3 para 4	5.98
App 4	5.18
App 4 para 3	2.8, 5.14
App 4 para 6	5.16
App 4 para 7	5.17, 5.18
App 4 para 8	5.22, 7.21
App 4 para 9	5.16
App 4 para 9c	2.9
App 4 para 13	5.20
App 4 para 14	5.20
Annex 1	2.9
Annex 2	5.18
Annex 2 para 2	5.18, 5.19
LAC(93)12	5.54
paras 9–11	5.54
LAC(93)18	6.126
LAC(94)1	8.75
paras 17, 18	8.70, 8.75
LAC(94)12	2.13
LAC(94)16 para 1	4.65
LAC(95)5	5.31, 5.81, 6.51, 6.81, 6.82, 6.100, 6.106–6.108, 6.114, 6.116, 6.122, 6.125, 6.126, 6.129
paras 17–24	6.125
paras 25–26	6.126
paras 27–31	6.129
Annex A p14	6.101, 6.107
Annex A p15	6.87
LAC(95)7 as amended, *Charging for Residential Accommodation Guide* ('CRAG')	1.25, 8.8–8.10, 8.20, 8.22–8.26, 8.31, 8.33, 8.35, 8.36, 8.48, 8.62–8.65
Chapter 6	8.18
para 1.015	8.10
paras 1.023–1.024	8.11
para 1.027	12.57
paras 2.001–2011	8.56
para 2.003	4.12
paras 3.004–3.004A	8.61
para 3.005	8.62
paras 3.006A–3.014	8.62
para 3.006A	8.62
para 4.001	8.14, 8.20
para 4.003	8.13
para 5.001	8.12
para 5.005	8.13
para 6.003	8.20
para 6.010	8.20
para 6.015	8.22
para 6.057	8.31
para 6.062	8.31
para 6.063	8.31
para 6.064	8.33
para 6.067	8.36
para 7.004	8.22
para 7.005	8.22
para 7.007	8.22
para 7.012–7016	8.23
para 7.012	8.24
para 7.014A	8.25
para 7.017	8.26
paras 8.005–8.020	8.16
para 8.024A	8.17
paras 8.031–8.032	8.16
paras 9.018–9.023	8.16
paras 11.001–11.025	8.65
para 11.005	8.64
para 11.006	8.64
Annex D	8.48
para 3A	8.48
para 3.5	8.48
LAC(95)12	1.25, 4.62
LAC(95)17	6.81, 6.125, 6.130
para 5	6.131
paras 6, 7	6.132
para 8	6.133
para 13	6.126
para 14	6.126, 7.60
para 16	6.134
paras 17–19	6.129

Local Authority Circulars *continued*
LAC(95)17 *continued*
  paras 2026 — 6.135
  paras 27–35 — 6.136
LAC(96)6 — 5.136
LAC(96)7 — 1.25, 6.65, 7.16, 7.18, 7.20, 7.24, 7.29
  para 5(a) — 7.35
  para 8 — 7.17
  para 10 — 7.18
  para 11 — 7.18
  para 16 — 7.23
  para 20 — 7.26
  paras 21–25 — 7.29
  para 29 — 7.24
  Annex 1 — 7.20
LAC(96)8 — 5.118, 5.128
LAC(97)6 — 4.19
LAC(97)11 paras 1516 — 5.143
LAC(98)8 — 4.5
  para 6 — 4.56
  para 7 — 4.5
  para 10 — 8.30
LAC(98)9 — 9.30, 9.31
LAC(98)19 — 3.25, 4.9, 8.21, 8.39
  para 10 — 8.21
LAC(98)19 para 8 — 3.16
  para 9 — 4.9
LAC(98)21 — 6.14
LAC(98)23 — 6.41
LAC(98)32 — 6.14
LAC(99)08 — 5.136
LAC(99)9 — 8.8
LAC(99)12 — 5.137

Department of Transport Circulars
3/91 — 5.59

Social Services Circulars
9/1988 — 5.113

Directions
Community Care Plans Directions 1991 — 2.13
Community Care Plans (Consultation) Directions 1993 — 2.13
Community Care Plans (Independent Sector Non-Residential Care) Directions 1994 — 2.13
Complaints Procedure Directions 1990 — 1.17, 12.5, 12.22
  direction 2(1) — 12.26
  direction 2(3) — 12.26
  direction 4(1) — 12.9
  direction 5(1) — 12.10, 12.12
  direction 5(2) — 12.17, 12.18
  direction 5(3) — 12.17
  direction 6(1) — 12.10, 12.19
  direction 7(1) — 12.23
  direction 7(2) — 12.10, 12.26
  direction 7(3) — 12.26
  direction 8(1) — 12.34
  direction 8(2) — 12.34
  direction 8(3) — 12.45
  direction 8(40 — 12.46
Directions to NHS Trusts, Health Authorities and Special Health Authorities for Special Hospitals on Hospital Complaints Procedures 1996 — 6.157
  direction 7(1)a — 6.165
  direction 10 — 6.161
  direction 11 — 6.159, 6.159
  direction 13 — 6.169
  direction 15(2) — 6.170
Miscellaneous Directions to Health Authorities for Dealing with Complaints 1996 — 6.157
National Health Service (Health Authorities) (Open Reporting of Nursing Home and Mental Nursing Home Inspections) Direction 1998 — 4.68

Directions *continued*

National Assistance Act 1948 (Choice
of Accommodation) Directions
1992   I.27, 1.17,
                             4.55, 9.5
  direction 2   4.55
  direction 3   4.55
  direction 4(2)   4.56
National Assistance Act 1948
(Choice of Accommodation)
(Amendment) Directions 1993
                             4.55

Executive Letters

EL(90)185   4.77, 6.51
EL(93)14   6.112, 6.114
  Annex C paras 1014   6.114
  Annex F   6.112
EL(94)14   6.112
EL(95)97   6.42, 6.74
EL(95)114   9.22
EL(95)121   6.157
EL(95)136   6.167
EL(96)8   6.94, 6.98,
                             6.104
  para 11   6.64
  para 16   6.90, 6.111,
                             6.114
EL(96)19   6.157
EL(96)58   6.157
EL(96)89   6.95, 6.99,
                             6.101
  Annex 1 para 4.14   6.95
  para 6   6.102
EL(97)1   5.135
  para 16   5.135

Guidance

Adjudication Officers Guidance
  para 11 (DSS, 1994)
                             4.7
*Balancing the Care Equation:
Progress with Community Care*
(HMSO, 1996)
  para 32   3.63
  para 40   3.91
Better Home Life
  s4.7   9.13

*Care Management and Assessment –
Managers' Guide* (HMSO, 1991)
                             3.31, 3.39,
                             5.132, 7.58
paras 2.43–2.46   7.59
para 2.43   3.39
para 2.44   3.39
paras 2.49–2.52   7.59
para 4.89   7.59
*Care Management and Assessment –
A Practitioners' Guide*
('The Practice Guidance',
HMSO, 1991)   2.20, 2.30,
                             3.31, 3.40,
                             3.45, 3.84,
                             3.99, 7.31,
                             9.5
para 1.2   2.20
para 1.3   2.20
paras 2.1–2.18   3.20
para 2.10   3.21
para 2.19   5.74
para 3.1   3.31
para 3.2   3.31
para 3.3   3.32
para 3.12   3.24
paras 3.12–3.15   3.34
para 3.17   3.40–3.42
para 3.22   7.31
paras 3.25–3.27   3.37
para 3.28   2.30,
                             3.37–3.38,
                             7.31
para 3.41   3.49
para 3.42   7.31
para 3.48   7.31
para 3.52   3.52
para 3.54   3.24, 3.54
paras 4.32–4.36   3.99
para 4.37   3.84
para 4.45   9.5
para 4.97   9.5
para 6.9   12.17
para 7   7.19, 7.22
paras 9–11   7.29
para 11   3.45
para 11 onwards   7.33
para 13   5.143
para 15.2   7.53

Guidance *continued*

The Practice Guidance *continued*

para 15.5	7.27, 7.31
para 16	3.45
para 17	7.51
para 20	5.143
para 22	3.31
para 23	5.143
para 32	5.143
para 33	5.143
paras 35–36	5.143
para 38	7.57
para 39	7.31
para 54	5.143

Caring for People (HMSO, 1989)

Cm 849	7.4
para 2.3	7.4
para 3.28	7.8

Code of Practice on the Identification and Assessment of Special Educational Needs: procedures within the Education, Health and Social Services (1994)

para 6.47	11.24

Community Care in the Next Decade and Beyond (LASSA Guidance, November 1990, HMSO, 'The Policy Guidance')

	3.35, 6.124, 7.30, 8.74, 9.5, 12.5, 12.30, 12.53
para 2.3	2.15
paras 2.7–2.10	2.13
para 2.11	2.15
para 2.22	2.14, 2.16
para 2.25	2.14, 2.19
para 3.3	3.24
paras 3.15–3.20	3.31
para 3.16	3.24, 3.35, 3.37, 7.30, 12.114
para 3.19	3.24
para 3.20	3.19
para 3.21	3.24
paras 3.24–3.26	3.85
para 3.24	3.86, 3.88, 3.95, 6.124
para 3.25	3.35, 3.90, 7.30, 12.114
paras 3.27–3.29	7.30
para 3.31	3.95, 8.74, 8.105
para 3.41	6.124
para 3.44	6.124
paras 3.51–3.53	3.101
para 5.3	4.65
para 5.13	4.66
para 5.17	4.67
para 5.18	4.67
para 5.24	4.71
para 5.25	4.70
para 6.5	12.7, 12.8
para 6.9	12.17
para 6.12	12.51
paras 6.15 onwards	12.9
paras 6.15–6.16	12.9
para 6.17	12.12, 12.18
para 6.19	12.23
para 6.22	12.34
para 6.30	12.10, 12.16, 12.52
para 6.31	12.56
para 6.32	12.53
para 6.33	12.53
para 6.34	12.2
para 6.35	12.2
para 8.4	9.1
para 8.5	9.22, 9.25
para 8.6	9.24, 9.25
App C.6–7	9.26
Annex A para 2	12.26, 12.27
Annex A para 3	12.27
Annex A paras 5–7	12.29
Annex A para 5	12.26
Chapter 2	2.15
Chapter 6 Annex A	12.34
Chapter 6 Annex A para 5	12.28
Chapter 6 Annex A para 6	12.30
Chapter 8	9.26

Department of Health Report Empowerment, Assessment, Care Management and the Skilled Worker (HMSO, 1993)

	7.8

Guidance *continued*
Empowerment, Assessment, Care
    Management and the Skilled
    Worker (HMSO, 1993)
                                3.31, 3.33
Guidance to Children Act 1989
    Vol 2   7.49, 11.8
        para 2.4   7.52
        para 2.7   11.8
        para 2.8   11.8
        para 2.11   11.20
        para 2.15   7.55
        paras 2.19–2.21   11.18
    Vol 3 paras 10.33 onwards
                                12.20, 12.58
    Vol 6   7.49, 11.9
        para 3.3   11.11
        paras 4.2–4.4   11.9
        para 5.4   11.25
Guidance to Housing Act 1996
    Pt VI   10.17, 11.16
    Pt VII   10.17, 11.16
    paras 2.14–2.19   10.18
    para 7.5   10.18, 11.18
    paras 14.5–14.10   10.17
    para 14.5   11.16
    para 14.10   11.17
Guidance to Mental Health (Patients
    in the Community) Act 1996
                                5.118, 5.128
    para 1.2   5.129
    para 27.2   5.129
Homelessness Code of Guidance
    (Third Edition)   10.16
    para 6.11   10.16
Laming Letter (CI(92)34) 1.30, 3.60
    para 13   3.60
    para 14   3.60
    para 15   3.85
    para 31   3.101
Mental Health Act 1983: Code of
    Practice (DoH, 1999)
                                5.134
    para 20.7   5.111
    para 22.12   5.134
    Chapter 27   5.134
    para 27.1   5.117
    para 27.2   5.134
    paras 27.4–27.12   5.134

    para 27.10(f)   5.117
    Chapter 28   5.134
    para 28.2   5.126
Modernising Social Services (1998)
    Cm 4169
    para 2.29   8.72
    para 2.31   8.72
NHS Priorities and Planning
    Guidance 1996/1997
                                6.101
NHS Priorities and Planning
    Guidance 1997/1998
                                6.101
Policy Guidance. See Community Care
    into the Next Decade and Beyond
    (HMSO, 1990)
Practice Guidance. See Care
    Management and Assessment –
    A Practitioners' Guide
Practice Guidance – Carers
    (Recognition and Services)
    Act 1995
    para 11.2   3.9
Purchasing Effective Treatment and
    Care for Drug Misusers (DOH)
    (March 1997)
    para 1.7   9.11
    para 5.1   9.7
    para 5.2   9.7
    para 5.5   9.7
Right to Complain (HMSO, 1991)
                                12.5, 12.17,
                                12.20, 12.21,
                                12.27
    para 3.3   12.9
    para 3.10   12.21
    para 3.16   12.21
    para 3.4   12.9
    para 4.2   12.12
    para 4.3   12.12
    para 4.4   12.13
    para 4.9   12.16
    para 4.10   12.18
    para 4.11   12.22
    para 4.12   12.20
    para 4.16   12.33
    para 4.23   12.27
    para 4.24   12.27
    para 4.32   12.13

Guidance *continued*
Right to Complain continued

paras 6.8–6.34	7.60
paras 7.1 onwards	12.52
para 7.19	12.55

Social Services Inspectorate (SSI) Guidance

CI(92)34. See *Laming Letter*	
CI(95)12	7.49
Annex A para 1.1	7.52
CIS 124/1990	8.32

Guidelines
Health Service Guidelines

HS(G) 104	4.83, 4.84
HSG(92)43	6.137, 6.146
Annex C	6.146, 6.148
para 1.7	6.148
HSG(92)50	6.114
HSG(94)5	5.134
HSG(94)27	5.132, 5.134
para 8	5.131
para 10	5.133
HSG(95)8	6.51, 6.81
HSG(95)39	6.81, 6.130
HSG(95)41	4.62
HSG(95)45	6.146, 6.150
Annex A para 4.1	6.150
HSG(96)11	5.128
HSG(96)11 para 18	5.118
HSG(96)34	6.70
HSG(96)53	6.70
HSG(97)22	6.12

Local Authority Social Services Letters

LASSL(90)11	5.129, 5.134, 10.17
LASSL(93)6	1.30
LASSL(94)4	5.132, 5.134
para 10	5.133
LASSL(96)1	8.51
LASSL(99)2	4.89, 7.4, 7.33, 7.45

LASSL(99)16	2.21
para 2.3	2.24
para 2.4	2.22, 2.24
paras 2.5–2.7	2.25
para 2.7	2.25
para 2.8 onwards	2.26
para 2.10	2.26
para 2.12	2.28
para 2.13	2.39
para 2.16	2.34
para 2.17	2.34
para 2.18	2.34
para 2.19	2.34
para 2.20–2.21	2.32
para 2.20	2.32
paras 2.25–2.28	2.36
para 2.32	2.32
para 2.37	2.36
para 2.39	2.37
LASSL(99)21	5.64, 10.21

Advice Notes
Notes on Good Practice (1995, SSI)

	12.5, 12.20

SSI Advice

para 2	8.110
para 5	8.82
para 7	8.76
paras 8–11	8.107
para 8.7	8.89
para 8.69 onwards	8.80
para 11	8.81
para 12	8.96
para 13	8.86
para 14	8.87
para 18	8.97
para 19	8.97, 8.98
para 20	8.107
para 21	8.90
para 23	8.89
para 24	8.89
para 26	8.105
para 28	8.84

Table of local government ombudsman complaints

Bedfordshire County Council
    Complaint No 94/B/3146   3.28
Bexley LBC
    Complaint No 97/A/4002   12.53
Bolton Metropolitan Borough Council
    Complaint No 98/C/1088   12.22
Bury MBC
    Complaint No 97/C/1614   12.8, 12.9, 12.31
    Complaint No 97/C/3668   12.54
Calderdale Metropolitan Borough Council
    Complaint 96/C/3868   6.56
Calderdale Metropolitan Borough Council
    Complaint No 98/C/1294   12.23
Camden LBC
    Report No 90/C/0336 (3 October 1991)   5.62
Case No E.1190/94-95   6.119
Case No E.264/94-95   6.80
Case No E.672/9495   6.127
Case No E.685/9495   6.127
Case No E.859/96-97   6.173
Case No E.918/96-97   6.173
Case No E.985/96, p61   6.117
Case No W.478/89-90   6.80
Cheshire County Council
    Complaint No 97/C/4618   3.37, 3.38, 12.23,
        12.24, 12.31
Cleveland County Council
    Complaint No 92/C/1042   12.29
Cleveland County Council
    Complaint No 94/C/0965   3.28
Clwyd County Council
    Complaint No 98/B/0341   5.123
Decision No 91/C/1246   5.26
Devon CC
    Complaint No 96/B/4438   12.15, 12.30, 12.31
East Sussex CC
    Complaint No 93/A/3738   12.44

Essex CC
  Complaints Nos 90A/2675, 2075, 1705, 1228, 1172   8.101, 12.57
Greenwich LBC
  Complaint No 91A/3782   8.76, 8.78, 8.85,
                                                       12.57
Hampshire CC
  Complaint No 97/B/2441   12.31
Haringey LBC
  Complaint No 92/A/3725   12.9
Hounslow LBC
  Complaint No 93/A/3007   12.32, 12.36
Hounslow LBC
  Complaint No 97/A/1082   12.32, 12.36
Leeds Health Authority
  Case No E62/93–94   6.78
    para 3   6.81
    para 22   6.78
Liverpool City Council
  Complaint No 96/C/4315   3.97
Liverpool City Council
  Complaint No 98/C/3591   12.18
Merton LBC
  Complaint No 97/A/3218   4.55, 4.58
Middlesbrough District Council
  Complaint No 94/C/0964   3.28
Northumberland CC
  Complaint No 99/C/1276   12.54
North Worcestershire Health Authority
  Complaint E.985/94-95   6.80
Nottingham City Council
  Complaint No 94/C/2959   12.8, 12.9
Rochdale Metropolitan Borough Council
  Complaint No 93/C/3660   3.28
South Bedfordshire District Council
  Complaint No 94/B/3111   3.28
Stockton-on-Tees Borough Council
  Complaint 98/C/0911   8.103
    para 153   8.71
Stockton-on-Tees Borough Council
  Complaints No 98/C/1166, 1975, 1977, 1978   8.103
Waltham Forest LBC
  Complaint No 97/A/2464   12.15
Wiltshire CC
  Complaint No 98/B/0341   5.123

Table of European Conventions

European Convention on Human Rights   12.78, 12.121
    article 2   3.83, 4.82, 8.54,
                    12.128
    article 3   3.83, 7.91, 8.54,
                    12.129–12.130,
                    12.132
    article 5   4.72, 12.131–
                    12.132, 12.134
    article 6   4.72, 12.59, 12.137
    article 8   4.64, 4.82, 12.133,
                    12.138–12.139,
                    12.141–12.143
    article 12   12.143
    article 14   2.29, 12.142–12.143
    First Protocol   12.145
    article 1   12.144

List of diagrams

1: Community care assessments – when is the duty triggered?   46

2: The three stages in assessment and care planning   51

3: Residential care entitlement   92

4: Non-accommodation services   131

5: NHS commissioning arrangements prior to April 1999   208

6: NHS commissioning arrangements post-April 1999   209

7: The rights of carers   274

8: Charging for residential accommodation   308

9: Charging for non-accommodation services   336

10: Complaints   409

Abbreviations

CCPs	community care papers
CI	Chief Inspectors' letter
CIBFA	Chartered Institute of Public Finance and Accountancy
COIN	circular on the internet
CPA	care programme approach
CRAG	Charging for Residential Accommodation Guide (LAC (95)7 as amended)
CRSA	Carers (Recognition and Services) Act 1995
CSDPA	Chronically Sick and Disabled Persons Act 1970
DGM	district general manager guidance
DHA	District Health Authority
DHSS	Department of Health and Social Security
DoH	Department of Health
DP(SCR)A	Disabled Persons (Services, Consultation and Representation) Act 1986
DSS	Department of Social Security
ECRs	extra contractual referrals
EL	executive letter
EMI	elderly mentally infirm
EPA	enduring power of attorney
FSHA	family health services authority
GP	general practitioner
HASSASSAA	Health and Social Services and Social Security Adjudications Act 1983
HImP	health improvement programme
HSC	health service circular
HSG	health service guidelines
HSPHA	Health Services and Public Health Act 1968
ILF	Independent Living Fund
LAC	local authority circular
LASSA	Local Authority Social Services Act 1970
LASSL	local authority social services letter
LEA	local education authority
LGA	Local Government Act 1972
MHA	Mental Health Act 1983
NAA	National Assistance Act 1948

NHS	National Health Service
NHSA	National Health Service Act 1946 & 1977
NHSCCA	National Health Service and Community Care Act 1990
OT	occupational therapists
PAYE	pay as you earn
PCTs	primary care trusts
RADAR	Royal Association for Disability and Rehabilitation
RHA	Registered Homes Act 1984
RMO	regional medical officer
SSD	social services department
SSI	social services inspectorate
STG	special transitional grant
WHC	Welsh health circular
WOC	Welsh Office circular

Introduction

I.1   When Sir William Beveridge declared war on the five giant evils in society he had in mind Giant Want; Giant Disease; Giant Ignorance; Giant Squalor and Giant Idleness. At the end of WWII legislation was brought forward with the purpose of slaying some of these monsters: the Education Act 1944, the NHS Act 1946 and the National Assistance Act 1948. Giant Squalor was to be slain by a concerted programme of slum clearance and the building, within ten years, of three million new houses.[1]

I.2   The neglect of disabled, elderly and ill people living in the community was in many respects the forgotten sixth giant. Part III of the 1948 Act did however contain the means by which Giant Neglect was to be slain, namely the provision of 'community care services for ill, elderly and disabled people' and indeed for anyone else who 'is in need of care and attention which is not otherwise available'.[2]

I.3   It is however difficult to lay down strict rules as to the nature of what today we call 'community care services'. In general they are provided by social services departments, although the NHS also has community care responsibilities (see Chapter 6); in general they are personal care services although social services departments may now provide the disabled person with cash by a direct payment (see para 5.138). While the service is primarily concerned with personal care rather than health care, on occasions it will involve the provision of general nursing (see para 6.90). Likewise, while community care is not primarily concerned with the provision of housing or education services, at its margins it does embrace obligations in both these areas (see para 4.41 and Chapter 10). At its heart community care is about the provision of accommodation in residential care homes and the provision 'in the community' of home helps, adaptations, day centres

1   N Timmins *The Five Giants* (Fontana, 1996).
2   NAA 1948 s21.

and meals on wheels. As an arm of the welfare state it commands over £11 billion per annum of public resources.[3]

I.4   The state's assumption of responsibility for the provision of community care services predates Beveridge, however, by almost 400 years and although National Assistance Act 1948 s1 boldly proclaims that the 'Poor Law is abolished', the present scheme bears many traits of its infamous forebear.

I.5   Sir William Holdsworth[4] considered that the poor law system commenced with a Statute of 1535–1536,[5] the preamble to which declared that the former Acts were defective because no provision was made in them for providing work for the unemployed. Sir William listed six principles, which he considered as underlying the early poor law development, namely:

1) the duty to contribute to the support of the poor was a legal duty of the state;
2) the parish (via the justices) was the administrative unit for assessing need and payments;
3) the impotent poor were to be supported in the places in which they were settled (but not necessarily where they were born – previously they would have been directed to return to their birth place);
4) the children of people who could not work had to be taught a trade to enable them to support themselves;
5) the able-bodied vagrant and beggar should be suppressed by criminal law;
6) the able-bodied should have work provided for them and it be compulsory for them to do that work.

I.6   We see, particularly in points 1 to 3, signs of this parentage today. The obligation still rests with local councils (albeit social services authorities rather than the parish). The concept of ordinary residence persists, as do the liable relative rules and the importance of the inter-relationship between community care and education, housing and employment. While categories 5 and 6 are of less relevance to our present welfare benefits system, they too are echoed in the concept of work fare, claimants' availability for work and indeed in NAA 1948 s51 under which it still remains a criminal offence to 'neglect to maintain oneself'.

---

3   *With Respect to Old Age* Royal Commission on Long Term Care Cm 4192–I (The Stationery Office, 1999).
4   Sir William Holdsworth in *A History of English Law* (3rd impression, 1977) Vol IV pp390 onwards.
5   27 Henry VIII c25.

I.7   With the abolition of the 'Poor Law' by NAA 1948 Pt I local resources (principally the workhouses) had to be redistributed. The best of these were absorbed into the fledgling NHS and the remainder were put to use in meeting the new obligations created by Pt III of the 1948 Act.[6]

I.8   Part II replaced the poor law system with a national means-tested benefits system known as national assistance administered by the National Assistance Board, rather than by local councils. In due course Pt II was repealed and national assistance replaced by supplementary benefit, which itself has been replaced by income support. Income support is, however, based upon essentially the same means-tested national principles which characterised national assistance.

I.9   Part III of the Act tackled the needs of vulnerable people for residential accommodation and community or home-based (domiciliary) care services. Section 21 obliged authorities to provide residential accommodation for elderly and disabled people as well as temporary residential accommodation for homeless people where their homelessness had arisen through unforeseen circumstances. The accommodation obligations were met by the use of workhouses: as hostels for the homeless and as 'homes' for the disabled and elderly. The residential accommodation obligations under s21 have changed little since 1948; it is still the statutory basis for the vast majority of local authority residential accommodation placements. In 1977 the primary duty to accommodate homeless people was transferred to housing authorities via Stephen Ross MP's private member's bill which became the Housing (Homeless Persons) Act 1977, and with it many of the appalling problems highlighted in the film 'Cathy Come Home'.

I.10   The only other significant change to s21 resulted from the National Health Service and Community Care Act (NHSCCA) 1990. The 1990 Act repealed a provision under NHSA 1977 Sch 8 which enabled social services authorities to provide residential accommodation for people who needed it through illness and by amendment this accommodation obligation was transferred to s21. The 1990 Act also amended s21 so as to enable social services authorities to provide nursing home accommodation in addition to residential care accommodation.

I.11   Despite the rationing and general shortages present in 1948, s21 placed a duty on authorities to provide residential accommodation for

6   For an excellent account of the evolution of 'community care' see R Means and R Smith *Community Care* (Macmillan, 1994).

such persons who were ordinarily resident in their area and who were in need of care and attention which was not otherwise available to them. This obligation, in addition to the other social welfare duties – the house building programme, the creation of the new NHS and the education reforms – represented a huge public spending commitment. Perhaps not surprisingly therefore, when it came to the provision of community or domiciliary care services, authorities were not obliged to provide these services, although they were given discretion to do so if they were able.

I.12   NAA 1948 s29 empowered[7] authorities to provide four general types of service:

- advice and guidance;[8]
- the preparation of a register of disabled people;
- the provision of 'occupational activities' (such as workshops) for disabled people; and
- facilities which assist disabled people to overcome limitations of communication or mobility.

I.13   The power to provide such services was limited to disabled people. This represented the concern in 1948 to ensure that those people who had sacrificed their health for peace be given priority when it came to the provision of scarce resources.[9] In 1948 there was in relative terms a greater number of younger disabled people – in the form of wounded soldiers returning home and those injured in the bombing. This legislative prioritisation of the needs of disabled people (as opposed to those of the temporarily ill or elderly) remains anachronistically today, albeit to a lesser extent.

I.14   Given the enormous obligations placed on authorities in the postwar austerity years, the community care services provided under s29 were in general modest. Authorities were not under a statutory duty to provide them and in any event the community care services available under s29 were vaguely expressed, eg, 'assistance in overcoming limitations of mobility or communication'. What was required therefore was a statutory provision (similar in nature to s21) which provided, as of right, specific community care services for all those in need.

I.15   Although the post-war austerity years gave way to the increasingly

---

7   These discretionary powers were subsequently converted to 'target duties' (see para 1.4) by directions issued as LAC (93)10, see Appendix B.

8   It is pursuant to this provision that most social services welfare rights units are still provided.

9   H Bolderson, *Social Security, Disability and Rehabilitation* (Jessica Kingsley, 1991) p115.

prosperous 1950s and the relatively affluent 1960s, the provision of community care services remained a Cinderella area in social welfare terms. The mid and late 1960s were also characterised by a change in social philosophical attitudes – with, for instance, the enactment of the Family Law Reform Act 1969, the Children and Young Persons Act 1969 and the creation of social services departments consequent upon the Seebohm Report. This attitude was at considerable variance with that which promoted NAA 1948 s29; the cross-heading to which section blandly states 'services for blind, deaf, dumb and crippled persons, etc.' While therefore the pressure for a change in the statutory framework of community care services was present by the mid-1960s, reform was slow in coming.

I.16   We will never again see major social welfare legislation of the type enacted during the period 1945–1951. Since that time, beneficial social welfare legislation has generally originated from one of two sources. The first is the European Court of Human Rights; into this category one might place the Mental Health Act 1983 and the Children Act 1989. In terms of community care, questions concerning physical or learning difficulties, age and (non-mental) ill health have attracted hardly any complaints to Strasbourg. The second source is Acts of Parliament which started life as private members' bills, such as the Housing (Homeless Persons) Act 1977.

I.17   On 6 November 1969 it was announced that Alf Morris MP had won first place in the annual ballot for private members' bills. He chose to promote his own bill (which he himself drafted), the Chronically Sick and Disabled Persons Bill. The Act received Royal Assent on 29 May 1970, the day that parliament was dissolved for the 1970 general election.[10] The most important section of that Act has proved to be s2. It is drafted so as to make the provision of services under NAA 1948 s29 obligatory (rather than discretionary) and in place of s29's vague wording, to spell out precisely what services are to be provided. The 1970 Act remains the finest community care statute, providing disabled people with private law rights to specific services.

I.18   Despite the significance of s2, however, history has shown it to have three defects. The first is that its services are only available to disabled people (as with NAA 1948 s29). Other statutory provisions are therefore required to cater for people who need such services not because they are 'permanently and substantially handicapped',[11] but

---

10 For an account of the passing of the Act, see *Be it enacted* . . . (RADAR, 1995).
11 The definition applied under the 1948 Act, see para 5.13.

because they are either frail elderly or ill (but not permanently ill). The second defect concerns two particular drafting imperfections with this section, which are considered below. The third is that the section has proved to be simply too generous – from the perspective of social services authorities. On any reasonable interpretation it entitles disabled people to receive high quality services 'as of right'. In 1970, at the end of the 'Golden Phase' of the twentieth century,[12] such rights were perhaps seen as a logical next step in the development of the welfare state. The subsequent turmoil in the west, precipitated by the oil crisis in the early 1970s, led to a general retreat from such specific and (in budgetary terms) open-ended welfare rights. As a consequence, subsequent community care legislation has been cloth of a duller weave; generally 'resource' rather than 'rights' oriented. Section 2 is, sadly, out of step with all the other community care legislation and this incongruity is becoming ever more obvious.

1.19   Section 2 provided disabled people with the right to good quality community care services. The need for elderly people to have such services (when they were not themselves 'permanently and substantially handicapped') was satisfied by the enactment of Health Services and Public Health Act 1968 s45 which enabled authorities to make similar arrangements for 'promoting the welfare of old people'.[13] Likewise authorities were empowered to provide such services for ill people (ie, those not 'chronically sick') by virtue of NHSA 1977 Sch 8. Thus by 1977 social services authorities were under varying degrees of obligation to provide an array of community care services to the three main client groups: ill, elderly and disabled people.

1.20   During the late 1970s and in the 1980s the closure of long-stay mental hospitals gathered pace, such that community care became linked in the public mind with the care of people with mental health difficulties in the community rather than by incarceration in isolated hospitals. Mental Health Act 1983 s117 accordingly made particular provision for community care services to be provided for certain patients on their discharge from hospital. Section 117 services are only available to a restricted number of people.[14] Most people with a mental health difficulty receive their community care services under s2 of the 1970 Act.

---

12 See E Hobsbawn *Age of Extremes* (Michael Joseph, 1994).
13 Sections 2 and 45 came into force on the same date, 29 August 1970.
14 People who are discharged after detention under s3 or one of the criminal provisions of MHA 1983, see para 5.100.

I.21   When the term 'community care services' is used today in its generic legal sense, it means (as defined by NHSCCA 1990 s46):

> ... services which a local authority may provide or arrange to be provided under any of the following provisions –
> '   – Part III of the National Assistance Act 1948;
>   – section 45 of the Health Services and Public Health Act 1968;
>   – section 21 of and Schedule 8 to the National Health Service Act 1977; and
>   – section 117 of the Mental Health Act 1983.

I.22   Although s46 does not mention services under Chronically Sick and Disabled Persons Act (CSDPA) 1970 s2 as being 'community care services', this is because the Department of Health has always considered s2 to be part of s29 of the 1948 Act. This somewhat confusing statement is explained at para 5.73 below. The question of the status of CSDPA 1970 s2 constitutes the first of its two drafting problems. The second concerns the question of when the duty under the Act crystallises in favour of a disabled person. Section 2 services are only owed to an individual when the authority is 'satisfied' that the services are necessary in order to meet his or her needs. What happens if the authority simply fails to decide whether or not it is 'satisfied' as to the person's need? In essence the provision of services requires a collateral duty to 'assess' a person's eligibility for that service. While Tom Clarke MP endeavoured (unsuccessfully) to fill this lacuna via his private member's bill in 1986,[15] it was only as a result of NHSCCA 1990 s47 that a comprehensive duty to assess potential service users for their possible need for services under the community care statutes was created.

I.23   A significant motivation for the 1990 Act was the soaring social security expenditure on residential care and nursing home accommodation; this had increased from about £10 million per annum in 1979 to £2.5 billion per annum in 1993. Hospitals were closing long-stay geriatric and psychiatric wards and discharging the patients into private nursing homes where the cost could be funded by the DHSS (as it then was), essentially, therefore, transferring the cost from one central government department's budget (the NHS) to another (social security). At the same time social services authorities were doing much the same, by closing their own funded residential care homes and transferring the residents to independent-sector homes, which again were capable of being funded via the DHSS, thus transferring the cost from local to central government.

---

15 Disabled Persons (Services, Consultation and Representation) Act 1986 s4.

1.24   The 1990 Act sought to cap this expenditure by transferring most of the funding responsibility to social services authorities and restricting access to residential and nursing homes if the person was to be supported by public funds. Access in such cases was to be conditional on the authority being satisfied that such a placement was appropriate. Social services authorities were provided with a 'special transitional grant' to compensate them for their extra costs in implementing the community care reforms and in particular for assuming responsibility for funding such accommodation. In the first full year of the reforms (1994–95) the grant amounted to £735.9 million of which 85 per cent was ring-fenced to the extent that it had to be spent on independent sector care services.[16]

1.25   The Act also endeavoured to bring together the disparate statutes which governed individual entitlement to community care services and, by various amendments, create a degree of coherence in this field of law. It was preceded by a white paper, *Caring for People* Cm 849 (1989), which owed much to a report prepared by Sir Roy Griffiths for the Secretary of State for Social Services, *Community Care: Agenda for Action* (1988). NHSCCA 1990 does not, however, convert into law many of the themes which infuse the white paper, the Griffiths report and many of the subsequent practice guides issued by the Department of Health. These documents received considerable publicity and a number of myths have arisen therefore about the legal entitlement of service users.

1.26   The white paper set out six key objectives in relation to the community care reforms. These were set out in the following way at para 1.11:

–   **to promote the development of domiciliary, day and respite services to enable people to live in their own homes wherever feasible and sensible.**
    Existing funding structures have worked against the development of such services. In future, the Government will encourage the targeting of home-based services on those people whose need for them is greatest;
–   **to ensure that service providers make practical support for carers a high priority.**
    Assessment of care needs should always take account of the needs of caring family, friends and neighbours;
–   **to make proper assessment of need and good case management the corner stone of high quality care.**

16   For further details see M Meredith *The Community Care Handbook* (ACE, 1995) pp165 onwards.

Packages of care should then be designed in line with individual needs and preferences;

- **to promote the development of a flourishing independent sector alongside good quality public services.**
  The Government has endorsed Sir Roy Griffiths' recommendation that social services authorities should be 'enabling' agencies. It will be their responsibility to make maximum possible use of private and voluntary providers, and so increase the available range of options and widen consumer choice;
- **to clarify the responsibilities of agencies and so make it easier to hold them to account for their performance.**
  The Government recognises that the present confusion has contributed to poor overall performance;
- **to secure better value for taxpayers' money by introducing a new funding structure for social care.**
  The Government's aim is that social security provisions should not, as they do now, provide any incentive in favour of residential and nursing home care.

1.27 NHSCCA 1990 was however largely silent on these themes. It provided no practical support for carers – this was left to Malcolm Wicks MP and his private member's bill which became the Carers (Recognition and Services) Act 1995. As to the emphasis on individual choice (or 'preferences'), this concept appears nowhere in any of the legislation, with the exception of the National Assistance Act 1948 (Choice of Accommodation) Directions 1992.

1.28 Community care law is a hotchpotch of conflicting statutes, which have been enacted over a period of 50 years; each statute reflects the different philosophical attitudes of its time. Community care law is in much the same state as was the law relating to children in the 1980s. The law was in a mess; there were no unifying principles underlying the statutes; there were many different procedures for essentially similar problems (for instance, the umpteen different ways a child could end up in local authority care or a custody or maintenance order could be made, and so on). A great deal of this confusion and nonsense was swept away by the Children Act 1989, which repealed many statutes, in full or in part, and replaced them with a unified procedure underscored by a set of widely accepted basic principles. It takes no great genius to realise that community care law is crying out for similar treatment.

CHAPTER 1

Social services statutes, regulations and guidance

1.1   Introduction

1.2   **Statutory duties and powers**

1.10 Local Authority Social Services Act 1970

1.13 **Regulations**

1.15 **Directions and guidance**

1.17 Directions

1.20 Guidance

Types of guidance • Social services policy guidance • Social services practice guidance • NHS guidance

Introduction

1.1   Social services authorities are the creatures of statute, being created in 1970 by the Local Authority Social Services Act (LASSA) 1970. The statute brought into effect a reorganisation of the various welfare departments recommended by the Seebohm report.[1] The Act remains the primary statute governing such authorities. Being statutory bodies, they have no inherent powers, and are therefore obliged to restrict their activities to actions specifically authorised by statute. These permitted actions (or 'functions') are listed in the first Schedule to LASSA. The list is regularly kept up to date. These functions are normally either expressed as being obligatory (ie, a statutory duty) or discretionary (ie, a statutory power).

Statutory duties and powers

1.2   In general therefore the use of words such as 'can' and 'may' are interpreted as conferring a permissive power rather than a duty. Conversely, the appearance of the words 'shall' or 'must' in a legal document are in general construed as creating a duty – an obligation on the undertaker of the duty to do or refrain from doing something. This is not, however, always the case. As de Smith points out,[2] a local authority empowered to approve building plans has been held to be obliged to approve plans that were in conformity with its bylaws,[3] whereas a local authority required by statute to provide suitable alternative accommodation for those displaced by a closing order has been held not to be obliged to place them at the top of the housing waiting list.[4]

1.3   Where an authority has a power to act, but not a duty, it must (when the possible use of that power arises) exercise its discretion in each case (albeit subject to general guidelines if necessary). Authorities are generally free to refuse to use a power, provided they reach such a decision in accordance with the principles of administrative law. A fixed policy of never using a power would constitute a fetter on their discretion and be unlawful.

---

1   Report of the Committee on Local Authority and Allied Personal Social Services (Cmnd 3703).
2   De Smith, Woolf and Jowell *Judicial Review of Administrative Action* (5th edn, Sweet & Maxwell, 1995) p301.
3   *R v Newcastle upon Tyne Corporation* (1889) 60 LT 963.
4   *R v Bristol Corporation ex p Hendy* [1974] 1 WLR 498.

1.4 Authorities are required to act when they are under a legal duty so to do. Statutory duties owed by public bodies can be divided into two categories, public law duties and duties owed to individuals. The main difference between these two is in the legal consequences which flow from an authority's breach of the duty. A failure to comply with a private law duty (ie, one owed to an individual rather than expressed in the statute as owed to the public in general) may entitle an aggrieved party to obtain damages ancillary to an application for judicial review. A failure to comply with a general public law duty (known as a target duty), however, renders the decision susceptible to judicial review, but not to a claim for damages.

1.5 A notable example of a general public law duty is to be found in the National Health Service Act (NHSA) 1977 s1 which places a duty on the secretary of state 'to continue the promotion in England and Wales of a comprehensive health service'. This type of duty has come to be termed a 'target duty'. Inevitably, it is not always clear whether a particular obligation falls into the specific or target category.

1.6 On this question Sedley J stated in *R v Islington LBC ex p Rixon*:[5]

> Some of the relevant legislation contains what are known as 'target duties'. This is a phrase coined by Woolf LJ in *R v Inner London Education Authority ex p Ali* (1990) 2 Admin LR 822, 828, in relation to the duty created by s8 of the Education Act 1944 for every local education authority to secure that there are in their area schools of sufficient number, character and equipment to afford education to pupils of all ages, abilities and aptitudes. The metaphor recognises that the statute requires the relevant public authority to aim to make the prescribed provisions but does not regard failure to achieve it without more as a breach.

1.7 Many of the community care statutes are phrased in target duty terms, although some appear to be of more specific application. For instance, the National Assistance Act (NAA) 1948 ss21 and 29 and the Health Services and Public Health Act (HSPHA) 1968 s45 require local authorities to 'make arrangements' for a class of people in general. These then are generally assumed to be more akin to 'target duties'. In contrast the Chronically Sick and Disabled Persons Act (CSDPA) 1970 s2, and the Mental Health Act (MHA) 1983 s117 expressly refer to the needs of a particular person being met and appear therefore to create binding rights enforceable by individuals.

1.8 In the *Rixon* decision,[6] Sedley J reiterated that CSDPA 1970 s2

5 (1998) 1 CCLR 119.
6 Ibid.

created specific individual private law duties.[7] The point had earlier been decided by McCowan LJ in *R v Gloucestershire CC ex p Mahfood*,[8] holding that once an authority had decided that it was under a duty to make arrangements under s2, it is 'under an absolute duty to make them. It is a duty owed to a specific individual and not a target duty'.[9] The duty under MHA 1983 s117 has also been held to be an individual private law duty. In *R v Ealing District HA ex p Fox*,[10] Otton J held that 'the duty is not only a general duty but a specific duty owed to the applicant'.

1.9   In *R v Islington LBC ex p Rixon* (above) the applicant's counsel sought to argue that the target duty under NAA 1948 s29 crystallised into a private law duty once services under that section had been identified as being required by an assessment under NHSCCA 1990 s47.[11] Sedley J rejected the argument thus:

> Miss Richards' [the applicant's counsel] submission that the two in combination make it unlawful to fail to provide under s29 the resources identified in the assessment of need under s47, rather than bringing the broad s29 duty within the purview of the court, brings the argument back to the personal duties generated under s29 by the Secretary of State's directions and by Parliament in s2 of the Act of 1970.

Local Authority Social Services Act 1970

1.10   Although (as noted above) LASSA 1970 details the general framework of social services authority functions, it does not go into detail as to how social services departments should be organised except that, by s6, they must have a director of social services, and there must be adequate staff to assist the director in the discharge of the department's functions:

> 6(1) A local authority shall appoint an officer, to be known as the director of social services, for the purposes of their social services functions.
> (2) Two or more local authorities may, if they consider that the same person can efficiently discharge, for both or all of them, the functions of director of social services for both or all of those

---

7   Ibid at 125H described as 'the duties brought into being by s2 of the Chronically Sick and Disabled Persons Act 1970 and owed to the individual'.
8   (1997) 1 CCLR 7.
9   Ibid at 16G.
10 [1993] 3 All ER 170 at 181.
11 A variant of the argument put forward by R Gordon in *Community Care Assessments* (Longman 1993) p70.

authorities, concur in the appointment of a person as director of social services for both or all those authorities.

(3), (4) [. . .]¹²

(5) The director of social services of a local authority shall not, without the approval of the Secretary of State (which may be given either generally or in relation to a particular authority), be employed by that authority in connection with the discharge of any of the authority's functions other than their social services functions.

(6) A local authority which has appointed, or concurred in the appoint-ment of, a director of social services, shall secure the provision of adequate staff¹³ for assisting him in the exercise of his functions . . .

The local authorities concerned are county councils, the London and metropolitan boroughs, other unitary authorities and the City of London (s1).

1.11   While authorities will be given a wide discretion by the courts in deciding what is an 'adequate' staff (for the purposes of s6(6)), the question may be raised in judicial review proceedings, particularly where the applicant is challenging the non-provision of a service dependent upon 'human resources'.¹⁴ For instance, in *R v Hereford and Worcester CC ex p Chandler*,¹⁵ leave to seek judicial review was granted on several grounds, including the argument that the applicant had not received the service he needed (a one-to-one carer) because the authority had inadequate staff, in breach of its statutory duty under s6. Where however the complaint concerns the interrup-tion of services due to unpredictable staff absences, judicial review is unlikely to be appropriate. Thus in *R v Islington LBC ex p McMillan*,¹⁶ the complaint concerned the interruption of home care assistance to the applicant due to (among other things) staff illness. The court did not consider this to be in breach of the duty owed (and in any event not something that would warrant any remedy). Where however the complaint concerns a repeated failure of the service due to predictable interruptions, then this would seem at least a matter of maladminis-tration and amenable to remedy via the complaints system.

---

12 Repealed by Local Government Planning and Land Act 1980 s194.

13 As well as the parallel duty, under NHSA 1977 s21 and Sch 8, to provide 'sufficient' approved social workers for the purposes of MHA 1983, see para 5.96.

14 To establish a case under this ground, useful evidence can be obtained from social services committee minutes; which not infrequently record unsuccessful requests by the director for extra staff.

15 Unreported but see September 1992 *Legal Action* 15: settled on terms that the applicant receive the assessed service.

16 (1997) 1 CCLR 7, at 10.

1.12   The lack of detail in LASSA 1970 as to how social services departments are to be organised and run is addressed in specific cases by the
relevant statute giving to the secretary of state the power to issue
regulations or directions concerning the way the particular function
is to be applied. In general terms, LASSA ss7B–7E are also concerned
with the powers of the secretary of state in relation to social work
functions, and are considered elsewhere in this text.[17]

Regulations

1.13   Regulations, rules and orders are the most common forms of delegated legislation encountered in social services law. They flesh out the
bare bones of the duty or power imposed by the primary statute. In
relation to charges for residential accommodation, for instance, NAA
1948 s22(1) requires authorities to charge for such accommodation
and s22(5) authorises the secretary of state to issue regulations detailing how this shall be done. This was accomplished on 30 November
1992 with the making of the National Assistance (Assessment of
Resources) Regulations 1992 SI No 2977.

1.14   Such delegated legislation has the force of law. The procedure by
which statutory instruments are created is set out in the Statutory
Instruments Act 1946, as modified in relation to Wales by the Government of Wales Act 1998. The Acts detail the requirements for publication and the various types of procedures by which the legislation is
laid before Parliament or the Assembly and so on. Such legislation
must be within the ambit of the statutory provision which enables it
to be made. In the example of the 1948 Act above, the subsequent
regulations must be restricted to the question of assessing charges
for accommodation. Judicial review will lie where the statutory instrument exceeds such limits.[18] Statutory instruments must not derogate
from provisions in the enabling legislation; thus where rights are
conferred by a statute, then any regulations made under that Act must
not detract from those rights.[19]

---

17   Section 7B concerns the complaints process and is dealt with in Chapter 12; s7C
     concerns the secretary of state's powers to convene inquiries; s7D concerns the
     secretary of state's default powers and is dealt with at para 12.116; s7E concerns
     the secretary of state's powers to make specific grants to authorities and is dealt
     with at para 5.136 and para 9.26.
18   See, eg, *Re Ripon* [1939] 2 KB 838 and *Dunkley v Evans* [1981] 1 WLR 1522.
19   See, eg, *King v Henderson* [1898] AC 720.

Directions and guidance

1.15   As mentioned above, LASSA 1970 ss7(1) and 7A require social services authorities to be run under the general supervision of the secretary of state.[20] The provisions state as follows:

> *Local authorities to exercise social services functions under guidance of Secretary of State*
>
> 7 (1) Local authorities shall, in the exercise of their social services functions, including the exercise of any discretion conferred by any relevant enactment, act under the general guidance of the Secretary of State . . .
>
> *Directions by the Secretary of State as to exercise of social services functions*
>
> 7A(1) Without prejudice to section 7 of this Act, every local authority shall exercise their social services functions in accordance with such directions as may be given to them under this section by the Secretary of State.
>
>   (2) Directions under this section –
>   shall be given in writing; and
>   may be given to a particular authority, or to authorities of a particular class, or to authorities generally.

1.16   As will be seen, the distinction between 'directions' and 'guidance' is the distinction between having to act 'in accordance with' directions as opposed to having to act 'under' guidance.

Directions

1.17   Directions are mandatory, and are phrased as such. The power of the secretary of state to issue directions, contained in LASSA 1970 s7A(1) is replicated in many other statutes, and as noted at para 6.40, such a power also exists in relation to the health service under NHSA 1977 s13. In relation to social services functions, however, examples of such directions include the Complaints Procedure Directions 1990 and the National Assistance Act (Choice of Accommodation) Directions 1992. These have the force of law and are set out as would be any statutory instrument. Directions are nevertheless problematical constitutional instruments; if they were statutory instruments, they would be laid before parliament in accordance with the constitutional convention that it is parliament which makes law rather than the

---

20 Ie, the Secretary of State for Health in England and the Assembly in Wales.

executive. They would also be published as statutory instruments[21] and accessible to the general public, whereas it is often difficult to discover whether a direction has in fact been issued and then equally difficult to discover from whom a copy may be obtained.

1.18   While directions are usually published separately, they may appear as appendices to guidance issued by the Department of Health or Welsh Assembly. In this context important directions were issued as appendices to local authority circular LAC(93)10/Welsh Office Circular WOC35/93 (concerning NAA 1948 Pt III and NHSA 1977 Sch 8[22]), and DHSS Circular 19/71 (concerning Health Services and Public Health Act 1968 s45[23]).

1.19   In *R v North Derbyshire Health Authority ex p Fisher*,[24] the court had to decide whether a circular issued by the secretary of state was 'guidance' or a 'direction'. Dyson J agreed with the respondents' proposition that:

> If it is the intention of the Secretary of State to give directions which attract a statutory duty of compliance, then he should make it clear that this is what he is doing. The difference between a policy which provides mere guidance and one which the . . . authority is obliged to implement is critical. Policy which is in the form of guidance can be expressed in strong terms and yet fall short of amounting to directions.

He went on to analyse the particular circular and having regards to its language and substance, the absence of the word 'direction' and the use of the word 'guidance', he concluded that it did not constitute a direction from the secretary of state.

Guidance

1.20   Guidance can take many forms. Most frequently in social services law it is issued in the form of a circular and generally identified by a reference such as 'LAC(93)10'.[25] This means that it was the tenth local authority circular issued by the Department of Health in 1993. There are two basic types of social services guidance:

---

21 Directions are only published in the form of a statutory instrument if this requirement is stipulated in the primary Act: see for instance NHSA 1977 s18(1).

22 See paras 5.25 and 5.84 where these directions are considered in detail.

23 See para 5.34 where this direction is considered in detail.

24 (1998) 1 CCLR 150, 154.

25 Equivalent guidance issued in respect of the NHS is often referenced 'HSG' (Health Service Guidelines). Where a particular circular refers both to the NHS and Social Services, it will have both an LAC and an HSG number.

formal guidance (often referred to as 'policy guidance') issued by the secretary of state specifically declaring that it is issued under LASSA 1970 s7(1) (ie, s7(1) guidance);

general guidance (often called 'practice guidance') of the classic form, ie advice which an authority should have regard to when reaching a decision, but which it is not required to follow slavishly.

Types of guidance

1.21 The Department of Health and Welsh Assembly[26] issue a large amount of guidance to health and social services authorities relevant to community care. The most common types are listed overleaf.

1.22 Copies of all English guidance can be obtained free of charge from the Department of Health, PO Box 777, London SE1 6XH; Fax: 01623 724524; e-mail: doh@prologistics. Such guidance, issued since 1 January 1995, is also available on the Internet at a site known as COIN (Circular on the Internet)[27] although frequently only the covering letter to a circular (rather than the annex with the meat in it) is published. The site is however extremely useful for browsing to see if any new guidance has been issued. The text of all pre-1995 current local authority circulars (LACs) and local authority social services letters (LASSLs) are separately available on the Department of Health's web page.[28]

1.23 A list of all Welsh Assembly guidance issued since June 1999 can be found on the Assembly's website at www.assembly.wales.gov.uk. At the time of writing, the full text of the circulars cannot be read on the Internet, but provision is made for copies to be ordered by e-mail (or post). Welsh office guidance prior to July 1999 is not however so easy to obtain. Copies can be requested from the relevant department via the Welsh Assembly, Crown Buildings, Cathays Park CF10 3NQ, although this presupposes awareness that such guidance has been issued. There is still no Internet site listing the extant guidance.

1.24 Guidance can, of course, itself be the subject of judicial review if it contains an error of law, particularly if it is likely to be acted upon by those to whom it is addressed.[29] It can, in addition, be struck down if

---

26 Until 1 July 1999, the Welsh Office.

27 http://www.doh.gov.uk/coinh.htm. The site can be accessed via the Open Government Site; then via Department of Health/publications/circulars/COIN.

28 http://www.doh.gov.uk/public/letters/lasslh.htm.

29 *R v Secretary of State for Health ex p Pfizer Ltd* (1999) 2 CCLR 270; *Gillick v West Norfolk Area Health Authority* [1986] AC 112.

DoH – social services

LAC   Local Authority Circular: the most important social services guidance.

LASSL   Local Authority Social Services Letter: guidance of lesser importance and issued by the Chief Inspector of the Social Services Inspectorate (or her deputy).

CI   A Chief Inspector's letter: again this is guidance of lesser importance issued by the Chief Inspector of the Social Services Inspectorate.

Welsh Assembly – social services

WOC   Welsh Office Circular: the most important social services guidance. Generally the Welsh Office (the predecessor to the Welsh Assembly) did not draft different guidance to that of the Department of Health, but merely issued the same (or virtually the same) guidance but labelled 'WOC' rather than an 'LAC'.

Department of Health – health

HSG   Health Service Guidance: the most important health guidance. Since 1998 this guidance has been discontinued and is now issued under the label 'HSC' (see below).

HSC   Health Service Circular: since 1998 the most important health guidance (see above).

EL   Executive Letter: Guidance of lesser importance issued by the Chief Executive of the NHS Executive (or his deputy).

Welsh Assembly – health

WHC   Welsh Health Circular: the most important health guidance. Generally the Welsh Office did not draft different guidance to that of the Department of Health, but merely issued the same (or virtually the same) guidance but labelled 'WHC' rather than an 'HSG' or 'HSC'.

DGM   District General Manager Guidance: Guidance of lesser importance and generally equivalent to the Department of Health's 'EL' guidance.

COIN (see below) provides the text of Department of Health guidance since 1 January 1995.

its purpose is, in reality, to circumvent a statutory provision.[30] In *R v Secretary of State for Health ex p Pfizer Ltd*,[31] Collins J held that HSC 1998/158, which suggested that GPs should not prescribe Viagra, was unlawful in that it (among other things) sought to restrict GPs' statutory duty to provide patients with all necessary and appropriate personal medical services.[32]

Social services policy guidance

1.25   Policy guidance is a higher-status form of guidance and is thus generally labelled as such and frequently it is then stated 'this guidance is issued under s7(1) Local Authority Social Services Act 1970'. Examples of such guidance include policy guidance issued concerning the Carers (Recognition and Services) Act 1995 as LAC(96)7[33] (see para 7.16); policy guidance concerning the accommodation obligations of authorities before 1 April 1993, issued as LAC(93)6 (see para 8.54); policy guidance concerning the charging for residential accommodation rules, generally known as CRAG, which is composed of many circulars (see para 8.8); and policy guidance concerning the regulation of residential care homes, issued as LAC(95)12. Such guidance covers the breadth of social services responsibilities; thus a series of volumes of s7(1) guidance have been issued concerning the implementation of the Children Act 1989 (see para 11.8).

1.26   In *R v Islington LBC ex p Rixon* (1996)[34] Sedley J held:

> In my judgment Parliament in enacting s7(1) did not intend local authorities to whom ministerial guidance was given to be free, having considered it, to take it or leave it. Such a construction would put this kind of statutory guidance on a par with the many forms of non-statutory guidance issued by departments of state. While guidance and directions are semantically and legally different things, and while 'guidance does not compel any particular decision' (*Laker Airways Ltd v Department of Trade* [1967] QB 643, 714 per Roskill LJ), especially when prefaced by the word 'general', in my view Parliament by s7(1) has required local authorities to follow the path charted by the Secretary of State's guidance, with liberty to deviate from it where the local authority judges on admissible grounds that

30   *Pfizer* (above) and *R v Worthing BC ex p Birch* (1985) 50 P&CR 53.
31   (1999) 2 CCLR 270.
32   Under NHS (General Medical Services) Regulations 1992 SI No 635 Sch 2 para 12(1).
33   WOC 16/96 and WHC (96)21 in Wales.
34   (1998) 1 CCLR 119, at 123; (1996) *Times* 17 April.

there is good reason to do so, but without freedom to take a substantially different course.

This view was reiterated in *R v Gloucestershire CC ex p Barry*,[35] where Hirst LJ contrasted the binding nature of policy guidance with other social services guidance which he considered to be merely of 'persuasive authority on the proper construction of the legislation'.[36]

1.27   The consequences of failing to take into account s7(1) policy guidance were spelt out by Sedley J in *Rixon* (above):

> . . . if this statutory guidance is to be departed from it must be with good reason, articulated in the course of some identifiable decision-making process even if not in the care plan itself. In the absence of any such considered decision, the deviation from statutory guidance is in my judgment a breach of law . . .

It follows that if a local authority decides not to follow policy guidance it must give clear and adequate reasons for its decision and its departure from the guidance must be as limited as is possible in the particular circumstances.

Social services practice guidance

1.28   The majority of guidance issued by the Department of Health/Welsh Assembly concerning community care is not issued under s7(1), but is general guidance. Authorities are not therefore required to 'act under' it. Such guidance is advice as to how an authority might go about implementing or interpreting a particular statutory responsibility. It is often said that policy guidance tells an authority what it must do, whereas practice guidance suggests how it might go about doing it. Practice guidance is generally issued by the Social Services Inspectorate (the 'SSI' – part of the department of health) or the Welsh SSI (part of the Office of the Welsh Assembly).

1.29   Administrative law requires authorities, when reaching a decision, to have regard to all material factors. Relevant practice guidance obviously falls into such a category, and therefore a failure to have regard to it (rather than a failure to follow it) may result in the subsequent decision being quashed. In *Rixon* (above) Sedley J referred to practice guidance in the following terms:

> While such guidance lacks the status accorded by s7(1) of Local Authority Social Services Act 1970, it is, as I have said, something to which regard must be had in carrying out the statutory functions.

35 (1997) 1 CCLR 19, at 24; 4 All ER 421, CA.
36 Hirst LJ's dissenting opinion was approved by the majority in the House of Lords: (1997) 1 CCLR 40.

While the occasional lacuna would not furnish evidence of such a disregard, the series of lacunae which I have mentioned does . . .[37]

1.30 Practice guidance takes many forms. It may be by way of a circular, eg LAC(93)2, which gives advice on alcohol and drug services within community care. It may be by way of a department letter to the senior officer of an authority, in which case it is often referred to as a 'local authority social services letter'; thus LASSL(93)6 is the sixth such letter sent in 1993 (and it contained advice on the implementation of the independent living fund). Guidance can also be issued by way of a letter or advice note from the SSI. Thus an important early advice letter on the implementation of the community care reforms was sent by Herbert Laming (then Chief Inspector of the SSI); this is often referred to as the 'Laming Letter', although its official title is CI(92)34, ie the 34th such letter sent by the Chief Inspector that year.

NHS guidance

1.31 The main types of health circular which concern community care are detailed at para 1.21 above). While NHSA 1977 s13 empowers the secretary of state to issue directions to NHS bodies in much the same way as s/he can to social services departments under LASSA 1970 s7A, there is no specific provision in the 1977 Act concerning the issuing of guidance. The nature and relevance of NHS guidance is considered at para 6.39 below.

---

37 (1998) 1 CCLR 119 at 131E.

CHAPTER 2

The duty to plan and to inform

2.1   Introduction

2.3   The social services duty to plan

2.4   Registration

2.10   The social services' duty to prepare community care plans

        Planning and the social services/NHS interface • NHS community care planning duties

2.17   The duty to inform

2.21   Data Protection Act 1998

        Access to information by or on behalf of children • Access to information on behalf of an adult lacking mental capacity • Access procedures • Third party information • Statutory exemptions from disclosure • Appeals procedure • Request made through another person (an agent)

Introduction

2.1   For individuals to receive appropriate community care services, they must either know of (and then request) their entitlement, or they must be identified by social services and then provided with the necessary assistance. Those in need must therefore be informed of their rights and authorities must (by the preparation of plans) develop systems to ensure that those in need of services receive them.

2.2   In general, the community care client group is a vulnerable client group. It includes many individuals with communication and mental capacity difficulties; many who are elderly or ill; and many who are unassertive. It is for this reason that in certain situations there is a positive obligation on the authority to act regardless of a request from the individual in need (most importantly, the duty to assess under NHSCCA 1990 s47(1) – see para 3.8 below).

The social services duty to plan

2.3   The duties upon social services authorities to plan, can be subdivided into a specific obligation to compile registers about the needs of individuals in their area, and a more general duty to prepare strategic plans as to how best to deliver services to those 'in need' within their area.

Registration

2.4   In consequence of NAA 1948 s29(1)(g) and the secretary of state's directions[1] under that section, social services authorities are obliged to keep a register of disabled adults who are ordinarily resident in their area.[2]

2.5   The purpose of such registers is to facilitate the obligation on social services authorities to inform 'persons to whom [s29] relates of the services available for them [under s29]'.[3]

2.6   The guidance[4] explains that, for certain statutory purposes (ie, to establish a right to certain social security and tax benefits)[5] uncon-

---

1   LAC(93)10 App 2 para 2(2).
2   See para 4.28 for the definition of 'ordinary residence'.
3   LAC(93)10 App 2 para 2(1)(2) and s29(4)(g).
4   Ibid para 2 onwards.
5   Various benefits for blind persons are dependent upon registration – most

nected with s29, there is a need to keep a register of the persons who come within the s29 client group. The guidance points out that in addition the registers serve an important community care planning role, by helping to ascertain the demand and potential demand for domiciliary care services. Although the form of the registers is not prescribed, the guidance makes it clear that they need to contain sufficient information to produce the annual statistical returns required by the Department of Health.[6] The register aims at recording all persons who come within the s29 client group – including mentally disordered persons.

2.7   In many authorities the maintenance of a register of disabled people is seen as an administrative chore of little practical value. Potentially, these registers could be important pro-active tools for disseminating information about new services and resources and as databases to facilitate consultation exercises, mail-shots and so on.

2.8   For community care purposes the register is purely a planning tool; where a person comes within the s29 client group and is assessed as requiring domiciliary services, then those services must be provided irrespective of whether s/he is registered. Indeed, the guidance makes clear that an individual has the right not to have his/her name included on the formal register if s/he so chooses.[7]

2.9   The s29 client group comprises 'persons aged eighteen or over who are blind, deaf or dumb or who suffer from mental disorder of any description, and other persons aged eighteen or over who are substantially and permanently handicapped by illness, injury, or congenital deformity'. The meaning of these terms is considered in detail at para 5.13 below. The guidance however requires social services authorities to divide their registers of 'substantially and permanently handicapped' persons into three categories,[8] namely:

1) *Very severe handicap*
    This category includes those persons who:
    a) need help going to or using the WC practically every night. In addition, most of those in this group need to be fed and dressed

notably an extra income tax allowance; in addition such persons are exempt from the 'all work test' for incapacity benefit, and severe disablement allowance together with other miscellaneous benefits such as certain income support premiums and relief from non-dependent deductions for income support, housing benefit and council tax benefit, certain car parking concessions, a small reduction in the TV licence and access to free NHS eye examinations.

6   LAC(93)10 App 2 para 2 onwards.
7   LAC(93)10 App 4 para 3.
8   LAC(93)10 App 4 para 9c and Annex 1.

or, if they can feed and/or dress themselves, they need a lot of help during the day with washing and WC, or are incontinent; or

b) need help with the WC during the night but not quite so much help with feeding, washing, dressing, or, while not needing night-time help with the WC, need a great deal of daytime help with feeding and/or washing and the WC; or

c) are permanently bedridden or confined to a chair and need help to get in and out, or are senile or mentally impaired, or are not able to care for themselves as far as normal everyday functions are concerned, but who do not need as much help as categories a) and b) above.

2) *Severe or appreciable handicap*
This category includes those persons who:

a) either have difficulty doing everything, or find most things difficult and some impossible; or

b) find most things difficult, or three or four items difficult and some impossible; or

c) can do a fair amount for themselves but have difficulty with some items, or have to have help with one or two minor items.

3) *Other persons*
This category is not defined, save only that it includes such persons as those suffering from a less severe heart or chest condition or from epilepsy.

An equivalent registration duty in relation to disabled children is found in the Children Act 1989 Sch 2 Pt I para 2 – see para 11.9.

The social services' duty to prepare community care plans

2.10   CSDPA 1970 s1(1) sought to increase the planning obligation on social services authorities by making them take a more pro-active role. The section requires the authority to 'inform themselves' of the number of disabled people in its area (rather than passively waiting for people to register themselves as disabled). Section 1(1) is, however, still restricted to disabled people. It provides as follows:

> It shall be the duty of every local authority having functions under section 29 of the National Assistance Act 1948 to inform themselves of the number of persons to whom that section applies within their area and of the need for the making by the authority of arrangements under that section for such persons.

2.11 DHSS Circular 12/70[9] explained the planning purpose underlying s1(1) thus:

> . . . it requires the authorities concerned to secure that they are adequately informed of the numbers and needs of substantially and permanently handicapped persons in order that they can formulate satisfactory plans for developing their services . . . It is not a requirement of the Section that authorities should attempt 100% identification and registration of the handicapped. This would be a difficult, expensive and time-consuming exercise, diverting excessive resources from effective work with those who are already known, involving a restrictive and artificial definition and likely to be counter-productive.

2.12 The need for a more effective planning obligation was highlighted by the White Paper *Caring for People*[10] which stated the government's intention that authorities would be required to draw up and publish plans for community care services, in consultation with health authorities and other interested agencies.[11] The intention was realised via NHSCCA 1990 s46 which provides:

46 (1) Each local authority –
    (a) shall, within such period after the day appointed for the coming into force of this section as the Secretary of State may direct, prepare and publish a plan for the provision of community care services in their area;
    (b) shall keep the plan prepared by them under paragraph (a) above and any further plans prepared by them under this section under review; and
    (c) shall, at such intervals as the Secretary of State may direct, prepare and publish modifications to the current plan, or if the case requires, a new plan.
(2) In carrying out any of their functions under paragraphs (a) to (c) of subsection (1) above, a local authority shall consult –
    (a) any Health Authority the whole or any part of whose district lies within the area of the local authority;
    (b) [*repealed*]
    (c) in so far as any proposed plan, review or modifications of a plan may affect or be affected by the provision or availability of housing and the local authority is not itself a local housing authority, within the meaning of the Housing Act 1985, every such local housing authority whose area is within the area of the local authority;

9 Para 5.
10 HMSO, November 1989, Cm 849.
11 At para 5.3.

(d) such voluntary organisations as appear to the authority to represent the interests of persons who use or are likely to use any community care services within the area of the authority or the interests of private carers who, within that area, provide care to persons for whom, in the exercise of their social services functions, the local authority have a power or a duty to provide a service;

(e) such voluntary housing agencies and other bodies as appear to the local authority to provide housing or community care services in their area; and

(f) such other persons as the Secretary of State may direct.

(3) In this section –

'local authority' means the council of a county, a county borough, a metropolitan district or a London borough or the Common Council of the City of London;

'community care services' means services which a local authority may provide or arrange to be provided under any of the following provisions –

a) Part III of the National Assistance Act 1948;

b) section 45 of the Health Services and Public Health Act 1968;

c) section 21 of and Schedule 8 to the National Health Service Act 1977; and

d) section 117 of the Mental Health Act 1983.

'private carer' means a person who is not employed to provide the care in question by any body in the exercise of its function under any enactment.

2.13   Every social services authority is required to prepare and publish an annual community care plan.[12] The Community Care Plans (Consultation) Directions 1993 (and accompanying guidance)[13] detail the obligation on authorities to consult with any local representative provider organisation which requests in writing to be consulted.[14] The directions also require that the plan specifically includes details of how such organisations and the other consultees mentioned in NHSCCA 1990 s46(2) would be consulted. The importance attached by the government to the involvement of the independent sector in the provision of community care services was further emphasised by the Community Care Plans (Independent Sector Non-Residential

12 Community Care Plans Directions 1991. The accompanying guidance [LAC(91)6] recommends (at para 2.18) that the plans be in a form which is readily understandable and in languages and formats relevant to the local population.

13 LAC(93)4.

14 The obligation to consult is the subject of further guidance in the Policy Guidance at paras 2.7–2.10.

Care) Directions 1994 and the accompanying guidance[15] which require the plan to include details of the authority's proposals for purchasing non-accommodation services from the independent sector.

2.14   Para 2.25 of the Policy Guidance deals with the essential ingredients of community care plans. To this brief list must be added those items the subject of specific directions (as detailed above).

In their plans SSDs should identify:

Assessment
- the care needs of the local population, taking into account factors such as age distribution, problems associated with living in inner city areas or rural areas, special needs of ethnic minority communities, the number of homeless or transient people likely to require care;
- how the care needs of individuals approaching them for assistance will be assessed;
- how service needs identified following the introduction of systematic assessment will be incorporated into the planning process.

Services
- the client groups for whom they intend to arrange services. The Department does not wish to be prescriptive about how these are categorised but grouping should show evidence of a balanced consideration of the needs of such groups as dependent elderly people, those with disabilities whether of a learning, physical or sensory nature and those whose need for social care may be intermittent such as those affected by HIV/AIDS or women suffering domestic violence. Plans should include services for people with multiple and low incidence disabilities and will be required to include services for mentally ill people (including those with dementia), and those who misuse drugs and/or alcohol;
- how priorities for arranging services are determined;
- how they intend to offer practical help, such as respite care, to carers;
- how they intend to develop domiciliary services.

Quality
- the steps they are taking to ensure quality in providing and purchasing services;
- how they intend to monitor the quality of services they have purchased or provided;
- the setting-up and role of inspection units;
- the setting-up and role of complaints procedures.

15 LAC(94)12.

Consumer choice
- how they intend to increase consumer choice;
- how they intend to stimulate the development of a mixed economy of care.

Resources
- the resource implications, both financial and human, of planned future developments;
- how they intend to improve the cost effectiveness of services;
- their personnel and training strategy for meeting both short and longer term developments.

Consultation
- how they intend to consult on plans with DHAs, FSHAs, housing authorities, voluntary organisations representing service users, voluntary organisations representing carers, voluntary housing agencies and other bodies providing housing or community care services in their area (as required by Section 46(2) of the Act).

Publishing Information
- what arrangements they intend to make to inform service users and their carers about services;
- how and when they intend to publish CCPs in the following year.

The Department of Health monitors all English social services authority plans and the Welsh Assembly monitors those in Wales. Ultimately, if a plan were 'out of line with national policies and priorities' then the secretary of state's powers under LASSA 1970 s7A could be invoked.[16]

Planning and the social services/NHS interface

2.15   Chapter 2 of the Policy Guidance gives general advice on what authorities are expected to achieve through planning, and throughout it lays considerable emphasis on the need for partnership and collaboration between authorities and the NHS:

> 2.3 Joint planning will be essential if the new planning agreements are to work. Many authorities believe there should be joint plans by LAs, [health authorities and primary care trusts] as this would most effectively ensure the 'seamless' service which they wish to achieve. The Department recommends that where ever possible joint plans are produced but recognises that in some areas problems exist (not least where authorities do not have coterminous boundaries) which mean that this objective would not be realistic at least in the short term. However, all authorities are expected to take a joint approach to planning and ensure their plans are complementary. Plans will be monitored to ensure this joint approach.

16   Policy Guidance para 2.22.

and at para 2.11 the point is again emphasised:

At an early stage [social services and health authorities/primary care trusts] should draw up joint resource inventories and analyses of need which enable them to reach agreement on key issues of 'who does what' for whom, when, at what cost and who pays.

The crucial importance of social services and health authorities developing common procedures for recording information and 'mapping' the needs of their service users has been emphasised on many occasions, including in the highly influential Audit Commission Report, *The Coming of Age*,[17] which stressed that 'Health authorities, trusts and social services departments must map needs and the services available to meet them. They should share this information with each other as the basis for joint planning and commissioning.'

NHS community care planning duties

2.16   Health authorities are under similar strategic planning obligations, most notably their duty to compile annual continuing care statements and to promote health improvement programmes. These functions are considered in detail at paras 6.83 and 6.47 below. Health authorities' plans are monitored by the NHS Executive.[18]

The duty to inform

2.17   NAA 1948 s29(1)(a) empowers authorities to make arrangements 'for informing' disabled adults 'of the services available for them' under that section. The secretary of state's directions[19] confirm authorities' power to so inform (but do not create a duty to do so).

2.18   CSDPA 1970 s1(2) converts the discretionary power into an obligation and spells out in greater detail the nature of that duty. The provision only applies to disabled people and leaves considerable discretion as to the way in which the information is published. It remains, however, the most important statutory provision in relation to the duty to provide general information. It provides as follows:

(2) Every such local authority –
  (a) shall cause to be published from time to time at such times and in such manner as they consider appropriate general information as to the services provided under arrangements

17   (1997) Recommendation 1 p77.
18   Policy Guidance para 2.22.
19   LAC(93)10 App 2 para 2(1).

made by the authority under the said section 29 which are for the time being available in the area; and

(b) shall ensure that any such person as aforesaid who uses any of those services is informed of any other service provided by the authority (whether under any such arrangements or not) which in the opinion of the authority is relevant to his needs and of any service provided by any other authority or organisation which in the opinion of the authority is so relevant and of which particulars are in the authority's possession.

2.19   DHSS Circular 12/70 at para 5 explains the purpose of s1(2) as ensuring that 'those who might benefit by help, and their families, should know what help is available to them and this is to be secured both by general publicity and by personal explanations'. While the duty to provide information to an individual service user is an essential part of the assessment process under NHSCCA 1990 s47, the general duty to publicise services is not specifically addressed by the 1990 Act. The Policy Guidance only deals with this issue as an aspect of community care planning, at para 2.25, requiring that plans include details of what arrangements authorities intend to make to inform service users and their carers about services.

2.20   *Care Management and Assessment – A Practitioners' Guide*[20] states (at para 1.2) that 'a greatly increased emphasis on the sharing of information' is 'an essential feature' of community care planning and that this should include the publishing of information on the resources/services available and the assessment and review procedures. In this context it advises:

> 1.3 It is the responsibility of the practitioner to ensure that this published information reaches potential users and carers who are considering seeking assistance. The availability of such material should help practitioners in their task but will also mean that they will be more open to public challenge on the quality of service they provide.

A parallel duty to prepare plans and to inform in relation to services for disabled children and other children in need exists in Children Act 1989 Sch 2 Pt I para 1.

Data Protection Act 1998

2.21   The Data Protection Act 1998 came into force on 1 March 2000 and covers all social services and health records, repealing the previously applicable law under the Access to Files Act 1987, the Access to

20 HMSO, 1991.

Health Records Act 1990 and the Data Protection Act 1984. General guidance on the Act has been issued by the Data Protection Commissioner,[21] in addition to which specific social services guidance has been published by the Department of Health as LASSL (99)16[22]; paragraph references below being to this circular (unless the context indicates otherwise). Any dispute concerning the refusal of access to information may be appealed to the Commissioner (or the courts); the Commissioner has, in addition, certain enforcement powers.

2.22   The 1998 Act applies to all 'accessible public records', no matter when they were compiled and includes electronic and manual data. An accessible public record is a record which contains any personal information held by the health body or social services department for the purposes of their health / social services functions, irrespective of when the information was recorded (s68). The information held may include factual material as well as 'any expressions of opinion, and the intentions of the authority in relation to the individual' (para 2.4).

2.23   The Act applies eight basic principles to the disclosure of information. These essentially require data to be processed fairly, legally and accurately, and that the information be retained no longer than necessary; they restrict the transfer of data as well as unnecessary reprocessing of data, and require organisations holding such information to take appropriate measures to restrict unauthorised access to it.

2.24   Where joint records are held, for example, by social services and an NHS trust in a community mental health team, a request for access to that information can be made to either body (paras 2.3 and 2.4).

2.25   The Act gives a right of access by individuals to any personal information held by the authority about them. Where the information concerns other individuals (for instance a local authority file on an entire family) one member is not in general entitled to see information about another member without that person's consent (paras 2.5–2.7). The Act permits the disclosure of information notwithstanding that it has been provided by a third party and that party has not consented to the disclosure, although in deciding whether to agree to disclosure regard is to be had to various factors, including the duty of confidence to the third party; the steps taken to obtain his or

21 'The Data Protection Act 1998 – An Introduction' obtainable from the Data Protection Commissioner's Office, Wycliffe House, Water Lane, Wilmslow, Cheshire, SK9 5AF.

22 Which repeals the previous guidance under LAC(87)10, LAC(88)16, LAC(88)17 and LAC(89)2. Further guidance has been issued as LASSL(2000)2.

her consent (and whether s/he is capable of giving such consent) as well as the reasons for any refusal given by the third party (s7(4); para 2.7 of the guidance).

Access to information by or on behalf of children

2.26   The guidance (at para 2.8 onwards) makes clear that where a person under 18 seeks access to their records the authority must decide whether or not s/he has 'sufficient understanding to do so', which means 'does he or she understand the nature of the request'. If the requisite capacity exists then the request for access should be complied with. If however insufficient understanding exists, the request may be made by a person with parental responsibility who can make the request on the child's behalf. Disclosure to parents in such cases should only occur after the authority has satisfied itself:

a)   that the child lacks the necessary capacity to make the request in his or her own name; and

b)   that the disclosure would not result in serious harm (para 2.10)

Access to information on behalf of an adult lacking mental capacity

2.27   A general outline of the law concerning adults who lack mental capacity is contained at para 7.63 below.

2.28   The Act makes no special arrangements for access to be made on behalf of an adult who lacks sufficient understanding to make the request in his or her own name. The guidance however states (at para 2.12) that 'if a person lacks capacity to manage their affairs, only a person acting under an order of the Court of Protection or acting within the terms of a registered enduring power of attorney (EPA) can request access on her or his behalf'. The failure of the Act to deal with this issue and the inadequacy of the guidance on this point has been the subject of considerable criticism.

2.29   For many people, most obviously those with a profound learning difficulty, the option of an EPA is not available. The guidance states, in such situations, that the only option is for the person seeking to gain access to the information to be acting under a power of attorney. Such a procedure is expensive, cumbersome and inappropriately orientated solely towards the disabled person's 'property and (financial) affairs'.[23] The guidance would appear to ignore (or seek to limit) the common law power of authorities to disclose information in such

23   *Re F* [1990] 2 AC 1.

cases,[24] albeit that in *R v Mid Glamorgan Family Health Services ex p Martin*[25] it was expressed as being a qualified right with a presumption against disclosure to third parties. The current legal position would appear to be contrary to article 8 (in combination with article 14) of the European Convention on Human Rights.[26]

2.30   Authorities should bear in mind, however, that their general duty of confidentiality exists, not for their own protection, but for the benefit of the disabled person. Accordingly, there must be occasions where the general interests of the disabled person require that information be disclosed, notwithstanding that s/he lacks the necessary mental capacity. In this respect, for instance, the Practice Guidance on Care Management and Assessment requires that advocates be given access to relevant information concerning the person for whom they advocate and are enabled to consult with appropriate individuals in order to establish the best interests of that person.[27]

Access procedures

2.31   Section 7(2)(a) of the Act requires all requests for access to information to be in writing and s7(8) requires the information to be disclosed 'promptly' and in any event within 40 days. All information must be disclosed, unless subject to any of the exceptions detailed below (most notably where the data includes information about another person).

2.32   The information should not be altered in any way (para 2.20) and should be the information which the authority held at the time of the request. Any amendment or deletion made between the time of request and supply should however be noted (if the changes would have occurred regardless of the request (paras 2.20–2.21). The Act contains procedures by which applicants can apply to have inaccurate information corrected.[28]

2.33   Section 8(2) stipulates that the information should generally be provided in the form of a permanent copy although a copy need not be provided if this is not possible, or would involve disproportionate effort or the applicant has agreed otherwise.

24 *R v Mid Glamorgan Family Health Services ex p Martin* [1995] 1 WLR 110.
25 Ibid.
26 Particularly where an application for pre-action discovery of documents is not possible (*Harris v Newcastle Health Authority* [1989] 1 WLR 96) or subject to a claim of public interest immunity. See *Gaskin v Liverpool CC* [1980] 1 WLR 1549, *Gaskin v UK* (1989) 12 EHRR 36.
27 *Care Management and Assessment – A Practitioners' Guide* (HMSO, 1991) para 3.28 and see also LAC(2000)7 *No Secrets* para 5.8.
28 Section 14 and see also para 2.32 onwards of the guidance.

2.34   The 40-day time period for disclosure is subject to certain restrictions, namely:

1) *Sufficient description of information sought*
The applicant must provide the authority with sufficient information to enable it to identify the person about whom the information is sought and where that information is likely to be held. Authorities are permitted to provide a standard request form for this purpose but are not permitted to insist on its use (para 2.16).

2) *Payment of the appropriate fee*
Authorities are permitted to charge a fee for the provision of information, which must not however exceed the statutory maximum of £10, including the cost of supplying copies. The guidance requires authorities to advise applicants promptly of the need to pay a fee (if one is charged) and advises that procedures should exist for waiving the fee where the applicant's means or any other circumstances dictate such a course (para 2.17). Since the 40-day period only commences when the fee has been paid, it may be appropriate to include payment in the initial letter of request (see Appendix C below for a precedent letter of request).
The guidance advises (at para 2.18) that where authorities do not have the requested information, applicants should be informed as quickly as possible, and a decision then made as to whether the fee should be returned. In so deciding it should consider the applicant's circumstances, the effort involved in discovering that there was no data and its own policy on charging.

3) *Repeated requests*
Section 8(3) provides that access can be refused where the authority has previously complied with an identical or similar request from the applicant, unless a reasonable interval separates the requests.[29]

Third party information

2.35   Section 7(4) of the 1998 Act states that where an authority is unable to comply with a request for information without disclosing information relating to another individual (who can be identified from that information) then it is not obliged to comply with the request, unless, either:

29 Para 2.19 of the guidance gives advice on what amounts to a 'reasonable interval'.

a) the other individual has consented to the disclosure; or
b) it is reasonable in all the circumstances to comply with the request without the consent.

In deciding whether or not it is reasonable to make a disclosure without the third party's consent, s7(6) requires the authority to have particular regard to the following factors:

a) any duty of confidentiality owed to that other individual;
b) any steps taken [by the authority] with a view to seeking the consent of the other individual;
c) whether the other individual is capable of giving consent;
d) any express refusal of consent by the other individual.

2.36   The guidance makes the following observations:

> 2.25 Section 7(6) is likely to be of particular relevance when a request is received for access to very old files and the possibility of tracing any third party is remote.
>
> 2.26 An authority should set itself a sensible timescale, within the 40 days allowed, in which to seek any third party consent. The 40 day period does not commence until the authority has received the written request, the appropriate fee, and if necessary, the further information required to satisfy itself as to the identity of the person making the request, and to locate the information sought.
>
> 2.27 If consent is not given by a third party within 40 days, an authority should give as much information as possible without identifying the third party (see DPA, section 7(5)). An authority should explain why some of the information requested has not been given. Where consent is or cannot be given and the authority considers it reasonable to comply with the request without consent then the authority may be required to justify its actions . . .
>
> 2.28 Where the authority is satisfied that the data subject will not be able to identify the other individual (the third party source) from the information, taking into account any other information which the authority reasonably believes is likely to be in or to come into the possession of the [applicant] then the authority must provide the information.

In addition to the above factors, the statutory exemptions detailed below also apply to decisions about disclosure, most importantly where it is considered that disclosure could result in serious harm to the other individual. Indeed, if the third party is a social worker, access cannot be refused unless the 'serious harm test' applies (para 2.37).

Statutory exemptions from disclosure

2.37　Part IV of the Act provides that authorities do not have to disclose information in certain situations. The principal grounds of relevance for the purposes of community care are (in summary):

1) *The prevention or detection of crime (s29)*
Where the authority considers that disclosure would be likely to prejudice criminal investigations, or crime prevention, it is exempt from the duty to disclose, although the guidance (para 2.37) advises that this only applies if there is a 'substantial chance' rather than a 'mere risk'.

2) *Information about physical or mental health conditions (s30(1))*
Social services are prohibited from disclosing any information without first consulting an appropriate health professional.[30]

At the time of writing the guidelines concerning the disclosure of health-related material by health professionals have not been issued. They are likely, however, to follow the previous provisions in the Access to Health Records Act 1990, namely that authorities can refuse to disclose any material which it believes likely to cause the individual serious physical, mental or emotional harm.[31]

3) *Where disclosure is prevented by another enactment*
This category includes such examples as adoption records and reports, parental order records and reports under Human Fertilisation and Embryology Act 1990 s30, etc.[32]

4) *Specific social services exemptions*
Information held for the purposes of social work is exempt from disclosure if it would be likely to prejudice the carrying-out of social work, by causing serious harm to the physical or mental health (or condition) of the applicant or another person (Data Protection (Subject Access Modification) (Social Work) Order 2000 SI No 415).

30　The guidance lists who this might be, but in general this will be a GP, psychiatrist or other consultant. The final regulations and guidance have not been issued in relation to the period in which the social services department must make their request to the health professional, although the previous regulations (under the 1987 Act) stipulated 14 days. The relevant detail is contained in the Data Protection (Subject Access Modification) (Health) Order 2000 SI No 413.

31　But authorities were obliged to disclose as much information as could be supplied without causing such serious harm. See also HSC 2000/019.

32　These exemptions are listed in the Data Protection (Miscellaneous Subject Access Exemptions) Order 2000 SI No 419.

If any of these exemptions are to be relied upon, the applicant must be notified as soon as practicable and in writing, even where the decision has also been given in person; reasons should also be given (para 2.39).

Appeals procedure

2.38   If disclosure is refused the applicant may apply either to the Data Protection Commissioner or to the courts; the choice of remedy is up to the applicant.

Request made through another person (an agent)

2.39   The guidance (para 2.13) advise that persons who have sufficient understanding to make a request, can do so via an agent, although such agents should provide evidence (usually in writing) of their authority and identity and their relationship to the applicant.

CHAPTER 3

The duty to assess and the provision of services

3.1   Introduction

3.8   The duty to assess: when does it arise?

3.18   The nature of an assessment

3.19   Screening assessments

3.23   The minimum criteria for an assessment

3.26   Timescale for assessments

3.31   Practice guidance
3.32   Negotiate scope of assessment
3.34   Choose an appropriate setting
3.35   User involvement
3.37   Potential service users with communication or mental capacity difficulties

3.43   The meaning of 'need' under s47(1)(a)

3.50   Delegation of duty to assess

3.51   Assessment under s47(2)

3.52   The written record of the assessment

3.56   Community care assessments and disabled children

3.57   The service provision decision: what needs must be satisfied by the provision of services?

continued

3.59   Eligibility criteria and the question of resources

3.70   Constraint 1

3.71   Constraint 2 ·

3.75   Constraint 3
Waiting lists/physical resource shortages

3.82   Constraint 4

3.84   The provision of services and the care plan

3.88   The objectives of a care plan

3.89   Choosing between alternative care packages

3.98   A refusal of services

3.99   Unmet need

3.101   Reviews and reassessments

3.102   Provision of services without an assessment

Introduction

3.1   The public provision of community care services is dependent in each case on a public authority making an administrative decision that the particular individual could not only benefit from the service, but also that the service should be provided. The decision-making procedure is known as the assessment process.

3.2   The assessment process commences with the potential service user coming to the notice of the social services authority and ends with a decision as to whether or not s/he is entitled to services. If services are required, then the next stage is the preparation of a care plan which details and quantifies the services and specifies how (and by whom) they are to be delivered. The first part of this chapter is concerned with assessments and the second part with the care plans. The duty to assess carers is considered separately in Chapter 7.

3.3   Arguably, there has always been an implied duty on authorities to assess potential service users. Because of doubt about the extent of this obligation, in relation to the provision of services under CSDPA 1970 s2, the Disabled Persons (Services, Consultation and Representation) Act 1986 (DP(SCR)A) s4 gave to disabled people (and their carers) the right to request an assessment. The circular accompanying the 1986 Act (LAC(87)6) explained the position thus:

> 3. However, s2(1) does not make it explicit whether a local authority has a duty to determine the needs of a disabled person. It was suggested in the course of debates in Parliament on the Disabled Persons (Services, Consultation and Representation) Bill that as the duty to 'make arrangements' could be interpreted as applying only after the local authority are satisfied that such arrangements are necessary in order to meet particular needs, local authorities might refuse to come to a view as to what are those needs as a means of avoiding the obligation to make arrangements. It has never been the Government's view that subsection 2(1) should be interpreted in that way, and it is clear that this is shared by the vast majority of local authorities. However, it was agreed that the matter should be put beyond doubt.

> 4. Section 4 of the 1986 Act accordingly makes it clear that local authorities have a duty to decide whether the needs of a disabled person call for the provision of services under section 2 of the 1970 Act, if they are requested to do so by a disabled person (section 4(a)) or by anyone who provides care for him or her (section 4(c)) in the circumstances mentioned in section 8 of the 1986 Act.

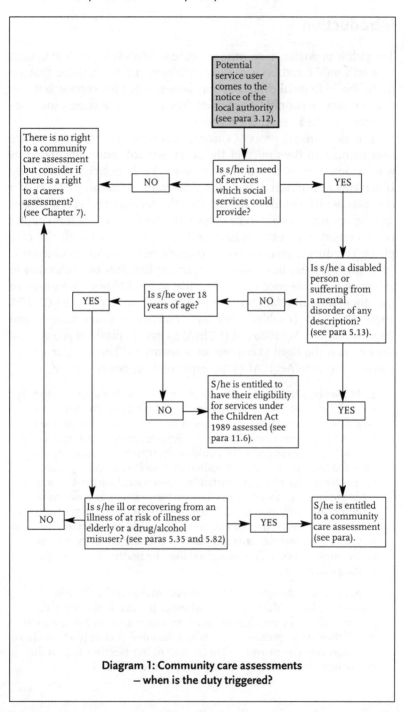

**Diagram 1: Community care assessments
— when is the duty triggered?**

3.4   Section 4 of the 1986 Act provides:

> When requested to do so by –
> a disabled person,
> (b) . . .[1]
> (c) any person who provides care for him in the circumstances
>   mentioned in section 8,[2]
> a local authority shall decide whether the needs of the disabled
> person call for the provision by the authority of any services in
> accordance with section 2(1) of the 1970 Act (provision of welfare
> services).

3.5   The right to request an assessment proved to be an unsatisfactory
mechanism for disabled people to access services under the 1970 Act
as it required people to know of the existence of their right to services
before they could access those services. As most people did not know
of their rights under that Act, they were obviously unable to make the
necessary request under the 1986 Act s4. What was required, therefore, was a duty to assess regardless of any request from the potential
service user. The duty had also to extend not only to services under
the 1970 Act s2, but to all services under all the community care
statutes.

3.6   The intention to create such a general duty to assess was
announced in the 1989 white paper *Caring for People* (Cm 849) which
at para 3.1.3 stated that social services authorities would be responsible for:

> carrying out an appropriate assessment of an individual's need for
> social care (including residential and nursing home care), in
> collaboration as necessary with medical, nursing and other agencies,
> before deciding what services should be provided.

3.7   The effect of the changes has been to make social services departments the 'gate-keepers', controlling access to state-supported
community care services. Such services can only be provided at
public expense after an assessment of need has occurred[3] and a
decision made by the social services authority that, having regard to
the assessment of need, services should be provided.

---

1   This provision, which related to requests by 'authorised representatives' has not
    at the time of going to press been brought into force.
2   Ie, someone 'who provides regular and substantial care for the disabled person'
    – see para 7.18.
3   Except in emergencies – NHSCCA 1990 s47(5), see para 3.102.

The duty to assess: when does it arise?

3.8   NHSCCA 1990 s47(1) provides:

> Subject to subsections (5) and (6) below, where it appears to a local authority that any person for whom they may provide or arrange for the provision of community care services may be in need of any such services, the authority –
> (a) shall carry out an assessment of his needs for those services; and
> (b) having regard to the results of that assessment, shall decide whether his needs call for the provision by them of any such services.

3.9   Section 47(1) obliges social services authorities to carry out an assessment of an individual's needs for community care services even where the individual has made no request for an assessment. All that is required in order to trigger the assessment obligation is that:

a) the individual's circumstances have come to the knowledge of the authority;

b) the individual appears to be a member of one of the client groups for whom community care services can be provided, eg, s/he appears to be disabled, elderly or ill; and

c) the individual might benefit from the provision of community care services.

In such situations there is an obligation on the social services authority to assess. In reality, of course, authorities have difficulty assessing all individuals who have requested an assessment, let alone those who have not (or indeed those who do not want to be assessed). The point, however, is of importance in several respects: most obviously, as will be seen below, carers have the right in certain situations to a separate assessment under the Carers (Recognition and Services) Act 1995, when the person for whom they care is also being assessed; if that person could refuse an assessment, then s/he could deny the carer their right to an assessment under that Act.[4]

3.10   The duty to assess, accordingly arises, irrespective of:

a) any request by the potential service user; or

b) whether there is any prospect of the potential service user actually qualifying for any services;[5] or

4 Para 11.2 of the practice guidance to the Carers (Recognition and Services) Act 1995 suggests that users can refuse an assessment; while this may be a statement of practice, as a matter of law it is clearly incorrect. All an individual can do is not co-operate and if needs be, refuse any services which are offered.

5 See *R v Bristol CC ex p Penfold* discussed at para 3.14, although in such cases the assessment may be rudimentary.

c) the financial circumstances of the service user; or

d) whether the service user is ordinarily resident[6] in the local authority's area.[7]

3.11 In *R v Gloucestershire CC ex p RADAR*[8] it was held that the local authority could not discharge its obligation to potential service users (who had in fact previously received services) simply by writing to them asking them to reply if they wanted to be considered for assessment. Carnwath J stated:

> The obligation to make an assessment for community care services does not depend on a request, but on the 'appearance of need' . . . Of course, the authority cannot carry out an effective reassessment without some degree of co-operation from the service user or his helpers. However, that is a very different thing from saying that they can simply rest on having sent a letter of the type to which I have referred.

In reaching this decision the court emphasised the essential frailty of many of the potential service users:

> In some areas of law that might be an adequate response, where those affected can be assumed to be capable of looking after their own interests, and where silence in response to an offer can be treated as acceptance or acquiescence. However, that approach cannot be and is not valid in the present context.[9]

3.12 Clearly it will be a question of fact and degree, whether a local authority has, in any particular situation, sufficient knowledge of a potential service user, so as to trigger the duty to assess. In *R v Bexley LBC ex p B*,[10] for instance, the court held that:

> Authorities are, however, under an obligation to make provision . . . whenever they are satisfied that the relevant conditions have been met. A request by or on behalf of a disabled person is not one of those conditions. It seems to me that the Court should look at the reality of the situation. In the present case, although no formal request was made by the applicant's mother for an assessment of the applicant's needs, that was the effect of what happened in the early months of 1994.

---

6 See para 4.28 where 'ordinary residence' is considered in greater detail.

7 See *R v Berkshire CC ex p P* at para 3.17, although in general this will only be necessary for a local authority to carry out an assessment of someone who is not ordinarily resident in their area, if the person's residence is disputed or s/he has no settled residence.

8 (1998) 1 CCLR 476; [1996] COD 253.

9 Ibid p482D.

10 (2000) 3 CCLR 15.

3.13   Not only is the duty to assess triggered by the 'appearance of need' rather than a request, it is also the case that the duty is triggered when it is the local authority who has this knowledge, not necessarily the social services department. Thus, where a local authority is considering the needs of a disabled child for special educational provision, this will almost certainly trigger the duty to assess; because the 'local authority' is aware of the need and it is the local authority's duty to assess (not the social services department's[11]). Likewise, in a unitary authority (which has responsibility for both housing and social services), the duty to assess will in general also be triggered when a 'vulnerable'[12] person presents him/herself as homeless.

3.14   *R v Bristol CC ex p Penfold*[13] concerned a 52-year-old single mother who suffered from anxiety and depression. She was accepted as being homeless by the respondent council who offered her two properties, although she refused both as neither were in the part of the city where her family (and support network) lived. Her solicitors then asked the authority to carry out a community care assessment of her needs, on the basis that she either be offered accommodation under NAA 1948 s21[14] or, if she moved elsewhere, that she would need support to replace her family.

3.15   The authority refused to carry out a community care assessment on the ground (among others) that there was no prospect of meeting any needs that might have emerged in the course of the assessment (because their eligibility criteria were so tightly drawn, only people at severe risk were likely to be offered services). In relation to this argument, Scott Baker J held:

1) Where there is an apparent need for community care services which a local authority is empowered to provide then the authority must undertake an assessment under NHSCCA 1990 s47(1)(a).

2) Even if it were the case that a service user has no sensible prospect of being awarded services because of constraints upon resources, that does not absolve the local authority from conducting a s47(1)(a) assessment.

3) The discharge by a housing authority of its obligations under the homelessness legislation does not preclude the need for a community care assessment.

11   See para 3.56 concerning the right of disabled children to community care assessments.
12   Under Housing Act 1996 s189.
13   (1998) 1 CCLR 315.
14   See para 4.41 where this aspect of the case is considered.

1 Information gathering
The social services department obtain sufficient information in order to make a decision about the most appropriate way of meeting the person's community care needs (see para 3.23).

Note
Depending on the extent of the person's care needs, this may be a brief process, or more complex, potentially requiring input from carers (see Chapter 7), and others with relevant information such as health (see para 6.57) and housing (see para 10.8). It may also require consideration of factors such as the person's emotional, cultural and psychological needs and preferences (see para 3.46).

2 Service provision decision
The social services department decides which of the 'needs' and 'requirements' that have been identified in the assessment 'call for the provision of services' (see para 3.57).

Note
The social services department may not consider that it is 'necessary' to provide everything which is identified in the assessment as being of potential benefit to the person. In general it will only provide services which are essential or for which the assessed need meets its 'eligibility criteria',

3 Care plan
The social services department now prepares a 'care plan' which explains what 'care needs' must be met and details the services that are to be provided in order to do this (see para 3.84). The care plan also explains what health or housing services are to be provided by the housing or health authority (if any). The plan will take account of the user's preferences and also identify those 'unmet needs' which do not qualify for services (see para 3.99).

Diagram 2: The three stages in assessment and care planning

3.16   Of particular relevance, the judgment states as follows:[15]

> It seems to me that Parliament has expressed Section 47(1) in very
> clear terms. The opening words of the subsection, the first step in the
> three stage process, provide a very low threshold test. The reference
> is to community care services the authority *may* provide or arrange
> for. And the services are those of which the person *may* be in need. If
> that test is passed it is mandatory to carry out the assessment. The
> word *shall* emphasises that this is so. The discretionary element
> comes in at the third stage when the authority decides, in the light of
> the results of the assessment what, if any, services to provide.
>
> Usually, but not inevitably, the section will be triggered by, or on
> behalf of, a person claiming to have a need. But the initiative could
> come from the local authority. In practice however only those who
> think they have a need will ask for a community care assessment. As
> a matter of logic it is difficult to see how the existence or otherwise of
> resources to meet a need can determine whether or not that need
> exists. The practical reality of success of the Applicant's argument is
> that the potentially deserving cases will be prioritised in terms of:
> (i)   assessed needs that are to be met;
> (ii) assessed needs that must remain current but will be recorded in
>   the local authority's records for planning purposes; and
> (iii) aspirations that following assessment turn out not to be a need.
>
> I do not, therefore accept [the] submission that Parliament cannot
> have intended expenditure to a pointless end when it was clear that
> any established need could not be met. Even if there is no hope from
> the resource point of view of meeting any needs identified in the
> assessment, the assessment may serve a useful purpose in
> identifying for the local authority unmet needs which will help it to
> plan for the future. Without assessment this could not be done.
>
> If the Respondent's argument on construction is accepted, the
> consequence will be that not only can authorities set wholly disparate
> eligibility criteria for services they intend to provide but they may also
> utilise such criteria as a basis for whether they will undertake a
> community care assessment at all. This cannot be right. The mere
> fact of unavailability of resources to meet a need does not mean that
> there is no need to be met. Resource implications in my view play no
> part in the decision whether to carry out an assessment.

The financial circumstances of a person are irrelevant for the purposes of assessment; para 8 of LAC(98)19 advises local authorities
that they are under a legal duty to carry out community care assessments regardless of the person's financial resources.

---

15   (1998) 1 CCLR 315 at 322.

3.17 Strictly speaking the duty to assess is triggered in relation to persons who may not be ordinarily resident in the local authority's area. In *R v Berkshire CC ex p P*,[16] the respondent local authority refused to assess the applicant, because it claimed that he was not 'ordinarily resident' within its area. The court held that the duty to assess arises whenever the authority possesses the legal power to provide or arrange for the provision of community care services.[17] Accordingly the duty to assess is not conditional upon whether the service user is resident in the authority's area or indeed whether the local authority is prepared to exercise its discretion to make any such services available. The rationale behind this decision is that without such a duty, persons whose residence was disputed by two or more authorities would effectively be in limbo until their residence was resolved.

The nature of an assessment

3.18 Despite the central importance of the assessment process in community care law, there is no effective legislative description of what the process actually consists of. NHSCCA 1990 empowers the secretary of state to give directions as to the form assessments should take; but no such directions have been issued.[18] In the absence of such a direction, s47(4) provides that assessments are to be carried out in such manner and take such form as the local authority considers appropriate. The assessment process was defined with some precision by Disabled Persons (Service, Consultation and Representation) Act 1986 s3, but this section has not been brought into force and the secretary of state has indicated that it will be long delayed (if indeed ever brought into force) because of its 'resource and administrative implications'. However, given that such procedures have received royal assent, it may be difficult for the executive to issue directions that are radically different to the scheme prescribed by the 1986 Act.[19]

---

16 (1998) 1 CCLR 141.
17 Social services authorities have the power under NAA 1948 s29 to provide services for people who are not ordinarily resident in their area, see para 5.12.
18 Section 47(4); see also Carers (Recognition and Services) Act 1995 s1(4), where a similar provision applies, and likewise no directions have been issued.
19 See, eg, *R v Secretary of State for Home Department ex p Fire Brigades Union* [1995] 2 All ER 244, where 'the Secretary of State could not validly . . . resolve to give up his statutory duty to consider from time to time whether or not to bring the statutory scheme into force' (per Lord Browne-Wilkinson at 256b) and so could not introduce a conflicting non-statutory criminal injuries compensation scheme.

Screening assessments

3.19   The Policy Guidance advises (at para 3.20) that:

> Assessment arrangements should normally include an initial screening process to determine the appropriate form of assessment. Some people may need advice and assistance which do not call for a formal assessment, others may only require a limited or specialist assessment of specific needs, others may have urgent needs which require an immediate response. Procedures should be sufficiently comprehensive and flexible to cope with all levels and types of need presented by different client groups.

3.20   The Practice Guidance[20] refers to screening procedures in terms of responding to approaches from the public and then deciding on one of the following responses:

1) providing information and advice (essentially redirecting inappropriate enquiries);
2) providing simple, direct services, such as a bus pass, without the necessity for a 'complex assessment';
3) collecting basic information to enable a referral for a more detailed assessment (and possibly referral also to another agency such as health or housing).

3.21   The guidance explains (at para 2.10) that the aim of this process is to 'establish as quickly and as sensitively as possible, the urgency, level and complexity of needs to inform the allocation decision. This will determine the speed and type of assessment response, including whether assessment by any other care agency is required'.

3.22   Many local authorities, however, are using screening assessments as a way of weeding out, at an early stage, potential service users. Effectively, such applicants are advised after a short telephone conversation that they are not entitled to services and nothing further occurs. In principle there appears nothing wrong with such an approach provided the screening assessment complies with certain minimum criteria. Indeed such procedures enable authorities to conserve their limited human resources and target scarce officer time on more detailed assessments of those in most need.

---

20 *Care Management and Assessment – A Practitioners' Guide* (HMSO, 1991) paras 2.1–2.18.

The minimum criteria for an assessment

3.23 As is noted below (see para 3.32), community care assessments may be simple or complex; sometimes involving many agencies and taking many months to complete. It is clear however that certain basic matters must be considered in even the most rudimentary interview for it to amount to an assessment. In *R v Bristol CC ex p Penfold*,[21] the respondent sought to argue that a mere consideration by the council of an applicant's request for an assessment was itself an assessment; in rejecting this Scott Baker J held that an assessment 'cannot be said to have been carried out unless the authority concerned has fully explored the need in relation to the services it has the power to supply. In some cases the exercise will be very simple; in others more complex'.[22]

3.24 When screening procedures of this type are employed by an authority, they must comply with certain minimum criteria, since the actual screening assessment may be the only 'community care assessment' the applicant receives. It would appear therefore that an assessment must, at the very minimum, be structured in such a way that it seeks to obtain the following information from the potential service user:

1) His /her name and contact details.

2) His/her choice of the setting for the assessment. If content, then the assessment could take place by questioning etc over the telephone but it would appear essential that any person being assessed has the option of a face-to-face interview. This requirement arises not merely from the Practice Guidance[23] (see below), but also from an appreciation that many potential service users may have communication problems, mental capacity difficulties, limited knowledge of the relative severity of their own circumstances; an inability to express their needs succinctly over the phone, etc.

3) His/her need for an interpreter or other facilitator[24] which may include an advocate (see para 7.58 below).

4) His/her care needs. This requires (in the absence of good reasons):

21 (1998) 1 CCLR 315
22 Ibid at 321C
23 *Care Management and Assessment – A Practitioners' Guide* (HMSO, 1991) para 3.12 onwards.
24 Policy Guidance para 3.21.

a) His/her involvement and (with his/her consent) the involvement of any carer.[25]

b) That the full spectrum of potential needs be considered. In *R v
Haringey LBC ex p Norton*,[26] the respondent council, when
carrying out its assessment, only considered its obligation to
provide 'personal care needs' rather than other needs such as
social, recreational and leisure needs. The court held this to be
unlawful; the assessment had to investigate all potential needs.

c) The potential service user's opinion as to his/her needs and
wishes be ascertained.[27]

d) The potential service user's opinion as to what choice s/he
would make as to any service that may be offered as a result of
the assessment be ascertained.[28] In *R v North Yorkshire CC ex p
Hargreaves*,[29] the court held that the potential service user had
not communicated her preferences as to service provision
during the assessment process and accordingly held the
assessment unlawful.

e) The particular risk factors that the potential service user faces
as well as his/her aptitudes, abilities and access to existing
social support networks be assessed.[30]

5) Whether there is any carer who may potentially be entitled to an
assessment under the Carers (Recognition and Services) Act 1995
and/or services under the Carers and Disabled Children Act
2000.[31]

6) Any associated health or housing difficulties s/he may have. If
such exist then there must be a referral to the health or housing
authority and it would seem therefore that the assessment cannot
be finally concluded until a response has been received to that
referral and the contents of that response fully considered.[32]

7) The potential service user should also be advised of his/her right
to have a written copy of the assessment forwarded to him/her.[33]

25   Ibid para 3.16
26   (1998) 1 CCLR 168.
27   Policy Guidance para 3.16.
28   Ibid para 3.3.
29   (1997) 1 CCLR 104.
30   Policy Guidance para 3.19.
31   See Chapter 7.
32   NHSCCA 1990 s47(3) and Policy Guidance para 3.19; see paras 6.57 and 10.8
     below.
33   *Care Management and Assessment – A Practitioners' Guide* (HMSO, 1991) para
     3.54; see para 3.54 below.

3.25   LAC(98)19 makes clear that the duty to assess arises irrespective of the financial status of the potential service user, stating:

> 8. Local authorities are under a legal duty under the NHS and Community Care Act 1990 to assess the care needs of anyone who, in the authority's view, may be in need of community care services. It is the Department's view that the law does not allow authorities to refuse to undertake an assessment of care needs for anyone on the grounds of the person's financial resources, eg because they have capital in excess of the capital limit for residential accommodation. Even if someone may be able to pay the full cost of any services, or make their own arrangements independently . . . they should be advised about what type of care they require, and informed about what services are available.[34]

Timescale for assessments

3.26   A problem with the absence of a statutory description of how the assessment process should be carried out, is that there is no specific time limit for the carrying out of assessments.

3.27   As a matter of statutory interpretation, where a provision is silent on the time for compliance, the law implies that it be done within a reasonable time, and that what is a 'reasonable time' is a question of fact, depending on the nature of the obligation and the purpose for which the computation is to be made.[35]

3.28   Authorities frequently adopt a priority scheme for assessments; for instance (put crudely) assessment within 24 hours for a person at serious risk of immediate and significant harm, assessment within 14 days for medium levels of non-immediate risk and 28 days for low-risk categories. Despite such aims (which are usually detailed in the authority's community care plan), chronic delay characterises many authorities' assessment procedures. This is particularly so in relation to assessments for home adaptations, which have been the subject of repeated criticism by the local ombudsman (see para 5.62). By way of example, in a 1996 report[36] a delay of six months in assessing a disabled person's needs was held to be maladministration and another

---

34   The circular is expressed as being issued under LASSA 1970 s7(1); see also para 8.21 below where it is further considered.

35   See, for instance, *Re North ex p Hasluck* [1895] 2 QB 264; *Charnock v Liverpool Corporation* [1968] 3 All ER 473.

36   Complaints against South Bedfordshire District Council and Bedfordshire County Council Nos 93/B/3111 and 94/B/3146.

1996 report found seven months for an assessment and a further four months' delay by the authority in processing the disabled facilities grant approval to be maladministration.[37] In this complaint the local ombudsman reiterated her view that if the authority has a shortage of occupational therapists, then it should not use them for assessment purposes if this will result in unreasonable delay, stating, 'If such expertise is not available, councils need to find an alternative way of meeting their statutory responsibilities'. While the local ombudsman has approved in principle the idea of prioritising certain assessments, she has criticised the way such a scheme is administered. In a 1995 complaint[38] she stated:

> [The complainants' disabled daughter's] prospective assessment was prioritised as complex. As such, the case was on a larger waiting list than the lists for emergency cases and simple cases. The Council considered it was not possible to regard the case as an emergency when it was compared with other children's needs at the time. However, the Council has no issue with the College of Occupational Therapist's alarm that a child in [her] situation was not listed as an urgent case. The Council's system of priorities is over-simple. Within the category of 'complex' cases there is no provision for relatively simple solutions to tide people over until a full assessment can be made. Also, there will be cases which cannot be described as 'emergencies' but need to be dealt with more urgently within the 'complex' category than others. The Council's over-simple system of priorities resulted in a failure to meet [her] needs promptly and I consider that to be an injustice resulting in maladministration.

3.29   The idea of a scheme setting priorities for assessment is to a degree itself anomalous, given that in general the object of assessment is to identify the extent and urgency of need. Provided there is not an unreasonable delay built into such schemes, they are in principle both lawful and sensible. LAC(93)2 (although primarily aimed at the particular needs of persons who misuse alcohol and/or drugs) makes a number of observations of more general application to assessments[39] and to a degree supports the idea of some assessments being carried out faster than others, stating that authorities 'should have criteria for determining the level of assessment that is appropriate to the severity or complexity of the need' (at para 14). It further advocates

---

37 Complaints against Middlesbrough District Council and Cleveland County Council Nos 94/C/0964 and 94/C/0965.

38 Complaint against Rochdale Metropolitan Borough Council No 93/C/3660.

39 See, eg, paras 26–27 concerning the applicability of its observations to the needs of homeless people, quoted at para 4.38 below.

the need for authorities to develop 'fast-track assessment' procedures (at paras 16–20). The circular is considered in detail in Chapter 10.

3.30   Where there is unreasonable delay in assessing (or an intimation that there will be), the potential service user should consider making a complaint about the delay. The effect of this, if it is coupled with a request that the complaint enter at Stage 2 of the complaints process,[40] is that the 28-day timescale is triggered and, hopefully, this should ensure a rapid acceleration in the assessment process. The complainant should emphasise (if it be the case) that the duty to assess commenced when his/her potential needs first came to the notice of the authority rather than at the time of any later request s/he may have made to be assessed.

Practice guidance

3.31   In contrast to the absence of a statutory definition of how an assessment should be conducted, and only rudimentary policy guidance,[41] detailed practice guidance has been issued,[42] the most quoted of which is *Care Management and Assessment: A Practitioners' Guide*, which is referred to henceforth in this chapter as the 'Practice Guidance'. The Practice Guidance mirrors the statutory requirements of s47(1) by emphasising the importance of treating the assessment of need as a separate exercise from consideration of service response, stating (at para 3.1):

> It is easy to slip out of thinking 'what does this person need?' into 'what have we got that he/she could have?' The focus on need is most clearly achieved where practitioners responsible for assessment do not also carry responsibility for the delivery or management of services arising from that assessment [at para 22 of the guide's summary].[43]

The assessment process should, according to the Practice Guidance (at para 3.2), include the following elements:

40 See para 12.6.
41 See, eg, paras 3.15–3.20 of the Policy Guidance.
42 *Care Management and Assessment: A Practitioners' Guide* (HMSO, 1991) ; *Care Management and Assessment: A Managers' Guide* (HMSO, 1991); and see also *Empowerment, Assessment, Care Management and the Skilled Worker* (HMSO, 1993).
43 In *R v Islington LBC ex p Rixon* (1998) 1 CCLR 119 at 129B Sedley J put it thus: 'The practice guidance . . . counsels against trimming the assessment of need to fit the available provision'.

Negotiate scope of assessment

3.32   In order to decide whether an individual is entitled to community care services, the authority is required to consider all relevant matters. It follows that an authority has a wide discretion in determining the extent to which it investigates an individual's circumstances and the other relevant facts before coming to the service provision decision. The Practice Guidance states (at para 3.3) that the:

> scope of an assessment should be related to its purpose. Simple needs will require less investigation than more complex ones. In the interests of both efficiency and consumer satisfaction, **the assessment process should be as simple, speedy and informal as possible.**

3.33   The Practice Guidance suggests that authorities may develop guidelines on the levels of assessment they consider appropriate for different types of needs – and that these guidelines should include the timescales considered reasonable for the completion of each type of assessment. Six models of assessment are illustrated, ranging from a 'simple assessment' (for instance, an assessment of eligibility for a bus pass or disabled parking badge), through a 'multiple assessment' (ie, an assessment for assistance with meals, chiropody and basic nursing), to a 'comprehensive assessment' (ie, an assessment which results in such services as family therapy, substitute care or intensive domiciliary support). An alternative and more social work theory-based analysis of various assessment models is given by the Department of Health publication *Empowerment, Assessment, Care Management and the Skilled Worker.*[44] Unfortunately, the Practice Guidance suggests that all people being assessed under NHSCCA 1990 s47(2) are entitled to a comprehensive assessment of the type detailed above (see para 3.51 where s47(2) is further considered). This advice stems in part from the general confusion over the status of services under CSDPA 1970 s2. For both legal and practical reasons the advice is wrong. From a practical viewpoint, it obviously makes little sense for a social services authority to have to undertake a comprehensive assessment purely because a person is 'disabled' rather than because his or her needs are complex. The misunderstanding underlying the guidance was considered by Carnwath J in *R v Gloucestershire CC ex p RADAR*,[45] where (referring to the Practice Guidance) he held:

44   HMSO, 1993.
45   (1998) 1 CCLR 476, at 484: CO/2764/95.

I have some sympathy with those trying to write these sort of guides since the complexity of the legislative chain, combined with the length of the titles of most of the Acts, makes short and accurate exposition particularly difficult. However, if what is intended is to define the legal obligation in respect of the disabled, then it can only be intended as a reference to the decision referred to in s4 Disabled Persons (Services, Consultation and Representation) Act 1986, that is, as to the range of services required under s2 of the 1970 Act. I take that to be the intended meaning of the word 'comprehensive'. If it is intended to mean anything else, it is misleading.

Choose an appropriate setting

3.34   The Practice Guidance (at paras 3.12–15) emphasises the importance of the assessment being conducted in an appropriate location, as this may have a material effect on the outcome of the assessment. It points out that office interviews, while administratively convenient and less costly than domiciliary assessments, may give false results if the interviewee is not at ease; and that the applicant is more likely to relax in the home setting. The following important points are also made:

> 3.13 Where the assessment is concerned with the maintenance of a person at home, the assessment should take place in that setting. If users are considering admission to residential or nursing home care, involving irreversible loss of their home, they should always be given the opportunity of experiencing that setting before making their final decision.

> 3.14 There may be advantages to some part of the assessment being undertaken in settings external to the home, for example, day or residential care settings, so that staff have longer contact with the individual. In such circumstances, assessors will be working in close collaboration with service providers.

> 3.15 In considering such options, care should be taken to avoid exposing individuals to unnecessary disruption. In addition, it is necessary to avoid assuming that behaviour will be replicated in other settings. Such considerations may, occasionally, affect assessment arrangements for hospital discharges.

User involvement

3.35   The Policy Guidance stresses the importance of involving users in the assessment process so that the resulting services fully take into account their preferences (and so far as possible those of their carers).[46] The Practice Guidance also highlights this point, emphasising the need for the assessor to establish a relationship of trust and to clarify what the assessment will entail. In most cases these will be straightforward, uncontroversial aims; the user will be seeking services and capable of articulating his or her needs. The user's evidence will be highly relevant information, so that a failure to have regard to it will in many cases vitiate any subsequent service provision decision, on the basis that it was arrived at without regard to a relevant factor. In *R v North Yorkshire CC ex p Hargreaves*,[47] the social services authority came to a service provision decision without taking into account the preferences of the disabled person – largely because (in Dyson J's opinion) her carer was very protective and probably considered by the social services authority as obstructing its ability to communicate with the disabled person. Nevertheless this did not discharge the authority's obligation to discover what her preferences were, and accordingly the decision was quashed.

3.36   Individual involvement in the assessment process becomes a more difficult question where the potential service user is unable to participate fully due to lack of ability to communicate or mental capacity. The issue becomes controversial where the potential service user chooses not to participate in (or actively objects to) the assessment.

Potential service users with communication or mental capacity difficulties

3.37   The Policy Guidance states that 'where a user is unable to participate actively [in the assessment] it is even more important that he or she should be helped to understand what is involved and the intended outcome'.[48] The Practice Guidance requires local authorities to ensure that such service users have access to an independent advocacy scheme (and requires authorities to 'encourage the development' of such schemes).[49] There is however no specific statutory right to have an advocate; the only statutory reference to such a service is found in DP(SCR)A 1986 ss1 and 2, but the government has indicated that it will not bring these provisions into force for resource reasons. The Practice Guidance states, however, that where it is clear that a user or

---

46 At paras 3.16 and 3.25.
47 (1997) 1 CCLR 104.
48 At para 3.16.
49 At para 3.28; see para 7.57.

carer would benefit from independent advocacy, s/he or they should be given information about any schemes funded by the authority or run locally. It goes on to state that it is consistent with the aims of basing service provision on the needs and wishes of users that those who are unable to express their views (for example, those with severe learning disabilities or dementia, or those who have been previously disadvantaged, such as those from minority ethnic groups) should, as a matter of priority, be supported in securing independent representation. This applies particularly to those users who have no acceptable friend or relation to speak on their behalf. Such users are likely to require an advocate or befriender on a long-term basis, whereas others may only require such assistance on a short-term basis, for example, in devising the original care plan or in the event of disagreement with the practitioner or agency.[50] The importance of advocacy when 'assessing the needs and planning the care of vulnerable, highly-dependent people who cannot easily communicate for themselves' has also been emphasised by the local government ombudsman.[51]

3.38   Despite the general rules of confidentiality under which social service authorities operate, the Practice Guidance requires that advocates are given access to relevant information concerning the person for whom they advocate and are enabled to consult with appropriate individuals in order to establish the best interests of that person.[52] The local government ombudsman has also suggested that 'confidentiality' should not be used as a reason for not disclosing relevant information in such cases. In criticising a council for not sharing information with the parents of a 24-year-old man with serious learning difficulties, she commented:

> I accept that this would not be regular practice when the Council is looking after an adult: the privacy of the individual demands that the parents be kept at some distance. But [the user] had such a high level of dependency that the Council should have been willing to reconsider its approach to parental involvement in this case.[53]

3.39   More detailed comment on the role of advocates is contained in *Care Management and Assessment: A Managers' Guide.*[54] At para 2.43 the

50 See paras 3.25–3.27.
51 Local Government Ombudsman Complaint No 97/C/4618 against Cheshire CC (1999).
52 Para 3.28 and see also LAC(2000)7 para 5.8.
53 Local Government Ombudsman Complaint No 97/C/4618 against Cheshire CC (1999).
54 HMSO, 1991.

Guide states that one of the major objectives of the community care reforms was 'to give users and carers a more powerful voice in expressing needs and influencing the services they receive'. In addition to ensuring that users are given every assistance in representing their own interests, the use of interpreters, communicators and the development of self-advocacy or self-help support groups, the Guide continues:

> 2.44 However there remain the users who, because of their disability, are unable to express their own views and/or who wish or need to have independent representatives to act on their behalf. This will include those suffering from dementia or severe learning disability. These users will be disadvantaged if the authority/agency confines itself to the promotion of self-advocacy.

The Guide's observations on the various forms of advocacy schemes are set out at para 7.57.

3.40   The Practice Guidance makes it clear that an individual's involvement in the assessment process may be involuntary (at para 3.17) and that any individual can withdraw at any stage from active involvement. As detailed above, the social services authority's duty to assess exists regardless of whether the proposed service user agrees to or objects to the assessment. The effect of such 'wilful lack of co-operation' may however be that the social services authority finds it impossible to ascertain the preferences of the user and/or carer.[55]

3.41   On this issue the Practice Guidance at times clouds the important distinction between assessment and service delivery. At para 3.17 it suggests that the assessment process might be a coercive exercise, whereas this valid observation is better made in respect of any subsequent attempt to enforce service delivery on an unwilling person. The assessment process is merely an information-gathering exercise to enable the authority to make a properly informed decision as to whether the individual requires services; if needs be, this exercise can take place without any direct contact with the potential service user – although in such cases the data obtained may be sketchy and insufficient to enable the authority to be 'satisfied' that a need for services exists. The provision of services is, however, a quite separate process and in general authorities are unable to force anyone to accept services against their will.

3.42   Subject to this caveat, para 3.17 makes a number of important observations, as follows:

---

55 Per Dyson J in *R v North Yorkshire CC ex p Hargreaves* (1997) 1 CCLR 104 at 16D.

3.17 Individuals who enter voluntarily into the assessment process should also be made aware of their entitlement to withdraw at any stage. Where the assessment is on an involuntary basis, for example as a prelude to possible compulsory admission to psychiatric hospital, it is even more important that the individuals are helped to understand, as far as they are able, the nature of the process in which they are engaged. It is less clear cut where practitioners are dealing with someone, with failing capacities, for example, relapse of a psychotic illness, where intervention has been on a voluntary basis but, at a certain threshold of risk or vulnerability, it is likely to tip over into compulsory admission. That threshold should be clearly defined in policy terms and agreed with other relevant agencies, for example, police and health authorities. All practitioners should be clear on the distinction between using assessment as an instrument of social support as opposed to social control. The former offers choices to the user while the latter imposes solutions. The one should not be allowed to shade into the other without all parties appreciating the full implications of that change.

The meaning of 'need' under s47(1)(a)

3.43   For the purposes of s47(1)(a) need is dependent on the individual circumstances of the potential user. At the next stage of the assessment process (under s47(1)(b)) the authority is required to undertake a relative assessment of need; comparing how the individual's need compares to that of others. In essence, the first stage of the assessment process focuses on the individual and the second attempts to contextualise this need in terms of the general needs and priorities of the community.

3.44   The assessment under s47(1)(a) obliges authorities to identify those needs which could potentially be satisfied by the provision of a community care service. Thus someone who is no longer able to cook for him/herself and is at risk of falling and suffering injury may be in need of the provision of meals at home or elsewhere, the provision of practical assistance in the home or the provision of a place in a residential care home; all of which are community care services. Likewise a person who is in need of an increased income may benefit from welfare rights advice which is again a community care service (NAA 1948 s29 – see para 5.26). On the other hand, if the assessment suggests that a person may benefit from (for example) medical or housing assistance, then these are requirements which are not capable of being satisfied by the provision of community care services and accordingly not 'needs' for the purposes of s47(1)(a). Where the assessment discloses a possible housing or medical need, s47(3) obliges the authority to notify the relevant housing or health authority.[56]

3.45   When using the word 'need', the Practice Guidance uses it in a looser, practitioner-oriented context, allowing it to encompass requirements which cannot be satisfied by the provision of community care services. Subject to this qualification, however, certain of its comments are illuminating:

> 11. Need is a complex concept which has been analysed in a variety of different ways. In this guidance, the term is used as a shorthand for the requirements of individuals to enable them to achieve, maintain or restore an acceptable level of social independence or quality of life, as defined by the particular care agency or authority.
>
> 16. . . . Need is a multi-faceted concept which, for the purposes of this guidance, is sub-divided into six broad categories, each of which should be covered in a comprehensive assessment of need:
> - personal/social care
> - health care
> - accommodation
> - finance
> - education/employment/leisure
> - transport/access.

3.46   Need is a subjective and objective, complex, multi-faceted concept. For instance, a person of profound religious conviction who is assessed as requiring residential accommodation may have a concomitant need for that accommodation to be sufficiently close to a church to enable him or her to enjoy a full religious life. That is a relevant need, as it is one which can be met in terms of 'community care services'. The need should therefore be recorded in the assessment process under s47(1)(a), although this does not mean that the authority is then bound to cater for it when making its decision under s47(1)(b).

3.47   In *R v Avon CC ex p M*,[57] the court was concerned, not with religious need, but with an individual's psychological need. The applicant M had Down's syndrome and a symptom of this was that he had formed an entrenched view that he wanted to go to a particular

---

56 The consequent obligations on the health and housing authorities are considered below at paras 6.57 and 10.8 respectively. Although there is no duty on the notified authority to respond following notification, the service user will benefit where parallel duties are triggered.

57 (1999) 2 CCLR 185; [1994] 2 FLR 1006; [1994] 2 FCR 259.

residential home even though an alternative, cheaper home objectively catered for all his other needs. The authority, in deciding what accommodation he needed, had regard to a psychologist's report which stated that M's entrenched position was typical of and therefore caused by the Down's syndrome. The authority refused to fund the more expensive home on the ground that it would set a precedent by accepting psychological need as being part of an individual's needs which could force it to pay more than it would usually expect to pay in such cases. Rejecting this argument, Henry J held:

> The law is clear. The council have to provide for the applicant's needs. Those needs may properly include psychological needs. Where they do, it is not right to describe the payment in meeting those needs as 'forcing the authority to pay more than the usual amount it would be prepared to pay for the individual concerned'. The authority would simply be paying what the law required, and not being forced to pay more. So the introduction of the question of precedent in this context is, in my judgment, potentially misleading.

and:

> The [local authority's report] . . . proceeds on the basis that the psychological need can simply be 'excluded': . . . M's needs are thus arbitrarily restricted to the remainder of his needs, which are then described as 'usual'. Meeting his psychological needs is then treated as mere 'preference', a preference involving payments greater than usual.

3.48   In *R v Kirklees MBC ex p Daykin*,[58] Collins J observed that it was 'not always easy to differentiate between what is a need and what is merely the means by which such need can be met'. The case concerned a disabled person who had been assessed as being unable to manage the stairs to his council flat. Collins J considered the 'need' in this case was to be able to get into and out of his dwelling. In this case, 'the means by which this need could be met' included, among other things, the provision of a stairlift. Not infrequently local authorities will be able to meet an assessed 'need' in more than one way, and this issue is considered further at para 3.89 below.

3.49   Need may not only vary in nature, it may also vary with time. In *R v Mid-Glamorgan CC ex p Miles*,[59] the applicant was a prisoner whose only realistic chance of obtaining parole depended on the local authority agreeing to fund his placement at a drug rehabilitation

---

58 (1998) 1 CCLR 512.

59 (1993) unreported, but see January 1994 *Legal Action* 21 and see *Social Services and Child Care Encyclopaedia*, section D1 p485.

hostel; the issue concerned whether the authority's duty to assess could be triggered by such a potential need (rather than a present existing need). The case was compromised on terms that the authority did carry out the assessment. The Practice Guidance (at para 3.41) also distinguishes between immediate needs, acute short-term needs and chronic long-term needs. The issue of future need is most apparent in relation to persons in hospital who are not yet ready for discharge. They have no immediate need for any community care services, but clearly it is important that the assessment process commences as soon as possible. The *Hospital Discharge Workbook* states that the assessment process for community care services (ie, future needs) should commence well before any decision to discharge is taken (see para 124).

Delegation of duty to assess

3.50   The duty to assess under NHSCCA 1990 s47 is a social services obligation and there is no express power for the authority to delegate that function to a third party or other agency. In practice authorities often request third parties to carry out a key function in the assessment (for instance, occupational therapists in assessing the need for home adaptations). Frequently an authority will be bound by that third party's view on need, especially if it has expertise which the social services authority lacks. Nevertheless, the authority is ultimately charged with making the assessment decision. LAC (93)2 gives guidance on the use of third parties in such situations, and clearly these principles have wider application.

> 14 ... LAs should ensure that:
> • arrangements have been agreed with all the agencies in their area to which misusers are likely to present for help, which will enable those agencies to initiate assessment procedures where in their view they are indicated;
> • arrangements are in place to facilitate the assessment of a person by another authority where that person is ordinarily resident in that other authority's area, for example by agreeing with another LA to undertake an assessment on that authority's behalf;
> • individuals who are of no settled residence are not excluded from assessment by means of eligibility criteria which require duration of residence ...
>
> 25. Some alcohol and/or drug misusing clients of the Probation Service will continue to seek access to residential and non-residential

care, and LAs should liaise with probation services to ensure that these needs can be considered within the community care arrangements. Attention should be given to establishing joint assessment or common assessment procedures, such as those LAs have developed with other client groups . . .

27. As with alcohol and drug misusers, LAs should have flexible systems of assessment and care management that allow such people [homeless people with other needs] access to the services they need in a way that meets their special circumstances. Their homelessness may in itself mean that an urgent response is called for. LAs will be aware that there are a wide variety of agencies which specialise in providing care for homeless people. As with specialist alcohol and drug providers, these agencies may be in a position to assist in assessment procedures.

Assessment under s47(2)

3.51   As noted above (see para 3.33) Carnwath J in *R v Gloucestershire CC ex p RADAR*,[60] found that the Department of Health had misunderstood the effect of NHSCCA 1990 s47(2) when issuing its Practice Guidance. Indeed, s47(2) is either an enormously confusing and unnecessary subsection or a modest provision aimed at flagging up the duty to provide services under CSDPA 1970 s2. In the House of Lords decision in *Barry*, Lord Clyde inclined to the latter point of view, explaining the purpose of s2 thus:

> So far as the twofold provision in s47(1) and (2) is concerned the obligation on the local authority introduced by s47(1) was to carry out an assessment on its own initiative and the separate provision made in subs (2) cannot have been intended merely to achieve that purpose. It seems to me that there is sufficient reason for the making of a distinctive provision in subs (2) in the desire to recognise the distinctive procedural situation relative to the disabled. But it does not follow that any distinction exists in the considerations which may or may not be taken into account in making an assessment in the case of the disabled as compared with any other case.

The practical application of s47(2) is therefore very limited, and its existence is probably attributable to 'ex abundanti cautela' (from excessive caution).

---

60 (1998) 1 CCLR 476 at 484.

The written record of the assessment

3.52   The Practice Guidance suggests that all assessments are likely to be recorded on some kind of pro forma, but advises that such documents be used with discretion (para 3.52); 'they should act as a help and not a hindrance to the process of understanding'.

3.53   There is, however, no statutory format to assessments; indeed an assessment may not be recorded at all, or merely evidenced in a conversation or as a scribbled note on the corner of a social worker's contact sheet. Many simple assessments (for instance, the provision of a disabled person's parking badge) may be evidenced by little more than performance: the handing over of the badge, etc.

3.54   The Practice Guidance states (at para 3.54) that a 'copy of the assessment of needs should usually be shared with the potential service user, any representative of that user and all other people who have agreed to provide a service. Except where no intervention is deemed necessary, this record will usually be combined with a written care plan'. There is, however, (subject to the comments detailed below) no statutory obligation upon authorities to comply with this guidance. Many authorities do not appear to provide copies of assessments or care plans in the absence of a specific request.

3.55   Where a service-user has difficulty obtaining a copy of his/her assessment and/or care plan, s/he can make a request for the file to be copied to him/her (see para 2.25). The assessment and care plan will be part of a person's social services file and therefore accessible via this process.

Community care assessments and disabled children

3.56   The duty to assess arises when a potential service-user comes to an authority's attention who may be in need of community care services (as defined by NHSCCA 1990 s46). Not uncommonly it is suggested that community care services are only available to persons aged over 18. This is not, however, the case. The age restriction for each s46 community care service is considered in detail in Chapter 5, but suffice it to say, only NAA 1948 s29 services are available solely to adults. By way of example, home help services under NHSA 1977 Sch 8 para 3 are unquestionably community care services and they can be provided in any case where a household has someone (of any age) suffering from illness, lying-in, an expectant mother, aged, or handicapped as a result of having suffered from illness or by congenital deformity. In such a case, if the person in question were a child, the duty to assess under s47(1) would still be triggered.

The service provision decision: what needs must be satisfied by the provision of services?

3.57 Once the authority has gathered together all the evidence it considers necessary (reports, interviews etc), it is obliged to decide what the individual's community care needs are. Section 47(1)(a) does not require the authority to assess an individual's 'needs' but his/her 'need for community care services'. The assessment process may reveal many services or other items which would enrich the individual's life; the local authority's statutory obligation is however initially limited to identifying those community care services which the individual 'needs'. In this context 'need' has a meaning more akin to 'could benefit from' rather than 'must have'. This distinction is important because, even if the assessment identifies a person as having a need for community care services, it does not follow that these services must be provided; under s47(1)(b) the authority must make a separate decision whether all or some of the assessed needs call for the provision of any community care services.

3.58 Although the Court of Appeal decision in *R v Gloucestershire CC ex p Barry*[61] was reversed by the House of Lords,[62] the following observations of Swinton-Thomas LJ concerning the effect of s47(1) were in no way contradicted by the Lords:

> Section 47(1)(a) provides for the provision of Community Care Services generally, the need for such services, the carrying out of an assessment and then, Section 47(1)(b) gives the Local Authority a discretion as to whether to provide those services. The discretion in making the decision under s47(1)(b) arises by reason of the words 'having regard to the results of that assessment'. In making that decision they will be entitled to take into account resources.

61 [1996] 4 All ER 421; (1997) 1 CCLR 19, CA.
62 [1997] AC 584; (1997) 1 CCLR 40, HL.

Eligibility criteria and the question of resources

3.59 Once an authority has assessed the needs of a potential service user (under s47(1)(a)), s47(1)(b) then requires that it decide whether that person's needs are such that they 'call for the provision by them of any such services'. Section 47(1)(b) obliges the authority to 'have regard to' the results of the assessment, rather than obliging it to provide services to meet all the identified needs.

3.60 Under s47(1)(b) an authority decides whether the individual's assessed needs are such that services should be provided. In order to take this decision, the authority will frequently have regard to a locally agreed scale of need, known as the 'eligibility criteria'. Need must often be put in the context of the community care implications of not providing that need. This process has been described, in guidance, in the following way:[63]

> 13. An authority may take into account the resources available when deciding how to respond to an individual's assessment. However, once the authority has indicated that a service should be provided to meet an individual's needs and the authority is under a legal obligation to provide it or arrange for its provision, then the service must be provided. It will not be possible for an authority to use budgeting difficulties as a basis for refusing to provide the service.

> 14. Authorities can be helped in this process by defining eligibility criteria, ie a system of banding which assigns individuals to particular categories, depending on the extent of the difficulties they encounter in carrying out everyday tasks and relating the level of response to the degree of such difficulties. Any 'banding' should not, however, be rigidly applied, as account needs to be taken of individual circumstances. Such eligibility criteria should be phrased in terms of the factors identified in the assessment process.

3.61 Eligibility criteria are generally based on a risk or harm assessment; for instance, in relation to home care assistance an authority might adopt a system of relative priorities for services. This at its crudest might be based upon the following criteria.

---

63 CI(92) 34; although the guidance was expressed as being cancelled on 1 April 1994, Sedley J accepted that 'in the sense that it gives plainly sensible advice' its content is still relevant although not mandatory – see *R v Islington LBC ex p Rixon* (1998) 1 CCLR 119 at 127B.

Example[64]

Priority 1 Persons who are likely to suffer serious physical harm within 72 hours if the service is not provided.

Priority 2 Persons who are likely to suffer serious physical harm within 28 days if the service is not provided.

Priority 3 Persons who are likely to suffer measurable harm (which is not minor) within three months if the service is not provided.

Priority 4 Persons who, although not at risk of physical harm, are likely to suffer serious social isolation if a service is not provided.

3.62   The authority might then state as a matter of general policy (always open to be displaced where exceptional circumstances exist) that it will only provide domiciliary services (ie, home-based services) to priority groups 1 and 2 and that groups 3 and 4 would only be eligible for community-based services such as day centres and workshop placements. The legal basis for such a policy is that the authority in general only considers a person as having a 'need which calls for the provision of services' (under s47(1)(b)) when his or her requirement for services comes within the description of the relevant priority category.

3.63   The need for central guidance on eligibility criteria (eg, on what minimum needs must always be met) has been mentioned by many commentators; the Audit Commission, for instance, stated:

> The effect of all this is to produce a maze of different criteria which are complex and difficult for people to understand. People who qualify for care in one authority may not qualify in another. The price of freedom of local decision-making is considerable variation in access to services between areas. Authorities may be able to reduce the worst effects of the inequities that result by comparing approaches and, here again, guidance may be useful.[65]

64 This example is deliberately crude; a set of criteria as basic as these would be vulnerable to challenge as unlawful. The use of eligibility criteria based on an assessment of 'likely harm' is particularly problematical in relation to children's cases; although children can of course suffer actual harm if services are not provided, they can also fail to make their next appropriate developmental milestone (Children Act 1989 s17(10)(a)). Risk assessment is also a question of family dynamics in children's cases, whereas in adults' cases there is a tendency to focus more on the user and less on the family.

65 *Balancing the Care Equation: Progress with Community Care* (HMSO, 1996) para 32.

3.64   The system has merit for a number of underlying policy and planning reasons. It most importantly gives authorities the possibility of resolving the fundamental contradiction within community care law: the fact that they are legally obliged to meet 'need', which (potentially) is almost unlimited, from finite resources. The point was made by Sedley J in *R v Islington LBC ex p Rixon*:[66] 'Even an unequivocal set of statutory duties cannot produce money where there is none or by itself repair gaps in the availability of finance'.

3.65   Authorities are required therefore to construct community care plans[67] based on detailed information about the potential care needs of their communities. Much of this information is already available via the register of disabled people, the data on hospital discharges, the census information on the elderly and so on. Authorities should therefore be able to predict the likely demand for services. They should then balance this expected demand against the available budget for community care services by constructing suitable eligibility criteria. Where budgets are squeezed, the criteria will be more restrictive and vice versa. Criteria cannot, however, be drawn so tightly that persons in great need are denied services. In *R v Gloucestershire CC ex p Mahfood*,[68] McCowan LJ stated:

> I should stress, however, that there will, in my judgment, be situations where a reasonable authority could only conclude that some arrangements were necessary to meet the needs of a particular disabled person and in which it could not reasonably conclude that a lack of resources provided an answer. Certain persons would be at severe physical risk if they were unable to have some practical assistance in their own homes. In those situations, I cannot conceive that an authority would be held to have acted reasonably if it used shortage of resources as a reason for not being satisfied that some arrangement should be made to meet those persons' needs.[69]

3.66   In *R v Gloucestershire CC ex p Barry*,[70] the House of Lords considered the legality of eligibility criteria. The case arose because the authority had its resources for community care drastically cut by an unexpected change in the size of the grant made by the Department of Health.

---

66   (1998) 1 CCLR 119 at 126D.
67   NHSCCA 1990 s46, and see para 2.10.
68   (1997) 1 CCLR 7; 94 LGR 593, DC.
69   94 LGR 593 at 605. Although McCowan LJ's decision concerning the duty to provide services under CSPDA 1970 s2 was reversed by the Court of Appeal and upheld by the House of Lords, both appellate courts echoed his comments in respect of a minimum basis for need.
70   (1997) 1 CCLR 40; [1997] AC 584.

The authority wrote to those people (about 1,500, it seems) on its lowest priority level advising them it had decided that their home care service would be reduced or withdrawn. Some of the people who were affected and (crucially) were receiving their services under CSDPA 1970 s2 sought a judicial review of the decision. Their basic argument was straightforward; their condition had not changed and so their need for services remained. How could the state of an authority's finances make their individual need no longer a need? The solution adopted by the House of Lords was that authorities can change their eligibility criteria and if they then become more austere, they can reassess existing service users against these new criteria. If on such a reassessment it is found that they are no longer eligible for assistance, then the service can be withdrawn. Accordingly Gloucestershire had acted unlawfully, by not reassessing before coming to a decision as to whether the service should be withdrawn or reduced.

3.67   Lord Clyde, who gave the leading judgment of the majority, held that:

> The words 'necessary' and 'need' are both relative expressions, admitting in each case a considerable range of meaning . . . In deciding whether there is a necessity to meet the needs of the individual some criteria have to be provided. Such criteria are required both to determine whether there is a necessity at all or only, for example, a desirability, and also to assess the degree of necessity . . . In the framing of the criteria to be applied it seems to me that the severity of a condition may have to be matched against the availability of resources.

3.68   The majority decision has been justly criticised as being confused and inconsistent[71] and indeed the Lords themselves have sought to restrict the impact of the decision. Subsequently, in *Re T (A Minor),*[72] a differently constituted House of Lords held that 'resource arguments' in the *Barry* decision were in large measure restricted to cases concerning CSDPA 1970 s2, the statutory construction of which the Lords held to be a 'strange one'. Indeed the court found certain aspects of the majority's reasoning in *Barry* to be 'with respect . . . very doubtful . . . '. A similar line was taken by the Court of Appeal in *R v Sefton MBC ex p Help the Aged,*[73] where the Master of the Rolls felt

---

71   See, eg, L Clements 'The collapsing duty' and B Rayment '*Ex p Barry* in the House of Lords' both in *Judicial Review* Vol 2 issue 3 and L Clements 'Case note' (1998) 20(1) JSWFL 86.
72   (1998) 1 CCLR 352.
73   (1997) 1 CCLR 57.

'compelled' to follow the reasoning of the majority in the *Barry* decision, but only to a limited degree. The Court of Appeal effectively distinguished the *Barry* decision, as one peculiar to the situation under CSDPA 1970 s2. This line was also adopted by Scott Baker J in *R v Bristol CC ex p Penfold*,[74] when he rejected the respondent's argument that its resource problems justified its refusal to carry out a community care assessment. It was also followed by Dyson J in *R v Birmingham CC ex p Taj Mohammed*,[75] where he held that housing authorities were not entitled to take resources into account when deciding whether or not to approve a disabled facilities grant.

3.69   The effect of the House of Lords judgment, however, means that social services authorities can (to a greater or lesser degree) take their available resources into account, when coming to a decision as to whether a persons 'need' for services is such that it is necessary to provide those services. This principle is, however, subject to four significant constraints.

Constraint 1

3.70   When such authorities make their eligibility criteria more severe, existing service users must be the subject of a full individual community care re-assessment before any decision can be taken on the withdrawal of services (see para 3.66 above).

Constraint 2

3.71   The extent of an authority's available resources can only be taken into account during the assessment process and in deciding whether it is necessary to provide the disabled person with the services s/he has been assessed as needing. Once, however, it has been decided that the services should be provided, then they must be provided, regardless of resource constraints. This principle is illustrated by the following decisions.

3.72   In *R v Wigan MBC ex p Tammadge*,[76] the applicant lived with her four children, three of whom had severe learning disabilities. Over a considerable period of time she sought a larger property in order to be able to better provide for their needs. In due course a complaints panel concluded that the family needed a larger property and asked

---

74   (1998) 1 CCLR 315.
75   (1998) 1 CCLR 441.
76   (1998) 1 CCLR 581.

the director of social services to investigate the possibility of one being found. Following the hearing, a social worker visited the applicant on 22 October and made it clear that the social services department accepted the panels recommendations. Subsequently on 15 November a multi-disciplinary meeting was convened where it was again agreed that a larger property was needed. The matter was then referred to a meeting of senior officers and councillors. This meeting decided however that 'it was not appropriate to commit the authority to the purchase or adaptation of a larger property'.

3.73   In quashing that decision, Forbes J held that by 22 September at the latest Wigan's 'own professionally qualified staff and advisors' had concluded that her need for larger accommodation had been established.

> Once the duty had arisen in this way, it was not lawful of Wigan to refuse to perform that duty because of shortage of or limits upon its financial resources.

3.74   *R v Sutton LBC ex p Tucker*[77] concerned a 32-year-old learning-disabled applicant who had sensory impairments and who was in an NHS trust unit awaiting discharge for over two years. The local authority had accepted that her needs called for the provision of 'non-institutional accommodation' shared with other similarly disabled persons with support provided by a specialist charity. The cost of providing this was likely to be very large and the local authority there-fore (in the opinion of the court) delayed unreasonably. Hidden J declared that the council had acted unlawfully in breach of the Policy Guidance in failing to make a service provision decision under NHSCCA 1990 s47(1)(b) once it was satisfied that the applicant had a need for services that it was necessary to meet.[78]

Constraint 3

3.75   Resource availability alone cannot be 'determinative'. In the *Barry* decision Lord Clyde held that Gloucestershire's actions 'amounted to treating the cut in resources as the sole factor to be taken into account, and that was, in my judgment, unlawful'. Hirst LJ (in the Court of Appeal) had held that resources were 'no more than one factor in an overall assessment, where no doubt the objective needs of the indi-vidual disabled person will always be the paramount consideration'.

---

77 (1998) 1 CCLR 251.
78 See para 3.87 below where the case is considered further.

3.76   This principle appears to be violated by the procedures followed by many social services 'allocation panels'. Such panels meet regularly and have responsibility for deciding how many people get a place in a residential or nursing home. Typically, after carrying out a community care assessment a social worker will advise the elderly person that although the criteria for obtaining a place in a home appear to be satisfied, the actual decision can only be made by the 'allocation panel'. The elderly person is told therefore that his or her name will be put forward for consideration at the next panel meeting.

3.77   The panel is sometimes composed only of senior officers although sometimes councillors may also be present. The panel meeting is typically advised as to how much money is available that week/month for new places in homes. At its crudest it is told that (for instance) six residents have died in the last two weeks so the panel can allocate six new places, although normally the issues considered are apparently more sophisticated. Nevertheless, no matter how the question is dressed up, all that is happening is that the service provision decision is being made solely on the basis of resources (and if no money is available that week, the person in need has to wait until the next such meeting).

Waiting lists/physical resource shortages

3.78   In *R v Gloucestershire CC ex p Barry*[79] and in *R v Sefton MBC ex p Help the Aged*[80] the distinction was drawn between the assessment of need and the provision of services to meet that need. A local authority's financial resources could be taken into account when deciding whether a person had a need and whether that need should be met. However once a need had been identified which the authority had decided it should meet, then at this stage the extent of an authority's financial resources ceased to be relevant. Lord Clyde, in the *Gloucestershire* case stated that a disabled person's right to services under CSDPA 1970 s2:

> was a right to have the arrangements made which the local authority was satisfied were necessary to meet his needs. The duty only arises if or when the local authority is so satisfied. But when it does arise, then it is clear that a shortage of resources will not excuse a failure in the performance of the duty.

3.79   The courts have taken a different approach where the resource short-

79   (1997) 1 CCLR 40; [1997] 2 All ER 1.
80   (1997) 1 CCLR 57.

age concerns physical or human resources as opposed to financial. In such cases the courts have generally adopted a realistic approach; provided the authority is taking reasonable steps to resolve the problem the court will not intervene. Thus in *R v Lambeth LBC ex p A1 and A2*,[81] the Court of Appeal held that provided the authority was making a 'sincere and determined' effort to resolve the physical resource problem, then it would not intervene.

3.80   However where an authority makes no such effort to resolve such a shortage, the situation will be otherwise. In *R v Islington LBC ex p Rixon*,[82] for instance, Sedley J considered that a local authority could not assess someone as needing a service (for instance, a day centre placement) and then fail to provide it, merely because none was available. This reason alone would be insufficient. He asserted:

> There are two points at which, in my judgment, the respondent local authority has fallen below the requirements of the law. The first concerns the relationship of need to availability . . . the local authority has, it appears, simply taken the existing unavailability of further facilities as an insuperable obstacle to any further attempt to make provision . . .

3.81   It is in this context that the court will examine the legality of a waiting list. In *R v Liverpool CC ex p Winter*,[83] leave was given to challenge an authority's practice of placing people (who it had assessed as requiring a service) on a waiting list; immediately prior to the substantive hearing the authority withdrew its defence and agreed to provide the assessed service and pay the applicant's full costs. While the efficient use of resources dictates that authorities may operate a relatively short waiting list (in chronological terms), a longer list will be open to challenge, unless the authority is making 'sincere and determined' efforts to resolve the shortage.

Constraint 4

3.82   Resource availability will not be a relevant factor where a disabled person would not be at severe physical risk if the services were not provided. In such a case, McCowan LJ held that he could not 'conceive that an authority would be held to have acted reasonably if it used shortages of resources as a reason [for not providing the service]'.

---

81 (1998) 1 CCLR 336 and see also *R v Islington LBC ex p McMillan* (1997) 1 CCLR 7 at 17.

82 (1997) 1 CCLR 7.

83 (1997) unreported but see (1997) 1 CCLR 5 and (1998) 1 CCLR 118.

3.83   When the issue of 'severe physical risk' arises, the obligation on the local authority stems not so much from the community care legislation as from the Human Rights Act 1998. The duty to protect life (article 2) and prevent degrading treatment (article 3) requires that positive action be taken.

The provision of services and the care plan

3.84   Once an authority has made a decision under NHSCCA 1990 s47(1)(b) that a person's need is such that community care services are called for, then the authority must make arrangements for those services to be provided.[84] The Practice Guidance describes this final phase of the assessment process as 'care planning'. Good practice requires that the authority specify in a care plan what services the individual is entitled to receive, their frequency, duration and so on.

3.85   A care plan is essentially a statement of the arrangements that are necessary in order that the services be delivered to the qualifying individual. The Practice Guidance states, as follows:[85]

> Care plans should be set out in concise written form, linked with the assessment of need. The document should be accessible to the user, for example, in Braille or translated into the user's own language. A copy should be given to the user but it should also, subject to constraints of confidentiality, be shared with other contributors to the plan. The compilation and distribution of such records has implications for the necessary levels of administrative support.
>
> A care plan should contain:
> - the overall objectives
> - the specific objectives:
>   – users
>   – carers
>   – service providers
> - the criteria for measuring the achievement of these objectives
> - the services to be provided by which personnel/agency
> - the cost to the user and the contributing agencies
> - the other options considered
> - any point of difference between the user, carer, care planning practitioner or other agency

84 In cases of emergency the services can be provided before the assessment: s47(5).

85 *Care Management and Assessment: A Practitioners' Guide* (HMSO, 1991) para 4.37; and see generally CI(92)34 para 15 (para 1.30 above) and Policy Guidance at paras 3.24–3.26.

- any unmet needs with reasons – to be separately notified to the service planning system
- the named person(s) responsible for implementing , monitoring and reviewing the care plan
- the first date of the first planned review.

3.86 In *R v Islington LBC ex p Rixon*,[86] Sedley J accepted the respondent's submission that 'nowhere in the legislation is a care plan, by that or any other name required' and that 'a care plan is nothing more than a clerical record of what has been decided and what is planned'. However he held that this:

> . . . far from marginalising the care plan, places it at the centre of any scrutiny of the local authority's due discharge of its functions. As paragraph 3.24 of the policy guidance indicates, a care plan is the means by which the local authority assembles the relevant information and applies it to the statutory ends, and hence affords good evidence to any inquirer of the due discharge of its statutory duties. It cannot, however, be quashed as if it were a self-implementing document.

3.87 In *R v Sutton LBC ex p Tucker*,[87] Hidden J held that a document put forward by the respondent as a care plan, was not, since (among other things):

> There are no stated overall objectives in terms of long-term obligations, carers' obligations or service providers, there are no criteria for the measurement of objectives because the objectives themselves are not recorded in any care plan. There are no costings, no long-term options, no residential care options considered, there are no recorded points of difference, there is no reference to unmet need and there is no reference to a next date of review.

The objectives of a care plan

3.88 The Policy Guidance, at para 3.24 states as follows:

> Once needs have been assessed, the services to be provided or arranged and the objectives of any intervention should be agreed in the form of a care plan. The objective of ensuring that service provision should, as far as possible, preserve or restore normal living implies the following order of preference in construing care packages which may include health provision, both primary and specialist, housing provision and social services provision:

86 (1998) 1 CCLR 119 at 128.
87 (1998) 1 CCLR 251.

- Support for the user in his or her own home including day and domiciliary care, respite care, the provision of disability equipment and adaptations to accommodation as necessary;
- A move to more suitable accommodation, which might be sheltered or very sheltered housing, together with the provision of social services support;
- A move to another private household, ie, to live with relatives or friends or as part of an adult fostering scheme;
- Residential care;
- Nursing home care;
- Long-stay care in hospital.

Accordingly in *Tucker* (above) the local authority's failure to develop an effective option for the applicant's discharge from hospital even though she was fit to leave was held to be unlawful.[88]

Choosing between alternative care packages

3.89   The assessment process may identify needs which are capable of being met by two alternative care packages. It is in respect of such situations that the choice of accommodation provisions apply (see para 4.55). Obviously there will be occasions when the two packages are not, on analysis, equivalent; in *R v Avon CC ex p M*[89] for instance, the court held that the package put forward by the authority was not equivalent because it did not meet the applicant's psychological needs.

3.90   Where the authority can meet the assessed need by two or more different care packages, it is not unreasonable for the cost of the options to be taken into account by the authority. The Policy Guidance puts the point as follows:

> 3.25   The aim should be to secure the most cost-effective package of services that meets the user's care needs, taking account of the user's and carers' own preferences. Where supporting the user in a home of their own would provide a better life, this is to be preferred to admission to residential or nursing home care. However, local authorities also have a responsibility to meet needs within resources available and this will sometimes involve difficult decisions where it will be necessary to strike a balance between meeting the needs identified within available resources and meeting the care preferences of the individual. Where agreement between all parties is not possible, the points of difference should be recorded. Failure to

88   Ibid at 274H.
89   (1999) 2 CCLR 185; [1994] 2 FLR 1006; [1994] 2 FCR 259.

satisfy particular needs can result in even greater burdens on particular services, for example where a person becomes homeless as a result of leaving inappropriate accommodation which has been provided following discharge from hospital.

3.91 While no one would dispute much of this statement, it does skate over a number of particular difficulties, most obviously the question of how one can compare the relative cost of two alternative services. This difficulty has been expressed by the Audit Commission thus:

> The financial incentive for authorities to use residential care remains strong. In nearly all situations it is substantially cheaper for local authorities to place people in residential care, even where there is no difference between the gross cost of residential care and care at home.[90]

3.92 The principal reasons for this apparently surprising situation can be illustrated by considering the example of an elderly widow living on income support in the community. The community care assessment might show that she has a need to be helped with many activities, getting up, in the bathroom, dressing, feeding and that there is a need for someone to keep an eye on her. Most obviously the local authority could construct two care plans to meet that assessed need; the first would be for home care or meals on wheels and possibly a night sitting service. This might be very expensive. The alternative would be a placement in a residential care home, where all the various identified needs could also be met. If the gross cost of the care home option is £220 per week and the cost of home care to the local authority is £10 per hour, then it might decide that if the package requires more than 22 hours home care (or a total cost of £220) per week, then it will expect the care home option to be adopted. However the net cost in this case to the local authority would be less, in fact approximately half, taking account of the income support, residential and other allowances.[91]

3.93 The local authority might then state that if the package requires more than 11 hours (or a total cost of over £110) per week it will expect the care home option to be adopted. In fact if the widow owns her own

---

90 *Balancing the Care Equation* (HMSO, 1996) at para 40.

91 The effect of the 'residential care allowance' in subsidising residential care home placements over domiciliary placements was noted in the White Paper *Modernising Social Services* (1998) para 7.25 and will be abolished from April 2002, *The NHS Plan: The Government's Response to the Royal Commission on Long-term Care* para 2.33, Cm 4818-II, July 2000.

home, it will always be cheaper to opt for a RCH, since the local authority could then sell the home and incur no costs.

3.94   The courts have yet to decide what is meant by the 'cheaper option'; is it the gross cost (ie, the cost borne by the UK plc) or the net cost (ie, the cost borne by the local authority) or the actual cost, (ie, taking into account the cost borne by the individual). The local authority can however only begin to consider the cheaper care home option if it is a real alternative. If, for instance, the widow's GP has written to the local authority stating that her patient would suffer a nervous breakdown if she were forced into a care home, then there would not generally be any option; the home care package would meet her needs, whereas the care home package would make her ill. In such a case the local authority would be required to fund *all* the home care costs it felt necessary in order to meet her assessed needs.

3.95   Given that one of the six objectives of the community care reforms was to 'enable people to live in their own homes wherever feasible and sensible',[92] the cost argument needs to be approached with caution. The authority must, it is submitted, when considering the relative costs, ignore any contribution it will be receiving from the user[93] or the DSS. It should also 'act under' the Policy Guidance para 3.24, quoted above, namely endeavour where possible to promote independence and the most 'community based option' feasible.

3.96   In principle, however, an authority is entitled to choose the cheaper option where there are two equally suitable ways of meeting an assessed need. In *R v Lancashire CC ex p Ingham*,[94] Hidden J held:

> In taking the decision the respondent was deciding that under s47(1)(b) of the 1990 Act the provision of residential care within s21 to s27 of the 1948 Act, rather than 24-hour care in the home, was called for and that under s2 of the 1970 Act it was not necessary to meet the applicant's needs by [practical assistance in the form of 24-hour care service being provided], as her needs were best met by the provision of residential care under the 1948 Act.
>
> In so far as the Council had regard to the fact that the residential placement was a more cost-effective means of meeting needs than 24-hour care in the home, it was entitled to do so. It was always aware

---

92 *Caring for People* para 1.11.
93 Policy Guidance para 3.31 states that 'the provision of services . . . should not be related to the ability of the user . . . to meet the costs' and that 'assessment of financial means should, therefore, follow the assessment of need and decisions about service provision'.
94 (1995) 5 July, QBD, CO/774 and 108/95 (unreported).

that identified needs must be met, but that cost-effective use of resources might be relevant to the type of service provision.[95]

Hidden J's judgment was upheld by the Court of Appeal,[96] where Swinton Thomas LJ held:

It is true that resources played a part in the decision that was made as to placement, but I am not persuaded that the Lancashire County Council behaved in any way improperly or unlawfully in carrying out the duties laid on them by Section 2 of the 1970 Act.

Likewise, in *R v Kirklees MBC ex p Daykin*,[97] the disabled person had been assessed as being unable to manage the stairs to his council flat. Collins J considered the 'need' in this case was to be able to get into and out of his dwelling. He held that it was not unreasonable for the authority to decide that this need could either be met by the provision of a stair lift, or by re-housing and for it to take into account the respective costs of both options, in deciding how to meet this need.

3.97   What local authorities are not able to do, is to adopt a rigid policy of not funding care packages in the community where the cost exceeds a certain arbitrary figure. In her report concerning a complaint against Liverpool City Council,[98] the local ombudsman considered the council financial ceiling (of £110 pw) on the level of domiciliary care provided, which reflected the average cost to the council for an older person in residential care. The ombudsman found that in setting the limit the council had fettered its discretion. She found no evidence that the council had ever in fact exercised its discretion to exceed the limit and that such a fees policy was unfair and unreasonably discriminated against elderly people (as opposed to other service users).

A refusal of services

3.98   Disabled people are entitled to refuse to accept services, either explicitly or by their behaviour. In *R v Kensington and Chelsea RLBC ex p Kujtim*,[99] for instance, the Court of Appeal held that the duty to provide accommodation (under NAA 1948 s21 see para 4.1 below)

---

95 From the uncorrected draft transcript of the judgment.

96 *R v Lancashire CC ex p RADAR* [1996] 4 All ER 421.

97 (1998) 1 CCLR 512.

98 Complaint 96/C/4315, 20 August 1998; (1999) 2 CCLR 128. A sum of £10,000 compensation was recommended by the ombudsman.

99 (1999) 2 CCLR 340 at 354I.

can be treated as discharged if the applicant 'either unreasonably refuses to accept the accommodation provided or if, following its provision, by his conduct he manifests a persistent and unequivocal refusal to observe the reasonable requirements of the local authority in relation to the occupation of such accommodation'. The same would presumably hold true of a disabled person who behaved offensively to a home care assistant or refused to comply with the reasonable requirements of a day centre etc; although in deciding whether to withdraw the service the applicant's mental health and its treatability may be relevant factors.[100]

Unmet need

3.99   The Practice Guidance advises that unmet need be recorded in a care plan. Some uncertainty has arisen over whether this is indeed unlawful. In relation to 'need' as the word is used in NHSCCA 1990 s47(1), there is no legal problem with the concept of unmet need. Under s47(1)(a) authorities have to assess a person's need for community care services, whereas s47(1)(b) clearly envisages that not all of these needs will call for the provision of services. This aspect is considered in detail above (under 'eligibility criteria'). Those services which a person is assessed as 'needing', but for which s/he does not score sufficiently highly on the scale of eligibility, will be needs which do not 'call for the provision' of services. Accordingly these could quite reasonably be recorded as 'unmet need', ie, services that the authority would provide if it had more liberal eligibility criteria (more resources available). However, the Practice Guidance (at paras 4.32–4.36) appears to use the phrase 'unmet need' as if it meant services which the authority had failed to provide even when it was under an obligation to do so. If this is what it is indeed saying, it must be wrong.

3.100   As noted (see para 3.14) the recording of unmet need is also an essential component of a local authority's strategic planning obligations. In *R v Bristol CC ex p Penfold*,[101] Scott Baker J. held that the duty to assess was not predicated upon the likelihood of a service being provided, stating:

> I do not, therefore accept [the] submission that Parliament cannot have intended expenditure to a pointless end when it was clear that

100   See *Croydon LBC v Moody* (1999) 2 CCLR 92 and para 10.6 below.
101   (1998) 1 CCLR 315, 322.

any established need could not be met. Even if there is no hope from the resource point of view of meeting any needs identified in the assessment, the assessment may serve a useful purpose in identifying for the local authority unmet needs which will help it to plan for the future. Without assessment this could not be done.

Reviews and reassessments

3.101   The duty to assess need carries with it a concomitant and implicit obligation to keep the individual's assessment of need (and any consequent care plan) under review. The Policy Guidance states as follows:

> 3.51 Care needs, for which services are being provided, should be reviewed at regular intervals. This review, especially where it relates to complex needs, should, where possible, be undertaken by someone, such as a care manager, not involved in direct service provision, to preserve the needs-led approach. The projected timing of the first review should be stated in the original care plan. However, reviews may take place earlier if it is clear that community care needs have changed. Reviews may also be needed of services already being provided before the introduction of the new arrangements.

> 3.52 The purpose of the review is to establish whether the objectives, set out in the original care plan, are being, or have been met and to increase, revise or withdraw services accordingly. Reviews should also take account of any changes in needs or service delivery policies. The other purposes of reviews are to monitor the quality of services provided and, in particular, to note the views of service users and carers and any changes in their wishes or preferences. These views should be fed back into service planning, together with any identified shortfalls in provision.

> 3.53 The type of review will vary according to need but all these involved in the original care planning should be consulted. Large-scale review meetings should rarely be necessary. All relevant agencies, service users and carers should be notified of the results of the review, subject to the same constraints of confidentiality as the care plan.

In this respect, Guidance CI(92)34, states:

> 31. The care plans of all users should be subject to regular review. For frail people in the community, frequent reviews and adjustments of their care plans are likely to be needed. Before any changes in services are made for existing users, they should be re-assessed. In

those cases where assessments have been undertaken, particularly under s2(1) of the CSDP Act 1970, authorities must satisfy themselves, before any reduction in service provision takes place that the user does not have a continuing need for it. So long as there is a continuing need, a service must be provided although, following review, it is possible that an assessed need might be met in a different way.

Provision of services without an assessment

3.102   Where an individual's need is so pressing that there is not time even to carry out a 'fast-track' assessment, then a service can be provided without an assessment. NHSCCA 1990 s47(5) provides:

> (5) Nothing in this section shall prevent a local authority from temporarily providing or arranging for the provision of community care services for any person without carrying out a prior assessment of his needs in accordance with the preceding provisions of this section if, in the opinion of the authority, the condition of that person is such that he requires those services as a matter of urgency.

While authorities are not obliged by s47(5) to make such provision, it would be an unlawful fettering of discretion for authorities to reach a policy decision prohibiting the provision of any community care service without a prior assessment. The guidance suggests that the power under s47(5) should be used sparingly.[102]

---

102   See for instance LAC(93)2 para 17 but cf paras 21–22.

CHAPTER 4

Residential and nursing accommodation

4.1   Introduction

4.2   **Accommodation under NAA 1948 s21**

4.5   Care and attention

4.6   'Not otherwise available to them'

4.10   Client group

         Age • Illness • Disability • Expectant or nursing mothers • Any other circumstance • Asylum-seekers and other persons who are 'destitute'

4.21   Powers and duties

         Duty • Mental disorder • Alcoholic or drug-dependent • Power

4.28   **Ordinary residence**

4.34   Ordinary residence and the Children Act 1989

4.35   Disputed 'ordinary residence'

4.37   No settled residence

4.39   Urgent need

4.40   **The nature of residential accommodation**

4.41   Ordinary housing

4.44   Accommodation in residential care or nursing homes

4.45   Residential care homes

4.49   Nursing homes

4.54   Dual registration

4.55   **Choice of accommodation**

continued

4.62   **Inspection duties**
4.63   Inspection of residential care homes
4.68   Inspection of nursing and mental nursing homes
4.70   Collaboration between health and social services authorities

4.72   **NAA 1948 s47: local authority's removal powers**

4.75   **NAA 1948 s48: duty to protect property**

4.76   **Closure of residential and nursing homes**

4.83   **Health and safety issues**
4.84   Manual handling

4.90   **Residential accommodation services and the NHS overlap**

4.91   **Accommodation under MHA 1983 s117**

4.93   **Accommodation under NAA 1948 s29(4)(c)**

4.95   **Accommodation under Children Act 1989 s17**

Introduction

4.1 The powers and duties of social services departments to provide residential accommodation (which may be in a residential or nursing home) are primarily dealt with in Part III of the National Assistance Act (NAA) 1948, and in particular in s21. There is a parallel duty on the NHS to accommodate in certain situations and this responsibility is considered separately at para 4.90 (as well as in Chapter 6); additionally accommodation services can be provided under the Mental Health Act (MHA) 1983 s117, NAA 1948 s29(4) and the Children Act (CA) 1989 s17; these are considered below at paras 4.91, 4.93 and 4.95 respectively.

Accommodation under NAA 1948 s21

4.2 NAA 1948 s21(1) as amended reads as follows:

(1) Subject to and in accordance with the provisions of this Part of this Act, a local authority may with the approval of the Secretary of State, and to such extent as he may direct shall, make arrangements for providing:
(a) residential accommodation for persons aged eighteen or over who by reason of age, illness, disability or any other circumstances are in need of care and attention which is not otherwise available to them and
(aa) residential accommodation for expectant and nursing mothers who are in need of care and attention which is not otherwise available to them.
(1A) A person to whom section 115 of the Immigration and Asylum Act 1999 (exclusion from benefits) applies may not be provided with residential accommodation under subsection (1)(a) if his need for care and attention has arisen solely –
(a) because he is destitute; or
(b) because of the physical effects, or anticipated physical effects, of his being destitute.
(1B) Subsections (3) and (5) to (8) of section 95 of the Immigration and Asylum Act 1999, and paragraph 2 of Schedule 8 to that Act, apply for the purposes of subsection (1A) as they apply for the purposes of that section, but for the references in subsections (5) and (7) of that section and in that paragraph to the Secretary of State substitute references to a local authority.

It follows that social services authorities have no power to make any arrangements under s21 unless and until the Secretary of State has

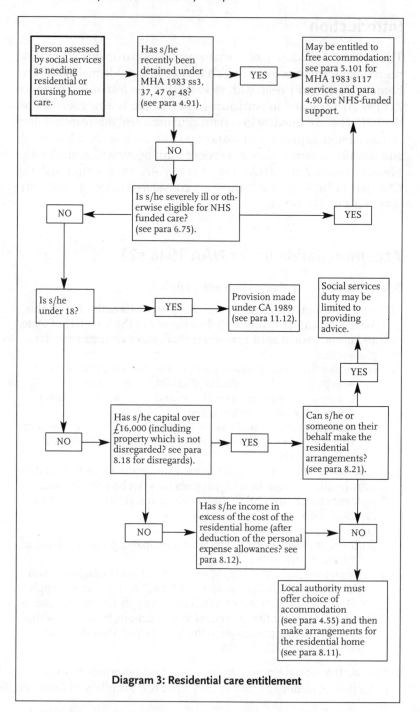

Diagram 3: Residential care entitlement

issued a direction specifying the arrangements which may be made (are 'approved') and those which must be made (are 'directed' to be made).

4.3 The secretary of state's most recent direction in England is found at Appendix 1 to LAC(93)10[1] and came into force on 1 April 1993 (see Appendix B below for the full text of the direction).

4.4 Section 21 specifies two hurdles which a person must (with one exception) surmount before being considered by a social services authority for residential accommodation. The exception relates to expectant and nursing mothers, for whom the age requirement does not apply (see below). The two requirements are:

a) the person must be 18 or over, and
b) the person must be in need of care and attention which is not otherwise available.

Care and attention

4.5 Care and attention are not defined, but presumably encompass a wide range of needs.[2] The phrase would appear to embrace far wider activities than the term 'personal care', which is defined in Registered Homes Act 1984 as including assistance with bodily functions where such assistance is required.[3] Personal care has been held to mean more 'than the mere provision of assistance with bodily functions'. Assistance with bodily functions had to be provided where it was required, but it did not have to be provided where not required and was not the criterion whether a person was or was not in need of personal care.[4] It however connoted a need for 'constant and regular attendance'.[5] In a series of cases concerning asylum-seekers (considered below) the court has however emphasised that a need for care and attention may arise simply because a person is destitute.[6] LAC(98)8 drew attention to the Income Support October 1997

---

1 WOC 35/93 in Wales; since the texts are virtually identical the English direction is referred henceforth.
2 For instance the need for board – this is defined in National Assistance (Assessment of Resources) Regulations 1992 reg 2 as including at least some cooked or prepared meals, cooked or prepared by someone other than the resident (or a member of his/her family) and eaten in the accommodation. See also para 8.57.
3 Section 20(1).
4 *Harrison v Cornwall CC* (1992) 90 LGR 81, CA.
5 Ibid at 93.
6 *R v Hammersmith and Fulham LBC ex p M* (1997) 1 CCLR 69, CA.

amendments which clarified the definition of personal care for entitlement to the residential allowance[7] by removing references to 'assistance with bodily functions' (at para 7); the purpose behind the amendment was to confirm entitlement to the allowance by certain groups of people (eg, those with learning difficulties and drug and alcohol dependency).

'Not otherwise available to them'

4.6   The social services' obligation to provide residential accommodation only arises when the care and attention that a person needs is 'not otherwise available'. Other options may of course include a package of domiciliary care services to enable the person to remain in his or her own home, and/or the provision of accommodation under the Housing Act 1996[8] or assistance from the NHS under its continuing care responsibilities.[9]

4.7   The interpretation of this phrase has been considered by the courts in *Steane v Chief Adjudication Officer*,[10] which concerned the payment of attendance allowance to persons placed in independent residential accommodation by social services authorities but whose residential home fees were not being funded by the authority.[11] The effect of this decision was to confirm that accommodation is not being provided under s21 if the resident is paying for the accom- modation without any support from the local authority (and making direct payment to the home owner). In effect, therefore, the duty on the social services authority to provide residential accommodation is one of last resort.[12]

4.8   The proposition that local authorities did not owe a duty to provide residential accommodation for 'self-funders'[13] was tested in *R v Sefton MBC ex p Help the Aged*.[14] Here the authority decided that it would not

---

7   See para 8.27 below.

8   See Chapter 10.

9   See para 6.75 and Chapter 6 generally.

10 (1998) 1 CCLR 538, HL and see also *Chief Adjudication Officer v Quinn and Gibbon* (1998) 1 CCLR 529, HL.

11 Social Security (Attendance Allowance) (No 3) Regulations 1983 reg 4(1)(c) provided that attendance allowance is not payable for any period during which a person is living in accommodation provided in circumstances in which the cost of the accommodation may be borne wholly or partly out of public funds.

12 As stated in *Adjudication Officers Guidance* (DSS 1994) para 11 concerning the payment of attendance allowance and disability living allowance.

13 Ie, persons already in such accommodation who were paying their own fees.

14 (1997) 1 CCLR 57.

accept responsibility for any person already in residential care or nursing home accommodation until such time as his/her capital fell below £1,500 (notwithstanding that the charging rules required capital below £10,000 to be absolutely disregarded). The Court of Appeal held such a policy to be unlawful, and that 'care and attention is not to be regarded as "otherwise available" if the person concerned is unable to pay for it according to' the charging rules.

4.9　In order to put the matter beyond question, the Community Care (Residential Accommodation) Act 1998 s1 amended NAA 1948 s21 by providing that for the purposes of deciding whether care and attention are otherwise available to a person, a local authority shall disregard so much of the person's capital as does not exceed the capital limit for the purposes of section 22 of this Act (ie, at present £16,000[15]). The Guidance which accompanies the Act[16] makes it clear that even if a person's capital exceeds the statutory limit, there will nevertheless be situations where they cannot decide that care and attention is not required (for instance because of lack of mental capacity).[17]

Client group

4.10　Section 21 lists the criteria which may cause a person to be considered in need of the necessary care and attention, namely:

- age
- illness
- disability
- being an expectant or nursing mother
- any other circumstances.

The list should be contrasted with that under s29 (which deals with domiciliary services – see para 5.13). The s29 list does not include age as a qualifying criterion and is generally more restrictive in its requirements (for instance, an illness must substantially and permanently handicap the person before s/he qualifies).

Age

4.11　Age is usually taken as a reference to the frail elderly. It also includes a class often referred to as EMI; elderly mentally infirm people. Age

15　See para 8.21 and NAA 1948 s21(2A), the full text of which is at Appendix A.
16　LAC(98)19; WOC 27/98 in Wales (both being 'policy guidance').
17　Ibid, para 9; and see para 8.21 below, where this issue is considered in greater detail.

is, of course, frequently accompanied by disabling conditions or illness, which may in fact be the actual cause for the person requiring the care and attention which is not otherwise available. The NHS has responsibilities for very frail elderly people (particularly for respite and rehabilitation services) and this obligation is considered in greater detail at para 6.75 below.

Illness

4.12   Illness is not defined by NAA 1948, although by NHSA 1977 s128 it is defined as including mental disorder within the meaning of MHA 1983 and any injury or disability requiring medical or dental treatment or nursing. The care and attention may be required not merely because the person is ill; it may arise in order to prevent that person becoming ill, or by way of after-care.[18] The residential accommodation duties parallel the obligations under NHSA 1977 Sch 8 para 2, which enable social services authorities to provide domiciliary services for people who are or have been ill (or for the prevention of illness – see para 5.95). The criterion of 'illness' was inserted into s21 by NHSCCA 1990 s42(1)(a). Prior to this amendment the social services authority accommodation duties to persons in residential accommodation arose from NHSA 1977 Sch 8 para 2.[19] This power to accommodate was generally used to provide accommodation for people who were able to live more independently than those accommodated under s21, but who nevertheless required some degree of care and support. These were mostly (but not always) people under pension age.[20]

Disability

4.13   Unlike in NAA s29, disability is not qualified in s21. It would appear to follow that the condition need not necessarily be substantial or permanent.

Expectant or nursing mothers

4.14   The Secretary of State's direction specifically states that residential accommodation can be provided for expectant and nursing mothers of any age, ie, irrespective of whether or not they are over 18.[21]

---

18 LAC(93)10 App 1 para 2(5).
19 Duties under this head repealed by NHSCCA 1990 Sch 10.
20 See charging for residential accommodation guidance (CRAG) para 2.003 – discussed at para 8.56 below.
21 LAC(93)10 App 1 para 3.

Any other circumstance

4.15 The secretary of state's direction[22] does not limit the potential client group entitled to services under s21 (as the direction also refers to persons whose need arises as a result of any other circumstance). The direction nevertheless specifically refers to two categories of condition:

Mental disorder	Residential accommodation can be provided for persons who are or have been suffering from mental disorder, as well as for the purpose of the prevention of mental disorder – see below.[23]
Alcohol or drug dependency	In this case however the residential accommodation is for those actually dependent (rather than for prevention).[24] The provision of accommodation for persons who are alcohol or drug-dependent is considered in greater detail in Chapter 9.

Asylum-seekers and other persons who are 'destitute'

4.16 Until the enactment of the Immigration and Asylum Act 1999 Pt IV, asylum-seekers had formed a significant group of persons who had been held to qualify for accommodation under s21 within the 'any other circumstance' category. While their entitlement to assistance is now in general dealt with by the Asylum and Immigration Act 1999, the case-law remains of importance for two reasons. First, because persons who are not asylum-seekers who are 'destitute' may still come within the provisions of s21 and secondly because asylum-seekers may still be entitled to assistance under s21 provided their need does not arise solely because they are 'destitute'.[25]

4.17 *R v Hammersmith LBC ex p M*[26] concerned the extent to which social services authorities were liable to provide residential accom-

22 LAC(93)10 App 1.
23 Ibid at para 2(3).
24 Ibid at para 2(6).
25 NAA 1948 s21(1A)A. The 1999 Act applies to 'Asylum' seekers (and their dependants) who have applied for asylum on the ground that they have a 'well-founded fear of persecution'. It does not, for instance, apply to persons solely because they are subject to immigration control.
26 (1997) 1 CCLR 69, which decision was upheld by the Court of Appeal as *R v Hammersmith and Fulham LBC ex p M* (1998) 30 HLR 10.

modation under s21, for destitute asylum-seekers, many of whom (because of the Asylum and Immigration Act 1996) were unable to receive any housing or social security assistance. In finding for the applicants, Collins J held that s21:

> ... does impose a duty upon [LAs] to provide for the applicants if satisfied that any of them have no other means of support and therefore are in need of care and attention, since such a need may exist where a person is unable to provide for himself.

The *ex p M* decision was upheld by the Court of Appeal,[27] although it stressed that NAA 1948 s21 is not a 'safety net' provision on which anyone who is short of money and/or short of accommodation can rely'.[28] What local authorities must do is arrange or provide accommodation when individuals (because of the lack of any other available means of obtaining the care and attention they require) are at risk of illness or disability. They do not need to wait until the person's health has been so damaged, but should anticipate this and avoid such deterioration by the provision of accommodation.[29] However, that does not mean that a duty is owed to every destitute person, particularly if the applicant is physically and mentally well and legally entitled to work.[30] In assessing whether a duty is owed, the authority must focus on the specific practical difficulties faced by the applicant and not on whether, in the abstract, the person is able to fend for him/herself.[31]

4.18   The court emphasised, however, that if the destitute person was illegally present in the United Kingdom (for instance, by being an illegal immigrant or illegal over-stayer) then in general there will be no entitlement to any assistance under s21, unless his/her health is so poor that to travel would risk serious damage to health or life[32] (or if otherwise prevented from leaving by factors beyond his or her control[33]).

4.19   As an immediate consequence of the *ex p M* decision the government brought forward a special grant[34] to compensate local author-

---

27 (1997) 1 CCLR 85.

28 Ibid at 94K.

29 Ibid at 95D. The local authority must focus on the practical realities of the situation and not the theoretical possibility that the applicant might be able to fend for herself, *R v Southwark LBC ex p Hong Cui* (1998) 2 CCLR 86.

30 *R v Newham LBC ex p Plastin* (1998) 1 CCLR 304.

31 *R v Southwark LBC ex p Hong Cui* (1999) 2 CCLR 86.

32 *R v Brent LBC ex p D* (1998) 1 CCLR 234.

33 *R v Lambeth LBC ex p Sarhangi* (1999) 2 CCLR 145.

34 Special Grant Report No 24 (5 March 1997) pursuant to Local Government Finance Act 1988 s88B(5).

ities for their extra expenditure under s21. The scope of the grant is explained in LAC(97)6 which at para 15 emphasises that under s21 it is not permissible to make cash payments. It however expressed the view that it was lawful for authorities to make arrangements with a supermarket to enable asylum-seekers to obtain by pre-arrangement food and other necessities not provided in their accommodation. The validity of this guidance was challenged in *R v Secretary of State for Health ex p Hammersmith and Fulham LBC, M and K*.[35] In rejecting the application, Laws J held that the expression in NAA 1948 s21 'to make arrangements for providing' meant:

> That the outcome of any such arrangements is that their beneficiaries should, in consequence of them, directly receive in kind the forms of provision contemplated by the statute, and nothing else . . . Payment of money for persons to buy their own necessities leaves them to make the arrangements to get what they need . . . and in my judgment, lies outside the statutory purpose.[36]

It has further been held that s21 does not permit local authorities to make cash payments[37] and that it is unlawful for them to provide food vouchers without the provision of accommodation.[38]

4.20   As noted above, the right of asylum-seekers to services under s21 or any other community care statute has now been removed, if the need arises solely because they are destitute.[39] By virtue of the Immigration and Asylum Act 1999 s95(3) a person is destitute if:

a) he does not have adequate accommodation or any other means of obtaining it (whether or not his other essential living needs are met); or

b) he has adequate accommodation or the means of obtaining it, but cannot meet his other essential living needs.

In such circumstances Part IV of the Act creates an alternative scheme for the provision of the necessary accommodation. While the detail of this scheme is outside the scope of this text, it essentially provides powers to the secretary of state to make the necessary provision throughout the United Kingdom (ie, for the geographical

---

35 (1997) 1 CCLR 96; and on appeal as *R v Secretary of State for Health ex p M and K* (1998) 1 CCLR 495, where the judgment of Laws J was upheld.

36 Ibid at 103C.

37 *R v Secretary of State for Health ex p Hammersmith and Fulham LBC, M and K* (1997) 1 CCLR 96.

38 *R v Newham LBC ex p Gorenkin* (1998) 1 CCLR 309.

39 NAA 1948 s21(1A)a as inserted by Immigration and Asylum Act 1999 s116 and s117 makes corresponding amendment to Health Services and Public Health Act 1968 s45 and NHSA 1977 Sch 8.

dispersal of asylum-seekers) and gives him/her power to compel local authorities, registered social landlords and others to co-operate in this process. The Act gives the secretary of state power to finance local authorities and voluntary organisations who provide support services under the Act.

Powers and duties

4.21   The differences between statutory powers and duties are considered at para 1.2 above. Certain of the accommodation obligations placed on authorities by s21 are discretionary (ie, powers), whereas the majority are mandatory (ie, duties); these two categories are dealt with separately below.

Duty

4.22   As a result of the secretary of state's direction contained in Appendix 1 to circular LAC(93)10, the social services authorities are under a duty to provide residential accommodation for all of the categories of persons described in NAA 1948 s21(1)(a), namely persons aged 18 or over who by reason of age, illness, disability or any other circumstance are in need of care and attention not otherwise available to them. The duty does not therefore extend to expectant or nursing mothers *per se* (although presumably they may nevertheless come within the ambit of any other circumstance). Furthermore, the secretary of state's direction additionally restricts the general duty to such persons who are either:

a) ordinarily resident in the social services authority's area, or
b) in urgent need of residential accommodation.

Both these terms are considered in greater detail below.

4.23   In *R v Kensington and Chelsea RLBC ex p Kujtim*,[40] the Court of Appeal held that the duty can be treated as discharged if the applicant 'either unreasonably refuses to accept the accommodation provided or if, following its provision, by his conduct he manifests a persistent and unequivocal refusal to observe the reasonable requirements of the local authority in relation to the occupation of such accommodation'.

4.24   **Mental disorder** In relation to persons who are or who have been suffering from mental disorder (or for the purpose of the prevention

---

40   (1999) 2 CCLR 340 at 354I and see para 10.7 below.

of mental disorder) the duty to provide residential accommodation is specifically stated as including those with no settled residence who are in the authority's area.[41]

4.25 **Alcoholic or drug-dependent** The secretary of state's direction specifically refers to persons who are alcoholic or drug-dependent as being persons for whom a social services authority is empowered to provide residential accommodation.[42] It would appear to follow that there must in consequence be a duty to provide residential accommodation for such persons when they are ordinarily resident in the authority's area and have been assessed as needing care and attention not otherwise available to them. NAA 1948 s21 sets out the full extent of the potential client group. The secretary of state cannot add new categories to the list; s/he can merely select who from this group is to qualify. As the direction states that social services authorities have a potential to accommodate all of the categories of persons specified in NAA 1948 s21(a), it must therefore follow that this includes persons who are alcoholic or drug dependent.

Power

4.26 Social services authorities have the power (but not the duty) to provide residential accommodation for persons described in NAA 1948 s21(1)(a) and (aa) who are ordinarily resident in the area of another local authority, provided that the other authority agrees.[43]

4.27 The secretary of state's direction empowers (but does not direct) social services authorities to provide residential accommodation for expectant and nursing mothers.[44] There is not therefore *per se* a duty to accommodate such persons, although if the woman is over 17, 'some other circumstance' would appear to include being an expectant or nursing mother; in which case she may then come within the ambit of s21(1)(a) rather than s21(1)(aa) of the Act.

Ordinary residence

4.28 The provision of residential accommodation is a local authority service, and accordingly it is necessary for the legislation to spell out

41 LAC(93)10 para 2(3).
42 Ibid at para 2(6).
43 Ibid at para 2(1)(a) and see NAA 1948 s24(4).
44 LAC(93)10 App 1 para 3.

which particular authority is responsible in each case. The device adopted by the Act is the concept of a person's ordinary residence.[45] NAA 1948 s24 lays down the basic rules for determining responsibility but fails to provide a statutory definition for the term. The Department of Health has issued interpretative guidance in circular LAC(93)7, which includes reference to a number of reported decisions in which the meaning of the term has been considered.

4.29   Ordinary residence for the purposes of MHA 1983 s117 has a slightly different interpretation and this is considered separately at paras 4.36 and 5.113 below. The key to the term is in the word residence; it will generally be the place where a person's normal residential address is to be found. The circular states that the phrase involves questions of fact and degree, and factors such as time, intention[46] and continuity.

4.30   The leading case on ordinary residence is the House of Lords' decision in *Shah v Barnet LBC*,[47] although it concerned the interpretation of the phrase as it appeared in the Education Act 1962. In Lord Scarman's judgment a person's long-term future intentions or expectations are not relevant; the test is not what is a person's real home[48] but whether a person can show a regular, habitual mode of life in a particular place, the continuity of which has persisted despite temporary absences.[49] A person's attitude is only relevant in two respects; the residence must be voluntarily adopted, and there must be a settled purpose in living in the particular residence. 'Ordinary residence' is to be given its 'ordinary and natural meaning', namely 'a man's abode in a particular place or country which he had adopted voluntarily and for settled purposes as part of the regular order of his life for the time being, whether of short or long duration'.[50]

---

45 Similar but distinct from the device of local connection used under Housing Act 1996 Pt VII; in this respect, see LAC(93)7 paras 16–17.
46 In view of the comments of Lord Scarman in *Shah* (see para 4.30 below), intention must be given a restrictive interpretation.
47 [1983] 1 All ER 226.
48 Ibid at 239.
49 Ibid at 236.
50 Ibid at 235.

Residential accommodation

For persons in need of care and attention not otherwise available to them

Ordinarily resident	No settled residence	Not ordinarily resident
POWER		
Expectant or nursing mothers (although they may come within the ambit of 'any other circumstance' if over 18).		Persons aged 18 or over who by reason of age, illness, disability or any other circumstance AND the other authority agrees.
DUTY		
Persons aged 18 or over who by reason of age, illness, disability or any other circumstance (which includes mental disorder of any description and alcohol or drug dependent persons).	Persons aged 18 or over who by reason of age, illness, disability or any other circumstance AND are living in the authority's area when the need arises.	Persons aged 18 or over who by reason of age, illness, disability or any other circumstance AND who are in urgent need.

4.31   *R v Waltham Forest LBC ex p Vale*[51] concerned a 28-year-old applicant with profound learning disabilities such that she was totally dependent on her parents. In these circumstances the court held that 'concepts of voluntarily adopted residence and settled purpose did not arise'. Importing principles from child care law,[52] it determined that her ordinary residence was that of her parents, not because it was her real home, but because it was her 'base'. The court further held that a person's ordinary residence could result after a stay in one place of only short duration; and that there was no reason why one month should be adjudged too short.

4.32   The *Waltham Forest* decision was tested in *R v Redbridge LBC ex p East Sussex CC*,[53] which concerned two adult male autistic twins with profound learning disabilities who were boarded at a school in East Sussex, but whose parents lived in Redbridge. Applying the principles enunciated in the *Waltham Forest* decision, the court held that the twins were at law ordinarily resident in Redbridge.

---

51 (1985) *Times* 25 February, QBD.
52 See, eg, *Re P (GE) (an infant)* [1965] Ch 568.
53 (1992) *Times* 31 December; [1993] COD 265, QBD.

Subsequently, however, the parents went to live in Nigeria. It was held that when this occurred the twins ceased to have any settled residence and accordingly became the responsibility of East Sussex. LAC(93)7 advises, however, that except in cases involving persons with severe learning difficulties, 'an adult with learning disabilities should be regarded as capable of forming his own intention of where he wishes to live'.[54]

4.33　Where a person is provided with residential accommodation by a social services authority, s/he is deemed to continue to be ordinarily resident in the area in which s/he was ordinarily resident immediately before the residential accommodation was provided.[55] Likewise where a person is in NHS care s/he is deemed to be ordinarily resident in the area in which s/he was ordinarily resident immediately before admission as a patient to the NHS facility.[56] Where a person was not ordinarily resident in any area prior to admission, then the responsible social services authority will be the one in whose area s/he is at that time.[57] The guidance suggests that these principles should also be followed when assessing responsibility for people leaving prisons, resettlement units and other similar establishments.[58]

Ordinary residence and the Children Act 1989

4.34　The social services' duty to provide services for disabled children under CA 1989 s17 is owed to children (ie, persons under 18 years of age) 'within their area'. In *R v Lambeth LBC ex p Caddell*[59] the applicant had been placed by the respondent London borough with paid carers who lived in Kent. When he became 18 years of age, the borough determined that he had ceased to be their responsibility since he was no longer a child, and accordingly the ordinary residence rules under the 1948 Act applied. Kent County Council contended however, that the borough was still the responsible authority since CA 1989 s24 allowed for social services authorities to continue to provide advice and assistance to young persons who had been in care

---

54　LAC(93)7 para 12.
55　NAA 1948 s24(5). The situation will generally be otherwise where the person has independently admitted him/herself to the home and without financial assistance from the local authority – see LAC(93)7 paras 10 and 15.
56　NAA 1948 s24(6).
57　NAA 1948 s24(3).
58　LAC(93)7 para 14.
59　[1998] 1 FLR 235.

once they achieved their majority. Connell J rejected this line of argument, holding that the duty under s24 was owed by the authority in whose area the young person resided, ie, Kent.

Disputed 'ordinary residence'

4.35 Where two or more social services authorities are in dispute over a person's ordinary residence, NAA 1948 s32(3) provides that the question is to be determined by the secretary of state. This procedure is however only available for disputes which concern potential services under the 1948 Act. LAC(93)7 Part II sets out the procedure to be followed by authorities in such cases, namely:

a) Before the secretary of state is approached, one of the authorities must provisionally accept responsibility and be providing services.

b) An agreed written statement of facts, signed by all authorities involved, must be sent, together with the application for determination. The statement should include:
   - full information about the person whose ordinary residence is in dispute;
   - details relating to the prior residence of the person;
   - details of the statutory provisions under which services have been provided.

   Copies of all relevant correspondence between the authorities should be annexed to the agreed statement.

c) In addition each authority may also send separate written representations concerning the agreed statement (ie, a legal submission).

4.36 In *R v Kent CC ex p Salisbury and Pierre*,[60] a dispute arose as to the potential service user's ordinary residence and the council argued that the court could not determine this question since s32(3) provided for this to be decided by the minister. The dispute arose, however, in the context of services under CSDPA 1970 and not NAA 1948. Latham J held:

> The difficulty with this submission is that . . . it is raised not under the National Assistance Act 1948, but under the 1970 Act. There is no equivalent provision in this latter Act. The reference to section 29 of the 1948 Act is not, in my judgment, sufficient to justify the conclusion that the provisions of section 32(3) of that Act apply to the determination of any issue under section 2 of the 1970 Act. The

60 (2000) 3 CCLR 38.

phrase 'are satisfied in the case of any person to whom that section applies' does not involve consideration of ordinary residence. It is a reference to the nature of the disabilities which trigger consideration of the question whether a person is one to whom the duty under section 2 of the 1970 Act is owed. That is why it was necessary to include the phrase 'who is ordinarily resident in their area' in that section. That being so, it seems to me that the present claim requires me to determine whether or not [the service user] is ordinarily resident in Kent.

The judge then determined the question of ordinary residence on the basis of the existing legal authorities. The service user had learning difficulties, but these were not so severe as those considered in *Vale* (see para 4.31), and accordingly it was held that:

In the present case, the papers show that [the service user] has expressed a clear and consistent desire to stay with [her paid carers who lived in Kent]. I think that is sufficient to justify the conclusion that she is in her present abode voluntarily, and with a settled intention to remain there for the time being. Her disabilities do not appear to be such as to prevent her from having the requisite understanding for both mental elements. That is sufficient to justify the conclusion that she is ordinarily resident in Kent. If I am wrong, she is nonetheless to be treated, in my view, as if [her paid carers] were her parents, and she were a child. This would produce the same result.

It follows that when services are being provided under MHA 1983 s117 or CSDPA 1970 s2 (or indeed under CA 1989), the procedures laid down by NAA 1948 s32(3) will not be available to determine ordinary residence disputes.

No settled residence

4.37   When a person presents him/herself to a social services authority and claims to be of no settled residence or of no fixed abode, the authority is advised that it should normally accept responsibility.[61] If this were not the case, authorities could argue that they owed no duty to such persons, as the secretary of state's direction in LAC(93)10 Appendix 1 (with one exception)[62] limits their duty to those ordinarily resident in the area, or in urgent need. It is submitted therefore that if a person has no settled residence, his/her ordinary residence is the place

---

61   LAC(93)7 para 16.
62   LAC(93)10 App 1 para 2(3).

where s/he is actually living (or perhaps (in extreme cases) the place where the previous night was spent).

4.38 Guidance on the special needs of homeless people has been given in LAC(93)2, including the following:

RESIDENTIAL CARE FOR HOMELESS PEOPLE WITH OTHER NEEDS

26. There may be other vulnerable people who are homeless and who are in need of residential care. Many of the above considerations apply to them as much as to alcohol and drug misusers. Like any other section of the population, homeless people may be in need of care because of frailty, physical disability, mental disorder of any description or a combination of any of these. They may have complex needs which also include alcohol and drug misuse. Their needs may be hard to classify by standard client groups.

27. As with alcohol and drug misusers, LAs should have flexible systems of assessment and care management that allow such people access to the services they need in a way that meets their special circumstances. Their homelessness may in itself mean that an urgent response is called for. LAs will be aware that there are a wide variety of agencies which specialise in providing care for homeless people. As with specialist alcohol and drug providers, these agencies may be in a position to assist in assessment procedures. Some of these homes receive additional support from the Home Office specifically to reserve places for vulnerable offenders and ex-offenders whose care needs require residential support. As above, LAs will need to collaborate with the Probation Service to make best use of these resources.

Other guidance of relevance to homeless persons with community care needs is considered at para 10.14 below.

Urgent need

4.39 The secretary of state's direction places a duty on authorities to make arrangements not only for persons ordinarily resident in their area, but also for 'other persons who are in urgent need thereof'.[63] Urgent need is not defined; in this context however it is only relevant when the person is ordinarily resident in another authority's area. It is submitted therefore that the duty to persons in urgent need will almost invariably be a short-term duty, only subsisting during the currency of the urgency, and even then, only until such time as the other authority assumes responsibility.

63 Ibid at para 2(1)(b), and see also NHSCCA 1990 s47(5) concerning the provision of community care services in cases of urgency.

The nature of residential accommodation

4.40   The duty under s21 is to make arrangements for providing 'residential accommodation'. While typically this will be in a residential care or nursing home, the duty is not limited to the provision of such accommodation.

Ordinary housing

4.41   In *R v Newham LBC ex p Medical Foundation for the Care of Victims of Torture*,[64] the respondent argued that under s21 it was unlawful to provide residential accommodation in the form of simple bed and breakfast accommodation, or indeed ordinary private sector flats or houses. In rejecting this assertion, Moses J held that the word 'residential' meant no more than 'accommodation where a person lives'. In his judgment, an authority might be obliged to provide accommodation under s21 notwithstanding that it had decided that the person did not need board or any other services. A similar argument was rejected by Scott Baker J in *R v Bristol CC ex p Penfold*,[65] where he held that s21 can:

> In appropriate circumstances extend to the provision of 'normal' accommodation. 'Normal' housing can be provided . . . when it is the answer to a need which would otherwise have to be met by other community care services.

4.42   In *Penfold*, the court further held that discharge by a housing authority of its obligations under the homelessness legislation does not preclude the need for a community care assessment. It follows therefore that a person may be entitled to housing under the community care legislation notwithstanding that s/he has been refused such accommodation under the homelessness legislation. In general however (as was the case in *Penfold*), the mere fact that a person is entitled to a community care assessment is no guarantee that their 'assessed need' will be sufficient to warrant such a service.

4.43   The interface between local authorities' community care and housing obligations is further considered at para 10.14 below.

---

64 (1998) 1 CCLR 227.
65 (1998) 1 CCLR 315; see also *R v Wigan MBC ex p Tammadge* (1998) 1 CCLR 582, where the respondent did not dispute that s21 permitted the provision of 'normal' or 'bare' accommodation, ie, without any board or services; at 584A.

Accommodation in residential care or nursing homes

4.44   As noted above, the duty under s21 is generally discharged by social services authorities making arrangements for the provision of accommodation in a registered residential care or nursing home. This accommodation may be provided by:

a) the social services authority itself;[66]
b) another social services authority;[67]
c) a voluntary organisation;[68] or
d) a private for-reward provider.[69]

A key aim of the community care reforms was the promotion of a flourishing independent sector (providing services such as residential accommodation) alongside good quality public services.[70] To encourage social services authorities to contract with the private sector, they were required to spend 85 per cent of their special transitional grant (STG)[71] on the purchase of non-local authority services. Despite the aim of the reforms being to maintain a mixed economy of care, it has been held that the legislation does not in fact require authorities to provide directly any public provision of residential accommodation, provided there is sufficient private or independent provision.[72]

Residential care homes

4.45   The Registered Homes Act (RHA) 1984 presently provides for the regulation of residential care and nursing homes. The Act will be repealed by the Care Standards Act 2000 when it comes into force. The 2000 Act creates an entirely new and independent regulatory scheme. Since the 2000 Act is unlikely to come into force until late 2001 at the earliest, the law as it currently applies under the 1984 Act is considered. RHA 1984 s1 defines a residential care home as follows:

66 NAA 1948 s21(3).
67 Ibid.
68 NAA 1948 s26(1).
69 Ibid.
70 White paper *Caring for People* (1989) para 1.11.
71 The Treasury grant which was paid to compensate local authorities for the transfer to them of the previous DSS responsibility for funding residential and nursing care (see also para 1.24 above). The STG was paid for the first six years after April 1993; from 1 April 1999 the compensation monies have been added to the general block funding.
72 *R v Wandsworth LBC ex p Beckwith* [1996] 1 WLR 60, HL.

... an establishment which provides or is intended to provide, whether for reward or not, residential accommodation with both board and personal care for persons in need of personal care by reason of old age, disablement, past or present dependence on alcohol or drugs, or past or present mental disorder.

4.46   Independent residential care homes must (with few exceptions)[73] be registered.[74] There are special rules for the registration of small homes (defined as homes providing for fewer than four people).[75] The social services authority is the registration authority for residential care homes within its area and is required to establish 'arm's length' registration and inspection units to oversee its responsibilities under RHA 1984 Pt I.

4.47   The registration is in the name of the manager or person in control of the home.[76] Registration is dependent upon the applicant establishing:[77]

a) that the persons concerned in carrying on the home are fit to do so;
b) that having regard to its situation, construction, state of repair, accommodation, staffing and equipment, the premises are fit to be used; and
c) that the home will provide the services and facilities reasonably required.

4.48   The actual services which are required to be provided for any person in a residential care home will vary in each case, depending on the authority's assessment of need. LAC(93)10 specifies the range of services which a social services authority must arrange for residents when the need is identified.[78] The Residential Care Homes Regulations 1984 reg 10 specifies the facilities and services which must be provided in all such homes.[79]

Nursing homes

4.49   RHA 1984 s21 defines a 'nursing home' as:

(a) any premises used, or intended to be used, for the reception of, and the provision of nursing for, persons suffering from any sickness, injury or infirmity;

73   See RHA 1984 s1(5).
74   Local authority homes are exempt from registration: RHA 1984 s1(5)(j).
75   RHA 1984 s1(4).
76   Ibid s3.
77   Ibid s9.
78   LAC(93)10 App 1 para 4.
79   SI No 1345: guidance on reg 10 is given in LAC(86)6 paras 7–8.

(b) any premises used, or intended to be used, for the reception of pregnant women, or of women immediately after childbirth . . . and

(c) any premises not falling within either of the preceding paragraphs which are used, or intended to be used, for the provision of all or any of the following services, namely –

(i) the carrying out of surgical procedures under anaesthesia;

(ii) the termination of pregnancies;

(iii) endoscopy;

(iv) haemodialysis or peritoneal dialysis;

(v) treatment by specially controlled techniques.

4.50   By RHA 1984 s22 a 'mental nursing home' is defined as:

> . . . any premises used, or intended to be used, for the reception of, and the provision of nursing or other medical treatment (including care, habitation, and rehabilitation under medical supervision) for one or more mentally disordered patients . . .

NHS or local authority premises (and certain other premises) are specifically excluded from these definitions.[80] Nursing and mental nursing homes must be registered. The health authority is the registration authority for such homes within its area[81] and is required to establish an 'arm's length' registration and inspection unit to oversee its responsibilities under the RHA 1984 Part II.

4.51   As with residential care homes, it is not the establishment itself which is registered, but the person who has responsibility for ensuring that the home complies with the registration conditions. The person who is actually in charge of the home must be named, and must be a registered medical practitioner or a qualified nurse (or in the case of a maternity home, a registered midwife).[82] The criteria for registration are much the same as for residential care homes (ie, the applicant is a fit person, the premises are suitable and will not be used in any improper or undesirable way),[83] although in addition the authority must be satisfied that there will at all times be sufficient suitably qualified staff in attendance.[84]

4.52   The services which are required to be provided in a nursing home will include those required in residential care homes (as detailed above) but in addition there will be others related to the residents'

---

80   RHA 1984 ss21(3) and 22(2).

81   RHA 1984 s23 and see NHS (Functions of Health Authorities and Administration Arrangements) Regulations 1996 SI No 708.

82   RHA 1984 s25(1)(f); the person registered may nevertheless be the same person as the person in charge.

83   Ibid s25(1).

84   Ibid s25(3).

medical and health needs. The range of services is specified in the Nursing Homes and Mental Nursing Homes Regulations 1984 SI No 1578 reg 12. Responsibility for some of these services may, however, rest with the NHS and this is discussed in greater detail below.

4.53   Before a social services authority can make arrangements to place a person in a nursing home, it must (except in cases of urgency)[85] obtain the consent of the responsible health authority.[86] In general this will be the one in which the service user is usually resident. Guidance on the appropriate health authority to contact has been issued as LAC(92)22, which states at para 5 that arrangements between the social services authority and the health authority will need to be 'sufficiently flexible so that there is a minimum of delay in the necessary consent being given. This will be particularly important for some client groups, eg, people without a settled way of life, drug and alcohol misusers'.

Dual registration

4.54   There is no restriction upon an establishment applying for registration both as a residential care home and as a nursing home. In such cases the home will have to satisfy (and be subject to) both of the registration/inspection authorities.[87]

Choice of accommodation

4.55   When a social services authority has assessed[88] a person as requiring residential accommodation under NAA 1948 s21, then it is obliged to make arrangements for accommodating that person at a place of his/her choice in England, Wales or Scotland[89] (if any choice of preferred

---

85   NAA 1948 s26(1D).
86   Ibid s26(1C).
87   HC(84)21 Annex B and LAC(84)15.
88   Under NHSCCA 1990 s47(1).
89   National Assistance Act 1948 (Choice of Accommodation) Directions 1992 direction 2, extended to Scotland by National Assistance Act 1948 (Choice of Accommodation) (Amendment) Directions 1993. Proposals were made to extend the Directions to cover Northern Ireland (see *Community Care* 2–8 November 1995) but do not appear as yet to have been implemented. It has been argued that the restriction of the Directions to England and Scotland may discriminate against other EU nationals contrary to Treaty of Rome article 6 – (1996) *Independent* 4 March. Guidance on the 1992 Directions is contained in LAC(92)27 (WOC 12/93 in Wales and WOC 47/93 in relation to 1993 Scottish amendment).

accommodation has been indicated) provided that the conditions specified in direction 3 of the National Assistance Act 1948 (Choice of Accommodation) Directions 1992 are satisfied. The directions are set out in Appendix 2. The conditions which need to be satisfied are:

- the preferred accommodation appears to the authority to be suitable[90] in relation to his or her needs as assessed by it;
- the cost of making the arrangements at the preferred accommodation would not require the authority to pay more than it would usually expect to pay having regard to the assessed needs;
- the preferred accommodation is available; and
- the persons in charge of the preferred accommodation provide it subject to the authority's usual terms and conditions, having regard to the nature of the accommodation, for providing accommodation for such a person under NAA 1948 Pt III.

It will be maladministration if a local authority fails to explain clearly to clients and their carers what their rights are under the Directions, or if it puts the onus on them to find accommodation at an acceptable cost to the authority.[91]

4.56   Where a person's preferred accommodation is more expensive than the accommodation proposed by the authority, then s/he may nevertheless require the authority to support him/her in that accommodation, provided a third party[92] agrees to top up the difference (and that third party can reasonably be expected to pay the sum for the duration of the proposed placement).[93] The amount of top-up is calculated as the difference between:

a) the cost which the authority would usually expect to pay for the accommodation having regard to the person's assessed need; and

b) the full standard rate for the accommodation.[94]

4.57   The guidance emphasises that it is the usual cost that must be used

---

90 Accommodation will not necessarily be unsuitable simply because it fails to conform with the authority's preferred model of provision – see LAC(92)27 para 7.2.

91 Complaint No 97/A/3218 against Merton LBC (1999) 25 October.

92 Special restrictions exist where the third party is a spouse – see direction 4(2) and LAC(92)27 para 11.13 – and residents are not entitled to 'top-up' their own residential costs (LAC(98)8 para 6). There is nothing in principle, however, to stop a resident transferring capital to a third party to enable that person to make the top-up payments (provided the transfer does not amount to a deprivation designed to reduce the residents liability for residential fees (see para 8.29 below).

93 LAC(92)27 para 4.1.

94 As specified in NAA 1948 s22(2) or pursuant to s26(2) and (4) of that Act.

for comparative purposes,[95] and that in certain situations this may be the cost in another part of the country, ie, there may be circumstances where an authority might judge the need to move to another part of the country to be an integral part of the individual's assessed needs.[96] The type of care may also affect the usual cost, for instance the cost an authority might usually expect to pay for respite care might be different from its usual cost for permanent care.[97] Local authorities are not, however, obliged to accommodate service users in the least expensive available accommodation commensurate with that person's assessed needs.[98]

4.58   The local ombudsman has stressed that since councils have a discretion to exceed the normal amount that they are willing to contribute to the costs of residential care, they must not fetter thus discretion; they must have regard to the particular circumstances of each case.[99]

4.59   The right to exercise choice over accommodation extends not only to prospective residents, but also to existing residents who wish to move to different or more expensive accommodation.[100]

4.60   While the Choice of Accommodation Directions enable an individual to opt for more expensive accommodation (and for a third party to pay the difference), this only applies if the usual cost figure used by the authority would genuinely secure the person a placement in a less expensive home which met his/her assessed needs (including in certain situations psychological needs).[101] The directions do not mean that authorities may set an arbitrary ceiling on the amount they are willing to contribute towards residential care and require third parties routinely to make up the difference. If challenged, an authority would need to be able to demonstrate that its usual cost was sufficient to allow it to provide people with the level of service they could reasonably expect if the possibility of third party contributions did not exist.[102]

4.61   There is a duty on social services authorities to explain to residents and prospective residents (and their carers) their rights under the

---

95 LAC(92)27 para 7.4.

96 Ibid para 7.6.

97 Ibid para 7.7.

98 Ibid para 4.3.

99 Complaint No 97/A/3218 against Merton LBC (25 October 1999).

100 LAC(92)27 para 13.

101 *R v Avon CC ex p M* [1994] 2 FCR 259; (1999) 2 CCLR 185; [1994] 2 FLR 1006, QBD.

102 LAC(92)27 para 10.

direction.[103] In addition, authorities are advised to have a written agreement with the resident, third party and the person providing the accommodation when they seek to exercise their right to use more expensive accommodation. It is suggested that the agreement specifies:[104]

a) that failure to keep up payments will normally result in the resident having to move to other accommodation;
b) that an increase in the resident's income will not necessarily lessen the need for a contribution, since the resident's own income will be subject to charging by the authority in the normal way;[105]
c) that a rise in the accommodation fees will not automatically be shared equally between authority and third party; and
d) that if the accommodation fails to honour its contractual conditions, the authority must reserve the right to terminate the contract.

Patients in NHS-funded nursing homes do not have a statutory right of choice; the government expects however that before any placement there will be 'considerable consultation with the patient and his or her family and [hospitals should] take account of the patient's wishes'.[106]

Inspection duties

4.62   In this section brief reference is made to the inspection requirements that exist in relation to residential care and nursing homes; detailed analysis of which is beyond the scope of this book. As noted in para 4.45 above, the regulatory scheme is to be substantially reformed when the Care Standards Act 2000 comes into force. Further guidance on nursing home regulation has been issued as HSG(95)41 and on residential care home regulation as LAC(95)12.

Inspection of residential care homes

4.63   The community care reforms reinforced and extended local authority inspection duties under RHA 1984. Under the initial scheme of the

---

103 Ibid para 17.
104 Ibid para 11.9.
105 See Chapter 8.
106 Statement to Health Committee, recorded at para 79 of *First Report into Long-Term Care* (HMSO, 1995).

1984 Act, independent residential care homes with fewer than four residents were not required to register. The Registered Homes (Amendment) Act 1991 required such homes to register, although subject to less stringent conditions.[107] The local authority was in turn given a power (but not a duty)[108] to inspect such small homes.

4.64   A harsh application of the administrative requirements of the 1991 Act might result in a violation of European Convention on Human Rights article 8 and this issue is considered at para 12.140 below.

4.65   Inspection is defined as a process of external examination intended to establish whether a service is managed and provided in conformity with expected standards.[109] The purpose of the inspection process is to check that the professional services that the public receive are delivered in the most effective way possible and genuinely meet the needs of those whom they serve.[110] Inspection units are required to develop objective and subjective standards against which service providers can be assessed. Guidance on this process has been issued by the Social Services Inspectorate.[111]

4.66   Inspection and registration units are required to operate at arm's length from the social services management of their own services[112] and to inspect, not only independent care homes, but also all local authority homes.[113] The power to inspect has been further extended to include any premises in which community care services are (or are proposed to be) provided by the local authority or an independent provider.[114]

4.67   A primary purpose of such free-standing inspection units is to ensure that local authority homes, although exempt from the registration requirements, are subjected to the same rigour of scrutiny as independent homes.[115] Inspection units are required to publish an

---

107 Registered Homes (Amendment) Act 1991 s1, amending RHA 1984 ss1(4) and 4.

108 RHA 1984 s17 and Residential Care Homes Regulations 1984 SI No 1345 reg 18(1) which place a duty on local authorities to inspect other homes at least twice a year in every period of 12 months.

109 Policy Guidance para 5.3.

110 LAC(94)16 para 1.

111 *Inspecting for Quality: Guidance on practice for inspection units in social services departments and other agencies; Principles, issues and recommendations, SSI* (HMSO, 1991); and see *Guidance on standards for residential homes for elderly people, SSI* (HMSO, 1990).

112 White paper *Caring for People* para 1.12.

113 Policy Guidance para 5.13.

114 NHSCCA 1990 s48.

115 Policy Guidance para 5.17.

annual report of their work (which should be available to the public) which includes specific information about care homes (both public and private).[116]

Inspection of nursing and mental nursing homes

4.68 The responsibility for registration and inspection of nursing homes rests with the Secretary of State for Health.[117] These duties have, however, been delegated to health authorities,[118] which are required to set up inspection and registration units which operate on a similar basis to the equivalent local authority units. These units must also operate at arm's length from the day-to-day NHS management, whose duties may include the purchase of services from such nursing homes.[119] Nursing homes must also be inspected at least twice a year[120] and the inspection reports must be available for public inspection.[121]

4.69 A policy decision by a registration authority affecting nursing home proprietors is amenable to judicial review if it is taken without proper consultation.[122]

Collaboration between health and social services authorities

4.70 As detailed above, the legislation requires similar registration and inspection units to be established by health authorities and by social services authorities. Their respective roles most obviously overlap in respect of homes which have dual registration. In such cases the two units are advised to co-ordinate their inspections[123] by agreeing and adopting a joint inspection strategy.[124]

4.71 Overlap will also occur in relation to independent nursing homes with which local authorities contract to provide care (under NAA 1948

116 Ibid para 5.18.
117 RHA 1984 s23.
118 NHS (Functions of Health Authorities and Administration Arrangements) Regulations 1996 SI No 708 reg 3(1).
119 See HC(81)8 and HC(86)5.
120 Nursing Homes and Mental Nursing Homes Regulations 1984 SI No 1578 reg 11.
121 See HSC 1998/047 (WHC(98)5 in Wales) National Health Service (Health Authorities) (Open Reporting of Nursing Home and Mental Nursing Home Inspections) Directions 1998.
122 *R v Kingston and Richmond Health Authority ex p Paxman* [1995] COD 410.
123 LAC(84)15 para 16.
124 Policy Guidance para 5.25

s21) but in respect of which the health authority is the registration and inspection authority. Before the social services authority places a person in such a home, it must obtain health authority consent (see para 4.53 above). The guidance also requires that the health authority be informed of the terms under which the contract has been placed.[125]

NAA 1948 s47: local authority's removal powers

4.72   Environmental health departments have power under NAA 1948 s47 to apply to a magistrates' court for an order removing chronically sick, disabled or elderly persons to more suitable accommodation. This anachronistic power was primarily aimed at facilitating slum clearance and is unlikely to survive the implementation of the Human Rights Act 1998.[126]

4.73   The application for removal requires that the vulnerable person or 'some person in charge of him' be given seven days' notice of the intended application, unless the case is urgent, in which case an ex parte application is permitted to a single justice.[127]

4.74   The requirements for a removal order to be made are:

1) that the respondent is either suffering from grave, chronic disease or being aged, infirm or physically incapacitated is living in unsanitary conditions (thus the 'unsanitary conditions' requirement does not apply to persons suffering from grave or chronic disease);
2) is 'unable to devote to himself and is not receiving from other persons proper care and attention'; and
3) the community physician has provided an appropriate certificate.[128]

---

125 Ibid para 5.24.
126 Section 47 (as amended) enables a person to be detained for up to three weeks on the authority of only the most limited of medical evidence without having any prior notice of the application or right to be heard. The certifying doctors need have no particular knowledge of the detained person. It is doubtful that this provision complies with articles 5 and 6 of the European Convention on Human Rights.
127 National Assistance (Amendment) Act 1951; it appears that nearly all applications for compulsory removal under s47 are now made using these ex parte powers.
128 Essentially that s/he is satisfied that it is either in the interests of the person concerned; or for the prevention of injury to the health of, or serious nuisance to other persons; and that it is necessary to remove the person concerned from the premises in which he is residing. In addition, if the application is made ex parte, that it is in the interests of the person concerned that s/he be removed without delay.

Where the court is satisfied it can order the removal of the person concerned to a suitable hospital or other place[129] for a period of up to three months, and the order can be renewed indefinitely.

NAA 1948 s48: duty to protect property

4.75 Where a person is provided with accommodation under NAA 1948 s21 or removed from their home by the local authority using its powers under s47 of the 1948 Act, s48 obliges the authority to take steps to protect that persons property, if there is a danger of loss/ damage to it and no other suitable arrangements have been made to protect it. Authorities are empowered to enter premises in order to take steps to protect property and to recover from the resident any reasonable expenses incurred in taking such action.

Closure of residential and nursing homes

4.76 The closure of residential homes for the elderly has proved to be one of the more controversial effects of the community care changes. The period 1990–1995 saw a 25 per cent reduction in the number of local authority homes in England (amounting to almost 40,000 fewer residents). The decline in the NHS provision of long-term geriatric beds has been no less dramatic, with the loss of 30 per cent of such beds between 1983 and 1993.[130]

4.77 In relation to the closure of long-stay NHS accommodation, there is now an obligation on health authorities to consult with the appropriate social services authority (see para 6.51 below) and community health council.[131]

4.78 *R v Devon CC ex p Baker and Durham CC ex p Curtis*[132] concerned the proposed closure of residential homes in Devon and in Durham. The Court of Appeal held that (in respect of the procedure followed by Durham County Council) the decision to close a particular home was

---

129 Which hospital or other place (usually a residential or nursing home) has also been given seven days' notice of the intended application.

130 T Harding et al *Options for Long Term Care* (HMSO, 1996) p8.

131 Community Health Council Regulations 1996 SI No 640 and see also EL (90)185. See also *R v North East Devon HA ex p Pow* (1998) 1 CCLR 280 and *R v North East Devon HA ex p Coughlan* (1999) 2 CCLR 285 considered at paras 6.51 and 6.91 below.

132 [1995] 1 All ER 72, CA at 91.

unlawful; the council had failed to consult the residents properly. The court approved the proposition that consultation contained four elements,[133] namely:

First, that consultation must be at a time when proposals are still at a formative stage. Second, that the proposer must give sufficient reasons for any proposal to permit of intelligent consideration and response. Third, that adequate time must be given for consideration and response and, finally, fourth, that the product of consultation must be conscientiously taken into account in finalising any statutory proposals.

The court also approved the proposition that if a resident is to be transferred from one home to another (for whatever reason), s/he must be consulted over his or her removal from the existing home as well as over the home to which s/he is to be transferred.[134]

4.79   In *R v Wandsworth LBC ex p Beckwith*,[135] a proposal by the respondent council to close all its residential care homes for the elderly was challenged by an elderly resident on the ground that the council was under a legal duty under NAA 1948 ss21 and 26 to maintain some accommodation for the elderly under its own management. The House of Lords rejected the argument. Provided there is sufficient residential accommodation in the local authority's area, there is no requirement that any be actually provided by the authority; it can consist entirely of arrangements made with voluntary organisations or other persons. Although LAC(93)10 para 4 states that authorities are required to maintain some public provision, this was in the Lords' judgment 'simply wrong'.

4.80   The importance of consultation before deciding on a home closure is reinforced by the emerging evidence that relocating institutionalised elderly people to a new residence may have a dramatic effect on their mental health and life expectancy,[136] some research studies suggesting that the increase in mortality rates might be as high as 35 per cent.[137]

4.81   In response to a particular incident at an NHS facility, guidance on the 'transfer of frail elderly patients to other long stay settings'

133 These elements first being propounded in *R v Brent LBC ex p Gunning* (1986) 84 LGR 168.

134 At 86.

135 [1996] 1 All ER 129; [1996] 1 WLR 60, HL.

136 See, eg, *International Journal of Geriatric Psychiatry* (1993) Vol 8, 521; also see (1994) *Times* 7 July, 'Elderly patients die within weeks of transfer'.

137 'Relocation of the aged and disabled: A mortality study' *Journal of American Geriatric Society*, Vol 11, 185.

(HSC 1998/048) was issued on 2 April 1998. Although primarily aimed at NHS bodies, the circular was copied to all directors of social services in England (and is considered at para 6.52 below).

4.82 Under article 2 of the European Convention of Human Rights, each state is obliged to protect the right to life of all its citizens. The Commission and Court have always interpreted article 2 strictly and held that it includes an obligation on the state to take appropriate action to safeguard life.[138] Many residential home closures involve the relocation of extremely frail elderly people who have spent very many years in a particular home. In addition, in *R v North and East Devon Health Authority ex p Coughlan*,[139] the Court of Appeal held that a closure of the NHS facility in question amounted to an interference with the applicant's right to enjoy her home under article 8. With the implementation of the Human Rights Act 1998, challenges to such home closures will accordingly be able to argue violations of articles 2 and 8 in addition to alleging a flawed consultation process/failure to follow HSC 1998/048.

Health and safety issues

4.83 Detailed consideration of general health and safety issues in residential homes is beyond the scope of this text and reference should be made to guidance issued by the Health and Safety Executive in its booklet HS(G)104, *Health and Safety in Residential Care Homes*.[140] The guidance details the main heads of legal responsibility to employees and residents under the Health and Safety at Work Act 1974 as well as in tort and contract. The guidance gives practical advice on the handling and reporting of incidents; occupational health; training; the working environment; kitchen, laundry and outdoor safety; as well as covering other issues such as violence to staff.

Manual handling

4.84 Of increasing and particular concern, however, is the question of the avoidance of manual handling. This question arises not only in resi-

138 See, eg, Decisions and Reports (of the European Commission on Human Rights) Vol 14, 13.
139 (1999) 2 CCLR 285, CA.
140 Obtainable from HSE Books, PO Box 1999, Sudbury, Suffolk, CO10 6FS. Tel: 01787 881165.

dential care settings, but also in general domiciliary and community care situations. HS(G)104 emphasises the importance of proper manual handling arrangements, thus:

> 89. Almost four of every ten accidents reported in the health care sector arise from manual handling. In residential care homes there will be a range of manual handling tasks from the simple lifting of provisions to complicated lifts involving residents. Sprains and strains of backs and limbs are often sustained from manual handling. Injuries may also occur as a result of cumulative damage often sustained over a considerable period, which can result in physical impairment, or even permanent disability.

4.85 Because of the general prevalence of such injuries throughout all types of work environment, European Directive 90/269/EEC required all member states to take specific legislative action to reduce such injuries at work. In consequence, the Manual Handling Operations Regulations 1992 SI No 2793 were issued, which came into force on 1 January 1993. Detailed guidance on the regulations has been issued by the Health and Safety Executive under reference L23. Regulation 4 provides that:

> 4 (1) Each employer shall –
>   (a) so far as is reasonably practicable, avoid the need for his employees to undertake any manual handling operations at work which involve a risk of their being injured;
>   (b) where it is not reasonably practicable to avoid the need for his employees to undertake any manual handling operations at work which involve a risk of their being injured –
>   (i)   make suitable and sufficient assessment of all manual handling operations to be undertaken by them, having regard to the factors which are specified in column 1 of Schedule 1 to these Regulations and considering the questions which are specified in the corresponding entry in column 2 of that Schedule,
>   (ii) take appropriate steps to reduce the risk of injury to those employees arising out of their undertaking any such manual handling operations to the lowest level reasonably practicable,
>   (iii) take appropriate steps to provide any of those employees who are undertaking any such manual handling operations with general indications and, where it is reasonably practicable to do so, precise information on –
>   (aa) the weight of each load, and
>   (bb) the heaviest side of any load whose centre of gravity is not positioned centrally.
> (2) Any assessment such as is referred to in paragraph (1)(b)(i) of this

regulation shall be reviewed by the employer who made it if –
(a) there is reason to suspect that it is no longer valid; or
(b) there has been a significant change in the manual handling operations to which it relates;
and where as a result of any such review changes to the assessment are required, the relevant employer shall make them.

4.86 As the guidance L23 states, regulation 4 establishes a clear hierarchy of measures which an employer is required to adopt, namely:

a) avoid hazardous manual operations so far as is reasonably practicable;

b) assess any hazardous manual handling operations that cannot be avoided;

c) reduce the risk of injury so far as is reasonably practicable.

The very detailed guidance given by the Health and Safety Executive is of great practical importance, analysing the appropriate use of hoists and other possible lifting mechanisms when moving patients. What the regulations do not do, however, is prohibit the lifting of patients. Frequently, it appears that social services authorities and health authorities are adopting an extremely restrictive interpretation of the regulations which has the end result that a patient does not receive a service (such as a bath) because it involves some manual handling. The regulations, it is emphasised, do not prohibit unavoidable manual handling.

4.87 Where a person is assessed as requiring a service and the authority is obliged by statute to provide that service, then:

a) if there is no mechanical option (ie, the use of a hoist) or other safer procedure, and

b) the authority has carried out a proper risk assessment and fully investigated all the options,

the service must be provided manually.

4.88 In those cases where authorities are using the regulations as a reason for refusing to provide a service, they are often willing to admit that in consequence the task is carried out by a carer instead. Although such a person is not an employee for the purposes of the regulations and other health and safety at work legislation, s/he is someone to whom the authority prima facie owes a duty of care (respect for, and the support of, carers being at the heart of the community care reforms). If an authority fully conversant with the good practice and knowledge engendered by the regulations stands by and allows a carer to carry out tasks it believes to be unduly hazardous for its own employees, then it may well be liable in negligence for any injuries that result (unless, perhaps, it has taken steps to inform and/or train the carer in safe lifting techniques, etc).

4.89   Such health risks are clearly foreseeable, since research has shown that over 50 per cent of carers have suffered a physical injury such as a strained back since they began to care. In addition, the research reveals that caring also subjects carers to other health-related problems, with over half receiving treatment for stress-related illness since becoming carers.[141]

Residential accommodation services and the NHS overlap

4.90   Both social services authorities and the NHS have obligations to care for people who are disabled, ill or who have learning difficulties. In the particular situation of residential accommodation services, however, the overlap takes two forms: the duty on the NHS to deliver specific services to persons in accommodation secured by the social services authority, and the duty on the NHS in certain cases to secure at its own expense the actual nursing home or other accommodation. The overlap of responsibilities, and in particular the responsibility of the NHS in this area, is discussed in detail at para 6.75 below.

Accommodation under MHA 1983 s117

4.91   The duty to provide accommodation (and other community care services) under MHA 1983 s117 is a quite separate community care service to the duty under NAA 1948 s21.[142] The duty only applies in respect of persons who are detained under MHA 1983 s3,[143] or admitted to a hospital under s37[144] or transferred to a hospital under a transfer direction made under s47 or s48[145] and then cease to be detained and leave hospital.

4.92   The duty to provide accommodation under MHA 1983 s117 only arises after a social services authority has assessed the patient as

141 M Henwood *Ignored and Invisible? Carers' Experience of the NHS* (Carers National Association, 1998) cited in *Caring about Carers: A National Strategy for Carers*, LASSL (99)2.

142 NHSCCA 1990 s46(3).

143 Admission to hospital for treatment of a mental disorder.

144 A hospital order made in criminal proceedings.

145 Transfer to hospital of a prisoner suffering from a mental disorder.

requiring this service. Accommodation provided under MHA 1983 s117 differs from the service under NAA 1948 s21 in that local authorities are not permitted to charge for this service (see para 8.109). Section 117 services are considered in detail at para 5.100.

Accommodation under NAA 1948 s29(4)(c)

4.93   NAA 1948 s29(4) empowers social services authorities (subject to direction by the secretary of state) to provide hostel accommodation for disabled people engaged in workshops provided by the authority under that section. The secretary of state's direction empowers (but does not oblige) authorities to provide such facilities.[146]

4.94   The provision of workshop activities is considered in detail at para 5.26(5). The effect of s29(4A) is to make the hostel accommodation so provided subject to the same charging provisions as apply to residential accommodation services under s21; accordingly reference should be made to Chapter 8 for detailed consideration of this aspect.

Accommodation under Children Act 1989 s17

4.95   Children Act 1989 s17 requires social services authorities to safeguard and promote the welfare of children in need in their area; this includes the provision of an almost unlimited range of services, of which accommodation (in a care home or ordinary rented dwelling) may be one. The duties owed to children in need (including disabled children) are considered in detail at para 11.6 below.

146 LAC(93)10 App 2 para 2(4).

CHAPTER 5

Domiciliary services

5.1   **Introduction**

5.9   **Services under NAA 1948 s29**

5.12   18 or over and ordinarily resident

5.13   Client group

Blind • Deaf • Dumb • Suffering from a mental disorder of any description • Substantially and permanently handicapped • 'Illness, injury, or congenital deformity or such other disabilities as may be prescribed by the Minister'

5.24   Services under s29

Services which SSDs have a duty to provide • Services which SSDs have power to provide • Direct payments to service users under NAA 1948 s29 • Overlap with services under NHSA 1977 Sch 8

5.33   **Services under Health Services and Public Health Act 1968 s45**

5.35   Client group

Old people • Ordinarily resident

5.38   Services under s45

Powers to provide s45 services • Excluded groups

5.41   **Services under Chronically Sick and Disabled Persons Act 1970 s2**

5.43   'Ordinarily resident'

5.44   Client group

Disabled adults • Disabled children

continued

5.48   Services under s2

> *Practical assistance in the home • The provision of a wireless, TV, library, etc • The provision of recreational / educational facilities • Travel and other assistance • Home adaptations and disabled facilities • Holidays • Meals • Telephone and ancillary equipment*

5.73   CSDPA 1970 s2 and NAA 1948 s29

5.78   CSDPA 1970 s2 and CA 1989

5.80   Services under National Health Services Act 1977 Sch 8

5.82   Client group

> *Mothers • The ill • Mothers lying-in • The aged • The handicapped*

5.91   Excluded groups

5.92   Services under NHSA 1977 s21 and Sch 8

> *Services for expectant and nursing mothers • Services for the prevention of illness, etc • Home help and laundry services*

5.100   Services under MHA 1983 s117

5.103   Client group

> *Age • Reasons for detention • 'Ceases to be detained' • District or area of residence*

5.115   Services

> *The duration of the duty*

5.126   Mental Health (Patients in the Community) Act 1995

5.129   The care programme approach

5.136   Mental Health Grant

5.138   Direct payments

5.140   Third party schemes

5.142   Community Care (Direct Payments) Act 1996

5.144   Independent Living Fund

> *Independent Living (Extension) Fund • Independent Living (1993) Fund*

Introduction

5.1 Domiciliary and day care services constitute a range of services which are generally provided or secured by social services authorities with the aim of enabling those people who receive them to continue to live in the community (rather than in residential care or nursing homes). The services available include help in the home (personal care and domestic assistance); transport; disability equipment; home adaptations; day care (in day centres or workshops); leisure facilities; and other services aimed at providing support for individuals and carers.[1] Where such services are delivered to a person's home they are referred to collectively as 'domiciliary services', whereas services provided in a community setting are generally termed 'community based services', although in this text, unless the contrary intention is made clear, the phrase 'community care services' is generally used to embrace all non-accommodation services (ie, including domiciliary services).

5.2 The haphazard development of community care over the last 50 years has resulted in community care services for separate client groups (ie, 'elderly people', 'ill people' and 'disabled people') being dealt with by separate statutes.

5.3 The statutory provision of community-based services stems from NAA 1948 s29 which lists, in general terms, the range of services that local authorities are empowered to provide. The statutory shortcomings of s29 eventually led to the enactment of the Chronically Sick and Disabled Persons Act (CSPDA) 1970, which spells out in greater detail some of the services that must be provided.

5.4 The persons entitled to receive services under CSDPA 1970 and under NAA 1948 s29 are broadly the same. Certain vulnerable groups are not, however, covered by these provisions (for instance, the frail elderly and those recovering from an illness). Such groups are nevertheless entitled to receive various community care services as a result of separate legislative provisions (namely the Health Services and Public Health Act (HSPHA) 1968, the NHS Act (NHSA) 1977 and the Mental Health Act (MHA) 1983).

5.5 Although limited steps have been taken to harmonise these disparate statutory provisions, they still retain distinctive features – often incongruous and frequently overlapping.

5.6 With the enactment of the Children Act (CA) 1989, an attempt was made to make separate provision for disabled children; accordingly

---

1 See white paper *Caring for People* para 3.61.

community-based services for children are now primarily governed by CA 1989 Pt III and CSDPA 1970 s2. CA 1989 amended NAA 1948 ss21 and 29 so that, in general, services under these sections are not available to children. Accordingly the community care statutes are often considered to be restricted to providing services for adults. There are, however, exceptions to this rule (most significantly, services under NHSA 1977 Sch 8 para 3 are available for adult or child alike).

5.7   NHSCCA 1990 Pt III made a further attempt to introduce some logical structure into the various community care statutes with s46(3) defining (for the purposes of the Act) 'community care services' as being services under:

*   National Assistance Act 1948 Pt III
*   Health Services and Public Health Act 1968 s45
*   National Health Service Act 1977 s21 and Sch 8
*   Mental Health Act 1983 s117.

Confusingly, however, s46 does not refer to services provided under CSDPA 1970 s2. For the moment the Court of Appeal has determined that services under s2 are 'community care services' notwithstanding this omission. The particular difficulties caused by the wording of s2 in this respect are considered in detail at para 5.73.

5.8   These contradictions and inconsistencies run like fault lines through the community care legislation, which has been well described as a set of often incomprehensible and frequently incompatible principles. Nowhere is this statement truer than in relation to domiciliary and day care services; these services have developed erratically since the war, first by way of cautious general provisions (for example, NAA 1948 s29), and subsequently by way of more idealistic and specific rights (such as those granted in CSDPA 1970 s2). Fundamental contradictions have emerged between these statutes, as a result of both poor and hurried drafting and the absence of any coherent theory underlying the provision of community care. Put plainly, this is an area of law crying out for codification. In an effort to present the subject in a coherent way, this chapter will consider the relevant statutes separately, namely:

*   National Assistance Act 1948 Pt III
*   Health Services and Public Health Act 1968 s45
*   Chronically Sick and Disabled Persons Act 1970 s2
*   National Health Service Act 1977 s21 and Sch 8
*   Mental Health Act 1983 s117
*   Community Care (Direct Payments) Act 1996 s1

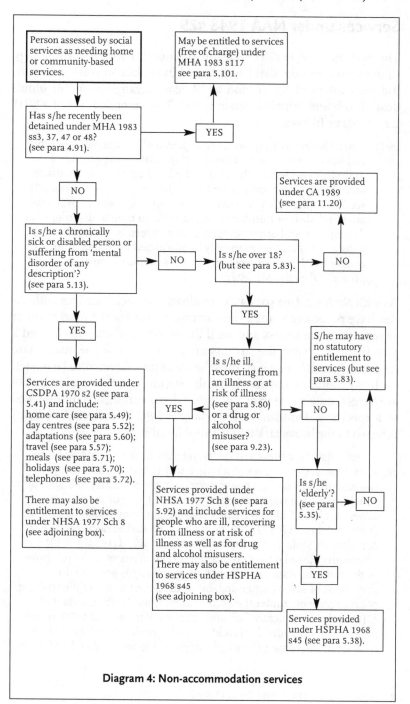

Diagram 4: Non-accommodation services

Services under NAA 1948 s29

5.9   The cross-heading to s29 reveals the profound change in terminology (if not social attitude) that has occurred in the last 50 years – describing the content of the section as 'Welfare arrangements for blind, deaf, dumb and crippled persons, etc'. The amended text of s29(1) now reads as follows:

> 29 (1) A local authority may, with the approval of the Secretary of State, and to such extent as he may direct in relation to persons ordinarily resident in the area of the local authority shall, make arrangements for promoting the welfare of persons to whom this section applies, that is to say persons aged eighteen or over who are blind, deaf or dumb or who suffer from mental disorder of any description, and other persons aged eighteen or over who are substantially and permanently handicapped by illness, injury, or congenital deformity or such other disabilities as may be prescribed by the Minister.

As with NAA s21 (see para 4.2), it follows that social services authorities have no power to make any arrangements for the promotion of anyone's welfare unless and until the secretary of state has issued a direction specifying the arrangements which may be made (are 'approved') and those which must be made (are 'directed' to be made).

5.10   It is generally considered that the statutory duties created by s29 are 'target' duties (see para 1.4) rather than creating any duties owed to a specific individual. In *R v Islington LBC ex p Rixon*,[2] Sedley J referred to the heavy task that counsel faced in:

> ... establishing a breach of the target duty under s29 of the Act of 1948. One of the features of a target duty is that it is ordinarily accompanied by default powers vested in the Secretary of State, to which in general courts defer save where a true question of law arises: see Woolf LJ in *R v Inner London Education Authority ex p Ali* (1990) 2 Admin LR 822, 829, citing his own earlier decision in *R v Secretary of State for the Environment ex p Ward* [1984] 1 WLR 849. Although counsel have drawn attention to no material default power in the National Assistance Act 1948, specificity is given to the provisions of s29, as amended, by (a) the power to direct the making of arrangements under the section and (b) the grafting onto it of s2(1) of the Chronically Sick and Disabled Persons Act 1970. In my judgement, the individual rights afforded under s29 of the 1948 Act (at least in the sense of a sufficient interest to seek judicial review of

2   (1998) 1 CCLR 119; (1996) *Times* 17 April.

failures of provision) militate against the existence of any locus standi to assert a failure in the target duty created by the section. If there has been such a failure, it will show, so far as material, in want of personal provision which is separately justiciable.

While the obligations created by s29 are target rather than private law duties, the deficiencies in this respect have (as Sedley J points out) been partially remedied by CSDPA 1970 s2 which was enacted with the purpose of creating individual rights to certain specified domiciliary services for the s29 client group.

5.11   The secretary of state's most recent direction in respect of s29 is found at Appendix 2 to LAC(93)10[3] and came into force on 1 April 1993 (the full text of the direction is in Appendix 2 below).

18 or over and ordinarily resident

5.12   Section 29 services are only available if they promote the welfare[4] of persons who are 18 or over. The duty to provide s29 services[5] applies only to persons who are ordinarily resident in the local authority's area, whereas a power exists to provide services for other persons.[6] There are no exceptions to these two basic requirements (for example, no exception for cases of urgency). Ordinary residence has the same meaning as in relation to s21 (see para 4.28) with a minor exception under s29(7) in relation to certain service users who are (or have been) employed in a workshop or an equivalent occupational activity promoted by the social services authority.

Client group

5.13   In order to be eligible for any of the services available under s29, a person must be:

a) blind, or
b) deaf, or
c) dumb, or
d) suffering from mental disorder of any description, or
e) substantially and permanently handicapped by 'illness, injury,

3   WOC35/93 in Wales.
4   The wording of s29(1) is such that the service need not be provided *to* the disabled person, ie, a service provided to a carer may be an 'arrangement which promotes the welfare of the disabled person'.
5   LAC(93)10 App 2 para 2(1); albeit that it is only a target duty, see para 1.4.
6   *R v Berkshire CC ex p P* (1998) 1 CCLR 141.

congenital deformity or such other disabilities as may be prescribed by the Minister'.

The list should be contrasted with that under s21 (see para 4.10) which deals with local authorities' duties to provide residential accommodation. The s21 list is less restrictive, including such groups as the frail elderly, expectant mothers and disabled persons (without having to establish that their 'handicap' is either permanent or substantial (to quote the language of s29)).

5.14   As already noted s29 places a duty on social services authorities to maintain registers of people in their area who may be entitled to its services (at para 2.4 above). The test, however, of whether a person qualifies for services under s29 is independent of whether or not s/he is on a particular authority's register, ie, registration is not a prerequisite to obtaining assistance.[7]

Blind

5.15   Although s29 makes no reference to partially sighted persons, previous guidance[8] confirms that the phrase 'other persons who are substantially and permanently handicapped' covers persons who are partially sighted.

5.16   Social services authorities have well-established procedures for determining whether a visually impaired person is blind or partially sighted and thus whether the terms of s29(1) (and registration) apply. The procedure is initiated by a consultant ophthalmologist completing the relevant form (a substantial form known as BD8).[9] The form is completed in collaboration with the patient, who is provided with a copy of the first part only (relating to the consultant's certification of sight loss). The patient has a right to seek a review of the assessment.[10] The circular guidance advises that the effective date of registration should be the same as that of certification.[11] The guidance further recommends that social services authorities have separate sections in their register for each of the groups of persons to whom s29 applies (ie, that blind and partially sighted persons be separately recorded).[12]

7   LAC(93)10 App 4 para 3.

8   LAC 13/74 para 11(i).

9   BP1 in Scotland and A655 in Northern Ireland.

10   For further information see LASSL(90)1 and generally para 4.7 of the 'In Touch' handbook (BBC).

11   LAC(93)10 App 4 para 6.

12   Ibid at para 9.

Deaf

5.17 Although s29 makes no specific reference to partially deaf persons, previous guidance[13] confirms that the phrase 'other persons who are substantially and permanently handicapped' covers persons who are hard of hearing.

5.18 There are no formal examination procedures for determining whether a person is deaf for the purposes of s29.[14] Social services authorities are advised that all persons who suffer from a disabling loss of hearing should be regarded as being deaf for the purposes of s29.[15] The guidance suggests, however, that this single class should be subdivided into three categories:[16]

Deaf without speech: Those who have no useful hearing and those whose normal method of communication is by signs, finger spelling or writing.

Deaf with speech: Those who (even with a hearing aid) have little or no useful hearing but whose normal method of communication is by speech and lip-reading.

Hard-of-hearing: Those who (with or without a hearing aid) have some useful hearing and whose normal method of communication is by speech, listening and lip-reading.

The guidance in LAC(93)10 Appendix 4 annex 2 makes a number of general statements concerning the importance the government attaches to services for the deaf; these statements are directed principally at the training and duties of specialist social workers in this field rather than being specific statements about the type of services to be provided.

Dumb

5.19 The guidance gives no advice as to the criteria for determining whether or not a person with limited speech comes within the scope of s29 (other than by reference to persons who are 'deaf without speech', see above). By implication, however, persons who have little or no useful speech must come within the scope of the phrase 'substantially and permanently handicapped'.[17]

13 LAC 13/74 para 11(i); see also LAC(93)10 App 4 para 7.

14 LAC(93)10 App 4 para 7.

15 Ibid at Annex 2 para 2.

16 Ibid.

17 See LAC 13/74 para 11(i) and LAC(93)10 App 4 Annex 2 para 2.

Suffering from a mental disorder of any description

5.20   Persons suffering from a mental disorder of any description (ie, within the ambit of MHA 1983 s1) are included in the s29 client group.[18] However, as is detailed below, s29 services cannot be provided to a person if the same service has been 'authorised or required' to be provided under NHSA 1977.[19] The relevant part of NHSA 1977 (and the secretary of state's direction issued under it) has been so drafted that s29 services are generally of little relevance to persons suffering from a mental disorder. The importance, however, of including such persons within s29 is that they are thereby included and eligible for services under CSDPA 1970 s2. Persons who suffer from a mental disorder are entitled to community care services under NHSA 1977 Sch 8 and/or under MHA 1983 s117 (see paras 5.96 and 5.101 respectively) in addition to s2 of the 1970 Act.[20]

5.21   Whereas all the other potential service users under NAA 1948 s29 (and/or CSDPA 1970 s2) are persons whose 'handicap' is permanent and substantial, this is not however a requirement for persons suffering from a mental disorder.

Substantially and permanently handicapped

5.22   Circular guidance[21] states:

It has not proved possible to give precise guidance on the interpretation of the phrase 'substantially and permanently handicapped'. However, as hitherto, authorities are asked to give a wide interpretation to the term 'substantial', which the Department fully recognises must always take full account of individual circumstances. With regard to the term 'permanent', authorities will also wish to interpret this sufficiently flexibly to ensure that they do not feel inhibited from giving help under s29 in cases where they are uncertain of the likely duration of the condition.

---

18 LAC(93)10 App 4 para 14.
19 NAA 1948 s29(6) see para 5.29 below.
20 LAC(93)10 App 4 para 13 incorrectly states that such services are generally provided under Health Services and Public Health Act 1968 s12 – this section has been repealed and reference should have been made to NHSA 1977 Sch 8 (although since CSDPA 1970 s2 applies to persons suffering from a mental disorder of any description, arguably this section is of greater importance).
21 LAC(93)10 App 4 para 8.

'Illness, injury, or congenital deformity or such other disabilities as may be prescribed by the Minister'

5.23 To qualify for services under s29 a person who is substantially and permanently handicapped must be so by virtue of an illness, an injury, or congenital deformity; no further disabilities have in fact been prescribed by the minister. Furthermore, people who are disabled as a result of an illness or congenital deformity will not be entitled to receive s29 services where those services are available under NHSA 1977.[22] It is undecided as to whether substantial and permanent handicap resulting from drug or alcohol misuse can be defined as arising out of illness or injury so as to qualify the person for s29 services; in practice domiciliary services to such persons will generally be delivered under NHSA 1977.

Services under s29

5.24 Section 29 leaves the secretary of state with the power to determine the type of domiciliary services which can be provided; the only limitations being:

a) that the purpose of the services must be the promotion of the welfare of the s29 client group;[23]

b) by virtue of s29(6)(a) that the direct payment of money to service users is not permitted under s29 (except if a payment for their work or produce, and see also para 5.142 concerning 'direct payments'); and

c) by virtue of s29(6)(b) that no accommodation or services can be provided under s29 if the accommodation or services have been 'authorised or required' to be provided under NHSA 1977.[24]

5.25 Although s29(4) contains an illustrative list of the type of services that may be made available, the Act leaves to the secretary of state the power to decide what services must and what services may be provided. The services referred to by s29(4) are:

(a) for informing persons to whom arrangements under that subsection relate of the services available for them thereunder;

(b) for giving persons instruction in their own homes or elsewhere in methods of overcoming the effects of their disabilities;

(c) for providing workshops where such persons may be engaged

---

22 NAA 1948 s29(6).

23 But see para 7.36 below.

24 The provision of accommodation is however specifically excluded from NHSA 1977 Sch 8, see para 5.92.

(whether under a contract of service or otherwise) in suitable work, and hostels where persons engaged in the workshops, and others to whom arrangements under subsection (1) of this section relate and for whom work or training is being provided in pursuance of the Disabled Persons (Employment) Act 1944, or the Employment and Training Act 1973 may live;

(d) for providing persons to whom arrangements under subsection (1) of this section relate with suitable work (whether under a contract of service or otherwise) in their own homes or elsewhere;

(e) for helping such persons in disposing of the produce of their work;

(f) for providing such persons with recreational facilities in their own homes or elsewhere

(g) for compiling and maintaining classified registers of the persons to whom arrangements under subsection (1) of this section relate.

The secretary of state's most recent directions in respect of s29 services were issued as Appendix 2 to LAC(93)10[25] in March 1993. The directions distinguish between services[26] which a social services department *may* provide (ie, has a power to provide – generally known as an 'approval') and those which it *must* provide (ie, is under a duty to provide).

Services which SSDs have a duty to provide

5.26   As noted above, the duty on social services departments to provide services under s29 is restricted to persons who are ordinarily resident in the authority's area. The services being:

1) *Social work service, advice and support* Social services authorities are required to 'provide a social work service and such advice and support as may be needed for people in their own homes or elsewhere' (LAC(93)10 App 2 para 2(1)(a)). This duty is complemented by Local Authority Social Services Act (LASSA) 1970 s6(6) which obliges local authorities to provide 'adequate staff for assisting' the director of social services in the exercise of his or her functions.[27] 'Advice and support' would cover such services as welfare rights advice[28] and counselling. Previous circular

25 The full text of which is at Appendix A below. The Directions were issued in Wales as WOC 35/93.

26 The local authority may provide the services alone, or in conjunction with another authority or by employing an independent or private provider: see NAA 1948 s30 and LAC(93)10 App 2 paras 3 and 4.

27 See para 1.11 above.

28 See the editor's comments at pD1–060 of the *Encyclopedia of Social Services and Child Care Law* (Sweet & Maxwell) on the extent of the welfare rights advice duty and reference to Local Government Ombudsman decision No 91/C/1246.

guidance[29] advised that the provision of advice and support would frequently necessitate offering advice and other help to the families of the disabled person; and that authorities should bear in mind the part which voluntary workers can play in delivering this service.

2) *Social rehabilitation or adjustment to disability* Social services authorities are required 'to provide, whether at centres or elsewhere, facilities for social rehabilitation and adjustment to disability including assistance in overcoming limitations of mobility or communication' (LAC(93)10 App 2 para 2(1)(b)). These services will generally be provided for a short or medium-term period covering the disabled person's rehabilitation or adjustment to his or her disability. The reference to 'social' rehabilitation makes the point that medical rehabilitation is either a service to be provided under the NHSA 1977 Sch 8 (and thus excluded from provision under s29)[30] or is one which should be provided by the NHS. The bundle of services referred to in this category covers, in many cases, services for which there is an overlapping responsibility between the NHS and the social services authority (see para 6.101).

The direction, in respect of these services, subsumes (and extends) the services referred to in s29(4)(b), which merely refers to arrangements for 'giving persons instruction in their own homes or elsewhere in methods of overcoming the effects of their disabilities'.

3) *Compiling and maintaining registers* Social services authorities are required to make arrangements 'for informing persons to whom [s29] relates of the services available for them [under s29]' (LAC(93)10 App 2 para 2(1)(2) and s29(4)(g)). The extent and nature of this duty is considered in detail at para 2.4 above.

4) *Occupational, social, cultural and recreational facilities* Social services authorities are required 'to provide, whether at centres or elsewhere, facilities for occupational, social, cultural and recreational activities and, where appropriate, the making of payments to persons for work undertaken by them' (LAC(93)10 App 2 para 2(1)(c)). These services will generally be provided on a continuing basis; being palliative rather than therapeutic in purpose. They include the day centre in its various forms, workshops,

29 DHSS Circular 13/74 para 11(ii) – cancelled by LAC(93)10.
30 NAA 1948 s29(6)(b).

recreational and educational activities, as well as art, sport, drama sessions and so on.

The direction, in respect of these services, overlaps with the workshop services referred to in s29(4)(c) and subsumes (and extends) the services referred to in s29(4)(f) which merely refers to arrangements for 'providing such persons with recreational facilities in their own homes or elsewhere'. In most cases services of this nature will in fact be provided to the eligible s29 service user via CSDPA 1970 s2(1)(c) (see para 5.52 below).

5) *Workshop and workshop hostel services* The provision of facilities for occupational activities often takes the form of a local authority workshop which provides employment (paid or otherwise) for particular user groups – frequently people with learning difficulties. In addition to the power to pay users employed in the workshops,[31] social services authorities are specifically empowered to help such persons dispose of the products of their work. The use of workshops continues the tradition of the segregated workhouse of the pre-welfare state. In the early post-war years many such workshops were former poor-law workhouses which continued to be devoted to menial mechanical tasks, and hence many are still to be found located on the old industrial estates.

The social services authorities' duty to provide workshops is coupled with the power to provide hostel accommodation (including board and other services, amenities and requisites)[32] for those engaged in the workshop or other occupational activity under to s29(4). Section 29(4A) applies the same charging rules for the provision of such accommodation as applies to residential accommodation provided under s21 (see Chapter 8 generally and para 8.56 specifically).

Services which SSDs have power to provide

5.27   The directions[33] give social services authorities the discretion to provide the following services (regardless of the potential service user's ordinary residence[34]).

---

31 LAC(93)10 App 2 para 2(1)(c) contains an express power for local authorities to pay disabled persons who undertake work in workshops.

32 NAA 1948 s29(4)(c) and LAC(93)10 App 2 para 2(4).

33 LAC(93)10 App 2 paras 2(3) and (4).

34 *R v Berkshire CC ex p P* (1998) 1 CCLR 141.

1) *Holiday homes* The discretion to provide holiday homes under s29 should be contrasted with the duty under CSDPA 1970 s2(1)(f) to facilitate the taking of a holiday (see para 5.70).

2) *Free or subsidised travel* 'Provide free or subsidised travel for all or any persons who do not otherwise qualify for travel concessions, but only in respect of travel arrangements for which concessions are available'. Travel concessions are dealt with under the Transport Act 1985,[35] s93(7) of which sets out the minimum eligibility requirements. The people concerned must be:
   a) men over 65 and women over 60; or
   b) persons under 16; or
   c) persons 16–18 undergoing full-time education; or
   d) blind persons; or
   e) people suffering from any disability or injury which, in the opinion of the authority, seriously impairs their ability to walk.
   Transport Act 2000 ss123–129 will (when they come into force) amend the 1985 Act by making provision for half-price travel concessionary schemes.

3) *Assistance in finding accommodation* 'Assist a person in finding accommodation which will enable him or her to take advantage of any arrangements made under s29(1) of the Act'. Social services authorities have been given the power to provide this service (and those detailed in (4) and (5) below) to meet the needs of disabled people, similar to the powers approved for elderly persons under DHSS Circular 19/71 para 4 (see para 5.39).

4) *Subsidy of warden costs* 'Contribute to the cost of employing a warden on welfare functions in warden assisted housing schemes'. For an equivalent power for elderly persons, see para 5.39.

5) *Warden services* 'Provide warden services for occupiers of private housing'. For an equivalent power for elderly persons, see para 5.39.

6) *Information on disability services* The power to inform persons to whom arrangements under s29 relate of the services available for them under s29.[36] The power under s29 to provide information services for disabled people has been subsumed into the wider duty set out in CSDPA 1970 (see para 2.18).

---

35 See also London Regional Transport Act 1984 and Transport Act 1985 (Extension of Eligibility for Travel Concessions) Order 1986.
36 NAA 1948 s29(4)(a) and LAC(93)10 App 2 para 2(4).

Direct payments to service users under NAA 1948 s29

5.28   Although s29(6)(a) prohibits authorities from making cash payments (under s29) to service users to enable them to procure their own care,[37] its impact has been largely neutralised by the provisions of the Community Care (Direct Payments) Act 1996, which Act is considered in detail at para 5.142 below.

Overlap with services under NHSA 1977 Sch 8

5.29   NAA 1948 s29(6)(b) excludes services being provided under s29 where such services 'are required to be provided' under NHSA 1977.

5.30   The use of the word 'required' suggests that it is only where there is an obligation to provide the service under NHSA 1977 that the provision must be under this statute (if at all) rather than under s29. A consideration of the similar exclusionary provision which exists in relation to accommodation services under NAA 1948 s21[38] supports this interpretation. The s21 provision was considered by the Court of Appeal in *R v North East Devon Health Authority ex p Coughlan*.[39] Amending the relevant judgment to accommodate the slightly different wording of s29(6)(b),[40] the court's interpretation would appear to be as follows:

> The subsection should not be regarded as preventing a local authority from providing any health services. The subsection's prohibitive effect is limited to those health services which, in fact, [are] . . . required to be provided under [NHSA 1977]. Such health services would not therefore include services which the Secretary of State legitimately decided under section 3(1) of the [NHSA 1977] it was not necessary for the NHS to provide . . . The true effect is to emphasise that [the NAA 1948] provision . . . is secondary to [the NHSA 1977] provision.

5.31   Physiotherapy and chiropody are examples of services which social services departments are probably prohibited from providing, by virtue of s29(6)(b), since these are specifically referred to as being health services under LAC(95)5.[41] Technically these are services

---

37 This provision is mirrored in NHSA 1977 Sch 8 para 2(2).

38 Section 21(8); although this subsection prohibits social services from providing any services which are *'authorised or* required' to be provided under NHSA 1977.

39 (1999) 2 CCLR 285.

40 Ie, by excluding reference to the phrase *'authorised or'*.

41 See para 6.116 below).

which local authorities might otherwise have been obliged to consider providing, in that they clearly come within the definition of services which help 'overcome limitations of mobility or communication' (LAC(93)10 App 2 para 2(1)(b)).

5.32   In *R v Gloucestershire CC ex p Mahfood*,[42] the council sought to argue that there was a further consequence which flowed from s29(6)(b). The argument hinged on whether or not services provided by virtue of CSDPA 1970 s2 are s29 services or free-standing s2 services.[43] This general question is considered in greater detail at para 5.73. In the context of s29(6)(b) McCowan LJ disposed of the respondent counsel's submissions as follows:

> His argument was that it is a pre-condition of the duty under section 2 of the 1970 Act that the local authority have power to provide the service under section 29 of the 1948 Act. If there is no power under section 29 there can be no duty under section 2. But section 29(6) of the 1948 Act positively provides that there is no power to exercise certain functions, in particular those which involve services which have to be provided under the National Health Service Act 1977. There is a duty to provide home helps for the aged and handicapped, but it is a duty under the 1977 Act. Therefore, the power to provide the service is excluded and home help services could not lawfully have been provided to Mr Mahfood and Mr Barry under section 2 of the 1970 Act.
>
> The submission is an unattractive one because it would follow that if the local authority were satisfied, by reason of the fact that general arrangements had not been made for home help under the 1977 Act, that arrangements should be made for home help, it would have no power and thus no duty to make these arrangements. The short answer to the point, however, is that section 29(6) of the 1948 Act merely states that 'nothing in the foregoing provisions of this section shall authorise or require'. What is authorising the local authority to make arrangements under section 2 is section 2. Thus the provisions which authorise the local authority to meet the needs of a disabled person if those needs are not being otherwise met are section 2 itself.[44]

---

42 (1997) 1 CCLR 7.
43 The respondent did not pursue this argument in the Court of Appeal or the House of Lords.
44 (1997) 1 CCLR 7 at 16K.

Services under Health Services and Public Health Act 1968 s45

5.33   NAA 1948 s29 enables social services authorities to provide domiciliary services for persons who are substantially and permanently handicapped by reason of illness, injury, or congenital deformity. It does not, however, permit the provision of such services to the elderly where their need arises not because of illness or 'handicap',[45] but solely because their age has made them frail. This lacuna is dealt with by HSPHA 1968 s45. Subsection (1) provides:

> A local authority may with the approval of the Secretary of State, and to such extent as he may direct, shall make arrangements for promoting the welfare of old people.

Section 45 is drafted to the same pattern as NAA 1948 s29, in that it does not authorise the provision of any services but leaves to the secretary of state the power to specify in directions what services may and what services must be provided.

5.34   The only (and current) directions that have been issued are contained in DHSS Circular 19/71 (see below). The circular explains (at para 3) that the purpose of s45 is to enable authorities to make approved arrangements for the elderly who are not substantially and permanently handicapped, and thus to promote the welfare of the elderly generally and so far as possible to prevent or postpone personal deterioration or breakdown.

Client group

Old people

5.35   Section 45 services are available to old people. The phrase 'old people' is not defined, and probably needs no definition. If a person requires domiciliary services for any reason other than the fact that age has made him/her frail, then statutory provisions exist to enable that service to be provided.[46] The phrase includes a class of persons often referred to as EMI, the elderly mentally infirm.

5.36   The circular guidance suggested however that in the early days of the power (ie, post-April 1971):

> it might prove desirable to start by identifying the needs of certain groups of the elderly who seem likely to be particularly vulnerable,

45   In the sense used by NAA 1948 s29.
46   Ie, under NAA 1948 s29, CSDPA 1970 s2, NHSA 1977 Sch 8 or MHA 1983 s117.

eg, (a) elderly people, especially the more elderly, who are housebound or living alone or recently bereaved or about to be discharged from hospital, and (b) other persons over, say, 75 living in the community, particularly where there are high concentrations of very elderly people in particular districts.[47]

Ordinarily resident

5.37 Neither the Act nor the Directions restrict s45 services to persons 'ordinarily resident' in the local authority's area. This again is not strictly necessary, in that the directions have been limited to authorising (but not directing) the provision of such services. Accordingly, social services authorities are entitled (but in no way obliged) to reach a general policy decision (without fettering their individual discretion) to limit the use of their powers to elderly persons ordinarily resident within their area.

Services under s45

5.38 The statutory framework for the provision of services under s45 is similar to that under NAA 1948 s29. As with s29, s45 leaves to the secretary of state the power to determine the type of domiciliary services which can be provided. As with s29, s45 services are subject to three basic limitations, which are (in the case of s45 services):

1) that the purpose of the service must be the promotion of the welfare of elderly people;[48]
2) by virtue of s45(4)(a) that the direct payment of money to 'old people' is not permitted (except if a payment for their 'work in accordance with the arrangements'); and
3) by virtue of s45(4)(b) that no accommodation or services can be provided under s45 if the accommodation or services could be provided under NHSA 1977.[49]

The secretary of state's only Direction in respect of s45 services was issued in DHSS Circular 19/71 para 4, in March 1971. Although the wording of s45 would allow the directions to place social services authorities under a duty to provide certain services, the direction

---

47 DHSS Circular 19/71 at para 7.
48 The wording of s45 is such that the service need not be provided *to* the disabled person; ie, a service provided to a carer may be 'an arrangement which promotes the welfare of an elderly person'.
49 See para 5.24 above.

merely empowers the provision of the specified services (ie, gives a discretion), without creating any obligation.

Powers to provide s45 services

5.39 The directions give social services authorities the discretion to provide[50] the services specified below. Authorities may provide services over and above those actually specified in the directions if they first obtain the secretary of state's specific approval.[51]

1) *'Meals and recreation in the home or elsewhere'* The guidance suggests that 'many of the elderly who are mobile or who can be transported will require social centres providing meals and oppor- tunities for occupation as well as companionship and recreation. For the housebound and the frailer elderly meals-on-wheels will also need to be developed'.[52] The services available under this direction include the provision of 'recreation'. This would include day centres, outings, the provision of a television in the home and so on. The equivalent services for disabled people (under CSDPA 1970 ss2(1)(c) and 2(1)(b) respectively) are considered at para 5.51 and para 5.52.

2) *Information on elderly services* 'To inform the elderly of services available to them and to identify elderly people in need of services'. The guidance cautions against attempts to develop a comprehen- sive register of the elderly.[53] It emphasises however that 'good services together with wide and continuing publicity about them are a pre-requisite of any scheme for finding out needs. The elderly and those who know of them cannot be expected to come forward if they do not know of any reason for doing so'.[54] The more specific duty to inform under CSDPA 1970 s1 is dealt with at para 2.17.

3) *Travel assistance to participate in s45 services* 'To provide facilities or assistance in travelling to and from the home for the purpose of participating in services provided by the authority or similar services'. The equivalent duty under CSDPA 1970 is dealt with at para 5.57.

50 The local authority may provide the services alone, or by employing independent or private providers – see HSPHA 1968 s45(3) and DHSS Circular 19/71 paras 5(b), 7 and 11 onwards.
51 DHSS Circular 19/71 at para 4.
52 Ibid at para 10.
53 Ibid at para 6(a).
54 Ibid at para 6(b).

4) *Assistance in finding boarding accommodation* 'To assist in finding suitable households for boarding elderly persons'. Social services authorities are given the power to provide this service (and those detailed in (7) and (8) below) to meet the needs of elderly people, similar to the powers approved for disabled people under NAA 1948 s29 in LAC(93)10 Appendix 2 para 3 (see para 5.27).

5) *Social work support and advice* 'To provide visiting and advisory services and social work support'. The guidance suggests that social visiting services should be given high priority and that they should be co-ordinated by local authorities but largely undertaken by voluntary workers or others after suitable preparatory training.[55]

6) *Home help and home adaptations* 'To provide practical assistance in the home, including assistance in the carrying out of any additional facilities designed to secure the greater safety, comfort or convenience'. The guidance states that 'home-help, including laundry services and other aids to independent living, should probably be high on any priority list'.[56] The equivalent (and more substantial) duties to provide such services under CSDPA 1970 s2, and under NHSA 1977 Sch 8 para 3 (home helps only) are dealt with at paras 5.49, 5.60 and 5.98 respectively.

7) *Subsidy of warden costs* 'To contribute towards the cost of employing a warden on welfare functions in warden-assisted housing schemes'.

8) *Warden services* 'To provide warden services for occupiers of private housing'.

Excluded groups

5.40   The effect of the Immigration and Asylum Act 1999 s117, by amending s45, is to exclude from services older people who are asylum seekers and are in need of community care services solely on account of being 'destitute'[57] (see para 4.16 above).

---

55   Ibid at para 10; and see also para 5.26 where the equivalent service under NAA 1948 s29 is considered.

56   Ibid at para 10.

57   Section 45(4A) as inserted by Immigration and Asylum Act 1999 s117.

Services under Chronically Sick and Disabled Persons Act 1970 s2

5.41   CSDPA 1970, sponsored by Alf Morris MP, is the first of a distinguished line of private members' Bills in this field[58] and represents an early marker in the continuing struggle by disabled people for full civil rights. Writing 25 years after its enactment, Alf Morris commented:

> It seems incredible and outrageous now, but from 1945–1964, there was not one debate in the Commons on disability. Westminster and Whitehall always had more pressing things to do than respond to the claims of people with disabilities. No one even knew how many disabled people there were in Britain. They were treated not so much as second-class citizens, more as non-people: seen or heard only by families or, if they were in institutions, by those who controlled their lives.[59]

5.42   The speed with which the Act was drafted resulted in ambiguities which have frustrated its interpretation; most significantly the extent to which CSDPA 1970 s2 is distinct from NAA 1948 s29; this question is considered in greater detail below. The underlying purpose of s2 was undoubtedly to convert the vaguely worded, generally discretionary services under NAA 1948 s29 into a set of specific services to which individual disabled people had an enforceable right. Section 2(1) reads as follows:

> Where a local authority having functions under section 29 of the National Assistance Act 1948 are satisfied in the case of any person to whom that section applies who is ordinarily resident in their area that it is necessary in order to meet the needs of that person for that authority to make arrangements for all or any of the following matters, namely –
> (a) the provision of practical assistance for that person in his home;
> (b) the provision for that person of, or assistance to that person in obtaining, wireless, television, library or similar recreational facilities;
> (c) the provision for that person of lectures, games, outings or other recreational facilities outside his home or assistance to that person in taking advantage of educational facilities available to him;

---

58   The Disabled Persons (Services, Consultation and Representation) Act 1986 was promoted by Tom Clarke MP and the Carers (Recognition and Services) Act 1995 was promoted by Malcolm Wicks MP.

59   DW Issues: June 1995.

(d) the provision for that person of facilities for, or assistance in, travelling to and from his home for the purpose of participating in any services provided under any arrangements made by the authority under the said section 29 or, with the approval of the authority, in any services provided otherwise than as aforesaid which are similar to services which could be provided under such arrangements;

(e) the provision of assistance for that person in arranging for the carrying out of any works of adaptation in his home or the provision of any additional facilities designed to secure his greater safety, comfort or convenience;

(f) facilitating the taking of holidays by that person, whether at holiday homes or otherwise and whether provided under arrangements made by the authority or otherwise;

(g) the provision of meals for that person whether in his home or elsewhere;

(h) the provision for that person of, or assistance to that person in obtaining, a telephone and any special equipment necessary to enable him to use a telephone,

then, [subject to the provisions of section 7(1) of the Local Authority Social Services Act 1970 (which requires local authorities in the exercise of certain functions, including functions under the said section 29, to act under the general guidance of the Secretary of State)], it shall be the duty of that authority to make those arrangements in exercise of their functions under the said section 29.

'Ordinarily resident'

5.43   Section 2 services are only available to persons who are ordinarily resident in the local authority's area. Ordinary residence has the same meaning as in relation to NAA 1948 s21 (see para 4.28), although the statutory procedure for resolving disputes about 'ordinary residence' (under NAA 1948 s32(3), see para 4.36 above) is not available where the disagreement concerns services under s2.[60]

Client group

5.44   CSDPA 1970 s2 services are available to both disabled children and disabled adults (unlike services under NAA 1948 s29, which are only available to disabled adults). Section 2 requires social services authorities to make arrangements 'for that person', whereas NAA 1948 s29

60   *R v Kent CC ex p Salisbury and Pierre* (2000) 3 CCLR 38.

speaks of the need to make arrangements to 'promote the welfare' of a class of people. It follows therefore that services under s2 must only be provided to the disabled person, whereas it is arguable that other domiciliary care services can be provided to third parties so long as they thereby 'promote the welfare' of the person in question.[61]

Disabled adults

5.45   Section 2 services are available to the same group of persons as specified in NAA 1948 s29, namely persons aged 18 or over who are blind, deaf, dumb or who suffer from mental disorder of any description, and other persons aged 18 or over who are substantially and permanently handicapped by illness, injury, or congenital deformity (see para 5.13 onwards, where these terms are considered in detail).

Disabled children

5.46   By virtue of CSDPA 1970 s28A, s2 services are additionally available to disabled children within the meaning of the Children Act 1989 s17(11), namely a child who is 'blind, deaf, dumb or suffers from mental disorder of any kind or is substantially and permanently handicapped by illness, injury or congenital deformity'. It will be seen that CA 1989 follows the wording used in NAA 1948 s29, and accordingly the comments made in respect of the adult client group apply equally to disabled children.

5.47   While CA 1989 itself makes provision for a wide range of services for disabled children (considered in greater detail at para 11.10 below), in general, if the service is capable of being provided under both Acts, then it will (as a matter of law) be provided under the 1970 Act.[62]

Services under s2

5.48   As already noted (see para 3.71 above), once a social services authority has carried out an assessment of the needs of a disabled person and decided that the provision of services under s2 is necessary in order to meet that person's needs, then the authority is under an absolute duty to provide that service.[63] The services detailed in s2 are described below.

---

61 See para 7.36 below.
62 *R v Bexley LBC ex p B* (2000) 3 CCLR 15, see para 5.79 below where this question is considered in greater detail.
63 *R v Gloucestershire CC ex p Barry* (1997) 1 CCLR 40; [1997] AC 584.

Practical assistance in the home

5.49 'The provision of practical assistance for that person in the home' (s2(1)(a)). The potential services covered by this paragraph include those primarily concerned with the maintenance of the home (eg, house-cleaning, ironing, decorating, etc) and those concerned with the personal care of the disabled person (eg, help with getting out of and into bed, dressing, cooking, laundry, etc). While a rigid policy of not providing the former services under s2 would amount to a breach of statutory duty, it is the case that personal care will generally be of higher priority in any system of eligibility criteria. Where (for instance) carers are providing significant personal care to the disabled person, assistance with house-cleaning, etc may become a higher priority – in that the provision of this service may free the carers to provide an equivalent amount of additional personal care.

5.50 There is appreciable overlap between the duty under s2(1)(a) and that under NHSA 1977 Sch 8 para 3, which places a duty on social services authorities to provide home help for households where such help is required owing to the presence of a person who is suffering from illness, lying in, an expectant mother, aged, or handicapped as a result of having suffered from illness or by congenital deformity (see para 5.98).The main differences between these two provisions are:

a) The NHSA service is available to a wider client group (ie, the 'handicap' need not be permanent or substantial; expectant mothers, the temporarily ill and the elderly are covered), but it does not cover persons handicapped as a result of injury.

b) The service under NHSA 1977 is generally regarded as a target duty, whereas the duty under s2 can create an individual right to the service (see para 1.4).

c) The NHSA service is provided to 'households' (ie, a direct beneficiary may be the carer), whereas the s2 service can only be provided to the disabled person (ie, a carer could only be an indirect beneficiary).

d) The NHSA 1977 uses the phrase 'home help' whereas s2(1)(a) refers to 'practical assistance' in the home – although it is difficult to see whether anything of significance can be discerned from this difference.

In *R v Islington LBC ex p McMillan*,[64] the applicant complained that, among other things, although he had been assessed as needing

64 (1997) 1 CCLR 7 at 17.

regular home care assistance, this had on occasions not materialised (because of staff being on leave or ill). The court held that this did not amount to a breach of duty since the applicant had been notified in the care plan that the service might suffer from such interruptions and, given his comparative need, that this was not unreasonable.[65]

The provision of a wireless, TV, library, etc

5.51 'The provision for that person of, or assistance to that person in obtaining, wireless, television, library or similar recreational facilities' (s2(1)(b)). The service described consists of the social services authority actually providing (or helping with the acquisition of) equipment to satisfy a recreational need; it clearly includes such an item as a personal computer, hi-fi system, etc.

The provision of recreational/ educational facilities

5.52 'The provision for that person of lectures, games, outings, or other recreational facilities outside his home or assistance to that person in taking advantage of educational facilities available to him' (s2(1)(c)). In *R v Haringey LBC ex p Norton*,[66] the respondent council, when carrying out its assessment, only considered its obligation to provide 'personal care needs' rather than other needs such as social, recreational and leisure needs (such as those available under s2(1)(c)). The court held this to be unlawful; the assessment had to investigate all potential needs.

5.53 Section 2(1)(c) requires social services authorities to provide two separate types of service, namely:

1) *Recreational facilities*

This service is complementary to the home-based service detailed in (2) above, and must be provided outside the person's home. Included within this provision are traditional day centres and 'drop-in' clubs as well as such recreational activities as outings and so on.

Where a person is assessed as needing a place in a day centre, and his/her name is put on a waiting list because no such places are currently available, then in effect the authority will be failing to meet assessed need. If the waiting list is reasonably short, then this may be acceptable. If, however, it is a chronic problem, the authority will be liable to challenge, unless it is taking expeditious steps to increase the number of available places. This aspect was

65   See para 3.79 above where this issue is considered in greater detail.
66   (1998) 1 CCLR 168.

considered by Sedley J in *R v Islington LBC ex p Rixon*,[67] where he held:

> The duty owed to the applicant personally by virtue of section 2(1) of the Chronically Sick and Disabled Persons Act 1970 includes the provision of recreational facilities outside the home to an extent which Islington accepts is greater than the care plan provides for. But the local authority has, it appears, simply taken existing unavailability of further facilities as an insuperable obstacle to any further attempt to make provision. The lack of a day care centre has been treated, however reluctantly, as a complete answer to the question of provision for Jonathan's needs. As McCowan LJ explained in the *Gloucestershire* case, the section 2(1) exercise is needs-led and not resource-led. To say this is not to ignore the existing resources either in terms of regular voluntary care in the home or in budgetary terms. These, however, are balancing and not blocking factors.

In *R v Liverpool CC ex p Winter*,[68] leave was given to challenge an authority's practice of placing people (who it had assessed as requiring a service) on a waiting list; immediately prior to the substantive hearing the authority withdrew its defence and agreed to provide the assessed service and pay the applicant's full costs.

2) *Educational facilities*

The educational service required in this case may be either home-based or otherwise. The wording suggests that the service provided by the authority consists of enabling the disabled person to have access to an (already existing) educational facility, rather than the provision of the educational facility itself. Potentially the scope of the educational obligation created by s2(1)(c) is wide. For instance in *R v Hereford and Worcester CC ex p Chandler*,[69] a stroke-disabled adult was assessed as requiring a 'one to one carer', it being agreed that with this assistance he might be able (among other things) to attend a special course at a local technical college. On the applicant's behalf it was argued that the provision of a one to one carer constituted 'assistance to that person in taking advantage of educational facilities available to him'.

5.54   In particular, the subsection appears to enable the provision of:

1) services for which there is an overlapping NHS responsibility (eg, communication assistance via speech synthesisers, speech therapy, hearing and writing aids, etc); and

---

67   (1998) 1 CCLR 119, at 130F.
68   (1997) unreported, but see (1997) 1 CCLR 5 and (1998) 1 CCLR 118.
69   (1992) unreported, but see September 1992 *Legal Action* 15.

2) services to support disabled (adult) students. LAC(93)12[70] gives specific guidance on these responsibilities, and in particular stresses that s2(1)(c) covers funding the personal care requirements of such students so as to enable them to pursue their studies (even if those studies are undertaken outside the local authority's area). The relevant part of the circular stating as follows:

> 9. SSDs have been reminded of their duty under s2(1)(c) of the Chronically Sick & Disabled Persons Act 1970 to make arrangements for assisting a disabled person who is ordinarily resident in their area in taking advantage of educational facilities available to him/her, (even where provision is made outside that local authority's area), if they are satisfied that it is necessary in order to meet that person's needs. Such assistance might, in appropriate cases include the funding by the local authority of the personal care required to enable the student in question to pursue his/her studies. It is, of course, for the authority to decide, in each case, what the individual's needs are, and how they are to be met.

> 10. Disabled students attending higher education courses may be eligible to receive up to three Disabled Students Allowances from the local education authority, as part of their mandatory award. These allowances are for a non-medical helper, major items of special equipment, or minor items such as tapes or Braille paper. They are aimed at helping students with costs related to their course, and are not intended to meet other costs arising from their disability which would have to be met irrespective of whether or not they were in a course. For those attending further education courses, similar support may be provided at the discretion of the LEA.

> 11. There may be occasions where the social services department is asked to consider the provision of additional care support for an individual who will receive a Disabled Students Allowance or discretionary support from the LEA. It will, therefore, be appropriate in some circumstances for the support for an individual's personal care needs to be provided jointly by the SSD and the LEA.

5.55 The *Rixon* judgment (above) also considered the interplay between the duties owed under s2(1)(c) and the general duty under Education Act 1944 s41[71] which obliges education authorities to secure adequate

---

70 See paras 9–11.
71 As substituted by Further and Higher Education Act 1992 s11. See also DFE Circular 1/93 *The Further and Higher Education Act 1992 Guidance* [WOC 15/93 in Wales] and *Duties and Powers: The Law Governing the Provision of Further Education to Students with Learning Difficulties and/or Disabilities* (HMSO, 1996).

further education facilities for (among others) adults who have learning difficulties. Sedley J observed that for persons with the gravest learning difficulties the s41 duty might be met by the provision of facilities under s2. He suggested, however, that if this was the case then the appropriate remedy for an alleged breach of the s41 duty was (in the first instance) via the secretary of state procedures under s68 or s99 of the 1944 Act.

5.56   *R v Further Education Funding Council and Bradford MBC ex p Parkinson*[72] concerned a 20-year-old applicant with severe mental and physical impairments. He was unable to take advantage of a place at a further education college without first being able to communicate to the required standard. He sought to compel the respondents to provide the necessary facilities either under Education Act 1944 s41 or Further and Higher Education Act 1992 Sch 2. In dismissing the application, Jowitt J observed that although 'purely education facilities' could not be provided under the community care legislation, the applicant might be eligible for services under CSDPA 1970 s2(1)(c) 'as providing assistance to take advantage of education facilities which are available to him'.

Travel and other assistance

5.57   'The provision for that person of facilities for, or assistance in, travelling to and from his home for the purposes of participating in any services provided under any arrangements made by the authority under the said section 29 or, with the approval of the authority, in any services provided otherwise than as aforesaid which are similar to services which could be provided under such arrangements' (s2(1)(d)). While social services authorities are empowered (but not obliged) to charge for such transport services (see para 8.67), in assessing a person's ability to pay, his/her mobility component of disability living allowance (if received) must be ignored.[73]

5.58   In general, where transport is required in order that a disabled child attend a school specified in a special educational needs statement, it will be for education departments to provide this.[74]

5.59   CSDPA 1970 s21 (as subsequently amended) requires motor vehicle badges to be made available for the benefit of disabled people

---

72 (1996) *Times* 31 October.
73 Social Security Contributions and Benefits Act 1992 s73(14).
74 This may even be the case where the statement provides that 'the mother to be responsible for transport to and from the school at her own expense', see *R v Havering LBC ex p K* (1997) *Times* 18 November.

and for regulations to be issued concerning the operation of this scheme, now generally known as the Orange Badge Scheme. The scheme is the subject of guidance issued by the Department of Transport as Circular 3/91, 'The Orange Badge Scheme of Parking Concessions for Disabled and Blind People'. The circular lists the relevant regulations which now apply. Travel assistance is also available under NAA 1948 s29 (see para 5.27).

Home adaptations and disabled facilities

5.60   'The provision of assistance for that person in arranging for the carrying out of any works of adaptation in his home or the provision of any additional facilities designed to secure his greater safety, comfort or convenience' (s2(1)(e)). Section 2(1)(e) is in two parts; one relating to adaptations (ie, significant works, possibly of a structural nature) and the other to the provision of additional facilities (ie, works involving the provision of fixtures and fittings and equipment).

5.61   In relation to 'additional facilities', the duty on the authority is to provide these ('the provision of'), whereas in relation to adaptations the duty is stated as being the 'provision of assistance . . . in arranging for the carrying out of'. Whether the difference in wording is legally significant is not clear. The subsection does not oblige social services authorities to carry out (or otherwise provide) the adaptations, merely to provide assistance for that person in arranging for the carrying out of the works. Arguably this might be no more than assistance in finding a suitable architect or builder or assistance with a grant application form. The circular guidance in relation to disabled facilities grants (see below) suggests, however, that the duty is more substantial, namely a duty to ensure that appropriate works are carried out including, for instance, financial assistance.

5.62   The carrying out of such adaptations has been frequently characterised by delay, not least because of a shortage of occupational therapists (OT), and the local ombudsman has produced a number of reports on this issue.[75] In her report No 90/C/0336 (3 October 1991) she dealt with a situation where the complainant had (among other things) waited nine months for an OT assessment. In finding maladministration, she commented:

> The Council say that they suffered from a shortage of OTs during 1989; while I recognise that this is a national problem, nevertheless the Council still retain their responsibility to assess their client's

---

75 See para 12.60 below where the ombudsman's role is considered.

needs. If sufficient OTs are not available, they may need to find another way of assessing those needs.

Her finding in this case does not of course mean that delays of less than nine months are acceptable. Her finding means that any council, knowing that the use of OTs for an assessment will cause a substantial delay, is guilty of maladministration when it opts to use OTs (ie, it is maladministration the moment such a procedure is adopted).

5.63   Frequently an overlapping responsibility for the provision of such works exists between the social services authority (whose duty arises under s2(1)(e)) and the housing authority which is obliged under the Housing Grants, Construction and Regeneration Act 1996 Pt I to provide disabled facilities grants for such works (subject to a means test[76]). The procedures for securing such grants are considered in detail at para 10.19 below, but they are primarily available to owner-occupiers/tenants for the purpose of:

- facilitating a disabled person's access to:
  - the dwelling;
  - a room usable as the principal family room, or for sleeping in;
  - a WC, bath, shower, etc (or the provision of a room for these facilities);
- facilitating the preparation of food by the disabled person;
- improving/providing a heating system to met the disabled person's needs;
- facilitating the disabled person's use of a source of power;
- facilitating access and movement around the home to enable the disabled person to care for someone dependent upon him/her;
- making the dwelling safe for the disabled person and others residing with him/her.

This dual responsibility has led to considerable confusion and resulted in numerous complaints to the local ombudsman. Section 2(1)(e) places a specific duty on the social services authority to help a disabled person arrange for adaptations to his/her home to be carried out. Frequently the social services department (in providing this assistance) requires the disabled person to make an application to the housing authority for a disabled facilities grant. At this stage delay may arise due to the housing authority's failure;[77] this does not

---

76   The means test for disabled facilities grants depends upon the financial resources of the disabled person and his/her partner. If the disabled person is under 18 his/her parents' means are assessed.

77   See para 5.62 above for the ombudsman's comments on such delay.

however discharge the social services department from its separate (and separately enforceable) duty under s2(1)(e).

5.64   When such delay occurs, the appropriate response from a social services department to assist the disabled person in resolving the problem, by actively intervening in the process if needs be. Likewise, the refusal of a grant application by the housing authority does not of itself absolve the social services authority from its separate responsibility under s2(1)(e). This point is emphasised in circular LAC(90)7,[78] which refers to the social services department as the 'lead body', and states that its duty to act remains regardless of the housing authority's actions.[79]

5.65   **Adaptations** Typically, home adaptations concern such matters as stair lifts, ground-floor extensions, doorway widening, ramps and wheelchair-accessible showers. Unlike under Housing Grants, Construction and Regeneration Act 1996 Part I (see para 10.19 below), CSDPA 1970 imposes no requirement that work be either 'appropriate' or 'reasonable and practicable'. All the 1970 statute requires is that the social services authority be satisfied that the works are necessary in order to meet the needs of the disabled person (by securing his/her greater safety, comfort or convenience).

5.66   Department of Health guidance, LAC(90)7, illustrates this difference of approach (at paras 15–17 and also at para 58):

> 15. The existing responsibilities of [social services authorities] under s2 of the CSDP Act are unchanged. In cases of their duty to make arrangements for home adaptations, under s2(1)(e), the responsibility will, in many instances, be effectively discharged on their behalf by the housing authority, by the giving of a disabled facilities grant. However the [social services authority's] duty to act remains, and they may be called upon to meet this duty in two ways. The first is where the needs as assessed by the [social services] authority exceed the scope for provision by the housing authority under s114(3) of the 1989 [Local Government and Housing] Act[80] and where the authority decline to use their discretionary powers under s114(4). If the [social services] authority deem the need to be established, then it will be their responsibility in these circumstances to make arrangements for this need to be met under s2 of the CSDP Act.

78 At para 14. LAC(90)7 was issued jointly as Department of the Environment Circular 10/90. Whilst DoE Circular 10/90 has been withdrawn (and superseded by new guidance, Circular 17/96) LAC(90)7 remains in force (see DoE 4/98 and LASSL(99)21).

79 LAC(90)7 para 15.

80 Now Part I of the Housing Grants, Construction and Regeneration Act 1996, see para 10.19 below.

16. Such a responsibility might arise when for instance the [social services] authority considers there is need related to the individual's social needs that demands a greater level of provision than is required for the disability alone, and where the housing authority chooses not to exercise its discretionary powers. This may occur, for example, where the size of a bedroom for a disabled child is required to be greater than is necessary for sleeping, because it needs to fulfil the role of bed/sitting room to provide more independent social space.

17. The second instance where the [social services] authority may find they have a continuing duty to provide assistance concerns cases where a disabled person asks the [social services] authority for financial assistance, under section 2(1)(e) of the CSDP Act, with that part of the costs of an adaptation which he is expected to finance himself in the light of the test of resources for the disabled facilities grant. On occasion, this could be as much as the total costs of the adaptation. In such cases, the [social services] authority still has a duty to assist. However, in order to maintain consistency with the new arrangements for disabled facilities grants, the [social services] authority may wish to use their existing powers to charge for their services (under section 17 of the [Health and Social Services and Social Security Adjudications] Act 1983) to recover the full cost of any assistance given, provided that they consider that the client is able to afford to repay this. In examining the question of financial assistance, [social services] authorities are recommended to bear in mind that the amount of grant approved will have been calculated on the basis of a test of resources (described in more detail in paragraphs 64 and 65 and Appendix II below). [Social services] authorities should not try to make their own separate assessment of what a grant applicant is expected to pay; but they might consider whether, in their opinion, the meeting of those costs would cause hardship.[81] The method of charging or of recovery of costs is for the [social services] authority to decide; but alternatives which might be considered include loans, with or without interest, possibly secured in either case by a charge on the property[82] or the placing of a charge on the property for a set period.

5.67   The Department of the Environment guidance, Circular 17/96, deals

---

81   Charging for domiciliary services is considered in detail at para 8.67. The reference to 'hardship' in the circular is unhelpful: HASSASSAA 1983 s17 merely requires that the disabled person satisfy the authority that his/her means are insufficient for it to be reasonably practicable for him/her to pay for the service.

82   Such a charge could presumably only be secured on the property with the owner's consent as HASSASSAA 1983 s17 does not empower authorities to create such charges (unlike s22).

with the interface between the two statutory obligations in the following terms:

Role of the social services authority to assist with adaptations
5. Social services authorities' responsibilities under s2 Chronically Sick & Disabled Persons Act 1970 to make arrangements for home adaptations are not affected by the grants legislation. Where an application for DFG has been made, those authorities may be called upon to meet this duty in two ways:
(a) where the assessed needs of a disabled person exceeds the scope for provision by the housing authority under section 23 of the 1996 Act; and
(b) where an applicant for DFG has difficulty in meeting his assessed contribution determined by the means test and seeks financial assistance from the authority.

6. In such cases, where the social services authority determine that the need has been established, it remains their duty to assist even where the local housing authority either refuse or are unable to approve the application. Social services authorities may also consider using their powers under section 17 of the Health and Social Services and Social Security Adjudications Act 1983 to charge for their services where appropriate.

5.68   **Additional facilities** Section 2(1)(e) also covers the provision of 'additional facilities' designed to secure the disabled person's greater safety, comfort or convenience. This includes all manner of fittings and gadgets such as handrails, alarm systems, hoists, movable baths, adapted switches and handles, and so on. Circular LAC(90)7 states (at para 19) that:

. . . equipment which can be installed and removed with little or no structural modification to the dwelling should usually be considered the responsibility of the [social services] authority. However, items such as stair lifts and through-floor lifts, which are designed to facilitate access into or around the dwelling would, in the view of the Secretaries of State, be eligible for disabled facilities grant. With items such as electric hoists, it is suggested that any structural modification of the property – such as strengthened joists or modified lintels – could be grant aidable under the disabled facilities grant, but that the hoisting equipment itself should be the responsibility of the [social services] authority. [Social services] authorities can, under s17 of the HASSASSA Act, charge for the provision of equipment. If the [social services] authority choose to make only a revenue charge (for example to cover maintenance), or not to charge at all, they would retain ownership of the equipment, and be able if they so wished to re-use it in another property if no longer required by the original recipient. [Social services] authorities are encouraged to make maximum use of their opportunities to recover and re-use equipment such as stairlifts, and to foster local arrangements for direct provision of such equipment where this can be done effectively and economically.

5.69 The Department of the Environment guidance, Circular 17/96 complements this advice, in the following terms:

Funding considerations
7. It is for housing authorities and social services authorities between them to decide how particular adaptations should be funded either through CSDP Act or through a DFG.

8. However, since DFG's were introduced in 1990 under the Local Government and Housing Act 1989, it has been common practice that equipment which can be installed and removed fairly easily with little or no structural modification of the dwelling is normally the responsibility of the social services authority.

9. For larger items such as *stairlifts* and *through floor lifts* which normally require such structural works to the property, help is normally provided by housing authorities through DFG. However, some routine installations, may not involve structural work. To ensure that such adaptations are progressed quickly, the respective authorities should jointly agree a standard line on the installation of lifts which will apply unless there are exceptional circumstances. Authorities will wish to include arrangements for routine servicing, maintenance, removal and possible re-use.

Holidays

5.70 'Facilitating the taking of holidays by that person, whether at holiday homes or otherwise and whether provided under arrangements made by the authority or otherwise' (s2(1)(f)). The power of social services authorities to provide holiday homes under NAA 1948 s29 (see para 107) is complemented by the duty under CSDPA 1970 s2(1)(f) to facilitate the taking of holidays by disabled persons. In *R v Ealing LBC ex p Leaman*,[83] the council refused to consider a request made by the applicant for financial assistance in taking a privately arranged holiday, on the ground that it would only grant such assistance for holidays which it itself had arranged or sponsored. In quashing the council's decision Mann J held that:

The effect of the general policy adumbrated by the council is, in my judgement, to excise the words 'or otherwise' where they second

83 (1984) *Times* 10 February, QBD.

occur in section 2(1)(f). Accordingly, the London Borough were wrong in declining to consider any application which the Applicant might have made for assistance with his private holiday. Whether, having regard to a proper consideration of a person's needs, those needs required the making of a grant to a private holiday is an entirely different question. It is a question wholly within the province of the local authority. However, it was quite wrong for them to deprive themselves of the opportunity of asking that question.[84]

In appropriate cases, the local authority will have to fund the full cost of such a holiday, and not merely the additional costs attributable to the user's impairment. This may include the cost of a carer's attendance if that is the only way to 'facilitate the taking of the holiday', *R v North Yorkshire CC ex p Hargreaves (No 2).*[85]

Meals

5.71   'The provision of meals for that person whether in his home or elsewhere' (s2(1)(g)). Section 2(1)(g) covers the provision of meals at day centres (or indeed anywhere) as well as meals in the disabled person's home such as meals-on-wheels. The equivalent service for the elderly is governed by HSPHA 1968 s45 (see para 5.39).

Telephone and ancillary equipment

5.72   'The provision for that person of, or assistance to that person in obtaining, a telephone and any special equipment necessary to enable him to use a telephone' (s2(1)(h)). Section 2(1)(h) may cover the installation of a telephone line as well as the provision of an appropriate handset, loud telephone bell (or a flashing visual or vibrating signal), amplifiers, inductive couplers for personal hearing aids and visual transmission machines such as minicoms, faxes and possibly modems for computer e-mail transmission, etc.

CSDPA 1970 s2 and NAA 1948 s29

5.73   The rapid drafting[86] of s2 has led to considerable confusion as to its status. The section commences with the clause 'Where a local author-

---

84 From pages 4–5 of the transcript of the judgment.

85 (1998) 1 CCLR 331.

86 For a description of the speed with which the bill was drafted see *Be it Enacted* (RADAR, 1995). Unfortunately there is nothing in the *Hansard* reports on the passage of the bill through parliament to elucidate the confusing references to s29.

ity having functions under section 29 of the National Assistance Act 1948 are satisfied . . . ' and concludes 'it shall be the duty of that authority to make those arrangements in exercise of their functions under the said section 29'. It is not surprising therefore that s2 has been considered as an extension to s29 – to the extent that services identified under s2 are in fact s29 services, ie, delivered as 'arrangements in exercise of . . . s29'.

5.74   The Department of Health holds this view. Accordingly, when Health and Social Services and Social Security Adjudication Act (HASSASSAA) 1983 s17 was drafted (which section authorises charges to be levied for non-accommodation services), no reference was made to services under s2; not because it was intended that these be free of charge, but because s2 services 'are arranged by local authorities in exercise of their functions under s29 of the 1948 Act'.[87] Likewise, although s2 services are not specifically listed as being community care services in NHSCCA 1990 s46, this again has been explained by the Secretary of State for Health as being unnecessary since the reference in s46 to services under NAA 1948 Pt III includes s2 services because such services are discharged by an authority as part of its functions under s29 of the 1948 Act.[88] If this is the case, then no little confusion has been caused by NHSCCA 1990 s47(2), which appears to create a different assessment procedure for s2 services to those under the s46 community care statutes. The explanation advanced for this difference of treatment by the Department of Health (namely that s47(2) assessments are required to be 'comprehensive'),[89] was however rejected by Carnwath J in *R v Gloucestershire CC ex p RADAR.*[90]

5.75   Elaborate arguments have been deployed to establish that s2 is part of s29, although the cases which have been decided suggest that this view is open to considerable doubt. In *R v Gloucestershire CC ex p Mahfood,*[91] the respondent sought to argue that in consequence of s2 being part of s29 it followed that a home help service could not be provided under s2 notwithstanding that s2(1)(a) is concerned with precisely such a service. The argument turned upon NAA 1948 s29(6), which prohibits services being provided under s29 if they can

87   Footnote 2 to the SSI advice note on non-accommodation charges, January 1994 – see para 8.70.
88   *Hansard* (HC) Standing Committee E (15 February 1990) cols 1055 et seq.
89   See Practice Guidance para 2.19.
90   (1998) 1 CCLR 476. See para 3.33 above.
91   (1995) 1 CCLR 7; (1996) 160 LG Rev 321.

be provided under NHSA 1977. The 1977 Act makes provision for a home help service.[92] The argument was described as unattractive by McCowan LJ and rejected; services under s2 were provided under s2.

5.76 An additional difficulty with the Department of Health's view stems from the differences between the s2 and s29 client groups. Section 2 includes all disabled people, whereas s29 applies only to disabled people over 18 years of age. Clearly children's services under s2 cannot be provided under s29. In *R v Bexley LBC ex p B*[93] (referred to in detail below), Latham J held that such services were provided under s2 itself (rather than under CA 1989, as was argued by the respondent council).[94]

5.77 In *R v Powys CC ex p Hambidge*,[95] the Court of Appeal decided that local authorities were entitled to charge for services provided under s2 notwithstanding that s17 of the 1983 Act did not specifically authorise such charging. The court took a reasonably robust approach to the ambiguous relationship between s2 and s29 and decided, essentially on public policy grounds, that services provided in consequence of the duty under s2 were actually delivered as arrangements in exercise of the local authority's functions under NAA 1948 s29. The court did not deal with the major problem of the different client groups served by s2 and s29, on the ground that Mrs Hambidge was not under 18.

CSDPA 1970 s2 and CA 1989

5.78 CSDPA 1970 s28A[96] provides that:

> This Act applies with respect to disabled children in relation to whom the local authority have functions under Part III of the Children Act 1989 as it applies in relation to persons to whom section 29 of the National Assistance Act 1948 applies.

The effect of s28A is that disabled children have the same right to services under s2 of the 1970 Act as disabled adults. Such services cannot, however, be provided as part of an authority's functions under s29, since s29 specifically excludes services being given to people under 18 years of age.

---

92 This aspect is also considered at para 5.32.
93 (2000) 3 CCLR 15.
94 At p23B.
95 (1998) 1 CCLR 458.
96 Inserted by CA 1989 s108(5), Sch 13 para 27.

5.79   The other principal route by which disabled children receive services is under CA 1989 (see Chapter 11 for further consideration of these services). *R v Bexley LBC ex p B* (above) concerned the provision of care services for a severely disabled boy of 10. The respondent council sought to argue (among other things) that his home care services were being provided under CA 1989 rather than under s2. Latham J rejected the argument, reasoning as follows:

> The relationship between the Children Act 1989 and the Chronically Sick and Disabled Persons Act 1970 is an uneasy one. The provisions of the Children Act 1989 are in general terms; and the duties are of a type which Woolf LJ described as 'target duties' in *R v Inner London Education Authority ex p Ali* (1990) 2 Admin LR 822. An assessment of a disabled child's needs pursuant to paragraph 3 of Schedule 2 to the Act does not appear to give rise to any specific duty pursuant to the Act itself, which is the point made by the respondents. They accept, however, that section 2(1) of the Chronically Sick and Disabled Persons Act 1970 will impose a specific duty to provide, for example, practical assistance for a disabled person in his home, if they are satisfied that it is necessary to provide that in order to meet his needs. But, as I have already said, their argument is that no such assessment was made because there was no request for such an assessment. If this is a proper analysis, it would result in an Authority being able to avoid the specific duty under the Chronically Sick and Disabled Persons Act 1970 by purporting to act simply under the Children Act 1989. The same problem does not arise in relation to adults. Section 47 of the National Health Service and Community Care Act 1990 provides that an Authority is under an obligation to carry out an assessment of a person's needs wherever it appears to the Authority that he may be in need of community care services, and if it concludes that the person is a disabled person, it is under obligation to make a decision as to what services, if any, he requires under section 2(1) of the Chronically Sick and Disabled Persons Act 1970. This section does not apply to children because services provided pursuant to the Children Act 1989 are not community health services for the purposes of the Act.[97]
>
> Authorities are, however, under an obligation to make provision

---

97 The phrase used here, 'community health services', is clearly a mistake, and should read 'community care services'. The judge is also mistaken in relation to the ambit of s47. As detailed at para 3.56 the duty to assess under NHSCCA 1990 s47(1) is activated when, *inter alia*, an authority is aware of a potential service user possibly being in need of community care services. The definition of community care services under s46 of the 1990 Act includes services under NHSA 1977 Sch 8; home help services under para 3 of which can be supplied to disabled adults or disabled children; thus the assessment duty under s47(1) will generally be triggered for all disabled people regardless of age.

under the Chronically Sick and Disabled Persons Act 1970 whenever they are satisfied that the relevant conditions have been met. A request by or on behalf of a disabled person is not one of those conditions. It seems to me that the Court should look at the reality of the situation. In the present case, although no formal request was made by the applicant's mother for an assessment of the applicant's needs, that was the effect of what happened in the early months of 1994. As a result, it seems to me that the respondents were satisfied that it was necessary to provide practical assistance for him in the house in order to meet his needs. [The social worker] clearly decided that to expect his mother to go on meeting those needs without further help would be to the applicant's disadvantage. He had a need for full time care of a quality which one person could not be expected to continue to provide in the way the applicant's mother was then providing it. The only conclusion which a reasonable Authority could reach in that situation was that it was under a duty pursuant to section 2(1) of the Chronically Sick and Disabled Persons Act 1970 to provide practical assistance in his home. The respondents, in so far as they considered that they were simply exercising their general duties pursuant to the Children Act 1989, were wrong, and in breach of their duty under the Chronically Sick and Disabled Persons Act 1970.[98]

The difference between s2 services and CA 1989 services is recognised in the Carers (Recognition and Services) Act 1995 s1(2)(a) and it would seem, therefore, that when one is dealing with services for disabled children (at least), s2 services are provided under s2 and nothing else.

Services under National Health Services Act 1977 Sch 8

5.80   Most disabled people receive their domiciliary/community based services from social services departments under CSDPA 1970 s2. These services, however, are only available to people who are 'substantially and permanently handicapped,'[99] or who 'suffer from a mental disorder of any description'. Section 2 services are not therefore available to persons whose impairment is not 'permanent', notwithstanding it may be substantial. Domiciliary and community-based services for such persons are generally provided by social services authorities pursuant to duties under NHSA 1977 s21 and

98   P22E–23C.
99   See para 5.13 where this definition is considered in detail.

Sch 8. Frequently the persons covered by these provisions are referred to as 'ill people', ie, people who are substantially impaired by an accident or severe illness, but whose prognosis is that they will make a full recovery (and will not therefore be 'permanently handicapped'). The Act, however, also covers services for a wider client group including elderly people, expectant mothers, drug and alcohol misusers as well as disabled people.

5.81 In discussing the provision of care services for ill people, one enters the minefield that marks the medical/social divide; a subject discussed in greater detail in Chapter 6. The 1977 Act attempts to demarcate the duties of the NHS and the social services authorities. Sections 1–5 spell out the general nature of the NHS obligation as it applies to the prevention of disease, and the care and after-care of ill people. At s21 the Act outlines the services which are the responsibility of the social services authorities, these being amplified in Sch 8. Sections 22–28 contain empowering provisions designed to foster co-operation between the two agencies. The texts of s21(1) and Sch 8 paras 1–3 as amended are set out below.

21 (1) Subject to paragraphs (d) and (e) of section 3(1)[100] above, the services described in Schedule 8 to this Act in relation to –
(a) care of mothers,
(b) prevention, care and after-care,
(c) home help and laundry facilities,
are functions exercisable by local social services authorities, and that Schedule has effect accordingly.

Schedule 8: Local Social Services Authorities
Care of mothers and young children
1 (1) A local Social Services Authority may, with the Secretary of State's approval, and to such extent as he may direct shall, make arrangements for the care of expectant and nursing mothers (other than for the provision of residential accommodation for them).

Prevention, care and after-care
2 (1) A local Social Services Authority may, with the Secretary of State's approval, and to such extent as he may direct shall, make arrangements for the purpose of the prevention of illness and for the care of persons suffering from illness and for the after-care of persons who have been suffering and in particular for –

---

100 It is s3(1) which enables the secretary of state to direct that certain facilities for the care, the prevention of illness and the after-care of the 'ill' and for nursing or expectant mothers are the responsibility of the health service rather than social services authorities – see, eg, LAC(95)5 and Chapter 6 below.

(a) ...

(b) the provision for persons whose care is undertaken with a view to preventing them from becoming ill, persons suffering from illness and persons who have been so suffering, of centres or other facilities for training them or keeping them suitably occupied and the equipment and maintenance of such centres;

(c) the provision, for the benefit of such persons as are mentioned in paragraph (b) above, of ancillary or supplemental services; and

(d) for the exercise of the functions of the Authority in respect of persons suffering from mental disorder who are received into the guardianship under Part II or III of the Mental Health Act 1983 (whether the guardianship of the local Social Services Authority or of other persons).

Such an Authority shall neither have the power nor be subject to a duty to make under this paragraph arrangements to provide facilities for any of the purposes mentioned in section 15(1) of the Disabled Persons (Employment) Act 1944.

(2) No arrangements under this paragraph shall provide for the payment of money to persons for whose benefit they are made except –

(a) in so far as they may provide for the remuneration of such persons engaged in suitable work in accordance with the arrangements, of such amounts as the local social services authority think fit in respect of their occasional personal expenses where it appears to that Authority that no such payment would otherwise be made.

(2A) No arrangements under this paragraph may be given effect to in relation to a person to whom section 115 of the Immigration and Asylum Act 1999 (exclusion from benefits) applies solely –

(a) because he is destitute; or

(b) because of the physical effects, or anticipated physical effects, of his being destitute.

(2B) Subsections (3) and (5) to (8) of section 95 of the Immigration and Asylum Act 1999, and paragraph 2 of Schedule 8 to that Act, apply for the purposes of subsection (2A) as they apply for the purposes of that section, but for the references in subsections (5) and (7) of that section and in that paragraph to the Secretary of State substitute references to a local social services authority.'

(3) The Secretary of State may make regulations as to the conduct of premises in which, in pursuance of arrangements made under this paragraph, are provided for persons whose care is undertaken with a view to preventing them from becoming sufferers from mental disorder within the meaning of that Act of 1983 or who are, or have been, so suffering, facilities for training them or keeping them suitably occupied.

(4A) This paragraph does not apply in relation to persons under the age of 18.

(4AA) No authority is authorised or may be required under this paragraph to provide residential accommodation for any person.

Home help and laundry facilities

3 (1) It is the duty of every local Social Services Authority to provide on such a scale as is adequate for the needs of their area, or to arrange for the provision on such a scale as is so adequate, of home help for households where such help is required owing to the presence of a person who is suffering from illness, lying-in, an expectant mother, aged, handicapped as a result of having suffered from illness or by congenital deformity, and every such Authority has power to provide or arrange for the provisions of laundry facilities for households for which home help is being, or can be, provided under this sub-paragraph.

Client group

5.82   NHSA 1977 requires social services authorities to provide a variety of services for a diverse client group, certain services being restricted to particular client groups. There is no requirement that the persons be ordinarily resident within the social services authority's area.

5.83   The potential client group is wide, in that services can be provided for any adult in order to prevent illness – to which everyone is, of course, vulnerable. The provision of home help under Sch 8 para 3 has no age restriction on the person whose need triggers the service (ie, it applies to children as well as adults). It should also be noted that the provision of home helps is specified as being for the benefit of the 'household', rather than merely for the qualifying individual within the home.

5.84   Paragraphs 1 and 2 of Sch 8 are subject to directions issued by the Secretary of State (presently Appendix 3 to LAC(93)10[101] – see below).

Mothers

5.85   The client group is restricted to 'expectant and nursing mothers (of any age)'.[102] The services available are without restriction, save only that the provision of accommodation is not permitted. The accommodation needs of such mothers are covered by NAA 1948 s21(1)(aa) (see para 4.14).

101 WOC35/93 in Wales.
102 LAC(93)10 App 3 .

The ill

5.86   NHSA 1977 s128(1) defines illness as including mental disorder within the meaning of MHA 1983 and any injury or disability requiring medical or dental treatment or nursing. Persons who are alcoholic or drug-dependent are specifically included.[103] Services can also be provided for the purpose of preventing illness and for the after-care of persons who have been so suffering; the client group is therefore limited only by the size of the adult population.

5.87   The client group is generally restricted to persons aged 18 or over.[104] The exception to this general rule being that home help and laundry services (under para 3) are available to ill adults or children alike.

Mothers lying-in

5.88   At first sight it might appear incongruous that separate reference be made to mothers 'lying-in' (literally, 'the being in childbed'), when nursing mothers are already included as a category. The reason for this is related to the different services available. Where the need exists, there is a duty to provide home help for mothers lying in, whereas the other services available to expectant and nursing mothers are discretionary. The mother may be of any age (ie, over or under 18).

The aged

5.89   No definition is provided for 'aged', and there is probably no need.[105] The overlap with the corresponding provision under HSPHA 1968 s45 (see para 5.33 is presumably explained on the basis that (where need for home help is assessed) s45 services are discretionary whereas the NHS provision is obligatory.

The handicapped

5.90   The disabled person may be of any age (ie, over or under 18). The handicap need be neither substantial nor permanent (unlike the requirement in NAA 1948 s29; see para 5.22 above); it must, however, result from either illness or congenital deformity. Excluded, there-

---

103   Ibid para 3(g); see para 9.23 where services for alcohol and drug misusers are considered in greater detail.

104   NHSA 1977 Sch 8 para 4A.

105   See NAA 1948 s21, where no definition is given of 'age' and likewise HSPHA 1968 s45, which uses the phrase 'old people' – dealt with at para 4.11 and para 5.35 above respectively.

fore, are those whose handicap results from injury (s29 covers this category if the injury is permanent and substantial). The apparent lacuna is however largely academic – the NHSA's definition of illness (as detailed above) includes an injury which requires medical or dental treatment or nursing – and the Act covers the provision of services for the after-care of such persons.

Excluded groups

5.91   The effect of the Immigration and Asylum Act 1999 s117, by amending NHSA 1977 Sch 8, is to exclude from services older people who are asylum seekers and are in need of community care services solely on account of being 'destitute'[106] (see para 4.16 above).

Services under NHSA 1977 s21 and Sch 8

5.92   Before the implementation of NHSCCA 1990, the services that could be provided under NHSA 1977 Sch 8 included the provision of accommodation. The 1990 Act by amendment[107] removed this power, and all social services authority community care accommodation obligations for adults are now dealt with under NAA 1948[108] (or in limited situations under MHA 1983 s117 – see para 5.100 below).

5.93   Paragraphs 1, 2 and 3 of NHSA 1977 Sch 8 deal with three separate services:

Paragraph 1 Services for expectant and nursing mothers.

Paragraph 2 Services for the prevention of illness, and the care and after-care of sufferers.

Paragraph 3 Home help and laundry services.

Paragraphs 1 and 2 follow the traditional community care drafting convention; they do not authorise the provision of any services but leave to the secretary of state the power to specify in directions what services may and what services must be provided. The most recent directions in this respect were issued on 17 March 1993 as Appendix 3 to LAC(93)10.[109] Paragraph 3 is, however, a free-standing statutory provision which is not the subject of any direction. These three categories of services are dealt with separately below.

106   Sch 8 para 2A as inserted by Immigration and Asylum Act 1999 s117.
107   NHSCCA 1990 Sch 9 para 18(4). See also para 8.56.
108   NAA 1948 s21 as amended by NHSCCA 1990 s42 (see LAC(93)10 para 6) – and the provision of certain hostel accommodation under NAA 1948 s29 – see para 4.93.
109   WOC35/93 in Wales.

Services for expectant and nursing mothers

5.94   The directions merely state[110] that 'the Secretary of State approves the making of arrangements . . . for the care of expectant and nursing mothers (of any age) other than the provision of accommodation for them'.[111] For mothers under the age of 18 there is of course an over-lapping responsibility under CA 1989 Pt III (if the mother or child are considered to be 'in need' – see Chapter 11). No circular or other guidance has been given concerning the nature or extent of these services – they remain at the discretion of the social services authority. There is no reason why the service provided by the social services authority should not include the giving of assistance in kind or, in exceptional circumstances, in cash.[112] The only restrictions (which follow from the actual wording of the direction) are that the service must be a 'care' service and that the service must be for the care of the mother (ie, not for the infant or any one else in the house-hold).

Services for the prevention of illness, etc

5.95   Detailed directions have been issued in relation to the range of services that can be provided for the prevention of illness and the care and after-care of those who have been ill (see Appendix B for the full text). While the directions oblige social services authorities to provide services for the prevention of mental disorder (or for the care of persons who have been suffering from mental disorder) they leave the provision of services for the alleviation of 'non-mental disorder' illness to the discretion of the social services authority. These two services are therefore dealt with separately below. The services are, in both cases, only available to adults and (subject to the specific exceptions detailed below) may not include the payment of money to the service user (NHSA 1977 Sch 8 para 2(2) unless under the Direct Payments legislation – see para 5.142 below).

5.96   **The duty to provide services to alleviate mental disorder**   The secretary of state's directions oblige social services authorities to make domiciliary care arrangements (detailed in (a) and (b) below) for the purpose of preventing mental disorder, as well as for persons who are

---

110 LAC(93)10 App 3 para 2.
111 Accommodation services being covered by NAA 1948 s21(1)(aa).
112 The general prohibition on making payment to service users under the community care legislation does not apply in this case; cf NAA 1948 s29(6)(a) and NHSA 1977 Sch 8 para 2(2) and cf CA 1989 s17(6).

or who have been suffering from mental disorder[113] (see Appendix B for full text). The directed services are the provision of:

a) Centres (including training centres and day centres) or other facilities (including domiciliary facilities), whether in premises managed by the local authority or otherwise, for training or occupation of such persons; including the payment of persons engaged in suitable work at the 'centres or other facilities'.[114]

b) Social work and related services to help in the identification, diagnosis, assessment and social treatment of mental disorder and to provide social work support and other domiciliary and care services to people living in their own homes and elsewhere.

The directions would appear to be so widely drafted as to cover most of the commonly encountered domiciliary care services, ie, day centres, drop-in centres, educational, occupational and recreational facilities, transport, meals,[115] home helps and so on. Accommodation services are, however, specifically excluded by NHSA 1977 Sch 8 para 2(4AA). The directions additionally require local authorities to appoint sufficient social workers in their area to act as approved social workers for the purposes of MHA 1983 and to make arrangements to enable them to exercise their guardianship functions under the 1983 Act. As has been noted above (see para 5.29), NAA 1948 s29(6)(b) excludes services being provided under s29 where such services are 'required to be provided' under NHSA 1977. The inclusion of the phrase 'mental disorder of any description' within NAA 1948 s29 and in the secretary of state's direction relating to services under NHSA 1977 Sch 8, would tend to suggest that s29 is of limited relevance to persons suffering from a mental disorder. It is, however, unlikely that this exclusion applies to services under CSDPA 1970 s2 (for the reasons stated by McCowan LJ noted at para 5.32 above). The tortuous relationship between the almost irreconcilable provisions in these three Acts is so unsatisfactory, that only primary legislation can lead to a rational resolution.

5.97 **The power to provide services to alleviate 'illness'** The secretary of state's direction empowers (but does not oblige) social services

113 LAC(93)10 App 3 para 3(2).

114 Ibid at para 3(3)(b) – but subject to NHSA 1977 Sch 8 para 2(2)(a), which provides that the amount of such remuneration shall be limited to payment of such persons' occasional personal expenses if their work would not normally be remunerated.

115 Meals and meals-on-wheels for housebound people are specifically included by virtue of LAC(93)10 App 3 para 3(3)(a).

authorities to make the domiciliary care arrangements detailed below. In each case the service can only be provided for the purpose of either preventing illness, or for the care or after-care of a person suffering or recovering from an illness. The directed services are the provision of:

a) Centres or other facilities for training such persons or for keeping them suitably occupied (and the equipment and maintenance of such centres), together any other ancillary or supplemental services for such persons.[116] The services provided by a social services authority may include the payment of 'persons engaged in suitable work at the centres or other facilities'.[117] The equivalent services for disabled people (under CSDPA 1970 s2) are considered at para 5.52 and for elderly people (under HSPHA 1968 s45) at para 5.39.

b) Meals at the centres referred to in (a) above, or at other facilities (including domiciliary facilities) and meals-on-wheels for house-bound people, provided they are not available under HSPHA 1968 s45(1)[118] or from a district council under HASSASSAA 1983 Sch 9 Pt II para 1.[119] The equivalent services for disabled people (under CSDPA 1970) are considered at para 5.71 and for elderly people (under HSPHA 1968) at para 5.39.

c) Social services (including advice and support) for the purposes of preventing the impairment of physical or mental health of adults in families where such impairment is likely, and for the purposes of preventing the break-up of such families, or for assisting in their rehabilitation; the equivalent services for disabled people (under NAA 1948 s29) are considered at para 5.26.

d) Night-sitter services. Such a service is a specific form of 'practical assistance within the home' (as covered by CSDPA 1970 s2(1)(a)) and 'home help' (as covered by NHSA 1977 Sch 8 para 3 – see below). The inclusion of specific reference to this service is therefore probably unnecessary.

e) Recuperative holidays. CSDPA 1970 s2(1)(f) covers holidays for

---

116 LAC(93)10 App 3 paras 3(1)(a) and (b).
117 See n112 above.
118 See para 5.39.
119 The paragraph empowers a district council to make arrangements (or employ a suitable voluntary organisation to make these arrangements) for providing meals and recreation for old people in their homes or elsewhere, see Appendix A below.

disabled people (see para 5.70) and NAA 1948 s29 enables authorities to provide holiday homes (see para 5.27).

f) Facilities for social and recreational activities; this is an equivalent
power to the duty under CSDPA 1970 s2(1)(c) (see para 5.52) and
under HSPHA 1968 (see para 5.39).

g) Services specifically for persons who are alcoholic or drug-
dependent. Such services are considered separately in Chapter 9.

Home help and laundry services

5.98 **Home helps** NHSA 1977 requires social services authorities to
provide[120] a home help service for households where such help is
required owing to the presence of a person who is suffering from illness, lying-in, or is an expectant mother, aged, or handicapped as a
result of having suffered from illness or by congenital deformity.[121]
The potential extent of the service, as well as the overlap (and
differences) between this provision and that under CSDPA 1970
s2(1)(a) has been noted above (see para 5.50). The NHSA home help
service is not restricted to adults, unlike the CSDPA 1970 service,
which is so restricted (with the exception of disabled children); the
1970 Act service can only be provided for the benefit of the disabled
service user, whereas the NHSA home help service is provided for the
benefit of 'the household'.

5.99 **Laundry service** Social services authorities are empowered (but not
obliged) to provide[122] a laundry service for households where they
assess it as being required owing to the presence of a person who is
suffering from illness, or lying-in, an expectant mother, aged, or
handicapped as a result of having suffered from illness or by congenital deformity. Laundry services can therefore be provided in any
situation where NHSA 1977 enables the provision of home help: they
are not, however, dependent on the household actually receiving that
home help service – most obviously this would arise where the
household had a need for extra laundry help due to a person's illness,
but was otherwise able to cope with the general domestic chores.

120 The services may either be provided by the authority or arranged by the
authority but provided by another authority, a voluntary organisation or private
person – see LAC(93)10 App 3 para 4.
121 NHSA 1977 Sch 8 para 3.
122 See n120 above.

Services under MHA 1983 s117

5.100   Most non-accommodation services that authorities provide for people with a mental health difficulty are delivered under CSDPA 1970 s2. These services are available to persons 'who suffer from a mental disorder of any description'.[123] Likewise, most accommodation services that authorities provide for people with a mental health difficulty are delivered under NAA 1948 s21.

5.101   Only a small minority of people who receive community care services are entitled to their services under s117. For such people, however, as s117 services are virtually unlimited in nature (including where appropriate the provision of accommodation) and (potentially) give users specific individual legal rights,[124] the availability of those services under other Acts is in reality academic. From a service user's perspective, the receipt of services under s117 has the added advantage that social services authorities are not empowered to charge for them (see para 8.109).

5.102   MHA 1983 s117 (as amended) reads as follows:

(1) This section applies to persons who are detained under section 3 above, or admitted to a hospital in pursuance of a hospital order made under section 37 above, or transferred to a hospital in pursuance of a hospital direction made under s45A above or a transfer direction made under section 47 or 48 above, and then cease to be detained and (whether or not immediately after so ceasing) leave hospital.

(2) It shall be the duty of the Health Authority and of the local social services authority to provide, in co-operation with relevant voluntary agencies, after-care services for any person to whom this section applies until such time as the Health Authority and the local social services authority are satisfied that the person concerned is no longer in need of such services but they shall not be so satisfied in the case of a patient who is subject to after-care under supervision at any time while he so remains subject.

---

123 In addition, services are also available under NHSA 1977 Sch 8 for, *inter alia*, persons who are, or have been, suffering from an illness.

124 In *Clunis v Camden and Islington Health Authority* (1998) 1 CCLR 215, CA, it was held (applying *X v Bedfordshire CC* [1995] 2 AC 633) that s117(2) does not give rise to a private law action for breach of statutory duty. This decision may not apply after the Human Rights Act 1998 comes into force on 2 October 2000, in that *Bedfordshire* is arguably contra article 6 of the European Convention on Human Rights. See Application No 29392/95 *X v United Kingdom* (the Strasbourg reference for the *Bedfordshire* decision, and *Barrett v Enfield LBC* (1999) *Times*, 18 June, HL.

(2A) It shall be the duty of the Health Authority to secure that at all times while a patient is subject to after-care under supervision –

(a) a person who is a registered medical practitioner approved for the purposes of section 12 above by the Secretary of State as having special experience in the diagnosis or treatment of mental disorder is in charge of the medical treatment provided for the patient as part of the after-care services provided for him under this section; and

(b) a person professionally concerned with any of the after-care services so provided is supervising him with a view to securing that he receives the after-care services so provided.

(2B) Section 32 above shall apply for the purposes of this section as it applies for the purposes of Part II of this Act.

(3) In this section 'the Health Authority' means the Health Authority and 'the local social services authority' means the local social services authority for the area in which the person concerned is resident or to which he is sent on discharge by the hospital in which he was detained.

Client group

Age

5.103 While there is no minimum age limit for admission to hospital under MHA 1983, the nature (and timescale) of the Act's detention process means that s117 service users will generally be adults. Persons subject to the Mental Health (Patients in the Community) Act 1995 (see below) must be over 16, however.

Reasons for detention

5.104 **Section 3** Persons are detained under MHA 1983 s3 when admitted for treatment (as opposed to being detained under s2 (admission for assessment, whether or not accompanied by any treatment)).

5.105 **Section 37** Persons may only be detained under MHA 1983 s37 by order of a criminal court after being convicted of an offence (punishable by imprisonment) in criminal proceedings and the court being satisfied (among other things) that at the time of conviction the offender was suffering from a specific mental disorder.

5.106 **Section 45A**[125] Under s45A, and subject to certain restrictions, the Crown Court may, when sentencing a person who suffers from a

---

125 Inserted by Crime (Sentences) Act 1997.

psychopathic disorder to a term of imprisonment, direct that they be detained in a specified hospital.

5.107   **Section 47** Persons may only be detained under MHA 1983 s47 if they are serving a sentence of imprisonment (in a prison) and the secretary of state is satisfied (among other things) that they are suffering from a specific mental disorder (ie, mental illness, psychopathic disorder, mental impairment or severe mental impairment) and should in consequence be removed and detained in a hospital.

5.108   **Section 48** Detention under MHA 1983 s48 arises in the same circumstances as under s47, except that s48 applies to persons who, although detained, are not serving a sentence of imprisonment (eg, they are on remand pending trial, are civil prisoners or being detained under the Immigration Act 1971), and the person must be suffering from a mental illness of severe mental impairment.

'Ceases to be detained'

5.109   The duty to provide after-care services under s117 only applies to persons detained by virtue of ss 3, 37, 45A, 47 or 48 of the Act; the duty crystallises when the person 'ceases to be detained'. The nature of the duty under s117, and the meaning of the phrase 'ceases to be detained' was considered in *R v Ealing District Health Authority ex p Fox*,[126] in which Otton J held:

> I consider s117(2) as mandatory: 'It shall be the duty of the district health authority to provide after-care services for any person to whom the section applies . . .' The duty is not only a general duty but a specific duty owed to the applicant to provide him with after-care services until such time as the district health authority and local social services authority are satisfied that he is no longer in need of such services. I reject the submission that this duty only comes into existence when the applicant is discharged [from Broadmoor]. I consider a proper interpretation of this section to be that it is a continuing duty in respect of any patient who may be discharged and falls within s117, although the duty to any particular patient is only triggered at the moment of discharge.

5.110   In relation to the above decision, Scott Baker J in *R v Mental Health Review Tribunal ex p Hall*[127] commented:

> It is of note that Otton J rejected the submission that the health authority's duty only arose on the patient's discharge from hospital.

126   [1993] 3 All ER 170, QBD.
127   (1999) 2 CCLR 361.

A similar submission was made to me in the present case . . . and likewise I reject it. If effective aftercare services are to be provided, it is necessary for them to be planned and arranged before the patient leaves hospital.

5.111 The particular meaning ascribed to the phrase 'ceases to be detained' is well illustrated in relation to MHA 1983 s17. Section 17 provides that a 'responsible medical officer' can authorise leave of absence to patients detained under Part II of the Act (ie, under non-criminal detention). If the patient is detained under s3 of the Act, then s/he has a right to services under s117 during the 'leave of absence'. This entitlement, which is noted in the Code of Practice to the 1983 Act,[128] was confirmed by Sullivan J, in *R v Richmond LBC ex p Watson*.[129]

5.112 This entitlement arises because s117 services are provided to a person who is detained under (among other things) s3 'and then ceases to be detained and (whether or not immediately after so ceasing) leave hospital'. A person can therefore be entitled to services under s117 even though still formally detained under s3, since the crucial question is whether or not s/he is 'detained' (ie, physically detained in a hospital rather than legally 'subject to be detained' under s3).

District or area of residence

5.113 The duty to provide s117 services is the joint responsibility of the health authority, and the social services authority for the area in which the person concerned is resident or to which s/he is sent on discharge by the hospital in which s/he was detained.[130] Where doubt arises as to a person's area of residence, non-statutory guidance exists on determining the responsible district health authority and social services authority[131] (as the statutory procedure for determining ordinary residence under NAA 1948 s32(3) does not apply to disputes under s117, see para 4.36). The social services guidance deals with issues of good practice and sets out in detail the rules for determining which authority is responsible in any given case for funding the aftercare services. The basic rule being that the responsible authority is the

128 Para 20.7 asserts that the 'duty to provide after-care under s117 includes patients on leave of absence', Code of Practice 1 April 1999.
129 (1999) 2 CCLR 402, QBD and see [2000] LGR 318, CA. See also para 5.121 below for further consideration of this decision.
130 MHA 1983 s117(3).
131 See the Joint Association of Metropolitan/County Councils' guidance 'AMA/Social Services Circular 9/1988' and guidance letter 4.10.89 (which merely confirms that the effective date for 9/1988 is 11/2/88).

one within whose area the person concerned was ordinarily resident at the time of admission, whether the arrangements were made by that local authority or by another. The guidance also provides for a procedure for resolving disputes between authorities over responsibility.

5.114　In *R v Mental Health Review Tribunal ex p Hall*,[132] Scott Baker J considered (among other things) the question of the applicant's ordinary residence for the purposes of s117(3). He noted:

> The word 'or' in subsection (3) clearly envisages an alternative so that there is always some authority that will be responsible when a patient is discharged; if not that of his residence that of the place to which he is sent. One or the other authority is responsible but not both; otherwise there would be a recipe for disaster with the prospect of endless disagreements and failures to make arrangements. Section 117 does not provide for multi social services department or health authority responsibility. The words 'or to whom he is sent on discharge from Tribunal' are included simply to cater for the situation where a patient does not have a current place of residence. The subsection does not mean that a placing authority where the patient resides suddenly ceases to be 'the local social services authority' if on discharge the Applicant is sent to a different authority.

Services

5.115　In *R v Mental Health Review Tribunal ex p Hall*,[133] the Divisional Court held that the duty to provide after care services under s117(2) was jointly shared by the health and social services authority in which the patient was resident at the time he was detained. It is therefore up to individual health and social services authorities to decide among themselves how they will discharge these joint responsibilities.

5.116　Section 117 places no restriction upon the type of services that can be provided.[134] All that is required is that the person concerned must need these services. 'After-care' services under s117 include therefore all the traditional community care services such as advice, guidance and counselling; occupational, social, cultural or recreational activities as well as day centre and drop-in centre provision; domiciliary

---

132　(1999) 2 CCLR 361. Although the case went to the Court of Appeal (1999) 2 CCLR 383, the question of the responsible department was not argued in that court.

133　Ibid.

134　In co-operation with the relevant voluntary agencies – MHA 1983 s117(2).

care[135] as well as laundry and other such services; residential care accommodation and so on.

5.117   Only limited guidance on the nature and extent of s117 services has been issued. The Code of Practice to the Mental Health Act (April 1999) at paragraph 27.1 notes, however, that 'a central purpose of all treatment and care is to equip patients to cope with life outside hospital and function there successfully without danger to themselves or other people'. At paragraph 27.10(f) it suggests that the user's care plan should identify various needs, including, 'day time activities or employment, appropriate accommodation, out-patient treatment, counselling and personal support and assistance in welfare rights and managing finances'.

5.118   Guidance on the Mental Health (Patients in the Community) Act 1995[136] suggests that s117 services may include[137] 'appropriate day-time activities, accommodation, treatment, personal and practical support, 24-hour emergency cover and assistance in welfare rights and financial advice' as well as 'support for informal carers'.

5.119   The list of potential services described in the above guidance is illustrative rather than exhaustive, but nevertheless of assistance in confirming the breadth of the potential help that can be provided.

The duration of the duty

5.120   The services provided under s117 must continue to be supplied until the authorities are satisfied that s/he is no longer in need of them.

5.121   In *R v Richmond LBC ex p Watson*,[138] (a case concerning the lawfulness of charging for services under s117 – see para 8.109 below) Sullivan J held that after-care provision under s117 does not have to continue indefinitely, although it must continue until such time as the health authority and the local authority are satisfied that the individual is no longer in need of such services.

5.122   In his judgment he considered the following question. What are the local authorities' duties under s117 towards a person who, because of old age, illness or other circumstances, has been provided with residential accommodation under s21 of the 1948 Act, then becomes mentally unwell, is detained under s3, is discharged from

135 Including, for instance, such services as are detailed in CSDPA 1970 s2.
136 Which Act enables specific restrictions to be placed upon certain persons receiving s117 services – see below.
137 LAC(96)8/HSG (96)11 para 18.
138 (1999) 2 CCLR 402, upheld by the Court of Appeal [2000] LGR 318.

hospital and returns to his or her former accommodation as part of their after-care package? He held,

> I can see no reason why such a person should be in any worse position than the patient who has not previously been provided with accommodation under s21. On leaving hospital, the local authority will owe them a duty under s117. There may be cases where, in due course there will be no more need for after care services for the person's mental condition, but he or she will still need social services provision for other needs, for example, physical disability. Such cases will have to be examined individually on their facts, through the assessment process provided for by s47. In a case . . . where the illness is dementia, it is difficult to see how such a situation could arise.

5.123   The issue was also considered by the local ombudsman in a complaint against Clwyd.[139] The facts were that the resident had been detained under MHA 1983 s3 from which she was discharged and eventually moved to an EMI nursing home. Steps were then taken by the local authority to assess her liability for residential care charges and in due course the authority placed a charge on her home.

5.124   After the resident's daughter questioned the authority's power to levy such charges the hospital consultant met with the relevant social worker and purported to discharge the s117 after-care. Neither the resident nor her daughter were aware of the discharge meeting or decision.

5.125   The ombudsman considered all these matters, but in particular the decision to discharge the s117 arrangements. In his decision he held:

1) The council had a duty to provide after-care services at no cost to the resident from the moment she was discharged from hospital until such time as it was satisfied that she was no longer in need of such services.

2) In deciding that she no longer needed after-care under s117 the council had failed to address the relevant question which was whether she needed and whether she continued to need after-care services. The ombudsman concluded that if the council had asked itself the relevant question, it would have had to conclude that

---

139   19 September 1997: (1998) 1 CCLR 546; and see also Report No 98/B/0341 from the English local ombudsman against Wiltshire CC (2000) 3 CCLR 60, where a similar finding was made coupled with a recommendation that the cases of other people who might have had to pay for services inappropriately also be reviewed.

she was in need of the specialist care provided at a home for the elderly mentally infirm.

3) The ombudsman concluded that the council's maladministration had been exacerbated by a number of factors including their failure to take account of the daughter's views before ceasing to provide after-care services under s117.

Mental Health (Patients in the Community) Act 1995

5.126   The 1995 Act introduced the possibility of 'after-care under supervision', generally referred to as supervised discharge. While the specific requirements for supervised discharge are outside the scope of this text,[140] its purpose has been described thus:[141]

> After-care under supervision is an arrangement by which a patient who has been detained in hospital for treatment under the provisions of the Act may be subject to formal supervision after he or she is discharged. Its purpose is to help ensure that the patient receives the after-care services to be provided under section 117 of the Act. It is available for patients suffering from any of the four forms of mental disorder in the Act but is primarily intended for those with severe mental illness.

5.127   For such a supervised discharge to take place, it must be shown:

a) that unless aftercare services under s117 are provided there will be:
   i) a substantial risk of serious harm to the health or safety of the patient or the safety of others, or
   ii) a risk that the patient will be seriously exploited; and
b) in any event that placing the patient under supervised discharge is likely to help ensure that s/he will receive the relevant after-care services.

5.128   Guidance on the 1995 Act has been issued in the form of Circular LAC(96)8/HSG(96)11.[142] In relation to the amendments made to s117 the guidance states:

> 18. The arrangements for after-care under supervision will need to be drawn up as part of the normal discharge planning process, following the principles of the Care Programme Approach in

---

140 For detailed analysis see R Jones *Mental Health Act Manual* (Sweet & Maxwell, 1999).

141 Code of Practice to the Mental Health Act (April 1999) para 28.2.

142 WHC(96)11 in Wales.

England and WHC(95)40 in Wales and in accordance with the formal consultation requirements in the Act (see below). Chapter 27 of the Code is also relevant. The professional team providing care in the community will need to consider and plan the services to be provided, including as may be appropriate daytime activities, accommodation, treatment, personal and practical support, 24-hour emergency cover and assistance in welfare rights and financial advice. They will also need to consider how often the patient is likely to need particular services. Support for informal carers should not be overlooked as the care plan may be to some degree dependent on their role.

19. The Act defines requirements which may be imposed when a patient is subject to supervised discharge. These are:
- that the patient should live in a particular place;
- that the patient should attend a particular place at set times for medical treatment, occupation, education or training;
- that the supervisor, or a person authorised by the supervisor, should be allowed access to the patient at his or her place of residence (see paragraph 51 below).

The reasons for imposing requirements should be explained to the patient, and details of them should be included in the care plan. A requirement to attend for medical treatment does not carry with it any power to impose medication or other treatment against the patient's wishes.

The care programme approach

5.129   The care programme approach (CPA) was introduced by the joint health/social services Circular HC(90)23/LASSL (90)11 and applies in both England and Wales.[143] Health authorities were given lead responsibility for implementing the policy introduced by the circular, although there was an obligation on health and social services authorities to reach formal and detailed inter-agency agreements to ensure its full implementation.[144] Social services authorities were required to collaborate with health authorities in introducing the approach, and as 'resources allow, to continue to expand social services care services to patients being treated in the community'.[145]

---

143 In *R v Mental Health Review Tribunal ex p Hall* [1999] 3 All ER 132; (1999) 2 CCLR 361, it was argued that the CPA did not apply in Wales: Scott Baker rejected this, citing (among other things) paras 10, 11 and 14 of WHC95(40); and paras 1.2 and 27.2 of the Code of Guidance.

144 See *Social Services Departments and the Care Programme Approach: An SSI Inspection Report* (Department of Health, 1995) para 4.3.11.

145 Ibid at para 3.2.

5.130　The NHS Executive announced changes to the CPA in October 1999[146] including an intention to integrate the CPA and care management procedures, by (among other things) having one unified health and social care assessment process; and ensuring that service users 'had access through a single process to the support and resources of both health and social care'.

5.131　The care programme approach applies whether or not a patient has been detained under MHA 1983 and therefore the vast majority of cases covered by the programme will involve the discharge arrangements for voluntary or informal patients, or those detained for assessment under the 1983 Act.[147] The approach is however dominated by 'risk assessment' issues and accordingly especially concerned with the patients entitled to services under s117.

5.132　Since its introduction, the Department of Health has emphasised the importance it attaches to the care programme approach[148] and the original joint circular advice of 1990 was updated in May 1994 with the publication of *Guidance on the Discharge of Mentally Disordered People and their Continuing Care in the Community* as HSG(94)27/ LASSL(94)4.

5.133　The essential elements of the programme are described as:[149]

a) systematic assessment of health and social care needs (including accommodation), bearing in mind both immediate and longer-term requirements;

b) a care plan agreed between the relevant professional staff, the patient and his or her carers, and recorded in writing;

c) the allocation of a key worker whose job (with multi-disciplinary managerial and professional support) is:
   • to keep in close contact with the patient;
   • to monitor that the agreed programme of care is delivered; and
   • to take immediate action if it is not;

d) regular review of the patient's progress and of his or her health and social care needs.

5.134　The Code of Practice to the Mental Health Act (April 1999) describes

---

146　Via 'Effective care co-ordination in mental health services: modernising the care programme approach: a policy booklet'.

147　Ie, under ss2, 4, 5 or 136 of the 1983 Act; see also HSG(94)27 para 8.

148　See *Care Management and Assessment: Managers' Guide* (HMSO 1991) p93; *Health of the Nation: Key Area Handbook: Mental Illness* (1993) App 9.3; (1995) Chapters 9 and 11.

149　HSG(94)27 para 10 and see *Social Services Departments and the care programme approach: An SSI Inspection Report* (Department of Health, 1995) para 3.4 and HSG(94)27/LASSL(94)4 para 10.

the objectives of the care programme at Chapter 27. The relevant portions of which being:

27.2 These objectives apply to all patients receiving treatment and care from the specialist psychiatric services, whether or not they are admitted to hospital and whether or not they are detained under the Act. They are embodied in the Care Programme Approach (CPA) set out in Circular HC(90)23/LASSL(90)11, and in the Welsh Office Mental Illness Strategy (WHC(95)40).[149A] The key elements of the CPA are:

• systematic arrangements for assessing people's health and social care needs;
• the formulation of a care plan which addresses those needs;
• the appointment of a key worker to keep in close touch with the patient and monitor care;
• regular review and if need be, agreed changes to the care plan.

27.4 NHS Managers and Directors of Social Services should ensure that all staff are aware of the CPA and related provisions. Further guidance on the discharge of mentally disordered people and their continuing care in the community is given in HSG(94)27/LASSL(94)4 and WHC(95)7 and WHC(96)26. The relationship between the CPA, section 117 after-care and local authority arrangements for care management is more fully explained in *Building Bridges – A Guide to arrangements for inter-agency working for the care and protection of severely mentally ill people* (Department of Health, 1995).

27.5 Before the decision is taken to discharge or grant leave to a patient, it is the responsibility of the RMO to ensure, in consultation with the other professionals concerned, that the patient's needs for health and social care are fully assessed and the care plan addresses them. If the patient is being given leave for only a short period a less comprehensive review may suffice but the arrangements for the patient's care should still be properly recorded.

27.6 The RMO is also responsible for ensuring that:
• a proper assessment is made of risks to the patient or other people;
• in the case of offender patients, the circumstances of any victim and their families are taken into account;
• consideration is given to whether the patient meets the criteria for after-care under supervision, or under guardianship (see Chapter 13 and 28); and
• consideration is given to whether the patient should be placed on the supervision register established in accordance with HSG(94)5.

149A WHC(95) 40 was in fact a draft document and the correct reference should have been to WOC 19/96
150   *R v Ealing District Health Authority ex p Fox* [1993] 3 All ER 170, QBD.

Mental Health Review Tribunals and managers' hearings

27.7 The courts have ruled[150] that in order to fulfil their obligations under section 117 health authorities and local authority social services authorities must take reasonable steps to identify appropriate after-care facilities for a patient before his or her actual discharge from hospital. In view of this, some discussion of after-care needs, including social services and other relevant professionals and agencies, should take place before a patient has a Mental Health Review Tribunal or managers hearing, so that suitable after-care arrangements can be implemented in the event of his or her being discharged (see para 22.12).

Who should be involved

27.8 Those who should be involved in consideration of the patient's after-care needs include:
- the patient, if he or she wishes and/or a nominated representative;
- the patient's RMO;
- a nurse involved in caring for the patient in hospital;
- a social worker/care manager specialising in mental health work;
- the GP and primary care team;
- a community psychiatric/mental health nurse;
- a representative of relevant voluntary organisations;
- in the case of a restricted patient, the probation service;
- subject to the patient's consent, any informal carer who will be involved in looking after him or her outside hospital;
- subject to the patient's consent, his or her nearest relative;[151]
- a representative of housing authorities, if accommodation is an issue.

27.9 It is important that those who are involved are able to take decisions regarding their own and as far as possible their agency's involvement. If approval for plans needs to be obtained from more senior levels (for example, for funding) it is important that this causes no delay to the implementation of the care plan.

Considerations for after-care

27.10 Those concerned must consider the following issues:
a. the patient's own wishes and needs, and those of any dependents;
b. the views of any relevant relative, friend or supporter of the patient;
c. the need for agreement with authorities and agencies in the area where the patient is to live;
d. in the case of offender patients, the circumstances of any victim and their families should be taken into account when deciding where the patient should live;

151 There are special considerations governing consultation with the nearest relative of a patient subject to after-care under supervision; see Chapter 28 of the Code of Practice.

  e. the possible involvement of other agencies, eg probation,
      voluntary organisations;
  f. the establishing of a care plan, based on proper assessment and
      clearly identified needs, including:
      • day time activities or employment,
      • appropriate accommodation,
      • out-patient treatment,
      • counselling, and personal support,
      • assistance in welfare rights and managing finances,
      • a contingency plan should the patient relapse.
  g. the appointment of a key worker (see para 27.2) from either of the
      statutory agencies to monitor the care plan's implementation,
      liaise and co-ordinate where necessary and report to the senior
      officer in their agency any problems that arise which cannot be
      resolved through discussion;
  h. the identification of any unmet need.

27.11 The professionals concerned should establish an agreed
outline of the patient's needs, taking into account his or her social
and cultural background, and agree a time-scale for the
implementation of the various aspects of the plan. All key people
with specific responsibilities with regard to the patient should be
properly identified. Once plans are agreed it is essential that any
changes are discussed with others involved with the patient before
being implemented. The plan should be recorded in writing.

27.12 The care plan should be regularly reviewed. It will be the
responsibility of the key worker to arrange reviews of the plan until it
is agreed that it is no longer necessary. The senior officer in the key
worker's agency responsible for after-care arrangements should
ensure that all aspects of the procedure are followed.

5.135 The 'Patients' Charter on Mental Health Services' gave further
guidance on the level of service that can be expected by persons with
a mental health problem.[152] It states that persons referred to the
specialist mental health services by a GP should be seen within four
weeks and informed of the outcome of their assessment within a
further two weeks (para 16). The Charter states that users receiving
hospital in-patient treatment from the psychiatric services have an
entitlement to an after-care planning process which includes:
a) a needs assessment;
b) a named person who is responsible for deciding when discharge
   should occur;
c) an assurance that, if continuing care is needed outside hospital,
   discharge will not take place until appropriate arrangements have
   been made for that care;

152 EL(97)1.

d) (subject to the patient's agreement) his/her GP will be informed of the discharge as well as anyone else involved, eg, the CPN or social worker;

e) a named person who will be responsible for his/her care outside hospital;

f) an assurance that any community care services required will commence immediately upon discharge from hospital;

g) (together with his/her carer – provided the user consents) being fully informed and involved in plans for discharge and continuing care;

h) being advised what to do and who to contact in the event of problems occurring (including outside office hours).

Mental Health Grant

5.136 Specific central government grant support for mental health services is delivered by the Mental Health Grant (which from April 1999 replaced the previous mental illness specific grant although its purpose remains the same[153]). The grant is a combined grant paid for both social services and the NHS and guidance on its application has been issued as LAC(99) 08/HSC 1999/038.[154]

5.137 In addition to the grant, specific central government funding initiatives in this area are generally channelled via supplementary credit approvals under Local Government and Housing Act 1989 s54.[155]

Direct payments

5.138 There is substantial research which suggests that the making of direct payments to certain people in need of community care services can result in much improved user satisfaction, and indeed cost savings to

---

153 The mental illness specific grant was first introduced as a result of Local Authority Social Services Act 1970 s7E; LAC(96)6 explained its objective was to enable local authority social services departments to improve the social care of people with a mental illness who need specialist psychiatric care. It supports the care programme approach including the introduction of supervision registers for the provision of community care for all in-patients considered for discharge, and all new patients accepted by the specialist psychiatric services.

154 'Modernising mental health services; NHS modernisation fund for mental health services and mental health grant 199/2002'.

155 See, eg, LAC(99)12/HSG 1999/050 'Mental health supplementary credit approvals 1999/2000 for developing social care services for people with mental illness'.

local authorities.[156] Kestenbaum has, for instance, shown the high value placed by service users on choice and control and that in general this could not be provided by local authorities:

> It is not simply a matter of resource levels, though these are significant. As important are the qualities that any large-scale service providing organisation would find hard to deliver: choice of care assistant, flexibility, consistency, control of times and tasks, etc.[157]

5.139   The power of social services authorities to make direct cash payments to adults in need of community care services has been limited. Since March 1997, however, they have had the power in certain situations to make such payments to disabled adults, by virtue of the Community Care (Direct Payments) Act 1996. In addition disabled people are able to receive direct payments via the Independent Living Fund (ILF). Payments under the 1996 Act and ILF are considered separately below. Direct payments have, however, always been permitted 'in exceptional circumstances under the Children Act 1989 and these powers are considered separately at para 11.10 below.

Third party schemes

5.140   Prior to the implementation of the 1996 Act social services departments were (with very minor exceptions[158]) subject to a specific prohibition against making payments of cash to disabled people, in lieu of services.[159] They were however permitted to pay third parties (such as independent home care service providers) that had undertaken to deliver the assessed services. A number of authorities accordingly developed 'third party' schemes whereby they made payments to an intermediary (an individual, a trust fund or brokerage scheme) which then worked closely with the disabled person in the purchasing of his or her care. Such schemes gave the disabled person effective control over the purchasing of his/her care services and also provided assistance with the administrative obligations inherent in any employment situation (recruitment and appointment of carers, employment contracts, grievance procedures, PAYE, etc).

5.141   Although cash payments can now be made directly to disabled

---

156 See, eg, A Kestenbaum *Independent Living: a Review* (Joseph Rowntree Foundation, 1996).

157 Ibid p77.

158 See, for instance, para 5.94 above.

159 Most particularly by virtue of NAA 1948 s29(6)(a) [see para 5.28 above] and NHSA 1977 Sch 8 para 2(2)(a).

people in certain situations by virtue of the 1996 Act, there remain however a number of instances whereby third party schemes are still of value. Most notably, because they would appear to enable payments to be made in situations which are not permitted by the 1996 Act, for instance:

- to third parties on behalf of service users who lack the necessary mental capacity[160] to make decisions concerning their care arrangements; and
- to carers who are living in the same household as the disabled person.

During the bill's passage through parliament, the minister was asked to confirm that the new possibilities created by the Act would not affect the status of these pre-existing third-party schemes. He confirmed that such 'schemes that are in place now should not be affected. We are not seeking to undermine such schemes'.[161]

Community Care (Direct Payments) Act 1996

5.142   The general prohibition against direct payments for disabled adults was partially removed by the 1996 Act, s1(1) of which provides:[159A]

1 (1) Where –
(a) an authority have decided under section 47 of the National Health Service and Community Care Act 1990 (assessment by local authorities of needs for community care services) that the needs of a person call for the provision of any community care services, and
(b) the person is of a description which is specified for the purposes of this subsection by regulations made by the Secretary of State, the authority may, if the person consents, make to him, in respect of his securing the provision of any of the services for which they have decided his needs call, a payment of such amount as, subject to subsections (2) and (3) below, they think fit.

As will be seen, the Act is primarily an enabling statute. The statutory detail has been provided by the Community Care (Direct Payments) Regulations 1997 SI No 734 (referred to as the 'regulations' below). Revised Policy and Practice Guidance has been issued as LAC(2000)1. Direct payments are ignored for the purpose of calculating entitlement to social security benefits.

159A Section 1 of the 1996 Act will be amended by Carers and Disabled Children Act 2000 s5.
160   Required by the 1996 Act, see para 5.143 below.
161   John Bowis at *Hansard* (HC) (6 March 1996) col 380.

5.143   The main rules concerning entitlement can be set out as follows:

1) **The scheme is discretionary**
It is for the local authority to decide whether to offer a particular service user the option of receiving direct payments (section 1). If the authority decide on this option, it only becomes effective if the service user consents.

However, once a local authority has decided to offer a particular individual a direct payment, public policy would require (in the absence of cogent reasons) that authority to offer persons in a similar situation the same option. The Department of Health has advised that 'whilst local authorities may pursue broad policies they should be careful not to fetter their discretion. Our view has always been that a local authority should consider each application for a direct payment on its own merits'.[162]

Both the service user and the local authority have the right to terminate the direct payment arrangement, although LAC(2000)1 para 55 stresses that authorities 'should not automatically assume when problems arise that the solution is to discontinue' the payments. The termination of the direct payment arrangement should normally be subject to a minimum period of notice by both the user and the local authority (LAC(2000)1 para 56).

2) **Direct payments must relate to the user's community care assessment**
The money paid over by the authority must be spent on purchasing services to meet the need, which that authority has assessed (as a result of a community care assessment).

The local authority has, therefore, power to define precisely how the direct payment must be applied. However, the imposition of such restriction would in general defeat much of the purpose (and philosophy) underlying the legislation. Accordingly, LAC(2000)1 advises at para 6 that local authorities should seek to leave as much choice as possible in the hands of the individual and allow people to address their own needs in innovative ways while satisfying themselves that the person's assessed needs are being met.

3) **The ability of the direct payment recipient to 'manage'**
Direct payments may only be made to persons who can manage (alone or with assistance) such payments (reg 2(1)(b)).

162 A local authority that fettered its discretion, to the extent that it decided (explicitly or by its actions) not to implement the Act would also be open to challenge on similar grounds to those employed in *R v Secretary of State for Home Department ex p Fire Brigades Union* [1995] 2 All ER 244.

The previous practice guidance, LAC(97)11 at paras 15–16 listed seven questions the local authority might consider in determining whether or not a potential payee has sufficient ability to manage direct payments. It suggested that if 'the answer to either of the first two questions is "No", then that person is unlikely to be able to manage direct payments. Negative answers to the remaining questions may raise doubts, but local authorities should consider what assistance would enable the person to manage that aspect'. The first two questions, being:

• Does the person understand the nature of direct payments? and
• Can the person express preferences (with assistance to communicate their views if necessary) between different types of service?

If the user satisfies these questions, but needs assistance with such matters as keeping records, management of day-to-day relationships with staff or the operation of PAYE, then authorities are encourage to facilitate this (as well as offering training to assist payees to manage themselves and by providing advocacy support[163]).

As noted above, 'third party' schemes may be of benefit in situations whereby the social services department wishes to make direct payments to a carer or other intermediary on behalf of a service user who lacks the necessary mental capacity.

4) **Excluded service users**

Direct payments under the 1996 Act can only be made to persons 'to whom s29 National Assistance Act 1948 applies'[164] (reg 2(1)). The client group for this section is considered at para 5.13. Most importantly however it only applies to persons aged 18 or over. Direct payments will become available to disabled children aged 16 and 17 and to adults caring for disabled children, once the Carers and Disabled Children Act 2000 comes into force (see para 7.38 below). In the meantime there appears to be no reason why social services departments should not use their existing powers under CA 1989 to make such payments (see para 5.139 above).

Regulation 2 (as amended by the Community Care (Direct Payments) Amendment Regulations 2000[165]) specifies that direct

---

163 Practice Guidance paras 35–36.
164 Direct payments to carers will also be possible once the Carers and Disabled Children Act 2000 comes into force, see para 7.38 below.
165 Which removed the previous prohibition upon making direct payments to persons aged 65 or over.

payments cannot be offered to certain people whose liberty to arrange their care is restricted by certain mental health or criminal justice legislation, essentially being:

- patients detained under mental health legislation who are on leave of absence from hospital;
- conditionally discharged detained patients subject to Home Office restrictions;
- patients subject to guardianship under the mental health legislation;
- people receiving after-care under supervision (under MHA 1983 s25A) or after-care (including supervision/treatment) in consequence of a compulsory court order;
- offenders serving a probation or combination order subject to a requirement to undergo treatment for a mental health condition or for drug or alcohol dependency.

The policy guidance explains (at para 14) that such persons 'are required to receive specific community care services. Offering them direct payments in lieu of those services would not give a sufficient guarantee that the person would receive the services required'.

5) **Excluded service providers**

Section 1(4) of the Act stipulates that the recipients of direct payments cannot use the money to buy care from certain categories of people. Regulation 3 then prevents people using direct payments to secure services from their partners or a close relative living in the same household. A close relative is defined as a parent or parent-in-law, a son or daughter, son-in-law, daughter-in-law, stepson or stepdaughter, brother or sister, aunt or uncle, grandparent, or the spouse or partner of any of these.

LAC(2000)1 Policy Guidance para 24 states that local authorities should not allow people to use direct payments to secure services from a close relative living elsewhere or from someone else living in the same household as the direct payment recipient (except employed live-in personal assistants who are not close relatives). The guidance however states that 'a local authority may decide that an exception to this general rule is justified, if it is satisfied that that is the most appropriate way of securing the relevant services'.

As noted above, it does appear to be legally permissible for local authorities to make payments under 'third party' schemes to the carers of a disabled person notwithstanding that they are related or living in the same household. In many cases, however, there may well be good practice reasons why such an arrangement may not be appropriate.

6) **Prohibited services**

Direct payments can be used for the purchase of any 'community care services', including for instance aids and adaptations,[166] with two exceptions;

i) LAC(2000)1 para 32 states that direct payments cannot be used to purchase local authority provided services, although an individual could receive both direct payments, and services provided by the local authority in the normal way, within his or her care package.

ii) Regulation 4 prohibits the use of direct payments for the purpose of purchasing permanent residential care. It however permits the purchase of respite residential care provided that it is limited to a cumulative total of four weeks in any 12-month period. However, in calculating the cumulative period, only periods of residential care less than four weeks apart are added together to make a cumulative total.

By way of example, if a person purchases two weeks' residential care then spends five weeks living at home and then purchases a further two weeks residential care (and so on) s/he would be able to continue this process without falling foul of the four-week maximum period. The reason being that, because the periods in the residential home are separated by more than four weeks, they are not aggregated for the purpose of calculating the four weeks' maximum period.

7) **The amount of the payment**

The calculation of the appropriate amount of a direct payment may, in some cases, be complex. Advice on how this should be done is given in the practice guidance and in specialist guidelines produced by CIBFA for local authorities.[167] The practice guidance however makes the following comments:

---

166 LAC(2000)1 para 33, which goes on to suggest that 'direct payments will only rarely be appropriate for purchasing complex and expensive pieces of equipment, although they may well make sense for smaller, less specialised items'.

167 'Community Care (Direct Payments) Act 1996; accounting and financial management guidelines'. Chartered Institute of Public Finance and Accountancy (1998).

35. It is up to each local authority to decide on the amount of a direct payment but it must be enough, taking into account any contribution which the individual is expected to make to the cost of his or her care package, to enable the recipient legally to secure the relevant service to a standard which the local authority considers is acceptable.

The guidance emphasises that direct payments should only be used if they are a cost effective way of delivering the service.[168] Local authorities are however reminded that they have a discretion to increase the amount 'so as to enable the person to secure his or her preferred service if it is satisfied that the benefits of doing so outweigh the costs and that it still represents best value'.[169]

Section 2 of the 1996 Act replicates the provisions of HASSAS-SAA 1983 s17 (see para 8.67 below), such that any direct payment will be net of any reasonable charge that local authority decides to levy. The guidance advises that 'in considering whether, and if so how, to ask individuals to make a financial contribution to the cost of their care package, local authorities should treat people who receive direct payments as they would have treated them under the authority's charging policy if those people were receiving the equivalent services'.[170]

8) The obligations upon the recipient of direct payments

In some cases direct payments will place a considerable administrative burden on the payee; requiring detailed records and accounts to be kept (as the local authority will need to audit these) as well as obligations in relation to employment contracts, grievance procedures, the payment of PAYE and national insurance, VAT and so on. Local authorities are advised to provide advice and assistance to help payees cope with these obligations (including, as noted above, access to an advocacy scheme). A detailed and practical booklet on these questions has been issued by the Department of Health as *A Guide for People who Receive Direct Payments* (1998).

The recipient of direct payments is liable to repay any unspent (or misspent) monies. Practice guidance para 54 advises, however, that the discretion to seek a recovery of misapplied monies 'is intended to enable [local authorities] to recover money which has

168 Ibid.
169 LAC(2000)1 para 35.
170 LAC(2000)1 para 27.

been diverted from the purpose for which it was intended, or which has simply not been spent at all. It is not intended to be used to penalise honest mistakes'.

Independent Living Fund

5.144   The Independent Living Fund was established by the DHSS in 1988 as an independent trust[171] to provide a weekly payment to severely disabled people who suffered significant financial loss as a result of the abolition of supplementary benefits 'additional requirements' payments in that year.[172] The fund is financed by the government, but administered by seven independent trustees.

Independent Living (Extension) Fund

5.145   The original trust was wound up in 1993 as part of the community care reforms with the fund monies being transferred to local authorities via the special transitional grant. However the payments that were being made to disabled people at the time it was wound up, have been preserved and are paid from what is known as the Independent Living (Extension) Fund.

5.146   There is provision for payments made from the Independent Living (Extension) Fund to be increased to recipients if they experience a 'significant change in their circumstances', and although payments are suspended during any period when the disabled person is accommodated in a hospital residential or nursing home, the payments can be reinstated when s/he returns to live independently in the community.

Independent Living (1993) Fund

5.147   After the original fund was wound up in 1993, a new fund, known as the Independent Living (1993) Fund, was created for new applicants. The entitlement terms of the trust were, however, more stringent and the benefits less generous.

5.148   In order to qualify for a grant from the fund, an applicant must:

1) be at least 16 and under 66 years of age; and
2) be receiving the highest rate of the care component of disability living allowance; and

171   The trust deeds for the various funds are held by the solicitor to the Department of Social Security; the original trust deed being dated 8 June 1988 and the Independent Living (Extension) Fund, 25 February 1993.
172   R Means and R Smith *Community Care Policy and Practice* (Macmillan, 1994).

3) be at risk of entering residential care (or currently be in residential care and wish to leave and live independently); and

4) live alone or with people who cannot fully meet the care needs; and

5) be on income support; or

6) have an income at or around income support levels after care costs paid; and

7) have savings of less than £8,000.

The Fund works in partnership with local authorities, in that it will only make payments (to a maximum of £300) if the social services department agrees to provide services and/or cash to a minimum value of £200 net a week. The combined value of the Local Authority and the 1993 Fund provision must not exceed £500 a week; the top up monies from the fund are paid directly to the user.

5.149   Although applications can be made directly to the Fund (see below) in general the social services department should first carry out a full community care assessment and agree to support the application to the fund on the basis that:

1) it will contribute money or services to the value of £200 per week; and

2) it is satisfied that the total care package should not exceed £500 per week; and

3) the monies from the Fund will be used to employ one or more people as care assistants (Fund monies cannot be used for other purposes such as equipment, heating bills, home adaptations and transport costs); and

4) the applicant is capable of independent living in the community for at least six months.

If an applicant appears to meet all the criteria, the Fund will arrange for an assessment visit to be made. The visit will be carried out jointly, by one of the Fund's visiting social workers together with a local authority social worker.

5.150   Applicants are required to contribute towards the overall cost of the care package:

- all of their severe disability premium and special transitional addition (if these additions to income support are received);
- half of their disability living allowance; and
- any income above income support level that is not already being used for care.

5.151   The contact address for the Independent Living Funds is PO Box 183, Nottingham, NG8 3RD Tel: 0115 942 8191/8192. The web address is http://www.dss.gov.uk/ba/GBI/5a58b13.htm.

CHAPTER 6

NHS responsibilities for community care services

6.1   **Introduction**

6.4   **Health care and the NHS – historical overview**

6.11   Primary care groups/trusts

6.19   Wales

Local health groups

6.16   **NHSA 1977**

6.26   Hospital and community health services: Part I

6.33   Family health services: Part II

6.35   Section 1: the duty to promote a 'comprehensive' health service

6.39   NHS Guidance

Access to circulars

6.45   **The medical/social divide**

6.46   The duty to co-operate

Health improvement programmes • Hospital closures • Specific duties to collaborate

6.62   **NHS primary health care responsibilities**

6.62   General practitioner services

GPs' obligation to provide general medical services • GPs' obligation to prescribe drugs and appliances • GPs' obligation to provide medical certificates

6.72   Hospital consultant services

continued

6.75   NHS's continuing care responsibilities

6.75   Introduction

6.81   NHS continuing care guidance

6.82   NHS responsibilities for meeting continuing health care needs

Mental health, learning disability and children's services • Continuing in-patient care

6.101   Rehabilitation and recovery

6.106   Respite health care

6.112   Palliative health care

6.116   NHS specialist or intensive services for people in nursing homes

Specialist medical equipment • Incontinence supplies

6.122   NHS discharge procedures

Discharge planning and the duty to inform • Patient's right to seek a review of a discharge decision

6.137   Learning disability services

6.138   Health authority payments to social services

6.140   Budget sharing arrangements under NHSA 1977 s28A

6.143   Partnerships arrangements under Health Act 1999 s31

6.145   Other partnership arrangements

6.146   Budget sharing arrangements prior to the Health Act 1999

Joint finance • Dowry payments • Other payments

6.153   Code of Practice on Openness in the NHS

6.157   NHS complaints

6.159   Who may complain?

6.161   Time limits

6.163   Complaints personnel

Complaints manager • Convenor

6.165   Excluded matters

6.166   Stage 1

Trusts and health authorities • GP complaints • Completion of stage 1 procedure

6.170   Stage 2: the independent review panel
The panel

6.180   Health Service Ombudsman

Introduction

6.1   This chapter considers the community care responsibilities of the NHS and the obligation upon it and local authorities to work together in order to promote the health and well being of community care service users. While the NHS spends in excess of £8 billion per annum on long-term care,[1] this represents only one of the many functions of this enormously complex institution. The NHS is the single biggest organisation in Western Europe; it employs a million people, and spends £1,000 every second.[2] What follows, therefore, is a brief overview of those aspects of the NHS of relevance to community care users and practitioners.

6.2   At no time since the formation of the NHS over 50 years ago, has there been a clear separation between its responsibilities for health services and those of the local authorities for care services.

6.3   Until 1990, successive governments sought, by simultaneous amendment[3] of the community care and NHS legislation, to transfer most health functions from local authorities to the NHS. During this period, however, perceptions as to what was a 'health function' changed. In consequence the NHS concentrated upon the provision of acute health care and sought to shed its responsibilities for the long-term health care needs of people with mental health problems. During the 1980s responsibility for people who would formerly have been resident in a long-stay mental hospital or geriatric ward was in large measure transferred to the social security budget, leading to a substantial increase in the number of private residential and nursing homes. Accordingly the legislative changes of the last ten years have been dominated by the tripartite tension between these three agencies. The National Health Service and Community Care Act (NHSCCA) 1990 radically altered the respective responsibilities of the Benefits Agency and local authorities, but left virtually unchanged the interface between the NHS and local authorities. In contrast, however, the present reforms of the NHS seek to redraw the relationship between the NHS and local authorities, indeed in relation to primary care services, they may result in an effective merger of the two responsibilities.

1   Health Committee 3rd report on *Long-term Care* Vol 1 HC 59–I (1996) para 111.
2   *The New NHS Modern Dependable* Cm 3807 (December 1997) paras 1.1 and 9.1.
3   The NHS Act (NHSA) 1946 and the National Assistance Act (NAA) 1948 came into force on the same day, as did the Health Services and Public Health Act (HSPHA) 1968 and the Local Authority Social Services Act (LASSA) 1970; as did the Local Government Act (LGA) 1972 and the NHS Reorganisation Act 1973.

Health care and the NHS – historical overview

6.4 At the beginning of the 20th century the majority of institutional health and social care was provided via the poor law boards. Gradually as the century progressed local authorities assumed greater responsibilities for both functions. The 1929[4] poor law reforms led to the creation of local authority health committees, which took control of the better poor law hospitals (then known as public health hospitals). The remaining poor law institutions, workhouses and basic poor law hospitals were also transferred away from the poor law boards and became the responsibility of the county and county borough councils.

6.5 The creation of the NHS in 1946 did not initially wrest responsibility for health services from local authorities. Although today it is convenient to see NHSA 1946 and NAA 1948 as demarcating the responsibilities of what we now call social services departments and the NHS, this separation of responsibilities has in fact developed largely as a consequence of subsequent legislation. The 1946 Act stipulated that many services we would today label as 'health services', such as ambulances (s27), midwifery (s23), health visitors (s24), were to be the responsibility of local authority health committees (called 'local health authorities').[5] Indeed NAA 1948 s21(7)(b), as originally enacted, authorised the provision by local authorities of 'health services, not being specialist services or services of a kind normally provided only on admission to hospital'.[6]

6.6 While minor changes to the health/social care responsibilities of NHS/local authorities occurred over the next 25 years,[7] major reform did not take place until 1974, when LGA 1972 and the NHS Reorganisation Act 1973 came into force. The 1973 Act sought to transfer all nursing functions (whether in hospital, at home or elsewhere) to the NHS. It abolished local health authorities (ie, local authority health committees) and in their place created free-standing regional, area and district health authorities.

6.7 In 1977 NHSA 1946 was repealed and replaced by a consolidating Act, NHSA 1977. Although the 1977 Act has itself been much amended, it remains the primary statute governing the NHS.

---

4 LGA 1929.
5 NHSA 1946 Sch 4 Pt II.
6 Including nursing services by virtue of NHSA 1946 s25.
7 Most notably HSPHA 1968 which transferred to local health authorities responsibility for health visitors and nursing other than in a person's home; and LASSA 1970 which in its first schedule sought to delineate the responsibilities of local authority social services departments.

6.8   In 1990[8] major reform of the NHS was effected by the creation of GP fundholding practices and by the removal of health authority responsibility for providing hospital, community health and ambulance services. The responsibility for the management and running of these services was placed in hands of an entirely new institution, the NHS trust. Health authorities henceforth became purchasers of health care.[9] Secondary and tertiary health care (ie, general and specialist hospitals) were to be provided by acute trusts, while primary care (ie, community health and GP services) was to be provided by fundholding and non-fundholding GPs and community NHS trusts.

6.9   In 1996 district and regional health authorities were abolished[10] by the Health Authorities Act 1995 and replaced by the present single tier health authority system, which, in England, receives funding from the executive branch of the Department of Health known as the NHS Executive. In Wales responsibility for funding health authorities has devolved to the Welsh Assembly.

6.10   In 1997 the government published its plans for reform of the NHS in England, as *The New NHS: Modern, Dependable.*[11] The proposals for Wales were published as *NHS Wales: putting patients first.*[12] The Welsh proposals are very similar to those proposed for England, but the main differences are outlined separately below. Many of the proposals for reform have now been introduced via the Health Act 1999. The Act (among other things):

- abolished GP fundholding and provides for the creation of new statutory bodies to be known as primary care trusts;
- created new duties of partnership within the NHS and between NHS bodies and local authorities in England and Wales;
- provides for local strategies to be developed for improving health via 'Health Improvement Programmes';
- created new powers which enabled NHS bodies and local authorities to share budgets and enter into joint arrangements for the purchase or provision of health and health-related services (eg, social care).

---

8 Via NHSCCA 1990.

9 This separation of purchaser/provider is known as the 'internal market'.

10 Largely because the 1990 legislation had stripped away many of their responsibilities.

11 Cm 3807, December 1997.

12 The Stationery Office, January 1998.

Primary care groups/trusts

6.11 At the heart of the reform plan is the idea of promoting primary care groups and primary care trusts as the alternative to GP fundholding[13]. The aim is to create a primary care-led commissioning process which would redress the present imbalance of NHS expenditure; where over 70 per cent of the whole NHS budget is spent on secondary and tertiary health care.[14]

6.12 Diagram 5 depicts the NHS commissioning arrangements prior to April 1999. The main funding for the NHS, voted by parliament, was at that time transferred by the Department of Health and Welsh Office to the NHS Executive who then apportioned the monies between the 100 health authorities in England and Wales. Each health authority entered into block contracts with their local trusts for the provision of the general health services required by their population.[15] Unusual 'one-off' treatments were dealt with by a separate procedure known as 'extra contractual referrals' (ECRs).[16] About half the GP practices[17] in the United Kingdom opted to become fundholders; this entitled them to approximately 20 per cent extra financial support from which they were expected to purchase certain services[18] (such as elective surgery, physiotherapy, etc) for their patients. Patients of non-fundholding GPs however had to rely upon their health authority's block contract for such treatments.

6.13 Fundholding was abolished by the Health Act 1999 largely because of its enormous administrative expense.[19] It had however proved effective in a number of respects, including:

1) GPs were able to purchase from any trust in England or Wales and so could seek value for money in a way not possible for health

---

13 Fundholding practices were wound up in April 1999; and the system was formerly abolished by Health Act 1999 s1.

14 *The New NHS: Modern, Dependable* Cm 3807 (December 1997) para 6.1.

15 These contracts are now known as 'Service Agreements', and are subject to detailed guidance, see HSC 1998/198.

16 ECRs were abolished in April 1999 and have been replaced by commissioning arrangements known as 'Out of Area Treatments', guidance for which was issued as HSC 1998/198.

17 At April 1999 there were approximately 3,500 fundholding practices: *The New NHS: Modern, Dependable* Cm 3807 (December 1997) para 9.2.

18 The services were specified in 'The Approved List of Goods and Services' issued by the NHS Executive; see, eg, HSG(97)22.

19 The government estimates that its abolition will save £1 billion over the life of the present parliament: *The New NHS: Modern, Dependable* Cm 3807 (December 1997) para 9.25.

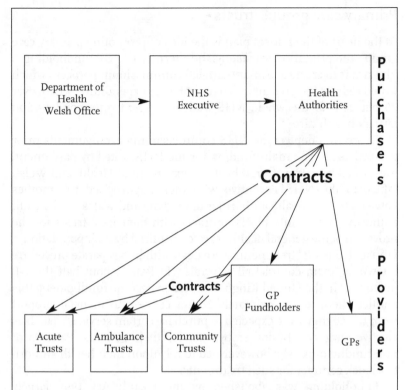

Diagram 5: NHS commissioning arrangements prior to April 1999

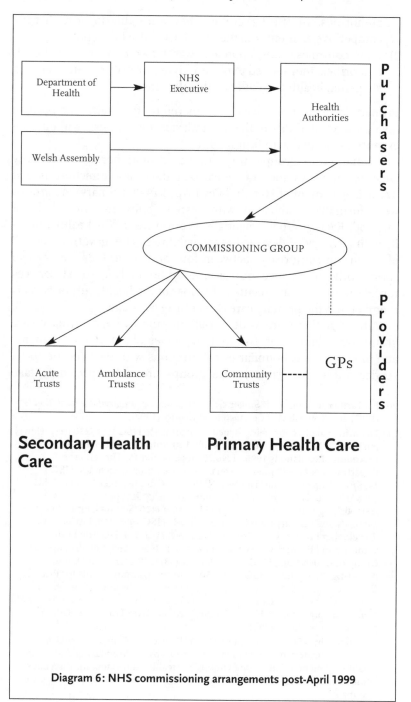

Diagram 6: NHS commissioning arrangements post-April 1999

authorities. In effect therefore they were able to bring a truly competitive element into the 'purchaser/provider' split.

2) GPs' commissioning approach was different to that of health authorities; they tended to place a higher priority on such services as mental health than did health authorities.

Primary care groups/trusts aim therefore to retain the positive involvement of GPs in the commissioning process without the expense associated with fundholding.[20]

6.14   Primary care groups are administrative rather than statutory creatures; they owe their existence to guidance and directions issued by the Department of Health.[21] On 1 April 1999, primary care groups were formally established with responsibility for the whole of England. Each group is essentially a committee of the health authority with advisory or devolved responsibilities. The 'governing board' of the group comprises[22] between four and seven GPs, one or two community or practice nurses and additionally a social services representative, a non-executive member of the health authority, a lay member and the primary care chief officer/manager.

6.15   Although there are wide variations, the average primary care group has a budget of £60 million, serves about 100,000 patients and in general has boundaries coterminous with those of the social service authority. Primary care groups are not expected to take

20 For further reading see R Singer *GP Commissioning: an inevitable revolution* (1997) and K Walsh et al *Contracting for Change* (1997).

21 The principal direction being issued as an annex to HSC 1998/230 (see below) , pursuant to NHSA 1977 s17 and Health Authorities (Membership and Procedure) Regulations 1996 SI No 707 regs 14 and 15. The relevant Department of Health guidance on primary care groups includes: HSC 1998/021 Implementing 'The New NHS' and 'Our Healthier Nation'; HSC 1998/030 'Guidance notes for GP Commissioning Groups'; HSC 1998/065 'Establishing Primary Care Groups'; HSC 1998/120 'Setting Unified health authority and Primary Care Group baselines'; HSC 1998/139, LAC(98)21 'Developing Primary Care Groups'; HSC 1998/171 'Guidance on health authority and Primary Care Group allocations'; HSC 1998/190 'Primary Care Group remuneration'; HSC 1998/228, LAC(98)32 'Primary Care Groups: delivering the Agenda'; HSC 1998/230 'Governing arrangements for Primary Care Groups'; HSC 1999/048 'Corporate governance health authorities and Primary Care Groups standing orders'; HSC 1999/167 'Primary Care Trusts application procedures'; HSC 1999/207 'Primary Care Trust consultation proposals to establish a PCT'.

22 As detailed in HSC 1998/139, LAC(98)21 'Developing Primary Care Groups' and now obligatory pursuant to the 'Directions by the Secretary of State as the Establishment of Primary Care Groups by Health Authorities' the directions being Annex A to HSC 1998/230 'Governing arrangements for Primary Care Groups'.

responsibility for specialist mental health or for learning disability services.

6.16   Primary care groups can take one of two forms, namely:

1) at a minimum, the group supports the health authority in commissioning care for its population, acting in an advisory capacity;

2) at its more evolved stage, it takes devolved responsibility for managing the budget for healthcare in their area, formally as part of the health authority.

6.17   Once these groups have acquired commissioning and budgeting expertise it is proposed that they develop into primary care trusts (PCTs). The Health Act 1999 provides for the creation of these 'free standing' bodies (ss2–12). Trusts will take two forms, namely:

1) The PCT will be primarily responsible for the management of its budget, although accountable to the health authority for commissioning care.

2) At its more evolved stage it will take on the added responsibility for the provision of community health services for the population effectively by acquiring the responsibilities and facilities of the existing NHS community health trust within its area. Not only will such PCTs run community hospitals and other community services, they will also be encouraged to use the NHS (Primary Care) Act 1997 to initiate such new local services.

6.18   Diagram 6 depicts the present NHS commissioning process. The commissioning group (known in England as a primary care group or primary care trust) will be representative of all GPs in its area, and will gradually absorb all the community trust facilities within that area. Initially (as noted above) funding will continue to be via the health authority, although it seems likely that in time health authorities may cease to exist and funding would then come directly from the regional office of the NHS Executive.

Wales

6.19   The White Paper 'NHS Wales' differs from the English White Paper, in relation to the way that the new locality commissioning schemes will operate, and in the future roles of health authorities and trusts. In part this difference can be seen as reflecting:

- the significantly different local and health authority configurations in Wales – large health authorities coterminous with several smaller unitary local authorities;

- the perceived need for a rationalisation of the numerous NHS trusts in Wales;
- the impact of the Welsh Assembly which will create a political landscape quite distinct to that in England.

Local health groups

6.20   Local health groups will be coterminous with unitary authority boundaries. Initially they will be established as sub-committees of health authorities, but they will be responsible for commissioning local services and will be able to take decisions about resource use.

6.21   Welsh Office guidance 'Establishing Local Health Groups' (1999) provides for the creation of local health group executive committees which will in general comprise two GPs (one of whom will normally be the Chair), and a representative from the health authority and the local authority as well as a 'responsible officer'.[23] The executive committee is part of the larger local health group management board which in addition comprises up to four GPs, a pharmacist, dentist, optometrist, two nursing representatives and a second health authority representative. The board is a sub-committee of the health authority.

6.22   The future evolution of local health groups in Wales is largely dependent upon the direction that the Welsh Assembly wishes them to take. The Government of Wales Act 1998 gives the Assembly power to (effectively) take over all health authority functions.

NHSA 1977

6.23   The principal statute governing the health service is NHSA 1977. The structure of the Act reflects the fact that the NHS in reality contains two quite different systems. Part I is primarily concerned with the provision of health care in hospitals and 'community health services', for example, the services provided by district nurses, midwives or health visitors in clinics or individuals' homes, and the provision of medical services to pupils in state schools. The responsibility for securing the provision of these services rests with the secretary of state in England and the Assembly in Wales. Under s13 this responsibility has, in large measure, been delegated to health authorities.

---

23   The most senior official employed by the health authority specifically to work in the local health group.

6.24   The second aspect of the NHS, sometimes described by the government as 'the NHS in the high street' is dealt with under Part II of the 1977 Act. This governs the arrangements made by health authorities for the provision of services by GPs, dentists, opticians and chemists.

6.25   The separateness of these two systems has been slightly blurred by the National Health Service (Primary Care) Act 1997 which enables (in essence) doctor and dentist services to be provided under Part I of the Act, via a salaried service.[24]

Hospital and community health services: Part I

6.26   NHSA 1977 s1 places the general NHS duty upon the secretary of state in England and the Assembly in Wales.[25] The extent and nature of the duty under s1 is dealt with in detail below (see para 6.35), however the Act provides:

> (1) It is the Secretary of State's duty to continue the promotion in England and Wales of a comprehensive health service designed to secure improvement –
>   (a) in the physical and mental health of the people of those countries, and
>   (b) in the prevention, diagnosis and treatment of illness,
>   and for that purpose to provide or secure the effective provision of services in accordance with this Act.
> (2) The services so provided shall be free of charge except in so far as the making and recovery of charges is expressly provided for by or under any enactment, whenever passed.

6.27   Section 2 confers wide-ranging powers for the secretary of state to provide such services as are appropriate, namely:

> Without prejudice to the Secretary of State's powers apart from this section, he has power –
>   (a) to provide such services as he considers appropriate for the purpose of discharging any duty imposed upon him by this Act; and
>   (b) to do any other thing whatsoever which is calculated to facilitate, or is conducive or incidental to, the discharge of such a duty.

6.28   Section 3 sets out those general services which it is the secretary of state's duty to provide to such extent as he considers necessary to meet all reasonable requirements. Most of the services that may be

---

24 See HSC 1999/116 'NHS primary care walk-in centres'.
25 Government of Wales Act 1998 and the National Assembly for Wales (Transfer of Functions) Order 1999 SI No 672.

described as hospital and community health services are included under this section.

6.29   Section 3(1) provides:

(1) It is the Secretary of State's duty to provide throughout England and Wales, to such extent as he considers necessary to meet all reasonable requirements –
(a) hospital accommodation;
(b) other accommodation for the purpose of any service provided under this Act;
(c) medical, dental, nursing and ambulance services;
(d) such other facilities for the care of expectant mothers and young children as he considers are appropriate as part of the health service;
(e) such facilities for the prevention of illness, the care of persons suffering from illness and the after care of persons who have suffered from illness as he considers are appropriate as part of the health service;
(f) such other services as are required for the diagnosis and treatment of illness.

6.30   Section 4 imposes a specific duty on the secretary of state to provide high-security psychiatric services.[26]

6.31   Section 8 of the Act provides for the creation of health authorities which have responsibility for defined geographic areas.[27] Under s13 the secretary of state may devolve his/her responsibilities to health authorities although s13 also enables the secretary of state to control the exercise of these functions, providing for a power to issue 'directions'.[28]

6.32   As noted above, the responsibility for actual provision of services under Part I of the Act was, as a result of NHSCCA 1990, transferred to NHS trusts. Trusts are semi-autonomous bodies set up to assume responsibility for the ownership and management of hospitals or other establishments or facilities previously managed or provided by a health authority.[29] NHS trusts do not receive funding in the way that

26 Managed by special health authorities established under NHSA 1977 s11.
27 The areas being defined in the 'establishment orders' under which they are created.
28 The main directions have been issued as the National Health Service (Functions of Health Authorities and Administration Arrangements) Regulations 1996 SI No 708. Sch 1 to those Regulations lists those 'specified health service functions' of the secretary of state that s/he has delegated to health authorities. The secretary of state has directed health authorities to exercise most of his/her functions under Part I, in particular ss2, 3, and 5.
29 A trust's functions are conferred by its establishment order made under NHSCCA 1990 s5(1) and Sch 2.

health authorities do, but rather through obtaining orders for their services from health authorities.[30]

Family health services: Part II

6.33   Part II of the Act regulates the NHS in so far as it relates to GPs, dentists, opticians, and chemists.

6.34   Section 29 of the 1977 Act requires health authorities to arrange 'general medical services' for all persons in the area. Health authorities discharge this duty by entering into separate statutory arrangements with GPs, dentists, opticians, and chemists for the provision of their services. GPs are not therefore health authority employees, but independent professionals. The terms of their contractual relationship with the health authority are set out in regulations, namely the National Health Service (General Medical Services) Regulations 1992 SI No 635 as amended. The community care responsibilities of GPs are considered in detail below at para 6.62.

Section 1: the duty to promote a 'comprehensive' health service

6.35   As has been noted above, in contrast to the detailed legislative duties laid on social services authorities, the statutory duties placed upon the NHS are general and indeterminate. Accordingly the courts have been reluctant to disturb NHS administrative decisions where these general public law duties are involved. In *R v Cambridge Health Authority ex p B*,[31] the decision in question concerned 'the life of a young patient'. At first instance Laws J criticised the authority's justification for its decision not to fund any further chemotherapy treatment for the child as consisting 'only of grave and well-rounded generalities', stating that 'where the question is whether the life of a 10-year-old child might be saved, however slim a chance, the responsible authority . . . must do more than toll the bell of tight resources . . . they must explain the priorities that have led them to decline to fund the treatment'. The Court of Appeal felt unable to sustain this line, holding instead:

> Difficult and agonising judgements have to be made as to how a limited budget is best allocated to the maximum advantage of the

30 Under NHSCCA 1990 s4, these 'NHS contracts' (now called 'service agreements' see n15 above) are not legally enforceable but are subject to arbitration by the secretary of state/Welsh Assembly.

31 [1995] 2 All ER 129, CA.

maximum number of patients. That is not a judgement which the court can make. . . . It is not something that a health authority . . . can be fairly criticised for not advancing before the court . . . It would be totally unrealistic to require the authority to come to court with its accounts and seek to demonstrate that if this treatment were provided for B then there would be a patient, C, who would have to go without treatment. No major authority could run its financial affairs in a way which would permit such a demonstration.

6.36   The *ex p B* decision should not be seen as an abrogation by the court of its duty to scrutinise 'anxiously' questions which engage fundamental human rights. In the case the court heard evidence of the lengths to which the health authority had gone to weigh up the likelihood of the treatment being successful, the adverse effects of the treatment and had consulted with the family. The court accepted that it was a bona fides decision taken on an individual basis and supported by respected professional opinion. In such cases, where the key consideration is expertise that the court does not possess, even with the enactment of the Human Rights Act 1998, the courts will inevitably hesitate to substitute its opinions. The situation will however be otherwise where the issue concerns questions of law or logic.

6.37   Health bodies must, therefore, comply with the law, respect fundamental human rights and ensure that their decisions are reached in accordance with established public law principles. They must not, for instance, ignore circular guidance,[32] operate a perverse policy which (in practice) fetters its discretion to fund the treatment for a particular illness,[33] or fail to consult before reaching certain decisions. In *R v North East Devon HA ex p Pow*,[34] the health authority, faced with severe cash shortages, decided to close certain hospitals without consulting the community health council (which consultation is required where substantial changes to services are contemplated). In quashing the decision to close the units Moses J held:

> It would seriously undermine the purpose of Regulation 18 [Community Health Council Regulations 1996] . . . if a Health Authority could allow time to pass to the point where matters were so urgent that there was no time left for consultation.
>
>   I was told . . . that if I grant relief it will not be possible to use the closure of the hospitals as a means of making savings at all. . . . Even though, the task [of making budget savings] . . . is far harder, in my view the importance of the duty to consult is such that I do not think

---

32   *R v North Derbyshire HA ex p Fisher* (1998) 1 CCLR 150 (see below).
33   *R v North West Lancashire HA ex p A* (1999) *Times* 24 August.
34   (1998) 1 CCLR 280.

the greater burden of the task facing the Health Authority, caused by its own error in law, justifies the refusal of relief.

6.38 The core provisions of NHSA 1977 ss1 and 3 were subjected to considerable scrutiny by the Court of Appeal in *R v North and East Devon HA ex p Coughlan*.[35] There the court noted that:

> Section 1(1) does not place a duty on the Secretary of State to provide a comprehensive health service. His duty is 'to continue to promote' such a service. In addition the services which he is required to provide have to be provided 'in accordance with this Act'.[36]

and

> the Secretary of State's section 3 duty is subject to two different qualifications. First of all there is the initial qualification that his obligation is limited to providing the services identified to the extent that he considers that they are *necessary* to meet *all reasonable requirements* . . .[37]

and

> 24. The first qualification placed on the duty contained in section 3 makes it clear that there is scope for the Secretary of State to exercise a degree of judgment as to the circumstances in which he will provide the services, including nursing services referred to in the section. He does not automatically have to meet all nursing requirements. In certain circumstances he can exercise his judgment and legitimately decline to provide nursing services. He need not provide nursing services if he does not consider they are reasonably required or necessary to meet a reasonable requirement.
>
> 25. When exercising his judgment he has to bear in mind the comprehensive service which he is under a duty to promote as set out in section 1. However, as long as he pays due regard to that duty, the fact that the service will not be comprehensive does not mean that he is necessarily contravening either section 1 or section 3. The truth is that, while he has the duty to continue to promote a comprehensive free health service and he must never, in making a decision under section 3, disregard that duty, a comprehensive health service may never, for human, financial and other resource reasons, be achievable. Recent history has demonstrated that the pace of developments as to what is possible by way of medical treatment, coupled with the ever increasing expectations of the public, mean that the resources of the NHS are and are likely to continue, at least in the foreseeable future, to be insufficient to meet demand.

35 (1999) 2 CCLR 285.
36 Ibid para 22.
37 Ibid para 23.

26. In exercising his judgment the Secretary of State is entitled to take into account the resources available to him and the demands on those resources. In *R v Secretary of State for Social Services and Ors ex parte Hincks* [1980] 1 BMLR 93 the Court of Appeal held that section 3(1) of the Health Act does not impose an absolute duty to provide the specified services. The Secretary of State is entitled to have regard to the resources made available to him under current government economic policy.

NHS Guidance

6.39   The main types of health circular which concern community care are detailed at para 1.21 above. For the purpose of its community care responsibilities the most influential NHS guidance is (in order of importance) an 'HSC'[38] (health service circular) and an 'EL'[39] (executive letter), ie, a letter written by the chief executive (or deputy) of the NHS Executive.

6.40   While NHSA 1977 s13 empowers the secretary of state to issue directions to NHS bodies in much the same way as s/he can to social services departments under LASSA 1970 s7A, there is no specific provision in the 1977 Act concerning the issuing of guidance. It is however generally assumed that HSC (or their predecessor guidance, HSG) circulars carry significant weight probably equivalent to social services policy guidance (considered at para 1.25 above).

6.41   Under NHSA 1977 s2(b) the secretary of state has power to do 'anything whatsoever which is calculated to facilitate or is conducive or incidental to, the discharge of' the duty to promote a comprehensive health service. Such a power clearly authorises the issuing of guidance. In all other respects however the Act is silent on the effect of such guidance. It would appear however that such guidance must, in certain situations, be equivalent to the policy guidance issued to social services, ie, by obliging the health body 'to follow the path charted by the Secretary of State's guidance, with liberty to deviate from it where the ... authority judges on admissible grounds that there is good reason to do so, but without freedom to take a substantially different course'.[40] By way of example, the guidance given to health authorities (and other health bodies) concerning the preparation of health improvement programmes as HSC 1998/176 was also

---

38 Prior to 1998 HSCs were known as HSGs – Health Services Guidance. In Wales the equivalent guidance being a WHC (see para 1.21 above).

39 However since 1998 the use of EL guidance has become restricted.

40 *R v Islington LBC ex p Rixon* (1998) 1 CCLR 119 at 123.

issued as LAC(98)23 to social services authorities. Since the circular was primarily aimed at health authorities, it is not unreasonable to assume that its legal force was no less in relation to them than it was to social services authorities, especially as the circular states that it is 'policy guidance'[41] in so far as it applies to social services.

6.42   In *R v North Derbyshire HA ex p Fisher*,[42] Dyson J had to decide whether an Executive Letter (EL(95)97 – which concerns the prescribing of Beta-Interferon drugs to people with MS) was a 'direction' under NHSA 1997 s13, and if not, how much weight a health authority was required to afford it. He held that directions could be contained in such a circular, but that the wording of the circular was not sufficiently mandatory to be a 'Direction'. Accordingly it was to be construed as 'strong guidance'. This meant that the health authority, although not obliged to follow the circular, could only depart from it by giving clear reasons for so doing and that those reasons would be susceptible to a *Wednesbury* challenge. In finding against the health authority the judge held that it had failed to properly understand the circular and therefore its actions were defective (as if it had had no regard to the circular at all).

6.43   In *R v Secretary of State for Health ex p Pfizer Ltd*,[43] Collins J held that HSC 1998/158 which suggested that GPs should not prescribe Viagra was unlawful in that it sought (among other things) to restrict the GPs' duty to provide patients with all necessary and appropriate personal medical services pursuant to the NHS (General Medical Services) Regulations 1992 Sch 2 para 12(1) (these regulations are considered below at para 6.62).[44]

Access to circulars

6.44   The procedure for obtaining access to circular guidance is outlined at para 1.22 above. In addition to the postal and internet access arrangements, details of new health circulars are announced in the 'Communications Summary' issued monthly by the NHS Executive, Quarry House, Quarry Hill, Leeds, LS2 7EU.

---

41 See para 1.25 above for an explanation as to the effect of 'policy guidance'.
42 (1998) 1 CCLR 150. See also *Blackpool Corporation v Locker* [1947] 1 KB 349.
43 (1999) 2 CCLR 270.
44 Accordingly, the Regulations were subsequently amended via NHS (General Medical Services) Amendment (No 2) Regulations 1999 SI No 1627; see HSC 1999/115.

The medical/social divide

6.45   The conflict between health and social care is not a new one. What is a social need and what is a medical need is an intractable problem. It is only of practical importance to community care service users because a service provided by the NHS is generally free at the point of need, whereas a service provided by the social services department is generally subject to a means-tested charge. Help with bathing is therefore free if provided in a person's home by the district nurse (or NHS auxiliary), whereas if provided by a social services care assistant it may be subject to a charge. The argument is repeated in a hundred different ways with such items as walking sticks, hoists, commodes and speech therapy. Exhortations to organisations, professionals and other producer interests to work together more closely and effectively litter the policy landscape, yet the reality is all too often a jumble of services fractionalised by professional culture and organisational boundaries and by tiers of governance.[45]

The duty to co-operate

6.46   There are a number of statutory duties on local authorities and 'health bodies' (ie, health authorities, NHS trusts and primary care trusts) to work together constructively. These obligations (which are explored in greater detail below) fall into two broad categories, namely:

1) the obligation to co-operate at the strategic level, ie, in the preparation of plans for the improvement of the health of the general population and in relation to the closure of hospitals or other facilities; and

2) the obligation on a general day-to-day level requiring co-operation in the delivery of services to individuals who are disabled, elderly or ill.

45 Webb *Policy and Politics* (1991) Vol 19.4, p29; quoted in Means and Smith *Community Care* (Macmillan 1994). There has been considerable criticism of successive governments' concentration upon creating administrative joint planning structures, on creating coterminosity, and other organisational devices to promote joint working. The research evidence suggests however that 'where mutual trust has existed between senior officers from health and local authorities, the relationship has appeared to be far more important than joint planning machinery'. R Davidson and S Hunter *Community Care in Practice* (1994); see also L Clements and P Smith *A Snapshot' Survey of Social Services' Responses to the Continuing Care Needs of Older People in Wales* (1999)

Health improvement programmes

6.47 As noted at para 2.10 above, local authorities must, when preparing their community care plans, consult with the health authority.[46] A reciprocal (and more substantial) duty rests with health authorities in the preparation of their health improvement programmes.

6.48   Health Act 1999 s28(1) obliges every health authority to prepare a health improvement programme (HImP) for its area. The need for such programmes was introduced in consequence of the white paper *The New NHS: Modern, Dependable.*[47] The white paper explained that the programmes should span a three-year period and cover:

- the most important health needs of the local population and how these are to be met by the NHS and its partner organisations through broader action on public health;
- the main healthcare requirements of local people, and how local services should be developed to meet them either directly by the NHS, or where appropriate jointly with social services;
- the range, location and investment required in local health services to meet the needs of local people.

6.49 Health authorities are responsible for monitoring the implementation of the HImPs by NHS trusts and primary care groups/trusts and have 'reserve powers'[48] to ensure that 'major investment decisions' taken by such bodies are consistent with the programme. The key role of the local authority in the development and implementation of the programme is underscored by the creation of the new duty under Health Act 1999 s27 requiring co-operation between health bodies and local authorities (see below 6.54).[49]

6.50   HSC 1998/167 explained that HImPs are in essence the 'local plan of action to improve health' and directed that the process of preparing the programmes should:

- bring together the local NHS with local authorities and others, including the voluntary sector, to set the strategic framework for improving health, tackling inequalities, and developing faster, more convenient services of a consistently high standard;
- be action focused, setting out high-level objectives and a summary of the commitments of the local players to deliver these;

46 NHSCCA 1990 s46(2)(a).
47 Cm 3807 (December 1997).
48 Under NHSA 1977 ss17A and 17B as inserted by Health Act 1999 s12.
49 The white paper, at para 4.8, emphasised that this duty of co-operation would be underscored by a duty to 'promote the economic, social and environmental well being of their areas', now enacted as Local Government Act 2000 s2.

- include measurable targets for improvement, demonstrating how resources are to be used to improve the health and well-being of the population and modernise the NHS.

The emphasis here is collaboration by the local authority as a whole, recognising that the causes of ill-health are related to social, economic, environmental, housing, education and transport factors and their alleviation are not merely the responsibility of social services and the NHS.[50]

Hospital closures

6.51   LAC(95)5/HSG(95)8 emphasises that health authorities should not proceed with any plans to reduce continuing health care services without the prior agreement of the relevant local authority(s). In addition, where a health authority is contemplating any substantial change to its service it must consult with the appropriate community health council.[51] The importance of this duty was highlighted in *R v North East Devon HA ex p Pow*[52] and in *R v North East Devon HA ex p Coughlan*,[53] which decisions are considered in detail at paras 6.37 and 6.91 respectively.

6.52   In response to a particular incident at an NHS facility, guidance on the 'transfer of frail elderly patients to other long stay settings' (HSC 1998/048) was issued on 2 April 1998. The circular emphasises the key importance (prior to any transfer being activated) of (1) consultation; (2) the preparation of a project plan; (3) the careful assessment of the needs of the patient and relatives or carers; (4) the process of transfer and the role of the receiving setting; and (5) arrangements for follow-up monitoring.

6.53   The law as it relates to the closure of residential care homes is considered separately at para 4.76 above, including the relevance of the Human Rights Act 1998 to such cases.

Specific duties to collaborate

6.54   **NHSA 1977 s22**   Health Act 1999 s27 amended s22 of the 1977 Act by substituting a more extensive duty to co-operate. The notes of

---

50   'Our Healthier Nation' Department of Health, Cm 3852 (February 1998).
51   Community Health Council Regulations 1996 SI No 640 and see also EL(90)185.
52   (1998) 1 CCLR 280.
53   (1999) 2 CCLR 285.

guidance to the 1999 Act explained that the purpose of the amendment was to extend the duty of partnership in order to:

> . . . secure and advance the health and welfare of the people of
> England and Wales, to cover Primary Care Trusts and NHS trusts as
> well as Health Authorities and Special Health Authorities. This
> recognises the need to work in partnership in commissioning and
> delivering care, as well as at the strategic planning level. Welfare is
> used in its wide general sense and is designed to cover functions
> relating to social services, education, housing and the environment.

6.55   Section 22 as amended, provides:

> (1) In exercising their respective functions NHS bodies (on the one
>   hand) and local authorities (on the other) shall co-operate with one
>   another in order to secure and advance the health and welfare of the
>   people of England and Wales.
> (1A) In this section 'NHS body' means–
>   (a) a Health Authority;
>   (b) a Special Health Authority;
>   (c) a Primary Care Trust; or
>   (d) an NHS trust.

6.56   Where a community care user suffers as a result of an inter-agency
dispute, it is generally appropriate for complaints to be made against
each authority primarily on the basis that they have failed to 'work
together' in violation of their specific statutory obligations. The
ombudsman has repeatedly criticised authorities for failing to provide services while they squabbled over their respective obligations. A
recent complaint concerned the failure of a health authority and
social services department to co-operate. Although the local ombudsman considered that the health authority's involvement had been
'reluctant, if not unhelpful' she nevertheless found the social services
authority guilty of maladministration. In her opinion, having accepted that a need existed, social services should have 'grasped the nettle'
and secured the provision, before entering into protracted negotiations with the NHS on liability for the care costs.[54]

6.57   **NHSCCA 1990 s47(3)** A specific duty to co-operate exists under
s47(3) of the 1990 Act which provides:

> If at any time during the assessment of the needs of any person
> under subsection (1)(a) above, it appears to a local authority –
> (a) that there may be a need for the provision to that person by such

---

54 Complaint 96/C/3868 against Calderdale MBC.

Health Authority as may be determined in accordance with regulations of any services under the National Health Service Act 1977, or

(b) that there may be the need for the provision to him of any services which fall within the functions of a local housing authority (within the meaning of the Housing Act 1985)[55] which is not the local authority carrying out the assessment,

the local authority shall notify that Health Authority or local housing authority and invite them to assist, to such extent as is reasonable in the circumstances, in the making of the assessment; and, in making their decision as to the provision of services needed for the person in question, the local authority shall take into account any services which are likely to be made available for him by that Health Authority or local housing authority.

6.58   It follows that where during the assessment process an NHS need is disclosed, the assessing authority is obliged to notify the health authority and at the same time to specify what assistance that authority is requested to provide in order to facilitate the assessment. The health authority is not however under any statutory duty to respond or co-operate.[56] Presumably, however, a failure to respond – or failure to respond within a reasonable time or in a reasonable manner – would be vulnerable to challenge as maladministration. The same applies to a housing authority where a housing need is disclosed (see para 10.8).

6.59   During the passage of the Health Bill through parliament, an attempt was made to insert an amendment which would have required a positive response from health authorities to any request for assistance by a local authority (of a similar nature to that required under CA 1989 s27). On the amendment being withdrawn, the government gave an assurance that guidance would be issued requiring health and local authorities to publish details as to how they will work together to ensure that all the assessment needs of individuals are met.[57]

---

55 A 'housing function' is defined by Housing Act 1985 s8 onwards and covers the wide range of activities connected with the provision of housing.

56 Unlike the equivalent duty under CA 1989 s27.

57 Lord Hunt of Kings Heath: *Hansard* (HL) (18 March 1999) col 851. This guidance was to be issued as part of the guidance on the 'Better Services For Vulnerable People Initiative' and Lord Hunt confirmed that this initiative would 'set out the requirement for health and local authorities to develop a framework for multi-disciplinary assessment in their first joint investment plans'.

6.60   **MHA 1983 s117(2)** In the field of mental health, specific co-operation is required by s117(2) of the 1983 Act, which stipulates that it shall be the duty of the health authority and the local social services department to provide, in co-operation with the relevant voluntary agents, after-care services for any such person until satisfied that the person concerned is no longer in need of such services.

6.61   In *R v Mental Health Review Tribunal ex p Hall*,[58] the Divisional Court held that the duty to provide after-care services under s117(2) was jointly shared by the health and social services authority in which the patient was resident at the time he was detained. See para 5.100 where s117 services are considered in detail.

NHS primary health care responsibilities

General practitioner services

6.62   NHSA 1977 s29 places a duty on each health authority to arrange with medical practitioners to provide personal medical services for all persons in the area who wish to take advantage of the arrangements. These services are described as 'general medical services'. As with hospital services, it is not the health authority itself which provides the service, instead, it enters into separate statutory arrangements with independent practitioners for the provision of those services. GPs are therefore not employees of the health authority, they are independent professionals who undertake to provide general medical services in accordance with Regulations which govern that activity, currently the NHS (General Medical Services) Regulations 1992 SI No 635 (as amended). The regulations are of particular relevance in three specific respects.

GPs' obligation to provide general medical services

6.63   Schedule 2 paragraph 12 of the 1992 Regulations requires GPs to render to their patients all necessary and appropriate medical services of the type usually provided by GPs including:

a) giving advice, where appropriate, to a patient in connection with the patient's general health, and in particular about the significance of diet, exercise, the use of tobacco, the consumption of alcohol and the misuse of drugs or solvents;

58 [1999] 3 All ER 132; (1999) 2 CCLR 361. Although the case was appealed, this issue was not re-argued before the Court of Appeal.

b) offering to patients, consultations and, where appropriate, physical examinations for the purpose of identifying, or reducing the risk of disease or injury;

c) offering to patients, where appropriate, vaccination or immunisation against measles, mumps, rubella, pertussis, poliomyelitis and tetanus;

d) arranging for the referral of patients, as appropriate, for the provision of any other services under NHSA 1977; and

e) giving advice, as appropriate, to enable patients to avail themselves of services provided by a local social services authority.

Considerable concern has been expressed about the general performance of GPs in fulfilling their community care obligations, primarily the responsibility of ensuring that people in need of community care services are provided with the necessary assistance to obtain them.[59]

6.64   The obligation created by paragraphs (d) and (e) above includes more than merely advising patients of the availability of the community care services for which the social services department is responsible. This obligation nevertheless presupposes that GPs properly inform themselves of the social services' community care responsibilities. Where the patient may be entitled to other services under NHSA 1977, the obligation on the GP is not merely to advise; it is to refer, to enable the patient to receive the service. This must mean that a GP is required to refer patients to social services authorities where they may be entitled to receive the wide range of community care services available under NHSA 1977 Sch 8 (see para 5.80).

6.65   In those cases where the patient lacks mental capacity or it is otherwise unlikely that s/he will respond to such advice or referral, there will frequently be an equivalent duty owed to the patient's carer. This will most obviously be the case where the carer is also a patient of the GP (as s/he will also be entitled to many of the same services). LAC(96)7 stresses this aspect, thus:

> 30. Primary care staff, including GPs and community nurses through their contact with users and carers, are in a good position to notice signs of stress, difficulty or rapidly deteriorating health particularly in carers. The provisions of the [Carers (Recognition and Services) Act 1995] will help primary care staff to meet the medical and nursing needs of their patients who are carers. When making a

59 See, eg, EL(96)8 para 11.

referral for a user's assessment they should be able to inform the carer that they may also have a right to request an assessment and will be well-placed to encourage patients whom they consider will benefit most to take up the opportunity. Social services departments should make sure that primary care staff have relevant information about social services criteria and know who to contact to make referral.

6.66 The NHS (General Medical Services) Regulations 1992 Sch 2 para 16 stipulates that (in relation to patients over 75) GPs must offer each of them a domiciliary visit every 12 months with a view to assessing whether the patient requires personal medical services; the assessment must take into account a variety of factors which might affect the patient's health, including his or her mobility and social environment.

GPs' obligation to prescribe drugs and appliances

6.67 The obligation on GPs to render general medical services for their patients brings with it a need to prescribe. This requirement is dealt with in Sch 2 para 43 of the 1992 Regulations which provides:

43(1) Subject to paragraph 44, a doctor shall order any drugs or appliances which are needed for the treatment of any patient to whom he is providing treatment under these terms of service by issuing to that patient a prescription form, and such a form shall not be used in any other circumstances.

6.68 The prescription powers of GPs are subject to specific restrictions in relation to the provision of controlled drugs.[60] In addition under Sch 2 para 44 of the 1992 Regulations GPs are prohibited from prescribing certain drugs and other substances (which are listed in Sch 10 of the regulations). These are items which it is thought that patients should obtain at their own expense, and are for the large part proprietary medicines which are generally bought over the counter at chemists. If the government wishes to circumscribe the duty on GPs to prescribe any drug 'needed for a patient's treatment' it must do so through the medium of regulatory amendment and not guidance.[61]

6.69 In addition to the power to prescribe drugs, reg 43 enables GPs to prescribe 'appliances', ie, medical aids, dressings, pads, etc, as well as

---

60 Ie, drugs listed in Misuse of Drugs Regulations 1985 SI No 2066 Sch 2; National Health Service (General Medical Services) Regulations 1992 SI No 635 Sch 2 para 43(3) as amended.

61 *R v Secretary of State for Health ex p Pfizer Ltd* (1999) 2 CCLR 270.

basic equipment to help overcome the effects of disability. In relation to disability equipment there is frequently an overlap of responsibility with the local social services department's community care duties (see para 5.68 above). It is therefore common practice for health and social services to arrange joint equipment stores which can be accessed by both social services and the relevant NHS trust.

6.70   The appliances which a GP can prescribe are detailed in two lists known as the 'Drug Tariff' and the 'Appliance List'.[62] The lists enable GPs to provide a range of general items:

- Stoma and some incontinence care equipment. See also para 6.119 below where health authority responsibility for incontinence supplies is considered.

- Equipment for people with diabetes.

- Elastic hosiery, dressings, bandages, trusses, etc.

- Respiratory equipment (including oxygen cylinders and oxygen concentrators).

- Chiropody appliances. GPs can refer patients to NHS chiropodists and consultants for more specialist equipment. Health authorities must also ensure that adequate chiropody services are available to residents placed by social services in nursing home accommodation (see para 6.116 below).

- Wheelchairs for permanent use. Wheelchairs may also be obtained from NHS trusts for temporary use on discharge from hospital. In general the disabled person will be referred to an occupational therapist, physiotherapist or consultant for assessment as to the most suitable wheelchair. If the patient has difficulty using a manual wheelchair the trust can supply an electric model (including one for outdoor use if appropriate).[63] The NHS operates a 'wheelchair voucher scheme' that gives users the option of purchasing from an independent supplier or from the wheelchair service. In either case the user can top up the voucher cost (which covers only the cost of a 'standard' wheelchair to meet the user's needs) to enable a more expensive model to be acquired. However if the chair is purchased from an independent supplier it is owned by the user who is responsible for its maintenance and repair,

---

62 The 'Drug Tariff' is a statement published from time to time under National Health Service (Pharmaceutical Services) Regulations 1992 SI No 662 reg 18. The 'Appliance List' contains the details of appliances which have been approved by the Secretary of State for the purposes of NHSA 1977 s41.

63 HSG(96)34.

whereas if the 'wheelchair services' option is chosen, the trust retains ownership but is also responsible for its maintenance.[64]

If more specialist equipment is needed, this may be obtained via a hospital consultant (see para 6.72).

GPs' obligation to provide medical certificates

6.71 GPs have an important role in providing certificates for the purpose of contributory benefits and non-contributory social security benefits. Accordingly Sch 2 para 37(1) of the 1992 Regulations provides that GPs are required to issue free of charge to their patients (or their personal representatives) any medical certificate which is reasonably required for certain specified purposes; these being set out in the 1992 Regulations Sch 9.

Hospital consultant services

6.72 As noted above, NHS trusts are the major providers of secondary health services in hospitals and similar institutions. Doctors and consultants working for such trusts[65] are directly employed by the trusts under an employment contract; a quite different arrangement to the 'independent' provider status of GPs.

6.73 Such a doctor/consultant may prescribe any drug, appliance or piece of equipment which s/he considers necessary for a patient's treatment. In general their employment contract with the NHS trust will restrict this prescribing power, or at least make the provision of expensive items subject to validation by the trusts' managers.

6.74 In certain situations it may be unlawful for a health authority to restrict the availability of specialist drugs. In *R v North Derbyshire HA ex p Fisher*,[66] for instance, the court held that the respondent authority had failed, without good reason, to follow government guidance[67] on the prescription of Beta-Interferon drugs to people with MS, and accordingly its actions were unlawful.

---

64 HSG(96)53.
65 Ie, consultants or junior doctors (which description includes senior registrars, registrars, senior house officers and house officers).
66 (1998) 1 CCLR 150.
67 Executive Letter EL(95)97.

NHS's continuing care responsibilities

Introduction

6.75   The NHS was initially seen as the main provider of residential long-term care for the elderly (in geriatric long-stay hospital wards). This arrangement became less common after 1979, when supplementary benefit (and later income support) payments became available to cover the cost of private nursing home accommodation. This situation led to the closure of many NHS continuing care wards.[68] At the same time social services authorities saw the same advantage (of making considerable savings) by encouraging persons on low income to move into independent residential care homes and thus be subsidised by the DHSS (as it then was), rather than move into Part III accommodation subsidised by the rates.

6.76   On 1 April 1993 the higher-rate income support payments for nursing and residential care homes were withdrawn and the social services authorities became the 'gate keepers' for such community placements. This led to a general, but incorrect, assumption that the NHS no longer had the same responsibility for funding long-term care. The fact that social services authorities were (for the first time) empowered to make payments towards the cost of independent nursing home placements also encouraged the view that the NHS was no longer an agency responsible for making similar payments. In fact, the responsibility for the care of persons in need of nursing home accommodation is an overlapping one between the two authorities.

6.77   The effect of this shift in the provision of continuing care was commented upon by the Audit Commission, which noted a significant rise in local authority funding for nursing home placements (over and above what would have been predicted), describing this trend as 'worrying' and suggesting that it was due to 'a combination of rising demand from within the community and increasing pressure from hospitals'.[69]

6.78   Many individuals, their carers and relatives were required to pay substantial sums to private nursing homes in situations where previously the care would have been provided by the NHS. This

---

68   Between 1983 and 1993 there was a 30 per cent (17,000) reduction in number of long-term geriatric and psychogeriatric NHS beds: Harding et al *Options for Long Term Care* (HMSO, 1996) p8.

69   Audit Commission report *Taking Stock* (December 1994), commenting on the pattern of hospital discharges (at para 32).

aspect came prominently to the fore with the publication by the Health Service Ombudsman of a highly critical report into a premature hospital discharge by the Leeds Health Authority. The complaint concerned a patient who was discharged from a neuro-surgical ward in the Leeds General Infirmary, forcing his wife to pay for his continuing care in a private nursing home.[70] The ombudsman in his conclusion made the following statement (at para 22):

> The patient had been in the care of the Infirmary for over 18 months under a contract made by Leeds Health Authority. No one disputes that by August 1991 his condition had reached the stage where active treatment was no longer required but that he was still in need of substantial nursing care, which could not be provided at home and which would continue to be needed for the rest of his life. Where was he to go? Leeds Health Authority's policy, as explained by their chief executive, was (and still is) to make no provision for continuing care at NHS expense either in hospital or in private nursing homes. In particular I note that the contract for neurosurgical services makes no reference to continuing institutional care. This patient was a highly dependent patient in hospital under a contract made with the Infirmary by Leeds Health Authority; and yet, when he no longer needed care in an acute ward but manifestly still needed what the National Health Service is there to provide, they regarded themselves as having no scope for continuing to discharge their responsibilities to him because their policy was to make no provision for continuing care. The policy had the effect of excluding an option whereby he might have the cost of his continuing care met by the NHS. In my opinion the failure to make available long-term care within the NHS for this patient was unreasonable and constitutes a failure in the service provided by the Health Authority. I uphold this complaint. I recommend that Leeds Health authority make an ex gratia payment to the complainant to cover those costs which she has already had to incur and to provide for her husband's appropriate nursing care at the expense of the NHS in the future. I recommend that the Authority review their provision of services for the likes of this man in view of the apparent gap in service available for this particular group of patients.

6.79   The Health Service Ombudsman was so concerned about the situation disclosed by the Leeds complaint that he took the exceptional step of having his report separately published.[71] In response, the government undertook to issue guidance, indicating:

---

70 Health Service Commissioner Second Report for Session 1993–94; Case No E62/93–94 (HMSO).

71 Usually only an abbreviated selection of his reports is published twice yearly.

If in the light of the guidance, some health authorities are found to have reduced their capacity to secure continuing care too far – as clearly happened in the case dealt with by the Health Service Commissioner – then they will have to take action to close the gap.[72]

6.80   The Health Service Ombudsman has commented in similar terms in relation to other complaints concerning continuing care. In 1996 he published a short digest of investigations his office had made into complaints concerning long-term care.[73] A number of complaints have concerned health authorities who made no provision for continuing care arrangements[74] or whose arrangements were inadequate. Complaint E.985/94–95,[75] for example, concerned an elderly patient who suffered a stroke and became unable to swallow and was fed by means of a gastric tube. After her condition had stabilised in hospital her husband felt compelled to acquiesce in her discharge although she remained ill and incapacitated, and indeed died shortly after her admission to the nursing home. Although the husband had had contact with the consultant, the ward staff, the hospital social worker and the GP, no one had properly explained the various options available[76] including the possibility that she would meet the criteria for NHS-funded continuing care in a nursing home. As a result of the Ombudsman's intervention the health authority agreed to accept responsibility for the nursing home fees.

NHS continuing care guidance

6.81   In February 1995, as a consequence of the Health Service Ombudsman's 'Leeds report',[77] continuing care guidance was published as a first step towards defining with greater precision the boundaries between the responsibilities of the NHS and social services authorities for continuing care. The Department of Health guidance is

---

72   Virginia Bottomley, Secretary of State for Health, 4 November 1994.

73   Fifth Report for session 1995–96, *Investigations of Complaints about Long-Term NHS Care* (HMSO).

74   See, eg, No E.264/94–95 which concerned a 55-year-old stroke patient (in the selected investigations April–September 1995); W.478/89–90 which involved the failure to provide NHS after-care to a woman who had suffered severe brain injuries (in the selected volume for October 1990–March 1991).

75   Against North Worcestershire health authority, selected volume for April–September 1996.

76   See para 6.126 below for details of the duty to provide information on hospital discharge.

77   At para 3 it states that the guidance 'addresses a number of concerns raised in the report made last year by the Health Service Ombudsman'.

LAC(95)5/HSG(95)8[78] 'NHS Responsibilities for Meeting Continuing Health Care Needs'. As part of this process the guidance also announced proposals to change the procedures by which patients were discharged from in-patient hospital care (by giving them a general right to have such discharge decisions reviewed). More detailed guidance on the discharge review procedures has subsequently been issued in LAC(95)17/HSG(95)39. The continuing care guidance and the discharge procedures are considered separately below.

NHS responsibilities for meeting continuing health care needs

6.82   The circular guidance LAC(95)5 (in this section referred to as the '1995 guidance') commences with an important introductory statement:

> 1. The arrangement and funding of services to meet continuing physical and mental care needs are an integral part of the responsibilities of the NHS. This includes, but is not limited to, the responsibility to arrange and fund an appropriate level of care from the NHS under specialist clinical supervision in hospital or in a nursing home. It also includes equally important responsibilities around rehabilitation, palliative health care, respite health care, community health services support and specialist health care support in different settings. All health authorities . . . must arrange and fund a full range of these services to meet the needs of their population.

6.83   The 1995 guidance also required health authorities to publish annual statements of their local policies and eligibility criteria for continuing health care. Before finalising these annual continuing care statements, health authorities are obliged to consult with local authorities and 'other relevant parties'.[79] These statements are the starting point for any disagreement over whether an individual is entitled to NHS continuing care services.

6.84   Paragraph 10 of the 1995 guidance gives examples of the range of health services which all health authorities must arrange and fund to meet the needs of their population:

- specialist medical and nursing assessment;
- rehabilitation and recovery;
- palliative health care;

78   WOC 16/95 and WHC(95)7 in Wales.
79   At para 9.

- continuing inpatient care under specialist supervision in hospital or in a nursing home;
- respite health care;
- specialist health care support to people in nursing homes or residential care homes or the community;
- community health services to people at home or in residential care homes;
- primary health care;
- specialist transport services.

The 1995 guidance amplifies the nature and extent to which these services should be provided by health authorities. While the circular leaves to health authorities the decision over the balance, type and precise level of services, it specifies (in Annex A) 'a number of key conditions which all health authorities . . . must be able to cover in their local arrangements' (para 12).

Mental health, learning disability and children's services

6.85   The 1995 guidance stressed that its comments did not detract in any way from the requirements set out in previous guidance for other specific client groups, and in particular for children, adolescents and adults with a mental illness or with learning disabilities.

6.86   The duties of the NHS for the continuing care of adults with a mental illness, including the care programme approach guidance are considered in detail at para 5.115 above. The duties in relation to persons with learning disabilities are considered at para 6.137 below.

Continuing in-patient care

6.87   Health authorities are required to arrange and fund an adequate level of service to meet the needs of people who:[80]

> because of the nature, complexity or intensity of their health care needs will require continuing inpatient care arranged and funded by the NHS in hospital or in a nursing home.

6.88   This will include[81] arranging and funding continuing inpatient care, on a short or long-term basis, for people:

- Where the complexity or intensity of their medical, nursing care or other clinical care or the need for frequent not easily predictable

---

80   LAC(95)5 Annex A p15.
81   Ibid.

interventions requires the regular (in the majority of cases this might be weekly or more frequent) supervision of a consultant, specialist nurse or other NHS member of the multidisciplinary team.

- Who require routinely the use of specialist health care equipment or treatments which require the supervision of specialist NHS staff.
- Have a rapidly degenerating or unstable condition which means that they will require specialist medical or nursing home supervision.
- In addition patients who have finished acute treatment or in-patient palliative care in a hospital or hospice, but whose prognosis is that they are likely to die in the very near future should be able to choose to remain in NHS-funded accommodation, or where practicable and after an appropriate and sensitive assessment of their needs, to return home with appropriate support.

6.89   The point is reiterated in Circular LAC(92)24, which states that where a patient's need is primarily for health care, any placement (in a nursing home or elsewhere) must be fully funded by the health authority (Annex A para 7).

6.90   **Specialist care** Considerable concern has been expressed over the repeated use of undefined terms such as 'specialist'. For instance, EL (96)8 at para 16 criticised continuing care statements which placed an 'over-reliance on the needs of a patient for specialist medical supervision in determining eligibility for continuing in-patient care' and specifically referred to the fact that this was not considered by the ombudsman in the Leeds case as an acceptable basis for withdrawing NHS support.

6.91   In *R v North and East Devon HA ex p Coughlan*,[82] the Court of Appeal commented (at paras 41 onwards):

> The distinction between general and special or specialist services does provide a degree of non technical guidance as to the services which, because of their nature or quality, should be regarded in any particular case as being more likely to be the responsibility of the NHS. Where the issue is whether the services should be treated as the responsibility of the NHS, not because of their nature or quality, but because of their quantity or the continuity with which they are provided, the distinction between general and specialist services is of less assistance. The distinction certainly does not provide an

82 (1999) 2 CCLR 285.

exhaustive test. The distinction does not necessarily cater for the situation where the demands for nursing attention are continuous and intense. In that situation the patient may not require in-patient care in a hospital under the new policy, but the nursing care which is necessary may still exceed that which can be properly provided as a part of social services care provision.

The court went on to emphasise (at para 42) that:

> the fact that the resident at a nursing home does not require in-patient treatment in a hospital does not mean that his or her care should not be the responsibility of the NHS.

6.92   The importance of ensuring that residential and nursing homes did not become a second-tier means-tested health service was emphasised in the original guidance which accompanied the coming into force of the Registered Homes Act 1984 (Circular LAC(84)15). The annex to that circular referred to (and quoted) previous relevant guidance, namely para 3 of the Memorandum on Health Care issued with LAC(77)13:

> 3. Residential homes are primarily a means of providing a greater degree of support for those elderly people no longer able to cope with the practicalities of living in their own homes even with the help of domiciliary services. The care provided is limited to that appropriate to a residential setting and is broadly equivalent to what might be provided by a competent and caring relative able to respond to emotional as well as physical needs. It includes, for instance, help with washing, bathing, dressing, assistance with toilet needs; the administration of medicines and, when a resident falls sick, the kind of attention someone would receive in his own home from a caring relative under guidance of a general practitioner or nurse member of the primary health care team. However, the staff of the home are not expected to provide the professional kind of health care that is properly the function of the primary health care services. Nor should residential homes be used as nursing homes or extensions of hospitals (unless the home is dually registered).

6.93   The respective responsibilities of the two authorities are the subject of further guidance in LAC(92)24, which emphasises at para 2:

> 2. Local authority contracts for independent sector residential care should not include provision of any service which it is the responsibility of the NHS to provide. It will continue to be the responsibility of the NHS to provide where necessary community health services to residents of LA and independent residential care homes on the same basis as to people in their own homes. These services include the provision of district nursing and other specialist

nursing services (eg, incontinence advice) as well as the provision, where necessary, of incontinence and nursing aids, physiotherapy, speech and language therapy and chiropody. Where such services are provided they must be free of charge to people in independent sector homes as well as to residents of local authority Part III homes.

The guidance further reminds health authorities that they continue to have the power to enter into a contractual arrangement with a nursing home where a patient's need is primarily of health care. Such placements must be fully funded by the health authority.[83] The financial consequences of this division of responsibility are of prime importance to service users; the NHS has no power to charge for such nursing home accommodation, whereas social services authorities are under a duty to charge; see Chapter 8.

6.94 **'Complex, intense or unpredictable'** The 1995 guidance as it relates to 'continuing in-patient care', refers to patients who have complex, intense or unpredictable conditions. EL(96)8 was critical of a number of continuing care statements which, rather than being sensitive to the complexity *or* intensity *or* unpredictability of a person's needs, placed too much emphasis on the need for people to meet multiple criteria for NHS-funded care.

6.95 EL(96)89[84] noted with concern that of the 25 Health Authority Continuing Care Statements considered, ten required individuals to meet at least two or more criteria. It criticised, by way of example, a statement which required adults to fulfil all these criteria:

- unable to initiate purposeful movements even with aids;
- poor physical condition which requires constant observation or active intervention supported by technical means and a clinical specialist;
- needs feeding by technical means;
- requires on-going supervision at least weekly by a specialist health professional, either NHS consultant or specialist nurse.

6.96 In *R v North and East Devon HA ex p Coughlan*,[85] the Court of Appeal emphasised that a person could be entitled to continuing care funded by the NHS because of the overall quantity of health care required; and presumably therefore the word 'intense' should be interpreted to include this meaning. The court held (at para 30):

---

83 LAC(92)24 para 7.
84 Annex 1 at para 4.14.
85 (1999) 2 CCLR 285.

(d) There can be no precise legal line drawn between those nursing services which are and those which are not capable of being treated as included in such a package of care services.

(e) The distinction between those services which can and cannot be so provided is one of degree which in a borderline case will depend on a careful appraisal of the facts of the individual case. However, as a very general indication as to where the line is to be drawn, it can be said that if the nursing services are:

- merely incidental or ancillary to the provision of the accommodation which a local authority is under a duty to provide to the category of persons to whom section 21 refers and
- of a nature which it can be expected that an authority whose primary responsibility is to provide social services can be expected to provide, then they can be provided under section 21.

It will be appreciated that the first part of the test is focusing on the overall quantity of the services and the second part on the quality of the services provided.

The court went on to note (at para 31) that:

The Secretary of State accepts that, where the primary need is a health need, then the responsibility is that of the NHS, even when the individual has been placed in a home by a local authority.

6.97   Where there is a dispute between the health authority and social services as to whose responsibility it is to fund the care of a patient, it may be worthwhile to consider what would have happened prior to April 1993. At that time a person (on a low income) would only have been accepted by an independent nursing home if the income support allowance would have been sufficient to fund the care needed. The preserved entitlement rates for nursing homes as at April 2000 are detailed below[86] (for placements in Greater London a figure of £51 should be added). Since social services authorities only took over responsibility for the care of people who would otherwise have been funded by the DSS, it would seem logical that they should not be responsible for patients whose nursing care needs would cost substantially more than the scale rate.

Terminal illness		£330.00
Drug/alcohol		£331.00
Mental handicap		£337.00
Mental disorder		£331.00
Physically disabled	(< pension age)	£373.00
	(> pension age)	£330.00
Others		£330.00

---

86 See para 8.51 below for a consideration of the principles relating to 'preserved entitlement'.

6.98 **Likely to die in the near future** The final example in the 1995 guidance on 'continuing in-patient care', relates to patients who are likely to die in the very near future. Such patients should, it states, be able to choose to remain in NHS-funded accommodation, or where practicable and after an appropriate and sensitive assessment of their needs, to return home with appropriate support. In relation to such persons, EL (96)8 states that 'very short time limits (for instance of the order of a couple of weeks) are not appropriate and any time limits should be applied flexibly in the light of individual circumstances'. In general health authorities appear to interpret 'likely to die in the near future' as a period of between 6 and 12 weeks.

6.99 In a research report annexed to EL(96)89[87] it was noted that some health authorities were placing inappropriate limitations on this obligation, for instance suggesting that such a package would only be provided in unusual circumstances. It would also be inappropriate to suggest that such patients could only be provided with a package of health and social care at home if it was less expensive than the package if provided in a hospital or nursing home.

6.100 The 1995 guidance makes it clear that the NHS obligation applies to any patients 'who have finished acute treatment or inpatient palliative care in a hospital or hospice'. Accordingly, the duty applies to all patients in this category. It follows that a health authority policy, which confined this service merely to those patients dying of cancer, would appear therefore to be directly contrary to the 1995 guidance (and irrational). It might also constitute an unlawful discrimination contrary to Articles 14 and 8 of the European Convention on Human Rights.

Rehabilitation and recovery

6.101 Much of the continuing care guidance has been directed at the NHS providing after-care services where they help promote independent living. If with the assistance of rehabilitation or respite services, a patient can live independently in the community, then resources should be devoted towards this end.[88] Thus the 1995 guidance

---

87 M Henwood *Continuing Health Care: Analysis of a sample of final documents* (1996).

88 The Audit Commission noted however that '[r]ehabilitation is currently advocated by many as the 'missing factor' in the care of elderly people. What is clear is that many health authorities lack basic knowledge about the rehabilitation services for older people in their area' *Coming of Age* (Audit Commission, 1997).

suggested that 'the existence of good rehabilitation services and well-developed community health services and social care support may lessen, although not eliminate, the need for continuing inpatient care.[89] The importance of developing rehabilitation and recovery services was described as a 'crucial priority' in EL(96)89.[90]

6.102   The 1995 guidance required health authorities to take full account of the need for services:[91]

> to promote the effective recovery and rehabilitation of patients after acute treatment so as to maximise the chances of the successful implementation of long-term care plans. This is particularly important for older people who may need a longer period to reach their full potential for recovery and to regain confidence. Local policies should guard against the risk of premature discharge in terms of poorer experiences for patients and increased levels of readmissions.

6.103   The point is also emphasised in the *Hospital Discharge Workbook*,[92] which states:

> Under-provision of rehabilitation and convalescent facilities can not only delay discharge, but can reduce substantially outcomes and degree of achievable recovery . Steps need to be taken to ensure that patients are able to benefit from early rehabilitation, and that they are not discharged before such support can be provided. Investment in rehabilitation is one area in which the benefits may be particularly apparent to providers of community care services (both health and social care), and may therefore be an appropriate area for joint commissioning initiatives.

6.104   Follow-up guidance in February 1996 on the local eligibility criteria (EL(96)8) expressed concern over certain rehabilitation and recovery criteria, stating (at para 16) that they would be unduly:

> restrictive if they limit NHS responsibility for rehabilitation to post-acute care and do not take account of responsibilities to contribute to longer-term rehabilitative care which is needed as part of a care package for someone in their own home or in a residential care home or nursing home. Some eligibility criteria include time limits for rehabilitation or recovery. While perhaps helpful in ensuring that services are well focused, such limits will be restrictive if applied rigidly. They will usefully act as a trigger for reassessment.

---

89   Annex A p14.
90   Para 6; and this emphasis was underscored by its inclusion in the NHS Priorities and Planning guidance of 1996/97 and 1997/98.
91   Ibid.
92   Department of Health, 1994.

6.105   The reference to 'longer-term' rehabilitative care is of importance and is echoed by the 1995 guidance in relation to respite services (see below). Health authorities are required to provide rehabilitation services for persons with chronic conditions, as well as acute needs. In general this obligation is not fulfilled; while the NHS provides rehabilitation following an acute episode, such as a stroke, hip operation or accident, such services are not commonly available to the chronically sick. 'Active rehabilitation' for such patients can improve their ability to cope with daily living skills and so prolong their ability to live in the community and relieve some of the pressure on their carers.

Respite health care

6.106   In keeping with the policy of 'promoting independence' the 1995 guidance states that the NHS 'has important responsibilities' for arranging and funding respite care and that 'all health authorities ... must arrange and fund an adequate level of such care'.

6.107   Arranging and funding an 'adequate level' of such services presupposes that the health authority has assessed what the potential need for respite care is, within its area, and has then made a strategic decision as to what would be an adequate funding response to that need. In order to carry out such an assessment the 1995 guidance states that health authorities 'are expected to base purchasing decisions on a full assessment of the needs of their population, fully discussed and, if possible, jointly agreed with local authorities'.[93] This presupposes significant liaison by the health authority with relevant interest groups such as carers organisations, who will be able to assist in assessing the need for such services. All too often it appears that such a strategic approach is not occurring and indeed health authorities are unable to identify or quantify the respite provision they have purchased or indeed the criteria for accessing such a service.

6.108   The 1995 guidance gave three examples of the type of patient who ought to be able to access NHS-funded respite services, namely:

- people who have complex or intense health care needs and will require specialist medical or nursing supervision or assessment during a period of respite care;
- people who during a period of respite care require or could benefit from active rehabilitation; and

93 Annex A p14.

- people who are receiving a package of palliative care in their own homes but where they or their carer need a period of respite care.

6.109   As noted above, in relation to rehabilitation the reference to 'active rehabilitation' is of importance in that it is directed towards the needs of people whose condition is chronic rather than acute. By providing such persons with regular periods of respite when they also receive such services as intensive physiotherapy, speech and occupational therapy, the NHS can prolong their ability to live independently in the community and reduce the pressure on their carers.

6.110   The guidance emphasises that in making arrangements for respite care, health authorities should pay careful attention to the wishes of patients and their carers. In this context it must be assumed that the respite care is provided as an in-patient in a hospital or NHS-funded nursing home.

6.111   EL(96)8 at para 16 states that eligibility criteria will in general be too restrictive if they exclude any of the above three conditions and gives as one of its examples, 'where carers have been providing a level of health care which is not reasonably available in a residential setting'.

Palliative health care

6.112   Health authorities receive substantial funding each year from the NHS Executive to enable them to make contributions towards the running costs of voluntary hospices and similar organisations. The guidance (EL(93)14 and EL(94)14) urges authorities to work closely with the voluntary sector (ie, hospices), and provide palliative care services.[94] Palliative care must be distinguished from the care of 'terminally ill people', who are defined by the Department of Health (at EL(93)14 Annex F) as people with an active and progressive disease for which curative treatment is not possible or not appropriate and whose death can reasonably be expected within 12 months.

6.113   The guidance expressly requires health authorities to provide:

- palliative health care, on an inpatient basis, fully funded by the NHS in hospital, hospice or in a limited number of cases in nursing homes capable of providing this level of care;

94   The World Health Organisation defines palliative health care as 'The total active care of patients whose disease is not responsive to curative treatment. Control of pain, and other symptoms of psychological, social and spiritual problems is paramount. The goal of palliative care is achievement of the best quality of life for the patients and their families'.

- specialist palliative health care to old people already in nursing homes;
- palliative health care support to people in their own homes or in residential care.

6.114   In relation to the community care overlap between social services and health authorities, EL(93)14 gives the following guidance (at Annex C paras 10–14):

> 10. Under the wider community care reforms, from April 1993, local authorities will be responsible for assessing people's needs for care, including residential care and nursing home places. Where people have health as well as social needs, appropriate NHS staff will be involved in these assessments.

> 11. Where assessment reveals that a person is terminally ill and requires specialist in-patient palliative care, it will be for the health authority to arrange that, whether in a voluntary hospice, an NHS facility or an independent sector nursing home capable of providing such care. This applies equally to respite palliative care.

> 12. Where it is decided on the basis of assessment that a person's needs make a placement in a residential care or nursing home appropriate, the local authority will generally be responsible for arranging such a placement (although precise responsibilities will have been agreed between local authorities and health authorities).[95] Although not in need of specialist in-patient palliative care at the time of their initial assessment and placement, some people placed in this way may eventually become terminally ill[96] or enter the terminal phase of a long-term condition. Some of these patients may come in time to require specialist palliative care. Health authorities will be responsible for providing such specialist care. Depending on the individual's needs, specialist palliative care could be provided by means of a placement for temporary or permanent specialist in-patient care elsewhere (for which new placement the health authority would bear the cost) or by additional specialist health care to the

95 The wording used here is tendentious. Whether a person has a health or a social need is in every case a question of fact and agreement; whether the majority of such persons end up as the responsibility of the NHS or social services cannot be relevant in an individual's case; the Executive Letter guidance is here echoing the wording used in the draft guidance which preceded LAC(95)5; the 1994 draft stated 'The expectation will be that the significant majority of people who require continuing care in a nursing home setting are likely to have their needs met through social services'. This draft was the subject of substantial criticism (see, eg, *Community Care* magazine, 29 September 1994 p24) and was in consequence heavily rewritten with this passage omitted.

96 That is, have, *inter alia*, a life expectancy of less than 12 months.

person in the home where they live (in which case the health authority would fund only the additional care).

13. There has been some confusion about whether nursing homes which currently attract the 'Terminal Illness' level of Income Support should, therefore, automatically look to health authorities for funding. This is not necessarily the case. Responsibility for funding depends on the care needs as described above.

14. HSG(92)50, issued to health authorities and Trusts in December 1992, sets out health authorities' responsibilities for the health care of people placed in residential care and nursing homes under local authority contracts. Broadly, health authorities would be expected to provide specialist palliative care to people in residential care homes as if they were living at home, and in nursing homes to provide any necessary additional specialist palliative health care in addition to general nursing (which will continue to be included in the local authority's contract with the home). Arrangements for this need to be agreed locally between health and local authorities. Local discussion and agreement are the key to seamless and responsive care.

EL(96)8 (at para 16) reminded authorities that eligibility criteria which applied time limits for palliative care would be inappropriate; such care should be provided by the NHS purely on the basis of clinical need.

6.115   Reference has been made above (para 6.98) to the duties owed by the NHS patients to patients 'likely to die in the very near future'.

NHS specialist or intensive services for people in nursing homes

6.116   It is a basic principle of the NHS that all medical and nursing services are provided free at the point of need. While this canon is curtailed in so far as it applies to the needs of residents in nursing homes not funded by the NHS, the limitation only applies to the general nursing needs of such residents. The 1995 guidance clarifies this distinction in the following terms:

> Some people who will be appropriately placed by social services in nursing homes, as their permanent home, may still require some regular access to specialist medical, nursing or other community health services. This will also apply to people who have arranged and are funding their own care. This may include occasional continuing specialist medical advice or treatment, specialist palliative care, specialist nursing care such as incontinence advice, stoma care or

diabetic advice or community health services such as physiotherapy, speech therapy and language therapy and chiropody. It should also include specialist medical or nursing equipment (for instance specialist feeding equipment) not available on prescription and normally only available through hospitals. It would not cover basic equipment such as incontinence supplies which should be included in the basic price charged by the home to the local authority or the person.

Assessment procedures and arrangements for purchasing care should take account of such needs and details should be identified in individual care plans. In such cases the NHS can either provide such services directly or contract with the home to provide the additional services required. Such additional services should be free at the point of delivery.

LAC(92)24 also defines specialist nursing as 'primarily continence advice and stoma care, but also other specialist nursing such as diabetic liaison and other community health services (primarily physiotherapy, speech and language therapy and chiropody'. It then makes clear that such services should be provided by the NHS to patients in local authority-funded nursing home accommodation.

Specialist medical equipment

6.117   The issue of 'specialist medical and nursing' equipment can cause problems. In general, however, a nursing home only has to provide the general equipment which is a prerequisite for its registration (by the health authority – see para 4.51 above). Thus, if a patient is in need of equipment which is not part of the basic registration requirement it may be argued that this is therefore 'specialist' in the sense that it ought to be funded by the health authority. The Health Service Ombudsman has, for instance, investigated a complaint[97] concerning an elderly nursing home resident who had to be fed by means of a gastric tube. Although the liquid feed was supplied on prescription she was required to pay for the tubes through which the feed was delivered (at £25 per week). The health authority accepted that this was incorrect and refunded the cost of the tubes.

6.118   The guidance states that specialist medical or nursing equipment not available on prescription (such as wheelchairs,[98] special beds, commodes, incontinence pads) may be supplied by the NHS to people living at home as part of its community health services.

---

97   Case No E985/94, p61, Selected Investigations April–September 1996.
98   See para 6.70 above.

Incontinence supplies

6.119   The Health Service Ombudsman has considered the responsibilities of health authorities for incontinence supplies.[99] He noted that health authorities are 'required to apply the same criteria with regard to funding incontinence supplies to people living in residential care homes as to those living in their own homes'.[100] The health authority in question had refused to pay for the incontinence supplies of all of the residents of a residential care home, albeit that it had a policy of providing these supplies free to people in their homes. Accordingly the policy was ruled inconsistent and the health authority refunded the home owner's expenses.

6.120   Where incontinence supplies are provided by the health authority to people in their own homes, free of charge; these may include incontinence pads, commodes, protective pants, bed linen and liners etc. A laundry service can also be provided by the health authority, although generally it is provided by the social services authority under their responsibilities under NHSA 1977 Sch 8 (see para 5.99).

6.121   As noted at para 6.78 above, the Health Service Ombudsman has taken the view that many self-funding nursing home residents are in fact entitled to have their fees paid by the health authority since they are entitled to continuing care services from the NHS. Department of Health guidance *Good practice in continence services*[101] has been issued which emphasises, among other things, that there 'is an unacceptable variation among NHS Trust in the type, quality and quantity of continence supplies made available to patients' (para 3.12) and that NHS bodies should note (at para 3.6):

(1) that older people living in long-stay accommodation should have the same access to services as those living in their own homes;

(2) that hospitals should have trained nurses to carry out initial management of incontinence among patients who are first identified with this problem while in hospital; and

(3) carers receiving help because they are finding their caring relationships stressful and tiring may reveal that incontinence is a major cause of concern to them.

---

99   See complaint E.1190/94–95, Annual Report 1996/97, p11.

100   LAC(92)24, also requires local authorities to ensure that where they fund nursing home care, their contracts with the independent sector include the provision of 'all general nursing care services (including incontinence services and aids but not specialist incontinence advice)' (para 2).

101   Issued 19 April 2000.

NHS discharge procedures

6.122 LAC(95)5 also introduced new procedures to deal with hospital discharge arrangements for people with continuing health or social care needs. The issue of premature discharge from NHS care had been highlighted by the Health Service Ombudsman (see above) but has also caused general concern as the average length of time an individual spends in hospital has progressively been getting shorter.[102]

6.123 Contrary to general belief, the discharge decision is not the prerogative of the consultant. The *Hospital Discharge Workbook*[103] explains the situation as follows:

> The decision that a patient is medically fit for discharge can only be made by a consultant (or by someone to whom the consultant has delegated his authority), or by another doctor who is responsible for the care of an individual patient (such as a general practitioner responsible for GP beds). However, the decision to discharge a patient should be the result of a jointly agreed, multi-disciplinary process in which social services are responsible for assessing the needs of people for social care.

6.124 The workbook emphasises that discharge planning should commence with the patient's admission to hospital, and that the decision to discharge 'should not be the point at which discharge planning begins, rather it is the point at which all the planning is brought together and implemented'. The 'policy guidance'[104] stresses that patients should not leave hospital until the 'supply of at least essential community care services has been agreed with them, their carers and all the authorities concerned' (para 3.44). It however makes clear that 'it is most undesirable that anyone should be admitted to, or remain in, hospital when their care could be more appropriately provided elsewhere' (para 3.41) and in general care plans should actively seek to promote independent living to the maximum realistic extent (para 3.24).[105]

6.125 LAC(95)5 gives the following guidance on the discharge procedures:

> 17. A minority of patients may need intensive support including the possibility of continuing NHS inpatient care, nursing home or

---

102 The average length of stay in all sectors has fallen from 8.6 days in 1982 to 5.7 days in 1991/92; the average length of stay in geriatric beds has halved in ten years: *Hospital Discharge Workbook* (DoH) p12.

103 Ibid at p1.

104 *Community Care into the Next Decade and Beyond* (HMSO, 1990).

105 See para 3.88 (Ch 2).

residential care or an intensive package of support at home.
Decisions about the discharge of these patients from NHS care and
on how their continuing needs might best be met should be taken
following an appropriate multi-disciplinary assessment of the
patient's needs. In many cases this will involve referral to a
consultant with specialist responsibility for continuing care
(including geriatricians or psycho-geriatricians or other consultants
responsible for continuing inpatient care) along with the other
specialist staff, including specialist nursing staff, working with them.
Such consultants, working with other specialist staff, will also be
normally responsible for assessing patients referred directly from the
community who may require NHS continuing inpatient care.

18. In all such cases social services staff should be involved at the
earliest appropriate opportunity. Hospitals and social services staff
should work together to ensure the most effective integration
between social services assessments and care management
procedures and hospital discharge arrangements.

19. The multi-disciplinary assessment should be co-ordinated
between key professional staff from health and social services. The
assessment process should involve consultation with the patient's
GP and where appropriate community health services or social
services staff who are familiar with the patient's circumstances.
Where a patient has no form of accommodation to go to or where
their housing is no longer suitable for their needs, staff from housing
authorities and housing providers should be fully involved at an early
stage. The assessment should also take account of the views and
wishes of the patient, his or her family and any carer.

20. Taking account of the results of the assessment and local
eligibility criteria, the consultant (or GP in some community
hospitals) in consultation with the multi-disciplinary team, and in
particular with nursing staff, should consider what the most
appropriate response to the patient's needs would be.

21. As a result the consultant (or GP in some community hospitals),
in consultation with the multi-disciplinary team, will decide whether:
a) The patient needs continuing inpatient care arranged and funded
by the NHS because:
  • either he or she needs ongoing and regular specialist clinical
    supervision (in the majority of cases this might be weekly or
    more frequent) on account of:
  • the complexity, nature or intensity of his or her medical,
    nursing or other clinical needs;
  • the need for frequent not easily predictable interventions;
  • or because after acute treatment or inpatient palliative care in
    hospital or hospice his or her prognosis is such that he or she is

likely to die in the very near future and discharge from NHS care would be inappropriate.

b) The patient needs a period of rehabilitation or recovery arranged and funded by the NHS to prepare for discharge arrangements breaking down.

c) The patient can be appropriately discharged from NHS inpatient care with:

- either a place in a nursing home or residential home or residential care home arranged and funded by social services or by the patient and his or her family;
- or a package of social and health care support to allow the patient to return to his or her own home or to alternatively arranged accommodation.

22. Where a patient meets the eligibility criteria for continuing NHS inpatient care but a bed is not available within the provision which has been contracted for, the agreement of the health authority should be sought for an extra contractual referral to another hospital or nursing home in the NHS or independent sector.

23. Health and local authorities should have in place clear agreements on how they will resolve disputes about responsibility in individual cases for meeting continuing care needs.[106]

24. Health authorities or local authorities should not place younger people inappropriately in inpatient, nursing or residential care intended for older people.

Discharge planning and the duty to inform

6.126   It is crucial that patients, who may be entitled to continuing care services from the NHS, are informed of this entitlement before they are discharged. Likewise it is essential that the obligations of carers and patients be spelt out at the earliest opportunity so that, if necessary, they can make representations via the complaints procedures. Accordingly the 1995 guidance placed specific duties upon social services and trusts to inform patients and their carers of all aspects of their discharge planning and of their rights in this process.

Information
25. Patients and their families and carers should be kept fully informed about how procedures for hospital discharge and assessment will work and should receive the relevant information (in writing and in other formats appropriate to their needs) they require to make decisions about continuing care. In particular:

106 See LAC(95)17 para 10 which confirms that the hospital discharge review procedure should not be used to resolve such disputes.

– **hospitals** should provide simple written information about how hospital discharge procedures will operate and what will happen if patients need continuing care.[107]

– **hospitals and social services staff** should ensure that patients, their families and any carers have the necessary information, where appropriate in writing, to enable them to take key decisions about continuing care.

– **social services staff** should provide written details of the likely cost to the patient of any option which he or she is asked to consider (including where possible and appropriate the availability of social security benefits).

– **hospital and social services staff** should ensure that patients receive written details of any continuing care which is arranged for them.[108] This should include a statement of which aspects of care will be arranged and funded by the NHS.

Direction on choice
26. Where a patient has been assessed as needing care in a nursing home or residential care home arranged by a local authority, he or she has the right, under the Direction on Choice [LAC(92)27 and LAC(93)18[109]] to choose, within limits on cost and assessed needs, which home he or she moves into. Where, however, a place in the particular home chosen by the patient is not currently available and is unlikely to be available in the near future, it may be necessary for the patient to be discharged to another home until a place becomes available.

6.127   In a number of investigations the Health Service Ombudsman has been critical of trusts who have failed to provide the required information, so that a right to challenge discharge from NHS-funded care was lost. He has stressed that where the duty to inform is a joint one with the social services, this does not excuse a failure by the trust to provide the information (ie, it cannot assume that social services will discharge its duty).[110] He has also criticised as inadequate the

---

107 See also LAC(95)17 para 14 which requires health authorities to ensure (via the nominated individual – see n108) that in appropriate cases an advocate is secured to enable the patient to use the review procedure.

108 LAC(95)17 para 13 requires in addition that the statement include the name of the 'nominated individual' (usually a member of the multi-disciplinary team who can talk clearly, impartially and sensitively) who can be approached if the patient or the family or any carer wish to discuss the result of the assessment or are unhappy with the discharge arrangements.

109 See para 4.61 above.

110 Fifth Report for session 1995/96, *Investigations of Complaints about Long-Term NHS Care* (HMSO) complaint E.685/94–95.

provision of general brochures to patients, or only limited advice on possible options by trust staff.[111]

6.128   If a patient is discharged without the detailed requirements of the discharge planning process being complied with, then it may be appropriate to make a formal complaint. In general this will be to the hospital (trust) although it may additionally be necessary to complain to the social services about any failure by that department and potentially also to the health authority if it is believed that the patient meets their continuing care criteria. This may necessitate three separate complaints. NHS complaints procedures are dealt with at para 6.157 below and social services complaints at para 12.5.

Patient's right to seek a review of a discharge decision

6.129   LAC(95)5 introduced the right of patients, their families and carers to seek a review of a hospital's decision that they be discharged from inpatient NHS care, namely:

> *Rights to refuse discharge to nursing home or residential care*
> 27. Where patients have been assessed as not requiring NHS continuing inpatient care, as now, they do not have the right to occupy indefinitely an NHS bed. In all but a very small number of cases where a patient is being placed under Part II of the Mental Health Act 1983, they do however have the right to refuse to be discharged from NHS care into a nursing home or residential care home.
>
> 28. In such cases the social services department should work with the hospital and community based staff and with the patient, his or her family and any carer to explore alternative options.
>
> 29. If these other options have been rejected it may be necessary for the hospital, in consultation with the health authority, social services department and, where necessary housing authority, to implement discharge to the patient's home or alternative accommodation, with a package of health and social care within the options and resources available. A charge may be payable by the person to the social services department for the social care element of the package.
>
> 30. As a final check before such a discharge is implemented, a patient and his or her family and any carer have the right to ask the health authority, in which the patient is normally resident, to review the decision which has been made about eligibility for NHS continuing inpatient care. The health authority should deal urgently with such a request and the patient and his or family and any carer

111 Ibid complaint E.672/94–95.

should expect a response in writing from the health authority, with an explanation of the basis of its decision, within 2 weeks of them making their request.[112]

31. In reaching a decision the normal expectation will be that the health authority will seek advice from an independent panel who will consider the case and make a recommendation to the health authority. The health authority, in consultation with the local authority, does have the right to decide, in any individual case, not to convene a panel, for instance in those cases where a patient's needs fall well outside the eligibility for NHS continuing inpatient care.[113] In those cases the health authority will be required to give the patient, his or her family and any carer a written explanation of the basis of its decision.[114]

6.130 The starting point for any discharge decision is that the most important persons involved in such a decision are the patients and their carers.[115] More detailed information on the actual procedures involved has been given in LAC(95)17/HSG(95)39[116] concerning the discharge procedures that must be followed, and in particular on the establishment and operation of the independent panels to undertake the review procedure.

6.131 The guidance confirms that the review procedure applies to all patients who have been receiving NHS in-patient care, whether in hospital, or arranged and funded by the NHS in a hospice, nursing home, or elsewhere, and to all client groups covered in local eligibility criteria (para 5).

6.132 The scope of the review procedure is described as being twofold:

a) to check that proper procedures have been followed in reaching the decisions about the need for NHS continuing in-patient care, and

b) to ensure that the health authority's eligibility criteria for NHS continuing in-patient care are properly and consistently applied

---

112 The period starts once any action to resolve the case informally has been completed, and may be extended if there are exceptional circumstances, eg, if unforeseen difficulties arise over the provision of clinical advice or in convening the panel, or public holidays have made the adherence to this timescale impossible, and during the review procedure the patient should remain in NHS-funded accommodation – see LAC(95)17 paras 17 and 18.

113 Before making this decision the health authority should seek the advice of the chairman of the panel – ibid para 19.

114 The letter should also contain a reminder of their rights under the NHS complaints procedure – ibid para 19.

115 *Hospital Discharge Workbook* p3.

116 WOC 47/95 and WHC(95)38.

(para 6). The procedure is not, however, a formal appeals mechanism or a complaints procedure, and does not therefore affect patients' rights under NHS or social services complaints procedures (para 7).

6.133 The procedure cannot be used to challenge the content (as opposed to the application) of the health authority's eligibility criteria; the type and location of any offer of NHS-funded continuing in-patient care; the content of any alternative care package offered; or such matters as the patient's treatment or any other aspect of his/her stay in hospital (para 8).

6.134 Each health authority is required to appoint a 'designated officer' who is responsible for the efficient operation of the review procedure. This will encompass checking (in liaison with the provider) that all appropriate steps have been taken to resolve the case informally as well as the collection of information for the panel, including interviewing patients, family members and any relevant carer(s) (para 16).

6.135 Health authorities are required to appoint and maintain a standing panel whose role is to review challenged discharge decisions. The panel comprises an independent chairman and single representatives from the health and local authorities (para 20). The chairman is appointed by the health authority. The guidance states that s/he must be seen to be free of bias towards either party, but then advises that although 'current non-executive directors of health authorities or LA members should not be considered . . . people who have formerly held such a position are eligible for consideration'. One would in general have thought that a former senior employee of one 'party' to the review could not objectively be 'seen' to be free from bias.[117]

6.136 The panel procedure is detailed by the circular guidance in the following terms:

> 27. The designated health authority officer is responsible for preparing information for the panel. The panel should have access to any existing documentation which is relevant, including the record of assessment. They should also have access to the views of the key parties involved in the case including the patient, his or her family and, if appropriate, carer, health and social services staff, and any other relevant bodies or individuals. It will be open to the key parties to put their views in writing or to request an interview with the health authority officer, or in exceptional circumstances with another person nominated by the panel.

---

117 Further detailed guidance on the appointment, composition and training of the panel is given at paras 20–26 of the guidance.

28. The panel must retain patient confidentiality at all times.

29. When interviewed by the health authority's officer, or other person nominated by the panel, a patient may have a representative present to speak on his or her behalf where they wish, or are unable to present their own views. The health authority must aim to ensure that the views of patients who are unable to speak for themselves, for whatever reason, are appropriately represented. This may be done by a relative or carer, but the health authority will need to ensure that it is not any person whose interests or wishes conflict with those of the patient.

30. The panel will require access to independent clinical advice which should take account of the range of medical, nursing and therapy needs involved in each case. There should be standing arrangements to provide this, which are reflected in contracts between the provider unit which employs the adviser(s) and the appropriate authority, to ensure consistency of advice. Such arrangements should not involve any providers with whom the authority most commonly contracts for services.

31. The role of the clinical advisers is to advise the panel on the original clinical judgements and on how those judgements relate to the health authority's eligibility criteria. It is **not** to provide a second opinion on the clinical diagnosis, management or prognosis of the patient.

32. The members of the panel should meet to consider individual cases. They may wish to invite the clinical adviser(s) and the health authority officer, or if appropriate the person nominated to take the views of the parties concerned, to attend their meetings. This should ensure that the panel has access to all the information it will require and to the views of all parties. It is not proposed that anyone else should attend the panel's meetings.

33. The role of the panel is advisory. However, while its decisions will not be formally binding, the expectation is that its recommendations will be accepted in all but very exceptional circumstances. If a health authority decides to reject a panel's recommendation in an individual case it must put in writing to the patient and to the chairman of the panel its reasons for doing so.[118]

---

118 The Health Committee *Report into Long-Term Care* (1995) noted at para 85 that the minister 'was unable to give us an example of circumstances in which a health authority was right to reject a panel's conclusions. He argued, nonetheless, that it was right to leave some discretion to the authority just in case "some quirk, some aberration in the proceedings, some unfairness arose which led to the authority being unable to accept the recommendation"'. (The Health Committee was not impressed.)

34. In all cases the health authority must communicate in writing to the patient the outcome of the review, with reasons. The relevant hospital, consultant or GP should also receive this information.

Health authorities are required to make publicly available on an annual basis a report containing general information on the number of cases considered by the panel and their outcomes (para 35).

Learning disability services

6.137 Circular guidance HSG(92)43 and LAC(92)17 has referred to the historically anomalous position of people with learning difficulties; essentially that although their needs are primarily social, historically the NHS has provided for people with learning difficulties and therefore the NHS has received the funding for the continuing care needs of such people. Thus, the guidance states that:

> it is well recognised that many people (ie people with learning difficulties) traditionally cared for in long-stay hospitals are predominantly in need of social care, and should be cared for in the community. In order to support in the community ex long-stay patients and people who might in earlier times have been cared for in long-stay hospitals, health finance may be spent on social services rather than on health services.

Until the large-scale almost closure of the large NHS hospitals specifically catering for people with learning disabilities, one-fifth of people with severe or profound learning disabilities received their care services from the NHS.[119] The guidance advocates, therefore, not only that the NHS transfer monies to social services for the present support of such persons (and their successors[120]) but also that it should develop new and innovative services to meet the social (as opposed to health) needs of such persons.

Health authority payments to social services

6.138 Historically, the ability of the NHS and social services authorities to pool budgets, or transfer resources from one to another, has been severely curtailed. In consequence it has been argued that innovation has been stifled and 'cost shunting' between authorities encouraged.[121]

119 LAC(92)15.
120 HSG(92)43/LAC(92)17.
121 'Partnership in Action' (Sept 1998) DoH discussion paper.

6.139   Health Act 1999 ss29–31 have relaxed the restrictions upon health and social services entering into 'partnership arrangements' albeit that initially such schemes will require specific approval (from the secretary of state in England and the Assembly in Wales).

Budget sharing arrangements under NHSA 1977 s28A

6.140   Prior to the Health Act 1999 the provision which regulated budget transfers between health and social services was NHSA 1977 s28A. This section has been amended by ss29 and 30 of the 1999 Act.

6.141   Section 29 amends NHSA 1977 s28A by extending the ability of health authorities to make payments to a local authority to allow payments to be made in respect of any local authority function that is health-related. It also allows primary care trusts to make similar payments to local authorities.

6.142   Section 30 introduces a new reciprocal power for local authorities to make payments to health authorities or primary care trusts. It gives the secretary of state powers to set conditions as to local authority payments to these health bodies and to set conditions for repayment of the money. The guidance to the bill states that 'it is intended that the conditions will provide that payments may only be made if doing so will improve the health of the people in the local authority's area'.

Partnership arrangements under Health Act 1999 s31

6.143   Section 31 allows the NHS and local authorities to pool their resources, delegate functions and resources from one party to another and enable a single provider to provide both health and local authority services. In effect, it permits:

- authorities to pool resources so that they will effectively 'lose their health and local authority identity', allowing staff from either agency to develop packages of care suited to particular individuals irrespective of whether health or local authority money is used;
- health authorities or primary care trust and local authority departments to delegate functions to one another. In the case of health and social care, this will allow, for example, one of the partner bodies to commission all mental health or learning disability services locally;
- the provision of health and local authority services from a single managed provider.

It is intended that use of the new arrangements will be subject, initially, to approval by the secretary of state. Regulations will flesh out the detail as to consultation, timescales, etc.

6.144   Section 31(5) confirms that the provisions do not affect local authorities' powers or duties to charge for services.

Other partnership arrangements

6.145   The government's discussion paper *Partnership in Action* noted that not all the perceived constraints to joint working were legislative, and that in 'many areas, health and social services authorities have not taken advantage of opportunities allowed within the existing framework'.[122] A detailed list of these legal mechanisms was provided in a 1998 Report *Pathways to Partnership: Legal Aspects of Joint Working in Mental Health*,[123] and included:

- *Housing and social services*
  Housing Act 1996 s213(1): the duty on a housing authority to respond to any request for assistance from a social services authority.

- *The duty to co-operate*
  NHS Act 1977 s22: the duty on health and local authorities to co-operate in order to advance the health and welfare of the people of England and Wales.

- *Sharing of staff*
  NHS Act 1977 s26: so far as is reasonably necessary and practicable health authority staff should be made available to enable local authorities to help them discharge their social services, education and public health functions.
  NHS Act 1977 s27: this provides a reverse obligation to s26, so far as it is reasonably necessary and practicable in order to enable health authorities to discharge their functions under NHSA 1977 and NHSCCA 1990.

- *Staff transfers*
  Local Government Act 1972 s113: enables local authority staff to be seconded to the NHS and vice versa.

- *Supply of goods and services*
  Local Authorities (Goods and Services) Act 1970: this Act enables local authorities to enter into agreements with health authorities for the supply of goods and services.

---

122 *Partnership in Action* (Sept 1998) DoH discussion paper, para 4.5.
123 Camilla Parker with Richard Gordon QC for the Sainsbury Centre for Mental Health.

Budget sharing arrangements prior to the Health Act 1999

6.146   Prior to its amendment by the Health Act 1999, NHSA 1977 s28A only permitted payments by health authorities to local authorities, housing associations and certain other bodies and voluntary organisations in respect of personal social services, education for disabled people and housing. Detailed guidance[124] and directions[125] were issued in relation to these payments; as will be seen below, the criteria under which the payments were made will remain of relevance for a number of years, notwithstanding that s28A of the 1977 Act has now been the subject of fundamental amendment.

6.147   A health authority was able to transfer resources under s28A when it had been decided that a service, or a major part of it, could be more appropriately provided by a social services department, for example, services for people with learning disabilities.[126] Guidance on such payments has been issued in LAC(92)17. Any payment made under s28A had to be approved by the appropriate joint consultative committee[127] (such committees were abolished by Health Act 1999 s32). The categories of payment under s28A comprised (i) 'joint finance' payments, (ii) 'dowry' payments, and (iii) other arrangements.

Joint finance

6.148   Joint finance expenditure was a complex subject, in that health authorities had a power to make such payments out of general allocations received from central government in addition to allocations made for specific joint finance schemes. Such special allocations were subject to specific conditions, such as the maximum length of time for which a health authority could support a project and the tapering of its contribution. Health authorities were able to enter into joint finance arrangements with local authorities only on the basis that the local authority assumed financial responsibility as soon as possible, 'to help get activities started or to prevent their premature abandonment'.[128] Directions[129] set out in detail the permitted periods

---

124   LAC(92)17, HSG(92)43 and HSG(95)45.
125   Directions under s28A being contained as Annex C to HSG(92)43.
126   LAC(92)17 Annex A para 3.
127   A committee appointed by the health authority under the Joint Consultative Committees Order 1985 SI No 305.
128   LAC(92)17 Annex B para 7.
129   Section 28A directions contained as Annex C to HSG(92)43.

for such health authority funding; briefly, however, payments can be made as follows:

a) in the case of projects designed to move people out of long-stay hospitals and into community care and services for drug mis-users, full revenue costs for up to ten years and part of the cost for up to 13 years; and

b) in respect of all other joint finance projects, full revenue costs for up to three years and part costs for up to seven years.[130]

Dowry payments

6.149   Dowry payments were used to facilitate the transfer of patients from long-stay hospitals into the community. They involved a lump-sum payment or annual payment to a local authority taking over the patient's care. The amount of the lump-sum or annual payment and the length of time for which annual payments were to be made being negotiated by the respective authorities.

6.150   HSG(95)45 stated (at Annex para 4.1) that:

> . . . in respect of people being discharged from long stay institutions, the NHS is responsible for negotiating arrangements with local authorities, including any appropriate transfer of resources which assist the local authority meeting the community care needs of such people **and of their successors** who may otherwise have entered the institution.

6.151   In relation to this issue, LAC(92)17 states (Annex A para 10) that:

> Where residential care arrangements in the community for a person who was formerly a patient in a long-stay hospital appear to be breaking down . . . then the LA .. should take the lead in seeing that the appropriate arrangements are secured . . . Where no agreement has been made between the DHA responsible for the hospital care before discharge and the LA about respective responsibilities, the HA should assist the LA . . . and if the resecuring or reprovisioning of care leads the LA to incur additional expenditure, the HA will be expected to use its powers under s28A to assist the LA to fund the care.

Other payments

6.152   The scope for payments under s28A was not restricted merely to joint finance and dowry arrangements. LAC(92)17 Annex A para 12, for

---

130 Both the three- and seven-year periods may be extended for a maximum of two years: direction 1(7).

instance, suggested that health authorities should also consider using such resource transfers to support personal social services and housing expenditure.

Code of Practice on Openness in the NHS

6.153 In 1993 the Government published a White Paper on 'Open Government', and as part of this programme in April 1995 published 'The Code of Practice on Openness in the NHS in England' and similar but separate codes in respect of Wales and Scotland. The health service commissioners were given responsibility for overseeing the codes and in particular for investigating complaints from members of the public that their requests for information under the codes had not been met.

6.154 The underlying principle of the codes is that information (not necessarily the documents from which the information derives) should be made available unless it can be shown to fall into one of the following exempt categories.

1) Personal information. People have a right of access to their own health records but not normally about other people.

2) Requests for information which are manifestly unreasonable, far too general, or would require unreasonable resources to answer.

3) Information about internal discussion and advice, where disclosure would harm frank internal debate, except where this disclosure would be outweighed by the public interest.

4) Management information, where disclosure would harm the proper and effective operation of the NHS organisation.

5) Information about legal matters and proceedings where disclosure would prejudice the administration of justice and the law.

6) Information which could prejudice negotiations or the effective conduct of personnel management or commercial or contractual activities. This does not cover information about internal NHS contracts.

7) Information given in confidence. The NHS has a common law duty to respect confidences except where it is clearly outweighed by the public interest.

8) Information which will soon be published or where disclosure would be premature in relation to a planned announcement or publication.

9) Information relating to incomplete analysis, research or statistics

where disclosure could be misleading or prevent the older from publishing it first.

6.155   The codes require that (i) each health body must publish the name of an individual in their employ responsible for the operation of the code, and (ii) how to request information through that individual should be publicised locally. Complaints about non-disclosure, or about delays in disclosure, or charges for information, should be made to that individual. The codes provide that if complainants are dissatisfied with the response they receive they should write to the Chief Executive of the health body concerned. Time limits are set for each stage. Complainants still dissatisfied after receiving a reply from the Chief Executive are entitled then to complain to the health service commissioner.

6.156   The health service commissioner has stated that unlike his practice with other complaints (where he expects individuals to show some prima facie reason for their claim to have suffered some hardship or injustice) in relation to complaints about non-disclosure he regards the refusal as of itself a ground on which to claim injustice or hardship. To date, he has taken a robust approach to the enforcement of the Codes and required the health body to establish with precision the specific exemption relied upon, in order to justify any refusal to disclose information.

NHS complaints

6.157   The legal basis for the NHS complaints system stems from directions[131] issued by the secretary of state. Guidance has been issued[132] on the working of the scheme, particularly as a Department of Health booklet *Complaints Listening, Acting, Improving: Guidance on implementation of the NHS Complaints Procedure* (March 1996) and in the remainder of this section any paragraph reference is a reference to this document, and any direction reference refers to the 1996 Directions to NHS Trusts.[133]

---

131 Directions to NHS Trusts, Health Authorities and Special Health Authorities for Special Hospitals on Hospital Complaints Procedures 1996; Miscellaneous Directions to Health Authorities for Dealing with Complaints 1996; given under NHSA 1977 s17, NHSCCA 1990 Sch 2 para 6(2)(a) and the NHS (Functions of Health Authorities) (Complaints) Regulations 1996 SI No 669.

132 Guidance EL(95)121; EL(96)19; EL(96)58.

133 See n131 above.

6.158   There are many parallels between the NHS and social services complaints procedures, the most significant difference being that the NHS system has only two stages – and the complainant has no automatic entitlement to progress from the first to the second stage.

Who may complain?

6.159   Complaints may be made by existing or former users of NHS trust services. People may complain on behalf of existing or former users where the trust (usually through its complaints manager) or the convenor at the independent review stage, accepts them as a suitable representative (para 4.7 and direction 11).

6.160   In relation to GPs the complainants may be existing or former patients, or people who have received services from that GP (para 4.8).

Time limits

6.161   The guidance states that a complaint should be made within six months of the event giving rise to it (or of the patient becoming aware of that event). There is, however, a discretion to extend the time limit where it would be unreasonable in the circumstances of a particular case for the complaint to have been made earlier and where it is still possible to investigate the facts of the case (para 4.11 and direction 10).

6.162   It is suggested (at para 4.12) that this power to vary the time limit should be used with flexibility and sensitivity.

Complaints personnel

Complaints manager

6.163   The complaints manager is the person in the GP's practice, the trust or health authority who is responsible for ensuring complaints are responded to and that the first-stage process is properly discharged. Such managers must be readily accessible to the public and the complaints managers for trusts and health authorities should not only have access to all relevant records; they should also be directly accountable to the chief executive (paras 4.16–4.18).

Convenor

6.164   A convenor must be appointed by each trust or health authority. The convenor must be a non-executive director and his or her function is to consider (and determine) requests made by complainants for their complaints to be referred to the independent review panel. Although not independent, s/he is advised to distance him/herself from those involved in the complaint and ensure that it is dealt with impartially (paras 4.22–4.24).

Excluded matters

6.165 The new procedure is concerned with resolving complaints and not with investigating disciplinary matters or criminal offences (paras 4.27 onwards) and the guidance gives advice on the procedure to be followed when a trust or health authority receives a complaint which raises such questions. If a complaint raises issues of negligence, the guidance states that the complaints procedure should not cease unless the complainant explicitly indicates an intention to take legal action in respect of the complaint (para 4.37 and direction 7(1)(a)). The mere fact that a complainant is seeking compensation in a complaint does not however exclude it from the scheme. This point has been confirmed by the NHS Executive, stating:

> There is nothing in the guidance or Directions to prevent a health authority (or NHS trust) from making an ex-gratia payment as part of the resolution of a complaint if it is deemed appropriate. Similarly, an independent review panel could recommend an ex-gratia payment in a report but it would be for the health authority (or NHS Trust) to agree to this and to decide what amount would be paid.[134]

Stage 1

Trusts and health authorities

6.166 The first stage of the complaints procedure requires that trusts and health authorities establish a clear local resolution process, whose 'primary objective . . . is to provide the fullest possible opportunity for investigation and resolution of the complaint, as quickly as is sensible in the circumstances, aiming to satisfy the patient, while being scrupulously fair to staff' (para 5.2).

6.167 The guidance makes the following points concerning the Stage 1 process:

> 5.2 . . . The process should encourage communication on all sides. The aim should be to resolve complaints at this stage, and many

---

134 Private correspondence with the Complaints and Clinical Negligence Policy Unit, 28 September 1999.

should be capable of resolution orally. Local Resolution should not be seen simply as a run-up process to Independent Review: its primary purpose is to provide a comprehensive response that satisfies the complainant. Rigid, bureaucratic, and legalistic approaches should be avoided at all stages of the procedure, but particularly during Local Resolution . . .

5.7 When deciding whether or not to pass the complainant on to the complaints manager, front-line staff, for example in trusts, will need to take into account the seriousness of the complaint and the possible need for more independent investigation and assessment. While an important role of the complaints manager is to investigate written complaints and to satisfy complainants, this must not preclude the complaints manager from advising front-line and other staff in the resolution of complaints . . .

5.10 The Patient's Charter gives patients the right to a written reply from the relevant trust/health authority chief executive in response to a written complaint. The Ombudsman has criticised chief executives of NHS bodies for failure to sign written responses to complainants who have made written complaints, and the Chief Executive of the NHS has reaffirmed the importance which he and Ministers attach to performance in this area (see EL(95)136). The reply might take the form of a full personally signed response or shorter letter covering a full report from another member of staff, which the chief executive has reviewed and is content with. Some oral complaints are sufficiently serious, or difficult to resolve, that they should be recorded in writing by the complaints manager. These complaints ought also receive a written response from the chief executive.

GP complaints

6.168 From 1 April 1996 service obligations require that GPs have in place practice-based complaints procedures which comply with minimal national criteria as follows:

- practices must give the procedures publicity;
- practices must ensure it is clear how to lodge a complaint and to whom;
- an initial response should normally be made within two working days;
- the person nominated to investigate the complaint should make all necessary inquiries such as interviews, if appropriate, of the complainant, GPs and practice staff; and
- an explanation should normally be provided within two weeks (ie, ten working days).

The guidance states that health authorities will have a role to play in the stage 1 process for GPs by, for instance, having lay conciliators where for some reason the complainant does not wish the complaint to be dealt with by the practice (para 5.14). Detailed advice as to how GPs should organise their complaints systems has been issued by the NHS Executive as *Practice-Based Complaints Procedures* (January 1996).

Completion of stage 1 procedure

6.169 The entire stage 1 process may be conducted orally. The guidance (at para 5.18 and direction 13) states, however, that where the complainant is dissatisfied with the oral response, or that s/he wishes to take the matter further, then:

> ... it is recommended that Local Resolution be best rounded off with a letter to the complainant. Any letter concluding the Local Resolution stage (whether signed by the chief Executive because it is a written complaint, or by some other appropriate person) should indicate the right of the complainant to seek an Independent Review of the complaint, or any aspect of the response to it with which the complainant remains dissatisfied, and that the complainant has twenty-eight days from the date of the letter to make such a request.

Stage 2: the independent review panel

6.170 Any request for an independent review panel hearing (whether made orally or in writing) must be passed to the convenor within 28 days (direction 15(2)). The convenor must acknowledge receipt in writing, and then:

> before deciding whether to convene a panel, the convenor must obtain a signed statement signed by the complainant setting out their remaining grievances and why they are dissatisfied with the outcome of Local Resolution (para 6.4).

6.171 Before deciding whether to convene the panel the convenor must:

- decide whether all opportunities for satisfying the complaint at stage 1 have been explored and fully exhausted (para 6.8);
- consult with one of the independent lay chairmen (ideally not the one who will actually chair the panel) in order to obtain an 'external independent view', although ultimately the decision to recommend the convening of a panel is the convenor's alone (para 6.9);

- take appropriate clinical advice (if any question of clinical judgment is involved in the complaint – para 6.15). Detailed guidance is given on this aspect of complaints and from whom such advice should be sought.

6.172   The cost of convening a panel is an irrelevant consideration in this decision (para 6.14). Paragraph 6.20 advises that convenors should not recommend the setting up of a panel where:

- any legal proceedings have been commenced, or there is an explicit indication of the intention to make a legal claim;
- they consider that all practical action has already been taken and that a panel would add no further value to the process;
- there is still further scope for action at the stage 1 process.

The complainant must be informed in writing of the convenor's decision and reasons must be given if s/he decides to advise that a panel should not be set up. In such cases the complainant must be advised of the right to complain to the ombudsman. The decision whether or not to convene a panel should be determined within 20 working days of the date the convenor first received the complainant's request (para 6.29).

6.173   Good practice guidance has been issued to convenors as HSC 1999/193. In addition the Health Service Ombudsman has issued a number of critical reports concerning the actions of convenors[135] and in his Annual Report 1997/98 he highlighted a number of the common problems, the most common of which being a failure to obtain appropriate clinical advice. However, even when clinical advice was taken, he found that some convenors and clinical advisers misunderstood the purpose of clinical advice at this stage of the complaints procedure; it being to assess the adequacy of the response to the clinical aspects of the complaint at the local resolution stage, and not to reassess the clinical events themselves. He also stressed that it was not appropriate for convenors to investigate the complaint themselves: their role is to consider whether it has been adequately answered locally, whether further local resolution is needed, or whether it should proceed to independent review.

6.174   He found a number of failings in relation to the letters of determination sent by convenors, most frequently their failure to address all the issues fully and a failure to provide an adequate explanation of

---

135   See, eg, E.859/96–97 and E.918/96–97, Annual Report 1996/97; the general comments at piii of the Report of Selected Investigations April–September 1996 and generally in his Annual Report 1996/97.

why s/he had decided against holding an independent review. Other areas of difficulty included:

- convenors failing to identify and refer matters back for local resolution;
- unreasonable delay in the convening process;
- failure to explain time limits (such as the requirement that a request for an independent review should be made within 28 days of the conclusion of independent resolution) or to exercise reasonable discretion in applying them;
- convenors failing to consult lay chairs;
- convenors unreasonably prejudging the effectiveness of independent review or misunderstanding the role of review panels;
- convenors making unreasonable assumptions about complainants' intention to resort to the law; and
- convenors failing to explain complainants' right of recourse to the NHS ombudsman.

The panel

6.175   The panel will comprise:

a) an independent chairman who must not be a present or past employee of the NHS or a member of any clinical profession nor have any previous formal links with the trust or health authority (para 7.2);

b) the convenor; and

c) either

   i) in the case of a trust panel, a representative of the purchaser;

   ii) in the case of a health authority, another independent person.

If the convenor considers the complaint to be a clinical complaint, then the panel will be advised by at least two independent clinical assessors (para 7.2). The guidance lays down detailed procedures for their selection, the submission of reports and the procedures to be followed if the panel disagrees with their reports.

6.176   The panel should be convened within four weeks of the convenor's decision to convene, and it should complete its work within 12 weeks (para 7.51). Its process should be informal, flexible and non-adversarial (para 7.9). No legal representation is permitted, although the complainant may be accompanied by a person of his/her choosing (para 7.10).

6.177   A draft of the panel's report should be sent to the relevant parties (to check its accuracy) 14 days before it is formally issued (para 7.30). The report is confidential, and should set out the results of the panel's investigations, outlining its conclusions with any appropriate comments or suggestions (para 7.32). Following receipt of the panel's report, the chief executive must write to the complainant informing him/her of any action the trust or health authority is taking as a result of the panel's deliberations and of the right of the complainant to take his or her grievance to the ombudsman if s/he remains dissatisfied (para 7.35).

6.178   In his Annual Report 1997/98 the Health Service Ombudsman made a number of comments concerning investigations into flawed panel hearings. While he noted that the directions/guidance gave considerable discretion as to the conduct of the panel stage and as to how evidence was taken, he stressed that the underlying principle was the need for panels to adopt procedures that enabled the facts to be examined fully and fairly. He specifically criticised panels whose decisions on procedure contributed to a failure to fulfil these essential functions, for example, by:

- failing to identify and take evidence from key witnesses or others able to assist the panel in reaching its conclusions;
- failing to take evidence from the parties to the complaint; and
- taking evidence of a clinical nature in the absence of one or more of the clinical assessors.

6.179   The Health Service Ombudsman also reminded panel chairpersons that they are required to report their findings in writing, and that their reports must include:

- findings of fact relevant to the complaint;
- the opinion of the panel on the complaint having regard to the findings of fact;
- the reasons for the panel's opinion;
- the report of the assessors and the panel's reasons for any disagreement with it.

Health Service Ombudsman

6.180   The Health Service Commissioner (generally called the Health Service Ombudsman) now has wide powers to investigate complaints concerning GPs, trusts and health authorities, including clinical practice. In general he cannot consider a complaint until the relevant NHS complaints procedures have been exhausted. He has however stated that:[136]

136 Health Service Commissioner, Annual Report 1997/98 Chapter 3.

In considering whether to investigate, I consider, case by case, what is the most appropriate way to resolve the particular complaint. If there is still scope for it to be done locally, then I shall continue to favour that. If, however, there is evidence of a breakdown of trust between the complainant and the NHS body, or if I believe that further local action would not satisfy the complainant, I may use my discretion to investigate the substance of the complaint when the matter first comes to me, even though it has not gone through all the possible stages of the NHS procedure.

Complaints should be made within one year of the date when the action complained about occurred. Complaints must concern issues of maladministration.

6.181   As noted above the Health Service Ombudsman has issued various important reports concerning the NHS's continuing care obligations (see para 6.78); recent reports are now available on the internet at http://www.health.ombudsman.org.uk/health.html. The Health Service Ombudsman's addresses in England and Wales are as follows:

The Health Service Commissioner for England
Millbank Tower, Millbank, London SW1P 4QP
tel: 020 7276 2035

The Health Service Commissioner for Wales
4th Floor, Pearl Assurance House, Greyfriars Road, Cardiff, CF1 3AG
tel: 029 2039 4621

CHAPTER 7

Carers, advocates and mental capacity

7.1   Introduction

7.3   **Carers**
7.7   Carer – definition
7.10   Carers' rights in the assessment process
7.11   Carers who provide regular and substantial amounts of care
        *Carer assessments and the DP(SCR)A 1986 • Carer assessments and
        CRSA 1995 • The carer's assessment*
7.30   Carers whose care is not regular and/or substantial
7.32   Services for carers
        *Services specifically for carers • Services prior to the implementation of
        the Carers and Disabled Children Act 2000 • Services customarily
        considered 'carers' services' • The Carers and Disabled Children Act 2000
        • Time off work to care for dependants • Parent carers • Young carers*

7.57   **Advocates**
7.60   Crisis advocacy
7.61   Citizen advocacy

7.63   **Decision making and mental capacity**
7.66   Capacity
7.69   Court of Protection
7.70   Powers of attorney
        General powers • Enduring powers
7.77   Social security appointees
7.80   Guardianship

continued

7.82   The court's inherent jurisdiction
7.86   Proposals for reform
        Decision-making powers • Adult abuse

Introduction

7.1 Community care service users rely to a greater or lesser extent upon the help provided by unpaid carers and advocates. A significant determinant upon the nature of this legal relationship is the extent of the service user's mental capacity.

7.2 The law as it relates to carers, advocates and mental incapacity is deficient. Until 1986, carers were not acknowledged in any legislation and even today their legal situation is profoundly unsatisfactory. There remains, however no (extant[1]) statutory recognition whatsoever of advocates, and the law as it relates to mental incapacity is universally recognised as being seriously defective.

Carers

7.3 There are six million 'carers' in Britain (one in eight people, one in six households), of whom 855,000 provide care for more than 50 hours a week. Half of all carers are in full or part-time work whereas only a quarter are retired. Carers are most commonly aged between 45 and 64 and nine out of ten care for a relative. One half of all carers look after someone aged over 75. Some 58 per cent of carers are women compared with 42 per cent who are men.[2] The task of providing care has subjected over half of all carers to a health-related problem (see para 4.89 above).

7.4 A key objective of the community care reforms was to ensure that 'service providers make practical support for carers a high priority'. The white paper[3] emphasised the crucial role played by carers in the provision of community care:

> The reality is that most care is provided by family, friends and neighbours. The majority of carers take on these responsibilities willingly, but the Government recognises that many need help to be able to manage what can become a heavy burden. Their lives can be made much easier if the right support is there at the right time, and a key responsibility of statutory service providers should be to do all they can to assist and support carers. Helping carers to maintain

---

1 The government has stated that the provisions of the Disabled Persons (Services, Consultation and Representation) Act 1986 which deal with 'authorised representatives' will not be implemented because of their 'resource and administrative implications'.

2 *Caring about Carers: A National Strategy for Carers*; LASSL(99)2.

3 *Caring for People* (HMSO, 1989) Cm 849, quotation from para 1.11.

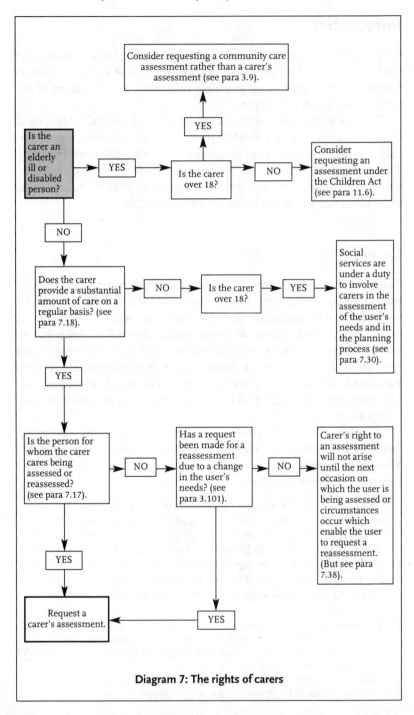

Diagram 7: The rights of carers

their valuable contribution to the spectrum of care is both right and a sound investment. Help may take the form of providing advice and support as well as practical services such as day, domiciliary and respite care.[4]

7.5 While the legislation recognises the need to support carers, the support provided is, however, generally aimed at maximising the quantity of free care they can provide. Carers have the right, therefore, to an assessment, but only limited entitlement to services in their own right (but see para 7.38 below). Where the disabled person lacks mental capacity, then the guidance designates the carer as his/her advocate or decision-maker for certain purposes (eg, in the complaints process (see para 12.7) or in making a choice as to appropriate residential accommodation (see para 4.55)).

7.6 The legislation acknowledges that the ability of carers to provide care is affected by the type of services received by the disabled person. If there is no shared care (respite care), no night-sitting service, no home-help etc, then it is more likely that the carer will have difficulty managing, with the risk that s/he might withdraw from the caring role in part or altogether. For this reason the legislation requires social services authorities (when requested) to carry out a separate assessment of the carer's ability to provide and to continue to provide care. Any service deficiency highlighted by this assessment can however only be addressed by the provision of extra services for the disabled person, not the carer (but see para 7.38 below). To this extent, therefore, carers remain in the penumbra with the legislative spotlight focusing upon the people for whom they care. Thus in *R v Secretary of State for the Home Department ex p Zakrocki*,[5] Carnwath J ruled that the Home Secretary had acted unlawfully when deciding to deport two full-time carers, not because of their circumstances, but because of the impact deportation would have had upon the person for whom they cared.

Carer – definition

7.7 There is no single definition of a 'carer' although its use in this text (and in general community care usage) excludes persons who are under a contract of employment to provide the care.

7.8 NHSCCA 1990 s46 obliges each social services authority to prepare and publish a plan detailing the provision of community care

4 Ibid para 2.3.
5 (1998) 1 CCLR 374.

services in their area.[6] During the preparation of the plan the authority is required to consult with (among other things) voluntary organisations which represent the interests of private carers.[7] In this context s46(3) defines a private carer as:

> a person who is not employed to provide the care in question by any body in the exercise of its function under any enactment.

Such a definition includes non-resident carers and makes no stipulation as to the age of the carer or the quantity or quality of care provided. In general any reference to a 'carer' (unless the context shows otherwise) must therefore be to such a heterogeneous group; indeed the Policy Guidance makes clear that the term may encompass 'families, friends and neighbours'.[8] The common denominator for such carers is that they all provide some 'service', even though this might be, for instance, in the form of advocacy or emotional support, rather than a personal care service of the kind delivered by the social services authority.[9] Even if a person does not come within an authority's definition of 'carer', s/he may be a 'significant other' whose views should properly be taken into account in the assessment and decision-making process.[10]

7.9   'Carer' has a more restricted meaning when used in the context of certain aspects of the assessment process and this is dealt with in greater detail below.

Carers' rights in the assessment process

7.10   By virtue of Disabled Persons (Services, Consultation and Representation) Act (DP(SCR)A) 1986 s8 and the Carers (Recognition and Services) Act (CRSA) 1995, carers who 'provide a substantial amount of care on a regular basis' have a statutory right to be involved in the assessment process. Department of Health guidance states

---

6   See para 2.12 above.

7   NHSCCA 1990 s46(2)(d).

8   Para 3.28: the same phrase as used in *Caring for People*, see n1 above.

9   The DoH-commissioned report *Empowerment, Assessment, Care Management and the Skilled Worker* (HMSO, 1993) uses the term 'significant others' as a separate category from 'carer'; although neither term is defined, the report accepts the importance of involving 'members of the user's networks to negotiate and sustain arrangements which integrate resources from the statutory and independent sectors with the help given through family and/or neighbourhood networks'.

10   Ibid.

that the views and interests of carers who do not come within this category (ie, who do not provide substantial or regular care) should nevertheless be taken into account when an assessment is undertaken. These two categories of carer are dealt with separately below. Substantial changes to the legal position will occur when the Carers and Disabled Children Act 2000 (outlined in para 7.38 below) comes into force.

Carers who provide regular and substantial amounts of care

7.11 Both DP(SCR)A 1986 s8 and CRSA 1995 s1 contain a statutory right for carers who provide regular and substantial amounts of care to be involved in the assessment process. Although there is considerable overlap between the two statutory provisions, they differ in a number of respects:

DP(SCR)A 1986 s8	CRSA 1995 s1
Applies only when a disabled adult is being assessed	Applies during any assessment of a disabled adult or disabled child or during any other assessment under NHSCCA 1990 s47(1)
Duty of assessor to consider the ability of the carer arises irrespective of a request	Duty of assessor to consider the ability of the carer arises only if a request has been made by the carer
Social services merely required to 'have regard' to the ability of the carer to continue to provide, etc	Social services required to carry out an actual 'assessment' of the ability of the carer to provide care
The definition of 'carer' includes voluntary organisation volunteers and (probably) voluntary organisation employees who provide the care	Voluntary organisation employees and volunteers who provide the care are excluded from the definition of 'carer'
Only applies where the carer is already providing a substantial amount of care on a regular basis	Applies where a person 'intends' to provide the care (ie, to those not as yet providing such care)
Does not cover carers who care for a person receiving care services under MHA 1983 or HSPHA 1968 (ie, the frail elderly)	Covers carers who care for persons receiving care services under MHA 1983 and HSPHA 1968 (ie, the frail elderly)

Carer assessments and DP(SCR)A 1986

7.12   DP(SCR)A 1986 s8(1)[11] provides that where:

(a) a disabled person is living at home and receiving a substantial amount of care on a regular basis from another person (who is not a person employed to provide such care by any body in the exercise of its functions under any enactment), and

(b) it falls to a local authority to decide whether the disabled person's needs call for the provision by them of any services for him under any of the welfare enactments,

the local authority shall, in deciding that question, have regard to the ability of that person to continue to provide such care on a regular basis.

The 1986 Act gives less substantial rights to carers than CRSA 1995 (discussed below), but nevertheless remains of importance in certain situations. Most obviously (and in contrast to the 1995 Act) the obligation imposed by the 1986 Act (to have regard to the ability of such carers) exists in all cases and does not have to be triggered by a request from the carer. Guidance on the 1986 Act is given in Circular LAC(87)6. A number of the terms used in s8 have been adopted in the drafting of CRSA 1995 s1 (such as 'regular' and 'substantial' and 'ability of carer') and these are considered next.

Carer assessments and CRSA 1995

7.13   CRSA 1995 s1 provides:

(1) Subject to subsection (3) below, in any case where –

(a) a local authority carry out an assessment under section 47(1)(a) of the National Health Service and Community Care Act 1990 of the needs of a person ('the relevant person') for community care services, and

(b) an individual ('the carer') provides or intends to provide a substantial amount of care on a regular basis for the relevant person,

the carer may request the local authority, before they make their decision as to whether the needs of the relevant person call for the provision of any services, to carry out an assessment of his ability to provide and continue to provide care for the relevant person; and if he makes such a request, the local authority shall carry out such an assessment and shall take into account the results of that assessment in making that decision.

11   This subsection of the Act came into force on 1 April 1987; subsections (2) and (3) are still not in force.

(2) Subject to subsection (3) below, in any case where –

    (a) a local authority assess the needs of a disabled child for the purpose of Part III of the Children Act 1989 or section 2 of the Chronically Sick and Disabled Persons Act 1970, and

    (b) an individual ('the carer') provides or intends to provide a substantial amount of care on a regular basis for the disabled child,

the carer may request the local authority, before they make their decision as to whether the needs of the disabled child call for the provision of any services, to carry out an assessment of his ability to provide and continue to provide care for the disabled child; and if he makes such a request, the local authority shall carry out such an assessment and shall take into account the results of that assessment in making that decision.

(3) No request may be made under subsection (1) or (2) above by an individual who provides or will provide the care in question –

    (a) by virtue of a contract of employment or other contract with any person; or

    (b) as a volunteer for a voluntary organisation.

7.14   The 1995 Act originated as a private member's bill[12] aimed at securing for carers recognition of their central importance as providers of community care services. This recognition is provided by requiring the social services authority (if so requested) to carry out a separate assessment of the carer at the same time as it assesses the person for whom the care is provided. The right of a carer to an 'assessment' under the 1995 Act is to be contrasted with the situation under the 1986 Act which merely requires the social services authority to 'have regard to' the carer's ability. This Act is misnamed, in that there is only one service it provides for carers, namely an assessment.[13]

7.15   Section 1(1) of the Act is aimed at carers (of whatever age) who care for adults and s1(2) at carers (of whatever age,[14] although generally adults) who care for children.

7.16   Policy guidance on the Act (under LASSA 1970 s7(1)) has been issued as circular LAC(96)7[15] as well as practice guidance (which is referred to in the rest of this section as the Practice Guidance). Carers, in order to be eligible for an assessment under the Act, must cross four hurdles:

---

12 Sponsored by Malcolm Wicks MP.

13 LASSA 1970 Sch 1 is amended to include the assessment under s1 of the 1995 Act as a social services authority function.

14 It would include young carers, for example, if caring for disabled siblings, etc.

15 WOC 16/96 and WHC(96)21 in Wales.

a) the person for whom they care must be 'being' assessed;
b) they must be providing (or intending to provide) a substantial amount of care on a regular basis;
c) they must not be under a contract to provide the care or doing so as a volunteer from a voluntary organisation; and
d) they must make a request for the carer's assessment.

7.17   **In conjunction with an assessment of the service user** Carers do not have a right to a 'free-standing' assessment (unless of course they are entitled to a community care assessment in their own right, by virtue of being an elderly, ill or disabled person). Carers only qualify for a carer's assessment under the 1995 Act, when the person for whom they care 'is being' assessed (but see para 7.38 below). The carer's assessment must therefore coincide with the service user's assessment. The Policy Guidance (at para 8) confirms that this will also arise:

> where a re-assessment of the service user is taking place, either as part of a review or because of a change in circumstances of either the user or carer arising for example, from a deterioration in the health of the user or a change in the carer's ability to continue to provide care.

7.18   **Providing (or intending to provide) a substantial amount of care on a regular basis** Circular LAC(96)7 is singularly unhelpful in advising on how this phrase should be interpreted,[16] stating (at para 11) that it is 'for local authorities to form their own judgement about what amounts to "regular" and "substantial"'. There is also a need to clarify the meaning of 'care'.

7.19   **'Care'** Care in the context of the Act will include not merely physical caring tasks but also general attendance on the service user to ensure s/he comes to no harm as well as emotional care in appropriate cases. Young carers with a parent who has a mental health difficulty, for instance, often provide little physical care but substantial emotional support. Such care (representing as it does a reversal of the traditional roles of a parent emotionally supporting a child) must on the face of it constitute care for the purposes of the Act.[17]

7.20   **'Substantial'** Circular LAC(96)7 fails to give any constructive guidance on how 'substantial' should be interpreted. The Practice Guidance, while adopting an equally detached tone on the subject, includes as Annex 1 a précis of various research which had been

16 See LAC(96)7 para 10.
17 See Practice Guidance para 7.

carried out on carers. The research most quoted in the annex looked at the number of hours each carer spent caring, and there is the implication that persons providing 20 hours or more a week are 'substantial carers'.[18] While this may indeed be the case, it cannot follow that persons who provide less than this are not also 'substantial carers'.

7.21   The Department of Health has elsewhere given advice on the interpretation of the word 'substantial' where it appears in a community care statute. In the context of NAA 1948 s29 it has stated that the word should be given a wide interpretation which fully takes into account the individual's circumstances;[19] essentially, therefore, that the word should be used subjectively. This must also be the case in the context of the 1995 Act. While it may be appropriate for an authority to start from the position of accepting a carer who provides more than (say) 15 hours' a week care as a 'substantial' carer, it must also look at the individual circumstances of a carer who fails to qualify on this ground. What may not be a substantial amount of care to a 25-year-old carer may be otherwise if provided by a seven or 87-year-old carer. Likewise if the caring task is physically demanding, then the question of what is or is not substantial will depend in part on the physical strength of the carer; again, if the carer has recently recovered from a serious mental illness, then even five hours' care may be substantial to him or her. A morning or evening caring task will be substantial to a carer who works nine to five but not necessarily for one who does not – and so on.

7.22   **'Regular'** 'Regular' should be distinguished from 'frequent'; it merely connotes an event which recurs or is repeated at fixed times or uniform intervals.[20] The Practice Guidance points out (at para 7) that:

> Some users with mental health or substance misuse problems or with conditions such as neurological disorders, dementia, cancer or HIV/AIDS will have care needs which vary over time but may present regular and substantial burdens for carers.

7.23   **'Intending to provide'** A carer may be entitled to a carer's assessment even if s/he is presently providing no care – provided the authority is

18 This is similar to the requirement of 35 hours' caring work in order to qualify for invalid care allowance.

19 This interpretation adopts the DoH guidance on how the word 'substantial' should be interpreted in the context of NAA 1948 s29 – see LAC(93)10 App 4 para 8. The word 'substantial' has been the subject of considerable judicial interpretation; see, eg, *R v Monopolies Commission ex p S Yorks Ltd* [1993] 1 WLR 23, HL at 29, and *Palser v Grinling* [1948] AC 291 at 317.

20 Definition taken from the *Shorter Oxford English Dictionary*.

satisfied that s/he is intending to provide a substantial amount of care on a regular basis for the user. This provision covers all such 'intending' carers, and is explained by LAC(96)7 (at para 16) thus:

> By including carers both providing or intending to provide care, the Act covers those carers who are about to take on substantial and regular caring tasks for someone who has just become, or is becoming, disabled through accident or physical or mental ill health. Local and health authorities will need to ensure that hospital discharge procedures take account of the provisions of the Act and that carers are involved once planning discharge starts.

7.24 The provision (although not restricted to such cases) is of particular relevance to potential users who are about to be discharged from hospital. The importance of good collaborative working practices between social services and the NHS is emphasised in LAC(96)7, suggesting at para 29 that local authorities should 'review with NHS commissioning agencies and NHS providers how they might best be involved in the carer's assessment', and then stating:

> 30. Primary care staff, including GPs and community nurses through their contact with users and carers, are in a good position to notice signs of stress, difficulty or rapidly deteriorating health particularly in carers. The provisions of the Act will help primary care staff to meet the medical and nursing needs of their patients who are carers. When making a referral for a user's assessment they should be able to inform the carer that they may also have a right to request an assessment and will be well-placed to encourage patients whom they consider will benefit most to take up the opportunity. Social services departments should make sure that primary care staff have relevant information about social services criteria and know who to contact to make a referral. GPs nurses and other members of multi-disciplinary teams may be able to assist in an assessment of a carer's ability to provide and continue to provide care.

7.25 **Employed and voluntary organisation carers** The Act excludes from consideration (at s1(3)) persons who provide the care by virtue of a contract of employment or as a volunteer for a voluntary organisation. This will not exclude carers who are in receipt of invalid care allowance[21] or similar social security benefits, but foster carers of disabled children or care assistants working in their capacity as part of a home care service (whether private or public) will be excluded.

---

21 A taxable, non-contributory benefit for people aged 16–65 caring for more than 35 hours a week for someone who is getting attendance allowance or the middle/higher rate care component of disability living allowance or certain rates of constant care allowance.

Anyone who is paid by the user (using their own money, direct payments from the authority or independent living funds) will also be excluded.

7.26 **The carer must request the assessment** LAC(96)7 at para 20 makes the important point that:

> Many carers with substantial caring responsibilities may not know about their right under the Act. Local authorities should ensure that it becomes part of routine practice to inform any carer who appears to be eligible under this Act of their right to request an assessment.

7.27 Young carers are in particular unlikely to know of their right to seek a carer's assessment, or to request one when told of their right. Accordingly the Practice Guidance states (at para 15.5) that even where no assessment is requested, 'the care manager should still consider whether there is a need to assist or relieve the child either through the provision of community care services for the user or through the provision of services to promote the welfare of the child'.

The carer's assessment

7.28 A carer's assessment under the 1995 Act differs markedly from a user's assessment. Under NHSCCA 1990 s47(1) the object of a user's assessment is to identify that person's need for community care services. The object of a carer's assessment is to identify his or her 'ability to provide and to continue to provide care' (CRSA 1995 s1(1) and (2)). Whilst carers have only limited rights to services (see para 7.36 below), the outcome of a carer's assessment under the 1995 Act may nevertheless be an increase in the community care services provided for the user. This can perhaps be best illustrated by an example.

Example

A carer in her 60s, still in full-time work, provides all the morning and evening care for her disabled husband, whose care needs are substantial. While she is at work, a care package involving a call by the district nurse, meals-on-wheels and a short visit by the home care service occurs. On the annual review of the care plan, the user assessment discloses that his condition has deteriorated slightly, but that the present care package meets his needs adequately. During her carer's assessment she discloses that her GP has recently told her that she has suffered a slight stroke and in the GP's opinion if she continues with the stressful routine of caring and working, then there is a risk of a significantly more serious stroke (in which case there will be two service users in the household). Having regard to the user's assessment, his need for services remains; having regard to the carer's assessment, her ability to continue to provide care is in jeopardy, such that some extra local authority services in the morning and evening may be required to ensure that she can otherwise continue to provide care. Essentially her assessment informs and amends the user's care package.

7.29   Section 1(4) of the Act enables the secretary of state to issue directions as to the manner in which a carer's assessment is to be carried out.[22] To date no such direction has been issued. LAC(96)7 gives limited and general advice on the form such assessments should take (at paras 21–25), whereas slightly more detail is provided in the Practice Guidance,[23] including:

> 9.1 The assessment is not a test for the carer. It should not be prescriptive but recognise the carer's knowledge and expertise. The assessment should listen to what they are saying and offer an opportunity for private[24] discussion in which carers can candidly express their views . . .

> 9.3 Carers often give most of the assistance needed by the person for whom they care, and may only want a fairly small amount of help to enable them to continue caring. A PSSRU study[25] found that some of the most cost effective care packages were where carers continued to perform caring tasks but were given sufficient support and respite to enhance their well being and maintain their own health. Equally it is important that care managers do not make assumptions about carers' willingness to undertake the range of caring tasks, particularly those related to intimate personal care. This is highlighted in a discussion of spouse carers[26] which emphasises the difficulties faced by some husbands or wives when their ability to cope with changed behaviour or personality and/or tasks involving physical intimacy is taken for granted . . .

> 9.8 In assessing the carer's ability to care or continue to care, care managers should not assume a willingness by the carer to continue caring, or continue to provide the same level of support. They will wish to bear in mind the distinction between caring *about* someone

22 Mirroring NHSCCA 1990 s47(4).

23 For adult carers at paras 9–11 and for young carers at para 16.

24 Authorities will need to ensure that the carer is aware that his or her comments may be placed on the user's file and accordingly advised of the right to withhold consent to them being copied to the user; see para 2.35.

25 D Challis et al *Care Management and Health Care of Older People* (Canterbury, 1995).

26 K Atkin, 'Similarities and Differences Between Informal Carers', in *Carers: Research and Practice* (HMSO, 1992).

and caring *for* them. Many carers continue to care deeply *about* a person even though their ability to care for them may change.

Carers whose care is not regular and/or substantial

7.30   As detailed above, the statutory rights enshrined in the 1986 and 1995 Acts only apply to carers who (among other things) provide a substantial amount of care on a regular basis. The Policy Guidance[27] sets out the way social services authorities should deal with all carers, ie, regardless of whether the care they provide is either regular or substantial. Paragraph 3.25 emphasises that assessments and care plans must take account of 'user's and the carer's own preferences', and (at para 3.16) that they 'must feel that the process is aimed at meeting their wishes'.[28] It continues:

Role of carers in assessment
3.27 Service users and carers should be informed of the result of the assessment and of any services to be provided. In the case of carers, due regard should be had to confidentiality, particularly where the carer is not a close relative. Where care needs are relatively straightforward the most appropriate way of conveying decisions can best be determined taking individual circumstances into account. A written statement will normally be needed if a continuing service is to be provided. Written statements should always be supplied on request.

3.28 Most support for vulnerable people is provided by families, friends and neighbours. The assessment will need to take account of the support that is available from such carers. They should feel that the overall provision of care is a shared responsibility between them and the statutory authorities and that the relationship between them is one of mutual support. The preferences of carers should be taken into account and their willingness to continue caring should not be assumed. Both service users and carers should therefore be consulted – separately, if either of them wishes – since their views may not coincide. The care plan should be the result of a constructive dialogue between service user, carer, social services staff and those of any other agency involved.

Carers' own needs
3.29 Carers who feel they need community care services in their own right can ask for a separate assessment. This could arise if the care

---

27 *Community Care in the Next Decade and Beyond* (HMSO, 1990).
28 And any failure to take into account user and carer preferences will normally render invalid any assessment, *R v North Yorkshire CC ex p Hargreaves* (1997) 1 CCLR 104.

plan of the person for whom they care does not, in their view, adequately address the carer's own needs.

7.31 The Practice Guidance issued by the Social Services Inspectorate[29] reinforces the Department of Health's view that carers should be encouraged to participate in the assessment process[30] and that:

> The contribution of carers should be formally recognised in new procedures for care management and assessment. Because the interests of users and carers may not coincide, both parties should be given the opportunity of separate consultation with an assessing practitioner. If necessary, carers should be offered a separate assessment of their own needs.[31]

The Practice Guidance (at para 15.5) emphasises in respect of young carers that even when it is decided that they are not providing substantial and regular care, nevertheless their caring tasks may be impairing their development to such an extent that they may be entitled to services under CA 1989 by virtue of being children 'in need' (see below).

Services for carers

7.32 The community care legislation concentrates on providing services for disabled people, the frail elderly and the ill. It is generally considered that (with only a few exceptions, detailed below) social services authorities are not empowered to provide services for carers unless they are themselves disabled, elderly or ill.[32] Thus, for instance, in *R v Kirklees MBC ex p Good*,[33] the court reaffirmed that the duty to facilitate adaptations under CSDPA 1970 s2 and the duty to pay a disabled facilities grant to assist with such adaptations are duties owed to disabled people and not to their carers.

7.33 As noted below, the Carers and Disabled Children Act 2000 will (once in force) enable local authorities to provide services for carers, including 'short-term break support'[34] and entitlement to direct payments in their own right (see para 5.143 above). However, in practice, the paucity of actual services for carers is seldom a

---

29 *Care Management and Assessment: A Practitioners' Guide* (HMSO, 1991).

30 Ibid, paras 3.22, 3.38, 3.42, 3.48 and in particular see pp58–59.

31 Ibid, p16 para 39.

32 45% of carers are themselves over retirement age; see also LAC(87)6 para 6.

33 (1998) 1 CCLR 506.

34 Paras 11 onwards, *Caring about Carers: A National Strategy for Carers*, LASSL(99)2.

cause of difficulty; almost any care provision which might be considered as a service to a carer, is in fact a service for the person for whom s/he cares – for instance, shared care (or respite care) is a service for a disabled person when it is not appropriate for that care to be provided by his or her carer. Below is a brief commentary on certain community care services which are frequently considered of most relevance to carers. In each case reference is made to the relevant part of this text where the service is discussed in greater detail.

Services specifically for carers

7.34   Until the Carers and Disabled Children Act (CDCA) 2000 comes into force, the only service specifically available for carers is the right to an assessment under CRSA 1995 s1. Such an assessment is itself a service.[35] The CDCA 2000 and the present possibility of providing community care services for carers are therefore considered separately below.

Services prior to the implementation of the Carers and Disabled Children Act 2000

7.35   The Department of Health has drawn attention to two statutory provisions (Local Government Act 1972 s111 and NHSA 1977 Sch 8 para 2(1))[36] which, it believes, enable local authorities to make services available for carers. At present, there appears to be scope for such services under the following sections:

Services under the Children Act 1989 By virtue of CA 1989 s17(3), services can be provided for the 'family of a particular child in need or any member of his family, if it is provided with a view to safeguarding or promoting the child's welfare'. See Chapter 11.

Home help under the NHSA 1977 NHSA 1977 Sch 8 para 3 obliges social services authorities to provide home helps for households which contain people with certain specified needs (see para 5.50).

General services to prevent illness under the NHSA 1977 As detailed above, the Department of Health considers that NHS Act 1977 Sch 8 para 2(1) empowers authorities to provide general carer support services (see para 5.86).

---

35   CRSA 1995 s1(7).
36   See LAC(96)7 para 5(a).

Services under NAA 1948 s29 Section 29 authorises authorities to make arrangements for promoting the welfare of certain disabled people; in theory the provision of a service to a carer could promote the welfare of such a person (see para 5.24 above).

LGA 1972 s111 Section 111 empowers authorities to 'do anything . . . which is calculated to facilitate, or is conducive or incidental to, the discharge of any of their functions'.

Services customarily considered 'carers' services'

7.36   **Respite care** Respite care (now generally called 'shared care') is not a service referred to as such by any statute. It is a generic term for temporary care; care which temporarily relieves a carer from his/her caring role (or put another way, gives the service-user the opportunity of a 'break' from his/her usual carer). If respite care takes place in the service-user's home it is 'practical assistance in the home, or home help' (ie, a service under CSDPA 1970 s2, or under NHSA 1977 Sch 8 para 3). If it consists of the service-user leaving his/her home for a short period then it may be provided by the NHS under the 1977 Act (see para 6.101) or by social services under NAA 1948 s21 (see Chapter 4).[37] The care may be by way of a recuperative holiday, in which case it will most probably be a service under NHSA 1977 Sch 8 para 2.[38]

Night-sitter service A night-sitter is a person who provides 'practical assistance in the home' or is a 'home help' and thus provision of a service under CSDPA 1970 s2 and/or under NHSA 1977 Sch 8 para 3. The service is also specifically referred to as one which can be provided under para 2 of the same Schedule.[39]

The Carers and Disabled Children Act 2000

7.37   It is anticipated that the CDCA 2000 will not come into force until April 2001 at the earliest. When in force the Act will provide as detailed below.

7.38   **Section 1 : Right of carers to assessment** Section 1 provides for 'free-standing carers assessments, that is, a carer can be assessed even if

---

37   For periods of up to eight weeks the authority has the power to waive charges for this service: NAA 1948 s22(5A).

38   As empowered by LAC(93)10 Appendix 3 para 3(3)(e); but it could be considered as a service under Chronically Sick and Disabled Persons Act 1970 s2(1)(f).

39   NHS Act 1977 Sch 8 para 3(3)(d).

the person for whom s/he cares refuses a community care assessment.[40] The requirements are that the carer is over 15 years of age, is caring for someone aged 18 or over and the carer requests an assessment. The assessment enables the local authority to decide whether to provide services to the carer under s2.

7.39 **Section 2: Services for carers** Section 2 enables the local authority to provide services to carers following a carer's assessment. Potentially, there is little restriction upon the services that can be made available, provided the service helps 'the carer care for the person cared for'. The explanatory notes to the bill indicated that these services may take the form of physical help, for example, assistance around the house, or other forms of support such as training or counselling for the carer. Guidance and regulations will detail the limits of these services. Section 2 makes provision for services to be delivered to a carer, notwithstanding that they could be delivered to the person cared for by way of community care services. This can only arise if both the carer and the person cared for agree and, in any event, may not include anything of an 'intimate nature' (which phrase will be defined in regulations and is likely to include such services as dressing, feeding, lifting, washing and bathing).

7.40 **Section 3: Vouchers** Section 3 makes provision for regulations to be issued which will enable local authorities to issue vouchers for short-term breaks (either at home or in residential accommodation).

7.41 **Section 4: Assessments and services for carer and disabled child** Section 4 is a complex and inelegant provision. Essentially, it enables the local authority (where it has identified a need for services that could either be provided to the carer as a carer's service under s2 or to the person cared for as a community care service) to make a determination whether the service is the carer's service or the user's. The government asserts that such a determination is necessary in order to clarify who can complain about a service failure, and whose means can be assessed for charging purposes.

7.42 **Section 5: Direct payments** Section 5 amends Community Care (Direct Payments) Act 1996 s1 enabling local authorities to make direct payments to carers in lieu of the services which they have been assessed as needing under s2.

40 The government's view being that such a provision is necessary to overcome the problem of a disabled person refusing an assessment under NHSCCA 1990 s47, and thereby denying the carer an assessment under the 1995 Act. This view appears flawed for the reasons detailed in paras 3.40–41 above.

7.43   **Section 6: Parent carer assessments**   Section 6 provides that a person with parental responsibility for a disabled child has the right to a carers assessment under s1 and that the local authority must take that assessment into account when deciding what services to provide under CA 1989 s17.

7.44   **Section 7: Vouchers/direct payments and disabled children**   Section 7 amends CA 1989 s17 by inserting new ss17A and 17B. The new s17A provides for regulations to be issued which will enable a local authority to make direct payments to the parents of disabled children (or the child him/herself if aged 16 or 17) in lieu of services under s17. The new s17B provides for regulations to be issued which will enable local authorities to issue vouchers for respite care in much the same way as in relation to disabled adults under s3 above.

7.45   **Section 8: Charging**   Section 8 enables local authorities to charge carers for the services they receive and HASSASSA 1983 s17 is amended accordingly.

Time off work to care for dependants

7.46   Employment Relations Act 1999 s8 and Sch 4 Pt II inserted a new section (s57A) into the Employment Relations Act 1996, subsection (1) of which provides:

> An employee is entitled to be permitted by his employer to take a reasonable amount of time off during the employee's working hours in order to take action which is necessary –
>
> (a) to provide assistance on an occasion when a dependant falls ill, gives birth or is injured or assaulted
> (b) to make arrangements for the provision of care for a dependant who is ill or injured,
> (c) in consequence of the death of a dependant,
> (d) because of the unexpected disruption or termination of arrangements for the care of a dependant, or
> (e) to deal with an incident which involves a child of the employee and which occurs unexpectedly in a period during which an educational establishment which the child attends is responsible for him.

'Dependant' is defined widely in relation to persons who live in the same household (s57A(3)) and there is a general obligation upon carers who take such time off work to tell the employer the reason for the absence as soon as practicable and how long the absence is likely to last (s57A(2)). It will be noted that the event which requires the carer to take time off need not be 'unexpected' in relation to the situations detailed in subsections (a)–(c). Any time off work claimed as a result of this statutory provision is taken as 'unpaid' leave.

Parent carers

7.47   In this context 'parent carer' means an adult who cares for an ill[44] or disabled child (within the meaning of CA 1989 s17(11) – see para 11.3). Such parent carers are themselves entitled to an assessment under CRSA 1995 s1(2),[45] and in any event to be considered under DP(SCR)A 1986 s1(2). The services available to disabled children are dealt with in Chapter 11. As it is self-evident that most parent carers provide a 'substantial amount of care on a regular basis' in general, therefore all parent carers will be entitled to a carer's assessment under the 1995 Act.

Young carers

7.48   The Carers (Recognition and Services) Act 1995 applies to all carers irrespective of their age. Carers who are under the age of 18 are generally referred to as 'young carers'. They are eligible, in addition to the benefits detailed above, to services in their own right.

7.49   There is no legislation which specifically refers to young carers. Recent guidance concerning young carers has, however, been issued by the Social Services Inspectorate.[46] The guidance adopts a definition of a 'young carer' as 'a child or young person who is carrying out significant caring tasks and assuming a level of responsibility for another person, which would usually be taken by an adult'. Such duties as are owed to young carers by a social services authority are primarily contained in CA 1989 and in the guidance issued by the Department of Health.[47]

7.50   CA 1989 s17(1) places a general duty on social services authorities to safeguard and promote the welfare of children within their area who are 'in need', and empowers authorities to provide almost un-

---

44   Ie, entitled to care services under NHSA 1977 Sch 8 paras 2 and 3.

45   Section 1(2) was inserted to deal with the question of parent carers; s1(1) is only activated where an assessment under NHSCCA 1990 s47(1) is carried out and such assessments are generally limited to persons over 18; this is not however always the case, eg, if the assessment concerns a child entitled to services under NHSA 1977 Sch 8 para 3 (which is a community care service under s46 of the 1990 Act).

46   Guidance letter 28 April 1995; CI(95)12.

47   Two volumes of guidance have been issued under the Children Act 1989 of relevance to young carers – Volume 2: *Family Support* and Volume 6: *Children with Disabilities* (both HMSO, 1991).

limited services towards this goal. The definition of a 'child in need' is therefore of key importance. Under CA 1989 s17(10) a child is 'in need' if:

> (a) he is unlikely to achieve or maintain, or to have the opportunity of achieving or maintaining, a reasonable standard of health or development without the provision for him of services by a local authority . . . ; or
>
> (b) his health or development is likely to be significantly impaired, or further impaired, without the provision for him of such services; or
>
> (c) he is disabled.

7.51   In relation to young carers, since they are not usually 'disabled children', it is necessary to establish that the child comes within category (a) or (b). Because of the prevalent resource shortages within social services authorities, the criteria for obtaining services or funding under s17 have become increasingly severe. In a number of authorities, the position was reached that they were only considering a non-disabled child to be in need if his or her name was on the child protection register. Such a high threshold for accessing services effectively ruled young carers out; the fear of social services' child protection powers was a major reason why many young carers and their families avoid making contact with such authorities.[48]

7.52   In order to improve the help available to young carers it was necessary for such restrictive definitions of 'in need' to be removed. The way this has been achieved is by the SSI issuing specific guidance[49] on young carers in April 1995. The guidance (among other things) refers to research which it states:

> . . . has demonstrated that many young people carry out a level of caring responsibilities which prevents them from enjoying normal social opportunities and from achieving full school attendance. Many young carers with significant caring responsibilities should therefore be seen as children in need.[50]

7.53   The key issue therefore is whether the young carer's caring responsibilities are 'significant'. In this respect the Practice Guidance points out (at para 15.2) that young carers should not be expected to carry out 'inappropriate' levels of caring (that is, inappropriate to their age, sex, culture, etc).

48   See, eg, Practice Guidance para 17.
49   Guidance letter CI(95)12 Annex A para 1.1.
50   See also para 2.4 of Volume 2 Guidance (see n47 above) which emphasises that 'the definition of "need" in the Act is deliberately wide to reinforce the emphasis on preventive support and services to families'.

7.54   If the young carer's caring responsibilities are significant, then s/he will be eligible for an assessment and possibly services under CA 1989. S/he will, in addition, almost certainly also be entitled to a carer's assessment (if the care provided is 'regular and substantial'). Obviously in such cases only one combined assessment will be carried out, although there will inevitably be policy and practice differences as to whether it is a children's team or adult care social worker who actually does the assessment.

7.55   CA 1989 assessment procedures and service provision arrangements for young carers are the same as for any other child in need, and are therefore considered generally in Chapter 11. Section 17(1)(b) emphasises that a principal purpose for the provision of services to children in need is to promote the upbringing of such children by their families. A fear often expressed by young carers and their disabled parents is that of child protection proceedings being initiated by social services were they to appreciate the extent of the child's caring responsibilities.[51]

7.56   A local authority can of course provide services for a sibling carer even if that child is not considered to be a 'child in need'. Section 17(3) specifically provides that social services may provide services to (inter alia) such a child 'if it is provided with a view to safeguarding and promoting the welfare' of the disabled child.

Advocates

7.57   Statutory references to advocates are even rarer than those to carers[52] although much of the guidance presupposes their existence – especially in the assessment process if the service user has communication difficulties and in the complaints process (see below). The local community care charters consultation document makes specific reference to an 'entitlement' to have an advocate involved in the assess-

---

51 See, eg, *Community Care* No 1020 p14, 'Lost Childhood'; 'There is a conspiracy of silence around young carers. This silence is often the result of fear, fear of separation from their families either by the institutionalisation of the care recipient or by the instigation of care proceedings'. Volume 2 Guidance para 2.15 (see n47 above) states: 'The Act gives a positive emphasis to identifying and providing for the children's needs rather than focusing on parental shortcomings in a negative manner'.

52 DP(SCR)A 1986 ss1–2, which was to put advocates ('authorised representatives') on a statutory footing, has not been implemented by the government because of 'its resource and administrative implications'.

ment process. The Practice Guidance[53] also stresses the importance
of advocates 'taking a full part in decision-making'.

7.58   The role of the advocate in the assessment process is considered at
paras 3.24 and 3.37 above. Further and more detailed comment on
the role of advocates is contained in Department of Health's *Care
Management and Assessment – Managers' Guide*.[54]

7.59   At para 2.43 the guide states that one of the major objectives of the
community care reforms was 'to give users and carers a more powerful voice in expressing needs and influencing the services they
receive'. In addition to ensuring that users are given every assistance
to represent their own interests (the use of interpreters, communicators and the development of self-advocacy/self-help support groups
is encouraged), the guidance continues:

> 2.44 However there remain the users who, because of their disability
> are unable to express their own views and/or who wish or need to
> have independent representatives to act on their behalf. This will
> include those suffering from dementia or severe learning disability.
> These users will be disadvantaged if the authority/agency confines
> itself to the promotion of self-advocacy.

> 2.45 Independent advocacy is being developed in a number of ways
> by
> • setting up local authority schemes to provide advocacy support that
> is separate from the assessing and service providing sectors of the
> authority
> • funding an existing voluntary organisation to expand its activities
> • establishing or grant-aiding a new agency responsible for providing
> independent advocacy.

> *Local Authority schemes*
> 2.46 The advantage of an internal scheme is that the local authority
> can target its advocacy support according to its own priority criteria
> and can validate those staff acting as advocates. However, local
> authorities will need to consider how best to assure users and carers
> of the independence of such schemes. The existence of users' rights
> officers or consumer relations officers within social services/work
> authorities can help to create a culture that is more sensitive to users'
> and carers' concerns. Either as an alternative or in addition, local
> authorities may recruit and train volunteers to give advice and
> support on request.

---

53 Para 38.
54 HMSO, 1991.

Existing voluntary organisations

2.49 Because advocacy will have to compete for funding with other departmental priorities, it is recognised that local authorities will wish to target their resources on those users with a priority need for such a service, for example:

- users unable to express their own views who have no acceptable friend or relative to act on their behalf,
- users who are in dispute with the agency,
- users who have been previously disadvantaged, for example, minority ethnic users or disabled people.

2.50 Especially for those users who are unable to request such assistance, there should be agreed criteria for triggering the involvement of advocacy support.

2.51 Independent agencies wishing to offer a universal service will have to raise funding from other sources or by charging.

2.52 Advocacy schemes should be characterised by their informality, flexibility and proven effectiveness in highlighting the needs, concerns and wishes of users and carers. To that end, local authorities will need to satisfy themselves about the quality of advocacy schemes and the suitability of any individuals who are acting as advocates . . .

4.89 A few authorities have experimented with partnership agreements with voluntary, not-for-profit bodies to perform an independent care management function. In the interests of empowering users and their carers to make choices, local authorities should welcome and promote the development of advocacy services in the independent sector, although any public funding may be confined to target groups.

Crisis advocacy

7.60 Advocates (often referred to as crisis advocates) are specifically referred to as being desirable in relation to challenged hospital discharges (see LAC(95)17 para 14 and para 6.129 above) and in relation to the social services complaints process (see *The Right to Complain* (1991) paras 6.8–6.34, considered at para 12.7 below). Their relationship with the disabled person is generally short term and limited to assistance in resolving a specific issue.

Citizen advocacy

7.61　Citizen advocacy involves the advocate developing a longer term relationship with the disabled person.[55] It is a form of advocacy where 'an ordinary citizen develops a relationship with another person who risks social exclusion or other unfair treatment because of a handicap. As the relationship develops, the advocate chooses ways to understand, respond to and represent the other person's interests as if they were the advocate's own'.[56]

7.62　The Law Commission, in its 1995 Report, stressed that as a matter of law, citizen advocates were not 'substitute decision-makers' and indeed that with their assistance many disabled people might never need a substitute decision-maker. It continued:

> There is thus no conflict between the advocacy movement and the need for substantive law reform. They address different issues. The advocacy movement cannot deal with the legal difficulty which arises when a legally effective decision is needed and the person concerned does not have the capacity to make that decision. An advocate might sometimes be the best person to gain the legal status which would enable him or her to take the substitute decision, but he or she would then have the choice of two distinct hats to wear as and when the need should arise.[57]

Decision making and mental capacity

7.63　The present state of our domestic law concerning the decision-making powers of third parties on behalf of people who lack the necessary mental capacity, is highly confused and inadequate. Substantial proposals for reform have been made and these are considered at para 7.86 below.

7.64　All adults are presumed to be capable of handling their own affairs unless the contrary is shown. The fact that (for instance) a person has been detained under MHA 1983 does not affect this presumption; in the absence of proof to the contrary, he or she will be assumed to retain their capacity to make informed decisions. Where an adult is incapable or considered 'vulnerable', then a variety of legal provisions can apply.

55　For an excellent account see A Dunning *Citizen Advocacy with Older People: a Code of Good Practice* (CPA, 1995).

56　See B Sang and J O'Brien *Advocacy: the United Kingdom and American experiences* (1984) p27, King's Fund Project paper No 51.

57　*Mental Incapacity* Law Commission Report No 231 (February 1995) para 2.44.

7.65   MHA 1983 is not primarily concerned with the needs of vulnerable adults. The central provision of the 1983 Act concerns the admission to hospital of any person suffering from a specified mental disorder 'of a nature or degree which makes it appropriate for him to receive medical treatment in a hospital' (s3(2)(a)). The Act is also concerned with the provision of treatment; s63 (subject to ss57 and 58) provides that 'the consent of a patient shall not be required for any medical treatment given to him for the mental disorder from which he is suffering'.

Capacity

7.66   The law is concerned with the ability of a person to perform a specific legal act, such as making a will; marrying; giving property away; or being able to manage his/her affairs. Whether or not a person does have mental capacity is a legal, not a medical question. Capacity will vary depending on the nature of the act that is to be undertaken. Frequently, the courts will place a great deal of weight on the evidence of a doctor, but ultimately it is a legal decision. A person may have mental capacity at law to conduct a simple transaction (for instance handle his/her social security monies) but not sufficient capacity for a complex matter, such as conducting medical negligence litigation. As noted above, it is presumed that a person is capable until the contrary is proved and then it is presumed that the person is mentally incapable until the contrary is proved. The standard of proof is 'the balance of probabilities'.

7.67   If a decision has to be made on behalf of a person who lacks mental capacity and that decision relates to the person's 'property' or 'affairs', then legal mechanisms such as enduring powers of attorney or the Court of Protection are available. Unfortunately these words 'property' or 'affairs' have been given a restrictive interpretation and in effect are limited to issues concerning 'business matters, legal transactions and other dealings of a similar kind'.[58]

7.68   Where the matter does not concern 'property or affairs' (for instance a decision has to be made where the person lives, or whether contact should be allowed with a third party), then in relation to persons over 18, the law is significantly deficient. Frequently all that can be done (legally) is to invoke the inherent jurisdiction of the High Court (considered below).

---

58 *Re F (mental patient: sterilisation)* [1990] 2 AC 1.

Court of Protection

7.69   The Court of Protection is an Office of the Supreme Court and is now governed by MHA 1983 Pt VII. The court has wide powers to 'do or secure the doing of all such things as appear necessary or expedient' concerning persons who lack mental capacity. The court can however only take action in relation to a person's property and affairs, and only after it has been satisfied (after considering medical evidence) of the necessary mental incapacity. The court can in particular take action:

1) for the maintenance or other benefit of the patient;
2) for the maintenance or other benefit of the patient's family;
3) for making provision for other persons or purposes for whom or which the patient might be expected to provide if he were not mentally disordered; or
4) otherwise, for administering the patient's affairs (s95).

Generally the court will do this by appointing a 'receiver' although in certain situations, this is not necessary, for instance when the patient's only assets consist of:

1) social security benefits;
2) a pension or similar payment from a government department or local authority;
3) entitlement under a discretionary trust;
4) property which does not exceed £5,000 in value (in such cases 'short Order' can be made avoiding the necessity of a receiver).

Where a receivership order has been made, the incapacitated person is generally referred to as a 'patient' of the Court of Protection. A separate administrative agency exists to manage the affairs of many patients, know as the Public Trust Office, whose address is the same as for the court, namely Stewart House, 24 Kingsway, London, WC2B 6JX, tel 020 7269 7300.

Powers of attorney

General powers

7.70   An individual has always had the power to appoint somebody else to act as his/her agent in regard to his/her financial affairs. The power may be in general terms or limited to specific acts. The power is presently contained in the Powers of Attorney Act 1971.

7.71   A power of attorney may be general in terms (allowing the attorney to do anything that the 'donor' could do) or it may be limited to a specific act (for instance, signing a contract for the sale of land).

7.72   The problem with ordinary powers of attorney is that the donor must be mentally capable when s/he gives the power and the authority of the attorney ceases immediately the donor ceases to have mental capacity. As noted above, powers of attorney can only be used to determine questions concerning a person's 'property and financial affairs'.

Enduring powers

7.73   The Enduring Powers of Attorney Act 1985 enables attorneys to be appointed whose powers would continue even after the donor had become mentally incapable of managing his/her affairs.

7.74   The procedure for creating such powers is straightforward. A pre-printed form is completed and signed by the donor and each attorney (their signatures are witnessed). The power can come into force immediately or only after the donor has lost his/her capacity.

7.75   The attorney is under a duty to apply to the Public Trust Office as soon as s/he has reason to believe that the donor is (or is becoming) mentally incapable. Before applying, the attorney must give notice of his/her intention to apply for registration of the enduring power, to the donor, the donor's relatives and any 'co-attorney'. At least three relatives must receive the notice (and the Act states the priority of relative). People served with these notices have the power to object to registration. Failing an objection, the registration takes effect (within about five weeks).

7.76   As noted above, enduring powers of attorney do not however enable the attorney to make long-term arrangements about health care matters or where the person should live or with whom s/he should have contact, etc.

Social security appointees

7.77   Social Security (Claims and Payments) Regulations 1987 SI No 1968 reg 33 allows for an appointee to be appointed where the claimant is 'unable for the time being to act'. Guidance suggests that a person is unable to act if they 'do not have the mental ability to understand and control their own affairs, for example because of senility or mental illness'. Appointees do not apply to people who are hospital in-patients.[59] The Benefits Agency is the responsible authority for the appointment, supervision and revocation of appointeeships. The

59 Social Security (Hospital In-patients) Regulations 1975 SI No 555 reg 16(2).

appointee is personally responsible for ensuring that the social security monies are applied in the patient's interests.[60]

7.78   In relation to home proprietors acting as appointees, the Age Concern publication *Residents' Money* (1996) states that 'although the home proprietor may be prepared to manage an individual's financial affairs, large groups of homes may have a specific Finance Department, it should be remembered that no available guidance recommends this. It should therefore be considered only as a last resort, and all the parties involved must ensure that the appropriate safeguards are observed'.

7.79   Where the home proprietor is a local authority, it often acts as the appointee or receiver for those living in its home.

Guardianship

7.80   MHA 1983 s7 provides for the making of a guardianship order in relation to mentally disordered people where 'it is necessary in the interests of the welfare of the patient or for the protection of other persons that' such an order be made. Guardianship orders can there- fore be made in relation to persons who do not lack mental capacity.

7.81   Under MHA 1983 s8 the guardian (usually the social services department, or rarely, a family member, has three limited powers, namely:

1) the power to require the patient to reside at a place specified;
2) the power to require the patient to attend at places for medical treatment, occupation, education or training; and
3) the power to require access to the patient to be given.

The court's inherent jurisdiction

7.82   The High Court has power (both inherent and statutory) to make a declaration as to whether an Act is lawful or not. The Law Commis- sion, when reviewing this power commented as follows:[61]

> . . . a declaration by the High Court does not answer the question 'who decides?' Nor does it answer the question 'what will be best?' It has been said that 'the essence of the jurisdiction is that the Court is

---

60   See CIS/12022/96 which concerned an appointee's failure to notify the DSS about an increase in the disabled person's savings; the consequent over- payment was held to be recoverable from the appointee in addition to the claimant.

61   'Mental Incapacity' (1995 No. 231).

like a camera photographing the relevant legal terrain. It registers what exists, and declares what it finds.'

7.83   In spite of the fact that the declaration cannot change anything, the court has expressed the view that certain serious procedures should always be referred to it for a declaration in advance (ie, sterilisation/withdrawal of artificial feeding). It has also expressed a willingness to respond to new and difficult dilemmas, such as those that may arise when a patient who has lost capacity appears to have refused consent to a particular procedure being performed.

7.84   The declaration procedure is used in cases concerning the cessation of artificial sustenance for a patient in persistent vegetative state[62] and to clarify the effect of purported refusals of treatment.[63] In *Re C (mental patient: contact)*,[64] it was invoked to determine a dispute concerning whether a disabled adult who lacked capacity should have contact with her mother. Although that case never came to a full hearing, Eastham J accepted that there was jurisdiction in the High Court to make a declaration about such a matter. In *Re S*,[65] declarations were sought as to whether a stroke victim should remain within the jurisdiction to receive treatment and care at his home in England.

7.85   In *R v Portsmouth Hospitals NHS Trust ex p Glass*,[66] the Court of Appeal indicated that in general where there was a dispute between the parties as to the 'best interests' of a mentally incapacitated person, application for a declaration in the Family Division was the appropriate course (as opposed to judicial review) but that the court would normally decline to make declarations concerning the legality of future, hypothetical events.

Proposals for reform

7.86   In 1995 the Law Commission, in its Report *Mental Incapacity*,[67] recommended a wholesale reform of the law as it applies to mentally incapacitated adults. The proposals covered a number of areas including the law concerning adult abuse and decision making. In 1997 the government invited comments on law reform in its consultation

---

62   *Airedale NHS Trust v Bland* [1993] AC 789.

63   *Re C (Adult: refusal of treatment)* [1994] 1 WLR 290.

64   [1993] 1 FLR 940.

65   [1995] 3 All ER 290.

66   (1999) 2 FLR 905; (1999) 50 BMLR 269.

67   February 1995 No 231.

paper *Who Decides?*[68] and in 1999 it published its conclusions as *Making Decisions.*[69] The proposed legislation is limited to reform of the decision-making powers available to third parties, be they carers, attorneys or the court.

Decision-making powers

7.87   The proposed legislation will clearly define incapacity, namely 'where a person is unable by reason of mental disability to make a decision on the matter in question; or unable to communicate a decision on that matter because he or she is unconscious or for any other reason' (para 1.6). Allied to this will be a basic requirement of 'best interests', namely that decisions taken by others on behalf of people without capacity must be made in their best interests (and the proposals set out six principles by which 'best interests' are to be assessed (para 1.11). Subject to these criteria carers will have general authority to make decisions on behalf of a person lacking capacity provided they are reasonable and the issue in question does not concern a certain prohibited issue (paras 1.14 onwards).

7.88   The law reform proposals include changes to enduring powers of attorney. These will be renamed 'continuing powers of attorney' and the powers of an attorney acting under such authority will be capable of covering welfare and health care issues. Where such an attorney has not been appointed, the court will have jurisdiction as at present, and it will be able to appoint a 'manager' to make decisions on behalf of the incapacitated person (including decisions concerning welfare and health care matters) although generally the court will ensure that the appointment limits the scope and duration of the managers powers so far as is possible (paras 3.5 onwards).

Adult abuse

7.89   The government has proposed no legislation to deal with the present imperfect state of the law as it applies to the protection of vulnerable adults from abuse.[70] The Law Commission in its 1995 paper recommended that social services departments be given limited powers to

---

68   Lord Chancellor's Department Cm 3803, December 1997.
69   Lord Chancellor's Department Cm 4465, October 1999.
70   The government has, however, issued inter-agency guidance as LAC(2000)7 *No Secrets: Guidance on developing and implementing multi-agency policies and procedure to protect vulnerable adults from abuse*. Although this guidance is issued under LASSA 1970 s7 (see para 1.25 above) it proposes no new legal measures to protect vulnerable adults.

intervene where they considered a vulnerable adult was suffering harm or exploitation. These powers were similar to those under CA 1989 in relation to emergency protection and assessment, but were to be strictly limited.

7.90 In the absence of a change in the law, there is only limited action that can be taken where it is believed that a vulnerable adult is suffering harm or exploitation. If sufficient evidence exists of a criminal offence having been committed the police may intervene and investigate. Powers also exist under MHA 1983 enabling a magistrate to issue a warrant to authorise access by a police officer to premises where it is believed that a person suffering from a mental disorder is being ill-treated or neglected (s135): such a warrant may also include a power of removal. Under s127 of the 1983 Act it is also an offence for anyone to (among other things) ill-treat or wilfully neglect a mentally disordered person who is in their custody or care. Local authorities also have limited powers under NAA 1948 s47 to remove vulnerable people who are not receiving proper care (see para 4.72 above).

7.91 It remains to be seen whether domestic law complies with article 3 of the European Convention on Human Rights. Article 3 places an obligation on the state to ensure that no one suffers inhuman or degrading treatment. The European Court of Human Rights has held that the obligation under article 3 requires minimum safeguards to be present in domestic law, and arguably this is not the case within England and Wales.[71]

---

71 In this respect see *A v United Kingdom* (1998) 27 EHRR 611; *X & Y v Netherlands* 8 EHRR 235 and the report of the European Commission of Human Rights in *Z v UK*, 10 September 1999.

CHAPTER 8

Charges for community care services

8.1   Introduction

8.2   Accommodation charges

8.4   Accommodation provided under NAA 1948 Pt III

8.9   The assessment of charges

Personal expenses allowance • The treatment of income • The treatment of capital • The treatment of residential property

8.27   Income support residential allowance

Example

8.29   Deprivation of capital

Timing of the disposal • Diminishing notional capital rule • Local authority responses to deliberate deprivations • Enforcement powers

8.51   Residents in local authority homes before April 1993

8.56   Less dependent residents

8.60   Temporary residents

8.63   Liable relatives

Seeking payments from liable relatives • Liable relative payments

8.66   Challenging charges

8.67   Charges for non-accommodation services

8.70   Guidance

The Good Practice Handbook

8.73   The discretion to charge

8.78   Local charging schemes: the duty to consult

8.80   The amount that can be charged

continued

8.83   Assessment of ability to pay

*Charging and income support • Charging and disability living
allowance/attendance allowance • Assessment of the 'user's' income*

8.99   Challenging the assessed charge

8.104   The consequences of non-payment

8.107   Services not directly provided by the social services authority

8.108   Charging for MHA 1983 and CSDPA 1970 services

Services under MHA 1983 • CSDPA 1970 s2

Introduction

8.1 Social services authorities are under a general duty to charge individuals for whom they provide residential care or nursing home accommodation. There is no equivalent obligation to charge for non-accommodation community care services; instead, such authorities have (in general) a discretion to charge for such services. Since the two charging systems are quite different they are dealt with separately below.

Accommodation charges

8.2 As will be clear from flow diagram 8, social services authorities are able to provide residential accommodation under various statutory provisions. The vast majority of residents are accommodated by social services under National Assistance Act (NAA) 1948 Pt III although their statutory authority for accommodating residents under 18 derives primarily from the Children Act (CA) 1989. In certain situations, however, where the resident was formerly a detained patient under the Mental Health Act (MHA) 1983, the accommodation is provided under s117 of that Act.

8.3 The charging rules relating to accommodation provided under NAA 1948 Pt III are considered below. The charging rules under the Children Act 1989 are considered at para 11.26 below, and those relating to accommodation provided under MHA 1983 s117 at para 8.109 below.

Accommodation provided under NAA 1948 Pt III

8.4 Local authorities are under a duty to charge for residential accommodation which they provide under NAA 1948 Pt III (except temporary accommodation[1]).

8.5 Section 22(1) places a general obligation on social services authorities to charge for residential accommodation. It refers to s26, which (as will be seen below) deals with the charging situation where the authority has provided residential accommodation in an independent home.

---

1 Local authorities are not obliged to charge for temporary periods of accommodation of less than eight weeks, NAA 1948 s22(5A).

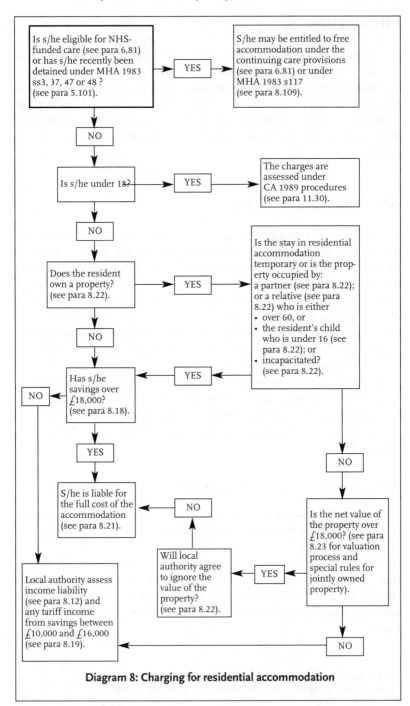

Is s/he eligible for NHS-funded care (see para 6.81) or has s/he recently been detained under MHA 1983 ss3, 37, 47 or 48 ? (see para 5.101).

→ YES → **S/he may be entitled to free accommodation under the continuing care provisions (see para 6.81) or under MHA 1983 s117 (see para 8.109).**

NO ↓

Is s/he under 18? → YES → **The charges are assessed under CA 1989 procedures (see para 11.30).**

NO ↓

Does the resident own a property? (see para 8.22). → YES → **Is the stay in residential accommodation temporary or is the property occupied by: a partner (see para 8.22); or a relative (see para 8.22) who is either
• over 60, or
• the resident's child who is under 16 (see para 8.22); or
• incapacitated? (see para 8.22).**

NO ↓

Has s/he savings over £18,000? (see para 8.18). ← YES ← [from above box]

NO → [to Local authority assess box]

YES ↓

S/he is liable for the full cost of the accommodation (see para 8.21). ← NO ← **Will local authority agree to ignore the value of the property? (see para 8.22).** ← YES ← **Is the net value of the property over £18,000? (see para 8.23 for valuation process and special rules for jointly owned property).**

[right box] NO ↓

Local authority assess income liability (see para 8.12) and any tariff income from savings between £10,000 and £16,000 (see para 8.19). ← NO ← [from net value box]

Diagram 8: Charging for residential accommodation

8.6   Section 22(2) stipulates that the maximum charge for such accommodation shall be fixed by the local authority but that this must be the full cost to the authority of providing that accommodation. From October 2001, it is intended that the charge in a nursing home will not include any of the costs for the registered nurses involved in the person's care.[2]

8.7   Section 22(3) requires that the charging provisions be means tested, and s22(4) directs that every resident must be allowed to retain (or receive) a minimum weekly personal allowance. The amount is laid down each year in the National Assistance (Sums For Personal Expenses) Regulations and is the same for each resident whether in a social services authority-run home or an independent-sector home (the personal allowance for April 2000 to March 2001 is £15.45 per week).[3] Section 22(4) additionally gives authorities a discretion to vary the allowance in certain situations. This provision enables authorities to reduce the severity of the otherwise rigid means testing laid down in the regulations (its relevance is considered below, under the heading 'discretion').

8.8   Most importantly, however, s22(5) stipulates that the way the means-tested charging system operates is to be specified in separate regulations made by the Secretary of State. The principal regulations in this respect are the National Assistance (Assessment of Resources) Regulations 1992 SI No 2977, although they are the subject of annual amendments. The assessment of resources under these regulations are similar in many respects to the resource assessments required by the Income Support (General) Regulations 1987 SI No 1967 for the income support claimants. Detailed guidance has been issued by the Department of Health on the interpretation of the Assessment of Resources Regulations (subsequently referred to in this section as 'the Regulations'). The guidance, known as CRAG (*Charging for Residential Accommodation Guide*) is available free of charge from the Department of Health, PO Box 777, London SE1 6XH; Fax: 01623 724524; e-mail: doh@prologistics. Annual amendments (by updating circulars) are generally issued in March/April of each year and can be checked by viewing the COIN web-site (see para 1.22 above). In March 1999 the entire CRAG guidance was re-issued as circular

2   Although 'people who can afford to do so will still have to make a contribution towards their personal care and accommodation costs while in a nursing home'; *The NHS Plan: The Government's Response to the Royal Commission on Long-term Care* para 2.10, Cm 4818-II July 2000.

3   National Assistance (Sums for Personal Requirements) Regulations 1996 SI No 391.

LAC(99)9. References in the following section to paragraph numbers are to paragraphs in CRAG unless otherwise stated. The details given below are those applying as at March 2000, incorporating the amendments in LAC(2000)11. The CRAG guidance specifically states that it is 'policy guidance' for the purposes of Local Authority Social Services Act (LASSA) 1970 s7(1). It is therefore guidance which local authorities must follow in all but the most exceptional of circumstances.[4]

The assessment of charges

8.9   Where a resident is unable to pay either the standard rate residential home charges or the actual cost incurred by the local authority (either for a local authority or independent home),[5] the authority is obliged to assess that person's ability to pay by reference to the Regulations and to CRAG. If, having carried out such an assessment, the authority is satisfied that the resident is unable to pay the standard rate (or in the case of an independent home, make a full refund of the fees), the authority must decide on the basis of the assessment what the person's contribution should be. If the resident refuses to co-operate with the financial assessment, then the authority will charge that person the full standard rate.

8.10   CRAG obliges authorities to ensure that residents are given a clear explanation (usually in writing) of how their assessed contribution has been calculated and why this figure may fluctuate, particularly where a new resident's charge may vary in the first few weeks of admission because, for instance, of the effect of benefit pay-days on income support or the withdrawal of attendance allowance (para 1.015).

8.11   Usually, residents will pay their assessed charge direct to the local authority. However, NAA 1948 s26(3A) provides for an exception to this rule for residents placed by local authorities in independent-sector homes: where the resident, the authority and the organisation or person managing the home all agree, the resident may pay the assessed charge direct to the home with the authority paying the remainder. The advantage of such an arrangement is not only administrative convenience; it also may enable the resident to have a clearer

---

4   See para 1.25 above for consideration of 'policy guidance'.
5   The standard rate for local authority homes is the 'full cost' to the authority of providing the accommodation (s22(2)); the standard rate for accommodation in homes not managed by the local authority is the gross cost to the authority of providing or purchasing the accommodation under contract with the independent-sector home (s26(2)).

contractual relationship with the home owner (rather than having to rely on the authority's contract). Despite such an arrangement, the authority remains liable to the home owner for any arrears, should the resident fail to pay the home as agreed (paras 1.023–1.024).

Personal expenses allowance

8.12   The basis of the charging provisions is that residents are required to pay all of their assessed income (above the personal allowance) towards the charge for the residential accommodation: 'The personal allowance is intended to enable residents to have money to spend as they wish, for example, on stationery, personal toiletries, treats and small presents for friends and relatives' (para 5.001). The amount in general allowed in the assessment for personal expenses is laid down each year in the National Assistance (Sums For Personal Requirements) Regulations (being £15.45 for April 2000–March 2001),[5A] although by virtue of NAA 1948 s22(4) there is power to allow a different amount from that prescribed for personal expenses in special circumstances (see below).

8.13   **Discretion** Under NAA 1948 s22(4) authorities have the power to allow a different amount from that prescribed for personal expenses in special circumstances. CRAG gives various examples[6] where it may be appropriate for an authority to consider allowing a different amount, including:

- where a person in residential accommodation has a dependent child, the authority should consider the needs of the child in setting the personal allowance;
- where a person temporarily in residential accommodation receives income support including an amount for a partner who remains at home;
- where the resident is the main recipient of an couple's overall income, the authority can use its discretion to increase the resident's personal expenses allowance in special circumstances to enable the resident to pass some of that income to the partner remaining at home (see also para 4.003);
- where the resident has a pension or retirement annuity contract etc, 50 per cent of which would be ignored had it been an occupational pension (see below), then the authority can use its discretion to enable a similar outcome.

5A   See SI 2000 No 798.
6   At para 5.005.

The treatment of income

8.14 Part II of the Regulations contains the procedure by which a resident's income (earned and unearned) is calculated; the provisions adopt many of the same rules used in the assessment of income for income support purposes[7] and are the subject of detailed guidance in sections 8 and 9 of CRAG. A major difference between the two assessment regimes is, however, that the income taken into account is that of the resident alone. Under NAA 1948, the authority has no power to assess a couple (whether or not married) according to their joint resources. Each person entering residential care should be assessed according to their individual means (para 4.001).

8.15 If, however, at the conclusion of the assessment process the local authority provide support for a resident in circumstances where it believes that the resources of his or her spouse are such that s/he ought to make a contribution, then the authority can invoke the quite separate 'liable relative' rules under NAA 1948 s42. Section 42 provides that it is the duty of spouses to maintain each other and s43 makes provision for local authorities to recover payments from such liable relatives. The liable relative rules only apply to spouses (ie, married partners) and are considered in greater detail at para 8.63 below.

8.16 **Income taken into account in full** In general, and like the income support assessment rules, income is taken into account in full. This includes, for instance, net earnings,[8] most social security benefits, annuity income, pensions, trust income, etc (paras 8.005–8.020).

Partially disregarded income Some income is partly ignored, for instance £10 of certain war pensions, up to half of occupational pensions (see below) and modest amounts of the income from lodgers/sub-letting (paras 8.031–8.032).

Income fully disregarded Some income is fully disregarded, for instance disability living allowance/attendance allowance for temporary residents, income from the independent living funds (see para 5.144 above) and social fund payments, DLA (mobility component) and mobility supplement.

8.17 **Occupational pensions** Where the resident spouse has an occupational pension and has a spouse who is not living in the same residential home, 50 per cent of the occupational pension should be dis-

---

7   Under the Income Support (General) Regulations 1987 SI No 1967.
8   Subject to a £5 or £15 disregard; see paras 9.018–9.023.

regarded, providing the resident is actually paying such a sum over to the spouse. The disregard only applies to *occupational* pensions; only between married partners and only where the spouse actually pays over at least 50 per cent of the pension. In all other cases the use of the 'discretion' detailed above should be considered (para 8.024A).

The treatment of capital

8.18 Part III of the Regulations deals with the capital entitlement rules. Capital is widely defined and includes all land and buildings (unless disregarded – see para 8.22 below). It also includes savings, shares, bonds and the like. It does not however include the surrender value of an insurance policy or annuity; or the value of any payment made from the social fund, independent living fund, payments 'in kind' from a charity, or student loans.

8.19 Where the capital of a resident is less than £10,000,[9] it is disregarded for the purpose of the means test. For so long as the resident's assessed capital exceeds £16,000 (£18,000 after March 2001[10]), then s/he is not entitled to receive any financial assistance from the local authority in respect of the payment of residential home fees. Capital of between £10,000 and £16,000 (£18,000 after March 2001) is taken into account by attributing a 'tariff income' of £1 per week for each £250 (or part of £250) from £10,000 to £16,000. Thus if a resident has £10,630 capital, £10,000 is disregarded and a tariff income of £3 per week is taken into account as income.

8.20 **Couples** As with income, the authority is only permitted to take into account the capital of the resident. CRAG is explicit on this point, stating:

> The LA has no power to assess a couple according to their joint resources. Each person entering residential care should be assessed according to their individual means, although liability of a married person to maintain their spouse (see below) should be considered in each case (para 4.001).

Where a resident is one of a couple, the resident is liable to pay the standard rate or full contracted fee if the resident has more than £16,000 in his/her own right; or if his/her share of the jointly held

9 While the capital rules broadly parallel those for income support entitlement for a person in permanent residential accommodation, the capital limits for income support differ for temporary stays; in such cases the capital limit is £8,000 with a notional income assumed for savings in excess of £3,000.

10 *The NHS Plan: The Government's Response to the Royal Commission on Long-term Care* para 2.20, Cm 4818-II July 2000.

capital is more than £16,000 (reg 20 and para 6.003). If the capital is in a joint account,[11] then there will be a presumption that it is owned in equal shares, thus if the account is held by the resident and his/her partner, it will be presumed that half of it is owned by the resident (para 6.010).

8.21   The Community Care (Residential Accommodation) Act 1998 makes clear that for the purposes of deciding whether care and attention 'is otherwise available' a local authority must disregard the person's capital up to the sum of £16,000. The guidance accompanying the Act, LAC(98)19,[12] goes on to make a number of important points, including:

1) *Local authorities are under a legal duty to carry out community care assessments regardless of whether the person has (or has not) capital in excess of £16,000.*
   The requirements of a community care assessment are considered at para 3.8 above. The duty to assess is not a 'resource dependent' duty.[13]

2) *If, after an assessment of a person's resources, a local authority determine that they exceed £16,000 this does not exempt the authority from its duty to make arrangements for those people who are themselves unable to make care arrangements and have no one to make care arrangements for them.*
   Thus, where a resident has capital in excess of £16,000, but lacks the ability to make the necessary arrangements, and there is no one available to do this on his/her behalf, then the social services department's duty remains. The guidance (at para 10) explains:

> It is the Department's view that having capital in excess of the upper limit of £16,000 does not *in itself* constitute adequate access to alternative care and attention. Local authorities will wish to consider the position of those who have capital in excess of the upper limit of £16,000 and must satisfy themselves that the individual is able to make their own arrangements, or has others who are willing and able to make arrangements for them, for appropriate care. Where there is a suitable advocate or representative (in most cases a close relative) it is the Department's view that local authorities should provide guidance

---

11 Different rules apply in relation to jointly owned interests in land.
12 LAC(98)19 is expressly stated as being 'policy guidance' for the purposes of LASSA 1970 s7(1) (see para 1.25 above).
13 *R v Bristol CC ex p Penfold* (1998) 1 CCLR 315.

and advice on the availability and appropriate level of services to meet the individual's needs. Where there is no identifiable advocate or representative to act on the individual's behalf it must be the responsibility of the local authority to make arrangements and to contract for the person's care.

It appears, however, that the local authority duty is very limited, when it is satisfied that the resident has more than £16,000 capital and sufficient ability to make the necessary arrangements (or has access to a person with these skills). The basis for this reasoning, being that the duty under NAA 1948 s21 only arises if the care and attention required is 'not otherwise available' and having the ability to pay for one's own accommodation may mean that it is 'otherwise available'.[14] The situation may also apply if the resident's capital is only 'notional' (see para 8.39 below).

3) *Local authorities should ensure that they have in place procedures to ensure that when the net capital of a resident (who is self-funding) reduces to £16,000 that they undertake an assessment and if necessary step in and take over funding arrangements to ensure that the resident is not forced to use capital below £16,000 (other than the notional income from that capital).*

Not infrequently, a self-funding resident will approach a local authority for assistance, having spent almost all of his or her savings on the home fees. Clearly in such cases the local authority may have had a duty to assist with the cost when the savings had fallen to £16,0000. In such a case the resident may have a claim against the local authority for a refund of the lost savings, if that authority had previously assessed his/her need and declined services because the savings were above the £16,000 threshold. It follows that local authorities should, when declining to provide services for this reason, also (as a minimum) state in writing that if the person subsequently enters residential accommodation, s/he should contact the social services authority in whose area they then reside when their savings have diminished to £16,000. Clearly if the resident is already in a home in the local authority's area, the duty will be greater and may require the authority to re-contact the resident when it believes it likely that the savings will have so diminished. It may also be that there is a duty (for the purposes of negligence) on residential and nursing home providers to advise their residents of the charging system.

---

14 See *Steane v Chief Adjudication Officer* (1998) 1 CCLR 538, HL and para 4.6 above where this issue is considered in greater detail.

The treatment of residential property

8.22   In general (after the first 3 months[15]) the capital value of a house is taken into account in full (less 10 per cent for disposal costs – para 6.015); there are however a number of circumstances in which it is disregarded indefinitely. These are:

a) The value of a dwelling normally occupied by a resident as his/her home should be ignored if his/her stay in a residential care or nursing home is temporary and:

   • s/he intends to return to that dwelling, and the dwelling is still available to him/her; or

   • s/he is taking reasonable steps to dispose of the property in order to acquire another more suitable property to return to.

   Only one dwelling can be disregarded in these circumstances.

b) Where the resident no longer occupies a dwelling as his/her home, its value should be disregarded where it is occupied in whole or in part by:

   • the resident's partner or former partner[16] (except where the resident is estranged or divorced from the former partner); or

   • a relative[17] of the resident or member of his/her family (ie, another person for whom the resident is treated as responsible) who:

      i)   is aged 60 or over, or

      ii) is aged under 16 and is a child whom the resident is liable to maintain, or

      iii) is incapacitated.[18]

---

15 From April 2001, the value of a home will be disregarded for the first 3 months of a person's stay in residential accommodation; *The NHS Plan: The Government's Response to the Royal Commission on Long-term Care* para 2.18, Cm 4818-II July 2000.

16 This need not therefore be a 'spouse' and CRAG does not provide any clarification as to how 'partner' should be interpreted.

17 'Relative' is specified as including: parents, parents-in-law, sons, sons-in-law, daughters, daughters-in-law, step-parents, step-sons, step-daughters, brothers, sisters, grandparents, grandchildren, uncles, aunts, nephews, nieces and the spouse or unmarried partner of any except the last five (para 7.004). The relevant point here is that this is an *inclusive* definition rather than an exclusive one.

18 The meaning of 'incapacitated' is not defined by the Regulations, but CRAG suggests that it includes a person receiving (or whose incapacity is sufficient to that required to qualify for) one of the following 'incapacity benefits, namely incapacity benefit, severe disablement allowance, disabled living allowance, attendance allowance, constant attendance allowance, or an analogous benefit'. Again this is an inclusive rather than an exclusive definition (see para 7.005).

c) Where the resident has acquired property which s/he intends eventually to occupy as his/her home, the value should be disregarded for up to 26 weeks from the date the resident first takes steps to take up occupation, or such longer period as is considered reasonable (Regulations Sch 4 para 16).

d) Local authorities have an overall discretion to disregard the capital value of premises, not covered by the above exceptions, in which a third party continues to live.[19] Paragraph 7.007 of CRAG suggests that:

> LAs will have to balance the use of this discretion with the need to ensure that residents with assets are not maintained at public expense. It may be reasonable, for example, to disregard a dwelling's value where it is the sole residence of someone who has given up their home in order to care for the resident, or someone who is an elderly companion of the resident particularly if they have given up their own home.

8.23 **Joint beneficial ownership of property** CRAG and the Regulations[20] deal with the procedure to be adopted in order to value property which is the subject of joint beneficial ownership. The general rule is that where a resident owns property, ie, s/he has the right to receive some of the proceeds of a sale, it is the resident's interest in the property which is to be valued as capital, and not the property itself. The value of this interest is governed by:

a) the resident's ability to re-assign the beneficial interest to somebody else; and

b) there being a market, ie, the interest being such as to attract a willing buyer for the interest.

8.24 CRAG suggests that in most cases there is unlikely to be any legal impediment preventing a joint beneficial interest in a property being re-assigned. But the likelihood of there being a willing buyer will depend on the conditions in which the joint beneficial interest has arisen. It goes on to advise (at paras 7.012 onwards) that where an interest in property is beneficially shared between relatives:

> the value of the resident's interest will be heavily influenced by the possibility of a market amongst his or her fellow beneficiaries. If no

---

19 Regulations Sch 4 para 18.
20 Reg 27(2) and paras 7.012–7.016 of CRAG.

other relative is willing to buy the resident's interest, it is highly unlikely that any 'outsider' would be willing to buy into the property unless the financial advantages far outweighed the risks and limitations involved. The value of the interest, even to a willing buyer, could in such circumstances effectively be nil. If the local authority is unsure about the resident's share, or their valuation is disputed by the resident, again professional valuation should be obtained.

8.25   CRAG provides local authorities with further advice (including the 'example' below) as to what action they should take in such situations (at para 7.014A):

> If the ownership is disputed and a resident's interest is alleged to be less than seems apparent from the initial information, the local authority will need written evidence on any beneficial interest the resident, or other parties possess. Such evidence may include the person's understanding of events, including why and how the property came to be in the resident's name or possession. Where it is contended that the interest in the property is held for someone else, the local authority should require evidence of the arrangement, the origin of the arrangement and the intentions for its future use. The law of equity may operate to resolve doubts about beneficial ownership, by deciding what is reasonable by reference to the original intentions behind a person's action, rather than applying the strict letter of the law.

> **Example**
> The resident has a beneficial interest in a property worth £60,000. He shares the interest with two relatives. After deductions for outstanding mortgage, the residual value is £30,000. One relative would be willing to buy the resident's interest for £5,000. Although the value of the resident's share of the property may be worth £10,000, if the property as a whole had been sold, the value of just his share is £5,000, as this is the sum he could obtain from a willing buyer. The amount to be taken into account as actual capital would be £4,500 because a further 10% would be deducted from the value of his share to cover the cost of transferring the interest to the buyer.

8.26   **Property owned but rented to tenants** CRAG provides[21] that where a resident owns property, the value of which takes the resident's total capital above £16,000, and the property is rented to tenants, the

---

21 At para 7.017, inserted as a result of the amending regulations (National Assistance (Assessment of Resources) (Amendment No 2) Regulations 1995 SI No 3054) which came into force on 20 December 1995.

resident will be assessed as able to pay the standard charge for the accommodation (because of the level of capital). It will then be for the resident to agree to pay the rental income (along with any other income) to the local authority in order to reduce the accruing debt. In such cases, authorities may chose to place a legal charge on the property and wait until the tenant dies before enforcing payment of the accrued debt (plus interest from the date of death) against the estate,[22] but they are not obliged to take this course (see para 8.48 below).

Income support residential allowance

8.27   It is beyond the scope of this book to consider the social security benefit rules relating to residential home placements.[23] However, there are situations whereby potential residents can be significantly better off if they do not seek financial help with their home care fees from the local authority. This is illustrated by the example detailed below. It should however be appreciated that the rates quoted are those current as at April 2000, that the benefit rules change frequently and the rates change annually. It is also likely that the 'residential allowance' will be phased out.[24]

Example

8.28   A 75-year-old disabled person enters a residential home on a permanent basis. Its weekly cost is £235. He has under £10,000 savings and a house (value £125,000) which is up for sale. The disabled person receives attendance allowance and is entitled to income support.

1) If he does not seek financial help from the social services department, he will be entitled to the following benefits:

---

22 See HASSASSAA s22 and s24.
23 Full details of resident's entitlement to such benefits are provided in specialist texts, such as the *Disability Rights Handbook* (Disability Alliance, annual), *Welfare Benefits Handbook* (CPAG, annual).
24 The residential allowance has been criticised as skewing commissioning in favour of independent homes (rather than Pt III accommodation) and favouring placements in residential homes over maintaining people in their own homes and will be abolished from April 2002; *The NHS Plan: The Government's Response to the Royal Commission on Long-term Care* para 2.33, Cm 4818-II July 2000.

Attendance allowance	£53.55
Income support	
Personal allowance	£52.20
Higher pensioner premium	£33.85
Severe disability premium	£40.20
Residential allowance	£61.30[25]
Total benefits received	£241.10

The house value will be ignored while the house is being sold, although once the proceeds of sale are received, entitlement to income support will cease.

2) If he seeks assistance from the social services department, his benefit entitlement will be as follows:

Attendance allowance	NIL	This benefit ceases four weeks after entry into the home. It would not cease if none of the cost of the home was not 'born by the local authority'.
Income support		
Personal allowance	£52.20	
Higher pensioner premium	NIL	This benefit ceases because of the loss of the attendance allowance.[26]
Enhanced pensioner premium	£28.95	Payable for persons aged 75–79.
Severe disability premium	NIL	This benefit ceases because of the loss of the attendance allowance
Residential allowance	£61.30	
Total benefits received	£142.15	

It can be seen that in such cases, while the resident's house is being sold, he will be substantially better off if he does not have any assistance from the local authority in the paying of home fees.

---

25 The residential allowance is £68.20 if the home is within Greater London.
26 The premium would remain if the resident was over 79 years old; the claimant receives in substitution the lesser, 'enhanced pensioner premium'.

Deprivation of capital

8.29 Regulation 25(1) of the Regulations provides that:

A resident may be treated as possessing actual capital of which he has deprived himself for the purpose of decreasing the amount that he may be liable to pay for his accommodation except –

(a) where that capital is derived from a payment made in consequence of any personal injury and is placed on trust for the benefit of the resident; or

(b) to the extent that the capital which he is treated as possessing is reduced in accordance with regulation 26 [the diminishing notional capital rule – see below].

8.30 In seeking to determine whether a deprivation has occurred, LAC(98)8 para 10 advised as follows:

Much information can be verified by reference to recent documentation provided by the client such as bank statements and building society account books. Authorities should also make use of information available to them from other departments within the authority or District Councils to verify client details, for example council tax benefit and housing records. They should also, as appropriate and with the consent of the client, undertake checks with other agencies such as the Benefits Agency, banks and private pension firms. Obviously it is not necessary for all information to be verified, and it is for authorities themselves to determine the extent and circumstances for verifying information.

8.31 CRAG explains[27] that where an authority feels that a resident has deliberately deprived himself or herself of a capital asset in order to reduce the accommodation charge, it may treat the resident as still possessing the asset. CRAG provides further guidance in the following terms:

6.062 There may be more than one purpose for disposing of a capital asset, only one of which is to avoid a charge for accommodation. Avoiding the charge need not be the resident's main motive but it must be a significant one.

6.063 If, for example, a person has used capital to repay a debt, careful consideration should be given to whether there was a need for the debt to be repaid at that time. If it seems unreasonable for the resident to have repaid that debt at that time, it may be that the purpose was to avoid a charge for accommodation.

27 At paras 6.057 onwards.

Examples (CRAG para 6.063)

[1] A person moves into residential accommodation and has a 50% interest in property which continues to be occupied by his spouse. The authority ignores the value of the resident's share in property while the spouse lives there but the spouse decides to move to smaller accommodation and so sells the former home. At the time the property is sold the resident's 50% share of the proceeds could be taken into account in the charging assessment but, in order to enable the spouse to purchase the smaller property, the resident makes part of his share of the proceeds from the sale available to the spouse. In these circumstances, in the Department's view, it would not be reasonable to treat the resident as having deprived himself of capital in order to reduce his residential accommodation charge.

[2] A person has £18,000 in the bank. He is about to move permanently to a residential care home, and before doing so, pays off £3,000 outstanding on a loan for home improvements. In these circumstances, in the Department's view, it would not be reasonable to treat him as having deprived himself of the £3,000 deliberately in order to reduce his residential accommodation charge.

[3] A resident has £12,000 in a building society. Two weeks before entering the home, he bought a car for £10,500 which he gave to his son on entering the home. If the resident knew he was to be admitted permanently to a residential home at the time he bought the car, it would be reasonable to treat this as a deliberate deprivation. However, all the circumstances must be taken into account. If he was admitted as an emergency and had no reason to think he would not be in a position to drive the car at the time he bought it, in the Department's view, it would not be reasonable to treat it as a deliberate deprivation.

8.32　As there have been few reported decisions on the scope of reg 25 of the Regulations, reference is generally made to the larger body of commissioners' decisions concerning the meaning of Income Support (General) Regulations 1987 reg 51, the equivalent 'notional capital' rule for income support purposes.[28] While the deprivation must have been made with the purpose of obtaining increased benefits, this does not have to be the person's predominant purpose, provided it was a 'significant operative purpose'.[29] The authority must establish that the resident actually knew of the capital limit rule[30] (or that given the person's background this can be inferred).

28　Reg 51(1) commences: 'A claimant shall be treated as possessing capital of which he has deprived himself for the purpose of securing entitlement to income support or increasing the amount of that benefit . . .'

29　R(SB)40/85.

30　CIS 124/1990.

Timing of the disposal

8.33 The length of time between the disposal and the application for financial assistance will generally be relevant; the longer the time between the disposal of an asset and a person's liability for accommodation charges, the less likely it is that the obtaining of the financial advantage was a foreseeable consequence of the transaction.[31] CRAG states that 'It would be unreasonable to decide that a resident had disposed of an asset in order to reduce his charge for accommodation when the disposal took place at a time when he was fit and healthy and could not have foreseen the need for a move to residential accommodation' (para 6.064).

8.34   In *Yule v South Lanarkshire Council*,[32] Lord Philip held that a local authority was entitled to take account of the value of an elderly woman's home transferred to her daughter over 18 months before the woman entered residential care. The court held that there was no time limit on local authorities when deciding whether a person had deprived themselves of assets for the purposes of avoiding residential care fees.

Diminishing notional capital rule

8.35 Where a resident is deemed to possess notional capital (such that s/he is deemed liable to pay some or all of the standard rate for the residential accommodation), then the diminishing notional capital rule means that over time s/he may nevertheless qualify for financial assistance from the authority in meeting the accommodation charges. Regulation 26 provides that where a resident has been assessed as having notional capital, that capital will have to be reduced each week by the difference between the rate which s/he is paying for the accommodation and the rate s/he would have paid if s/he was not treated as possessing the notional capital. CRAG gives the following example of the workings of such a calculation:

> A resident is assessed as having notional capital of £14,250 plus actual capital of £16,000. This results in him having to pay the standard charge of, eg, £200. If he did not possess the notional capital, his capital would not affect his ability to pay for the accommodation so, based on an income of £83 and a personal allowance of for example, £13 he would be assessed as paying a

---

31 For a general analysis of the relevant commissioners' decisions see Mesher *CPAG's Income-Related Benefits: The Legislation* (Sweet & Maxwell) and Philip Boyd 'Sheltering Properties' *Adviser* July/August 1995.

32 (1998) 1 CCLR 571; Scottish Court of Session.

charge of £70. The notional capital should be reduced by £130 per week ie, the difference between the sum he has to pay because of the notional capital (£200) and the charge he would have to pay if the notional capital did not exist (£70).

Local authority responses to deliberate deprivations

8.36   If the authority believes that the resident has disposed of capital in order to reduce the charge payable, it will have to decide whether to treat the resident as having the capital (notional capital) and assess the charge payable accordingly. It will then have to decide what if any action it should take. CRAG advises that there are two options, namely (para 6.067):

a)   to recover the assessed charge from the resident; or

b)   if the resident is unable to pay the assessed charge, to use the provisions of HASSASSAA 1983 s21 to transfer liability to the recipient of the asset for that part of the charges assessed as a result of the notional capital (see para 8.43 below).

It appears, however, that in addition to their enforcement powers under HASSASSAA 1983 s21 local authorities are able in certain situations to use powers provided by the Insolvency Act 1986. These options are considered at para 8.45 below.

8.37   Local authorities would also appear to have another effective response where it is believed that a deliberate deprivation has occurred. If the authority believes that in consequence, the resident has notional capital in excess of £16,000, it may decide that it need not provide or fund the accommodation at all.

8.38   Ellis v Chief Adjudication Officer [1998] 1 FLR 184 concerned a refusal of income support by the Benefits Agency to an elderly person who had transferred her house to her daughter. The principles are directly applicable to the situation where a local authority refuses to provide assistance under the residential accommodation charging procedures. Mrs Ellis had transferred her flat to her daughter on the condition that the daughter would (inter alia) look after her in the flat. Instead, the daughter evicted her and sold the flat. The Court of Appeal rejected Mrs Ellis' argument that the 'condition subsequent' was void for uncertainty. As a result it ruled that she was still the notional owner of the proceeds of sale of the property. Since this notional asset had been valued at £35,000 it followed that Mrs Ellis was not entitled to any assistance. As Otton LJ observed:

It may be that when the claimant has pursued the daughter she will recover capital in excess of the prescribed limit – in which case no injustice will be done to her. On the other hand it may transpire that the net proceeds of sale are, for whatever reason, less than the limit in which event she will no doubt be entitled to make a fresh application for benefit. The property was held on trust by the daughter for Mrs Ellis.

8.39   It would appear to follow, therefore, that where a local authority is satisfied that a potential (or actual) resident has:

1) notional capital in excess of £16,000, and
2) sufficient ability to make the necessary arrangements with a residential care or nursing home (or has access to a person with these skills and who is 'willing' to do so),[33]

then it is under no duty to provide the accommodation. It does not, therefore, need to take action against the third party to whom the asset has been transferred. In such a case, the potential (or actual) resident would seem to be restricted in the action that could be taken against the local authority. In an action for judicial review, for instance, it would appear that s/he would have to show (in the absence of a procedural flaw in the decision-making process) that the decision was *Wednesbury* unreasonable.[34] This proposition was endorsed in large measure by the Scottish Court of Session in its opinion on the judicial review proceedings in *Robertson v Fife Council* (2000) GWD 4-172 (available at www.scotcourts.gov.uk/index1.htm).

Enforcement powers

8.40   If the local authority decides to take action to recover the disposed property (or the proceeds of sale) it has a number of statutory provisions available to assist. It is also likely that authorities will be given extra powers to strengthen 'procedures to prevent and detect evasion of care charges'.[35]

8.41   While taking such action (or prior to its commencement) the authority will invoice the resident for his or her assessed contribution towards the care charges. It is frequently suggested that authorities are unlikely to take enforcement action for fear of (among other things) the adverse publicity such action might provoke. This will

33 By virtue of LAC(98)19, see para 8.21 above.
34 See para 12.91 for a general consideration of the grounds for judicial review.
35 See *A New Partnership for Care in Old Age*, para 3.2; a government consultation paper on the future funding of long-term care (HMSO, May 1996).

seldom be the case. In many cases an authority may defer such action (waiting until the resident dies before enforcing the debt against the estate). However, where an authority has an increasing debt, it will annually have to justify its inaction to its auditors, who may well require action to be taken to recover the outstanding monies.

8.42   Where the resident has transferred assets to other parties with the purpose of avoiding or reducing his or her liability for charges, then the options available to the authority will depend in part on when the transfer occurred.

8.43   **Transfers within six months of entering residential accommodation**
HASSASSAA 1983 s21(1) provides:

> Subject to the following provisions of this section, where –
> (a) a person avails himself of Part III accommodation; and
> (b) that person knowingly and with the intention of avoiding charges for the accommodation –
>   (i) has transferred any asset to which this section applies to some other person or persons not more than six months before the date on which he begins to reside in such accommodation; or
>   (ii) transfers any such asset to some other person or persons while residing in the accommodation; and
> (c) either –
>   (i) the consideration for the transfer is less than the value of the asset; or
>   (ii) there is no consideration for the transfer,
> the person or persons to whom the asset is transferred by the person availing himself of the accommodation shall be liable to pay the local authority providing the accommodation or arranging for its provision the difference between the amount assessed as due to be paid for the accommodation by the person availing himself of it and the amount which the local authority receive from him for it.

8.44   The effect of s21 is that where a resident transfers any asset to a third party at less than its full value, then the authority can take enforcement proceedings against the third party if:

a) the transfer takes place no more than six months before the resident enters the home, and

b) the authority can establish that the transfer was effected 'knowingly and with the intention of avoiding charges for the accommodation'.

Although s21 is differently worded to the notional capital rule under reg 25 of the Regulations ('knowingly and with the intention of' rather than 'for the purpose of'), it is difficult to see that any significant practical differences of interpretation emerge from the two phrases; where a deprivation of capital is assessed as having occurred, then it would seem that this is also sufficient for the purposes of s21.

8.45 **Transfers over six months before entering residential accommodation**
If an authority has determined that:

a) a resident has notional capital, and
b) the notional capital asset was transferred to a third party more than six months before the resident took up residence in the residential home, and
c) in order to recover its charges (or payments made on the resident's behalf) it needs to take proceedings to set aside the disposition of the notional capital asset,

then the authority has the option of using the enforcement procedures under the Insolvency Act 1986 by which the court is empowered in certain situations to set aside such transfers and restore the position to what it would have been if the resident had not entered into the transaction.

8.46 By virtue of Insolvency Act 1986 s339, where an individual is adjudged bankrupt and s/he has entered into a transaction at an undervalue, the trustee in bankruptcy may (subject to the following time limits) apply to the court for an order restoring the position to what it would have been had the transaction not occurred.[36] The relevant time limits are computed backwards from the day of presentation of the bankruptcy petition and are, in general:

5 years if the individual was insolvent[37] at the time of the transaction, or became insolvent in consequence of the transaction; or
2 years if the above criteria do not apply.

By virtue of Insolvency Act 1986 s423, where the court is satisfied that an individual entered into a transaction (inter alia) at an undervalue

---

36 The details given here are a simplified account of the actual provisions; 'transactions at an undervalue' are defined by s339 and are contrasted with 'preferences' (s340), for which slightly different rules apply.

37 Insolvency Act 1986 s341(3) states that an individual is insolvent if s/he is unable to pay his/her debts as they fall due, or the value of his/her assets is less than the amount of his/her liabilities, taking into account contingent and prospective liabilities. Section 341(2) creates a rebuttable presumption that an individual is insolvent where s/he enters into a transaction at an undervalue with an associate – see s435.

for the purpose of putting assets beyond the reach of a creditor or future creditor, then it may make such order as it thinks fit (including an order restoring the position to what it would have been had the transaction not been entered into).

8.47   The powers available to the court under s423 are without time limit and are exercisable without the need for bankruptcy proceedings[38] (or for the individual in question to be insolvent). What the authority must establish, however, is (unlike under s339) that the debtor's dominant purpose was to put assets beyond the reach of creditors (or more importantly in respect of local authority charges, a future creditor). The breadth of s423 has been explained thus:

> While the burden of proof remains on the applicant, establishing the necessary purpose should be less difficult to achieve than proving intent to defraud under the previous law . . . The inclusion of persons who 'may at some time claim' against the debtor envisages potential future creditors who, individually unknown to the debtor at the time of the transaction, become victims of a risky business enterprise against the consequences of failure of which the debtor seeks to protect himself at the outset. In extending the purposes of present or future claimants, the ambit of the section is made very wide . . .[39]

Where the resident has transferred the capital asset using a firm or business which specifically markets schemes designed to avoid the value of the asset being taken into account for residential fee purposes, this may, perversely, be used as evidence to establish the purpose behind the transaction.[40]

8.48   **Registering of a charge or caution on any interest in land which the resident may have (under HASSASSAA 1983 s22)**[41] Where a resident fails to pay an assessed charge for accommodation and has a beneficial interest in land, then HASSASSAA 1983 s22 enables the local authority to create a charge in its favour on that land.[42] CRAG advises that where a local authority is contemplating taking such a step, it should advise the resident to consult a solicitor about the procedure. Any charge so registered does not carry interest until the

---

38   See generally *Midland Bank v Wyatt* [1995] 1 FLR 697.

39   Berry et al *Personal Insolvency* (Butterworths, 1993).

40   See paras 3 and 12 in particular of the Law Society guidelines, *Gifts of Property: Guidelines for Solicitors* (September 1995). For a salutary decision on the courts' power to order disclosure of a solicitor's file in such cases, see *Barclays Bank v Eustice* [1995] 1 WLR 1238.

41   For guidance on the application of s22 see CRAG Annex D.

42   If the land is jointly owned, then the local authority cannot create a charge, but can register a caution (para 3.5 Annex D to CRAG).

resident's death, when HASSASSAA 1983 s24 provides for interest from that date 'at a reasonable rate' (determined by the local authority). While local authorities have no statutory power to charge interest,[43] there would appear to be nothing to stop them suing on the accumulated arrears and, in the normal course, such a judgment debt would then carry interest at the statutory rate.

8.49   Section 22 empowers, but does not oblige local authorities to place charges on property. In certain situations authorities may consider that the possession of a valuable asset (such as a house) is such that the resident has no need of assistance. The basis for this view being that the resident has capital in excess of £16,000 (ie, the house) and accordingly is able to pay their own way (by, for instance, raising a commercial loan secured on the property, pending its sale). The authority can then determine that the care and attention is 'otherwise available' and refuse to provide temporary financial support and to register a charge under s22.

8.50   As s22 is phrased in discretionary terms, authorities are in principle entitled, where the circumstances allow, to take such a course. Whether such a decision is reasonable in any particular case, will depend upon its specific facts. In general, a suggestion that a person take out a commercial loan (or obtain a home's agreement to defer payment until the sale of a property) assumes (at a minimum);

- the need for accommodation does not arise in an emergency (ie, sufficient time to arrange a loan); and
- that the person is of sufficient mental capacity/intelligence to arrange such a loan; and
- that in all the circumstances, the taking of a commercial loan in such a situation is something that would be a reasonable decision for him/her to take.

Residents in local authority homes before April 1993

8.51   A major aim of the community care reforms was the capping of income support expenditure on residential and nursing home fees. This aim was realised by transferring the means-tested funding responsibility for all new residents to social services authorities. In return, central government paid a special transitional grant (STG) to these authorities[44] to compensate them for their increased expend-

---

43   CRAG at para 3A Annex D specifically states that the general powers under Local Government Act 1972 s111 cannot be used for this purpose.

44   £418 million in 1996/97; see LASSL(96)1.

iture. The STG was payable until April 1999, since when the funding
has been distributed via the general central government grant
support to local authorities.

8.52   Residents in residential care or nursing homes on 31 March 1993
were unaffected by the funding changes and their entitlement to payments of income support at a higher level continued; this is so even if
the residents were not actually in receipt of such payments at that
time.[45] Such residents are described as having 'preserved rights'. The
income support changes were effected by the Social Security
(Amendments Consequential upon the Introduction of Community
Care) Regulations 1992 SI No 3147.

8.53   As part of this transfer of responsibility, it was considered important to keep the two funding regimes separate by prohibiting
social services authority funding of pre-April 1993 residents. This aim
was achieved by NHSCCA 1990 s43, which inserted s26A into NAA
1948. The new section provides:

(1) Subject to subsection (3) of this section, no accommodation may be
provided under section 21 or 26 of this Act for any person who
immediately before the date on which this section comes into force
was ordinarily resident in relevant premises.

(2) In subsection (1) 'relevant premises' means –
    (a) premises in respect of which any person is registered under the
        Registered Homes Act 1984;
    (b) premises in respect of which such registration is not required by
        virtue of their being managed or provided by an exempt body;
    (c) premises which do not fall within the definition of a nursing
        home in section 21 of that Act by reason only of their being
        maintained or controlled by an exempt body; and
    (d such other premises as the Secretary of State may by regulations
        prescribe;
    and in this subsection 'exempt body' has the same meaning as in
    section 26 of this Act.

(3) The Secretary of State may by regulations provide that, in such cases
and subject to such conditions as may be prescribed, subsection (1)
of this section shall not apply in relation to such classes of persons
as may be prescribed in [the Regulations].

(4) The Secretary of State shall by regulations prescribe the
circumstances in which persons are to be treated as being ordinarily
resident in any premises for the purposes of subsection (1) of this
section.

45 The only exception being residents of 'small homes' (ie, those with fewer than
    four residents), whose preserved entitlement only continued if they were
    actually getting the higher levels of income support on 31 March 1993.

(5) This section does not affect the validity of any contract made before the date on which this section comes into force for the provision of accommodation on or after that date or anything done in pursuance of such a contract.

8.54 While s26A prohibits social services authorities from making residential accommodation arrangements for such people, it provides for certain exceptions to this rule. These exceptions are set out in the Residential Accommodation (Relevant Premises, Ordinary Residence and Exemptions) Regulations 1993, and guidance[46] has been issued as LAC(93)6. The provisions are complex and are increasingly having the effect of forcing elderly persons out of suitable homes, purely because their funding needs have increased. A number of reports have highlighted the hardship caused to the diminishing group of residents who are subject to the preserved entitlement rules[47] and the government has announced that it will be abolished from April 2002.[48]

8.55 Local authorities can only 'top up' the residential home fees of residents with preserved entitlement where the person:

1) was already receiving a 'topping up' payment on 31 March 1993; or
2) is under pension age; or
3) is over pension age and faces eviction or the home is about to close (in which case the local authority can only assist with topping up payments if the resident moves to another home which is not owned or managed by the current home's proprietor).

Less dependent residents

8.56 The charging rules allow authorities to treat 'less dependent' residents in a different way, especially in relation to the amount of their standard personal expenses allowance. The reason for this difference in treatment is explained in CRAG at paras 2.001–2.011 (which are paraphrased below).

---

46 Issued under LASSA 1970 s7(1).
47 See *Preserved Rights to Income Support*, results of an Age Concern/Association of Charity Officers survey (July 1996).
48 *The NHS Plan: The Government's Response to the Royal Commission on Long-term Care* para 2.26, Cm 4818-II July 2000. See also 'Under threat of removal' *Community Care Journal* 6 April 2000 p28 which suggests that the current arrangements may violate European Convention on Human Rights articles 2 and 3.

8.57   For the purposes of the charging rules[49] a 'less dependent' resident is a person who lives in either:

a) private or voluntary sector accommodation which is not required to be registered under the Registered Homes Act 1984 as a residential care or nursing home, or

b) local authority accommodation that does not provide board.[50]

8.58   Before April 1993, social services authorities had powers to arrange for the provision of residential accommodation under NHSA 1977 Sch 8 as well as under NAA 1948 Pt III. The accommodation powers under NHSA 1977 were repealed by NHSCCA 1990 Sch 10. The 1977 Act powers were mainly used to accommodate people who were able to live more independently than those accommodated under the 1948 Act, but who nevertheless required some degree of care and support. These were mainly (but not always) people under pension age. Authorities were not required to charge for accommodation provided under NHSA 1977, although they were empowered to make a reasonable charge[51] where appropriate. This meant that the money left with residents for their personal use was not limited to the prescribed amount for personal expenses allowed for people accommodated under the 1948 Act. The reason for this difference in treatment was because less dependent residents were encouraged to live as independently as possible, often with a view to eventually living independently in the community. They needed extra money for items such as the cost of food or household expenses or travel to work.

8.59   From 1 April 1993 all adult residential accommodation placements made by social services authorities, including those for people who are less dependent, are made under NAA 1948, for which a charge must be made in accordance with the charging rules detailed above. The normal charging rules would not, however, be appropriate for 'less dependent' residents because they will frequently need to be left with more than the standard personal expenses allowance if they are to live as independently as possible. Regulation 5 accordingly enables authorities to continue to treat 'less dependent' residents differently where they consider it reasonable in the circumstances to do so. It enables authorities to disregard the resources of such residents, taking into account:

49 Regulations reg 2(1).

50 'Board' is defined in reg 2(1) as including at least some cooked or prepared meals, cooked or prepared by someone other than the resident (or a member of his/her family) and eaten in the accommodation, where the cost of the meals is included in the standard rate fixed for the accommodation.

51 Using their discretionary powers under HASSASSAA 1983 s17.

- the resident's commitments, ie, costs of necessities such as food, fuel, and clothing;
- the degree of the resident's independence, ie, the extent to which s/he should be encouraged to take on expenditure commitments; and
- whether s/he needs a greater incentive to become more independent, eg, s/he may be encouraged to take on paid employment if most or all of the earnings are disregarded.

Temporary residents

8.60   By virtue of NAA 1948 s22(5A), authorities are not obliged to apply the charging rules to temporary residents. The subsection provides:

> If they think fit, an authority managing premises in which accommodation is provided for a person shall have power on each occasion when they provide accommodation for him, irrespective of his means, to limit to such amount as appears to them reasonable for him to pay the payments required from him for his accommodation during a period commencing when they begin to provide the accommodation for him and ending not more than eight weeks after that.

Although s22(5A) specifies an eight-week period, clearly authorities cannot be certain in advance of the duration of a person's stay in residential accommodation. Accordingly, reg 2(1) allows an authority to regard a person's stay as temporary if it is likely to last for any period not exceeding 52 weeks, or, in exceptional circumstances, is unlikely to exceed that period substantially.[52]

8.61   CRAG advises (at paras 3.004–3.004A), where a stay which was expected to be permanent turns out to be temporary, that as soon as this is appreciated, it is unreasonable to continue to apply to that resident any adverse rules (ie, those which apply to permanent residents but not to temporary residents, such as the disregard of the value of dwellings). Conversely, where a stay which was initially expected to be temporary turns out to be permanent, then assessment as a permanent resident should begin from the date it is agreed that the stay is to become permanent.

8.62   Authorities have a discretion whether or not to apply the charging rules for the first eight weeks of a temporary stay. CRAG advises that

---

52 An authority's acceptance that a resident's stay is temporary will also have other consequences, most obviously the disregard of the value of any dwelling normally occupied by the resident (see above).

where the authority decides to make an assessment of ability to pay, then it should do so on the normal charging basis. Where it decides not to make such an assessment, then it is able to charge such amount as it considers reasonable for the resident to pay (para 3.005).[53] CRAG gives brief advice to authorities on general issues to bear in mind in assessing what is reasonable for temporary residents to pay, including the interaction of various social security benefits (at paras 3.006A–3.014).

Liable relatives

8.63   NAA 1948 s42 provides:

42 (1) For the purposes of this Act –
(a) a man shall be liable to maintain his wife and his children, and
(b) a woman shall be liable to maintain her husband and her children.
(2) Any reference in subsection (1) of this section to a person's children shall be construed in accordance with section 1 of the Family Law Reform Act 1987.

Thus, married couples are liable to maintain each other under NAA 1948 s42 as well as under the social security legislation.[54] CRAG advises that it is not worth the social services authority pursuing maintenance where income support is in payment to the resident.

Seeking payments from liable relatives

8.64   Where it appears to an authority appropriate to pursue a resident's spouse under s42, CRAG gives advice as to the procedure to be followed:

11.005. . . . LAs may ask a spouse to refund part or all of the authority's expenditure in providing residential accommodation for his/her husband or wife. LAs should note that this does not mean that an authority can demand that a spouse provide details of his/her resources. LAs should not use assessment forms for the resident which require information about the means of the spouse. LAs should use tact in explaining to residents and spouses the legal

53 Where a resident enters residential accommodation for a temporary period, income support is not payable if his/her capital exceeds £8,000. This may mean that, where the resident has capital of more than £8,000 but less than £16,000, the resident's contribution towards the cost of his/her accommodation will not include any income support (para 3.006A).
54 Social Security Administration Act 1992 ss78(6) and 105(3).

liability to maintain and point out that the extent of that liability is best considered in the light of the spouse's resources.

11.006. In practical terms, LAs may wish to proceed as follows:

i) assess the liability of the resident to pay based solely on his/her own resources. This establishes the charge the resident is able to pay without assistance from the liable relative;

ii) if the resident is unable to pay for his/her accommodation at the standard rate, the LA decides whether it is worth pursuing the spouse for maintenance towards the shortfall;

iii) if it is worth pursuing the spouse for maintenance, consider in each case what would be 'appropriate' for the spouse to pay by way of maintenance. This will involve discussion and negotiation with the spouse, and will be determined to a large extent by his/her financial circumstances in relation to his/her expenditure and normal standard of living. In the Department's view, it would not be appropriate, for example, to necessarily expect spouses to reduce their resources to Income Support levels in order to pay maintenance;

iv) ultimately, only the courts can decide what is an 'appropriate' amount of maintenance to pay. When negotiating maintenance payments with spouses the LA should therefore consider whether the amount being sought would be similar to that decided by the courts.

Liable relative payments

8.65 Where a resident receives money from his/her spouse or former (divorced) spouse, then CRAG provides procedures for deciding whether these payments are to be treated as capital or income. Where the payment is treated as income, it may be either:

- a periodical payment, in which case it is generally treated in the same way as any other income of the resident; or
- a non-periodical payment, in which case CRAG gives advice as to how the LA should go about calculating the period over which to take the payment into account.

The possible permutations for such payments are many, and the detailed guidance in CRAG should be referred to if such a problem is encountered (see paras 11.001–11.025).

Challenging charges

8.66 Complaints about the level of charges levied by an authority are subject to the usual social services complaints procedures; see Chapter 12.

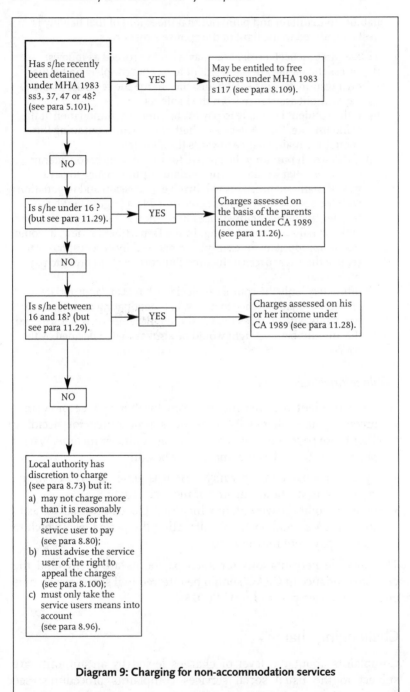

Has s/he recently been detained under MHA 1983 ss3, 37, 47 or 48? (see para 5.101).

YES → May be entitled to free services under MHA 1983 s117 (see para 8.109).

NO

Is s/he under 16 ? (but see para 11.29).

YES → Charges assessed on the basis of the parents income under CA 1989 (see para 11.26).

NO

Is s/he between 16 and 18? (but see para 11.29).

YES → Charges assessed on his or her income under CA 1989 (see para 11.28).

NO

Local authority has discretion to charge (see para 8.73) but it:

a) may not charge more than it is reasonably practicable for the service user to pay (see para 8.80);

b) must advise the service user of the right to appeal the charges (see para 8.100);

c) must only take the service users means into account (see para 8.96).

Diagram 9: Charging for non-accommodation services

Charges for non-accommodation services

8.67   Social services authorities have a discretionary power to charge for certain non-accommodation services. In relation to adult services this power presently[55] derives from HASSASSAA 1983 s17, which provides as follows:

(1) Subject to subsection (3) below, an authority providing a service to which this section applies may recover such charge (if any) for it as they consider reasonable.

(2) This section applies to services provided under the following enactments:

(a) section 29 of the National Assistance Act 1948 (welfare arrangements for disabled persons);

(b) section 45(1) of the Health Services and Public Health Act 1968 (welfare of old people);

(c) Schedule 8 to the National Health Service Act 1977 (care of mothers and young children, prevention of illness and care and after-care and home help and laundry facilities);

(d) section 8 of the Residential Homes Act 1980 (meals and recreation for old people); and

(e) paragraph 1 of Part II of Schedule 9 to this Act, other than the provision of services for which payment may be required under section 22 or 26 of the National Assistance Act 1948.

(3) If a person –

(a) avails himself of a service to which this section applies, and

(b) satisfies the authority providing the service that his means are insufficient for it to be reasonably practicable for him to pay for the service the amount which he would otherwise be obliged to pay for it,

the authority shall not require him to pay more for it than it appears to them that it is reasonably practicable for him to pay.

(4) Any charge under this section may, without prejudice to any other method of recovery, be recovered summarily as a civil debt.

8.68   Separate charging provisions relate to services provided to disabled children under CA 1989 Pt III, and these are considered separately at para 11.26. As noted below, however, disabled children will usually receive their non-accommodation services under CSDPA 1970 s2

---

55   The power was formerly to be found under NAA 1948 s29(5) which provided that '[a] local authority may recover from persons availing themselves of any service provided under this Section such charges (if any) as, having regard to the cost of the service, the authority may determine, whether generally or in the circumstances of any particular case'. Section 17 is to be amended when the Carers and Disabled Children Act 2000 comes into force, see para 7.45 above.

and it is doubtful if local authorities can make any charge for these services (see para 11.29).

8.69   The charging provisions for adult non-accommodation services differ in two significant ways from the provisions relating to residential accommodation charges:

a) Social services authorities are under no obligation to charge for non-accommodation services; whereas they are obliged to charge for residential accommodation (with the exception of temporary residential accommodation).[56]

b) There is no statutorily defined procedure for assessing non-accommodation charges, each authority being entitled to develop its own procedures.

Guidance

8.70   Only two paragraphs of circular guidance have been issued concerning non-accommodation charges, LAC(94)1 paras 17 and 18. The only significant non-circular guidance given in respect of such charges was issued by the Social Services Inspectorate in January 1994, ostensibly as advice to its own officers. The guidance is not therefore 'guidance' within the meaning of LASSA 1970 s7(1) (see para 1.28). Its status is no more than that of a 'relevant consideration' to which all authorities should have regard when drawing up or administering a charging policy. This guidance is referred to in the rest of this section as the 'SSI Advice'. Although helpful in a number of respects, the SSI Advice has been the subject of criticism, most importantly in a detailed commentary issued jointly by the Association of Metropolitan Authorities and the Local Government Information Unit in August 1994.[57] The lack of central guidance has been criticised by the Audit Commission[57A] as has the very wide variation in charging schemes, some of which leave 'people with less to live on than income support'.

Good Practice Handbook

8.71   The AMA/LGIU 'commentary' has now been superseded by a *Good Practice Handbook* (1996) issued by the Association of County Councils and the Association of Metropolitan Authorities. While this

56   NAA 1948 s22(5A) – see above.
57   Copies of which can be purchased from Local Government Information Unit, 1–5 Bath Street, London EC1V 9QQ, tel: 020 7608 1051.
57A   *Charging with Care* Audit Commission May 2000.

is not formal government guidance, the Local Ombudsman has stated that she would expect authorities to take account of this advice when devising charging policies.[58]

8.72 In its white paper *Modernising Social Services* (1998) the government committed itself to establish greater consistency and fairness in charging,[59] having acknowledged the wide local variations that exist under the present system, stating:

> The differences between these discretionary charges can be considerable. The amount that authorities recover in charges – as a percentage of their spending on these services – varies from 4% to 28%. And the charging systems vary enormously from one council to another. For instance, one council might charge a standard hourly rate which everyone – whatever their income – pays, so that the amount paid depends on the amount of care received. Whereas another council might operate a sliding scale of charges according to income, regardless of how much care is received. Taking as a random example, someone with an income of £115 and receiving 12 hours of care per week could pay £13 per week in one area, and £48 per week in the other.[60]

The discretion to charge

8.73 Social services authorities are under no statutory obligation to charge for non-accommodation services; HASSASSAA 1983 s17(1) merely states that they 'may recover such charges (if any)' as they consider reasonable. The fact therefore that s17(3) states subsequently that authorities cannot in any event charge more than it is 'reasonably practicable' for a person to pay, does not remove their overall discretion to waive charges for whatever reason (ie, not only on the ground of insufficient financial means).

8.74 Authorities are, however, under considerable pressure to operate a charging scheme. The Policy Guidance states that it 'is expected that local authorities will institute arrangements so that users of services of all types pay what they can reasonably afford towards their costs', although it then adds, that the provision of services should 'not be related to the ability of the user or their families to meet the costs' and that 'the assessment of means should, therefore, follow the assessment of need and decisions about service provision' (at para 3.31).

---

58 Para 153 Complaint 98/C/0911 and others against Stockton on Tees BC 29 July 1999.
59 Cm 4169 at para 2.31.
60 Ibid at para 2.29.

8.75   The pressure on authorities to levy charges is evident from LAC(94)1, which explains the position thus:

> 17. . . . The Government's view . . . has consistently been that users who can pay for such services should be expected to do so taking account of their ability to pay. The White Paper and Policy Guidance also make it clear that ability to pay should not influence decisions on the services to be provided, and the assessment of financial means should therefore follow the care assessment.

> 18. Authorities are locally accountable for making sensible and constructive use of the discretionary powers they have, in order to prevent avoidable burdens falling on council and national taxpayers. Authorities are reminded that the standard spending assessment formula for domiciliary care for elderly people does not take account of the level of income from charges actually received by each authority. This means that any authority which recovers less revenue than its discretionary powers allow is placing an extra burden on the local population or is foregoing resources which could be used to the benefit of the service . . .

8.76   At present, the standard spending assessment formula assumes that authorities are raising nine per cent of their non-residential care costs via charges. Charges can raise appreciable sums which can be used to enhance the services provided. They can, however, be administratively expensive to collect, in that this involves receiving and accounting for large numbers of small payments – even without the cost of chasing non-payers.[61] The levying of charges has two other significant consequences. The first is a reduction in demand for services, as many people in need refuse services (or do not request them) because of fear of the likely cost. The fear may indeed be misplaced due to the widespread confusion over the various systems – a confusion which has been the subject of Audit Commission criticism.[62] There appears to be, however, substantial evidence that charges do deter many people in need of services from receiving those services. The *Good Practice Handbook* accordingly advises local authorities (at p31) 'that a procedure should be put in place to monitor any instances where the user may have refused service, or requested a lower level of service, because of the charges involved'. The Local Government Ombudsman has specifically criticised a council that failed to follow

---

61 This point is emphasised in the SSI Advice para 7 where it states, 'The operating costs of a very complex system of financial assessment may reduce the net benefit of the charges collected'.

62 Audit Commission, *Balancing the Care Equation* (HMSO, 1996).

up clients who had cancelled the service because they could not afford to pay the new charges.[63]

8.77   The second effect becomes more significant as the charges begin to reflect the full cost of the service to the authority. When this occurs, it is usual that the private sector can undercut the charge and so divert users away from public-sector provision. This consequence furthers one of the main aims in the 1990 community care reforms – namely, the promotion of a mixed economy of care. Private providers have only appeared in the non-accommodation community care sector in appreciable numbers since the widespread increase in charges levied by authorities for these services.

Local charging schemes: the duty to consult

8.78   The *Good Practice Handbook* emphasises that consultation with service users on the development and piloting of charging procedures is crucial and that a realistic time scale needs to be set for the consultation process before any changes take place. It notes that 'the experience of local authorities suggests that consultation will take months'.[64] The local government ombudsman has been critical of charging schemes that have been introduced with undue haste, ie, before the procedures for their implementation were in place.[65]

8.79   The extent to which such consultation is a legal requirement is, however, uncertain. In *R v Powys CC ex p Hambidge (No 2)*,[66] the local authority decided upon a substantial increase in its charges, without any significant consultation of users who would be affected. The Court of Appeal dismissed the application without considering in detail the issue of consultation; namely that such users are generally so vulnerable and little able to assert their rights that there is an accordingly high requirement to consult prior to the imposition of any new scheme. In *R v Gloucestershire CC ex p RADAR*,[67] for instance, Carnwath J noted that what 'might be an adequate response, where those affected can be assumed to be capable of looking after their own interests, and where silence . . . can be treated as acceptance or acquiescence' cannot be so assumed where such assumptions cannot be made because of the vulnerability of the community care user group.

---

63 Complaint No 91A/3782 against Greenwich LBC (1993).
64 At pp16 and 25–27.
65 Complaint No 91A/3782 against Greenwich LBC (1993).
66 (2000) *Times* 16 March.
67 (1998) 1 CCLR 476, at 482.

The amount that can be charged

8.80 HASSASSAA 1983 s17(1) permits authorities to recover such charge as they consider reasonable (including no charge). Section 17(3) requires authorities to reduce or waive such a charge if satisfied in an individual case that the person's means are insufficient for it to be reasonably practicable for him or her to pay it. The test under s17(1) is an objective one, and considered in this section: the test under s17(3) is a subjective test of what an individual can afford, and is considered below at paras 8.69 onwards.

8.81 Section 17(1) is worded so as to allow authorities a wide scope in setting the basic charge for a particular service. The maximum charge would seem to be the portion of the total cost of the service that is attributable to the particular service user. Anything greater than this would result in the authority making a profit from the service, which is not permitted; as the SSI Advice puts it (at para 11), 's17 is not a provision which enables them to raise general revenue'. The minimum charge is nothing, as authorities do not have to charge for their services, and s17(1) clearly envisages this by using the phrase 'if any'.

8.82 The SSI Advice suggests that charges should be related to the overall cost of the service, stating,

> In the Government's view, in setting charges (whether flat rate or on a scale) authorities should take account both of the full cost of providing the service and within that of what recipients can reasonably be expected to pay ... In calculating the full cost of providing the service local authorities should take into account capital, managerial and other overheads directly attributable to provision, but not costs associated with the purchasing function and not the costs of operating the charging system. (para 5)

As detailed above, the SSI Advice is by no means binding on authorities and accordingly they are under no obligation to use the full cost of the service as a starting point for deciding what to charge. As long as the system adopted is based on reasonable and relevant criteria, it is most unlikely that a court would interfere with the exercise by an authority of its wide discretion in this field.

Assessment of ability to pay

8.83 HASSASSAA 1983 s17(3) provides that where a service user satisfies the authority that s/he has insufficient means for it to be reasonably practicable to pay for the service, then the authority must not charge that person any more than it is reasonably practicable for him or her to pay. This provision means that those authorities who do charge must have a means-testing system which enables charges to be reduced or waived altogether in appropriate cases. The phrasing of s17(3) makes it clear that authorities are entitled to levy their full standard charge for services until such time as the service user 'satisfies' them that his/her means are insufficient. Thus if an individual refuses to provide reasonable information about his/her finances, the authority is entitled to levy the full charge.[67A] In this respect the *Good Practice Handbook* advises (at p36) that financial assessment forms should contain a warning statement which explains that a failure to provide accurate financial information might lead an authority to decide 'that the user should be charged the maximum costs for the services provided in line with that authority's current charging policy'.

8.84   While the onus is on service users to provide the necessary information in order that the amount of the charge can be reviewed, there is a concomitant obligation on the authority to ensure that it gives clients accurate information about the charges they will face and information as to how they can challenge those charges if they believe that they are unreasonable. Paragraph 28 of the SSI Advice stipulates:

> Good practice requires that users should be given an accurate indication of the charges that they will incur before they are required to commit themselves to a particular care plan. Only exceptional circumstances can justify not doing so. They also should be given a written statement of their financial liability at the earliest opportunity, with access to advice and explanation as required.

8.85   This advice is echoed in the *Good Practice Handbook*, which states that authorities should ensure that:

- information about their charging policies for service users and carers is accurate, and that it contains a clear explanation as of the law and the authority's 'discretion' (p18);[68] and
- that copies of the financial information that the user has supplied should be made available to the user (p32).

67A   A point emphasised in *Avon CC v Hooper* (1998) 1 CCLR 366 (albeit that this was a highly unusual 'fact' case). The court also held that a person's 'means' was not limited to cash, but included other financial resources.

68   The importance of this information being available in appropriate languages was noted by the local government ombudsman in Complaint No 91A/3782 against Greenwich LBC (1993).

Charging and income support

8.86   Although a number of authorities do not charge service users who are on income support, many do.[69] The government initially indicated that it hoped that in time such people would be automatically exempt from charges[70] although the SSI Advice now contradicts this intention, stating that the government 'does not consider that there should be an automatic exemption from charges for people receiving [means-tested or disability benefits]. For them, as for other service users, authorities should have regard to the amount of charge in relation to their individual overall financial position' (para 13).

8.87   Given that income support represents no more than a subsistence level of income, it might appear self-evident that a person in receipt of it would have insufficient means for 'it to be reasonably practicable' for him/her to pay any significant charge.[71] Whether the levying of small charges to such persons is in any way cost-effective must be highly questionable. The fact that it is the government's view that such people should not be automatically exempt from charges in no way restrains authorities[72] from taking a contrary view. The straitened circumstances of such persons is recognised by the SSI Advice at para 14, stating, 'Representations from people receiving welfare benefits and those on very low incomes should, however, be given sympathetic consideration. Authorities will want to bear in mind that these benefits cannot be increased to enable the recipient to meet charges for care'.

---

69 The parallel charging provisions in relation to services for disabled children specifically exclude parents on income support or family credit: CA 1989 s29.

70 *Hansard* (HC) Vol 42 col 885 (1982): 'Local authorities will, as steadily as circumstances allow, move towards the elimination of charges to those on supplementary benefit'.

71 The costs of disability rise with the severity of the impairment. Average levels of disability-related costs for severely disabled people have been estimated to range from £20 per week (J Martin and A White *The Financial Circumstances of Disabled People Living in Private Households* (HMSO, 1988)) to £50 per week (R Berthoud, J Lakey and S McKay *The Economic Problems of Disabled People* (Policy Studies Institute and JRF Social Policy Research Findings 39, 1993)) to £100 per week (P Thompson, M Lavery and J Curtice *Short Changed by Disability*. (The Disablement Income Group, 1990)). In addition, as has been repeatedly stressed, disabled people suffer particularly severe poverty because of their (often permanent) lack of access to employment opportunities (see, eg, 'Disability, Household Income and Expenditure: Follow up Survey of Disabled Adults in the Family Expenditure Survey', DSS Research Support No 2 (HMSO, 1990) ix and p31).

72 Or, indeed, complaints panel members who ultimately will be required to consider an individual's complaint against the levying of a charge.

8.88   Where authorities are taking into account, for charging purposes, means-tested and non-means-tested benefits it is in their interests to maximise the receipt of these benefits by services users. Accordingly, the *Good Practice Handbook* suggests (at p33) that authorities should consider the introduction of welfare rights advice into the assessment process.[73]

Charging and disability living allowance/attendance allowance

8.89   The SSI Advice states that in assessing ability to pay authorities may take into account all types of income, with the exception of the mobility component of disability living allowance (DLA)[74] and any income which is being received from the Independent Living (1993) Fund.[75] Many authorities adopt a general charging policy which requires a portion of any DLA care component or attendance allowance to be contributed towards the cost of any home care service. In relation to this practice the joint AMA/LGIU commentary[76] states with considerable force (at para 8.7):

> It is essential to bear in mind that these benefits are not paid to pay for care but to reflect the extra costs of living which someone incurs if they have this level of need for care or supervision. Many disabled people cannot afford to spend this benefit on paying for care even when they need to because the money is already committed towards basic living expenses, such as heating and laundry.

8.90   The SSI Advice does, however, make the important point (at para 21) that authorities should have regard not only to the service user's income, 'but his/her overall financial circumstances'. In particular they should take into account any extra expenditure that may be incurred because of the service user's disability or frailty. The *Good Practice Handbook* accordingly recommends (at p34) that authorities should provide space on the financial assessment form for the service user to mention any existing financial commitments, 'including debts currently being paid off, and any extra disability-related expenditure'.

8.91   In *R v Calderdale DC ex p Houghton*,[77] leave to move for judicial review was granted to challenge the authority's procedures for assess-

---

73 The provision of welfare benefits advice by a social services department is done pursuant to their powers under NAA 1948 s29, see para 5.26.

74 Social Security Contributions and Benefits Act 1992 s73(14) requires this benefit to be disregarded in any charging scheme – see SSI Advice para 23.

75 SSI Advice para 24

76 See para 8.70 above.

77 (1999) unreported but see (1999) 2 CCLR 119.

ing the reasonableness of its charges. These procedures stipulated that the applicant had to establish that his/her 'expenditure was so exceptional' that it was not reasonable to charge the full amount. The case settled before a final hearing with the council accepting that this was an unreasonably high test to set.

8.92   The *Good Practice Handbook* emphasises this point, stating (at p32):

> authorities should be seen to consider the individual's circumstances. It is unlawful for local authorities to fetter their discretion by adhering to rigid criteria. Any criteria that are established should be flexible and should not include specific exclusions, such as not allowing certain expenditure. The set criteria should not be negative statements. This would conflict with the authority's duty to ensure that it has reasonably considered each individual user's ability to pay.

8.93   In *R v Powys CC ex p Hambidge (No 2)*,[78] the applicant submitted unsuccessfully that any scheme which separates out recipients of DLA or attendance allowance for higher charges is contrary to the Disability Discrimination Act 1995 in that it treats disabled people (ie, persons who receive DLA/attendance allowance) differently from non-disabled people (who are charged significantly less if they only receive income support and no DLA/attendance allowance).[79]

8.94   The argument is that since neither DLA nor attendance allowance can be awarded merely because a person needs general help in the home it is perverse and/or discriminatory to take them into account for charging purposes.

8.95   An alternative legal approach (which was not argued in the proceedings) appears to exist; such policies may constitute unlawful discrimination between disabled people themselves, in that:

a) Less than a third of disabled people who receive the middle rate

---

78 (2000) *Times* 16 March.
79 Contrary to Disability Discrimination Act 1995 s20(1), which provides that an organisation discriminates against a disabled person when for a reason which relates to that person's disability, it treats him less favourably than it treats (or would treat) others to whom the reason does not (or would not) apply, and this difference in treatment cannot be justified (within s20(4)). As Professor Doyle points out (*Disability Discrimination Law and Practice* (Jordans, 1996), para 5.5.5), the 'comparator is another member of the public (or hypothetical member of the public). This might include a person with a disability of a different kind from the complainant because the wording of the section does not appear to rule out the unlawfulness of differential treatment by service providers among disabled persons themselves.'

DLA or attendance allowance actually receive any home care from local authorities.[80]

b) Eligibility criteria target those most in need; ie, those with the greatest impairments.[81]

c) It follows that those in greatest need will almost certainly be the poorest; because the costs associated with their disability will generally be the greatest.[82]

d) Arguably it is perverse to adopt a charging policy that targets the poorest/most disabled people. If this is the case, such a local policy is capable of being struck down as ultra vires; being contrary to common law, in that it is 'manifestly unjust, partial and so gratuitous and oppressive that no reasonable person could think them justified' and deals unequally between citizens contrary to the principles enunciated in *Kruse v Johnson*.[83]

Assessment of the 'user's' income

8.96   In carrying out its means test, the local authority can only require the user to give information about his or her income; the SSI guidance states (at para 12) 'any means test must be confined to the means of the service user'.

8.97   Section 17(3) specifically refers to the means of 'a person' who 'avails himself of a service'. It follows that only the service user's financial means can be assessed. The SSI Advice is explicit on this point, stating, 'under s17, authorities may charge only the person receiving the service and should have regard only to that individual's means in assessing his/her ability to pay' (at para 18). Unfortunately this clear statement of what must unquestionably be the legal position is then muddied by the SSI Advice suggesting that in certain situations authorities may cast their gaze slightly wider. The relevant paragraph states:

19. In the Department's view this will normally mean that parents and other members of an adult user's family cannot be required to

---

80 There are about 2,036,000 disabled adults in the UK living in the community who are receiving these benefits, but only 612,000 get home care services (*With Respect to Old Age* Royal Commission Report on Long Term Care Cm 4192–I (1999) p9).

81 See, eg, *Balancing the Care Equation* Audit Commission (1996) '23. Authorities are tackling the need to devise a priority system in several ways. All involve grouping people into categories that are ranked in order of need. Some take into account dependency and risk, sometimes using complex scoring systems.'

82 See note 71 above.

83 [1898] 2 QB 91.

pay the charges, except to the extent that they may be managing the resources of the user, and that their own resources should not be taken into account. Local authorities may, in individual cases, wish to consider whether a client has sufficient reliable access to resources beyond those held in his/her own name for them to be part of his/her means for the purposes of s17(3). The most likely instances of this kind will arise in relation to married or unmarried couples. It will be for the authority to consider each case in the light of their own legal advice.

8.98   Paragraph 19 is a highly confused statement; it mixes two quite separate situations. The first is where a person's finances are being managed by another person, such as under a power of attorney, a receivership order or a simple trust arrangement. In such cases the assets, although administered by a third party, clearly belong to the service user and should be taken into account in the means test. Another example of such an arrangement is where the service user receives maintenance or a covenanted income. The second situation is quite different; here the assets being considered belong to a third party and there is the suggestion that somehow or other they can be treated as part of the service user's means. This must be wrong, and indeed the hesitant language used by the SSI suggests that the SSI too appreciate they are walking on thin ice. What might more productively have been said by the SSI concerns service users with apparently lavish lifestyles and buying power. In such cases, the authority might consider that this evidence was such as to cast doubt on the service user's assertion of 'insufficient means' such that it was not 'satisfied' that it was not reasonably practicable for him/her to pay the assessed charge.

Challenging the assessed charge

8.99   Where a service user wishes to challenge a non-accommodation charge, the usual procedure will be to pursue the matter through the local authority's complaints procedures (see para 12.5).[84]

8.100   The *Good Practice Handbook* states (at p32) that users should be fully aware that they have the right to make representations about the amount of the charge and about their ability to pay. It stresses that authorities should have review procedures that are capable of introducing flexibility into the process for special cases, and that 'an authority should be able to demonstrate that it will genuinely assess

---

84   The omission of HASSASSAA 1983 s17 from the list of social services 'functions' in LASSA 1970 Sch 1 has now been rectified via Care Standards Act 2000 s112, and see also Policy Guidance para 6.5.

an individual user's ability to pay by showing the criteria, in relation to ability to pay, that it will use to meet the requirements of section 17(3) of the 1983 Act'.

8.101   In similar vein the local government ombudsman has emphasised that appellants should be given clear information as to the criteria for having charges reduced or waived, and of their right to a hearing before an appeal panel if their initial challenge was unsuccessful. He has also stressed the need for panel decisions to be as consistent as possible and that clear reasons for their decisions should be given so that appellants can then decide whether or not to pursue the matter further.[85]

8.102   At any hearing it may be important to remind the panel that the authority's power to reduce or waive charges is not limited to a consideration of the service user's financial means. As the authority has an overall discretion whether or not to levy any charges, it must retain a discretion to waive or reduce charges on any ground. Such an overall discretion might be used where, for instance, the service user lacked mental capacity and the services were therefore being put in without consent, or where the service user is at risk of serious and immediate harm if the services are not provided, but refuses to have the services if s/he is charged for them.

8.103   It is important that advocacy assistance is available to persons challenging charges. The *Good Practice Handbook* states (at p29) that 'the principle that service users should be enabled to seek independent advice and advocacy is one which needs to underpin any charging policy or procedure', and the local ombudsman has specifically criticised the lack of proper advocacy assistance to appellants during the appeals process.[86]

The consequences of non-payment

8.104   Where the community care service is provided by the authority in consequence of a statutory duty (for instance, under CSDPA 1970 s2), then the service cannot as a matter of law be withdrawn merely because the service user is refusing to pay for it. This proposition derives from the fact that a duty to provide cannot be negated by a service user frustrating an authority's exercise of a discretionary power.

8.105   The Policy Guidance extends this principle to all services, stating

85 Complaints Nos 90A/2675, 2075, 1705, 1228 and 1172 against Essex CC (1990).
86 Complaint No 98/C/0911, 1166, 1975, 1977 and 1978 against Stockton on Tees BC (29 July 1999).

'the provision of services, whether or not the local authority is under a duty to make provision, should not be related to the ability of the service user or their families to meet the costs . . . The assessment of financial means should, therefore, follow the assessment of need and decisions about service provision' (at para 3.31). The SSI Advice likewise states, 'Once someone has been assessed as needing a service, that service should not be withdrawn even if he or she refuses to pay the charge required. The authority should continue provision of the service while pursuing the debt, if necessary, through the Magistrates' Court' (at para 26).

8.106   HASSASSAA s17(4) states that any charge levied 'may, without prejudice to any other method of recovery, be recovered summarily as a civil debt'. The use of the phrase 'summarily as a civil debt' is a reference to Magistrates' Courts Act 1980 s58(1). In principle it appears undesirable that such a procedure (normally reserved for the collection of overdue local taxes such as council tax) be used to collect such monies. A far more appropriate course would be the use of the small claims system in the county courts. It is unclear whether local authorities are able to use this option, although, as the magistrates' procedure is expressed as being 'without prejudice to any other method', it would in principle appear to be a possibility. Although this question would appear to have been a central issue in *Avon CC v Hooper* [1997] 1 All ER 532, CA; (1998) 1 CCLR 366 at 368J, the judgment indicates that it was not the subject of full argument. In that case the council issued proceedings in the High Court for the recovery of charges. The Court of Appeal judgment notes 'it is now accepted that the claim in the action is governed by Limitation Act 1980 s9 and that any cause of action which accrued more than six years before that date is statute barred'. The advantage of the county court process is that the case will be considered by a judge familiar with such civil concepts as lack of mental capacity and its legal consequences (a problem which is frequently an issue with frail service users) and the civil courts tend to be more realistic in setting appropriate repayment sums.

Services not directly provided by the social services authority

8.107   While the principles of charging for community care services are relatively straightforward in relation to services provided by a social services authority, they become more involved in relation to services delivered by independent providers and relatively complex in the case of jointly supplied services, such as those provided by a jointly funded NHS/social services arrangement. In relation to these issues, the SSI Advice states as follows:

8. Only local authorities are empowered by [HASSASSAA 1983] s17 to set and recover charges for the services arranged by the authority. Authorities should seek their own legal advice on the extent to which a provider contracted by the Authority can collect the charges which have been assessed by the Authority. The power to set charges and assess the charge paid by each user cannot be delegated. This means, for example, that providers may not vary or waive a charge which the Authority has decided to recover. Wherever practical, charges should be paid direct to the Authority. In all other circumstances it should be clear to the user that any collecting of the charges is being done on behalf of the Authority and any revenue collected is remitted to the Authority.

9. Where the provider is an NHS unit contracting with the local authority to provide social care, it is very important that the services provided are kept distinct from the NHS purchased service provision. As outlined above, only local authorities are empowered to set and recover charges and, if possible, LAs should be responsible for the collection of charges for services provided by NHS providers under contract to them to ensure that there is no confusion.

However, if the charge being made is relatively small (eg, for meals-on-wheels) it may be inefficient to arrange a separate collection of charges. Local authorities should obtain their own legal advice where it is proposed to make the NHS provider unit responsible for collecting charges. It should be made very clear to users that the collection is on behalf of the LA, for LA services, and the charges would be passed directly to the LA.

10. It is open to a provider contracted by an Authority for a particular level of service to offer to provide additional services to individuals among the group as a private arrangement. For all types of services, including non-residential as well as residential accommodation, the contract specification should clearly set out the services to be provided within the contract, and the authority should ensure that it is aware of any other services which the provider is making available to individual users at an additional price. It should be made clear to individuals that they have a choice whether to accept the offer to provide additional services.

Joint LA/HA Services
11. There are many different circumstances under which health and local authorities work together to purchase a service for users. Charging for services is a complicated area, and if charges are to be

made the details should be devised with advice from the local authority's own lawyers. In the Department's view local authorities are allowed to charge for services up to the level that the services cost. Local and health authorities may arrange jointly for social care services under s28A of the NHS Act 1977. Where this is so, it may be permissible for the local authority to recover from service users the full cost of the social care service even though a health authority has met some or all of the cost of the social care service. Local authorities must, however, bear in mind that s17 is not a provision which enables them to raise general revenue. If a local authority purchases social care and a health authority purchases health care services from the same provider, then, in the Department's view, charges to users may only be made for the social care element . . .

20. The proprietor of a residential care home, nursing home or other residential provision is responsible for the provision of whatever day time activities are specified in the residential care contract with the local authority for each resident. Depending on the contract agreed with the local authority these activities may be provided directly by the proprietor, or he may arrange them with another provider. If the residential care contract includes such activities, the costs should have been included in the contract price, and the resident's charging assessment for residential care will have been calculated against the contract price. In these circumstances the resident cannot be charged extra for these activities. If the proprietor arranges for some of the activities specified in the contract to be provided by another provider, this will be a private arrangement between these two parties, and again the resident should not be charged an extra sum. There may be instances where a local authority assesses a resident as requiring specialised activities which are not included in the residential care contract. In these circumstances if the local authority wishes to recover a charge for the service, they will need to charge the resident himself, bearing in mind the amount he will have remaining after his residential charge has been calculated and his other outgoings have been taken into consideration.

Charging for MHA 1983 and CSDPA 1970 services

8.108 Authorities are only empowered to charge for services provided under the statutes listed in HASSASSAA 1983 s17(2). This list does not mention MHA 1983 or CSDPA 1970 s2.

Services under MHA 1983

8.109 **Section 117 services** When a person who has been detained under s3 (or one of the criminal provisions) of MHA 1983 is discharged from hospital, s/he has a right to have their after-care services provided free of charge under MHA 1983 s117.

8.110   The SSI Advice states (at para 2) that services provided under MHA 1983 s117 are not subject to charging.

8.111   In *R v Richmond LBC ex p Watson*,[87] Sullivan J confirmed that it was unlawful for local authorities to charge for services under s117, including residential accommodation. This decision, and the nature of s117 services, are considered in greater detail at para 5.120 above. Guidance issued by the Department of Health as LAC(2000)3 confirms the government's view that charges for residential care under s117 are unlawful and that 'social services authorities still charging for after-care services provided under s117 should immediately cease charging since there is no power to do so'.

8.112   **Guardianship** MHA 1983 ss7–9 provide for the making of guardianship orders and for the powers of guardians. They do not however authorise or require the provision of any services. Accordingly, where residential or domiciliary care services are provided for a person the subject of a guardianship order, these services are made available under other statutory provisions (ie, NAA 1948 s21, CSDPA 1970 s2, MHA 1983 s117, etc). Whether or not a charge can be levied for such a service depends, of course, upon whether charging is permitted under the statute in question. Thus, if the user was formerly detained under s3 or one of the criminal provisions of the 1983 Act, services will be provided under s117 of the Act for which a charge cannot be raised.

8.113   The Department of Health has expressed the opinion[88] that the right to free services under s117 also applies to guardianship. Most probably the department was referring to guardianship under s19 (considered below), although it might be that the advice addresses the more general issue of the human rights predicament of users who are required by their guardian to live (against their wishes) at a residential or nursing home.

8.114   Such persons have no choice but to live at a specified address, and while this may not amount to a form of detention, it is clearly an infringement of the right to choose the type of home they live in. If

---

87 (1999) 2 CCLR 402, upheld by the Court of Appeal [2000] LGR 318.

88 In a letter of 18 January 1995 to Oldham Social Services. The letter states that 'until recently it had been assumed that local authorities could use an implied power to charge based upon s111 Local Government Act 1972, if they wished to charge for any services where they had no express power to charge. Following the decision in *R v Richmond LBC ex p McCarthy* [1992] 2 AC 48, it is now clear that this is not the case . . .'.

the state is requiring them to live in more expensive accommodation (a registered care or nursing home rather than rented accommodation) then the added requirement that they pay the additional cost may be a violation of their right to respect for their home (article 8) in combination with article 14 (non-discrimination).

8.115 Where however the guardianship order is pursuant to MHA 1983 s19, then, since the patient is in such circumstances also entitled to s117 services, it follows that these services must be provided without charge to the user.

CSDPA 1970 s2

8.116 Notwithstanding that s2 services are not listed in HASSASSAA 1983 s17(2), the SSI Advice states that charges can be recovered for services provided under that section, as 'these services are arranged by local authorities in exercise of their functions under s29 of the 1948 Act'.

8.117 This advice was upheld by the Court of Appeal, in *R v Powys CC ex p Hambidge*.[89] The relationship between CSDPA 1970 s2 and NAA 1948 s29 is however a difficult one. While the Court of Appeal decision confirms that local authorities are acting lawfully when they charge adults for the services they provide under s2, the judgment does not address the problem of the different client groups covered by the two sections. If services, assessed as being necessary under s2, are actually provided 'in exercise of functions under s29', it begs the question of the authority for providing disabled children with such services; s29 only applies to persons aged 18 or over. The Court of Appeal declined to respond to this question as Mrs Hambidge was aged over 18.

8.118 It appears likely, however, that local authorities have no power to charge for services provided to children under CSDPA 1970 s2 (and as noted in *R v Bexley LBC ex p B*,[90] most domiciliary services provided to disabled children are provided under the 1970 Act).

---

89 (1998) 1 CCLR 458.
90 (2000) 3 CCLR 15.

CHAPTER 9

Drug/alcohol and HIV/AIDS services

9.1   Introduction

9.5   Assessment procedures

9.6   The provision and commissioning of services

9.7   Purchaser consortia

9.10   Service user failure

9.12   **Residential care and nursing home accommodation**

9.14   Social services' obligations

9.18   NHS obligations

9.23   **Community care services**

9.26   **Drug and alcohol specific grant**

9.28   **People with HIV/AIDS**

9.31   HIV/AIDS Support Grant

Introduction

9.1   The white paper *Health of the Nation*[1] and the Policy Guidance confirm that an important objective of the community care reforms was to ensure that community care services were available to those whose need for them arose by reason of alcohol or drug misuse. The Policy Guidance (at para 8.4) emphasises the point thus:

> The Government attaches a high priority[2] to tackling the problems associated with the misuse of alcohol and drugs, and to ensuring the provision of a comprehensive network of services for alcohol and drug misusers.

9.2   In similar vein, in guidance on the housing and community care interface, LAC(92)12 makes the following point:

> Housing authorities will need to be aware that for some clients, such as alcohol and drug misusers, their care plan may include a planned progression from some form of residential care to a more independent lifestyle, possibly away from their original area of residence.[3]

9.3   In many cases this objective has been met by clarifying existing duties by issuing directions and guidance, although in addition there have been minor statutory amendments and the provision of a new and specific grant for such services. The main circular guidance is LAC(93)2, which requires 'LAs to attach a high priority to alcohol and drug misusers within community care. Alcohol and drug misuse is a problem both for individuals and for the public health' (para 1).

9.4   LAC(93)2 stresses the special circumstances surrounding the provision of services for people who misuse alcohol and/or drugs.

> 12. Addressing the needs of people with alcohol and drug problems will present a particular challenge to LAs. The aim must be to respond effectively and to offer a programme of care that will help the misuser make positive changes to his or her life. LAs will need to bear in mind that people who misuse alcohol and drugs may:
> - present to LAs with problems other than alcohol and/or drug misuse. LAs will need to ensure that the possibility of alcohol and drug misuse is covered in essential procedures;
> - have particularly complex needs including urgent workplace or family crises or difficulties with child care, which may not have been revealed to LA services;

---

1   (1993). See, eg, paras D.17–D.18.
2   The point is also made in the white paper *Tackling Drugs Together* (Cm 2846, 1995) at para B.55.
3   At para 2 of the Annex to the circular.

- move between areas frequently, and a significant proportion will have no settled residence or be living away from their area of ordinary residence;
- self-refer to agencies which are not in their home area, both because of their transient lifestyle and for therapeutic reasons, and many will need urgent help;
- avoid contact with statutory services; drug misusers in particular may be reluctant to become involved with statutory agencies because of the illegal nature of their drug-related activities;
- need to be provided with services several times before they succeed in controlling their alcohol or drug misuse;
- require residential treatment and rehabilitation as a positive treatment choice;
- sometimes behave unpredictably and may not fit easily into assessment and care management systems designed to meet the needs of other client groups.

Assessment procedures

9.5 Circular LAC(93)2 makes a number of important points concerning the need for authorities to adopt flexible assessment procedures in relation to people who misuse alcohol or drugs, and the related need in many cases to develop a close working relationship with the probation services.

13. People with serious and urgent alcohol and/or drug problems are likely to need a rapid response because of crises and to capture fluctuating motivation. Serious deterioration which may carry social, legal and care implications may ensue if there is delay before assessment or if assessment procedures are prolonged.

Eligibility for assessment
14. LAs should ensure that any criteria they may develop governing eligibility for assessment are sensitive to the circumstances of alcohol and drug misusers. As with all other user groups, the LA should have criteria for determining the level of assessment that is appropriate to the severity or complexity of the need. LAs should ensure that:
- arrangements have been agreed with all the agencies in their area to which misusers are likely to present for help, which will enable those agencies to initiate assessment procedures where in their view they are indicated;
- arrangements are in place to facilitate the assessment of a person by another authority where that person is ordinarily resident in that other authority's area, for example by agreeing with another LA to undertake an assessment on that authority's behalf;

- individuals who are of no settled residence are not excluded from assessment by means of eligibility criteria which require duration of residence. The Department proposes to issue guidance to LAs in 1993 about the resolution of disputes and the procedures to be adopted in the last resort where disputes cannot be resolved between the authorities concerned.[4] Disputes about ordinary residence should not prevent people receiving the care they need.

Adapting assessment to the special needs of alcohol and drug misusers
15. LAs will need to ensure that their assessment systems take full account of the different ways in which alcohol and drug misusers present for services, their different characteristics and their particular needs:

- standard LA assessment procedures and documentation should include consideration of substance misuse.
- LA staff will need to be able to identify the indications of substance misuse so that specialist agencies can be involved where appropriate.

Rapid assessment procedures ('fast-track' assessment)
16. There are a range of organisations and professionals who deal frequently with alcohol and drug misusers. A great many of the services, including virtually all residential services, are provided by the independent sector. There is, therefore, within the independent sector, a substantial reservoir of experienced professionals with skills to undertake assessment in this field. LAs should consider involving independent sector agencies in the assessment process. Practice guidance issued by the Department of Health Social Services Inspectorate[5] emphasises the importance of training to equip those people within LAs who undertake assessment with the necessary knowledge and skills. Policy guidance issued by the Department, *Community Care in the Next Decade and Beyond*[6] states that where a specialist service – for example a drug and alcohol service – is provided by an independent agency under arrangements with a social services department, it will be possible to include assessment of needs in relation to such services in contract arrangements. In these circumstances LAs will need to ensure that the specialist agency is aware of other potential needs for which LAs have a responsibility.

17. Residential placements should not normally take place without a comprehensive needs assessment. Where assessment is contracted to an independent specialist agency, decisions to commit resources and ultimate responsibility for the assessment remains with the LA.

---

4   This was effected via LAC(93)7 Pt II – see para 4.28 above.
5   *Care Management and Assessment – A Practitioners' Guide* (1991) see para 3.31 above. Referred to in this text as the Practice Guidance.
6   Referred to in this text as the Policy Guidance; see para 1.25 above.

18. Because many alcohol and drug misusers present or are referred to services outside their area of ordinary residence LAs are encouraged to work together to identify systems so that they can feel confident about committing resources on the basis of an assessment undertaken in another LA. This may be facilitated by the development of standard and agreed assessment procedures and forms and networks of named responsible officers within LAs.

19. The Department is encouraging local authority associations to work with the independent sector to establish rapid assessment procedures for alcohol and drug misusers and good practice guidance in out of area referrals which they can commend to local authorities.

20. Individual LAs and independent service providers should, together, ensure that rapid assessment procedures meet the needs of alcohol and drug misusers. In order to do so LAs and providers may want to determine the pattern of referrals of their residents/clients in order to establish contact and set up appropriate arrangements where regular flows exist. LAs and independent sector service providers will together wish to have regard to the Department's study examining good practice in care management and assessment for alcohol and drug misusers which will be available to local authorities shortly.

Emergency action
21. LAs need to be aware that alcohol and drug misusers may sometimes be in such urgent need that residential care will need to be provided immediately. *The Care Management and Assessment* practice guidance issued by the Department of Health covers the arrangements for urgent admission to both residential and nursing home care.[7]

22. LAs may contract with a provider to offer an emergency direct access service for people in urgent need, with assessment and a decision about longer term treatment following as soon as practicable. LAs may wish to contract with a voluntary organisation to provide direct access to residential care without assessment in these circumstances. In such cases of urgent need the area of ordinary residence of the person should not be a consideration.[8]

Out of area referrals
23. Because of the transient lifestyles of a significant proportion of drug and alcohol misusers LAs will be involved in negotiations about area of ordinary residence for people with alcohol and drug misuse problems to a greater extent than for others. Where people are ordinarily resident in the area of the LA undertaking the assessment,

7   Practice Guidance at para 4.45 for nursing homes and para 4.97 for residential homes.
8   NAA 1948 s24(3).

there may be therapeutic benefit in referring people to a residential service away from the area in which they are experiencing their alcohol and drug problems. LAs are reminded that the statutory direction on choice[9] of residential accommodation advises that people assessed as needing residential care should be able to exercise choice over the place where they receive that care. LAs should ensure that resources can be identified for out of area placements.

24. LAs should ensure that there are arrangements in place for responding to the following types of out of area referrals:
- where people are ordinarily resident outside the area of the LA undertaking the assessment, there will be a need to liaise with the LA in the area of ordinary residence to establish responsibility for funding the care package.
- where people are ordinarily resident outside the area of the LA but are in urgent need of residential care.[10]
- where it is impossible to identify a person's area of ordinary residence; in these circumstances the LA where they present for services should assume responsibility for arranging and providing the necessary services.[11]

Probation service
25. Some alcohol and/or drug misusing clients of the Probation Service will continue to seek access to residential and non-residential care, and LAs should liaise with probation services to ensure that these needs can be considered within the community care arrangements. Attention should be given to establishing joint assessment or common assessment procedures, such as those LAs have developed with other client groups. LAs will also need to be aware that there may be requests for resources to provide residential and non-residential care for persons whose alcohol or drug misuse comes to light through offending, appearance in court and/or involvement with probation services. LAs are reminded that the Criminal Justice Act 1991 which came into force on 1 October 1992 emphasises that it is preferable for offenders who misuse alcohol or drugs to be dealt with in the community rather than in custody.[12]

In this respect, the strategy paper, *Tackling Drugs To Build A Better Britain* (1998)[13] also highlighted the crucial role of inter-disciplinary working (particularly between health, social services, housing, education and employment services).

9   National Assistance Act 1948 (Choice of Accommodation) Directions 1992; see para 4.55 and Appendix B.
10   NAA 1948 s24(3)(b).
11   NAA 1948 s24(3)(a) and s32.
12   See Powers of Criminal Courts Act 1973 Sch 1A.
13   Cm 3945, p23.

The provision and commissioning of services

9.6   The strategy paper, *Tackling Drugs To Build A Better Britain*[14] makes specific reference to the 'growing evidence that treatment works' and 'in particular, harm reduction work over the last 15 years has had a major impact on the rate of HIV and other drug-related infections. And rehabilitation programmes have shown real gains in crime reduction'. It however went on to caution that 'the scope, accessibility and effectiveness of available treatments are inconsistent between localities and generally insufficient'. There is considerable insecurity about funding and disparity in provision. Consequently, there is rarely immediate access for a drug misuser to a treatment programme – given the urgency of the needs of drug misusers, this is unacceptable.

Purchaser consortia

9.7   The Department of Health publication *Purchasing Effective Treatment and Care for Drug Misusers* (March 1997, para 5.1) encouraged, whenever possible, joint commissioning between health, social services and other agencies, such as probation. It also advised on the benefits of forming consortia which could share information about needs, costs and quality, and which could pool specialist skills such as working with the prison service (para 5.3). From the purchasers perspective, membership of a consortium enables them to impose agreed service standards and prices. From a provider perspective the benefits are that they do not have to meet different service standards from the separate purchasers. Large consortia (such as the 29 local authority London consortia) however have such a dominant position in the market place that they can, in effect, create an unhealthy unbalanced market where they effectively dictate all the contractual terms (particularly price). The guidance cautions therefore that:

> Where purchasing intentions of health and local authorities change and funding is shifted from one service provider to another, purchasers should consult with other purchasers and funders of that service, and the service provider before a decision is made, to ensure that the impact of such shifts in funding is minimised for both provider and purchaser.[15]

9.8   It is possible that oppressive action by such consortia might constitute oppressive trade practices contrary to articles 81 and 82 of the EC Treaty (formerly articles 85 and 86) and more importantly, domes-

14 Ibid p22.
15 Ibid para 5.5.

tically contrary to Competition Act 1998 s18. Action by 'undertakings' which have the effect of distorting competition or amount to an abuse of a dominant position in the market place may violate s18 of the 1998 Act and articles 81 and 82 of the Treaty.

9.9   The crucial (and undecided) issue is whether consortia members constitute 'undertakings' within the meaning of the Treaty. Although the term is not defined, it has been held that in general member states and local authorities, when exercising public law powers, do not constitute undertakings for the purpose of the Treaty,[16] although if the local authority or other public body is involved in a quasi-commercial activity it may come within the definition.[17] The question may become of increasing relevance if primary care trusts become significant members of such consortia.

Service user failure

9.10   Drug and alcohol services can be relatively expensive, and the guidance (LAC(93)2 para 11) states, 'there is a comparatively rapid turnover' of such service users in residential accommodation due in part to the relatively high 'failure rate' experienced by people trying to rid themselves of an addiction.

9.11   The importance of this issue was re-emphasised in *Purchasing Effective Treatment and Care for Drug Misusers* (March 1997) which stated (at para 1.7):

> Drug misusers suffer relapses, and may need several periods of treatment before they achieve the ultimate aim of 'abstinence'. 'Instant' cures are relatively rare, partly because drug misuse is closely associated with many other problems. These include unemployment, family break up, homelessness and crime. Tackling drug misuse effectively may therefore involve a range of interventions by several agencies, for people at different stages of their drug misusing careers. If these are not properly co-ordinated resources will be wasted.

Residential care and nursing home accommodation

9.12   Where addiction is severe, the service user will often be seeking continuing care support from the NHS in addition to services (or a commitment to future services) from the social services authority. These are considered separately below.

16   C–159 and 160/91 *Poucet v Assurances Generales de France* [1993] ECR 637.

17   *Höfner & Elser v Macroton* [1991] ECR I–1079.

9.13   Registered Homes Act 1984 s1(1) requires (subject to general exceptions) the registration of homes which provide residential accommodation with board and personal care for persons in need of that care by reason of (among other things) 'past or present dependence on alcohol or drugs'.[18] Where the home provides in addition nursing or other treatment by specially controlled techniques, it will be subject to the nursing home registration requirements of the Act.[19]

Social services' obligations

9.14   The duty to provide residential care or nursing home accommodation under NAA 1948 s21 specifically includes a duty towards persons who are 'alcoholic or drug-dependent'.[20] The duties under s21 are considered in detail in Chapter 4.

9.15   The role of residential care facilities is the subject of guidance in LAC(93)2, which states:

> 10. Residential services are an important component of overall service provision for alcohol and drug misusers and have developed as a national network. There are many LAs without such an alcohol or drug service in their area. Residential services offer a number of different treatment approaches, and LAs will need to ensure that people are referred to a service best suited to their needs. LAs can obtain information about the network of residential service provision in publications from two national voluntary organisations, Alcohol Concern and SCODA.[21]

> 11. The length of treatment programmes in a residential setting varies between three and eighteen months. The comparatively rapid turnover of alcohol and drug clients in residential care mean that places will begin to become vacant on a relatively large scale after 1 April 1993. LAs will need to address issues of assessment and care management for these people now so that they are ready from 1 April 1993 to provide new applicants with the care they need.[22]

18 For detailed comment on this aspect see R Jones *The Registered Homes Act Manual* (Sweet & Maxwell, 1993) para 1–013 which refers to LAC(86)6 paras 12–16 and *Home Life: a code of practice for residential care* (Centre for Policy and Ageing, 1984, revised 1986) and *A Better Home Life* (Centre for Policy and Ageing, 1996) section 4.7 (which has a brief section on 'People recovering from drug addiction and alcohol abuse').

19 Registered Homes Act 1984 ss21 and 23.

20 LAC(93)10 App 1 para 2(6).

21 Standing Conference on Drug Abuse, Waterbridge House, 32–36 Loman Street, London SE1 0EE. Tel: 020 7928 9500.

22 LAC(93)2 was issued in January 1993.

9.16   A Social Services Inspectorate report, *Residential Care for People with Drug/Alcohol Problems* (1994), made the following general comments concerning the accommodation needs of such people:

- Drug/alcohol misusers often have a range of problems which may contribute to, or be exacerbated by, substance misuse; residential care is only one part of a continuum of services.
- Residential care may be the preferred option most appropriate to meet individual need for one of the following reasons:
  - the service user may need 'time out' from an environment which is not conducive to cessation of drug/alcohol misuse;
  - the service user many have a number of complex and inter-related problems which can be addressed only in a residential environment.
- A primary and major need of people, in other client groups, requiring residential care is usually for supervised accommodation; for drug/alcohol misusers, accommodation is often only one of a range of needs which require intensive support.
- The characteristics and needs of drug/alcohol misusers are different in some ways from those of other client groups who require residential care because they are unable, or do not feel able, to live independently in their home environment. Many drug/alcohol misusers are in their early adult years and residential care is required as an appropriate temporary environment in which to provide intensive therapeutic care as well as physical and social care. Residential care is rarely provided for drug/alcohol misusers as a permanent home.

9.17   The SSI report lists some of the residential care approaches which have been developed for people who misuse drugs/alcohol. The list is useful, as it is an indication of the range of possible services for which funding should be considered by authorities. On occasions some authorities have indicated that they are only prepared to fund services which aim at 'detox' and 'rehab', in other words, services whose specific aim is to stop the service user taking drugs by removing his or her physiological and/or psychological addiction and then promoting social rehabilitation. Given that the duties under s21 are not so restricted, such a policy may well amount to an unlawful fettering of the authority's discretion (if indeed it has any). The list includes a short description of the service. The following is an abbreviation of the information:

Dry houses
Dry houses represent the largest sector of residential care for alcohol/ drug misusers. The aim is to maintain an alcohol/drug free environment,

with a variety of relapse procedures. They offer a combination of individual counselling through a key worker system, supplemented by group work, social skills training and practical help to encourage the use of local community resources such as health, education, employment and recreational facilities.

Therapeutic communities
Therapeutic communities have a hierarchical structure and residents, in working through the programme (which includes intensive group therapy sessions), progress their way through the hierarchy.

Minnesota method units
A treatment based on the 12 steps of the Fellowship of Alcoholics/ Narcotics Anonymous and the belief that addiction/chemical dependency is a disease.

Christian philosophy houses
Houses which provide rehabilitation within a Christian ethos of care. Treatment usually involves some written or course work as well as structured teaching and counselling. Residents are required to participate in the daily routine of the community, which is the focus of therapeutic activity.

General houses
General houses are those which have a mixed and varied approach to the care of people with drug/alcohol problems. The emphasis is on individual care, and group work may be offered either as an option or as an integral part of the regime.

Heavy drinkers' houses
Also known as 'wet hostels', these provide support and care for long-term alcohol misusers who appear unable or unwilling to make use of other forms of supported accommodation. There is neither a formal programme nor an expectation that residents will work towards rehabilitation. The goal of most residents is a gradual improvement in their quality of life. Some stay for many years, seeing the house as their long-term home.

Residential units which focus on harm minimisation
There has long been concern for people who continue to misuse drugs and who remain vulnerable to the health and social problems which result from homelessness and a chaotic lifestyle. The advent of HIV infection and AIDS has further highlighted the need for services for this particular group. Pioneering projects have been developed which offer accommodation, support and nursing care for continuing drug users who receive a prescription from their GP, a Drug Dependency Unit or another specialist service. Priority is given to harm minimisation through controlled prescribing and the stabilisation of drug use.

NHS obligations

9.18   The effects of alcohol/drug misuse can be life threatening and frequently require specialist medical and nursing interventions. The NHS has a clear responsibility in this field, although it is, in relation to such matters as rehabilitation and recovery (see para 6.101 above), an overlapping responsibility with social services authorities. LAC(93)2 confirms[23] that 'the new community care arrangements do not affect health authorities' responsibilities for funding the health-care element of any alcohol and drug service. LAs will need to consider and draw up agreements with health authorities covering arrangements for funding treatment and rehabilitation services for people with alcohol and/or drug problems'.

9.19   There is some evidence that some health authorities have (since the implementation of the community care reforms) adopted rigid policies of only funding the 'detox' element of any nursing home placement and of limiting this to a fixed period; such a rigid policy would appear to be prima facie unlawful.

9.20   Where the original placement in a nursing home is made (and funded) by the social services authority, the prior consent of the district health authority to such a placement must be obtained[24] except in cases of urgency.[25] Guidance on identifying the appropriate health authority is given in LAC(92)22, which at para 5 states that social services/health authority liaison arrangements will need 'to be sufficiently flexible so that there is a minimum of delay in the necessary consent being given. This will be particularly important for some client groups, eg, people without a settled way of life, drug and alcohol misusers'.

9.21   The white paper *Tackling Drugs Together*[26] in referring to the role of health care services stated:[27]

> The Government's aim is to provide a comprehensive range and choice of local services to help drug misusers give up drugs and maintain abstinence. Such services also promote better health and reduce the risks of drug misuse, including infections associated with sharing injecting equipment such as HIV and hepatitis. These services include residential detoxification and rehabilitation, community drug dependency services, needle and syringe exchange

23   At para 7.
24   NAA 1948 s26(1C).
25   NAA 1948 s26(1D).
26   Cm 2846 (HMSO, 1995).
27   At para B.49.

schemes, advice and counselling, and after-care and support services. Facilities are provided by both statutory and independent agencies. General practitioners are also encouraged to address the needs of drug misusers. Guidelines on clinical management, *Drug Misuse and Dependence*[28] were issued to all doctors in 1991. Guidelines for the clinical management of substance misusers in police custody[29] were issued in March 1995.

9.22 EL(95)114 required health authorities to review and report on their arrangements for 'shared care' of drug misusers. The outcome of this review and advice on general health authority commissioning is contained in the Department of Health publication *Purchasing Effective Treatment and Care for Drug Misusers* (March 1997), Appendix C, which lists a number of specific health services that ought to be available for drug misusers. These include: hospital drug detoxification units,[30] providing urgent assessment and acute care as well as support, counselling and rehabilitation; methadone reduction programmes; hospital outpatient and community-based clinics; general counselling; and GP training and encouragement to 'identify drug misuse, promote harm minimisation and where appropriate refer to specialist services'. The publication expressed particular concern about failures of co-ordination between health and local authorities such that there were 'long waits for detoxification', noting that this may mean that drug misusers lose their motivation to continue with treatment (para 8.5).

Community care services

9.23 Services under NHSA 1977 Sch 8 para 2 are specifically available for persons who are 'alcoholic or drug-dependent' and these services are considered at para 5.80 above. In general, drug and alcohol misusers will only qualify for services under CSDPA 1970 s2 where their addiction is such as to bring them within the criteria of being 'substantially and permanently handicapped'.[31]

9.24 The description of possible arrangements which can be made

---

28 Department of Health (HMSO, 1991).
29 *Substance Misuse Detainees in Police Custody: Guidelines on Clinical Management* (DoH, 1995).
30 Or via specialist nursing home facilities.
31 This will be so even though such services are also available to persons suffering from a mental disorder of any description, since MHA 1983 s1(3) excludes persons whose disorder is solely attributable to dependence on alcohol or drugs.

under NHSA 1977 Sch 8 para 2 is so widely drafted as to be capable of encompassing virtually all the traditional domiciliary and community care services. The inclusion in the directions (Appendix 3 to LAC(93)10) of a separate category of potential service 'specifically for persons who are alcoholic or drug-dependent', is clearly designed to ensure that authorities are empowered to provide all the relevant services which may be required by alcohol or drug misusers. The Policy Guidance (at para 8.6) states that the range of services local authorities will need to consider 'include prevention and harm minimisation, advice and counselling, day care and residential rehabilitation'.[32]

9.25   *Purchasing Effective Treatment and Care for Drug Misusers* (March 1997), gives commissioning advice on various community and residential-based services, including outreach programmes and structured day care.[33] It however emphasised the central part played by counselling (both structured and general) in all drug misuse treatments (para 8.6) and the 'evidence that residential rehabilitation programmes can effectively help many drug misusers, particularly with chaotic lifestyles and severe problems related to their misuse (para 8.5).

Drug and alcohol specific grant

9.26   The cost of local authority drug and alcohol misuse services is for the most part covered by general community care funding although under LASSA 1970 s7E grant support is available to local authorities to enable them to support voluntary organisations providing care and services for persons who are, have been, or are likely to become dependent upon alcohol or drugs. In 1997/98 the grant amounted to £2.5 million. Advice on the application of the grant-making power is given in Chapter 8 of the Policy Guidance and the secretary of state's directions under LASSA 1970 s7E(b) are at Appendix C/6–7 to the Policy Guidance.

9.27   The situation is similar for health authorities, in that services are expected to be funded out of their mainstream budgets although a special grant also exists in the form of the 'Drug Misuse Services Special Allocation' which in 1997/98 amounted to £37 million.

32   See *New Options: Changing residential and social care for drug users* (SCODA, 1997), see n21 above.

33   See also *Structured Day Programmes: new options in community care for drug misusers* (SCODA, 1996), see n21 above.

People with HIV/AIDS

9.28 In contrast to the requirements of people who abuse alcohol or drugs, the needs of people with HIV or AIDS are not specifically mentioned in the community care legislation or directions. However, by virtue of their illness people with HIV/AIDS are potential community care users and therefore entitled to an assessment and, where appropriate, services. In general residential care or nursing home accommodation will be provided by social services departments under NAA 1948 s21 (see Chapter 4 above) and by health authorities under the continuing care obligations (see para 6.75 above).

9.29 In relation to non-accommodation services, the social services obligation under CSDPA 1970 s2 is owed to people who are already 'substantially and permanently handicapped'. These services are therefore only likely to be available for people who have developed the AIDS symptoms. In contrast the social services duty under NHSA 1977 Sch 8 is owed to people who have an illness (whether or not it has already resulted in them becoming permanently and substantially handicapped) or for people who are recovering from an illness or in order to prevent illness. These services, which are of primary relevance to people with HIV, but who have not yet developed the AIDS symptoms, are considered in detail at para 5.80 above.

9.30 The Department of Health has published guidance and issued a number of circulars concerning the social care needs of people with HIV infection and AIDS. These include:

1) HIV infection – The working interface between voluntary organisations and social services departments (1992).

2) Children and HIV – Guidance for local authorities (1992).

3) The health and social care of people with HIV infection and AIDS – Findings and good practice recommendations from research funded by the DoH 1986–1992 (1993).

4) Women and HIV (1993).

5) Inspection of local authority services for people affected by HIV/AIDS: Overview (1994).

6) Implementing Caring for People: Caring for People with HIV and AIDS (1994).

7) Support Grant for social services for people with AIDS 1998/99: LAC(98)9.

HIV/AIDS Support Grant

9.31   Each year the Department of Health provides to social services authorities a specific support grant to assist in the provision of services for people with AIDS. Circular guidance has been issued on the support grant scheme as LAC(98)9.

9.32   In 1998/99 a total grant of £13.7 million was made available. The scheme operates on a 70:30 basis with authorities providing at least 30 per cent of expenditure from their own resources.

9.33   The general aim of the scheme is to enable social services departments to draw up strategic plans, based on local population needs assessments, for commissioning social care for people with HIV/AIDS and to enable social services departments to finance provision of social care for people with HIV/AIDS (including their partners, carers and families).

9.34   The grant can be used to support the costs of HIV/AIDS training related to community care services as well as joint projects established to address the accommodation needs of people with HIV/AIDS as part of a co-ordinated strategy to facilitate community care needs (but not for the provision of housing alone).

9.35   The guidance recognises that HIV/AIDS prevalence remains concentrated in London and is low elsewhere. It emphasises the important role played by voluntary organisations in developing services for people with HIV/AIDS and the need for local authorities to work in conjunction with their respective health authorities.

CHAPTER 10

Housing and community care

10.1   Introduction

10.8   Collaboration in assessment and care planning

10.14   Housing homeless persons overlap

10.19   Disabled facilities grants

10.23   Role of the housing authority
         'Reasonable and practicable' • *'Necessary and appropriate'*

10.28   Grant-eligible works

10.29   Mandatory grants
         Making the dwelling safe • *Facilitating access and provision* • *Room usable for sleeping* • *Bathroom* • *Facilitating preparation and cooking of food* • *Heating, lighting and power* • *Dependent residents*

10.38   Discretionary grants

10.39   Ineligibility for grant and the social services overlap

10.41   Fixtures and fittings

10.42   Eligibility
         Means-testing

10.46   Timescales and loan deferment

Introduction

10.1   The importance of appropriate housing for people with community care needs is enormous. Over 1.3 million tenants and owner-occupiers are beneficiaries of housing-related community care services and over £2 billion is spent each year on the housing aspects of community care.[1] Disabled people place a high value on appropriate accommodation. A Help the Aged 'Independent Living Survey' in 1995 identified aids and adaptations, such as stairlifts and wheelchair ramps, as the most effective means to enable them to remain in their own homes and a 1998 Audit Commission report highlighted housing as the single most important service required by people with mental health problems to live independently in the community.[2]

10.2   The widespread neglect of housing in community care planning at local and central government level has been described in a Rowntree report in the following terms:

> Housing is more than a neglected dimension of community care. It is more, even, than a 'key component'. The logic of the 'new' community care entails the redefinition of housing as the basic requirement – the foundation – of community care. Anything less than this will reinforce past mistakes, expensive in human and financial terms, which have relegated so many people to less-than-ordinary lives in less-than-ordinary housing.[3]

10.3   While this chapter is primarily concerned with the obligations on housing authorities to provide disabled facilities grants and, to a lesser extent, the statutory obligations to house homeless people, it must be appreciated that the issue of appropriate accommodation is a fundamental theme in relation to almost all community care services. As the Audit Commission has noted, 'it is not simply the provision of a roof over people's heads that makes housing's contribution so important, it is the personal support to help vulnerable people cope with everyday living – for example, negotiating the complexities of rent payments or resolving problems with water, gas and electricity suppliers – that makes the difference between life in the community and institutionalisation'.[4] Many aspects of the housing contribution

1   *Home Alone* report into the role of housing in community care (Audit Commission, 1998) paras 6 and 8.

2   Ibid.

3   P Arnold et al *Community Care: The housing dimension* (Joseph Rowntree Foundation, 1993); and see also P Arnold and D Page *Housing and Community Care* (University of Humberside, 1992).

4   *Home Alone* report into the role of housing in community care (Audit Commission,) para 7.

to community care are therefore considered elsewhere in this book, most notably the provision of residential care accommodation, which is discussed in Chapter 4 above and home adaptations under the Chronically Sick and Disabled Persons Act (CSDPA) 1970 s2(1)(e) is considered in detail at para 5.60 above.

10.4   Housing authorities, in meeting their responsibilities under Housing Act 1985 s8 to consider housing conditions and provision in their area are required to have specific regard to the special needs of chronically sick and disabled persons in their area under their powers in CSDPA 1970 s3, including the provision or adaptation of existing accommodation for their own disabled tenants. In this respect Department of the Environment guidance Circular 17/96 (Annex I para 2) reminds authorities of their 'wide responsibilities in identifying disabled people who need help with essential adaptations arising out of their disability' and that they should 'consider the needs of the disabled person in the context of their wider life-style and desired activities'.

10.5   The community care needs of disadvantaged people will not infrequently come to the notice of the courts by way of possession proceedings founded upon their failure to pay rent or their behaviour. In such cases courts have power to adjourn to enable an urgent assessment of needs to be carried out. Such an assessment will inevitably involve the social services department liaising with the housing authority under National Health Service and Community Care Act (NHSCCA) 1990 s47(3). The courts have wide powers to adjourn possession proceedings in secure and assured tenancy cases.[5] However, in assured shorthold cases judges will need to rely on the power they have under County Courts Act 1984 s3 and the power to adjourn in the Civil Procedure Rules 3.1 and 3.2 in furtherance of the over-riding objective in rule 1 to enable the court to deal with the case 'justly'. Where the application for possession is brought by a housing department in the public sector, a failure to liaise with the social services department and the absence of a full assessment will be relevant to the question of 'reasonableness'.

10.6   In *Croydon LBC v Moody*,[6] the Court of Appeal concluded that in determining whether it was reasonable to make a possession order on the grounds of nuisance, relevant factors included the fact that the

5   Housing Act 1985 s85 and Housing Act 1988 s9. It will be maladministration for a local authority not to provide support (including welfare rights advice) for an existing client which could avoid his arrears/eviction, see complaint 98/A/0280 against Barnet LBC.

6   (1999) 2 CCLR 92.

defendant suffered from a personality disorder that was amenable to treatment and that he had agreed to this treatment, as well as his likely fate in the event of an eviction order being made.

10.7   In *R v Kensington and Chelsea RLBC ex p Kujtim*,[7] the Court of Appeal held that the duty to provide accommodation (under NAA 1948 s21, see para 3.98 above) can be treated as discharged if the applicant 'either unreasonably refuses to accept the accommodation provided or if, following its provision, by his conduct he manifests a persistent and unequivocal refusal to observe the reasonable requirements of the local authority in relation to the occupation of such accommodation'.

Collaboration in assessment and care planning

10.8   The need for housing authorities and social services authorities to co-operate fully in the community care planning and assessment process is obvious and is itself a statutory obligation on the social services authority.

10.9   NHSCCA 1990 s47(3) provides:

> (3) If at any time during the assessment of the needs of any person under subsection (1)(a) above, it appears to a local authority –
> (a) that there may be a need for the provision to that person by such Health Authority as may be determined in accordance with regulations of any services under the National Health Service Act 1977, or
> (b) that there may be the need for the provision to him of any services which fall within the functions of a local housing authority (within the meaning of the Housing Act 1985)[8] which is not the local authority carrying out the assessment,
> the local authority shall notify that Health Authority or local housing authority and invite them to assist, to such extent as is reasonable in the circumstances, in the making of the assessment; and, in making their decision as to the provision of services needed for the person in question, the local authority shall take into account any services which are likely to be made available for him by that Health Authority or local housing authority.

10.10   It follows that (in non-unitary authorities) where during the assessment process a housing need is disclosed, the assessing authority

---

7   (1999) 2 CCLR 340 at 354I.
8   A 'housing function' is defined by Housing Act 1985 ss228 onwards and covers the wide range of activities connected with the provision of housing.

is obliged to notify the housing authority and at the same time to specify what assistance that authority is requested to provide in order to facilitate the assessment. Although the housing authority is not under any statutory duty to respond or co-operate,[9] where the assessing authority notifies the housing authority of a housing need, separate parallel duties under the Housing Act 1996 may well be triggered. The housing authority will be under a duty to receive applications[10] and to make enquiries under Housing Act 1996 s184 in cases of homelessness and apparent priority need. As the application need not be in any particular form,[11] it may be argued in appropriate cases that notification of housing need amounts in itself to an application made on behalf of the assessed person.[12]

10.11   Presumably, a housing authority's failure to respond – or failure to respond within a reasonable time or in a reasonable manner – would be vulnerable to challenge as maladministration. Likewise, there must be an administrative obligation in unitary authorities for the housing and social services departments to liaise, notwithstanding that this is not required by Children Act (CA) 1989 s47(3) or s27. In *R v Lewisham LBC ex p Pinzon and Patino*,[13] Laws J held that the recommendations in the circular guidance that housing and social services authorities work together does not in itself convert that obligation into a legally enforceable duty.

10.12   The duty to co-operate has been reinforced by joint guidance issued by the Departments of Health and the Environment in LAC(92)12/DOE Circular 10/92, para 11 of which emphasises that in furtherance of this aim the authorities involve other housing providers, such as housing associations where they may be able to help. Further encouragement in the circular in the direction of joint working is given in paras 16 and 19 in particular:

> 16. Social services authorities and housing should construct an individual's care plan with the objective of preserving or restoring non-institutional living as far as possible, and of securing the most appropriate and cost-effective package of care, housing and other services that meets the person's future needs. For some people the

9   See Children Act 1989 s27 and *R v Northavon DC ex p Smith* [1994] 3 All ER 313, HL.

10   *R v Camden LBC ex p Gillan* (1988) *Independent* 13 October, DC.

11   *R v Chiltern DC ex p Roberts* (1990) 23 HLR 387, DC.

12   Disabled adults with insufficient mental capacity to make an application or authorise someone else to do so are not entitled to apply under Part VII of the 1996 Act – see *R v Tower Hamlets LBC ex p Begum* (1993) 25 HLR 319, HL.

13   (1999) 2 CCLR 152.

most appropriate package of care will be in a nursing or residential home, but in many cases this will be achieved by bringing in domiciliary support and making any necessary adaptations to the individual's existing home. The balance between these should be considered carefully. For example, where expensive or disruptive adaptations or improvements are being considered it may be more cost-effective to provide domiciliary care and support together with more minor works. In other cases adaptations or improvements (eg, to help people bathe or cook by themselves) may reduce or obviate the need for domiciliary support . . .

19. The new proposals will require effective relationships to be established and built upon between all parties involved. The aim should be to provide a seamless service for clients, with a mutual recognition of all authorities' responsibilities. This will require all the relevant agencies, including housing, health and social services authorities, to put an emphasis on discussion, understanding and agreement in the planning of services, rather than unilateral decision making. Joint working will be important to maximise the use of existing resources. Administrative systems will need to be developed, perhaps including joint planning structures, in order to monitor and plan effective use of services. Authorities may wish to set up pilot projects. In taking forward their role in community care, housing authorities in particular should have regard to the points made in the annex to this circular [which among other things expands upon what 'joint working' is likely to entail].

10.13   In relation to the processing of disabled facilities grants (see below), Housing Grants, Construction and Regeneration Act 1996 s24(3) imposes a duty on local housing authorities to consult social services authorities in coming to their view on whether the proposed works for which an application for a disabled facilities grant has been made, are 'necessary' and 'appropriate' to meet the needs of the disabled occupant. In this respect the relevant guidance (Department of the Environment Circular 17/96) states:

7.7.2 Within their statutory responsibilities, housing and social services authorities are expected to co-operate fully in carrying out the assessments under section 24(3) for the purposes of meeting the needs of disabled people in their area. In many areas, efficient and effective systems of consultation between the respective authorities have been developed locally in meeting these statutory responsibilities. This not only enables people needing help to receive the best possible service but also ensures that there are common practices for consultation with all those involved. It also ensures that there is wide consistency across the area covered by individual social services authorities.

Housing homeless persons overlap

10.14 The obligation to house homeless persons originated as National Assistance Act (NAA) 1948 s21(1)(b) being a power to provide temporary accommodation for persons who were homeless in circumstances that could not have been foreseen. The power was repealed by the Housing (Homeless Persons) Act 1977, although the relic duty to provide residential accommodation for persons 'in urgent need' remains under s21(1)(a) of the Act (see para 4.39). In *R v Bristol CC ex p Penfold*[14] and subsequent cases, the High Court confirmed that the duty under s21 can extend, in appropriate circumstances, to the provision of ordinary housing accommodation and this aspect is considered in greater detail at para 4.41 above. Likewise in relation to the needs of 'children in need' it has been held that CA 1989 empowers social services authorities to provide ordinary housing in appropriate circumstances, see para 11.12 below.

10.15 Many disabled, elderly or ill people will however also come within the provisions of Housing Act 1996 Pt VII provisions; not least because:

a) a person is homeless for the purposes of the Act if s/he has no accommodation which it would be reasonable for him or her to occupy (s175); and

b) a person is considered in priority need if s/he 'is vulnerable as a result of old age, mental illness or handicap or physical disability or other special reason, or is a person with whom such a person resides or might reasonably be expected to reside' (s189(1)(c)).[15]

10.16 The relationship between the housing authority homelessness obligations under Housing Act 1996 Pt VII and the community care obligations of social services authorities is considered by various circulars (eg, see para 4.38 above) but in particular at paras 3–4 of the Annex to LAC(92)12, namely:

> 3. Housing authorities should bear in mind their duties under the homelessness legislation to secure accommodation for applicant households who are unintentionally homeless and in priority need. Section 59(1) of the Housing Act 1985[16] defines priority need categories as including families with dependent children, households containing a pregnant woman, or people who are vulnerable through old age, mental illness or handicap or other special reasons.

14 (1998) 1 CCLR 315; see also *R v Wigan MBC ex p Tammadge* (1998) 1 CCLR 582, where the respondent did not dispute that s21 permitted the provision of 'normal' or 'bare accommodation, ie, without any board or services; at 584A.

15 As a cautionary note, see *Ortiz v City of Westminster* (1995) 27 HLR 364.

16 Now Housing Act 1996 s189(1).

4. Paragraph 6.11 of the Homelessness Code of Guidance (Third Edition) sets out the procedures to be followed in the case of those recently discharged, or about to be discharged, from psychiatric or learning difficulty (mental handicap) hospitals. In such cases, if the housing authority sees the need, they should establish whether the local social services authority has been involved and give consideration to referring cases for assessment if this seems appropriate.

10.17   The Code of Guidance on Housing Act 1996 (the 1996 Act) Pts VI and VII (7 March 1997) deals with the issue of vulnerability in the following way:

14.5 Section 198(1)(c) defines someone as being in priority need if s/he is vulnerable as a result of:
– old age;
– mental illness or handicap;
– physical disability; or
– other special reason.
The critical test is whether the applicant is less able to fend for him/herself so that s/he will suffer injury or detriment, in circumstances where a less vulnerable person would be able to cope without harmful effects. People who live or might reasonably be expected to live with a vulnerable person are also in priority need.

14.6. **Old age:** while age alone may not necessarily be sufficient for the applicant to be deemed vulnerable the authority should consider whether it is a factor which makes the applicant less able to fend for him/herself. All applications from people aged over 60 need to be considered carefully especially where the applicant is leaving tied accommodation. However, authorities should not use 60 as a fixed age beyond which vulnerability occurs automatically: each case will need to be considered on its individual circumstances.

14.7. **Mental illness or learning or physical disability:** authorities should have regard to any medical advice or social services advice that they obtain, but the final decision on the question of vulnerability will rest with the authority. Factors which an authority may wish to consider are:
– the nature and extent of illness which may render the applicant vulnerable; and
– the relationship between the illness or disability and the individual's housing difficulties.
Information about an applicant's illness or disability should be treated in strict confidence.

14.8. Health authorities have an express duty (advice contained in Department of Health circulars HC(90)23 and LASSL(90)11) to implement a specifically tailored care programme for all patients considered for discharge from psychiatric hospitals and all new patients accepted by the specialist psychiatric services. People discharged from psychiatric hospitals and local authority hostels for those with mental health problems may be vulnerable. Effective liaison between housing, social services and health authorities will assist in such cases but authorities also need to be sensitive to direct approaches from discharged patients who are homeless. Physical disability or long-term acute illness, such as those defined by the **Disability Discrimination Act 1995**, which impinge on the applicant's housing situation and give rise to vulnerability may be readily ascertainable, but advice from health or social services staff should be sought if necessary.

14.9. **Chronically sick, including AIDS and HIV:** chronically sick people, including people with AIDS and HIV related illnesses, may be vulnerable not only because their illness has progressed to the point of physical or mental disability (when they would anyway be vulnerable and in priority need under the 1996 Act) but because the manifestations or effects of their illness, or common attitudes to it, make it very difficult for them to find stable or suitable accommodation. This may be particularly true of people with AIDS, or even people who are infected with HIV without having any overt signs or symptoms if the nature of their infection is known.

14.10. **Other special reasons:** authorities should determine whether applicants are vulnerable for 'other special reason'. Authorities should consider the following:
Young people (16 or over): vulnerability should not automatically be judged on age alone but authorities should consider the extent to which a young person is 'at risk' and therefore vulnerable. Risks could arise from:
– fear of or actual violence or sexual abuse from a person with whom s/he is associated;
– the likelihood of drug or alcohol abuse; or
– prostitution.
Some young people may be less able than others to fend for themselves for example:
– those leaving or who have been in local authority care;
– juvenile offenders (including those discharged from young offender institutions);
– those who have been physically or sexually abused;
– those with learning disabilities;
– those who have been the subject of statements of special educational need;
– those who lack family contact and support.
These examples do not constitute a complete list: authorities are

advised to liaise with social services authorities when considering individual cases, for example through joint assessment or other procedures.

10.18   The Code of Guidance emphasises the importance of joint working and in particular the need for housing authorities to be 'fully involved in the development of community care plans and children's services plans (para 7.5). It further states:

> **Joint working with social services departments and other agencies**
> 2.14. Under the **National Health Service and Community Care Act 1990** (the 1990 Act), social services departments are required to carry out an assessment for any individual who may have a need for community care services. it is the intention of that legislation that the planning and assessment process should identify the full range of needs, including housing needs. **Section 47 of the 1990 Act** requires social service authorities to notify the housing authority if there appears to be a housing need when the assessment is carried out. The housing need may be for alternative accommodation, or for renovation or adaptation of the accommodation in which the individual is currently living.
>
> 2.15. A joint approach should be agreed between local housing and social services and health authorities, to include:
> – mechanisms and triggers for referral between housing, health and social services authorities in relation to housing and community care issues, and alerting relevant agencies to any difficulties;
> – co-ordination between housing and social services assessments;
> – communication and follow-up once a care plan has been implemented, for example between community psychiatric nurses, social workers or care managers, and housing officers;
> – the assessment of individuals who require emergency accommodation; and
> – identification of those clients with inter-dependent health, housing and social services needs.
>
> 2.16. Local authority housing, social services and health authorities should liaise over the best solution for each client, recognising, for example, that the provision of more appropriate housing may assist in the delivery of social services; and/or that increased support or care services may allow a person to remain in his/her current home rather than moving to new accommodation. Where clients' needs warrant varying levels of priority for different services, procedures should be in place for reaching agreement on how clients' needs should be addressed.
>
> 2.17. The Government is particularly keen to ensure the delivery of a full spectrum of care for people suffering from severe mental illness.

Research has shown that provision of suitable, stable housing is essential if community care is to be a reality for this vulnerable group of clients. A key element in the spectrum of care is the development of a care plan under the Government's care programme approach (CPA). The initial assessment under the CPA must include an assessment of an individual's housing needs. It is essential that housing authorities liaise closely with social services authorities so that any housing allocation is appropriate to the needs of the individual, and meshes in with the social and health care support that may be a part of the patient's care programme.

2.18. Timing can be critical when people have to move from long stay institutions, or from temporary accommodation. Again, procedures should be agreed between the local housing authority and the referring agencies, incorporating criteria for and the timing of referrals, and the action to be taken on them.

2.19. Under **s20 of the Children Act 1989**, a local social services authority must provide accommodation for a child in need in their area who requires it as a result of:
– there being no person who has parental responsibility for him/her;
– his/her being lost or having been abandoned; or
– the person who has been caring for him/her being prevented (whether or not permanently, and for whatever reason) from providing him/her with suitable accommodation.
In the Government's view, social services authorities should not accommodate children in public care as a result of his/her family's homelessness. This would separate children from their parents, and cut across the Government's objective that family breakdown should be avoided wherever possible.[17]

Disabled facilities grants

10.19 Disabled facilities grants are grants paid towards the cost of building works which are necessary in order to meet the needs of a disabled occupant. The housing authority is responsible for the administration and payment of the grant, although the original application may be instigated (and referred to it) by a social services authority after a community care assessment. The maximum mandatory grant is currently £20,000 although local authorities have the discretion to make higher awards.[18]

---

17 See para 11.12 below where this issue is considered further.
18 Disabled Facilities Grants and Home Repair Assistance (Maximum Amounts) Order 1996 SI No 2888.

10.20 The grant is only payable in respect of disabled occupants; ie, persons who are 'substantially and permanently handicapped' within the meaning of NAA 1948 s29 (see para 5.13). It is not therefore available for persons whose need arises solely through age or temporary (albeit prolonged) illness.[19] The grant is however payable to disabled occupants who are either owner-occupiers or tenants (including housing association, council tenants and certain licensees.).

10.21 The relevant statutory provision for disabled facilities grants is Housing Grants, Construction and Regeneration Act (HGCRA) 1996 Pt I upon which detailed guidance has been issued by the Department of the Environment as Circular 17/96. As has been noted above, at para 5.65, there is considerable overlap between the duties of the housing authority to process these grants, and the duties owed by social services authorities to facilitate such adaptations. Unfortunately this complex inter-play of duties has not been simplified by the existence of separate guidance from the Department of Health on the social services responsibilities, as LAC(90)7.[20] However all references to paragraphs in the following section are references to paragraphs of Department of the Environment as Circular 17/96 unless specifically stated to the contrary.

10.22 Housing Grants, Construction and Regeneration Act 1996 s23 provides:

> *Disabled facilities grants: purposes for which grant must or may be given.*
>
> 23 (1) The purposes for which an application for a disabled facilities grant must be approved, subject to the provisions of this Chapter, are the following –
>
> (a) facilitating access by the disabled occupant to and from the dwelling or the building in which the dwelling or, as the case may be, flat is situated;
>
> (b) making the dwelling or building safe for the disabled occupant and other persons residing with him;
>
> (c) facilitating access by the disabled occupant to a room used or usable as the principal family room;
>
> (d) facilitating access by the disabled occupant to, or providing for the disabled occupant, a room used or usable for sleeping;

19 Other housing grants are available from housing authorities for renovation and minor repairs and these are available to non-disabled people as well as disabled people (and can, eg, be used to carry out renovation work in addition to the installation of disabled facilities etc). These grants are discretionary and subject to the priorities set by each local authority.

20 LAC(90)7 was issued jointly as DoE Circular 10/90. Whilst DoE Circular 10/90 has been withdrawn (and superseded by new guidance, Circular 17/96) LAC(90)7 remains in force (see DoE 4/98 and LASSL (99)21).

(e) facilitating access by the disabled occupant to, or providing for the disabled occupant, a room in which there is a lavatory, or facilitating the use by the disabled occupant of such a facility;

(f) facilitating access by the disabled occupant to, or providing for the disabled occupant, a room in which there is a bath or shower (or both), or facilitating the use by the disabled occupant of such a facility;

(g) facilitating access by the disabled occupant to, or providing for the disabled occupant, a room in which there is a washhand basin, or facilitating the use by the disabled occupant of such a facility;

(h) facilitating the preparation and cooking of food by the disabled occupant;

(i) improving any heating system in the dwelling to meet the needs of the disabled occupant or, if there is no existing heating system in the dwelling or any such system is unsuitable for use by the disabled occupant, providing a heating system suitable to meet his needs;

(j) facilitating the use by the disabled occupant of a source of power, light or heat by altering the position of one or more means of access to or control of that source or by providing additional means of control;

(k) facilitating access and movement by the disabled occupant around the dwelling in order to enable him to care for a person who is normally resident in the dwelling and is in need of such care;

(l) such other purposes as may be specified by order of the Secretary of State.

(2) An application for a disabled facilities grant may be approved, subject to the provisions of this Chapter, for the purpose of making the dwelling or building suitable for the accommodation, welfare or employment of the disabled occupant in any other respect.

(3) If in the opinion of the local housing authority the relevant works are more or less extensive than is necessary to achieve any of the purposes set out in subsection (1) or the purpose mentioned in subsection (2), they may, with the consent of the applicant, treat the application as varied so that the relevant works are limited to or, as the case may be, include such works as seem to the authority to be necessary for that purpose.

Role of the housing authority

10.23 The housing authority is responsible for the administration of the disabled facilities grant, through all stages from initial enquiry (or referral by the social services authority) to post-completion approval.

Although the Act specifically requires housing authorities to consult with social services authorities over whether the proposed works are necessary and appropriate, nevertheless it is for housing authorities to decide in any particular case whether or not to approve a grant; they are not bound to follow the social services authority's advice, although the guidance suggests that this should in general be a rare occurrence (Annex I para 4).

'Reasonable and practicable'

10.24   Section 24(3)(b) of HGCRA 1996 charges the housing authority with the duty of deciding whether it is reasonable and practicable to carry out the proposed adaptation works. In making its assessment, a housing authority is specifically required to have regard to the age and condition of the dwelling or building. While s24(4) of the Act permits grants to be made even where on completion of the works the property would remain unfit for human habitation, the guidance advises as to what alternatives should be offered by the housing and social services departments to the disabled person if the final 'unfitness' of the property is considered to be such that it renders the proposed works unreasonable and impractical (Annex I para 51).[21] In determining whether the work is reasonable and practicable, the guidance refers to other relevant considerations, including the architectural and structural characteristics of the property, conservation considerations, the practicalities of carrying out work on smaller properties or older properties with limited access and the impact on other occupants of the proposed works (Annex I para 52).[22]

'Necessary and appropriate'

10.25   In deciding whether the proposed works are necessary and appropriate to meet the needs of the disabled occupant, the housing authority must consult the social services authority. On this aspect Annex I to the guidance makes the following points:[23]

---

21 Including the possibility of obtaining a discretionary renovation grant, reducing the amount of DFG work, and the possibility of re-housing the disabled person.

22 Ie, if the works would lead to substantial disruption to other tenants (eg, the noise of an air-compressor, in *R v Kirklees MBC ex p Daykin* (1998) 1 CCLR 512, or alternatively by of indirect benefit to neighbours as in *R v Kirklees MBC ex p Good* (1998) 1 CCLR 506.

23 Separate and at times slightly divergent guidance is given to social services in LAC(90) 7 paras 36 onwards; but since final responsibility rests with the housing authority, the DoE guidance is of more weight.

47. The housing authority must satisfy itself that the works are necessary and appropriate to meet the needs of the disabled person under s24(3)(a), and in doing so should consult the social services authority. They need to consider a number of factors. In particular whether the proposed adaptations or improvements:

- are needed to provide for a care plan to be implemented which will enable the disabled occupant to remain living in their existing home as independently as possible;
- would meet, as far as possible, the assessed needs of the disabled person taking into account both their medical and physical needs; and
- distinguish between what is desirable and possibly legitimate aspirations of the disabled person, and what is actually needed and for which grant support is fully justified.

48. In determining the needs of the disabled person consideration should be given to the particular household group in which the disabled occupant resides so that any adaptations being contemplated do not cause strain on the household which may lead to a breakdown of the present care arrangements. For instance, a relevant factor might be the continued privacy of the disabled person or carer following completion of works.

49. DFGs are designed to give the disabled person a degree of independence in the home. Consideration therefore needs to be given to the impact of adaptations on the level of care given to the disabled person and whether those tasks will be reduced or eased. Adaptation works would not have achieved their objective within a care package if the disabled person does not gain an acceptable degree of independence, where possible, or, where the disabled person remains dependent upon the care of others, where the adaptation does not significantly ease the burden of the carer.

10.26 The consideration of what 'meets' the assessed needs of a disabled person can take into account the issue of cost, where there are alternative ways of meeting the need. Thus, in *R v Kirklees MBC ex p Daykin*,[24] the disabled person was assessed as needing to be able to get into and out of his council flat. Collins J held that it was reasonable for the authority to decide that this need could either be met by the provision of a stair lift, or by re-housing and for it to take into account the respective costs of both options in deciding how to meet this need.

10.27 Further and detailed guidance on the housing authority's duty to collaborate with social services is given in Annex I to the guidance, including information on the findings of 'good practice' research commissioned by the DoE on this issue.

24 (1998) 1 CCLR 512.

Grant-eligible works

10.28   The guidance (at para 7.5.2) explains that:

> the prominent purpose for which mandatory disabled facilities grant is given is that of access and provision: this includes access into and around the dwelling, to essential facilities and amenities within the dwelling and the provision of certain facilities within the dwelling, such as making the building safe, where this is the only or most suitable option. The purposes for which discretionary disabled facilities grants are available are for works to make the dwelling suitable for the accommodation, welfare or employment of the disabled person. Discretionary grant is also available where a local authority decides to meet the cost of works which are mandatory in nature but in excess of the grant limit for mandatory assistance.

Mandatory grants

10.29   Section 23(1) of HGCRA 1996 details the purposes for which mandatory grants may be awarded. The duty is not a 'resource' dependent duty (see para 3.59 above); thus in *R v Birmingham CC ex p Taj Mohammed*,[25] Dyson J held that housing authorities were not entitled to take resources into account when deciding whether or not to approve a disabled facilities grant.

10.30   The work will generally be within a dwelling but may in certain situations be elsewhere, for instance, in the common parts of a building containing flats (Annex I para 30). The works eligible for mandatory grant support can be conveniently grouped as follows.

Making the dwelling safe

10.31   Annex I para 17 of the guidance explains that works under this heading may include 'the provision of lighting where safety is an issue of adaptations designed to minimise the risk of danger where a disabled person has behavioural problems which cause him to act occasionally or regularly in a boisterous or violent manner damaging the house, himself and perhaps other people'. It may also include enhanced alarm systems for people with hearing difficulties.

Facilitating access and provision

10.32   Annex I para 15 of the guidance explains that this includes works which remove or help overcome any obstacles which prevent the

25   (1998) 1 CCLR 441.

disabled person from moving freely into and around the dwelling and enjoying the use of the dwelling and the facilities or amenities within it. In particular, this includes works which enable the disabled person to prepare and cook food as well as facilitating access to and from the dwelling and to the following:

- the principal family room;
- a room used for sleeping (or providing such a room);
- a room in which there is a lavatory, a bath or shower and a wash-basin (or providing such a room).

Room usable for sleeping

10.33 Annex I para 20 of the guidance advises that a room 'usable for sleeping' should only be grant funded if the housing authority is satisfied that the adaptation of an existing room (or access to that room) is not a suitable option. It states, however, that where the disabled person shares a bedroom, grant funding may be given to provide a room of sufficient size 'so that the normal sleeping arrangements can be maintained'.

Bathroom

10.34 The guidance explains (Annex I para 21) that HGCRA 1996 separates the provision of a lavatory and washing, bathing and showering facilities, in order to clarify that grant support is available to ensure that the disabled person has access to each of these facilities (as well as facilitating their use).

Facilitating preparation and cooking of food

10.35 Eligible works under this heading include the rearrangement or enlargement of a kitchen to ease manoeuvrability of a wheelchair and specially modified or designed storage units, gas, electricity and plumbing installations to enable the disabled person to use these facilities independently (Annex I para 22). The guidance advises, however, that a full adaptation of a kitchen would not generally be appropriate, however, if most of the cooking and preparation is done by another household member.

Heating, lighting and power

10.36 The guidance (Annex I para 24) advises that although grant support may be made in order to provide (or improve, or replace) a heating system, this should only extend to rooms normally used by the disabled person and central heating should only be funded 'where the wellbeing and mobility of the disabled person would be otherwise adversely affected'. Works in relation to lighting and power may include the relocation of power points and the provision of suitably adapted controls.

Dependent residents

10.37   Grant support is available to cover work which improves a disabled person's access and movement around a dwelling in order to care for another person who normally resides there (s23(1)(k)). The guidance makes it clear that the dependent being cared for need not be a disabled person and need not be a relation.

Discretionary grants

10.38   Under HGCRA 1996 s23(2) local authorities have the discretion to award disabled facilities grants for works which make the dwelling suitable for the accommodation, welfare or employment of the disabled occupant in any other respect. The guidance (Annex I paras 32–36) explains what works of this nature might comprise:

Accommodation: this will generally comprise work which is more extensive than strictly necessary for the mandatory grant; for instance extending or enlarging a dwelling which is already suitable for the disabled occupant in all other respects.

Welfare: examples of such works might be to provide access to a garden adjacent to a property, or a safe play area for a disabled child especially if such work is carried out at the same time as work under a mandatory grant.

Employment: this might include adapting a room for the use of a disabled person who is housebound but nevertheless able to work from home.

Ineligibility for grant and the social services overlap

10.39   Cases arise where the social services authority assesses a need for the adaptation, but the housing authority refuses or is unable to approve the grant. This may arise because the works in question come under the discretionary rather than the mandatory scheme, or because the housing authority does not consider the proposed works to be reasonable or practicable.

10.40 The guidance (Annex I) expresses this as follows:

5. Social services authorities' responsibilities under section 2 of the Chronically Sick and Disabled Persons Act 1970 to make arrangements for home adaptations are not affected by the grants legislation. Where an application for DFG has been made, those authorities may be called upon to meet this duty in two ways:
(a) where the assessed needs of a disabled person exceeds the scope for provision by the housing authority under section 23 of the 1996 Act; and
(b) where an applicant for DFG has difficulty in meeting his assessed contribution determined by the means test and seeks financial assistance from the authority.

6. In such cases, where the social services authority determine that the need has been established, it remains their duty to assist even where the local housing authority either refuse or are unable to approve an application. Social Services authorities may also consider using their powers under section 17 of the Health and Social Services and Social Security Adjudications Act 1983 to charge for their services where appropriate.

In such situations the guidance reminds of the duties of social services authorities, namely:

7.4.1 The existing statutory duties of social services departments under Section 2(1)(e) of Chronically Sick and Disabled Persons Act 1970 to provide assistance to disabled people needing home adaptations and other facilities designed to secure the greater safety, comfort and convenience of a disabled person, remain. Such help is normally available in the form of financial assistance, including loans, to assist with equipment in the home but, under these powers, social services authorities have a duty to assist disabled people who, because of their particular circumstances, cannot afford the assessed contribution towards the cost of works for which a DFG has been approved by the housing authority. Resources are also available to fund adaptation work either from housing associations or from the Housing Corporation where the adaptation is required for a property in that sector and local authorities may wish, where appropriate, to ensure that this option is considered.

This question is considered at greater length at para 5.60 onwards.

Fixtures and fittings

10.41 While disabled facilities grants are available to cover (among other things) adaptations to the fabric of a building, questions do arise as to whether items of specialist equipment, etc, come within the scheme. In this respect the guidance advises:

> 7.6.1 Under arrangements agreed between the Secretaries of State for Health and the Environment, help with equipment which can be easily installed and removed with little or no modification to the dwelling, is normally the responsibility of the social services authority under its responsibilities under the 1970 Act with larger adaptations requiring structural modification of a dwelling normally coming within the scope of a disabled facilities grant. However, it is for housing authorities and social services authorities between them to decide how the particular adaptation needs of a disabled person should be funded. In taking such decisions authorities should not forget that the needs of the disabled occupant are **paramount within the framework of what can be offered.**

> 7.6.2 Close co-operation between the respective authorities is vital to ensure that those requiring help in paying for works for essential adaptations to meet their special needs, are given the most efficient and effective support.

Additional advice in the guidance, at Annex I, states:

> 7. It is for housing authorities and social services authorities between them to decide how particular adaptations should be funded either through CSDP Act or through a DFG.

> 8. However, since DFGs were introduced in 1990 under the Local Government and Housing Act 1989, it has been common practice that equipment which can be installed and removed fairly easily with little or no structural modification of the dwelling is normally the responsibility of the social services authority.

> 9. For larger items such as *stairlifts* and *through floor lifts* which require such structural works to the property, help is normally provided by housing authorities through DFG. However, some routine installations may not involve structural work. To ensure that such adaptations are progressed quickly, the respective authorities should jointly agree a standard line on the installation of lifts which will apply unless there are exceptional circumstances. Authorities will wish to include arrangements for routine servicing, maintenance, removal and possible re-use.

Eligibility

10.42   All owner-occupiers, tenants (both council, housing association and private) and licensees[26] are potentially eligible to apply for disabled

---

26   HGCRA 1996 s19(5) extends eligibility for a DFG to a range of licensees, eg, secure or introductory tenants who are licensees, agricultural workers and service employees such as publicans.

facilities grants as are landlords on behalf of disabled tenants. The guidance (Annex I para 11) advises that where a 'council tenant is seeking help with adaptations, it is for the authority to decide whether to carry out the works under its own resources for capital works or to advise the applicant to apply for a DFG. If the local authority decide to undertake the works from their own resources they should be carried out on the same terms as if a DFG has been awarded'. It however also advises that where the disabled person is a council tenant residing in an overspill estate, 'it should be borne in mind that an application for DFG can only be made to the local authority in whose area the dwelling, which is the subject of the application, is situated and not to the particular council whose tenant the applicant is'.

Means testing

10.43 Eligibility for a disabled facilities grant is dependent upon satisfying a means test. Only the financial circumstances of the disabled occupant[27] and his/her partner are assessed and not other members of the household. In the case of adaptations for a disabled child, the test takes into account the resources of the parents (or relevant person where the child does not live with his/her parents).

10.44 The details of the means test are determined by regulations,[28] are relatively complex and are set out in detail in the guidance (Annex J2). In many instances the calculation adopts housing benefit principles; thus the value of a person's savings is determined in the same way as for housing benefit and a tariff income of £1 per £250 is applied to any capital in excess of £5000 (there is no upper capital limit).

10.45 Income is also assessed on basic housing benefit principles and the person's relevant 'applicable amount' is the current housing benefit sum. Where the financial resources do not exceed the relevant applicable amount plus a 'grant premium' of £40, the disabled facilities grant will be the cost of the approved works. Where the financial resources are greater than the applicable amount, a staggered taper is applied to the surplus, designed to produce what the regulations term an 'affordable loan' (reg 10). The idea is that the contribution made by the applicant constitutes 'an affordable loan that could be raised based on the current standard national rate of interest, over repayment periods of 10 years for owner-occupiers and 5 years for tenants' (Annex J2, para 17).

---

27 The disabled occupant may or may not be the applicant.
28 Housing Renewal Grants Regulations 1996 SI No 2890.

Timescales and loan deferment

10.46   Under HGCRA 1996 s34 the housing authority must approve or refuse a grant application as soon as reasonably practicable and in any event not later than six months after the date of application. It is therefore essential that the completed application be lodged with the housing authority at the earliest opportunity, as time runs from that date. The guidance stresses that 'local authorities should not use pre application tests as a way of delaying applications or avoiding their statutory duty to process applications within 6 months' (Annex I para 45).

10.47   HGCRA 1996 s36 provides local authorities with a discretion to notify the grant applicant that payment of their mandatory disabled facilities grant will not be made until a date not more than 12 months following the date of the application. The guidance (at para 7.5.4) states that this:

> . . . should enable authorities to manage their resources better between financial years by prioritising cases. However, this power should be used only in exceptional circumstances and not where the applicant would suffer undue hardship. There is no expectation that the contractor would complete the work in advance of the date the grant has been scheduled for payment. The 12-month period for completion of grant assisted works is not affected although the date from which this runs will be the date in the notification of the authority's decision.[29]

---

29   Further guidance on this issue is given in Annex I.

CHAPTER 11

Children Act 1989 duties to children in need

11.1   Introduction

11.6   The assessment of children in need

11.9   Disabled children's register

11.10   Services for children in need

11.12   Housing and residential care services
        Homelessness

11.20   Domiciliary and community-based services

11.21   The transition into adulthood

11.26   Charging for children's services

11.26   Charging for domiciliary and community-based services

11.29   Charging for services under CSDPA 1970

11.30   Charging for accommodation services under CA 1989

Introduction

11.1   As has been seen above (at para 7.48), in relation to young carers, social services authorities are under a general duty, by virtue of Children Act (CA) 1989 s17(1), to safeguard and promote the interests of children 'in need' and in furtherance of this duty they are empowered to provide a wide range of services.

11.2   CA 1989 s17(10) provides that a child shall be taken to be 'in need' if:

a) he is unlikely to achieve or maintain, or to have the opportunity of achieving or maintaining, a reasonable standard of health or development without the provision for him of services by a local authority . . . ; or

b) his health or development is likely to be significantly impaired, or further impaired, without the provision for him of such services; or

c) he is disabled.

11.3   The definition of a disabled child (which closely follows the definition of a disabled adult set out in National Assistance Act (NAA) 1948 s29) is contained in CA 1989 s17(11), namely:

> For the purposes of this Part, a child is disabled if he is blind, deaf or dumb or suffers from mental disorder of any kind or is substantially and permanently handicapped by illness, injury or congenital deformity or such other disability as may be prescribed; and in this Part –
> 'development' means physical, intellectual, emotional, social or behavioural development; and
> 'health' means physical or mental health.

11.4   A child who is not 'substantially and permanently' handicapped may nevertheless be a child in need by virtue of s17(10)(a) or s17(10)(b) of the Act and therefore entitled to assistance (see para 7.51 above where this question is considered in detail in relation to young carers). Having identified the potential recipients of assistance under s17, the Act then follows a similar route to the community care legislation, namely an assessment of needs followed by a decision on whether services are called for.

11.5   CA 1989 also follows NAA 1948 s29 by requiring social services authorities to maintain a register of disabled children (under Sch 2 Pt I para 2).

The assessment of children in need

11.6 There is no duty to assess under CA 1989 equivalent to that found in National Health Service and Community Care Act (NHSCCA) 1990 s47; nevertheless there is a power to assess (which is strongly reinforced by guidance). In most cases disabled children will be entitled to a community care assessment under NHSCCA 1990 s47(1), in that they will (for instance) be potentially entitled to services under National Health Service Act (NHSA) 1977 Sch 8 para 3 (see para 3.56 above).

11.7 CA 1989 Sch 2 Pt I para 3 provides:

> Where it appears to a local authority that a child within their area is in need, the authority may assess his needs for the purposes of this Act at the same time as any assessment of his needs is made under
> –
> (a) the Chronically Sick and Disabled Persons Act 1970;
> (b) Part IV of the Education Act 1996;
> (c) the Disabled Persons (SCR) Act 1986; or
> (d) any other enactment.

11.8 CA 1989 guidance[1] amplifies what is required in such assessments:

> 2.7 Good practice requires that the assessment of need should be undertaken in an open way and should involve those caring for the child, the child and other significant persons. Families with a child in need, whether the need results from family difficulties or the child's circumstances, have the right to receive sympathetic support and sensitive intervention in their family's life . . .

> 2.8 In making an assessment, the local authority should take account of the particular needs of the child – that is in relation to health, development, disability, education, religious persuasion, racial origin, cultural and linguistic background, the degree (if any) to which these needs are being met by existing services to the family or the child and which agencies' services are best suited to the child's needs.

Disabled children's register

11.9 As noted above, social services departments are obliged to keep a register of children with disabilities,[2] as part of their duty to safeguard and promote the interests of disabled children. Volume 6 of the

---

1 Guidance to the Children Act 1989 Vol 2 (Family Support) para 2.7.
2 Sch 2 para 2; and see also Vol 6 para 4.2 of the Children Act Guidance (Children with Disabilities).

Children Act Guidance (Children with Disabilities) makes the following comments on the role of registers:

> 4.2 ... There is no duty on parents to agree to registration (which is
> a voluntary procedure) and services are not dependent upon
> registration. Registration can contribute positively to coherent
> planning of service provision for children with disabilities under the
> Children Act ...
>
> 4.3 SSDs ... will need to liaise with their education and health
> counterparts to achieve an understanding of disability which permits
> early identification; which facilitates joint working; which encourages
> parents to agree to registration and which is meaningful in terms of
> planning services for the children in question and children in
> general. The creation of a joint register of children with disabilities
> between health, education and social services would greatly facilitate
> collaboration in identification and a co-ordinated provision of
> services under the Act ...
>
> 4.4 Whichever agency is the first to identify a child as having a
> disability whether it is the LEA, SSD or child health services they
> should initiate discussions with the parents about services or
> procedures which might be beneficial to the child and family. This
> should include an explanation of what other agencies can provide
> and information about the register. The registration of children with
> disabilities will be effective and productive only if parents and
> children are regarded as partners in the assessment process and as
> experts in their own right, from whom professionals may have much
> to learn.

Services for children in need

11.10   Once a child has been accepted as being 'in need', and that need
identified by an assessment or otherwise, then CA 1989 specifies
that a range of support services be made available. Section 17(1)
provides:

> It shall be the general duty of every local authority (in addition to the
> other duties imposed on them by this Part) –
> (a) to safeguard and promote the welfare of children within their
>   area who are in need; and
> (b) so far as is consistent with that duty, to promote the upbringing
>   of such children by their families,
> by providing a range of services appropriate to those children's
> needs.

The range of services that can be provided, as part of a strategy to keep families together, is almost unlimited; including, by s17(6), the giving of assistance in kind or, in exceptional circumstances, in cash. Upon the implementation of the Carers and Disabled Children Act 2000, the powers under s17 will extend to direct payments and respite care vouchers (see para 7.44 above).

11.11   The guidance to CA 1989 conveniently summarises the breadth of powers available to social services authorities in such cases:[3]

> This general duty is supported by other specific duties and powers such as the facilitation of 'the provision by others, including in particular voluntary organisations of services' (section 17(5) and Schedule 2). These provisions encourage SSDs to provide day and domiciliary services, guidance and counselling, respite care and a range of other services as a means of supporting children in need (including children with disabilities) within their families. The Act recognises that sometimes a child can only be helped by providing services for other members of his family (section 17(3)) 'if it [the service] is provided with a view to safeguarding or promoting the child's welfare' . . . The SSD may make such arrangements as they see fit for any person to provide services and support 'may include giving assistance in kind, or in exceptional circumstances in cash' (section 17(6)). However, where it is the SSD's view that a child's welfare is adequately provided for and no unmet need exists, they need not act.

The duties owed to disabled children are underwritten by a requirement (in CA 1989 Sch 2 Pt I para 6) that authorities provide services designed to minimise the effect on disabled children within their area of their disabilities and to give such children the opportunity to lead lives which are as normal as possible.

Housing and residential care services

11.12   The range of services available under CA 1989 Pt III clearly encompasses the provision of housing and residential care.

11.13   In *R v Tower Hamlets LBC ex p Bradford*,[4] the court considered the housing and community care needs of a family which included a severely disabled mother and an 11-year-old son with special educational needs. Although the family members experienced particularly unpleasant harassment from their neighbours, their 'housing points' were insufficient to make them an 'overriding priority' for re-

3   Guidance Vol 6 para 3.3.
4   (1998) 1 CCLR 294.

housing. A judicial review challenging this decision was adjourned on grounds that the authority undertook various assessments, including under CA 1989 Pt III. When considering its duty to provide accommodation under the Act, the authority effectively confined its attention to s20, the cross-heading to which section states 'provision of accommodation for children: general'. This section (which is in effect what, prior to 1989, used to be called 'voluntary care') only arises where there is no one with parental responsibility, or where the child is lost or abandoned or where the parents are prevented from providing suitable accommodation or care. Since these factors were not present, the authority declined to provide accommodation under Part III of the Act. Dyson J held that the authority had fundamentally misunderstood its accommodation powers under the Act; in that any housing would be provided under s17 (and not s20). Section 17 enables authorities to provide an almost unlimited range of services including, in appropriate circumstances, housing.

11.14   The unlawful action of the authority in the *Bradford* decision, was not its failure to re-house, but its misunderstanding of its powers under Pt III of the Act. Accordingly the rights under CA 1989 Pt III do not trump all other rights, but they must be properly understood by a social services authority and decisions made in accordance with the principles of public law. Authorities cannot therefore (for example) fetter their discretion in relation to the use of these powers. Thus in *R v Hammersmith and Fulham LBC ex p Damoah*,[5] Kay J held that it was unlawful for a local authority to limit its powers by refusing to provide any services for a child in need unless its mother agreed to take steps which the authority considered to be in the child's best interest (in this case, that she leave the country).

Homelessness

11.15   A consequence of the social services' obligations under CA 1989 Pt III is that they will often need to consider providing accommodation for families who have been held to be intentionally homeless under the Housing Act 1996.[6] In *R v Barnet LBC ex p Foran*,[7] the Court of Appeal emphasised, however, that this does not mean that social services authorities are under an 'absolute' duty to house homeless children in need together with their families.

11.16   As has been noted above at para 10.17 the code of guidance to

5   (1999) 2 CCLR 18.
6   *R v Northavon DC ex p Smith* [1994] 3 All ER 313, HL.
7   (1999) 2 CCLR 329.

housing authorities concerning their duty towards homeless people[8] deals with the issue of 'vulnerability', advising (at para 14.5) that the 'critical test is whether the applicant is less able to fend for him/herself so that s/he will suffer injury or detriment, in circumstances where a less vulnerable person would be able to cope without harmful effects. People who live or might reasonably be expected to live with a vulnerable person are also in priority need'.

11.17   In relation to children and young people the guidance explains as follows:

> **14.10. Other special reasons:** authorities should determine whether applicants are vulnerable for 'other special reason'. Authorities should consider the following:
>
> **Young people (16 or over):** vulnerability should not automatically be judged on age alone but authorities should consider the extent to which a young person is 'at risk' and therefore vulnerable. Risks could arise from:
> – fear of or actual violence or sexual abuse from a person with whom s/he is associated:
> – the likelihood of drug or alcohol abuse; or
> – prostitution.
> Some young people may be less able than others to fend for themselves for example:
> – those leaving or who have been in local authority care;
> – juvenile offenders (including those discharged from young offender institutions);
> – those who have been physically or sexually abused;
> – those with learning disabilities'
> – those who have been the subject of statements of special educational need;
> – those who lack family contact and support.
>
> These examples do not constitute a complete list: authorities are advised to liaise with social services authorities when considering individual cases, for example, through joint assessment or other procedures.

11.18   The Code of Guidance also emphasises the importance of joint working[9] and in particular the need for housing authorities to be 'fully involved in the development of community care plans and children's services plans' (para 7.5) and in relation to the needs of children states:

---

8   Code of Guidance under Housing Act 1996 Pts VI and VII, 7 March 1997.
9   In this respect see also para 10.18 above.

2.19. Under **s20 of the Children Act 1989**, a local social services authority must provide accommodation for a child in need in their area who requires it as a result of:
– there being no person who has parental responsibility for him/her;
– his/her being lost or having been abandoned; or
– the person who has been caring for him/her being prevented (whether or not permanently, and for whatever reason) from providing him/her with suitable accommodation.
In the Government's view, social services authorities should not accommodate children in public care as a result of his/her family's homelessness. This would separate children from their parents, and cut across the Government's objective that family breakdown should be avoided wherever possible.

2.20. If the child who is accommodated under this duty is ordinarily resident in the area of another local authority, the latter authority may take over the provision of accommodation for the child within three months of being notified in writing that the child is being accommodated. Local authorities are also required to provide accommodation for a child in need who has reached the age of 16 if his/her welfare is otherwise likely to be seriously prejudiced. Section 20(4) of the 1989 Act empowers a local authority to provide accommodation for any child in their area if it would safeguard or promote his/her welfare.

2.21. Under **s27 of the Children Act 1989**, a local social services authority can ask a local housing authority to help in delivering services for children in need, and the housing authority must comply with such a request to the extent that it is compatible with their own statutory duties and other obligations, and does not unduly prejudice the discharge of any of their own functions.

11.19   The Education Act 1996 Part IV obliges local education authorities to provide residential accommodation for school-age disabled children with special needs, in restricted circumstances. Consideration of this duty is beyond the scope of this text, but see Read and Clements *Disabled Children and the Law* (Jessica Kingsley, 2000).

Domiciliary and community-based services

11.20   CA 1989 Sch 2 Pt I gives an illustrative list of the type of services which may be provided, but it is clear that this list is not exhaustive.[10] The list[11] comprises:

10 Guidance para 2.11 states '. . . this is not an exhaustive list; others may need to be provided according to the local authority's assessment of need in their own area'.
11 CA 1989 Sch 2 para 8.

a) advice, guidance and counselling;
b) occupational, social, cultural or recreational activities;
c) home help (which may include laundry facilities);
d) facilities for, or assistance with, travelling to and from home for the purpose of taking advantage of any other service provided under this Act or of any similar service;
e) assistance to enable the child concerned and his family to have a holiday.

Domiciliary and community-based services for disabled children are available not only under CA 1989, but also under Chronically Sick and Disabled Persons Act (CSDPA) 1970 s2 (by virtue of s28A of the 1970 Act). The relationship between the two Acts was considered in *R v Bexley LBC ex p B*[12] which is considered at para 5.78 above. In essence, however, most domiciliary and community-based services provided for disabled children are done, not under the 1989 Act, but under the 1970 Act.

The transition into adulthood[13]

11.21 It is tempting to see community care law as synonymous with 'adult care law' and CA 1989 as the statute which provides for the community care needs of disabled children. Many social services authorities divide their services for disabled people into 'adult care' and 'child care' services. While there may be good social work practice reasons for this division (eg, the need of disabled children for a 'childhood' and to share in the common development experiences of their peers), there is no significant justification for it at law.

11.22 Although in general services under CA 1989 cease to be available to disabled children when they reach the age of 18, their entitlement to services under CSDPA 1970 s2 and under NHSA 1977 Sch 8 para 3 remains. The practical effect of the judgment in *R v Bexley LBC ex p B* (as discussed at para 5.78) is to confirm that most home care services provided to disabled children are done under the 1970 Act rather than the 1989 Act.

11.23 There are of course dangers in separating adult and child care services and these often surface when the care responsibilities are being transferred from the child to the adult social work team; all too

---

12 (2000) 3 CCLR 15.
13 For a detailed consideration of these issues, see J Read and L Clements *Disabled Children, the Law and Good Practice* (Jessica Kingsley, 2000).

often at this stage the quality of the services deteriorates significantly or the child is effectively lost to the system and ceases to receive any continuing care. Such a transfer of responsibility often occurs when the young person's special education provision is also coming to an end.

11.24   Statutory provisions exist which endeavour to ensure that there is a smooth hand-over of responsibility from the education department (responsible for the special education provision) to the social services department responsible for the continuing community care needs[14] of the disabled person. Disabled Persons (Services, Consultation and Representation) Act 1986 ss5 and 6 require education authorities to consult social services authorities to establish whether a child over the age of 14 who has been 'statemented' under Education Act 1996 Pt IV, is likely to require support from the social services department when s/he leaves school. This duty has been reinforced by the Education (Special Educational Needs) Regulations 1994 SI No 1047, which requires the contribution of social services departments and others to a transitional plan which the education department is required to prepare on the annual review of a statement made when the student attains the age of 14. The essential aim of such a plan is to ensure a smooth transition for the young person into adult life.[15]

11.25   The Children Act guidance also stresses the social services' obligation to ensure such a smooth transition, stating:[16]

> The SSD's provision of services to children with disabilities should involve an initial assessment of need, a continuing process of reassessment and review of the plan for the child. Continuity should not be broken for reasons which concern organisational or administrative convenience rather than the welfare of the child or young person. A smooth transition, when the young person reaches 18 . . . should be the objective.

---

14 And possible social services obligations in relation to the provision of education: see para 5.54.

15 Described in para 6.47 of the Code of Practice. At the time of writing the relevant code is that to the previous (1993) Act, namely the Code of Practice on the Identification and Assessment of Special Educational Needs: procedures within the Education, Health and Social Services (1994).

16 Vol 6 para 5.4 of the Children Act Guidance (Children with Disabilities).

Charging for children's services

Charging for domiciliary and community-based services

11.26   As with most statutory adult care services, local authorities are empowered to charge for the services they provide under CA 1989. The CA 1989 charging provisions differ in a number of respects, most obviously perhaps in the fact that it is in general the carer's (ie, the parent's) means which are assessed rather than the service-user's.

11.27   CA 1989 s29(1) deals with charging for non-accommodation services, and empowers the authority to recover 'such charge as they consider appropriate'. This is subject to the following restrictions:

a) that no person can be charged while in receipt of income support, working families' tax credit or disabled person's tax credit (s29(3)); and

b) that where the authority is satisfied that a person's means are insufficient for it to be reasonably practicable for him or her to pay the charge, the authority cannot require him/her to pay more than s/he can reasonably be expected to pay (s29(2)). This provision follows closely the wording found in Health and Social Services and Social Security Adjudications Act 1983 s17, and reference should be made to paras 8.67 onwards where the issues of charge reduction or waiver are considered in detail.

11.28   The persons who can be charged are specified in s29(4), namely:

a) where the service is provided for a child under 16, each of his parents;

b) where it is provided for a child who has reached the age of 16, the child himself; and

c) where it is provided for a member of the child's family, that member.

As with charges for adult non-accommodation services, authorities are empowered to recover outstanding charges 'summarily as a civil debt'[17] and where a service is assessed as being required, the authority must provide it even if the liable person refuses to pay the assessed charge.

---

17   CA 1989 s29(5).

Charging for services under CSDPA 1970

11.29 As noted at para 8.116 above, it is doubtful if social services departments can charge for any services provided under CSDPA 1970 s2, and in general few if any attempt to do so.

Charging for accommodation services under CA 1989

11.30 CA 1989 Sch 2 Pt III empowers (but does not oblige) local authorities to charge for the cost of accommodating children. The rules are the same as for non-accommodation services, save only that (in addition):

1) the local authority cannot charge a sum greater than 'they would normally be prepared to pay if they had placed a similar child with local authority foster parents'; and

2) provision is made for the local authority to serve what is known as a 'contribution notice' which they are able to enforce through the magistrates' court if necessary; which court can also arbitrate on any dispute as to the reasonableness of such a notice.

CHAPTER 12

Remedies

12.1   Introduction

12.5   Local authority complaints procedures

12.6   Who can complain?

12.9   The structure of the complaints system
        The informal or problem-solving stage • The formal stage • The review stage • Subsequent action • Special cases • Disciplinary or grievance procedures

12.53   NHS overlap

12.56   Independent and private sector providers

12.57   Complaints concerning non-accommodation charges

12.58   Children procedures

12.59   Human Rights Act 1998

12.60   Local government ombudsman procedures

12.77   Judicial review

12.83   Complaint to local authority monitoring officer

12.85   Sufficient standing

12.87   An alternative remedy?

12.91   Grounds for judicial review
        Illegality • Procedural impropriety

12.116   Default procedures

continued

12.121   European Convention on Human Rights

12.128   The main rights

12.145   European Court of Human Rights

Introduction

12.1   Frequently, the most effective way of resolving a community care dispute will be through informal contact with the social services department or a local councillor; indeed contact with the local media (newspapers and radio/TV) can also be a very effective way of remedying a problem. The law however provides four principal procedures by which a failure in the provision of community care services may be challenged. These are:

a) a complaint to the responsible local authority or NHS body;
b) a complaint to the local government ombudsman or health service commissioner;
c) an application to the High Court for judicial review;
d) an application to the Secretary of State for Health or Wales to use his or her default powers under Local Authority Social Services Act (LASSA) 1970 s7D.

12.2   Other procedures or remedies may be available in certain specific cases. A failure to provide some types of service may give an applicant a right to initiate a private civil action for damages;[1] mentally disordered people and their carers continue to have direct access to the Mental Health Act Commission,[2] and individuals continue to have access to their elected representatives for assistance in any particular case.[3] In addition it should be noted that where judicial review proceedings fail to provide an adequate remedy, there remains the option of an application to the European Commission of Human Rights (this potential remedy is considered below in the judicial review section).

12.3   Although there are many exceptions, a complainant will in general be expected to give the local authority or NHS body the opportunity to remedy the problem before the court, ombudsman or secretary of state concerned will be prepared to consider a complaint. There will, however, be a number of situations where the ombuds-

---

1   It is probable that in addition an aggrieved individual may have an action for damages in certain situations, such as a failure to provide assessed services under Chronically Sick and Disabled Persons Act (CSDPA) 1970 s2 or under Mental Health Act (MHA) 1983 ss117; in each case however it will almost invariably be more appropriate to commence proceedings by way of a judicial review and therein to claim damages under RSC Order 53 r7. See R Gordon, *Community Care Assessments* (Longman, 1993) p70 for further discussion on this point.
2   Policy Guidance para 6.35.
3   Ibid para 6.34.

man or court will accept an application without the complaints process being utilised: these circumstances are discussed in the ombudsman and judicial review sections below.

12.4   The NHS complaints system is considered separately at para 6.157 above.

Local authority complaints procedures

12.5   LASSA 1970 s7B gives the secretary of state the power to require social services authorities to establish a complaints procedure.[4] This power was exercised via the Local Authority Social Services (Complaints Procedure) Order 1990 SI No 2244, which required each such authority to have in place a complaints system by 1 April 1991. The secretary of state has directed the form and the procedures which must be adopted by each authority, by issuing the Complaints Procedure Directions 1990 (the full text of which is in Appendix B) and by including a chapter of guidance in the Policy Guidance (see para 1.25). Additionally, the Department of Health has issued guidance on good practice, *The Right To Complain*.[5] The Social Services Inspectorate (SSI) has issued to all social services complaints officers *Notes on Good Practice* (1995).

Who can complain?

12.6   LASSA 1970 s7B(2) stipulates that a person is a 'qualifying individual' (and thus entitled to make a complaint) if the authority has a power or a duty to secure the provision of services for him or her and the person's needs or possible needs for such a service have (by whatever means) come to the attention of the authority.

12.7   The breadth of this provision is emphasised by the Policy Guidance, which explains that the intention of the Act is to allow access to the complaints process by anyone who is likely to want to make representations, including complaints about actions, decisions or apparent failings of a social services department; and to allow any other person to act on behalf of the individual concerned. The procedure excludes only those for whom the authority has no power or duty to provide a service (para 6.5).

---

4   Section 7B was inserted by National Health Service and Community Care Act (NHSCCA) 1990 s50.

5   HMSO, 1991.

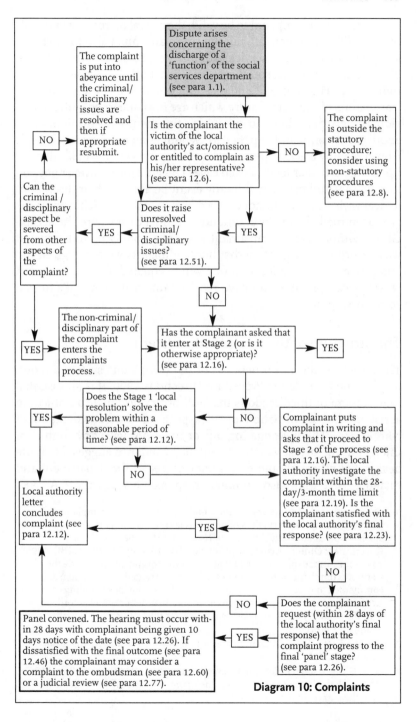

Dispute arises concerning the discharge of a 'function' of the social services department (see para 1.1).

The complaint is put into abeyance until the criminal/disciplinary issues are resolved and then if appropriate resubmit.

Is the complainant the victim of the local authority's act/omission or entitled to complain as his/her representative? (see para 12.6).

NO

The complaint is outside the statutory procedure; consider using non-statutory procedures (see para 12.8).

Can the criminal / disciplinary aspect be severed from other aspects of the complaint?

YES

Does it raise unresolved criminal/disciplinary issues? (see para 12.51).

YES

NO

YES

The non-criminal/disciplinary part of the complaint enters the complaints process.

Has the complainant asked that it enter at Stage 2 (or is it otherwise appropriate)? (see para 12.16).

YES

YES

Does the Stage 1 'local resolution' solve the problem within a reasonable period of time? (see para 12.12).

NO

Complainant puts complaint in writing and asks that it proceed to Stage 2 of the process (see para 12.16). The local authority investigate the complaint within the 28-day/3-month time limit (see para 12.19). Is the complainant satisfied with the local authority's final response? (see para 12.23).

NO

Local authority letter concludes complaint (see para 12.12).

YES

NO

Panel convened. The hearing must occur within 28 days with complainant being given 10 days notice of the date (see para 12.26). If dissatisfied with the final outcome (see para 12.46) the complainant may consider a complaint to the ombudsman (see para 12.60) or a judicial review (see para 12.77).

NO

YES

Does the complainant request (within 28 days of the local authority's final response) that the complaint progress to the final 'panel' stage? (see para 12.26).

Diagram 10: Complaints

12.8   In order for a complaint to be valid, the complainant must not only be a 'qualifying individual', but the complaint must also (by virtue of s7B(1)) relate to a social services authority's discharge of (or failure to discharge) any of its social services functions in respect of that individual. The Policy Guidance suggests that in consequence 'complaints of a general nature which are not concerned with an individual case are also likely to fall outside the statutory definition, as are anonymous complaints' (para 6.5). Whether such a conclusion flows from a reading of s7B is perhaps debatable, and will inevitably depend upon the particular facts of each case. The guidance however goes on to state that authorities will in any event be able (at their discretion) to deal with a complaint not covered by s7B (para 6.5). This point has also been made by the local ombudsman in a case where she accepted that although the complainant was not a qualifying individual, it was nevertheless important that her 'complaints were still given full and proper consideration in a way which equated to the standard of service a complaint would have received under the council's formal complaints procedure'.[6]

The structure of the complaints system

12.9   The structure and key timescales of the complaints system are outlined in the Complaints Procedure Directions 1990. It is an essential requirement of the directions that authorities designate an officer to assist in the co-ordination of all aspects of the consideration of complaints.[7] The investigating officer must not have any conflict of interest in the investigation.[8] The Policy Guidance suggests that the designated officer should be a senior officer of the department and that the post may also combine responsibility for the CA 1989

---

6   The complaint in fact concerned the Children Act (CA)1989 complaint procedures, but is nevertheless of no less relevance: see Report No. 94/C/2959 against Nottingham City Council; 28 November 1994. See also Local Government Ombudsman Complaint No 97/C/1614 against Bury MBC (1999) where the ombudsman accepted that part of the complaint lay outside the statutory complaints process but nevertheless warranted investigation, and commented 'it is hard to identify any aspect of the Council's handling of Mr Redfern's complaints which was in the proper manner or in full accordance with the statutory complaints procedure and/or the Council's own written complaints procedure'.

7   Direction 4(1); Policy Guidance paras 6.15 onwards; *The Right to Complain* para 3.4.

8   Local Government Ombudsman Complaint No 97/C/1614 against Bury MBC (1999), where the investigator was a line manager of the officer whose actions were the subject of the complaint.

complaints procedures.[9] The local ombudsman has stated that such a system can only function properly if the designated officer is of sufficient seniority to run the complaints system and to ensure that complaints are dealt with, not only within the statutory times, but also with sufficient commitment[10] and has commented in one report as follows:

> In my view the Council's procedures for dealing with complaints are seriously flawed. There seems to be no officer of sufficient seniority to run the complaints system and to ensure that complaints are dealt with, not only within the statutory times, but also with sufficient commitment.[11]

12.10   The directions require that the basic structure of all such complaints procedures be made up of three distinct stages:

1) the informal or problem-solving stage (direction 5(1));
2) the formal or registration stage (direction 6(1));
3) the review stage (direction 7(2)).

While authorities have no discretion in respect of the basic framework of the process, nevertheless the Policy Guidance stresses that 'an inflexible application of the complaints procedure in all cases would clearly be inappropriate. There will be cases where the earlier stages of the procedure should be bypassed; or an entirely different route taken'.[12]

12.11   Inevitably there will be certain types of complaint which raise particular problems requiring that they be subject to different procedures (such as complaints which involve an NHS/social services overlap of responsibilities or those which concern the discharge by a private operator of a community care function, or complaints which concern discretionary charging policies or which raise disciplinary questions). These are discussed below under the heading of 'special cases'.

The informal or problem-solving stage

12.12   Direction 5(1) states that where a local authority receives representations from any complainant, it must attempt to resolve the matter informally. At this stage there is no requirement that the complaint

---

9   Policy Guidance at paras 6.15–6.16; see also *The Right to Complain* para 3.3.
10   Complaint against Haringey LBC; Report No 92/A/3725.
11   Report against Nottingham City Council No 94/C/2659.
12   Policy Guidance para 6.30.

be in writing (Policy Guidance para 6.17). *The Right to Complain*[13] explains that:

> normal good practice should sort out, to the user's satisfaction, the queries and grumbles which are part of a social work department's daily workload. Stage 1 then alerts the relevant worker, supervisor or manager to the fact that there is a more fundamental problem, as perceived by the user or her or his representative. It gives users the right to decide whether or not to pursue the issue and ensures that it is taken seriously and not dismissed by busy staff. The fact, however, that this stage is not 'formal' does not mean that it is 'casual'.[14]

12.13   At the first stage, a complaint does not have to be registered (although many authorities do keep a written record of these:[15] it is simply an opportunity for the local authority to attempt 'problem-solving, conciliation and negotiation'.[16] The local government ombudsman has been critical of councils who have arbitrarily decided that a complaint is not a complaint but an 'issue' or some such other grumble which it could then ignore.[17]

12.14   A significant defect with the informal first stage (as opposed to the next two stages) is the lack of any statutory timescale for its completion. In practice many authorities specify in their local procedures maximum periods for this phase (often in the region of one to four weeks).

12.15   Local authorities should provide complainants with a simple explanation as to how the complaints process works and the relevant timescales. The provision of a leaflet with this information does not obviate the need to advise complainants (in correspondence at the appropriate times) of their rights at subsequent stages (ie, of the right to seek a panel hearing if dissatisfied with a stage 2 report, etc).[18] It will also be maladministration to fail to make it clear to a complainant at which particular stage of the process the complaint is currently being considered.[19]

---

13 Para 4.3.
14 Ibid paras 4.2–4.3.
15 Ibid para 4.32.
16 Ibid para 4.4.
17 Local Government Ombudsman Annual Report 1997/98 p10.
18 Local Government Ombudsman Complaint No 97/A/2464 against Waltham Forest LBC (1998).
19 Local Government Ombudsman Complaint No 96/B/4438 against Devon (1998).

The formal stage

12.16 This stage involves the formal registration of the complaint. A complainant is entitled to go straight to this stage (omitting the informal stage) if s/he so wishes.[20] Given the flexibility permitted by the guidance, it must follow that where a local authority considers it appropriate it too may skip the first 'informal' stage.[21]

12.17 Direction 5(2) of the Complaints Procedure Directions 1990 states that if the complaint cannot be resolved to the satisfaction of the complainant at the first (informal) stage, then the local authority shall give or send to the complainant an explanation of the complaints procedure and ask the complainant to submit a written representation if s/he wishes to proceed. Direction 5(3) requires authorities to offer assistance and guidance to the complainant on the use of the procedure (or an explanation as to where this assistance can be obtained). This point is amplified in *The Right to Complain*, which states that it is good practice to provide help to those who wish to make a complaint and stresses the importance of an advocacy service in this respect.[22]

12.18 Direction 5(2) is not worded so as to make it obligatory for complaints at the second stage to be in writing; indeed the Policy Guidance also uses the phrase 'should . . . be made in writing' (rather than 'must be').[23] *The Right to Complain* (at para 4.10), however, explains that at the second stage the complaint will need to be put in writing, either by the individual concerned or someone else on their behalf, to the designated complaints officer; and that:

> many people will need support and advice from someone they trust either from within or outside the department. Some people will need help in writing and sometimes formulating a complaint. Those who give help in writing down the complaint must ensure that it fully reflects what the complainant wishes to say and ask the complainant to sign it.

The mere fact that a complaint has progressed to the formal stage does not absolve the authority from its duty to try and resolve the problem.[24]

---

20 Ibid para 4.9.
21 Ibid para 4.9 and para 6.30 of Policy Guidance.
22 See para 6.9 Policy Guidance and the Practice Guidance which also refers to the role of advocacy.
23 At para 6.17.
24 Local Government Ombudsman Complaint No 98/C/3591 against Liverpool (1999).

12.19   Direction 6(1) directs the social services authority to consider the complaint and then formulate a response within 28 days of its receipt. If for any reason it is not possible to comply with the 28-day period, the authority must (within that period) explain to the complainant why this is so, and explain when the response will be given. In any event, the response must be forthcoming within three months.

12.20   Authorities have considerable latitude in how they investigate complaints at this stage (for instance, in relation to complaints about discretionary charges, they may decide to operate a restricted and standardised review, leaving those complainants who so choose the option of going to the panel (stage 3) if they wish to argue 'exceptional' (non-financial) grounds). The investigation should adhere to the principles of natural justice, expedition, competence and commitment expounded by the SSI in its *Notes on Good Practice*. Authorities may, if the need arises, appoint an independent person[25] at this stage to oversee the investigation (along the same lines as is required in the CA 1989 complaints procedures).[26] *The Right to Complain* explains that the significance of this stage of the complaints process is that other people (apart from the relevant worker, the supervisor or manager and the complainant) are involved in the consideration, discussion and, possibly, investigation of the complaint.[27]

12.21   *The Right to Complain* recommends that the designated complaints officer be given the power to postpone or stop decisions which are the subject-matter of the complaint (para 3.10). It also draws attention to the need in some investigations for 'expert advice' to be obtained (para 3.16).

12.22   While the Directions are phrased in mandatory terms as to the maximum length of the stage 2 investigation process (a response must be made within 28 days if possible, and if not within three months), frequently this may prove to be an unreasonably short period,[28] particularly where the complaint involves a number of

---

25 *The Right to Complain* para 4.12.

26 See Representations Procedure (Children) Regulations 1991 SI No 894 regs 5 and 6 and Children Act 1989 Guidance Vol 3 paras 10.33 onwards. Considered at para 12.58 below.

27 At para 4.11.

28 See, eg, K Simons, *I'm not complaining but . . .* (Joseph Rowntree Foundation, 1995) p23, concerning a prevalent view amongst social services authorities that the time-scales are unrealistic 'even in the most straightforward of cases': see, however, Complaint no 98/C/1088 against Bolton MBC in which the ombudsman acknowledged this problem, but stressed the need for councils to endeavour to meet the time-scales and provide full explanations when this proved impossible.

matters and its investigation requires several persons to be interviewed. Not unusually the complainant will (when clarifying the nature of the grievance) articulate what are in reality separate complaints; obviously the time for the investigation of these new matters runs from the date on which they were first articulated. While it has been suggested that a breach of the time limits alone may justify an application for judicial review,[29] it would have to be an extreme case for such action to serve any useful purpose (given the inherent delay involved in such proceedings). In general, authorities should be reminded of the time limits and asked to explain any failure to comply with them; provided the investigation is being conducted diligently, it is unlikely to be criticised either by the courts or the ombudsman.

12.23   Direction 7(1) requires the authority to notify the complainant in writing of the result of its investigation. In addition notification must also be sent to the person on whose behalf the complaint was made (unless the authority considers that that person is not able to understand it or it would cause him or her unnecessary distress). The authority should also notify any other person whom it considers to have sufficient interest in the case.[30] Complaints investigators should generally give complainants the opportunity to comment upon a draft of the investigator's report[31] (particularly in relation to any contra-allegations that may have been made[32]) prior to producing a final report.

12.24   Where possible, the investigator's report should distinguish between fact and conclusion, and 'all matters put forward as issues by the complainant should be dealt with: if they are considered unfounded or insignificant, the report should explain this'.[33]

12.25   There is no requirement at this stage for the authority to give reasons for its decision. As the Directions and Policy Guidance specifically require reasons to be given at the next stage, it may be argued that in general there is no enforceable obligation on the authority to give reasons at this point (unless there is something peculiar to the decision which in fairness calls for reasons to be given).[34] There is

---

29 See R Gordon *Community Care Assessments* (Longman, 1993) p50.
30 Para 6.19 of the Policy Guidance suggests that the aim should be to keep the number of those informed to an essential minimum.
31 Local Government Ombudsman Complaint No 97/C/4618 against Cheshire (1999).
32 Local Government Ombudsman report No 98/C/1294 against Calderdale MBC.
33 Local Government Ombudsman Complaint No 97/C/4618 against Cheshire (1999).
34 See, eg, *R v Higher Education Funding Council ex p Institute of Dental Surgery* [1994] 1 All ER 651, QBD at 667c; and cf *R v Bristol CC ex p Bailey and Bailey* (1995) 27 HLR 307, QBD.

also no requirement that a copy of the investigator's report (if any) be made available to the complainant. If, however, s/he takes the complaint to the next stage, it is difficult to see how the report can be kept confidential; it could not as a matter of natural justice be considered by the panel without being available to the complainant. Investigators should therefore ensure that they compile their reports in such a way as to facilitate early disclosure.

The review stage

12.26   The complainant may (if dissatisfied), within 28 days of receiving the decision, request that the complaint be referred to a panel for review (direction 7(2)). Such a request must be made in writing. In such cases the local authority is required to convene a panel hearing within 28 days of receipt of the complainant's request (direction 7(3)). The Policy Guidance requires that the complainant be notified in writing at least ten days beforehand of the time and place of the panel hearing, and be invited to attend.[35] Direction 2(1) requires the panel to comprise three persons, at least one of whom (the chairman)[36] must be an independent person, and direction 2(3) defines an 'independent person' as someone who is neither a member nor an officer of the authority, nor, where the authority has delegated any of its functions to an organisation, a person who is a member of or employed by that organisation, nor the spouse of any such person.

12.27   Complainants should be advised of the name and status of the panel members. There is no requirement that the wing members be independent; the Policy Guidance suggests that they may be independent persons or councillors or other persons whom the authority considers suitable,[37] although it stresses that where possible the persons appointed to the panel should have experience relevant to the subject-matter of the complaint.[38] In most cases authorities tend to appoint a councillor as one wing member and an officer as the other; obviously in such cases the panel is not 'independent', but this is an arrangement referred to without criticism by *The Right to Complain*.[39]

12.28   As soon as a complaint is referred to a panel, a complainant should ensure that sufficient details of the independent person's

35 Annex A para 5.
36 Ibid para 2.
37 Ibid para 3.
38 Ibid para 2, and see also *The Right to Complain* para 4.23: 'If a particular disability or minority group is involved, the panel should be convened so that the complainant's concerns are responded to sensitively and appropriately'.
39 At para 4.24.

curriculum vitae are provided to establish his/her independence.[40] The independence of such a person may be compromised for many reasons, for instance, s/he may be a past employee of the authority or have a connection with some other body (such as a health authority or local health trust) which has close contractual relations with the authority.

12.29 **Panel hearings** The basic procedure to be followed by the panel is detailed in the Policy Guidance (Annex A paras 5–7). Complainants should be told in advance which officers of the authority will be present. Complainants are entitled to make written submissions to the panel before the meeting and to make oral submissions at the meeting. They are entitled to be accompanied by another person who is entitled to be present at the whole meeting and to speak on their behalf. The guidance states that this person should not be a barrister or solicitor acting in a professional capacity.[41] Natural justice dictates that if the applicant is not entitled to have legal representation at a panel hearing, then the same applies to the local authority, and accordingly the local ombudsman has criticised the presence of a local authority's solicitor at a hearing, stating:

> I find it hard to see how a solicitor employed by the Council could be seen as an 'unbiased observer' and consider the way he joined at the outset in the in camera deliberations of the Panel to be unwise at the very least.[42]

12.30 The Policy Guidance requires that the panel:

> meeting should be conducted as informally as possible. The chairperson of the panel should open the meeting by explaining its purpose and the proposed procedure to be adopted for the hearing. In addition the participants should be reminded that the hearing is in private and of the need to respect the rules of confidentiality. The complainant (or a person accompanying him or her) should be given an opportunity to make an oral submission before the authority's representative does. Other people may attend the meeting to make oral submissions if requested to do so by the complainant, subject to

40 The Policy Guidance merely requires that 'complainants be informed of the name and status of the panel members': Chapter 6 Annex A para 5.
41 The Policy Guidance uses the word 'should' rather than 'cannot'; in certain instances legal representation may be desirable (as indeed occurred at the panel hearing the subject-matter of the judicial review in *R v Avon CC ex p M* [1994] 2 FLR 1006); if there is no lawyer present for the complainant, natural justice requires that this is also the case for the authority (see n54 below, where the ombudsman came to such a conclusion).
42 Complaint against Cleveland County Council No 92/C/1042.

the consent of the panel, but will normally only be allowed to be present for that part of the meeting. (Chapter 6 Annex A para 6).

The panel hearing must follow the rules of natural justice. If the complainant and/or his/her representative attend the hearing, the panel members should not talk to (or have lunch with) one party in the absence of the other.[43] The panel is however entitled to set reasonable time limits on the oral submissions to be made by the parties, provided these are used as 'guidelines rather than guillotines'.[44]

12.31   The local government ombudsman has made a number of criticisms about the conduct of panel hearings, including:

- A failure to ensure that key witnesses attended the panel hearing.[45]
- The panel interviewing witnesses at an adjourned hearing, in the absence of the complainant.[46]
- The failure of the local authority to ensure that the panel had clerical assistance: 'the job entrusted to Panels is complex and stressful enough and they need adequate administrative support to be able to perform efficiently and effectively'.[47]
- The introduction of new material by the local authority, at the hearing.[48]
- The need for independent advocates to assist complainants when the complaint is serious or particularly distressing (for instance involving bereavement).[49]
- The presence of a senior social services officer throughout a panel hearing as this may have 'inhibited junior staff from saying all they felt to be pertinent'.[50]
- The interviewing of several members of staff, at different levels of seniority, simultaneously.[51]

43 Local Government Ombudsman Complaint No 96/B/4438 against Devon (1998).
44 Ibid.
45 Local Government Ombudsman Complaint No 97/B/2441 against Hampshire (1999).
46 Ibid.
47 Ibid.
48 Local Government Ombudsman Complaint No 96/B/4438 against Devon (1998); although it will amount to serious maladministration for the local authority to suggest that evidence put forward by a complainant at a panel hearing is 'new material' when it is not, Local Government Ombudsman Complaint No 97/C/1614 against Bury MBC (1999).
49 Local Government Ombudsman Complaint No 97/C/4618 against Cheshire (1999).
50 Ibid.
51 Ibid.

12.32 If possible, the panel should have read key papers (and submissions) before the hearing. If on reading these the panel requires further information (for instance, a copy of a relevant assessment or details of the authority's eligibility criteria etc), it should endeavour to obtain this before the hearing if at all possible. Likewise any possible conflict on legal interpretation should be resolved before any hearing, as the panel is not qualified to make such determinations: ultimately, if the conflict persists, it will have little option other than to accept the local authority's view on such issues. A problem that has been identified on a number of occasions relates to the complainant's access to his or her social services file. The law allows 40 days for files to be prepared (see para 2.31 above), whereas the Directions require that a panel meet within 28 days; the local ombudsman has noted this problem and a possible solution, namely that 'information should be given about rights of access and timescales at the first stage of the procedure'.[52]

12.33 The role of the panel is to consider all the relevant evidence, weigh it up, and recommend a particular outcome. It is the panel's job to re-examine the previous decision;[53] it is the 'body entrusted with the basic fact-finding exercise under the complaints procedure'.[54]

12.34 Within 24 hours of the review hearing, the panel must reach a decision in writing and forward its recommendations (and reasons) to the local authority, the complainant (and his or her representative) and any other person who is considered to have sufficient interest (direction 8(1) and (2)). Policy Guidance para 6.22 suggests that members of the local authority staff with a direct interest in the complaint should receive an explanation of the outcome of the review. If a panel member disagrees with the majority recommendation, the decision letter should also record that member's view, and the reasons for it.[55]

12.35 A panel's recommendations can fall into four broad categories, namely:

1) recommendations of a factual nature;
2) recommendations concerning compensation;
3) recommendations of a policy nature;
4) recommendations of a legal nature.

---

52 Complaint No 93/A/3007 against Hounslow LBC (10 October 1995); and see also Complaint No 97/A/1082 where the need for local authority files to be made available, promptly, for inspection by complainants was emphasised.
53 *The Right to Complain* para 4.16.
54 *R v Avon CC ex p M* [1994] 2 FLR 1006; (1999) 2 CCLR 185; see para 12.48 below.
55 Policy Guidance Chapter 6 Annex A.

12.36   **Factual recommendations** The panel is, as stated above, the basic fact-finding body in the complaints process. Its task is to weigh up the evidence, evaluate witnesses, consider all the relevant facts, ignore irrelevant factors and apply these considerations reasonably in order to reach its recommendations. The panel should concentrate on resolving the complaint and endeavour to ensure (if appropriate) that any issues of wider significance arising out of the complaint are made known to the senior management of the authority (via the panel's recommendations). A panel's recommendations may be wide-ranging. The local ombudsman has, for instance, commented favourably on a panel's decision which (among other things) recommended that the local authority prepare a report 'in a year's time or earlier if appropriate, on what action had been taken [on the broad policy implications arising out of their findings]; and that a copy of the report be sent to the complainants'.[56]

12.37   The local government ombudsman expects local authorities to act on practical recommendations made by panels, and has noted that 'it is no use having a complaints procedure which provides for a thorough investigation but where no one acts upon its recommendations'.[57]

12.38   **Compensation** One of the defects of many local authority complaints procedures is their restricted powers to pay compensation, and in some cases authorities use this (and suggestions that it is not permitted by their insurers) as a reason for refusing all such payments. While ex gratia payments are not forbidden, local authorities must be able to justify any payments and satisfy elected members and the district auditor that the payment of compensation was appropriate. As a result of pressure from the ombudsman the government has agreed to introduce legislation to put beyond doubt the right of local authorities to pay compensation, although as yet such legislation has not been introduced.[58]

12.39   The local ombudsman has stressed that the possibility of compensation should be an element in a good complaints procedure[59] and expressed irritation with authorities who do not, in appropriate cases, offer to pay complainants compensation (or some other appropriate

56 Complaint against Hounslow (n52 above).
57 Local Government Ombudsman Digest of Cases 1996 p112; and see also similar criticism at p112 of the 1998 Digest of Cases.
58 Annual Report 1998/99 p7.
59 Guidance on Good Practice 1: 'Devising a Complaints System' (February 1992) App 2.

recompense) as part of their settlement.[60] He has emphasised that this is particularly important in relation to complaints panel recommendations.[61] Accordingly, in 1997 good practice guidance was issued, aimed at promoting greater consistency in the remedies recommended by local authorities.[62]

12.40 The guidance noted that an appropriate remedy may require a number of separate elements, including recommendations as to specific action that should be taken and as to an apology. On the question of compensation, however, it states that 'financial compensation may be appropriate, for example, if the council has taken the appropriate action but has delayed in doing so and the delay has caused injustice; or if there is no practical action which would provide a full and appropriate remedy; or if the complainant has sustained loss and suffering'. The guidance suggests that the calculation of what is appropriate may include consideration of:

- The effect of the complainant's own action.
- Reimbursement to the complainant of any money which is owing but unpaid (ie, unpaid housing benefit).
- Quantifiable loss; ie, 'paying for the additional help the parents procured for a child with special educational needs because the council delayed in drawing up a statement or fulfilling its provision'.
- Loss of a non-monetary benefit; ie, 'a council tenant has been unable to use one of the rooms in his or her flat for a period because of lack of repair.
- Loss of value; where something owned by the complainant has lost value.
- Lost opportunity; compensation for a lost opportunity may sometimes be a fairly small sum, because it is only the loss or opportunity which is certain and the actual outcome which would have obtained cannot be known.
- Distress 'including stress, anxiety, frustration, uncertainty, worry inconvenience etc'. 'This element may be a moderate sum of no more than a few hundred pounds or less but in cases where the distress has been severe and/or prolonged, a more substantial sum may be justified'. Generally it will be 'in the range of £200 to £1,000 for a year, with broadly pro rata sums for shorter or longer periods'.

60 Local Government Ombudsman Annual Report 1996/97 p11.
61 Local Government Ombudsman Annual Report 1998/99 p11.
62 Guidance on Good Practice, 6 'Remedies' (September 1996).

- Professional fees in pursuing the dispute; while the guidance advises that complainants usually do not need a solicitor or other professional to help them make a complaint, it may sometimes be appropriate. In such cases the recommendation may be for a contribution to costs rather than reimbursement of the whole of the expenditure.
- Time and trouble in pursuing the complaint (but this should not be confused with the question of distress (as above)). These 'normally fall into the range of £25 to £250'.
- Offsetting compensation; in circumstances where the complainant owes money to the council (eg, rent arrears) 'it would usually be appropriate for the compensation to be offset against the debt'.
- Interest.

12.41 **Policy recommendations** Panels will need to know (preferably before any hearing) the status of any policy matters relevant to the hearing (eg, eligibility criteria or charging policies and whether they are in draft form, approved or in the process of revision). Panels should be wary of making any recommendations which would be contrary to such general policies if they have been formulated and approved by the elected members (and especially if this was after the policies were the subject of proper consultation). The risk in such cases is of course that the panel is attempting to usurp the democratic community role of the council.

12.42   The local government ombudsman's guidance on good practice suggests, however, that in suitable cases the panel's recommendation can include advice that the authority review its practices, procedures or policies or give consideration to particular suggestions for improvements that have come to its notice.

12.43 **Legal recommendations** Where there is a straightforward disagreement between the complainant and the local authority about the law, then it is doubtful that the panel can do anything other than accept the authority's interpretation. While in such cases a complainant can use the complaints process, it is difficult to see that it can produce anything of value; the appropriate remedy in such a case is by way of a judicial review in order that the court can decide (see also para 12.87 below).

12.44   The panel must restrict itself to the relevant factors in the complaint and ignore the irrelevant. In a complaint to the local ombudsman involving East Sussex County Council,[63] the panel had decided

---

63 Local Government Ombudsman Complaint No 93/A/3738 against East Sussex County Council.

that because a council officer had given misleading advice (that the complainants were not eligible for certain benefits when they were), the complainants lost £4,220 in benefits. The panel recommended that they receive an ex gratia payment of £750, holding that it was not appropriate for the council to reimburse the unpaid benefit, as it was not the council's responsibility to issue such benefits but that of the DSS. The local government ombudsman held that the panel had considered an irrelevant factor, stating:

> The consequence of the misleading advice . . . was that they did not take up their entitlement to benefits. Accordingly, whether or not the Department itself was responsible for such benefits was not relevant to the Panel's consideration.

The ombudsman held that the full sum of unpaid benefit be paid by the council (plus £250 for the complainants' 'time and trouble' in making the complaint).

12.45   The panel is required to give reasons for its recommendation (direction 8(3)). The extent of this obligation is discussed below (in that the same obligation rests with the local authority when deciding its response to the recommendations).

Subsequent action

12.46   The local authority has 28 days from the date of the panel's recommendations to decide what action should be taken. It must notify in writing all the persons who received copies of the panel's recommendations; the notification must detail not only the authority's decision but also its reasons for taking that decision and of any action which it has in consequence taken (or which it proposes to take – direction 8(4)).

12.47   While a local authority is not bound to accept a panel's recommendation, it will in practice have to have extremely cogent reasons for deciding differently. Sedley J held in *R v Islington LBC ex p Rixon*[64] that 'a failure to comply with a review panel's recommendations is not by itself a breach of law; but the greater the departure, the greater the need for cogent articulated reasons if the court is not to infer that the panel's recommendations have been overlooked'.

12.48   The case of *R v Avon CC ex p M*[65] concerned the failure of a social services department to comply with the findings of its complaints review panel. Henry J held:

---

64   (1998) 1 CCLR 119.
65   [1994] 2 FLR 1006; (1999) 2 CCLR 185; [1994] 2 FCR 259, QBD.

I would be reluctant to hold (and do not) that in no circumstances whatsoever could the Social Services Committee have overruled the Review Panel's recommendation in the exercise of their legal right and duty to consider it. Caution normally requires the Court not to say 'never' in any obiter dictum pronouncement. But I have no hesitation in finding that they could not overrule that decision without a substantial reason and without having given that recommendation the weight it required. It was a decision taken by a body entrusted with the basic fact-finding exercise under the complaints procedure. It was arrived at after a convincing examination of the evidence, particularly the expert evidence. The evidence before them had, as to the practicalities, been largely one way. The Panel had directed themselves properly, in law, and had arrived at a decision in line with the strength of the evidence before them. They had given clear reasons and they had raised the crucial factual question with the parties before arriving at their conclusion . . . It seems to me that anybody required, at law, to give their reasons for reconsidering and changing such a decision must have good reasons for doing so, and must show that they gave that decision sufficient weight and, in my judgment, it failed to do. Their decision must be quashed.

12.49   The case was, however, distinguished by Dyson J in *R v North York-shire CC ex p Hargreaves*,[66] where he stated:

All that Henry J was saying was that where a panel has given a carefully reasoned decision adverse to the local authority on the subject of a complaint and the local authority rejects the panel's recommendation without itself giving a rational reason for doing so, then there is a strong prima facie case for quashing the local authority's decision as unlawful.

The local authority is (like the panel) required to give reasons for its decision. Such reasons must be 'proper, adequate and intelligible' and must deal with the substantial points raised by the complainant.[67] An unparticularised assertion that 'on the evidence' the panel makes certain findings and 'recommends . . .' will be considered inadequate.[68]

Special cases

12.50   Certain complaints will inevitably require a different investigative or

66   (1997) 1 CCLR 104.
67   *Westminster CC v Great Portland Estates PLC* [1985] 1 AC 661 at 673, HL and *In re Poyser and Mills' Arbitration* [1964] 2 QB 467 at 478.
68   *R v Secretary of State for Transport ex p Cumbria CC* [1983] RTR 129, QBD.

review procedure by virtue of their particular facts or the nature of the subject-matter.

Disciplinary or grievance procedures

12.51 The Policy Guidance (at para 6.12) stresses the importance of keeping complaints procedures separate from grievance procedures (which concern staff issues, ie, conditions of service) and disciplinary procedures (which apply to the actions of staff in relation to failures to comply with codes of conduct etc).

12.52 Where serious allegations are made, senior staff will need to be involved at the outset. Where such allegations suggest that a criminal offence may have been committed, the relevant local procedure, which may be contained in the authority's standing orders, should be followed. Where the allegation is serious and substantial, the police must be notified immediately.[69]

NHS overlap

12.53 The NHS complaints procedures, both in relation to general complaints and in respect of the specific procedure for challenging a discharge from NHS care (considered in detail in para 6.157 above), are quite separate from those applied by social services authorities. Occasionally, however, a complaint will concern a matter which is an overlapping responsibility of both authorities. The Policy Guidance suggests that in such cases it will be necessary to decide quickly which authority should deal with the complaint, and that the complainant should be informed at once when a complaint is transferred to the NHS system, together with an explanation as to the reason for the transfer and details of the person who will then be dealing with it (para 6.33). Where the complaint is lodged by a person being cared for in a nursing home under the terms of a contractual arrangement made between the home and a local authority, the complaint should initially be referred to the health authority registration officer responsible for registration and inspection of the home (para 6.32).[69A]

12.54 Not infrequently, a complaint concerns misbehaviour by both the social services department and the NHS. In such cases it is, unfortunately, necessary to make separate complaints to each body. If for instance the complaint concerns a faulty hospital discharge it may be

---

69 Policy Guidance para 6.30 and see *The Right to Complain* paras 7.1 onwards.
69A Although unltimately it may be the local authority's duty to investigate the complaint, see Complaint No 97/A/4002 against Bexley LBC.

necessary to make complaint to the social services department, the NHS trust and to the health authority. Thus (and absurdly) a complainant may need to maintain three separate complaints merely to remedy an injustice which may have arisen because the three bodies have failed to work with each other appropriately.[69B]

12.55   Specific collaboration is also required in such areas as hospital discharge procedures (see para 6.129 and *The Right to Complain* para 7.19).

Independent and private sector providers

12.56   The Policy Guidance states that, wherever possible, the service provider should handle complaints about care services provided in the voluntary and private sector with financial support from the local authority. Complainants who remain dissatisfied with the response to their complaints by the service provider may nevertheless choose to refer the matter to the social services department. Complaints received in such circumstances should be treated as registered complaints (para 6.31). Registered residential care homes are required by law to have a procedure for investigating complaints.[70]

Complaints concerning non-accommodation charges

12.57   Social services authorities have a discretion whether to levy charges for non-accommodation community care services (see para 8.67). It is implicit in the relevant statutory provision, Heath and Social Services and Social Security Adjudications Act (HASSASSAA) 1983 s17, that authorities must have a review process so that individuals can challenge charges on the grounds that their means are insufficient for it to be reasonably practicable for them to pay the assessed charge (or that notwithstanding this, that the authority's overall discretion not to charge should be applied in their particular case). Where an individual challenges any assessed charge (either for accommodation or non-accommodation charges), this should be dealt with by the complaints procedures.[71] Because of the relatively large number of

---

69B Although it may be maladministration for local authorities and health bodies not to have procedures for joint investigations in appropriate cases, see complaint No 97/C/3668 against Bury MBC and No 99/C/1276 against Northumberland CC.

70   Residential Care Homes Regulations 1984 SI No 1345 reg 17.

71   See CRAG para 1.027 and the local government ombudsman's criticisms of the failure of complaints procedures in the reports against Essex (No 90A/2675)

such complaints many authorities deal with them under a special procedure. On receiving the complaint the social worker reassesses the charge (by reference to the authority's local procedures) and if the assessment has been calculated correctly, the complaint is referred to a specific committee of officers who consider the complaint and review the authority's decision. This internal review is deemed to be stage 2 of the complaints process. If the complainant is dissatisfied with the committee's decision, s/he can request that the matter then be considered by the panel.

Children procedures

12.58 Complaints about the discharge by an authority of any of its functions under CA 1989 Pt III (which concerns services for children 'in need', including disabled children – see para 11.2) are dealt with under a similar but separate procedure.[72] The most significant difference between the two procedures is that at the equivalent (second) stage of the children's complaints procedure an independent person must be involved.

Human Rights Act 1998

12.59 Under article 6 of the European Convention on Human Rights a court is not independent if it does not have the power to give a binding decision. In general, this requirement will not cause problems in relation to the statutory complaints procedures (either under LASSA 1970 or Children Act 1989) since they do not in general consider matters which are 'civil' within the meaning of article 6. Nevertheless, the procedures prescribed by the Local Authority Social Services (Complaints Procedure) Order 1990 and the Representations Procedure (Children) Regulations 1991 do not require the final tribunal to be fully 'independent' (in the judicial sense) nor does it have the power to make binding decisions. Such panels do occasionally consider matters that concern 'civil' rights, for instance complaints concerning where a disabled person lives[73] or the refusal of a local authority to pursue rehabilitation of a child in care.[74] The

and others, and against Greenwich LBC (No 91/A/3782); but see para 8.99 note 84 above.
72 See Representations Procedure (Children) Regulations 1991 SI No 894 regs 5 and 6 and Children Act 1989 Guidance Vol 3 paras 10.33 onwards.
73 *R v North and East Devon HA ex p Coughlan* (1999) 2 CCLR 285, CA.
74 *R v Birmingham CC ex p A* [1997] 2 FLR 841.

situation is analogous to industrial tribunal wing members whose compliance with article 6 has been questioned.[75]

Local government ombudsman procedures

12.60   The commissioners for local administration in England and Wales (the local government ombudsmen) were established by (and remain governed by) Local Government Act (LGA) 1974 Pt III. By virtue of s25 of the Act they are empowered to investigate (among other things) any local authority. Section 26 stipulates that all complaints must be in writing and made by members of the public who claim to have sustained injustice in consequence of maladministration in connection with action taken by or on behalf of an authority. Complaints no longer have to be introduced by a local councillor, although this remains advisable where possible.

12.61   In *R v Commissioner for Local Administration ex p Eastleigh BC*,[76] Lord Donaldson MR commented:

> Maladministration is not defined in the 1974 Act, but its meaning was considered in *R v Local Comr for Administration for the North and East Area of England ex p Bradford MCC* [1979] 2 All ER 881. All three judges (Lord Denning MR, Eveleigh LJ and Sir David Cairns) expressed themselves differently, but in substance each was saying the same thing, namely that administration and maladministration, in the context of a local authority, is concerned with the *manner* in which decisions by the authority are reached and the *manner* in which they are or are not implemented.

12.62   The Health Service Ombudsman in his annual report for 1993/4 (para 1.4) commented on the nature of maladministration in the following terms:

> The terms given by Mr Richard Crossman in 1966 were 'bias, neglect, inattention, delay, incompetence, ineptitude, perversity, turpitude, arbitrariness and so on'. I have added:
> * rudeness (though that is a matter of degree);
> * unwillingness to treat the complainant as a person with rights;
> * refusal to answer reasonable questions;
> * neglecting to inform a complainant on request of his or her rights or entitlement;

---

75   *Smith v Secretary of State for Trade and Industry* (1999) *Times* 15 October, and see also *Starrs v Procurator Fiscal* (1999) *Times* 17 November, concerning the independence of temporary sheriffs.

76   [1988] 3 All ER 151, CA.

- knowingly giving advice which is misleading or inadequate;
- ignoring valid advice or overruling considerations which would produce an uncomfortable result for the overruler;
- offering no redress or manifestly disproportionate redress;
- showing bias whether because of colour, sex or any other grounds;
- omission to notify those who thereby lose a right of appeal;
- refusal to inform adequately of the right of appeal;
- faulty procedures; failure by management to monitor compliance with adequate procedures;
- cavalier disregard of guidance which is intended to be followed in the interest of equitable treatment of those who use the service;
- partiality; and
- failure to mitigate the effects of rigid adherence to the letter of the law where that produces manifestly inequitable treatment.

Complaints must in general be made to the local ombudsman (or the local councillor) within 12 months from the date on which the person aggrieved first had notice of the matters alleged in the complaint, although the local ombudsman has an overall discretion to extend time if s/he considers it reasonable to do so (s26(4)).

12.63   The local ombudsman cannot investigate a complaint unless it has first been drawn to the attention of the local authority in question, and that authority has been afforded an opportunity to investigate and reply to the complaint (s26(5)).

12.64   Unless the local ombudsman is satisfied that in the particular circumstances it is not reasonable to expect the aggrieved person to resort to such a remedy, complaints cannot be entertained where there exists an alternative remedy, for instance a right of appeal to a tribunal or to a minister of the Crown or a remedy by way of court proceedings. However, in general, relatively few complaints are rejected by the local ombudsman on these grounds (five per cent in 1998/99).

12.65   Only about three per cent of all complaints result in the local ombudsman preparing a final report; the most significant reasons for a complaint not resulting in a report being: (1) it discloses no maladministration; (2) the complaint is premature; (3) a local settlement results; and (4) the complaint is outside the ombudsman's jurisdiction.

12.66   An increasing (although still small) number of complaints are being received by the local ombudsman concerning the actions of social services authorities. In 1998/99 they amounted to seven per cent of all complaints (numerically 1,132 complaints received and 38 reports filed). The four most common reasons for a finding of malad-administration are (in decreasing order): (1) unreasonable delay, (2) taking incorrect action, (3) failure to provide adequate information, explanation or advice and (4) a failure to take appropriate action.[77]

12.67   The local ombudsman has produced many important reports on aspects of community care and these are referred to throughout this text in the appropriate chapters.

12.68   As detailed above, LGA 1974 s26(5) requires complainants to bring complaints to the notice of the local authority first before the local ombudsman will consider them. In general the ombudsman requires complainants to use the authority's complaints procedures before s/he will be prepared to investigate the matter. However, if the complaint is not investigated properly by the authority (for instance, if there was an unjustified breach of the timescales or a serious breach of the rules of natural justice), then the local ombudsman should accept the complaint even though it has not traversed the local authority's entire complaints process.

12.69   In his annual report for 1992/93 the local ombudsman, Mr G F Laws, commented on his general approach in this area:

> The recommendations of a statutory complaints panel to a director of social services are not binding. In assessing complaints that have been through the procedure and have then been rejected, I have looked at the investigation process; if it has been satisfactory, I have often adopted the recommendations of the panel and attempted to settle the matter. In this way I have been able to avoid the need for a further lengthy and costly investigation by my office.

12.70   While there can be no criticism of this as a general statement of sensible practice, the local ombudsman must of course also consider the approach adopted by the panel to its decision-making responsibilities: many panels, for instance, do not recommend any compensation payments because their social services authority has a practice of not making ex gratia payments.

12.71   As complaints to the local ombudsman are only (in general) accepted if no legal remedy is available, the judicial review and ombudsman procedures are separate, and in no way 'alternative options'.[78] In *R v Commissioner for Local Administration ex p PH*,[79] an

---

77 Annual Report 1998/99 p40.

78 Ombudsman decisions are, however, susceptible to judicial review; see, eg, *R v Parliamentary Commissioner ex p Dyer* (1993) *Times* 27 October and *R v Parliamentary Commissioner ex p Bachin* (1999) EGCS 78.

79 [1999] COD 382, as cited in Annual Report 1998/99 p7.

applicant commenced judicial review proceedings against a local authority on the grounds that it had delayed in carrying out a special educational needs assessment. As a consequence such an assessment took place. Subsequently, she complained to the ombudsman seeking compensation for the effect of the council's delay. The ombudsman decided, under LGA 1974 s26(6), that the complaint was outside his jurisdiction because the complainant had already sought a judicial review of the council's actions. In upholding the ombudsman's decision, Turner J held:

> It can hardly have been the intention of Parliament to have provided two remedies, one substantive by way of judicial review and one compensatory by way of the Local Commissioner . . . where a party has ventilated a grievance by way of judicial review it was not contemplated that they should enjoy an alternative, let alone an additional right by way of complaint to a local commissioner.

12.72 There are many advantages to a complainant in using the local ombudsman procedures. They are free to the complainant, they can result in the award of significant sums in compensation and the authority is required to publicise the ombudsman's report (LGA 1974 s30). The ombudsman has access to all the relevant files and other records, can require the authority to furnish additional information and has the same powers as the High Court in respect of the attendance and examination of witnesses and in respect of the production of documents (s29). Complaints to the local ombudsman are not subject to the same severe time limits as in judicial review (in general they must be made within 12 months of the maladministration, as detailed above).

12.73 The disadvantages include the apparent reluctance of the local ombudsman to accept many complaints, the fact that less than five per cent of all complaints actually result in a final report, and the length of time taken to complete the investigations (now averaging almost one and a half years). In spite of this, however, one has to accept that judicial review has many of the same failings.

12.74 The local ombudsman has a full web site with details of complaint forms, relevant publications and addresses. The Internet address is http://www.open.gov.uk/lgo/index.htm.

12.75 The regional offices of the local ombudsman are as follows (in England the office to use is generally the one closest to the relevant authority):

England
21 Queen Anne's Gate, London SW1H 9BU
   Tel: 020 7222 5622.
The Oaks, Westwood Way, Westwood Business Park, Coventry
CV4 8JB
   Tel: 024 6976-5999.
Beverley House, 17 Shipton Road, York YO3 6FZ
   Tel: 01904 630151.

Wales
Derwen House, Court Road, Bridgend, Mid-Glamorgan CF31 1BN
   Tel: 01656 661325.

Scotland
23 Walker Street, Edinburgh EH3 7HX
   Tel: 0131 225 5300.

12.76   Copies of all the local ombudsman's reports in England can be obtained from the London office. For a modest annual fee a subscription can be taken out to receive all copies of social services complaints reports – details can also be obtained from the same address.

Judicial review

12.77   Judicial review is a procedure by which the High Court reviews the lawfulness of decisions made by public bodies, such as the departments of state, local authorities and NHS bodies.

12.78   In general the law allows private individuals or businesses to behave unreasonably or make capricious decisions; public bodies however have no such freedom. They must act reasonably in reaching decisions, and (after 2 October 2000) must not act in any way which is incompatible with the European Convention on Human Rights.[80] If they fail to act in such a way, and significant injustice results, then the High Court may be prepared to quash the decision and require that it be considered again without the contaminant of unfairness.

12.79   What is 'reasonable' depends upon the nature of the decision and the context in which it is to be made. It will invariably require that in reaching a decision all relevant matters be considered; that all irrelevant matters are disregarded; and that the body correctly applies the relevant law (including that it has the power to make the decision). In certain situations reasonableness may require that, prior to making a

80   Human Rights Act 1998 s6.

decision, consultation takes place with persons who are likely to be affected. Likewise reasonableness may require that a particular decision-making procedure be followed, if affected parties have a 'legitimate expectation' that this will occur. Even if a public body adheres to all these principles, its ultimate decision will be capable of judicial challenge if it bears no sensible relationship to the material facts on which it was based (if it in essence 'defies logic') or if the decision amounts to an abuse of power.

12.80   The High Court, through the use of judicial review, seeks to improve the way public bodies make decisions and thus contribute to a fairer and more open administrative system. It does not seek to usurp the powers of these bodies. It follows therefore that the court will only get involved if the aggrieved party acts swiftly and produces significant evidence, not only of a 'flawed' decision-making process but also that as a consequence a real risk of injustice may result.

12.81   While decisions made by private or voluntary providers (such as independent nursing homes or voluntary sector day centres, etc) are not susceptible to judicial review (unless adopted by a responsible public body), they may constitute a breach of private law rights (eg, a breach of a contract with a nursing home).

12.82   In addition to their public law obligations, local authorities may have private law duties under the community care legislation. In *R v Bexley LBC ex p B*,[81] Latham J commented (obiter):

> The duty laid upon Authorities by [CSDPA 1970 s2(1)] was not merely a target duty, but was a duty owed to a specific individual. Prima facie, this points to the conclusion that breach is capable of giving rise to a remedy in tort. The very specific nature of the duty means that they [ie, damages] would be readily capable of evaluation in money terms. Parliament has not provided any specific remedy for breach. It, therefore, seems to me that these duties do fall into the category of those duties, breaches of which are capable of giving rise to a claim for damages in tort.

In such cases there is the option to commence a private law action for damages rather than by way of judicial review. Generally, however, it will be more appropriate to apply for judicial review under RSC Order 53, and in those proceedings to include a claim for damages.[82]

81 (2000) 3 CCLR 15; quoting from *R v Gloucestershire CC ex p Mahfood* (1997) 1 CCLR 7; 94 LGR 593.
82 Order 53 r7; and see *Roy v Kensington and Chelsea Family Practitioners Committee* [1992] 1 AC 625, HL; *R v Northavon DC ex p Palmer* (1995) 27 HLR 576, CA; and *X (Minors) v Bedfordshire CC* [1995] 3 All ER 353, HL.

Complaint to local authority monitoring officer

12.83   Where judicial review proceedings are contemplated, it is often advisable, as a preliminary step, to make a formal complaint to the local authority monitoring officer requesting that the impugned decision be reviewed. This may be in the form of (and constitute) the letter before action in appropriate cases. The duties of the monitoring officer are set out in Local Government and Housing Act 1989 s5 as follows:

(1) It shall be the duty of every relevant authority –

(a) to designate one of their officers (to be known as 'the monitoring officer') as the officer responsible for performing the duties imposed by this section; and

(b) to provide that officer with such staff, accommodation and other resources as are in his opinion, sufficient to allow those duties to be performed;

and the officer so designated may be the head of the authority's paid service but shall not be their chief finance officer.

(2) It shall be the duty of a relevant authority's monitoring officer, if it at any time appears to him that any proposal, decision or omission by the authority, by any committee, sub-committee or officer of the authority or by any joint committee on which the authority are represented constitutes, has given rise to or is likely to or would give rise to –

(a) a contravention by the authority, by any committee, sub-committee or officer of the authority or by any such joint committee of any enactment or rule of law or any code of practice made or approved by or under any enactment; or

(b) any such maladministration or injustice as is mentioned in Part III of the Local Government Act 1974 (Local Commissioners) or Part II of the Local Government (Scotland) Act 1975 (which makes corresponding provision for Scotland),

to prepare a report to the authority with respect to that proposal, decision or omission.

(3) It shall be the duty of a relevant authority's monitoring officer –

(a) in preparing a report under this section to consult so far as practical with the head of the authority's paid service and with the chief finance officer; and

(b) as soon as practicable after such a report has been prepared by him or his deputy, to arrange for a copy of it to be sent to each member of the authority.

Section 5 thus requires every authority to have such an officer who is responsible for reporting on any proposal, decision or omission made by the authority (or any of its committees or officers) which has given rise or is likely to give rise to a contravention of the law (or any code of practice made or approved by or under any enactment) or any maladministration or injustice as would fall within the investigative remit of the local government ombudsman.

12.84   The monitoring officer's duty is to prepare and circulate a report when it 'appears to' him/her that such a situation may exist; put another way, it is the fact of a situation (or the likely fact of it), in the view of the monitoring officer, which triggers the duty under s5.

Sufficient standing

12.85   In order to apply for judicial review, an applicant must have a sufficient interest in the matter to which the application relates (RSC Order 53 r3(7)).

12.86   In *R v Gloucestershire CC ex p RADAR*,[83] Carnwath J considered an application by the Royal Association for Disability and Rehabilitation (RADAR) for judicial review of a decision made by Gloucestershire County Council relating to a general procedure which the council had adopted for the reassessment of the community care needs of disabled people. Having considered the relevant authorities (such as *R v Foreign Secretary ex p World Development Movement*[84]) he held:

> the general principle, that the Authority is obliged to go through a process of reassessment in respect of all those affected by the 1994 decision [consequent on the decision in *R v Gloucestershire County Council ex p Mahfood*[85]] is one which can, in my view, properly and conveniently be asserted by a body such as RADAR. It cannot be in anyone's interests that it should be left to each individual separately to assert that right. No doubt other individual test cases can be bought, but there is always a risk that if the particular individual loses his direct interest, either because his circumstances change or because the Authority carry out a reassessment, then the proceedings will prove abortive. In my view, RADAR has a sufficient interest to entitle it to a declaration as to the position as I have outlined it.

Carnwath J, however, went on to suggest that it would 'be very rare that it would be appropriate for a coercive order such as an order for mandamus, to be granted to a body like RADAR'.

An alternative remedy?

12.87   Judicial review is not available where the applicant has failed to pursue an equally convenient, expeditious and effective remedy. This

---

83   (1998) 1 CCLR 476

84   [1995] 1 All ER 611, QBD.

85   (1997) 1 CCLR 7; 94 LGR 593.

will mean that, in the absence of cogent reasons, an applicant should first utilise the complaints procedures or seek to invoke an available 'default' remedy (see para 12.116 below). As a general rule disputes which are primarily factual are best suited to the complaints process and disputes which concern the interpretation of directions or guidance are suited to resolution via the default procedures.[86]

12.88　The court may be prepared to entertain a judicial review, notwithstanding that the applicant has not attempted to use the complaints or default procedures, if it can be shown that there are substantial reasons for believing that these remedies are not 'equally convenient, expeditious and effective'. Frequently this will be the case where:

a) the matter in issue is a clear-cut dispute of a legal definition;
b) what is in issue is a blanket practice or fixed policy;
c) there is an urgent need for the service (ie, a requirement for 'interim relief') or it can be otherwise shown that the complaints procedure would be incapable of adequately resolving the dispute.[87]

12.89　In *R v Gloucestershire CC ex p RADAR*, it was unsuccessfully argued that an application for judicial review could not be made until the alternative remedy of a local authority complaint under LASSA 1970 s7B had been pursued. Carnwath J held that in certain cases such a remedy might be appropriate, especially:

> where individual relief is being sought. However, in relation to a general issue of principle as to the authority's obligations in law, . . . I do not think that can be regarded as a suitable or alternative remedy to the procedure of judicial review.[88]

12.90　Likewise, in *R v Devon CC ex p Baker and Others*,[89] such an argument (not only that an alternative remedy via the complaints procedure existed, but also that under LASSA 1970 s7D the applicants should first have asked the secretary of state to use her default powers), was rejected on the grounds that:

> as the issue is entirely one in law in a developing field which is peculiarly appropriate for decisions by the Court rather than by the Secretary of State, I would hold that the Applicants in the Durham case were not precluded from making their application for Judicial

---

86　*R v Westminster CC ex p P* (1998) 1 CCLR 486 and see also *R v Kirklees MBC ex p Good* (1998) 1 CCLR 506.

87　See R Gordon *Community Care Assessments* (Longman, 1993) p61 onwards.

88　See also *Secretary of State for Education and Science v Tameside MBC ex p Ellerton* [1985] 1 WLR 749, and *R v Kent CC ex p Bruce* (1996) *Times* 8 February.

89　[1995] 1 All ER 73.

Review by the availability of another remedy; the case is one which it is proper for this Court to entertain.[90]

Grounds for judicial review

12.91 As noted above, judicial review generally concerns a challenge to the decision-making process (ie, the procedure followed in coming to the decision) rather than to the decision itself. In such 'procedural' challenges, applicants are required to show some substantial flaw in the process by which the public body reached its decision. In certain cases, however, the court will entertain a 'substantive' challenge to the actual decision itself; for instance on the basis that (given the process followed) the impugned decision is so absurd that in reaching it, the local authority must 'have taken leave of [its] senses'.[91]

12.92 The principles underlying judicial review are sophisticated and multi-faceted and are continually being refined and developed by the judiciary.

12.93 Thus, when in *Kruse v Johnson*,[92] the High Court indicated that it would be prepared to set aside local authority decisions which were 'manifestly unjust, partial, made in bad faith or so gratuitous and oppressive that no reasonable person could think them justified' it was merely outlining the type of situation which might provoke judicial intervention, not making any definitive statement of the potential grounds for review. Likewise, 50 years later, in *Associated Provincial Picture Houses v Wednesbury Corporation*,[93] when Lord Greene described what are now the classic '*Wednesbury*' principles, he was again only sketching out examples of administrative behaviour which might attract judicial censure, not seeking to compile an exhaustive list. In his judgment he instanced the following behaviour as being potentially justiciable:

- contravention of the law;
- a fettering of a discretion;
- unreasonableness in the sense of bad faith or dishonesty;
- failing to consider 'matters which he is bound to consider';
- failing to exclude matters which are irrelevant;
- reaching a decision that is 'so absurd that no sensible person could even dream that it lay within the powers of the authority'.

90 Per Dillon LJ at 87; and see also *R v Brent LBC ex p Sawyers* [1994] 1 FLR 203, CA.
91 *R v Secretary of State for the Environment ex p Nottinghamshire CC* [1986] AC 240, HL at 247.
92 [1898] 2 QB 91.
93 [1948] 1 KB 223.

12.94   Paragraphs 12.95–12.115 list some of the main principles which today are used by the courts, to test the validity of public law decisions. As indicated above, the labelling of these principles is not a taxonomic science, but merely an attempt to illustrate some of the more obvious characteristics of the jurisprudence in this field.

Illegality

12.95   A judicial review challenge on the grounds of illegality is based upon the notion that a 'decision-maker must understand correctly the law that regulates his decision-making power and give effect to it'.[94] De Smith[95] separates administrative decisions which are flawed for illegality into those which are either beyond the power which authorises the making of the decision, or those which pursue an objective other than that for which the power to make the decision was conferred. Illegality may present itself in a number of guises, for instance action by an authority which although within its power, has an ulterior and improper motive,[96] such as action designed to frustrate the purpose of a statute. Common examples are outlined below.

12.96   **Ultra vires**[97]   Social services, NHS bodies and health authorities are statutory creatures and only able to act in accordance with their powers under their enabling statute.

12.97   By way of example, certain actions are well established as being in general outside social services authority powers; for instance, the making of cash payments to asylum-seekers (see para 4.19 above). Certain areas, however, are less clear; for instance, it has been argued that local authorities are not empowered to change the address of adult persons who lack mental capacity, without authority of the High Court (and in situations where the person is not subject to a guardianship order under MHA 1983 s7).[98]

12.98   **Misdirection of law**   A decision may be challenged by way of judicial review if the authority can be shown to have misunderstood the relevant law in reaching its decision,[99] although the mere existence of

---

94   *Council of Civil Service Unions v Minister for the Civil Service* [1985] AC 374, HL at 410.

95   De Smith, Woolf and Jowell *Judicial Review of Administrative Action* (5th edn, Sweet & Maxwell, 1995).

96   De Smith, op cit p330 n69.

97   Action which is outside the public bodies' legal powers.

98   See para 7.82 above and *Re F (Mental patient; sterilisation)* [1990] 2 AC 1, HL; and *Re S (hospital patient: court's jurisdiction)* [1995] 3 All ER 290.

99   *R v Hull University Visitor ex p Page* [1993] AC 682, HL at 701–702.

a mistake of law does not vitiate the impugned decision unless it 'is a relevant error of law, ie, an error in the actual making of the decision which affected the decision itself'.

12.99   Given the confusing and complex nature of community care law, there is clearly wide scope for local authority decisions to be challenged on this ground; for instance, in *R v Tower Hamlets LBC ex p Bradford*,[100] the court held that the authority had fundamentally misunderstood its powers under CA 1989 Pt III and so quashed the decision it had reached.

12.100   An authority may make an error of law by misunderstanding the nature of its statutory obligation; it may, for instance, consider its obligation to be discretionary when it is in fact mandatory.

12.101   **Decision not made in accordance with the facts** The decision made by the authority must be in accordance with (and supported by) the evidence. Authorities cannot simply 'go through the motions' by paying lip service to the evidence but in reality having no regard to the individual merits of the case.[101] Accordingly, in *R v Avon CC ex p M*,[102] Henry J overruled a decision by the social services authority which directly conflicted with a recommendation made by the panel. In so doing, he stated:

> The evidence before [the panel] had, as to the practicalities, been largely one way. The panel had directed themselves properly at law, and had arrived at a decision in line with the strength of the evidence before them . . . the strength, coherence and apparent persuasiveness of that decision had to be addressed head-on if it were to be set aside and not followed. These difficulties were not faced either by the Respondent's officers in their paper to the Social Services committee or by the Social Services committee themselves. Not to face them was either unintentional perversity on their part or showed a wrong appreciation of the legal standing of that decision. It seems to me that you do not properly reconsider a decision when, on the evidence, it is not seen that the decision was given the weight it deserved.

12.102   **Relevant and irrelevant considerations** A basic tenet of the *Wednesbury* decision is that a decision-maker must take into account all relevant considerations before making his/her decision and must ignore the irrelevant. In *R v Avon CC ex p M* (above) the court found that the authority, in deciding which residential placement to support, had

---

100 (1998) 1 CCLR 294; see para 11.13 above.

101 *Hemns v Wheller* [1948] 2 KB 61 and *Sagnata Investments v Norwich Corporation* [1971] 2 QB 614, CA.

102 [1994] 2 FLR 1006; [1999] 2 CCLR 185; [1994] 2 FCR 259.

ignored the applicant's psychological needs. In so doing it failed to take account of a relevant (and in the court's view a 'crucial') consideration. In addition, the authority had decided that the applicant's preferred home should not be funded because (among other reasons) such a funding decision would 'set a precedent'. In this context the judge held that this was a misleading consideration; essentially whether or not the decision set a precedent was an irrelevant consideration. The same principle applies to the local ombudsman's decision[103] on a complaint against East Sussex County Council. The complaint concerned a panel's refusal to recommend the payment of compensation for benefits a service user lost as a result of wrong advice he received from the social services department. The ombudsman held that the refusal was based upon an irrelevant consideration (namely that it was the Benefits Agency, not the local authority, which was responsible for the payment of such benefits).

12.103   A further aspect of this decision-making principle is illustrated in the case of *R v Gloucestershire CC ex p Mahfood*.[104] In this case, the respondent council withdrew services to various disabled people solely because the council's resources had been cut. McCowan LJ considered that this was making one consideration determinative (ie, at the cost of and overruling all others) and in his view, 'this amounted to treating the cut in resources as the sole factor to be taken into account, and that was, in my judgment, unlawful'.

12.104 **Fettering of discretion** While an authority 'charged with exercising an administrative discretion is entitled to promulgate a policy or guidelines as an indication of a norm which is intended to be followed',[105] it is not entitled to fetter its discretion by approaching a decision with a pre-determined policy as to how all cases falling within a particular class will be treated. Accordingly in *R v Ealing LBC ex p Leaman*,[106] Mann J held that where a disabled person had applied to a local authority under CSDPA 1970 s2(1)(f) for financial assistance in taking a privately arranged holiday, it was an error of law for the authority to decline to consider the application on the ground that it would only grant such assistance for holidays which it itself had arranged or sponsored (as the Act specifically allows for the support of holidays 'provided under arrangements made by the authority or otherwise'). On this principle, it would also be unlawful for an author-

103 No 93/A/3738; see para 12.44 above.
104 (1997) 1 CCLR 7; 94 LGR 53.
105 See *R v Eastleigh BC ex p Betts* [1983] 2 AC 613, HL.
106 (1984) *Times* 10 February.

ity to have a fixed policy that it will not fund home help which consists solely of cleaning a house or ironing, etc (as no such limitation is imposed by s2(1)(a) of the 1970 Act); likewise fixed policies by health or local authorities in relation to drug rehabilitation, which either confine such rehabilitation solely to funding detoxification (as opposed to harm minimisation or stabilisation) or where there is a fixed policy only to fund detoxification for a fixed and limited period, would again amount to a fettering of discretion (given again, that no such limitations are imposed by the primary legislation).[107]

12.105   In *R v North West Lancashire HA ex p A*,[108] the Court of Appeal held that the respondent's policy of not providing treatment for gender reassignment 'save in cases of overriding clinical need', was 'non-sense' since the authority considered that there was no effective treatment for the condition, and accordingly an 'overriding clinical need' could not therefore arise. Auld LJ held:

> the stance of the authority, coupled with the near uniformity of its reasons for rejecting each of the respondent's requests for funding was not a genuine application of a policy subject to individually determined exceptions of the sort considered acceptable by Lord Scarman in *Findlay*.[109] It is similar to the over-rigid application of the neat 'blanket policy' questioned by Judge J in *R v Warwickshire County Council ex p Collymore* [1995] ELR 217, at 224 et seq 'which while in theory admitting exceptions, may not, in reality result in the proper consideration of each individual case on its merits'.

The court also made reference to *R v Bexley LBC ex p Jones*,[110] where Leggatt LJ held:

> It is . . . legitimate for a statutory body . . . to adopt a policy designed to ensure a rational and consistent approach to the exercise of a statutory discretion in particular types of case. But it can only do so provided that the policy fairly admits of exceptions to it. In my judgment, the respondents effectively disabled themselves from considering individual cases and there has been no convincing evidence that at any material time they had an exceptions procedure worth the name. There is no indication that there was a genuine willingness to consider individual cases.

---

107 NAA 1948 s21, subject to the directions in LAC(93)10 App 1 para 2(6) and under NHSA 1977 Sch 8 para 2, subject to the secretary of state's directions in LAC(93)10 App 3 para 3(3)(g).
108 (1999) *Times* 24 August.
109 *In re Findlay* [1985] 1 AC 316.
110 [1995] ELR 42 at 55.

12.106 **Unlawful delegation or dictation**

Decision-makers cannot avoid their duties by allowing themselves to be dictated to by, or simply accepting the decision of, another body. Further, decision-makers may not delegate their decisions to others unless they have specific power to do so and have done so properly.[111]

An example of this difficulty arises in relation to the duty on social services authorities to provide assistance for works of adaptation in a house, or the provision of additional facilities in the home (CSDPA 1970 s2(1)(e)). Not infrequently social services authorities allow their decision whether or not to provide assistance with such adaptations to be determined solely by whether the disabled person obtains a grant under Housing Grants, Construction and Regeneration Act 1996 s23 (a disabled facilities grant). In fact, the responsibility on the social services authority under s2 is independent of the question of whether or not a disabled facilities grant is awarded (although the award or refusal of a grant is a relevant consideration).[112]

Procedural impropriety

12.107 Procedural impropriety embraces a number of issues of natural justice.

12.108 **The duty to act fairly** Decision-makers must act fairly, must not be biased, must allow a party time to prepare his or her case, must ensure that a party has a proper opportunity to be heard, and in appropriate situations, must give reasons for their decisions.

12.109 Natural justice will most obviously come to the fore when authorities are discharging their duties to assess under NHSCCA 1990 s47(1) and during the complaints process, particularly at panel hearings. The complaints process specifically requires reasons to be given for the panel's recommendation and the local authority's subsequent decision (see para 12.46 above).

12.110 **Legitimate expectation and the abuse of power** Initially the courts developed the notion of 'legitimate expectation' as a facet of 'procedural impropriety' or the requirement of administrative fairness. As will be noted below, in relation to the *Coughlan* decision, the Court of Appeal has now signalled that the doctrine may also be of relevance in substantive challenges. The basic principle however, requires that no decision should be taken which will adversely affect an individual,

111 J Manning *Judicial Review Proceedings* (LAG, 1995) p48.
112 DoE Circular 10/90 para 15, see paras 5.65 and 10.16 above.

without that person being given an opportunity of making representations as to why the particular benefit or advantage should not be withdrawn.[113] Local authority eligibility criteria might probably fall into this category; so that an individual would have the legitimate expectation that authorities would not depart from these criteria.

12.111 In *R v North and East Devon HA ex p Coughlan*,[114] the Court of Appeal reviewed the development of the doctrine which it considered had 'emerged as a distinct application of the concept of abuse of power in relation to substantive as well as procedural benefits'. The court continued:

> Legitimate expectation may play different parts in different aspects of public law. The limits to its role have yet to be finally determined by the courts. Its application is still being developed on a case by case basis. Even where it reflects procedural expectations, for example concerning consultation, it may be affected by an overriding public interest. It may operate as an aspect of good administration, qualifying the intrinsic rationality of policy choices. And without injury to the *Wednesbury* doctrine it may furnish a proper basis for the application of the new established concept of abuse of power.[115]

and

> in relation to this category of legitimate expectation, we do not consider it necessary to explain the modern doctrine in *Wednesbury* terms, helpful though this is in terms of received jurisprudence . . . We would prefer to regard the *Wednesbury* categories themselves as the major instances (not necessarily the sole ones . . .) of how public power may be misused. Once it is recognised that conduct which is an abuse of power is contrary to law its existence must be for the court to determine.[116]

12.112 **The duty to consult** The principle of procedural propriety also appears, in certain situations, as a duty to consult. In *R v Devon CC and Durham CC ex p Baker*,[117] it was stated that the duty:

> encompasses those cases in which it is held that a particular procedure, not otherwise required by law in the protection of an interest, must be followed consequent upon some specific promise or practice. Fairness requires that the public authority be held to it.

12.113 In this case, the court quashed a decision by Durham County Council

---

113 *Council of Civil Service Unions v Minister for the Civil Service* [1985] AC 374, HL.
114 (1999) 2 CCLR 285, CA.
115 Ibid at 311.
116 Ibid at 315.
117 [1995] 1 All ER 89, QBD.

to close various residential care homes because the authority had not properly consulted (see para 4.78 above). The court approved an earlier judgment[118] where the duty to consult was formulated as consisting of four parts, the requirements being:

> First that the consultation must be at a time when proposals are still at a formative stage. Second that the proposer must give sufficient reasons for any proposal to permit of intelligent consideration and response. Third . . . that adequate time must be given for consideration and response and, finally, fourth, that the product of consultation must be conscientiously taken into account in finalising any statutory proposals.[119]

12.114 **The duty to act in accordance with mandatory or directory requirements** A further requirement of the duty to act fairly is that the decision-maker must comply with procedures laid down by parliament. This is sometimes known as the duty to act in accordance with 'mandatory or directory requirements'. In *R v North Yorkshire CC ex p Hargreaves*,[120] it was accepted that the respondent authority, in assessing the applicant's sister's needs, failed to take into account the preferences of the sister, contrary to the mandatory (or directory) requirements set out in the Policy Guidance.[121] As the Policy Guidance was made under LASSA 1970 s7(1) requiring authorities to act 'under' such guidance, a failure to do so rendered the decision unlawful. Dyson J held that the requirements of the Policy Guidance were mandatory and that the decision should, therefore, be quashed. See also *Secretary of State for Trade and Industry v Langridge*,[122] where guidance was given on the principles to be applied in deciding whether a particular duty is mandatory or directory.

12.115 **The duty to give reasons** Although there is no general duty on authorities to give reasons for their decisions, where the relevant statute, regulation or direction stipulates that reasons should be given, then the reasons must be 'proper, adequate and intelligible' and must deal with the substantial points raised by the complainant. An unparticularised assertion that 'on the evidence' the decision-maker makes certain findings 'and recommends . . .' will be considered inadequate.[123] An express duty to give reasons exists, for instance, in the Complaints

---

118 *R v Brent LBC ex p Gunning* (1986) 84 LGR 168.
119 [1995] 1 All ER 89 at 91.
120 (1997) 1 CCLR 104.
121 Paras 3.16 and 3.25; and see also *R v Islington LBC ex p Rixon* (1998) 1 CCLR 119.
122 [1991] 3 All ER 591.
123 See notes 67 and 68 above.

Procedure Directions (see para 12.45 above). In the absence of an express provision requiring the giving of reasons, they may nevertheless be required, if, for instance, the decision would otherwise be unintelligible, or would contravene the minimum standards of fairness.[124]

Default procedures

12.116 LASSA 1970 s7D[125] provides:

(1) If the Secretary of State is satisfied that any local authority have failed without reasonable excuse, to comply with any of their duties which are social services functions[126] (other than a duty imposed by or under the Children Act 1989,[127] he may make an order declaring that authority to be in default with respect to the duty in question.

(2) An order under subsection (1) may contain such directions for the purpose of ensuring that the duty is complied with within such period as may be specified in the order as appear to the Secretary of State to be necessary.

(3) Any such direction shall, on the application of the Secretary of State, be enforceable by mandamus.

12.117 On the face of it, a person aggrieved by a local authority decision may seek redress by making formal request to the secretary of state that s/he use this default power to remedy the particular injustice. In reality such executive powers are rarely if ever exercised. The power under s7D is no exception; it appears that it has never been used, and it is highly unlikely that it would be so exercised in anything but the most extreme of situations. The power can only be used where the authority has failed to exercise a 'duty' (rather than a 'power'); it only arises if the local authority has 'no reasonable excuse' for its failure; the secretary of state has to be 'satisfied' about the lack of any reasonable excuse; and even then s/he has wide discretion whether or not to take any such action.

12.118   In practice, when a complainant writes to the Department of Health referring to an apparent failure by an authority to comply with its statutory duty, the Department writes to the authority seeking an

---

124 *R v Secretary of State for Home Department ex p Doody* [1993] 3 WLR 154, HL.
125 Inserted by NHSCCA 1990 s50 and replacing an equivalent provision under NAA 1948 s36(1).
126 A function set out in LASSA 1970 Sch 1 other than a duty imposed by or under CA 1989.
127 An equivalent default power is found in CA 1989 s84.

explanation (see LASSL(96)12 which explains the procedure for such referrals). There is some evidence that this action in itself may lead to a resolution of the problem.[128]

12.119   In *R v Kent CC ex p Bruce*,[129] it was held that the secretary of state was not a 'tribunal of fact' and in considering whether to exercise the default procedure 'must properly be concerned with whether the local authority had misdirected itself in law or formed an irrational view of the facts'. In *R v Devon CC ex p Baker*,[130] an argument that the existence of the default procedure constituted an alternative remedy which thereby excluded the use of judicial review was, in this particular case, rejected (see para 4.78 above).

12.120   In *R v Westminster CC ex p P*,[131] four destitute asylum-seekers challenged the policy of various London boroughs to accommodate them outside London. Simon Brown LJ, in rejecting the application (on grounds that there was an alternative remedy, see para 12.87 above) held as follows:

> For my part I have reached the clear conclusion that the more 'convenient, expeditious and effective' course here is indeed that of applying to the Secretary of State to exercise his default powers under s7D. This is par excellence an area of administration in which the Secretary of State rather than the courts should be closely involved. In the first place it is the Secretary of State who funds the housing of asylum seekers under s21 of the 1948 Act. Secondly, it is the proper construction and application of his own Directions and Guidance which lie at the heart of the dispute. Thirdly, it was at the Secretary of State's insistence that the appeal from the Court of Appeal's decision in *R v Westminster CC ex p M*,[132] which was to be heard by the House of Lords last month, was adjourned, specifically because the Government are currently conducting a review of the treatment of asylum seekers and did not wish to risk a final judgment depriving asylum seekers of all protection until a decision had been made as to what (if any) alternative arrangements should be made.

---

128 See, eg, p5 onwards of *Putting Teeth into the Act*, a report produced by RADAR on attempts made between 1970–81 to enforce CSDPA 1970 s2.

129 (1986) *Times* 8 February.

130 [1985] 1 All ER 73.

131 (1998) 1 CCLR 486 and see also *R v Kirklees MBC ex p Good* (1998) 1 CCLR 506.

132 (1997) 1 CCLR 85, see para 4.17 above.

European Convention on Human Rights

12.121 The Human Rights Act 1998 will come into force on 2 October 2000. Although most community care lawyers have felt little or no need to familiarise themselves with the European Convention on Human Rights, it is an international treaty that has, for the last 40 years, been hugely influential in shaping UK legislation, from MHA 1983 to CA 1989.

12.122 The convention, once incorporated, will place respect for human rights at the centre of any legal dispute. To this extent it is a new and radical equity; as equity trumped the common law, convention submissions will now take precedence and render even primary statutes vulnerable to summary revision.[133]

12.123 The courts will be bound to interpret legislation so as to uphold the convention rights (s3) and this rule of construction will apply to past as well as future legislation. The higher courts will therefore be required to revisit and possibly reverse their previous decisions.

12.124 If subordinate legislation is found to be contrary to the convention, then the High Court will quash it (on much the same basis as it presently is able to quash 'ultra vires' delegated legislation). The High Court will not be able to quash primary legislation but will instead have power to declare it 'incompatible' with the convention (s4) which will automatically trigger parliamentary action leading to statutory amendment.

12.125 It will be unlawful for public authorities to act in a way which is incompatible with the convention (s6) and anyone who is materially affected by such an unlawful act will be able to bring proceedings against the authority including a claim for damages (s8).

12.126 The convention is concerned with individual liberty in its various manifestations; not least with personal integrity, privacy, the right to family life and the right to enjoy one's possessions – all concepts at the heart of community care law.

12.127 Although all the convention articles have potential impact on community care law, in practice the following have attracted most attention.

---

133 The High Court will not be able to quash primary legislation but will instead have power to declare it 'incompatible' with the convention (s4) which will automatically trigger parliamentary action leading to statutory amendment.

The main rights

12.128   **Article 2** places a positive obligation on the state to protect life. Cases are likely to occur concerning actions by health and social services authorities which might be harmful, such as the closure of dementia wards or residential care homes as well as decisions not to provide treatment for people with serious illness, ie, *R v Cambridge HA ex p B.*[134]

12.129   **Article 3** prohibits degrading treatment. Classically, this extends to corporal punishment but in *Patel v UK (the East Africans case)*[135] the commission considered that degrading treatment was not restricted to actual assaults but included acts of a serious nature designed to interfere with the dignity of a person.

12.130   Although racial discrimination was in issue in the *East Africans* case, the commission did not exclude the possibility that 'degrading aspects of sexual and other forms of discrimination' could violate article 3 (although it considered it unnecessary to investigate this aspect in relation to the particular complaint). In extreme cases, therefore, this could potentially extend to publicly humiliating and personally distressing treatment solely on the grounds of (for instance) disability, illness, age or habit of life.

12.131   **Article 5** lists the only situations in which the state is permitted to restrict a person's liberty. It specifically provides that no one shall be deprived of liberty unless this is done in accordance 'with a procedure prescribed by law' and (among other grounds) is to effect the lawful detention of a person of unsound mind.

12.132   In *Winterwerp v Netherlands*[136] and a series of subsequent cases,[137] the court has laid down a number of factors which must be satisfied before the detention of a person of unsound mind is lawful within the meaning of the convention, including:

1) The mental disorder must be reliably established by objective medical expertise.
2) The nature or degree of the disorder must be sufficiently extreme to justify the detention.
3) The detention should only last as long as the medical disorder (and its required severity) persists.

---

134   [1995] 2 All ER 129, CA.
135   (1973) 3 EHRR 76 Comm Rep; CM DH (77) 2. Publication of this case by the Council of Europe was long delayed because of its political sensitivity.
136   (1979) 2 EHRR 387; 24 October 1979, Series A No 33.
137   See, eg, *X v UK* (1981) 4 EHRR 188; 24 October 1981, Series A No 46 and *Ashingdane v UK* 7 EHRR 528; 28 May 1985, Series A No 93.

4) If the detention is potentially indefinite, then there must be a system of periodic reviews by a tribunal that has power to discharge.

5) The detention must be in a hospital, clinic or other appropriate institution authorised for the detention of such persons.[138]

In relation to point 3, the court has held that where an expert has found that a person is no longer suffering from mental illness, the authorities are not obliged to ensure his immediate and unconditional release from detention.[139] However, a violation of article 5(1) arose where the imposition of a condition that the person live in a suitable hostel led to a lengthy deferral of the applicant's release because of the inability of the authorities to satisfy this condition.[140]

12.133   It is doubtful whether the House of Lords judgment in *R v Bournewood Community and Mental Health Trust ex p L*[141] complies with the convention; if L was detained by virtue of common law, then it could not be said to be in accordance 'with a procedure prescribed by law'; if he was not detained then clearly the actions of the state interfered with his right to private life (ie, contact with his foster parents) under article 8 (see below).

12.134   While article 5 permits the detention of persons for the prevention of spreading infectious diseases, it does not appear to permit detention of the type provided for under NAA 1948 s47, namely of persons 'suffering from grave, chronic disease or being aged, infirm or physically incapacitated, living in unsanitary conditions'.

12.135   Section 47 has been amended by the National Assistance (Amendment) Act 1951 to enable ex parte applications to be made (to a single justice if no court is sitting); in such cases an additional certificate is required, signed by the community physician and one other doctor certifying that it is necessary and in the interests of the person concerned that s/he be removed without delay. No notice of the application need be given to the person affected by the order, and such order when made can last for up to three weeks.

---

138 *Ashingdane v UK*, Series A No 93 at para 44. In the case of *Micahel Aerts v Belgium* (1998) 29 EHRR 50, the Commission found a violation of article 5(1) in relation to the detention of the applicant in the psychiatric wing of a prison which was not an 'appropriate establishment' in view of the lack of qualified personnel. Commission Report adopted on 20 May 1997, pending before the Court. The failure to provide medical treatment to a person in detention under article 5(1)(e) could amount to inhuman treatment contrary to article 3. See above at para 12.129.

139 *Johnson (Stanley) v UK* (1997) *Times* 4 December.

140 Ibid.

141 [1998] 3 WLR 107; [1998] 3 All ER 289.

12.136   Although the s47 powers appear to be little used, they raise serious civil liberty implications. Section 47 (as amended) enables a person to be detained for up to three weeks on the authority of only the most limited of medical evidence without having any prior notice of the application or right to be heard. The certifying doctors may have no particular knowledge of the detained person and the community physician in particular is someone whose experience generally lies in the area of environmental rather than mental health.

12.137   **Article 6** entrenches the right of parties to a fair hearing when their civil rights are affected (or when charged with a criminal offence). It requires hearings to be within a 'reasonable time' which has in certain situations been held to require 'exceptional diligence' to ensure their early listing.[142] As noted in para 12.59 above, article 6 may require that local authority and NHS complaints review panels be reconstituted in certain instances so as to be truly independent and capable of delivering binding decisions.

12.138   **Article 8** specifically entrenches the rights of everyone to respect for their private and family life, home and correspondence.

12.139   *R v North and East Devon HA ex p Coughlan*[143] concerned the legality of the health authority's decision to close a hospital (Mardon House) in which the applicant had lived for very many years. It upheld the first instance judgment that the action violated article 8, in the following terms:

> The judge was entitled to treat this as a case where the Health Authority's conduct was in breach of Article 8 and was not justified by the provisions of Article 8(2). Mardon House is, in the circumstances described, Miss Coughlan's home. It has been that since 1993. It was promised to be just that for the rest of her life. It is not suggested that it is not her home or that she has a home elsewhere or that she has done anything to justify depriving her of her home at Mardon House. By closure of Mardon House the Health Authority will interfere with what will soon be her right to her home. For the reasons explained, the Health Authority would not be justified in law in doing so without providing accommodation which meets her needs. As Sir Thomas Bingham MR said in *R v Ministry of Defence ex parte Smith* [1996] QB 517 at 554E – 'The more substantial the interference with human rights, the more the court will require by way of justification before it is satisfied that the decision is reasonable . . .' or, we would add, in a case such as the present, fair.

As noted in para 2.29 above, complaints under article 8 have con-

142   *H v UK* (1987) 10 EHRR 95; see also *P & D v UK* [1996] EHRLR 526.
143   (1999) 2 CCLR 285, CA.

cerned access to official information (for instance social services files) and this area is likely to continue to be a significant area of conflict.[144]

12.140   In relation to older people's social care, it has been argued that the convention may be violated by the registration requirements for people living in 'small homes' (imposed by the Registered Homes (Amendment) Act 1991) and the closure of certain residential homes.[145]

12.141   Although the registration conditions are less stringent, they may in certain situations amount to an unwarranted intrusion into a person's private and family life. A literal interpretation of the Act would suggest that:

a) where a person who lives with (and cooks and cares for) another – perhaps out of friendship or in return for companionship, etc; and
b) where that other person needs personal care (by reason of age, disablement, past or present dependence on alcohol or drugs or past or present mental disorder); and
c) this help is provided free of charge; and
d) the two persons are not related/married and not living as common law spouses,

such an arrangement will be a criminal offence, unless the person doing the cooking/ caring is registered with the local authority. If this is the case then s1 of the 1991 Act may give rise to violations of article 8. The only apparent way of avoiding this construction of s1, would be for the word 'establishment' to connote a business type relationship between the two persons notwithstanding the phrase in s1 'whether for reward or not'.

12.142   **Article 14** does not prohibit discrimination 'per se'; it merely prohibits discrimination as regards the enjoyment of the rights and freedoms set out in the convention. Thus a violation of article 14 can only occur in combination with another article;[146] for instance the inferior inheritance rights of illegitimate children in Belgium (compared with legitimate children) were held to violate article 14 in conjunction with article 8[147] (right to family life). The court has been particularly forthright on the issue of sex discrimination, holding that '[t]he advancement of the equality of the sexes is today a major goal in the member-States of the council of Europe and very weighty reasons would have

144 *Gaskin v UK* 12 EHRR 36.
145 See para 4.63 above.
146 It may be that major improvement in this field will more likely flow from EU law, ie, the Amsterdam Treaty amendments.
147 *Marckx v Belgium* (1979) 2 EHRR 330.

to be put forward before such a difference of Treatment could be regarded as compatible with the Convention'.[148]

12.143   As has been noted above (para 7.91) the present law of mental capacity is particularly unsatisfactory and may well engage article 14. For instance the domestic law allows for significant restrictions upon the rights of people with learning disabilities to marry and have sexual relations (and indeed to found a family). These rights are generally protected by articles 8 and 12 of the convention and any unreasonable restriction on the enjoyment of these rights will amount to a violation of these articles in combination with article 14.

12.144   **Article 1 of the First Protocol** concerns the individual's right to enjoy his or her possessions. The restriction on the type and amount of possessions a resident is allowed in certain residential care homes might fall foul of article 1 of the first protocol as will discriminatory tax allowances.

European Court of Human Rights

12.145 A complaint can only be made to the European Court of Human Rights once all domestic remedies have been exhausted. The complainant must be an individual who claims to have actually suffered as a result of the measure in issue, and the complaint must be made within six months of the exhaustion of the last domestic remedy. The complaint must allege a violation of at least one of the principal articles of the European Convention on Human Rights (or the first protocol thereto).[149]

12.146   The address of the European Court is:

European Court of Human Rights, Council of Europe, F-67075 Strasbourg Cedex, France: tel 00 33 88 41 2000; fax 00 33 88 41 2792.

---

148 *Schuler-Zgraggen v Switzerland* 16 EHRR 405.

149 For detailed consideration of the law and procedures, see K Starmer *European Human Rights Law* (LAG, 1999) and L Clements *European Human Rights: Taking a Case Under the Convention* (2nd edn, Sweet & Maxwell, 1999).

APPENDICES

A Legislation: key provisions

National Assistance Act 1948 ss21–29

Health Services and Public Health Act 1968 s45

Chronically Sick and Disabled Persons Act 1970 ss1 and 2

Local Authority Social Services Act 1970 ss6, 7 and 7A–E

National Health Service Act 1977 ss1–3, 21, Sch 8 paras 1–3

Mental Health Act 1983 s117

Health and Social Services and Social Security Adjudications Act 1983 ss17, 21, 22, 24 and Sch 9, Pt II

Disabled Persons (Services, Consultation and Representation) Act 1986 ss4, 8 and 16

Children Act 1989 s17

National Health Service and Community Care Act 1990 ss46 and 47

Carers (Recognition and Services) Act 1995 s1

Housing Grants, Construction and Regeneration Act 1996 ss23 and 24

B Regulations and directions

LAC(93)10 Appendix 1

LAC(93)10 Appendix 2

LAC(93)10 Appendix 3

Complaints Procedure Direction 1990

National Assistance Act 1948 (Choice of Accommodation) Directions 1992

C Precedents

Community care assessment request

Access to information letter

Formal complaint letter

453

Legislation: key provisions

NATIONAL ASSISTANCE ACT 1948
Duty of local authorities to provide accommodation

21 (1) Subject to and in accordance with the provisions of this Part of this Act, a local authority may with the approval of the Secretary of State, and to such extent as he may direct shall, make arrangements for providing:

(a) residential accommodation for persons aged eighteen or over who by reason of age, illness, disability or any other circumstances are in need of care and attention which is not otherwise available to them and

(aa) residential accommodation for expectant and nursing mothers who are in need of care and attention which is not otherwise available to them.

(1A) A person to whom section 115 of the Immigration and Asylum Act 1999 (exclusion from benefits) applies may not be provided with residential accommodation under subsection (1)(a) if his need for care and attention has arisen solely –

(a) because he is destitute; or

(b) because of the physical effects, or anticipated physical effects, of his being destitute.

(1B) Subsections (3) and (5) to (8) of section 95 of the Immigration and Asylum Act 1999, and paragraph 2 of Schedule 8 to that Act, apply for the purposes of subsection (1A) as they apply for the purposes of that section, but for the references in subsections (5) and (7) of that section and in that paragraph to the Secretary of State substitute references to a local authority.

(2) In making any such arrangements a local authority shall have regard to the welfare of all persons for whom accommodation is provided, and in particular to the need for providing accommodation of different descriptions suited to different descriptions of such persons as are mentioned in the last foregoing subsection.

(2A) In determining for the purposes of paragraph (a) or (aa) of subsection (1) of this section whether care and attention are otherwise available to a person, a local authority shall disregard so much of the person's capital as does not exceed the capital limit for the purposes of section 22 of this Act.

(2B) For the purposes of subsection (2A) of this section –

(a) a person's capital shall be calculated in accordance with assessment regulations in the same way as if he were a person for whom accommodation is proposed to be provided as mentioned in subsection (3) of section 22 of this Act and whose ability to pay for the accommodation falls to be assessed for the purposes of that subsection; and

(b) 'the capital limit for the purposes of section 22 of this Act' means the amount for the time being prescribed in assessment regulations as the amount which a resident's capital (calculated in accordance with such regulations) must not exceed if he is to be assessed as unable to pay for his accommodation at the standard rate;

and in this subsection 'assessment regulations' means regulations made for the purposes of section 22(5) of this Act.

(3) [*repealed*]

(4) Subject to section 26 of this Act, accommodation provided by a local authority in the exercise of their functions under this section shall be provided in premises managed by the authority or, to such extent as may be determined in accordance with the arrangements under this section, in such premises managed by another local authority as may be agreed between the two authorities and on such terms as to the reimbursement of expenditure incurred by the said other authority, as may be so agreed.

(5) References in this Act to accommodation provided under this Part thereof shall be construed as references to accommodation provided in accordance with this and the five next following sections, and as including references to board and other services, amenities and requisites provided in connection with the accommodation except where in the opinion of the authority managing the premises their provision is unnecessary.

(6) References in this Act to a local authority providing accommodation shall be construed, in any case where a local authority agree with another local authority for the provision of accommodation in premises managed by the said other authority, as references to the first-mentioned local authority.

(7) Without prejudice to the generality of the foregoing provisions of this section, a local authority may –

(a) provide, in such cases as they may consider appropriate, for the conveyance of persons to and from premises in which accommodation is provided for them under this Part of the Act;

(b) make arrangements for the provision on the premises in which accommodation is being provided of such other services as appear to the authority to be required.

(8) Nothing in this section shall authorise or require a local authority to make any provision authorised or required to be made (whether by that or by any other authority) by or under any enactment not contained in this Part of this Act, or authorised or required to be provided under the National Health Service Act 1977.

Charges to be made for accommodation

22 (1) Subject to section 26 of this Act, where a person is provided with accommodation under this Part of this Act the local authority providing the accommodation shall recover from him the amount of the payment which he is liable to make.

(2) Subject to the following provisions of this section, the payment which a person is liable to make for any such accommodation shall be in accordance with a standard rate fixed for that accommodation by the authority managing the

premises in which it is provided and that standard rate shall represent the full cost to the authority of providing that accommodation.

(3) Where a person for whom accommodation in premises managed by any local authority is provided, or proposed to be provided, under this Part of this Act satisfies the local authority that he is unable to pay therefor at the standard rate, the authority shall assess his ability to pay, and accordingly determine at what lower rate he shall be liable to pay for the accommodation.

(4) In assessing for the purposes of the last foregoing subsection a person's ability to pay, a local authority shall assume that he will need for his personal requirements such sum per week as may be prescribed by the Minister, or such other sum as in special circumstances the authority may consider appropriate.

(4A) Regulations made for the purposes of subsection (4) of this section may prescribe different sums for different circumstances.

(5) In assessing as aforesaid a person's ability to pay, a local authority shall give effect to regulations made by the Secretary of State for the purposes of this subsection except that, until the first such regulations come into force, a local authority shall give effect to Part III of Schedule 1 to the Supplementary Benefits Act 1976, as it had effect immediately before the amendments made by Schedule 2 to the Social Security Act 1980.

(5A) If they think fit, an authority managing premises in which accommodation is provided for a person shall have power on each occasion when they provide accommodation for him, irrespective of his means, to limit to such amount as appears to them reasonable for him to pay the payments required from him for his accommodation during a period commencing when they begin to provide the accommodation for him and ending not more than eight weeks after that.

(6) [*repealed*]

(7) [*repealed*]

(8) Where accommodation is provided by a local authority in premises managed by another local authority, the payment therefor under this section shall be made to the authority managing the premises and not to the authority providing the accommodation, but the authority managing the premises shall account for the payment to the authority providing the accommodation.

(9) [*repealed*]

Management of premises in which accommodation provided

23 (1) Subject to the provisions of this Part of this Act, a local authority may make rules as to the conduct of premises under their management in which accommodation is provided under this Part of this Act and as to the preservation of order in the premises.

(2) Rules under this section may provide that where by reason of any change in a person's circumstances he is no longer qualified to receive accommodation under this Part of this Act or where a person has otherwise become unsuitable therefor, he may be required by the local authority managing the premises to leave the premises in which the accommodation is provided.

(3) Rules under this section may provide for the waiving of part of the payments due under the last foregoing section where in compliance with the rules

persons for whom accommodation is provided assist in the running of the premises.

Authority liable for provision of accommodation

24 (1) The local authority empowered under this Part of this Act to provide residential accommodation for any person shall subject to the following provisions of this Part of this Act be the authority in whose area the person is ordinarily resident.

(2) [*repealed*]

(3) Where a person in the area of a local authority –

(a) is a person with no settled residence, or

(b) not being ordinarily resident in the area of the local authority, is in urgent need of residential accommodation under this Part of this Act,

the authority shall have the like power to provide residential accommodation for him as if he were ordinarily resident in their area.

(4) Subject to and in accordance with the arrangements under section twenty-one of this Act, a local authority shall have power, as respects a person ordinarily resident in the area of another local authority, with the consent of that other local authority to provide residential accommodation for him in any case where the authority would have a duty to provide such accommodation if he were ordinarily resident in their area.

(5) Where a person is provided with residential accommodation under this Part of this Act, he shall be deemed for the purposes of this Act to continue to be ordinarily resident in the area in which he was ordinarily resident immediately before the residential accommodation was provided for him.

(6) For the purposes of the provision of residential accommodation under this Part of this Act, a patient in a hospital vested in the Secretary of State or an NHS trust shall be deemed to be ordinarily resident in the area, if any, in which he was ordinarily resident immediately before he was admitted as a patient to the hospital, whether or not he in fact continues to be ordinarily resident in that area.

(7) In subsection (6) above 'NHS trust' means a National Health Service trust established under Part I of the National Health Service and Community Care Act 1990 or under the National Health Service (Scotland) Act 1978.

25   [*repealed*]

Provision of accommodation in premises maintained by voluntary organisations

26 (1) Subject to subsections (1A) and (1B) below, arrangements under section 21 of this Act may include arrangements made with a voluntary organisation or with any other person who is not a local authority where –

(a) that organisation or person manages premises which provide for reward accommodation falling within subsection (1)(a) or (aa) of that section, and

(b) the arrangements are for the provision of such accommodation in those premises.

(1A) Subject to subsection (1B) below, arrangements made with any voluntary organisation or other person by virtue of this section must, if they are for the provision of residential accommodation with both board and personal care for such persons as are mentioned in section 1(1) of the Registered Homes Act 1984 (requirement for registration), be arrangements for the provision of such accommodation in a residential care home which is managed by the organisation or person in question, being such a home in respect of which that organisation or person –

(a) is registered under Part I of that Act, or

(b) is not required to be so registered by virtue of section 1(4)(a) or (b) of that Act (certain small homes) or by virtue of the home being managed or provided by an exempt body;

and for this purpose 'personal care' and 'residential care home' have the same meaning as in that Part of that Act.

(1B) Arrangements made with any voluntary organisation or other person by virtue of this section must, if they are for the provision of residential accommodation where nursing care is provided, be arrangements for the provision of such accommodation in premises which are managed by the organisation or persons in question, being premises –

(a) in respect of which that organisation or person is registered under Part II of the Registered Homes Act 1984, or

(b) which, by reason only of being maintained or controlled by an exempt body, do not fall within the definition of a nursing home in section 21 of that Act.

(1C) Subject to subsection (1D) below, no such arrangements as are mentioned in subsection (1B) above may be made by an authority for the accommodation of any person without the consent of such Health Authority as may be determined in accordance with regulations.

(1D) Subsection (1C) above does not apply to the making by an authority of temporary arrangements for the accommodation of any person as a matter of urgency; but, as soon as practicable after any such temporary arrangements have been made, the authority shall seek the consent required by subsection (1C) above to the making of appropriate arrangements for the accommodation of the person concerned.

(1E) No arrangements may be made by virtue of this section with a person who has been convicted of an offence under any provision of –

(a) the Registered Homes Act 1948 (or any enactment replaced by that Act); or

(b) regulations made under section 16 or section 26 of that Act (or under any corresponding provisions of any such enactment).

(2) Any arrangements made by virtue of this section shall provide for the making by the local authority to the other party thereto of payments in respect of the accommodation provided at such rates as may be determined by or under the arrangements and subject to subsection (3A) below the local authority shall recover from each person for whom accommodation is provided under the arrangements the amount of the refund which he is liable to make in accordance with the following provisions of this section.

(3) Subject to subsection (3A) below, a person for whom accommodation is provided under any such arrangements shall, in lieu of being liable to make payment therefor in accordance with section twenty-two of this Act, refund to the

local authority any payments made in respect of him under the last foregoing subsection:

Provided that where a person for whom accommodation is provided, or proposed to be provided, under any such arrangements satisfies the local authority that he is unable to make refund at the full rate determined under that subsection, subsections (3) to (5) of section twenty-two of this Act shall, with the necessary modifications, apply as they apply where a person satisfies the local authority of his inability to pay at the standard rate as mentioned in the said subsection (3).

(3A) Where accommodation in any premises is provided for any person under any arrangements made by virtue of this section and the local authority, the person concerned and the voluntary organisation or the other person managing the premises (in this subsection referred to as 'the provider') agree that this section shall apply –

(a) so long as the person concerned makes the payments for which he is liable under paragraph (b) below, he shall not be liable to make any refund under subsection (3) above and the local authority shall not be liable to make any payment under subsection (2) above in respect of the accommodation provided for him;

(b) the person concerned shall be liable to pay to the provider such sums as he would otherwise (under subsection (3) above) be liable to pay by way of refund to the local authority; and

(c) the local authority shall be liable to pay to the provider the difference between the sums paid by virtue of paragraph (b) above and the payments which, but for paragraph (a) above, the authority would be liable to pay under subsection (2) above.

(4) Subsections (5A), (7) and (9) of the said section twenty-two shall, with the necessary modifications, apply for the purposes of the last foregoing subsection as they apply for the purposes of the said section twenty-two.

(4A) Section 21(5) of this Act shall have effect as respects accommodation provided under arrangements made by virtue of this section with the substitution for the references to the authority managing the premises of a reference to the authority making the arrangements.

(5) Where in any premises accommodation is being provided under this section in accordance with arrangements made by any local authority, any person authorised in that behalf by the authority may at all reasonable times enter and inspect the premises

(6) [*repealed*]

(7) In this section the expression 'voluntary organisation' includes any association which is a housing association for the purposes of the Housing Act 1936, 'small home' means an establishment falling within section 1(4) of the Registered Homes Act 1984 and 'exempt body' means an authority or body constituted by an Act of Parliament or incorporated by Royal Charter.

Exclusion of powers to provide accommodation under this Part in certain cases

26A(1) Subject to subsection (3) of this section, no accommodation may be provided under section 21 or 26 of this Act for any person who immediately before the date on which this section comes into force was ordinarily resident in relevant premises.

(2) In subsection (1) 'relevant premises' means –

(a) premises in respect of which any person is registered under the Registered Homes Act 1984;

(b) premises in respect of which such registration is not required by virtue of their being managed or provided by an exempt body;

(c) premises which do not fall within the definition of a nursing home in section 21 of that Act by reason only of their being maintained or controlled by an exempt body; and

(d) such other premises as the Secretary of State may by regulations prescribe;

and in this subsection 'exempt body' has the same meaning as in section 26 of this Act.

(3) The Secretary of State may by regulations provide that, in such cases and subject to such conditions as may be prescribed, subsection (1) of this section shall not apply in relation to such classes of persons as may be prescribed in the regulations.

(4) The Secretary of State shall by regulations prescribe the circumstances in which persons are to be treated as being ordinarily resident in any premises for the purposes of subsection (1) of this section.

(5) This section does not affect the validity of any contract made before the date on which this section comes into force for the provision of accommodation on or after that date or anything done in pursuance of such a contract.

27 [repealed]

28 [repealed]

Welfare arrangements for blind, deaf, dumb and crippled persons, etc

29 (1) A local authority may, with the approval of the Secretary of State, and to such extent as he may direct in relation to persons ordinarily resident in the area of the local authority shall make arrangements for promoting the welfare of persons to whom this section applies, that is to say persons aged eighteen or over who are blind, deaf or dumb or who suffer from mental disorder of any description, and other persons aged eighteen or over who are substantially and permanently handicapped by illness, injury, or congenital deformity or such other disabilities as may be prescribed by the Minister.

(2) [repealed]

(3) [repealed]

(4) Without prejudice to the generality of the provisions of subsection (1) of this section, arrangements may be made thereunder –

(a) for informing persons to whom arrangements under that subsection relate of the services available for them thereunder;

(b) for giving such persons instruction in their own homes or elsewhere in methods of overcoming the effects of their disabilities;

(c) for providing workshops where such persons may be engaged (whether under a contract of service or otherwise) in suitable work, and hostels where persons engaged in the workshops, and other persons to whom arrangements under subsection (1) of this section relate and for whom work or training is being provided in pursuance of the Disabled Persons (Employment) Act 1944 or the Employment and Training Act 1973 may live;

(d) for providing persons to whom arrangements under subsection (1) of this section relate with suitable work (whether under a contract of service or otherwise) in their own homes or elsewhere;

(e) for helping such persons in disposing of the produce of their work;

(f) for providing such persons with recreational facilities in their own homes or elsewhere;

(g) for compiling and maintaining classified registers of the persons to whom arrangements under subsection (1) of this section relate.

(4A) Where accommodation in a hostel is provided under paragraph (c) of subsection (4) of this section –

(a) if the hostel is managed by a local authority, section 22 of this Act shall apply as it applies where accommodation is provided under s21;

(b) if the accommodation is provided in a hostel managed by a person other than a local authority under arrangements made with that person, subsections (2) to (4A) of section 26 of this Act shall apply as they apply where accommodation is provided under arrangements made by virtue of that section; and

(c) sections 32 and 43 of this Act shall apply as they apply where accommodation is provided under sections 21 to 26;

and in this subsection references to 'accommodation' include references to board and other services, amenities and requisites provided in connection with the accommodation, except where in the opinion of the authority managing the premises or, in the case mentioned in paragraph (b) above, the authority making the arrangements their provision is unnecessary.

(5) [*repealed*]

(6) Nothing in the foregoing provisions of this section shall authorise or require –

(a) the payment of money to persons to whom this section applies, other than persons for whom work is provided under arrangements made by virtue of paragraph (c) or paragraph (d) of subsection (4) of this section or who are engaged in work which they are enabled to perform in consequence of anything done in pursuance of arrangements made under this section; or

(b) the provision of any accommodation or services required to be provided under the National Health Service Act 1977.

(7) A person engaged in work in a workshop provided under paragraph (c) of subsection (4) of this section, or a person in receipt of a superannuation allowance granted on his retirement from engagement in any such workshop, shall be deemed for the purposes of this Act to continue to be ordinarily resident in the area in which he was ordinarily resident immediately before he was accepted for work in that workshop; and for the purposes of this subsection a course of training in such workshop shall be deemed to be work in that workshop.

HEALTH SERVICES AND PUBLIC HEALTH ACT 1968
Promotion, by local authorities, of the welfare of old people

45 (1) A local authority may with the approval of the Secretary of State, and to such extent as he may direct shall, make arrangements for promoting the welfare of old people.

(2) [*repealed*]

(3) A local authority may employ as their agent for the purposes of this section any voluntary organisation or any person carrying on, professionally or by way of trade or business, activities which consist of or include the provision of services for old people, being an organisation or person appearing to the authority to be capable of promoting the welfare of old people.

(4) No arrangements under this section shall provide –

    (a) for the payment of money to old people except in so far as the arrangements may provide for the remuneration of old people engaged in suitable work in accordance with the arrangements;

    (b) for making available any accommodation or services required to be provided under the National Health Service Act 1977.

(4A) No arrangements under this section may be given effect to in relation to a person to whom section 115 of the Immigration and Asylum Act 1999 (exclusion from benefits) applies solely –

    (a) because he is destitute; or

    (b) because of the physical effects, or anticipated physical effects, of his being destitute.

(4B) Subsections (3) and (5) to (8) of section 95 of the Immigration and Asylum Act 1999, and paragraph 2 of Schedule 8 to that Act, apply for the purposes of subsection (4A) as they apply for the purposes of that section, but for the references in subsections (5) and (7) of that section and in that paragraph to the Secretary of State substitute references to a local authority.

CHRONICALLY SICK AND DISABLED PERSONS ACT 1970
Information as to need for and existence of welfare services

1 (1) It shall be the duty of every local authority having functions under section 29 of the National Assistance Act 1948 to inform themselves of the number of persons to whom that section applies within their area and of the need for the making by the authority of arrangements under that section for such persons.

(2) Every such local authority –

    (a) shall cause to be published from time to time at such times and in such manner as they consider appropriate general information as to the services provided under arrangements made by the authority under the said section 29 which are for the time being available in the area; and

    (b) shall ensure that any such person as aforesaid who uses any of those services is informed of any other service provided by the authority (whether under any such arrangements or not) which in the opinion of the authority is relevant to his needs and of any service provided by any other authority or organisation which in the opinion of the authority is so relevant and of which particulars are in the authorities' possession.

Provision of welfare services

2 (1) Where a local authority having functions under s29 National Assistance Act 1948 are satisfied in the case of any person to whom that section applies who is ordinarily resident in their area that it is necessary in order to meet the needs of that person for that authority to make arrangements for all or any of the following matters, namely –

(a) the provision of practical assistance for that person in his home;

(b) the provision for that person of, or assistance to that person in obtaining, wireless, television, library or similar recreational facilities;

(c) the provision for that person of lectures, games, outings or other recreational facilities outside his home or assistance to that person in taking advantage of educational facilities available to him;

(d) the provision for that person of facilities for, or assistance in, travelling to and from his home for the purpose of participating in any services provided under arrangements made by the authority under the said section 29 or, with the approval of the authority, in any services provided otherwise than as aforesaid which are similar to services which could be provided under such arrangements;

(e) the provision of assistance for that person in arranging for the carrying out of any works of adaptation in his home or the provision of any additional facilities designed to secure his greater safety, comfort or convenience;

(f) facilitating the taking of holidays by that person, whether at holiday homes or otherwise and whether provided under arrangements made by the authority or otherwise;

(g) the provision of meals for that person whether in his home or elsewhere;

(h) the provision for that person of, or assistance to that person in obtaining, a telephone and any special equipment necessary to enable him to use a telephone,

then, subject to the provisions of section 7(1) of the Local Authority Social Services Act 1970 (which requires local authorities in the exercise of certain functions, including functions under the said section 29, to act under the general guidance of the Secretary of State) and to the provisions of section 7A of that Act (which requires local authorities to exercise their social services functions in accordance with directions given by the Secretary of State) it shall be the duty of that Authority to make those arrangements in exercise of their functions under the said section 29.

LOCAL AUTHORITY SOCIAL SERVICES ACT 1970
The director of social services

6 (1) A local authority shall appoint an officer, to be known as the director of social services, for the purposes of their social services functions.

(2) Two or more local authorities may, if they consider that the same person can efficiently discharge, for both or all of them, the functions of director of social services for both or all of those authorities, concur in the appointment of a person as director of social services for both or all of those authorities.

(3) & (4) [*repealed*]

(5) The director of social services of a local authority shall not, without the approval of the Secretary of State (which may be given either generally or in relation to a particular authority), be employed by that authority in connection with the discharge of any of the authority's functions other than their social services functions.

(6) A local authority which has appointed, or concurred in the appointment of, a director of social services, shall secure the provision of adequate staff for assisting him in the exercise of his functions.

Local authorities to exercise social services functions under guidance of Secretary of State

7 (1) Local authorities shall, in the exercise of their social services functions, including the exercise of any discretion conferred by any relevant enactment, act under the general guidance of the Secretary of State.

Directions by the Secretary of State as to exercise of social services functions

7A(1) Without prejudice to section 7 of this Act, every local authority shall exercise their social services functions in accordance with such directions as may be given to them under this section by the Secretary of State.

(2) Directions under this section –

(a) shall be given in writing; and

(b) may be given to a particular authority, or to authorities of a particular class, or to authorities generally.

Complaints procedure

7B(1) The Secretary of State may by order require local authorities to establish a procedure for considering any representations (including any complaints) which are made to them by a qualifying individual, or anyone acting on his behalf, in relation to the discharge of, or any failure to discharge, any of their social services functions in respect of that individual.

(2) In relation to a particular local authority, an individual is a qualifying individual for the purposes of subsection (1) above if –

(a) the authority have a power or a duty to provide, or to secure the provision of, a service for him; and

(b) his need or possible need for such a service has (by whatever means) come to the attention of the authority or if he is in receipt of payment from the authority under the Community Care (Direct Payments) Act 1996.

(3) A local authority shall comply with any directions given by the Secretary of State as to the procedure to be adopted in considering representations made as mentioned in subsection (1) above and as to the taking of such action as may be necessary in consequence of such representations.

(4) Local authorities shall give such publicity to any procedure established pursuant to this section as they consider appropriate.

Inquiries

7C(1) The Secretary of State may cause an inquiry to be held in any case where, whether on representations made to him or otherwise, he considers it advisable to do so in connection with the exercise by any local authority of any of their social services functions (except in so far as those functions relate to persons under the age of eighteen).

(2) Subsections (2) to (5) of section 250 of the Local Government Act 1972 (powers in relation to local inquiries) shall apply in relation to an inquiry under this section as they apply in relation to an inquiry under that section.

Default powers of Secretary of State as respects social services functions of local authorities

7D(1) If the Secretary of State is satisfied that any local authority have failed, without reasonable excuse, to comply with any of their duties which are social services functions (other than a duty imposed by or under the Children Act 1989), he may make an order declaring that authority to be in default with respect to the duty in question.

(2) An order under subsection (1) may contain such directions for the purpose of ensuring that the duty is complied with within such period as may be specified in the order as appear to the Secretary of State to be necessary.

(3) Any such direction shall, on the application of the Secretary of State, be enforceable by mandamus.

Grants to local authorities in respect of certain social services

7E The Secretary of State may, with the approval of the Treasury, make grants out of money provided by Parliament towards any expenses of local authorities incurred –

(a) in connection with the exercise of their social services functions in relation to persons suffering from mental illness; or

(b) in making payments, in accordance with directions given by the Secretary of State to voluntary organisations which provide care and services for persons who are, have been, or are likely to become dependent upon alcohol or drugs.

NATIONAL HEALTH SERVICE ACT 1977

Secretary of State's duty as to health service

1 (1) It is the Secretary of State's duty to continue the promotion in England and Wales of a comprehensive health service designed to secure improvement –

(a) in the physical and mental health of the people of those countries; and

(b) in the prevention, diagnosis and treatment of illness,

and for that purpose to provide or secure the effective provision of services in accordance with this Act.

(2) The services so provided shall be free of charge except in so far as the making and recovery of charges is expressly provided for by or under any enactment, whenever passed.

Secretary of State's general power as to services

2 Without prejudice to the Secretary of state's powers apart from this section, he has power –

(a) to provide such services as he considers appropriate for the purpose of discharging any duty imposed on him by this Act; and

(b) to do any other thing whatsoever which is calculated to facilitate, or is conducive or incidental to, the discharge of such a duty.

This section is subject to section 3(3) below.

Services generally

3 (1) It is the Secretary of State's duty to provide throughout England and Wales, to such extent as he considers necessary to meet all reasonable requirements –

(a) hospital accommodation;

(b) other accommodation for the purpose of any service provided under this Act;

(c) medical, dental, nursing and ambulance services;

(d) such other facilities for the care of expectant mothers and young children as he considers are appropriate as part of the health service;

(e) such facilities for the prevention of illness, the care of persons suffering from illness and the after care of persons who have suffered from illness as he considers are appropriate as part of the health service;

(f) such other services as are required for the diagnosis and treatment of illness.

(2) . . .

(3) Nothing in section 2 above or in this section affects the provisions of Part II of this Act (which relates to arrangements with practitioners for the provision of medical, dental, ophthalmic and pharmaceutical services).

CO-OPERATION AND ASSISTANCE

Local social services authorities

21 (1) Subject to paragraphs (d) and (e) of section 3(1) above, the services described in Schedule 8 to this Act in relation to –

(a) care of mothers and young children,

(b) prevention, care and after care,

(c) home help and laundry facilities,

are functions exercisable by local social services authorities, and that Schedule has effect accordingly.

(2) A local social services authority who provide premises, furniture or equipment for any of the purposes of this Act may permit the use of the premises, furniture or equipment –

(a) by any other social services authority, or

(b) by any of the bodies constituted under this Act, or

(c) by a local education authority.

This permission may be on such terms (including terms with respect to the services of any staff employed by the authority giving permission) as may be agreed.

(3) . . .

SCHEDULE 8: LOCAL SERVICES AUTHORITIES

Care of mothers and young children

1 (1) A local social services authority may, with the Secretary of State's approval, and to such extent as he may direct shall, make arrangements for the care of

expectant and nursing mothers (other than for the provision of residential accommodation for them).

Prevention, care and after-care

2 (1) A local social services authority may, with the Secretary of State's approval, and to such extent as he may direct shall, make arrangements for the purpose of the prevention of illness and for the care of persons suffering from illness and for the after-care of persons who have been suffering and in particular for –

(a) [repealed]

(b) the provision for persons whose care is undertaken with a view to preventing them from becoming ill, persons suffering from illness and persons who have been so suffering, of centres or other facilities for training them or keeping them suitably occupied and the equipment and maintenance of such centres;

(c) the provision, for the benefit of such persons as are mentioned in paragraph (b) above, of ancillary or supplemental services; and

(d) for the exercise of the functions of the Authority in respect of persons suffering from mental disorder who are received into the guardianship under Part II or III of the Mental Health Act 1983 (whether the guardianship of the local social services authority or of other persons).

Such an authority shall neither have the power nor be subject to a duty to make under this paragraph arrangements to provide facilities for any of the purposes mentioned in section 15(1) of the Disabled Persons (Employment) Act 1944.

(2) No arrangements under this paragraph shall provide for the payment of money to persons for whose benefit they are made except –

(a) in so far as they may provide for the remuneration of such persons engaged in suitable work in accordance with the arrangements, of such amounts as the local social services authority think fit in respect of their occasional personal expenses where it appears to that authority that no such payment would otherwise be made.

(2A) No arrangements under this paragraph may be given effect to in relation to a person to whom section 115 of the Immigration and Asylum Act 1999 (exclusion from benefits) applies solely –

(a) because he is destitute; or

(b) because of the physical effects, or anticipated physical effects, of his being destitute.

(2B) Subsections (3) and (5) to (8) of section 95 of the Immigration and Asylum Act 1999, and paragraph 2 of Schedule 8 to that Act, apply for the purposes of subsection (2A) as they apply for the purposes of that section, but for the references in subsections (5) and (7) of that section and in that paragraph to the Secretary of State substitute references to a local social services authority.

(3) The Secretary of State may make regulations as to the conduct of premises in which, in pursuance of arrangements made under this paragraph, are provided for persons whose care is undertaken with a view to preventing them from becoming sufferers from mental disorder within the meaning of that Act of 1983 or who are, or have been, so suffering, facilities for training them or

keeping them suitably occupied.

(4A) This paragraph does not apply in relation to persons under the age of 18.

(4AA) No authority is authorised or may be required under this paragraph to provide residential accommodation for any person.

(5) A local social services authority may recover from persons availing themselves of services provided in pursuance of arrangements under this paragraph such charges (if any) as the authority consider reasonable, having regard to the means of those persons.

Home help and laundry facilities

3 (1) It is the duty of every local social services authority to provide on such a scale as is adequate for the needs of their area, or to arrange for the provision on such a scale as is so adequate, of home help for households where such help is required owing to the presence of –

(a) a person who is suffering from illness, lying-in, an expectant mother, aged, handicapped as a result of having suffered from illness or by congenital deformity,

and every such Authority has power to provide or arrange for the provision of laundry facilities for households for which home help is being, or can be, provided under this sub-paragraph.

(2) A local social service authority may recover from persons availing themselves of help or facilities provided under this paragraph such charges (if any) as the authority consider reasonable, having regard to the means of those persons.

MENTAL HEALTH ACT 1983
After-care

117 (1) This section applies to persons who are detained under section 3 above, or admitted to a hospital in pursuance of a hospital order made under section 37 above, or transferred to a hospital in pursuance of a hospital direction made under section 45A above or a transfer direction made under section 47 or 48 above, and then cease to be detained and (whether or not immediately after so ceasing) leave hospital.

(2) It shall be the duty of the Health Authority and of the local social services authority to provide, in co-operation with relevant voluntary agencies, after-care services for any person to whom this section applies until such time as the Health Authority and the local social services authority are satisfied that the person concerned is no longer in need of such services but they shall not be so satisfied in the case of a patient who is subject to after-care under supervision at any time while he so remains subject.

(2A) It shall be the duty of the Health Authority to secure that at all times while a patient is subject to after-care under supervision –

(a) a person who is a registered medical practitioner approved for the purposes of section 12 above by the Secretary of State as having special experience in the diagnosis or treatment of mental disorder is in charge of the medical treatment provided for the patient as part of the after-care services provided for him under this section; and

(b) a person professionally concerned with any of the after-care services so provided is supervising him with a view to securing that he receives the after-care services so provided.

(2B) Section 32 above shall apply for the purposes of this section as it applies for the purposes of Part II of this Act.

(3) In this section 'the Health Authority' means the Health Authority and 'the local social services authority' means the local social services authority for the area in which the person concerned is resident or to which he is sent on discharge by the hospital in which he was detained.

HEALTH AND SOCIAL SERVICES AND SOCIAL SECURITY ADJUDICATIONS ACT 1983
Charges for local authority services in England and Wales

17 (1) Subject to subsection (3) below, an authority providing a service to which this section applies may recover such charge (if any) for it as they consider reasonable.

(2) This section applies to services provided under the following enactments –

   (a) section 29 of the National Assistance Act 1948 (welfare arrangements for blind, deaf, dumb and crippled persons etc.);

   (b) section 45(1) of the Health Services and Public Health Act 1968 (welfare of old people);

   (c) Schedule 8 to the National Health Service Act 1977 (care of mothers and young children, prevention of illness and care and after-care and home help and laundry facilities);

   (d) section 8 of the Residential Homes Act 1980 (meals and recreation for old people); and

   (e) paragraph 1 of Part II of Schedule 9 to this Act other than the provision of services for which payment may be required under section 22 or 26 of the National Assistance Act 1948.

(3) If a person –

   (a) avails himself of a service to which this section applies, and

   (b) satisfies the authority providing the service that his means are insufficient for it to be reasonably practicable for him to pay for the service the amount which he would otherwise be obliged to pay for it,

the authority shall not require him to pay more for it than it appears to them that it is reasonably practicable for him to pay.

(4) Any charge under this section may, without prejudice to any other method of recovery, be recovered summarily as a civil debt.

Recovery of sums due to local authority where persons in residential accommodation have disposed of assets

21 (1) Subject to the following provisions of this section, where –

   (a) a person avails himself of Part III accommodation; and

   (b) that person knowingly and with the intention of avoiding charges for the accommodation –

     (i) has transferred any asset to which this section applies to some other person or persons not more than six months before the date on which he begins to reside in such accommodation; or

(ii) transfers any such asset to some other person or persons while residing in the accommodation; and

(c) either –

(i) the consideration for the transfer is less than the value of the asset; or

(ii) there is no consideration for the transfer,

the person or persons to whom the asset is transferred by the person availing himself of the accommodation shall be liable to pay to the local authority providing the accommodation or arranging for its provision the difference between the amount assessed as due to be paid for the accommodation by the person availing himself of it and the amount which the local authority receive from him for it.

(2) This section applies to cash and any other asset which falls to be taken into account for the purpose of assessing under section 22 of the National Assistance Act 1948 the ability to pay for the accommodation of the person availing himself of it.

(3) Subsection 1(1) above shall have effect in relation to a transfer by a person who leaves Part III accommodation and subsequently resumes residence in such accommodation as if the period of six months mentioned in paragraph (b)(i) were a period of six months before the date on which he resumed residence in such accommodation.

(3A) If the Secretary of State so directs, subsection (1) above shall not apply in such cases as may be specified in the direction.

(4) Where a person has transferred an asset to which this section applies to more than one person, the liability of each of the persons to whom it was transferred shall be in proportion to the benefit accruing to him from the transfer.

(5) A person's liability under this section shall not exceed the benefit accruing to him from the transfer.

(6) Subject to subsection (7) below, the value of any asset to which this section applies, other than cash, which has been transferred shall be taken to be the amount of the consideration which would have been realised for it if it had been sold on the open market by a willing seller at the time of the transfer.

(7) For the purpose of calculating the value of an asset under subsection (6) above there shall be deducted from the amount of the consideration –

(a) the amount of any incumbrance on the asset; and

(b) a reasonable amount in respect of the expenses of the sale .

(8) In this Part of this Act 'Part III accommodation' means accommodation provided under sections 21 to 26 of the National Assistance Act 1948, and, in the application of this Part of this Act to Scotland, means accommodation provided under the Social Work (Scotland) Act 1968 or section 7 (functions of local authorities) of the Mental Health (Scotland) Act 1984.

Arrears of contributions charged on interest in land in England and Wales

22 (1) Subject to subsection (2) below, where a person who avails himself of Part III accommodation provided by a local authority in England, Wales or Scotland –

(a) fails to pay any sum assessed as due to be paid by him for the accommodation; and

(b) has a beneficial interest in land in England and Wales,

the local authority may create a charge in their favour on his interest in the land.

(2) In the case of a person who has interests in more than one parcel of land the charge under this section shall be upon his interest in such one of the parcels as the local authority may determine.

(2A) In determining whether to exercise their power under subsection (1) above and in making any determination under subsection (2) above, the local authority shall comply with any directions given to them by the Secretary of State as to the exercise of those functions.

(3) [*repealed*].

(4) Subject to subsection (5) below, a charge under this section shall be in respect of any amount assessed as due to be paid which is outstanding from time to time.

(5) The charge on the interest of an equitable joint tenant in land shall be in respect of an amount not exceeding the value of the interest that he would enjoy in the land if the joint tenancy were severed but the creation of such a charge shall not sever the joint tenancy.

(6) On the death of an equitable joint tenant in land whose interest in the land is subject to a charge under this section –

(a) if there are surviving joint tenants, their interests in the land; and

(b) if the land vests in one person, or one person is entitled to have it vested in him, his interest in it,

shall become subject to a charge for an amount not exceeding the amount of the charge to which the interest of the deceased joint tenant was subject by virtue of subsection (5) above.

(7) A charge under this section shall be created by a declaration in writing made by the local authority.

(8) Any such charge, other than a charge on the interest of an equitable joint tenant in land, shall in the case of unregistered land be a land charge of Class B within the meaning of section 2 of the Land Charges Act 1972 and in the case of registered land be a registrable charge taking effect as a charge by way of legal mortgage.

Interest on sums charged on or secured over interest in land

24 (1) Any sum charged on or secured over an interest in land under this Part of this Act shall bear interest from the day after that on which the person for whom the local authority provided the accommodation dies.

(2) The rate of interest shall be such reasonable rate as the Secretary of State may direct or, if no such direction is given, as the local authority may determine.

Schedule 9, Part II: Meals and recreation for old people

1   A district council shall have power to make such arrangements as they may from time to time determine for providing meals and recreation for old people in their homes or elsewhere and may employ as their agent for the purpose of this paragraph any voluntary organisation whose activities consist in or include the provision of meals or recreation for old people.

2   A district council may assist any such organisation as is referred to in paragraph 1 above to provide meals or recreation for old people –

(a) by contributing to the funds of the organisation;

(b) by permitting them to use premises belonging to the council on such terms as may be agreed; and

(c) by making available furniture, vehicles or equipment (whether by way of gift or loan or otherwise) and the services of any staff who are employed by the council in connection with the premises or other things which they permit the organisation to use.

3 (1) District councils shall exercise their functions under this Part of this Schedule (including any discretion conferred on them under it) in accordance with the provisions of any regulations of the Secretary of State made for the purposes of this paragraph; and without prejudice to the generality of this paragraph, regulations under this paragraph –

(a) may provide for conferring on officers of the Secretary of State authorised under the regulations such powers of inspection as may be prescribed in relation to the exercise of functions under this Part of this Schedule by or by arrangement with or on behalf of district councils; and

(b) may make provision with respect to the qualifications of officers employed by district councils for the purposes of this Part of this Schedule or by voluntary organisations acting under arrangements with or on behalf of district councils for those purposes.

(2) The power to make regulations under this paragraph shall be exercisable by statutory instrument which shall be subject to annulment in pursuance of a resolution of either House of Parliament.

DISABLED PERSONS (SERVICES, CONSULTATION AND REPRESENTATION) ACT 1986

4   When requested to do so by –

(a) a disabled person . . .

(c) any person who provides care for him in the circumstances mentioned in section 8,

a local authority shall decide whether the needs of the disabled person call for the provision by the authority of any services in accordance with section 2(1) of the 1970 Act (provision for welfare services).

8 (1) Where –

(a) a disabled person is living at home and receiving a substantial amount of care on a regular basis from another person (who is not a person employed to provide such care by any body in the exercise of its functions under any enactment), and

(b) it falls to a local authority to decide whether the disabled person's needs call for the provision by them of any services for him under any of the welfare enactments,

the local authority shall, in deciding that question, have regard to the ability of that other person to continue to provide such care on a regular basis.

16   In this Act –

. . .

disabled person' –

(a)   in relation to England and Wales, means

   (i)   in the case of a person aged 18 or over, a person to whom s29 of the National Assistance Act 1948 applies; and

   (ii)   in the case of a person under the age of 18, a person who is disabled within the meaning of Part III of the Children Act 1989.

CHILDREN ACT 1989
Provision of services for children in need, their families and others

17 (1)   It shall be the general duty of every local authority (in addition to the other duties imposed upon them by this Part) –

(a)   to safeguard and promote the welfare of children within their area who are in need; and

(b)   so far as is consistent with that duty to promote the upbringing of such children by their families,

by providing a range and level of services appropriate to those children's needs.

(2)   For the purpose principally of facilitating the discharge of their general duty under this section, every local authority shall have the specific duties and powers set out in Part I of Schedule 2.

(3)   Any service provided by an authority in the exercise of functions conferred on them by this section may be provided for the family of a particular child in need or for any member of his family, if it is provided with a view to safeguarding or promoting the child's welfare.

(4)   The Secretary of State may by order amend any provision of Part I of Schedule 2 or add any further duty or power to those for the tune being mentioned there.

(5)   Every local authority –

(a)   shall facilitate the provision by others (including in particular voluntary organisations) of services which the authority have power to provide by virtue of this section, or section 18, 20, 23 or 24; and

(b)   may make such arrangements as they see fit for any person to act on their behalf in the provision of any such service.

(6)   The services provided by a local authority in the exercise of functions conferred on them by this section may include giving assistance in kind or, in exceptional circumstances, in cash.

(7)   Assistance may be unconditional or subject to conditions as to the repayment of the assistance or of its value (in whole or in part).

(8)   Before giving any assistance or imposing any conditions, a local authority shall have regard to the means of the child concerned and of each of his parents.

(9)   No person shall be liable to make any repayment of assistance or of its value at any time when he is in receipt of income support, working families' tax

credit or disabled person's tax credit under Part VII of the Social Security Contributions and Benefits Act 1992 or of an income-based jobseeker's allowance.

(10) For the purposes of this Part a child shall be taken to be in need if –

   (a) he is unlikely to achieve or maintain, or to have the opportunity of achieving or maintaining, a reasonable standard of health or development without the provision for him of services by a local authority under this Part;

   (b) his health or development is likely to be significantly impaired, or further impaired, without the provision for him of such services; or

   (c) he is disabled,

and 'family', in relation to such a child, includes any person who has parental responsibility for the child and any other person with whom he has been living.

(11) For the purposes of this Part, a child is disabled if he is blind, deaf or dumb or suffers from mental disorder of any kind or is substantially and permanently handicapped by illness, injury or congenital deformity or such other disability as may be prescribed; and in this Part –

'development' means physical, intellectual, emotional, social or behavioural development; and

'health' means physical or mental health.

[The following provisions are inserted by Carers and Disabled Children Act 2000 s7 and will come into force on a date to be fixed (most probably in April 2001).]

Direct payments

17A(1) Instead of providing services in the exercise of functions conferred on them by section 17, a local authority may make to a person falling within subsection (2) (if he consents) a payment of such amount as, subject to subsections (5) and (6), they think fit in respect of his securing the provision of any of the services which the local authority would otherwise have provided

(2) The following fall within this subsection –

   (a) a person with parental responsibility for a disabled child;

   (b) a disabled child aged 16 or 17.

(3) A payment under subsection (1) shall be subject to the condition that the person to whom it is made shall not secure the provision of the service to which it relates by a person who is of a prescribed description.

(4) The Secretary of State may by regulations provide that the power conferred by subsection (1) is not to be exercisable in relation to the provision of residential accommodation for any person for a period exceeding a prescribed period.

(5) Except as mentioned in subsection (6) of this section, subsections (2) and (6) of section 1, and subsections (1) and (2) of section 2, of the Community Care (Direct Payments) Act 1996 apply in relation to payments under subsection (1) as they apply in relation to payments under section 1(1) of that Act, but as if –

   (a) the reference to 'subsection (4)' in section 1(6)(b) of that Act were a reference to subsection (3) of this section; and

(b) the references to 'the relevant community care enactment' in section 2 of that Act were to Part III of the Children Act 1989.

(6) Section 1(2) of the Community Care (Direct Payments) Act 1996 does not apply in relation to payments under subsection (1) to –

(a) a person with parental responsibility for a disabled child, other than a parent of such a child under the age of sixteen, in respect of a service which would otherwise have been provided for the child; or

(b) any person who is in receipt of income support, working families' tax credit or disabled person's tax credit under Part VII of the Social Security Contributions and Benefits Act 1992 or of an income-based jobseeker's allowance,

and in those cases the amount of any payment under subsection (1) is to be at a rate equal to the local authority's estimate of the reasonable cost of securing the provision of the service concerned.

Vouchers for persons with parental responsibility for disabled children

17B(1) The Secretary of State may by regulations make provision for the issue by a local authority of vouchers to a person with parental responsibility for a disabled child.

(2) 'Voucher' means a document whereby, if the local authority agrees with the person with parental responsibility that it would help him care for the child if the person with parental responsibility had a break from caring, that person may secure the temporary provision of services for the child under section 17.

(3) The regulations may, in particular, provide –

(a) for the value of a voucher to be expressed in terms of money, or of the delivery of a service for a period of time, or both;

(b) for the person who supplies a service against a voucher, or for the arrangement under which it is supplied, to be approved by the local authority;

(c) for a maximum period during which a service (or a service of a prescribed description) can be provided against a voucher.

(2) The reference to the Children Act 1989 in Schedule 1 to the National Assembly for Wales (Transfer of Functions) Order 1999 is to be treated as referring to that Act as amended by this section.

(3) Subsection (2) does not affect the power to make further Orders varying or omitting that reference

NATIONAL HEALTH SERVICE AND COMMUNITY CARE ACT 1990

Local authority plans for community care services

46 (1) Each local authority –

(a) shall, within such period after the day appointed for the coming into force of this section as the Secretary of State may direct, prepare and publish a plan for the provision of community care services in their area;

(b) shall keep the plan prepared by them under paragraph (a) above and any further plans prepared by them under this section under review; and

(c) shall, at such intervals as the Secretary of State may direct, prepare and publish modifications to the current plan, or if the case requires, a new plan.

(2) In carrying out any of their functions under paragraphs (a) to (c) of subsection (1) above, a local authority shall consult –

(a) any Health Authority the whole or any part of whose district lies within the area of the local authority;

(b) [*repealed*]

(c) in so far as any proposed plan, review or modifications of a plan may affect or be affected by the provision or availability of housing and the local authority is not itself a local housing authority, within the meaning of the Housing Act 1985, every such local housing authority whose area is within the area of the local authority;

(d) such voluntary organisations as appear to the authority to represent the interests of persons who use or are likely to use any community care services within the area of the authority or the interests of private carers who, within that area, provide care to persons for whom, in the exercise of their social services functions, the local authority have a power or a duty to provide a service;

(e) such voluntary housing agencies and other bodies as appear to the local authority to provide housing or community care services in their area; and

(f) such other persons as the Secretary of State may direct.

(3) In this section –

'local authority' means the council of a county, a county borough, a metropolitan district or a London borough or the Common Council of the City of London;

'community care services' means services which a local authority may provide or arrange to be provided under any of the following provisions –

(a) Part III of the National Assistance Act 1948;

(b) section 45 of the Health Services and Public Health Act 1968;

(c) section 21 of and Schedule 8 to the National Health Service Act 1977; and

(d) section 117 of the Mental Health Act 1983; and

'private carer' means a person who is not employed to provide the care in question by any body in the exercise of its function under any enactment.

Assessment of needs for community care services

47 (1) Subject to subsections (5) and (6) below, where it appears to a local authority that any person for whom they may provide or arrange for the provision of community care services may be in need of any such services, the authority –

(a) shall carry out an assessment of his needs for those services; and

(b) having regard to the results of that assessment, shall then decide whether his needs call for the provision by them of any such services.

(2) If at any time during the assessment of the needs of any person under subsection (1)(a) above it appears to a local authority that he is a disabled person, the authority –

(a) shall proceed to make such a decision as to the services he requires as is mentioned in section 4 of the Disabled Persons (Services, Consultation and Representation) Act 1986 without his requesting them to do so under that section; and

(b) shall inform him that they will be doing so and of his rights under that Act.

(3) If at any time during the assessment of the needs of any person under subsection (1)(a) above, it appears to a local authority –

(a) that there may be a need for the provision to that person by such Health Authority as may be determined in accordance with regulations of any services under the National Health Service Act 1977, or

(b) that there may be the need for the provision to him of any services which fall within the functions of a local housing authority (within the meaning of the Housing Act 1985) which is not the local authority carrying out the assessment,

the local authority shall notify that Health Authority or local housing authority and invite them to assist, to such extent as is reasonable in the circumstances, in the making of the assessment; and, in making their decision as to the provision of services needed for the person in question, the local authority shall take into account any services which are likely to be made available for him by that Health Authority or local housing authority.

(4) The Secretary of State may give directions as to the manner in which an assessment under this section is to be carried out or the form it is to take but, subject to any such directions and to subsection (7) below, it shall be carried out in such manner and take such form as the local authority consider appropriate.

(5) Nothing in this section shall prevent a local authority from temporarily providing or arranging for the provision of community care services for any person without carrying out a prior assessment of his needs in accordance with the preceding provisions of this section if, in the opinion of the authority, the condition of that person is such that he requires those services as a matter of urgency.

(6) If, by virtue of subsection (5) above, community care services have been provided temporarily for any person as a matter of urgency, then, as soon as practicable thereafter, an assessment of his needs shall be made in accordance with the preceding provisions of this section . . .

CARERS (RECOGNITION AND SERVICES) ACT 1995
Assessment of ability of carers to provide care: England and Wales

1 (1) Subject to subsection (3) below, in any case where –

(a) a local authority carry out an assessment under section 47(1)(a) of the National Health Service and Community Care Act 1990 of the needs of a person ('the relevant person') for community care services, and

(b) an individual ('the carer') provides or intends to provide a substantial amount of care on a regular basis for the relevant person,

the carer may request the local authority, before they make their decision as to whether the needs of the relevant person call for the provision of any services, to carry out an assessment of his ability to provide and continue to provide care for the relevant person; and if he makes such a request, the local authority shall carry out such an assessment and shall take into account the results of that assessment in making that decision.

(2) Subject to subsection (3) below, in any case where –

(a) a local authority assess the needs of a disabled child for the purpose of Part III of the Children Act 1989 or section 2 of the Chronically Sick and Disabled Persons Act 1970, and

(b) an individual ('the carer') provides or intends to provide a substantial amount of care on a regular basis for the disabled child,

the carer may request the local authority, before they make their decision as to whether the needs of the disabled child call for the provision of any services, to carry out an assessment of his ability to provide and continue to provide care for the disabled child; and if he makes such a request, the local authority shall carry out such an assessment and shall take into account the results of that assessment in making that decision.

(3) No request may be made under subsection (1) or (2) above by an individual who provides or will provide the care in question –

(a) by virtue of a contract of employment or other contract with any person; or

(b) as a volunteer for a voluntary organisation . . .

HOUSING GRANTS, CONSTRUCTION AND REGENERATION ACT 1996
Disabled facilities grants: purposes for which grant must or may be given

23 (1) The purposes for which an application for a disabled facilities grant must be approved, subject to the provisions of this Chapter, are the following –

(a) facilitating access by the disabled occupant to and from the dwelling or the building in which the dwelling or, as the case may be, flat is situated;

(b) making the dwelling or building safe for the disabled occupant and other persons residing with him;

(c) facilitating access by the disabled occupant to a room used or usable as the principal family room;

(d) facilitating access by the disabled occupant to, or providing for the disabled occupant, a room used or usable for sleeping;

(e) facilitating access by the disabled occupant to, or providing for the disabled occupant, a room in which there is a lavatory, or facilitating the use by the disabled occupant of such a facility;

(f) facilitating access by the disabled occupant to, or providing for the disabled occupant, a room in which there is a bath or shower (or both), or facilitating the use by the disabled occupant of such a facility;

(g) facilitating access by the disabled occupant to, or providing for the disabled occupant, a room in which there is a washhand basin, or facilitating the use by the disabled occupant of such a facility;

(h) facilitating the preparation and cooking of food by the disabled occupant;

(i) improving any heating system in the dwelling to meet the needs of the disabled occupant or, if there is no existing heating system in the dwelling or any such system is unsuitable for use by the disabled occupant, providing a heating system suitable to meet his needs;

(j) facilitating the use by the disabled occupant of a source of power, light or heat by altering the position of one or more means of access to or control of that source or by providing additional means of control;

(k) facilitating access and movement by the disabled occupant around the dwelling in order to enable him to care for a person who is normally resident in the dwelling and is in need of such care;

(l) such other purposes as may be specified by order of the Secretary of State.

(2) An application for a disabled facilities grant may be approved, subject to the provisions of this Chapter, for the purpose of making the dwelling or building suitable for the accommodation, welfare or employment of the disabled occupant in any other respect.

(3) If in the opinion of the local housing authority the relevant works are more or less extensive than is necessary to achieve any of the purposes set out in subsection (1) or the purpose mentioned in subsection (2), they may, with the consent of the applicant, treat the application as varied so that the relevant works are limited to or, as the case may be, include such works as seem to the authority to be necessary for that purpose.

Disabled facilities grants: approval of application

24 (1) The local housing authority –

(a) shall approve an application for a disabled facilities grant for purposes within section 23(1), and

(b) may if they think fit approve an application for a disabled facilities grant not for a purpose within that provision but for the purpose specified in section 23(2),

subject to the following provisions.

(2) Where an authority entertain an owner's application for a disabled facilities grant made by a person who proposes to acquire a qualifying owner's interest, they shall not approve the application until they are satisfied that he has done so.

(3) A local housing authority shall not approve an application for a disabled facilities grant unless they are satisfied –

(a) that the relevant works are necessary and appropriate to meet the needs of the disabled occupant, and

(b) that it is reasonable and practicable to carry out the relevant works having regard to the age and condition of the dwelling or building.

In considering the matters mentioned in paragraph (a) a local housing authority which is not itself a social services authority shall consult the social services authority.

(4) An authority proposing to approve an application for a disabled facilities grant shall consider –

(a) in the case of an application in respect of works to a dwelling, whether the dwelling is fit for human habitation;

(b) in the case of a common parts application, whether the building meets the requirements in section 604(2) of the Housing Act 1985,

and the authority shall take that into account in deciding whether it is reasonable and practicable to carry out the relevant works.

(5) A local housing authority shall not approve a common parts application for a disabled facilities grant unless they are satisfied that the applicant has a power or is under a duty to carry out the relevant works.

Regulations and directions

SECRETARY OF STATE'S APPROVALS AND DIRECTIONS UNDER SECTION 21(1) OF THE NATIONAL ASSISTANCE ACT 1948
(LAC(93)10 Appendix 1)

The Secretary of State for Health, in exercise of the powers conferred on her by section 21(1) of the National Assistance Act 1948, hereby makes the following Approvals and Directions –

Commencement, interpretation and extent

1 (1) These Approvals and Directions shall come into force on 1st April 1993.

(2) In these Approvals and Directions, unless the context otherwise requires, 'the Act' means the National Assistance Act 1948.

(3) The Interpretation Act 1978 applies to these Approvals and Direction as it applies to an Act of Parliament.

(4) These Approvals and Directions shall apply only to England and Wales.

Residential accommodation for persons in need of care and attention

2 (1) The Secretary of State hereby –

(a) approves the making by local authorities of arrangements under section 21(1)(a) of the Act in relation to persons with no settled residence and, to such extent as the authority may consider desirable, in relation to persons who are ordinarily resident in the area of another local authority, with the consent of that other authority; and

(b) directs local authorities to make arrangements under section 21(1)(a) of the Act in relation to persons who are ordinarily resident in their area and other persons who are in urgent need thereof,

to provide residential accommodation for persons aged 18 or over who by reason of age, illness, disability or any other circumstance are in need of care and attention not otherwise available to them.

(2) Without prejudice to the generality of sub-paragraph (1), the Secretary of State hereby directs local authorities to make arrangements under section 21(1)(a) of the Act to provide temporary accommodation for persons who are in urgent need thereof in circumstances where the need for that accommodation could not reasonably have been foreseen.

(3) Without prejudice to the generality of sub-paragraph (1), the Secretary of State hereby directs local authorities to make arrangements under section 21(1)(a) of the Act to provide accommodation –

(a) in relation to persons who are or have been suffering from mental disorder, or

(b) for the purposes of the prevention of mental disorder, for persons who are ordinarily resident in their area and for persons with no settled residence who are in the authority's area.

(4) Without prejudice to the generality of sub-paragraph (1) and subject to section 24(4) of the Act, the Secretary of State hereby approves the making by local authorities of arrangements under section 21(1)(a) of the Act to provide residential accommodation –

(a) in relation to persons who are or have been suffering from mental disorder; or

(b) for the purposes of the prevention of mental disorder,

for persons who are ordinarily resident in the area of another local authority but who following discharge from hospital have become resident in the authority's area.

(5) Without prejudice to the generality of sub-paragraph (1), the Secretary of State hereby approves the making by local authorities of arrangements under section 21(1)(a) of the Act to provide accommodation to meet the needs of persons for –

(a) the prevention of illness;

(b) the care of those suffering from illness; and

(c) the aftercare of those so suffering.

(6) Without prejudice to the generality of sub-paragraph (1), the Secretary of State hereby approves the making by local authorities of arrangements under section 21(1)(a) of the Act specifically for persons who are alcoholic or drug-dependent.

Residential accommodation for expectant and nursing mothers

3   The Secretary of State hereby approves the making by local authorities of arrangements under section 21(1)(aa) of the Act to provide residential accommodation (in particular mother and baby homes) for expectant and nursing mothers (of any age) who are in need of care and attention which is not otherwise available to them.

Arrangements to provide services for residents

4   The Secretary of State hereby directs local authorities to make arrangements in relation to persons provided with accommodation under section 21(1) of the Act for all or any of the following purposes –

(a) for the welfare of all persons for whom accommodation is provided;

(b) for the supervision of the hygiene of the accommodation so provided;

(c) to enable persons for whom accommodation is provided to obtain –

(i) medical attention,

(ii) nursing attention during illnesses of a kind which are ordinarily nursed at home, and

(iii) the benefit of any services provided by the National Health Service of which they may from time to time be in need,

but nothing in this paragraph shall require a local authority to make any provision authorised or required to be provided under the National Health Service Act 1977;

(d) for the provision of board and such other services, amenities and requisites provided in connection with the accommodation, except where in the opinion of the authority managing the premises their provision is unnecessary;

(e) to review regularly the provision made under the arrangements and to make such improvements as the authority considers necessary.

Arrangements for the conveyance of residents

5   The Secretary of State hereby approves the making by local authorities of arrangements under section 21(1) of the Act to provide, in such cases as the authority considers appropriate, for the conveyance of persons to and from premises in which accommodation is provided for them under Part III of the Act.

Duties in respect of residents in transferred accommodation

6   (1) Where a person is provided with accommodation pursuant to section 21(1) of the Act, and –

(a) the residential accommodation is local authority accommodation provided pursuant to section 21(4) of the 1948 Act; and

(b) the local authority transfer the management of the residential accommodation to a voluntary organisation who –

   (i) manages it as a residential care home within the meaning of Part I of the Registered Homes Act 1984, and

   (ii) is registered under that Part or is not required to be so registered by virtue of being an exempt body; and

(c) the person is accommodated in the residential accommodation immediately before and after the transfer,

while that person remains accommodated in that residential accommodation, the local authority shall remain under a duty to make arrangements to provide accommodation for him after any transfer to which paragraph (b) of this sub-paragraph refers.

(2) For the purposes of paragraph (c) of sub-paragraph (1), a person shall be regarded as accommodated in residential accommodation if –

(a) he is temporarily absent from such accommodation (including circumstances in which he is in hospital or on holiday);

(b) before 1st April 1993, that accommodation was provided under paragraph 2(1) of Schedule 8 to the National Health Service Act 1977.

(3) Where immediately before these Approvals and Directions come into force a local authority was under a duty to provide a person with accommodation by virtue of –

(a) the Secretary of State's former Directions under section 21(1) of the National Assistance Act 1948 contained in Annex 1 of Department of Health Circular LAC(91)12; or

(b) the Secretary of State's former Directions under paragraph 2 of Schedule 8 to the National Health Service Act 1977 contained in Annex 2 of Department of Health Circular LAC(91)12, while that person remains accommodated in that residential accommodation, the local authority shall remain under a duty to make arrangements to provide that person with accommodation from the date on which these Directions come into force.

Powers to make arrangements with other local authorities and voluntary organisations, etc

7   For the avoidance of doubt, these Approvals and Directions are without prejudice to any of the powers conferred on local authorities by section 21(4) and section 26(1) of the Act (arrangements with voluntary organisations, etc).

Dated 17/2/1993

SECRETARY OF STATE'S APPROVALS AND DIRECTIONS UNDER SECTION 29(1) OF THE NATIONAL ASSISTANCE ACT 1948
(LAC(93)10 Appendix 2)

The Secretary of State for Health, in exercise of the powers conferred on her by section 29(1) of the National Assistance Act 1948, hereby makes the following Approvals and Directions: –

Commencement, interpretation and extent

1   (1) These Approvals and Directions shall come into force on 1st April 1993.

(2) In these Approvals and Directions, unless the context otherwise requires, 'the Act' means the National Assistance Act 1948.

(3) The Interpretation Act 1978 applies to these Approvals and Directions as it applies to an Act of Parliament.

(4) These Approvals and Directions shall apply only to England and Wales.

Powers and duties to make welfare arrangements

2   (1) The Secretary of State hereby approves the making by local authorities of arrangements under section 29(1) of the Act for all persons to whom that subsection applies and directs local authorities to make arrangements under section 29(1) of the Act in relation to persons who are ordinarily resident in their area for all or any of the following purposes –

(a) to provide a social work service and such advice and support as may be needed for people in their own homes or elsewhere;

(b) to provide, whether at centres or elsewhere, facilities for social rehabilitation and adjustment to disability including assistance in overcoming limitations of mobility or communication;

(c) to provide, whether at centres or elsewhere, facilities for occupational, social, cultural and recreational activities and, where appropriate, the making of payments to persons for work undertaken by them.

(2) The Secretary of State hereby directs local authorities to make the arrangements referred to in section 29(4)(g) of the Act (compiling and maintaining registers) in relation to persons who are ordinarily resident in their area.

(3) The Secretary of State hereby approves the making by local authorities of arrangements under section 29(1) of the Act for all persons to whom that subsection applies for the following purposes –

(a) to provide holiday homes;

(b) to provide free or subsidised travel for all or any persons who do not otherwise qualify for travel concessions, but only in respect of travel arrangements for which concessions are available;

(c) to assist a person in finding accommodation which will enable him to take advantage of any arrangements made under section 29(1) of the Act;

(d) to contribute to the cost of employing a warden on welfare functions in warden assisted housing schemes;

(e) to provide warden services for occupiers of private housing.

(4) Save as is otherwise provided for under this paragraph, the Secretary of State hereby approves the making by local authorities of all or any of the arrangements referred to in section 29(4) of the Act (welfare arrangements, etc.) for all persons to whom section 29(1) applies.

Welfare arrangements with another local authority

3 The Secretary of State hereby approves the making by local authorities of arrangements under section 29(1) of the Act, where appropriate, with another local authority for the provision of any of the services referred to in these Approvals and Directions.

Welfare arrangements with voluntary organisations and otherwise

4 For the avoidance of doubt, these Approvals and Directions are without prejudice to the powers conferred on local authorities by section 30(1) of the Act (voluntary organisations for disabled persons' welfare).

Dated 17/3/1993

SECRETARY OF STATE'S APPROVALS AND DIRECTIONS UNDER PARAGRAPHS 1 AND 2 OF SCHEDULE 8 TO THE NATIONAL HEALTH SERVICE ACT 1977 (LAC(93)10 Appendix 3)

The Secretary of State for Health, in exercise of the powers conferred on her by paragraphs 1(1) and 2(1) of Schedule 8 to the National Health Service Act 1977, hereby makes the following Approvals and Directions –

Commencement, interpretation and extent

1 (1) These Approvals and Directions shall come into force on 1st April 1993.

(2) In these Approvals and Directions, unless the context otherwise requires, 'the Act' means the National Health Service Act 1977.

(3) The Interpretation Act 1978 applies to these Approvals and Directions as it applies to an Act of Parliament.

(4) For the avoidance of doubt, these Approvals and Directions apply only to England and Wales.

Services for expectant and nursing mothers

2 The Secretary of state hereby approves the making of arrangements under paragraph 1(1) of Schedule 8 to the Act for the care of expectant and nursing mothers (of any age) other than the provision of residential accommodation for them (services for the purpose of the prevention of illness etc.).

3 (1) The Secretary of State hereby approves the making by local authorities of arrangements under paragraph 2(1) of Schedule 8 to the Act for the purpose of the prevention of illness, and the care of persons suffering from illness and for the aftercare of persons who have been so suffering and in particular for –

   (a) the provision, for persons whose care is undertaken with a view to preventing them becoming ill, persons suffering from illness and persons who have been so suffering, of centres or other facilities for training them or keeping them suitably occupied and the equipment and maintenance of such centres;

   (b) the provision, for the benefit of such persons as are mentioned in paragraph (a) above, of ancillary or supplemental services.

(2) The Secretary of State hereby directs local authorities to make arrangements under paragraph 2(1) of Schedule 8 to the Act for the purposes of the prevention of mental disorder, or in relation to persons who are or who have been suffering from mental disorder –

   (a) for the provision of centres (including training centres and day centres) or other facilities (including domiciliary facilities), whether in premises managed by the local authority or otherwise, for training or occupation of such persons;

   (b) for the appointment of sufficient social workers in their area to act as approved social workers for the purposes of the Mental Health Act 1983;

   (c) for the exercise of the functions of the authority in respect of persons suffering from mental disorder who are received into guardianship under Part II or III of the Mental Health Act 1983 (whether the guardianship of the local social services authority or of other persons);

   (d) for the provision of social work and related services to help in the identification, diagnosis, assessment and social treatment of mental disorder and to provide social work support and other domiciliary and care services to people living in their homes and elsewhere.

(3) Without prejudice to the generality of sub-paragraph (1), the Secretary of State hereby approves the making by local authorities of arrangements under paragraph 2(1) of Schedule 8 to the Act for the provision of –

   (a) meals to be served at the centres or other facilities referred to in sub-paragraphs (1)(a) and (2)(a) above and meals-on-wheels for house-bound people not provided for –

      (i) under section 45(1) of the Health Services and Public Health Act 1968(a), or

      (ii) by a district council under paragraph 1 of Part II of Schedule 9 to the Health and Social Services and Social Security Adjudications Act 1983;

   (b) remuneration for persons engaged in suitable work at the centres or other facilities referred to in sub-paragraphs (1)(a) and (2)(a) above, subject to paragraph 2(2)(a) of Schedule 8 to the Act;

   (c) social services (including advice and support) for the purposes of preventing the impairment of physical or mental health of adults in families where such impairment is likely, and for the purposes of preventing the break-up of such families, or for assisting in their rehabilitation;

(d) night-sitter services;

(e) recuperative holidays;

(f) facilities for social and recreational activities;

(g) services specifically for persons who are alcoholic or drug-dependent.

Services made available by another local authority etc.

4 For the purposes of any arrangements made under these Approvals and Directions, the Secretary of State hereby approves the use by local authorities of services or facilities made available by another authority, voluntary body or person on such conditions as may be agreed, but in making such arrangements, a local authority shall have regard to the importance of services being provided as near to a person's home as is practicable.

Dated 17/3/1993
Signed on behalf of the Secretary of State for Health

COMPLAINTS PROCEDURE DIRECTIONS 1990

4 (1) The local authority shall appoint one of their officers to assist the authority in the co-ordination of all aspects of their consideration of the representations.

(2) The local authority shall ensure that all the members or officers involved in the handling of representations under s7B(1) are familiar with the procedures set out in these Directions.

5 (1) Where a local authority receives representations from any complainant they shall attempt to resolve the matter informally.

(2) If the matter cannot be resolved to the satisfaction of the complainant, the local authority shall give or send to him an explanation of the procedures set out in these Directions and ask him to submit a written representation if he wishes to proceed.

(3) The local authority shall offer assistance and guidance to the complainant on the use of this procedure, or give advice on where he may obtain it.

6 (1) The local authority shall consider the representations and formulate a response within 28 days of their receipt, or if this is not possible, explain to the complainant within that period why it is not possible and tell him when he can expect a response, which shall in any event be within three calendar months of receipt of the representations.

(2) The representations may be withdrawn at any stage by the complainant, in which case the procedures set out in these Directions (other than direction 9 and 11) shall no longer apply to that case.

7 (1) The local authority shall notify in writing the result of their consideration to –

(a) the complainant;

(b) the person on whose behalf the representations were made, unless the local authority consider that person is unable to understand it or it would cause him unnecessary distress;

(c) any other person who the local authority considers has sufficient interest in the case.

(2) If the complainant informs the local authority in writing within 28 days of the date on which the notification mentioned in paragraph (1) is sent to him that

he is dissatisfied with that result and wishes the matter to be referred to a panel for review, the local authority shall appoint a panel (including any independent person) to consider the matter which the local authority shall refer to it.

(3) The panel shall meet within 28 days of the receipt of the complainant's request for review by the local authority to consider the matter together with any oral or written submissions as the complainant or the local authority wish the panel to consider.

8 (1) Where a panel meets under direction 7, it shall decide on its recommendations and record them in writing within 24 hours of the end of the meeting.

(2) The panel shall send written copies of their recommendations to –
   (a) the local authority,
   (b) the complainant,
   (c) if appropriate, the person on whose behalf the representations were made, and
   (d) any other person who the local authority considers has sufficient interest in the case.

(3) The panel shall record the reasons for their recommendations in writing.

(4) The local authority shall consider what action they ought to take, and notify in writing the persons specified in paragraph (1)(b), (c) and (d) of the local authority's decision and of their reasons for taking that decision and of any action which they may have taken or propose to take within 28 days of the date of the panel's recommendation.

9 The local authority shall keep a record of each representation received, the outcome of each representation, and whether there was compliance with the time limits specified in directions 6(1), 7(3), and 8(1) and 8(4).

NATIONAL ASSISTANCE ACT 1948 (CHOICE OF ACCOMMODATION) DIRECTIONS 1992

The Secretary of State in exercise of the powers conferred by section 7A of the Local Authority Social Services Act 1970 and of all other powers enabling her in that behalf hereby makes the following Directions –

Citation, commencement and extent

1 (1) These Directions may be cited as the National Assistance Act 1948 (Choice of Accommodation) Directions 1992 and shall come into force on 1st April 1993.

(2) These Directions extend only to England.

Local authorities to provide preferred accommodation

2 Where a local authority have assessed a person under section 47 of the National Health Service and Community Care Act 1990 (assessment) and have decided that accommodation should be provided pursuant to section 21 of the National Assistance Act 1948 (provision of residential accommodation) the local authority shall, subject to paragraph 3 of these Directions, make arrangements for accommodation pursuant to section 21 for that person at the place of his choice within England and Wales (in these Directions called 'preferred accommodation') if he has indicated that he wishes to be accommodated in preferred accommodation.

Conditions for provision of preferred accommodation

3   Subject to paragraph 4 of these Directions the local authority shall only be required to make or continue to make arrangements for a person to be accommodated in his preferred accommodation if –

(a) the preferred accommodation appears to the authority to be suitable in relation to his needs as assessed by them;

(b) the cost of making arrangements for him at his preferred accommodation would not require the authority to pay more than they would usually expect to pay having regard to his assessed needs;

(c) the preferred accommodation is available;

(d) the persons in charge of the preferred accommodation provide it subject to the authority's usual terms and conditions, having regard to the nature of the accommodation, for providing accommodation for such a person under Part III of the National Assistance Act 1948.

Preferred accommodation outside local authority's usual limit

4   (1) Subject to sub-paragraphs (2) and (3), paragraph 3(b) of these Directions shall not apply to a local authority which makes arrangements which cost more than the local authority would usually expect to pay in order to provide a person with their preferred accommodation if a third party's contribution [towards the cost of that preferred accommodation, which is treated as a person's resources as assessed under the National Assistance (Assessment of Resources) Regulations 1992, is such that that person] can reasonably be expected to pay for the duration of the arrangements an amount which is at least equal to the difference between –

(a) the cost which the local authority would usually expect to pay for accommodation having regard to the person's assessed need, and

(b) the full standard rate for that accommodation as specified in section 22(2) of the National Assistance Act 1948 (liability to pay full cost of local authority accommodation) (the 'standard rate') or pursuant to section 26(2) to (4) of that Act (liability to pay full cost of other accommodation arranged by local authority).

(2) Sub-paragraph (1) shall not apply in respect of cases in which the third party's contributions are made by a person who is liable under section 42 of the National Assistance Act 1948 to maintain the person who wishes to be provided with preferred accommodation.

(3) Nothing in these Directions shall prevent a local authority from making or continuing to make arrangements for a person to be accommodated in his preferred accommodation where the cost of making such arrangements is more than the local authority would usually expect to pay having regard to the person's assessed needs.

GUIDANCE

Purpose

1   Under new community care arrangements social services authorities will increasingly be making placements in residential and nursing home care. This direction is intended to ensure where that happens that people are able to exercise a genuine choice over where they live.

2   It also gives people the right to enter more expensive accommodation than they would otherwise have been offered if there is a third party willing and able to pay the difference in cost.

3   This direction is intended to formalise the best practice which most authorities would in any case have adopted. It sets out the minimum that individuals should be able to expect. It is not, however, intended to mark the limits of the choice that authorities may be able to offer people. Even where not required to act in a certain way by this direction, authorities should exercise their discretion in a way that maximises choice as far as possible within available resources.

Summary

4   If after an assessment of need an authority decides to provide residential care for someone either permanently or temporarily, it will make a placement on their behalf in suitable accommodation.

5   If the individual concerned expresses a preference for particular accommodation ('preferred accommodation') within the UK, the authority must arrange for care in that accommodation, provided
   • the accommodation is suitable in relation to the individual's assessed needs
   • to do so would not cost the authority more than it would usually expect to pay for accommodation for someone with the individual's assessed needs
   • the accommodation is available
   • the person in charge of the accommodation is willing to provide accommodation subject to the authority's usual terms and conditions for such accommodation.

6   If a resident requests it, the authority must also arrange for care in accommodation more expensive than it would normally fund provided there is a third party willing and able to pay the difference between the cost the authority would usually expect to pay and the actual cost of the accommodation.

Preferred accommodation

7   As with all aspects of service provision, there should be a general presumption in favour of people being able to exercise choice over the service they receive. The limitations on authorities' legal obligation to provide preferred accommodation set out in the direction are not intended to deny people reasonable freedom of choice, but simply to ensure that authorities are able to fulfil their obligations for the quality of service provided and for value for money. The terms of the direction are explained more fully below. Where for any reason an authority decides not to arrange a place for someone in their preferred accommodation it must have a clear and reasonable justification for that decision which relates to the criteria of the direction.

Suitability of accommodation

7.1   Suitability will depend on the authority's assessment of individual need. Each case must be considered on its merits.

7.2   Consequently accommodation will not necessarily be suitable simply because it satisfies registration standards. On the other hand accommodation will not necessarily be unsuitable simply because it fails to conform with the authority's preferred model of provision, or meet the letter of a standard service specification.

7.3 This direction does not affect Section 26(1D) of the National Assistance Act 1948 as inserted by the NHS and Community Care Act 1990 which prevents an authority making arrangements for residential care with anyone convicted of an offence under the Registered Homes Act 1984. Similarly, the direction does not require an authority to contract with any accommodation where for any other reason it is prevented by law from doing so.

Cost

7.4 The test should be whether the cost of preferred accommodation is more than the authority would usually expect to pay for someone with the same assessed needs as the individual concerned. This is not necessarily the same as the cost that the authority would in fact have incurred had the particular individual not decided to exercise their right to choose, since that might be either higher or lower than the authority would usually pay. For example, the cost of one particular placement at a given time might be determined by the fortuitous availability for whatever reason of a place below the cost that an authority would usually expect to meet, or else by the temporary unavailability of accommodation at the authority's usual price.

7.5 The costs being compared should be gross costs before income from charging. Given the different amounts that authorities will recover from individuals by way of charges it would not be possible to determine a usual net cost an authority would expect to pay.

7.6 Costs will vary around the country. There may be circumstances where an authority might judge the need to move to another part of the country to be an integral part of an individual's assessed needs (eg, in certain cases to be near a relative), and therefore one of the factors to be considered in determining what the authority would usually expect to pay.

7.7 Costs may also vary according to the type of care. For example, the cost an authority might usually expect to pay for respite care might be different from its usual cost for permanent care.

Availability

7.8 A place in an individual's preferred accommodation may not always be available immediately. If the client wishes, authorities should where appropriate be willing to consider making temporary or intermediate arrangements until a place becomes available.

Conditions

7.9 In order to ensure that they are able to exercise proper control over the use of their funds, authorities need to be able to impose certain technical conditions, for example in relation to payment regimes, review, access, monitoring, audit, record keeping, information sharing, insurance, sub-contracting, etc.

7.10 The contract conditions required of preferred accommodation should be broadly the same as those it would impose on any other similar operation. Stricter conditions should never be used as a way of avoiding a placement. As with suitability, account should be taken of the nature and location of the accommodation. There may be reasons why it would be reasonable to adapt standard conditions and unreasonable not to. For example, authorities should take into account the fact that homes in other areas, or those which take residents from many areas, may have geared themselves to the normal requirements of other authorities.

7.11   In setting their usual terms and conditions authorities are reminded that Part II of the Local Government Act 1988 stipulates that they may not specify non-commercial considerations in contracts.

More expensive accommodation

8   The direction also places a duty on authorities to make placements in more expensive accommodation than they would usually expect to, provided there is a third party able and willing to pay the difference. A third party in this case might be a relative (but not a liable relative, see 11.13), a friend, or any other source.

9   This direction applies only where a resident explicitly chooses to enter accommodation other than that which the authority offers them, and where that preferred accommodation is more expensive than the authority would usually expect to pay.

10   This direction does not mean that authorities may set an arbitrary ceiling on the amount they are willing to contribute towards residential care and require third parties routinely to make up the difference. If challenged an authority would need to be able to demonstrate that its usual cost was sufficient to allow it to provide people with the level of service they could reasonably expect, did the possibility of third party contributions not exist.

11   Similarly, the direction is not intended to allow authorities to require third party contributions in cases where the authority itself decides to offer someone a place in unusually expensive accommodation, for example, where there is at the time in question no suitable accommodation available at the authority's 'usual cost'.

Responsibility for costs of accommodation

11.1   When making arrangements for residential care for an individual under the National Assistance Act 1948, an authority is responsible for the full cost of that accommodation. Therefore where an authority places someone in a more expensive accommodation it must contract to pay the accommodation's fees in full. The third party's contribution will be treated as part of the resident's income for charging purposes and the authority will be able to recover it in that way.

11.2   The prospective resident in these cases will therefore need to demonstrate that there is a third party able and willing to pay the difference between the authority's normal cost and the accommodation's actual fees.

11.3   In order to safeguard both residents and authorities from entering arrangements which are likely to fail, the third party must reasonably be expected to be able to continue to contribute for the duration of the arrangements. Authorities should assure themselves that there is every chance that that third party will continue to have the resources to make the required payments.

11.4   Authorities will be aware that under Section 26(3A) of the National Assistance Act 1948 (as inserted by the NHS and Community Care Act 1990) it is open to them to agree with both the resident and the person in charge of their accommodation that instead of paying a contribution to the authority, the resident may pay the same amount direct to the accommodation, with the authority paying the difference. In such a case the third party would also pay the accommodation direct on behalf of the resident. However, it should be noted that even where there is such an agreement for the resident to make direct payments, the authority continues to be liable to pay the full cost of the accommodation should either the resident or relative fail to pay the required amount.

11.5 Authorities should also note that because arrangements under section 26(3A) of the 1948 Act require the agreement of all parties, it would not be reasonable for them to refuse people their preferred accommodation on the grounds that they (or their preferred accommodation) would not enter such an arrangement.

The amount of the third party contribution

11.6 The amount of the third party contribution should be the difference between the actual fee for the accommodation and the amount that otherwise the authority would usually have expected to pay for someone with the individual's assessed needs. In determining this amount the authority should apply the same consideration as above (7.4–7.8), except that in these cases it will need to state a precise figure in each case.

11.7 The amount of the third party contribution should be calculated on gross costs, ie, the difference between the preferred accommodation's fees and the fees that an authority would usually expect to pay. The fact that residents might not have been able to meet the full cost of the accommodation that the authority would otherwise have arranged does not affect their ability to benefit from this part of the direction. When the third party's contribution has been taken into account, the cost net of charges to an authority of the more expensive accommodation should be the same as it would have been in accommodation at the authority's usual price.

Price increases

11.8 Arrangements between the authority, resident and third party will need to be reviewed from time to time to take account of changes to the accommodation's fees and also changes to the amount the authority would usually expect to pay. These may not change at the same rate, and residents and third parties should be told that there cannot be a guarantee that any increases in the accommodation's fees will automatically be shared evenly between the authority and third party should the particular accommodation's fees rise more quickly than the costs the authority would usually expect to pay for similar people. An authority may find it useful to agree with the resident and third party that the third party's contribution will be reviewed on a regular basis.

Responsibilities of residents and third parties

11.9 Authorities should make clear to residents and third parties the basis on which arrangements are to be made when they seek to exercise their right to more expensive preferred accommodation. It should be clear from the outset to the resident, third party and person providing the accommodation:

- that failure to keep up payments will normally result in the resident having to move to other accommodation;
- that an increase in the resident's income will not necessarily lessen the need for a contribution, since the resident's own income will be subject to charging by the authority in the normal way;

- that a rise in the accommodation's fees will not automatically be shared equally between authority and third party;
- that if the accommodation fails to honour its contractual conditions, the authority must reserve the right to terminate the contract.

11.10   Authorities may wish to consider making a binding legal agreement with the third party to this effect, though they should note there are restrictions on the ability of charitable contributors to enter into such contracts.

Suitability and conditions

11.11   The criteria of suitability, and willingness to provide on the basis of normal conditions should be applied in the same way as for other preferred accommodation (para. 7.1 ff).

11.12   An exception to this is that it would be reasonable to expect providers entering this kind of arrangement to agree to do so on the basis that the authority has the right, subject to notice, to terminate the contract should the third party's payment cease or cease to be adequate.

Liable relatives

11.13   Because they may already be obliged to contribute to the cost of accommodation, these arrangements do not apply to relatives liable to contribute to the cost of accommodation under section 42 of the National Assistance Act 1948. In other words, for the purposes of this direction such people cannot act as third parties for the care of the relative to whose care they are already obliged to contribute.

11.14   However, although the direction imposes no legal duty to do so, there is no reason why authorities should not enter into similar arrangements with liable relatives who have the resources both to meet their liability and make an additional third party payment. Indeed, there is no reason why authorities should not, at the request of the resident, arrange more expensive accommodation for someone who can from their own resources afford to pay the additional cost.[1]

People already resident in residential care

12   People already placed by an authority in residential accommodation have the same rights under this direction as those who have yet to be placed. An individual who wishes to move to different or more expensive accommodation may seek to do so on the same basis as anyone about to enter residential care for the first time.

People who are unable to make their own choices

13   There will be cases in which prospective residents are unable to express a preference for themselves. It would be reasonable to expect authorities to act on the preferences expressed by their carers in the same way that they would on the resident's own wishes, unless exceptionally that would be against the best interests of the resident.

---

1   The Department of Health has accepted that this final paragraph was 'misleading', and reaffirmed its view that the NAA 1948 does not permit a resident to use his/her own resources to pay for more expensive accommodation.

Effect on tendering, effect on block contracting

14   Many authorities will already be consulting on, or involved in formal tendering and contracting procedures. As this direction is intended simply to formalise best practice, there should be no conflict between it and arrangements authorities have already made.

15   However, authorities will need to review their arrangements to see if any further action is needed. In particular, where authorities have already published details of their contracting policies, they will need to inform prospective providers of any amendments to that policy required in the light of this direction.

16   For example, where authorities are conducting, or have completed exercises designed to draw up closed lists of approved suppliers they will need to make it clear that as a result of this direction such a list cannot now be regarded as an exhaustive statement of those providers with whom the authority will contract. It would not be reasonable for an authority to use as a test of the suitability of accommodation its presence on or absence from a previously compiled list of approved suppliers. The direction does not, however, prevent an authority having a list of preferred providers with which it will contract where a potential resident expresses no preference for particular accommodation, nor from recommending such providers to prospective residents.

Information

17   For individuals to be able to exercise genuine choice they need information about the options open to them. They should be given fair and balanced information with which to make the best choice of accommodation. Authorities should explain to individuals their rights under this direction. Individuals should be told explicitly that they may allow the authority to make a placement decision on their behalf, that they may choose from a preferred list (if the authority operates such a system) or if they wish that they are free to choose any accommodation which is likely to meet their needs subject to the constraints set out in this direction. Authorities might consider including this in a leaflet for prospective residents and their carers.

Complaints

18   Complaints about the application of this direction and decisions taken in individual cases will fall within the scope of authorities' statutory complaints procedures. As in all aspects of their activity, authorities should ensure that prospective residents are aware of the existence of the complaints procedure and of their rights under it.

Precedents

PRECEDENT 1
COMMUNITY CARE ASSESSMENT REQUEST

To: Director of Social Services / Health Authority / NHS Trust, etc
[address]

From: Applicant's name
[address]

Date

Dear Director of Social Services

Community Care Assessment
Mr Albert Smith [address]

I am the [solicitor/carer/agent/advocate] for the above named who has asked that I assist him in obtaining an assessment of his needs for community care services under s47 NHS & Community Care Act 1990.

Mr Smith is [insert] years of age being born on [insert if known] and is a [disabled/elderly/ill] person, in that he

[here detail as precisely as possible the impairments which have resulted in the applicant needing community care services].

The help that Mr Smith currently envisages as being necessary, is [here detail if possible the services which are required].

I understand that your care manager will wish to contact Mr Smith in order to investigate this complaint. He suggests that this be done by [here give a telephone contact number and the time/days the client or carer, etc, are usually available or some other convenient way that contact can be made]

Yours sincerely

PRECEDENT 2
ACCESS TO INFORMATION LETTER

To: Director of Social Services / Health Authority / NHS Trust, etc
[*address*]

From: *Applicant's name*
[*address*]

Date

Access to Personal Information
Data Protection Act 1998

REQUEST FOR INFORMATION

I formally request that you give me access to the personal information held by your authority relating to my personal circumstances, by copying the relevant information to [*me*] [*my agent, namely* . .] at [*insert address*].

The information I require to be disclosed is all personal information which your authority holds which relates to myself. [*If possible describe as precisely as possible the information that is sought, including for instance where the information is likely to be located, the nature of the information and the dates between which it was collected*].

I understand that I am entitled to receive this information within 40 days. I also understand that you may wish me to pay a fee for the processing and copying of this information and

[I confirm that I am willing to pay such reasonable sum as you may require (subject to the statutory maximum)] or

[in order to expedite matters I enclose a cheque in the sum of £10, being the statutory maximum, and would be grateful if you could refund to me, if appropriate, any excess[1]]

Please confirm receipt of this request.

....

---

1   The 40-day period runs from the date of receipt of the request and any necessary fee. Accordingly, provision should be expedited if the fee is actually enclosed.

PRECEDENT 3
FORMAL COMPLAINT LETTER

To: Director of Social Services
[*address*]

From: *Applicant's name*
[*address*]

Date

Dear Director of Social Services

Formal Complaint
Complaints Procedure Directions 1990

I ask that you treat this letter as a formal complaint concerning the discharge by your authority of its functions in respect of [*myself*] [*the person for whom I care – Mr/Mrs/Ms etc . . .*]

I require the complaint to be investigated under Stage 2 of the Complaints process in accordance with direction 6(1) of the above directions and paragraph 4.9 of 'The Right to Complain' (HMSO, 1991).

My complaint is:
[*here set out as precisely as possible:*

a)   what it is that is being complained about;
b)   the names of the key social workers whom the complaints investigator will need to speak to;
c)   the dates of the relevant acts/omissions.

If possible also enclose copies of any relevant papers.]

What I want to achieve by making this complaint is
[*here set out as precisely as possible what you want to be the result of your complaint: ie, an apology, a changed service provision, an alteration to practice, compensation, etc*]

I understand that your complaints receiving officer will wish to contact me in order to investigate this complaint. I suggest that this be done by [*here give a telephone contact number and the time/days you are normally available or some other convenient way you can be contacted*]

....

Index

Abuse of power, 12.110–12.111
Accommodation. *See also* Hostels,
Nursing homes, Residential
accommodation, Residential
care homes
assistance in finding, 5.27, 5.39
domiciliary services, 5.27, 5.39
Adaptations to the home
access, facilitating, 10.32
additional facilities, 5.68–5.69
alternatives, 10.24, 10.26
amenities, 10.32
assessment of needs, 10.26
assistance, 5.60–5.61
bathrooms, 10.23
bedrooms, 10.33
carers, 7.32
circulars, 5.64
delay, 5.62–5.64
dependants, 10.37
disabled people, 5.60–5.69, 7.32,
10.13, 10.19–10.47
domiciliary services, 5.39,
5.49–5.50, 5.60–5.69
employment, 10.38
fixtures and fittings, 10.39–10.40
food preparation, 10.35
grants, 5.63, 10.13, 10.19–10.47
guidance, 5.39, 5.61, 5.66–5.67,
5.69, 10.24, 10.27, 10.31
heating, 10.36
housing authorities, 5.63–5.64,
10.25–10.26, 10.39–10.40
judicial review, 12.106
kitchens, 10.35

lighting, 10.36
local government ombudsman,
5.62–5.63
maladministration, 5.62
'necessary and appropriate',
10.25–10.27
occupational therapists, 5.62
power, 10.36
reasonableness, 10.24
resources, 10.42
safe, making dwelling, 10.31
sleeping, rooms usable for,
10.33
social services authorities,
5.63–5.64, 5.66–5.67,
10.25–10.26, 10.39–10.40
Adjustment to disability, 5.26
Adult abuse, 7.89–7.91
Advice notes, 1.30
Advocacy, 7.1–7.2, 7.56–7.62
assessment of needs, 3.37, 3.39,
7.58
charges, 8.103
citizens, 7.61–7.62
crisis, 7.60
decision-making, 7.62
disabled people, 7.61–7.62
guidance, 7.57, 7.59
local authorities, 7.59
complaints procedure, 12.17
reform, 7.59
role, 7.58
After-care services
care in the community, 5.126
charges, 8.109

501

After-care services *continued*
mental hospitals, 5.109,
5.115–5.116, 5.124–5.125, 8.109
National Health Service, 6.61
supervision, 5.126
Age
domiciliary services, 5.12, 5.87
expectant or nursing mothers,
4.14
residential accommodation, 4.11,
4.14
AIDS/HIV
alcohol dependency, 9.17,
9.28–9.35
drugs, 9.17, 9.28–9.35
expenditure, 9.32
grants, 9.31–9.35
guidance, 9.30–9.31, 9.35
homelessness, 10.17
Alcohol dependency, 9.1–9.35
AIDS/HIV, 9.17, 9.28–9.35
assessment of needs, 9.5
Christian philosophy houses, 9.17
commissioning of services,
9.6–9.11, 9.25, 9.33
community care services,
9.23–9.25
competition, distortion of, 9.8–9.9
counselling, 9.25
directions, 9.3
domiciliary services, 5.23
emergency action, 9.5
expenditure, 9.26–9.27, 9.32
general houses, 9.17
grants, 9.3, 9.26–9.27, 9.31–9.35
guidance, 9.1–9.5, 9.10, 9.15,
9.20–9.21, 9.24, 9.26, 9.30–9.31,
9.35
health authorities, 9.18–9.22,
9.28, 9.35
heavy drinkers' houses, 9.17
illness, 5.97
Minnesota method units, 9.17
National Health Service,
9.18–9.22
nursing homes, 9.12–9.22, 9.28
probation, 9.5

provision of services, 9.6–9.11
purchaser consortia, 9.7–9.9
referrals, 9.5
rehabilitation, 9.17, 9.25
residential accommodation, 4.15,
4.25, 9.10
residential care homes, 9.12–9.22,
9.28
residential units focusing on
harm minimisation, 9.17
service user failure, 9.10–9.11
shared care, 9.22
social services authorities,
9.14–9.18, 9.20
therapeutic communities, 9.17
unfair trade practices, 9.8–9.9
Allocation panels, 3.76–3.77
Appeals
charges, 8.101–8.103
data protection, 2.38
Appliances, 6.67–6.70, 6.73
Assessment of needs, I.23,
3.1–3.102
adaptations to the home, 10.26
advocacy, 3.37, 3.39, 7.58
alcohol dependency, 9.5
appropriate settings, 3.34
care plans, 3.2, 3.55, 3.84–3.100,
10.8–10.13
carers, 3.9, 7.6, 7.10–7.29, 7.34,
7.54–7.55
charges, 8.21, 8.105
children, 3.56, 11.4, 11.6–11.9
circulars, 3.3
collaboration, 10.8–10.13
communication difficulties,
3.37–3.43
confidentiality, 3.38
copies, 3.55
criteria,
eligibility, 3.59–3.84
minimum, 3.23–3.25
day centres, 5.53
decision-making, 3.57–3.58
delay, 3.28–3.30
delegation, 3.50
delivery of services, 3.41

Assessment of needs *continued*
direct payments, 5.143
directions, 3.18
disabled people, 3.3–3.5, 3.35,
3.56, 5.48, 10.13
discretion, 3.32, 3.52, 3.102
domiciliary services, 5.48, 5.53
drugs, 9.5
fast-track, 3.102, 9.5
form of, 3.18, 3.53
general duty, 3.6
guidance, 3.19–3.21, 3.31–3.42,
3.50–3.55, 3.101
homelessness, 3.13–3.14
housing, 10.5, 10.8–10.13
implied duties, 3.3
information, 3.24, 3.41
interviews, 3.23
knowledge, 3.12–3.13
letters, 3.11
local government ombudsman,
3.37–3.38
maladministration, 3.28
mental disabilities, 3.37–3.43
National Health Service, 6.58
nature of, 3.18
negotiation scope of, 3.32–3.33
ordinary residence, 3.17
potential service users, 3.35–3.43,
3.54, 3.56
practice guidance, 3.31–3.42,
3.51–3.55
priorities, 3.28–3.29
process, 3.1–3.2, 3.18
reassessment, 3.101
refusal, 3.15, 3.68
requests, right, 3.5
resources, 3.25, 3.59–3.84
reviews, 3.101
risk assessment, 3.61
screening, 3.19–3.22, 3.24
settings, appropriate, 3.34
third parties, 3.50
time when duty arises, 3.8–3.17
timescale, 3.26–3.30, 3.33
triggering, 3.9, 3.12–3.13
user involvement, 3.35–3.36

withdrawal, 3.43
without assessment, provision
without, 3.102
written records, 3.52–3.55
Assistance
adaptations to the home,
5.60–5.61
domiciliary services, 5.49–5.50
Asylum-seekers
default procedure, 12.120
destitution, 4.5, 4.16–4.20, 5.40,
5.91
dispersal, 4.20
domiciliary services, 5.40, 5.91
vouchers, 4.19
Attendance allowance, 8.89–8.95

Bankruptcy, 8.46–8.47
Beveridge Report, I.13
Blind people, 5.15–5.16
Budget, I.3
alcohol dependency, 9.27
drugs, 9.27
National Health Service, 6.15,
6.17, 6.138, 6.140–6.142,
6.146–6.152
primary care trusts, 6.17

Capital
charges, 8.18–8.22, 8.29–8.50,
8.65
deliberate deprivation of,
8.36–8.50
deprivation of, 8.29–8.50
diminishing notional capital rule,
8.35, 8.44
disregard, 4.9, 8.19–8.21
enforcement powers, 8.40–8.50
guidance, 4.9, 8.31
liable relatives, 8.65
means-testing, 8.19
property, 8.22
residential accommodation, 4.9,
8.19–8.20, 8.43–8.47
spouses, 8.20–8.22
timing of the disposal, 8.33–8.34
transfers, 8.43–8.47
treatment of, 8.18–8.22

Car stickers, 5.59
Care and attention
  bodily functions, assistance with,
    4.5
  client group, 4.10–4.26
  needs, 4.5
  personal care, 4.5
  residential accommodation,
    4.5–4.27
Care in the community, I.20,
    5.126–5.137
  after-care, 5.126
  care programme approach,
    5.129–5.135
  circulars, 5.129, 5.132
  codes of practice, 5.134
  grants, 5.136–5.137
  guidance, 5.128, 5.136
  health authorities, 5.129
  Patients' Charter, 5.135
  social services authorities, 5.129
  supervision, 5.126–5.127
Care plans
  annual, 2.13
  assessment of needs, 3.2, 3.55,
    3.84–3.100, 10.8–10.13
  Audit Commission, 2.16
  carers, 7.8
  Caring for People, 2.12
  choice between alternative,
    3.89–3.97
  circulars, 2.11, 10.12
  collaboration, 10.8–10.13
  copies, 3.55
  definition, 3.85–3.87
  disabled people, 2.10,3.96, 3.98
  discretion, 3.97
  domiciliary care, 3.93, 3.97
  duty, 2.1, 2.3–2.16
  expenditure, 3.91–3.92, 3.97
  form of, 3.85
  guidance, 2.13–2.15, 3.84, 3.88,
    3.90, 3.95
  health authorities, 2.15
  housing, 10.8–10.13
    authorities, 10.8–10.13
  information, 2.19–2.20

  joint, 2.15
  National Health Service,
    2.15–2.16
  objectives, 3.88
  preparation, 2.10–2.14
  psychological needs, 3.89
  reforms, 3.95
  refusal of services, 3.98
  registration, 2.4–2.9
  resources, 3.65
  social services authorities, 2.1,
    2.3–2.16, 10.8–10.13
  unmet needs, 3.99–3.100
Carers, 7.1–7.56
  adaptations to the home, 7.32
  assessment of needs, 3.9, 7.6,
    7.10–7.31, 7.34, 7.54–7.55
  care plans, 7.8
  children, 7.27, 7.31, 7.36,
    7.47–7.56, 11.1
  client groups., 7.41
  definition, 7.7–7.9
  dependants, 7.46
  deportation, 7.6
  direct payments, 7.45
  directions, 7.29
  disabled people, 7.32, 7.39, 7.47
  domiciliary services, 5.49, 7.37,
    7.43
  emotional support, 7.19
  employed, 7.25
  expenditure, 7.35, 7.40
  guidance, 7.5, 7.8, 7.10, 7.12,
    7.16–7.24, 7.29–7.31, 7.49, 7.53
  illness, 7.38
  local authorities, 7.33, 7.56
  mental disabilities, 7.5
  National Health Service, 7.24
  needs, 7.30
  night-sitter services, 7.44
  number of, 7.3
  parents, 7.47
  reform, 7.45
  regular and substantial amounts
    of care, 7.11–7.29
  respite care, 7.33, 7.42
  services for, 7.32–7.56

Carers *continued*
 shared care, 7.33, 7.42
 short term breaks, 7.33
 social security benefits, 7.25
 social services authorities, 7.32,
  7.37, 7.49–7.50
 support for, I.27, 7.5, 7.19, 7.45
 time off work, 7.46
 voluntary organisations, 7.25
 white paper, 7.4
 young, 7.27, 7.31, 7.48–7.56
Cautions, 8.48–8.50
Charges, 8.1–8.118. *See also* **Fees**
 advocacy, 8.103
 after-care services, 8.109
 amount, 8.80–8.82
 appeals, 8.101–8.103
 arrears, 8.11
 assessment of, 8.9–8.26, 8.76,
  8.83–8.98
  needs, 8.21, 8.105
 attendance allowance, 8.89–8.95
 bankruptcy, 8.46–8.47
 capital, 8.65
  deliberate deprivation of,
  8.36–8.50
  deprivation of, 8.29–8.50
  diminishing notional capital
  rule, 8.35, 8.44
  enforcement powers, 8.40–8.50
  timing of the disposal,
  8.33–8.34
  transfers, 8.43–8.47
  treatment of, 8.18–8.22
 cautions, 8.48–8.50
 challenging, 8.66, 8.99–8.103
 charges, 8.48–8.50
 children, 8.68, 8.117–8.118,
  11.26–11.30
 circulars, 8.70
 client groups, 8.117
 complaints, 8.99
 consequences of, 8.76
 consultation, 8.78–8.79
 contributions, 8.9–8.11
 couples, 8.20–8.22, 8.63–8.65
 deterrence, 8.76

disability discrimination,
  8.93–8.95
 disability living allowance,
  8.89–8.95
 disabled people, 8.28, 8.68,
  8.89–8.95, 8.117–8.118
 discretion, 8.7, 8.13, 8.22, 8.62,
  8.67, 8.73–8.77, 8.102, 8.104,
  12.57
 disregard, 8.19
 domiciliary services, 5.77, 8.118,
  11.26–11.28
 duties, 8.1
 elderly people, 8.38, 8.54
 enforcement, 8.40–8.50, 11.28
 expenditure, 8.12–8.13, 8.90
 follow-up, 8.76
 Good Practice Handbook,
  8.71–8.72, 8.76, 8.78, 8.83–8.85,
  8.88, 8.90, 8.92, 8.100, 8.103,
  8.105
 grants, 8.51
 guardianship, 8.112–8.115
 guidance, 8.8, 8.31, 8.70–8.78,
  8.82–8.92, 8.96–8.100, 8.103,
  8.107, 8.110, 8.116
 hearings, 8.101–8.103
 human rights, 8.114
 income, 8.14–8.17, 8.26, 8.65,
  8.96–8.98
 income support, 8.32, 8.38, 8.51,
  8.86–8.88
  residential allowance, 8.27–8.28
 increase in, 8.79
 Independent Living Allowance,
  8.89
 information, 8.83–8.85, 8.96,
  8.101
 joint beneficial ownership,
  8,23–8.25
 less dependent relatives,
  8.56–8.59
 liable relatives, 8.15, 8.63–8.65
 local authorities, 8.4, 8.6, 8.9,
  8.11, 8.15, 8.21–8.22, 8.25, 8.34
  children, 11.26–11.27, 11.30
  complaints procedure, 12.57

Charges
local authorities *continued*
deliberate deprivation of capital,
8.36–8.50
residential homes, 8.51–8.55
local government ombudsman,
8.76, 8.78, 8.101
local schemes, 8.78–8.79
maximum, 8.6, 8.81
means-testing, 8.7–8.8, 8.19, 8.83,
8.88, 8.96–8.97
mental disabilities, 5.101
mental hospitals, 5.123–5.124,
8.2, 8.109–8.110
National Health Service, 6.45
non-accommodation services,
8.67–8.118
non-payment, consequences of,
8.104–8.106
nursing homes, 8.1, 8.52
occupational pensions, 8.17
pensions, 8.17
personal allowances, 8.7,
8.12–8.13, 8.56, 8.58–8.59
private providers, 8.77
profits, 8.81
property, 8.22–8.26, 8.48–8.50
reasonableness, 8.62, 8.73, 8.80,
8.82–8.83, 8.87, 8.91
recovery, 8.105–8.106
reduction, 8.102
reform, 8.51
regulations, 1.13, 8.8
relatives, 8.15, 8.63–8.65
residential accommodation,
8.1–8.66, 8.111
children, 11.30
less dependent residents,
8.56–8.59
temporary residents, 8.60–8.62
residential care homes, 8.52
residential property, 8.22–8.26
resources, 8.8, 8.21
self-funding, 8.21
small claims, 8.106
social security, 8.27–8.28, 8.32,
8.38, 8.51, 8.86–8.95

social services authorities,
8.1–8.2, 8.4, 8.54
services not provided by,
8.107
spouses, 8.20–8.22, 8.63–8.65
temporary residents, 8.60–8.62
tenants, 8.26
third parties, 8.98
topping up, 8.55
variation, 8.7
waiver, 8.102
withdrawal of services,
8.104–8.105
Children
adulthood, transition into,
11.21–11.25
assessment of needs, 3.56, 11.4,
11.6–11.9
carers, 7.27, 7.31, 7.36, 7.47–7.56,
11.1
charges, 8.68, 8.118, 11.26–11.30
Children Act 1989, 11.1–11.30
community-based services, 11.20,
11.26–11.28
continuing care under NHS,
6.85–6.86
data protection, 2.26
direct payments, 5.143
disabled people, 2.9, 3.56, 5.6,
5.46–5.47, 5.58, 5.78–5.79,
5.143, 7.47, 8.68, 8.118
adulthood, transition into,
11.21–11.22
assessment of needs, 11.6
definition, 11.3
domiciliary services, 11.20
register of, 11.5, 11.9
services for, 11.11
discretion, 11.14
domiciliary services, 5.6,
5.78–5.79, 8.118, 11.20,
11.26–11.28
education authorities, 11.24
guidance, 11.8–11.9, 11.11,
11.16–11.18, 11.25
homelessness, 10.14, 10.18,
11.5–11.19

Children *continued*
housing, 11.12–11.14
authorities, 11.18
local authorities, 11.26–11.27,
11.30
complaints procedure,
12.58–12.59
needs, 11.1–11.30
ordinary residence, 4.34
residential accommodation, 4.95,
11.30
residential care homes,
11.12–11.14
services, 11.10–11.20
social services authorities, 11.1,
11.14, 11.18, 11.24–11.25, 11.29
travel, 5.58
**Chronically Sick and Disabled
Persons Act 1970**, I.17–I.19,
I.22, 1.7–1.9, 5.3, 5.41–5.79
Circulars
access to, 6.44
adaptations to the home, 5.64
assessment of needs, 3.3
care in the community, 5.129,
5.132
care plans, 2.11, 10.12
carers, 7.18, 7.20
charges, 8.70
closure, 4.81
continuing care under NHS, 6.89,
6.92
data protection, 2.21
departing from, 6.42
directions, 1.19
disabled people, 10.13
domiciliary services,   5.34
guidance, 1.20
information, 2.19
National Health Service,
6.39–6.42, 6.44, 6.50
Orange Badge Scheme, 5.59
ordinary residence, 4.29
residential accommodation, 4.81
Citizen advocacy, 7.61–7,62
Clients
care and attention, 4.10–4.26

carers, 7.41
charges, 8.117
domiciliary services, 5.13–5.23,
5.35–5.37, 5.44–5.47, 5.76,
5.82–5.90
mental hospitals, 5.103
residential accommodation,
4.10–4.26
Closures
circulars, 4.81
consultation, 4.78, 4.80, 4.82, 6.51
continuing care under NHS, 6.75
decision-making, 6.37
elderly, 4.76, 4.79–4.82
European Convention on Human
Rights, 4.82, 12.128, 12.139
guidance, 6.62
hospitals, I.20, 6.37, 6.51–6.53,
6.137
learning disabilities, 6.137
long stay NHS accommodation,
4.77
mental hospitals, I.23
nursing homes, 4.76–4.82
residential accommodation,
4.76–4.82
residential care homes, 6.53
transfers, 4.78
Codes of practice
care in the community, 5.134
mental hospitals, 5.111
National Health Service,
6.153–6.156
openness, 6.153–6.156
Compensation
delay, 12.71
local authorities complaints
procedure, 12.38–12.40
local government ombudsman,
12.38–12.39, 12.70–12.71
Competition, 9.8–9.9
Complaints, 12.4. *See also* **Local
authorities complaints
procedure, Local government
ombudsman**
advice, 6.173
booklet on, 6.157

Complaints *continued*
charges, 8.99
complaints manager, 6.163
continuing care under NHS, 6.80,
    6.117, 6.126, 6.128
convenors, 6.164, 6.171–6.176
directions, 6.157
excluded matters, 6.166
expenditure, 6.172
general practitioners, 6.160, 6.168
guidance, 6.161, 6.166–6.169,
    6.173, 6.175
health authorities, 6.166–6.167
Health Service Ombudsmen,
    6.173, 6.178–6.181
independent review panels, 6.165,
    6.170–6.179
composition, 6.175
judicial review, 12.83–12.84,
    12.87–12.90
local authorities monitoring
    officers, 12.83–12.84
National Health Service,
    6.153–6.179
negligence, 6.166
personnel, 6.163–6.165
reports, 6.177–6.179
stage one, 6.166–6.169
stage two, 6.170–6.179
standing, 6.159–6.160
time limits, 6.161–6.162, 6.170,
    6.172
trusts, 6.166–6.167
Confidentiality
assessment of needs, 3.38
data protection, 2.30
Consultants, 6.72–6.74, 6.123
Continuing care under the NHS,
    6.75–6.137
children, 6.85
circulars, 6.89, 6.92
closure, 6.75, 6.137
complaints, 6.80, 6.117, 6.126,
    6.128
complex, intense or
    unpredictable, 6.94–6.97
consultants, 6.123

die in near future, likely to,
    6.98–6.100
directions, 6.126
discharge,
    planning, 6.126–6.128
    premature, 6.78, 6.122
    procedures, 6.78, 6.122–6.125
    reviews, 6.129–6.136
eligibility criteria, 6.83, 6.104,
    6.111, 6.133
funding, 6.77, 6.112
guidance, 6.81–6.85, 6.93,
    6.98–6.104, 6.108–6.118,
    6.124–6.131, 6.136–6.137
health authorities, 6.83–6.84,
    6.87, 6.93, 6.95–6.100, 6.107,
    6.113–6.121, 6.133–6.136
Health Service Ombudsman,
    6.78–6.80, 6.117, 6.119, 6.121,
    6.127
hospitals, 6.78, 6.126
income support, 6.76
incontinence supplies,
    6.119–6.121
information, 6.126–6.128, 6.130
in-patient care, 6.87–6.100
intensive services, 6.116–6.121
learning difficulties, 6.85–6.86,
    6.137
local authorities, 6.76, 6.93,
    6.135
long-term care, 6.76, 6.80, 6.105
medical equipment, 6.117–6.118
mental disabilities, 6.85–6.86
needs, 6.82–6.100
nursing homes, 6.76–6.80,
    6.92–6.93, 6.97, 6.116–6.121,
    6.129
palliative health care, 6.112–6.115
premature discharges, 6.78, 6.122
recovery, 6.101–6.105
rehabilitation, 6.101–6.105, 6.109
residential accommodation,
    6.92–6.93
residential care homes, 6.119,
    6.129
respite health care, 6.106–6.111

Continuing care under the NHS
continued
social services authorities, 6.81,
6.97, 6.114
specialist care, 6.90–6.93,
6.116–6.121
statements of local policies, 6.83
Correspondence, right to,
12.138–12.141
Costs. *See* **Charges, Expenditure**
Counselling, 9.25
Court of Protection, 2.28, 7.69
Criminal offences
adult abuse, 7.90
local authorities complaints
procedure, 12.52
mental disabilities, 7.90
mental hospitals, 5.105–5.108
staff, 12.52
Crisis advocacy, 7.60

Data protection, 2.21–2.39
access, 2.22–2.39
'accessible public records', 2.22
agents, 2.39
amendments, 2.32
appeals, 2.38
children, 2.26
circulars, 2.21
conditions of health, 2.37
confidentiality, 2.30
copies, 2.33
Court of Protection, 2.28
crime prevention or detection,
2.37
Data Protection Commissioner,
2.21, 2.38
data protection principles, 2.23
deletion, 2.32
disclosure, 2.25, 2.29–2.34
enduring powers of attorney,
2.28
exemptions, 2.36–2.37
guidance, 2.21, 2.28–2.30, 2.36
fees, 2.34
joint records, 2.24
mental disabilities, 2.27–2.30

people, requests made through
other, 2.39
procedure, 2.31–2.34
repeated requests, 2.34
social work, 2.37
third parties, 2.29, 2.35–2.36,
2.39
Damages, 1.4. *See also*
Compensation
Day centres, 5.53, 5.97
Deaf people, 5.17–5.18
Decision-making
advocates, 7.62
assessment of needs, 3.57–3.58
disabled people, 7.62
closure, 6.37
facts, not in accordance with,
12.101
judicial review, 12.77–12.83,
12.86, 12.91, 12.94–12.95,
12.99–12.103, 12.106,
12.113–12.115
mental disabilities, 7.63–7.91
mental hospitals, 7.64–7.65
National Health Service, 6.35
Default procedures, 12.116–12.120
asylum-seekers, 12.120
decision-making, 12.117
judicial review, 12.87–12.88
local authorities, 12.116–12.118
Secretary of State, 12.118–12.119
**Definition of community care
services,** I.3, I.21–I.22
Delay
adaptations to the home,
5.62–5.64
assessment of needs, 3.28–3.30
compensation, 12.71
local authorities complaints
procedure, 12.40
local government ombudsman,
12.71, 12.72
Delegated legislation, 1.13–1.14
Delegation
assessment of needs, 3.50
judicial review, 12.106
unlawful, 12.106

Dependants
adaptations to the home, 10.37
carers, 7.46
definition, 7.46
time off, 7.46
Destitution, 4.5, 4.16–4.20, 5.40,
5.91
Detention. *See* **Mental hospitals**
Direct payments
amount, 5.143
assessment of needs, 5.143
carers, 7.45
children, 5.143
disabled people, 5.140–5.143
discretion, 5.143
domiciliary services, 5.28,
5.138–5.151
exclusions, 5.143
guidance, 5.143
Independent Living Fund, 5.139,
5.144–5.151
managing, 5.143
powers, 5.139
prohibited services, 5.143
recipients, obligations of, 5.143
relatives, services from, 5.143
residential care homes, 5.143
social services authorities, 5.139
third parties, 5.140–5.141
Directions, 1.16–1.19
alcohol dependency, 9.3
assessment of needs, 3.18
carers, 7.29
circulars, 1.19
complaints, 6.157
domiciliary services, 5.9, 5.11,
5.25–5.27, 5.38, 5.84, 5.93,
5.95–5.96
drugs, 9.3
guidance and, 1.16, 1.19
illness, 5.95–5.97
local authorities complaints
procedure, 12.9–12.10, 12.12,
12.17–12.19, 12.22–12.26, 12.32
National Health Service, 6.148
complaints, 6.157
publication, 1.17–1.18

residential accommodation, 4.3,
4.55, 4.60–4.61
Secretary of State, 1.17
Director of social services, 1.10
Disability living allowance,
8.89–8.95
Disabled people. *See also* **Mental
disabilities**
adaptations to the home,
5.60–5.69, 7.32, 10.13,
10.19–10.47
adjustment to disability, 5.26
advocates, 7.61–7.62
assessment of needs, 3.3–3.5,
3.35, 3.56, 5.48, 10.13
blind people, 5.45–5.47
car stickers, 5.59
care plans, 2.10, 3.96, 3.98
carers, 7.32, 7.39, 7.47
charges, 8.28, 8.68, 8.89–8.95,
8.117–8.118, 8.68, 8.93–8.95,
8.118
children, 2.9, 3.56, 5.6, 5.46–5.47,
5.58–5.59, 5.78–5.79, 5.143,
7.47, 8.68, 8.118
adulthood, transition into,
11.21–11.22
assessment of needs, 11.6
definition, 11.3
domiciliary services, 11.20
register of, 11.5, 11.9
services for, 11.11
circulars, 10.13
deaf people, 5.17–5.18
decision-making, 7.62
direct payments, 5.140–5.143
discrimination, 8.93–8.95, 10.17
domiciliary services, 5.6,
5.15–5.23, 5.26–5.27, 5.41–5.99,
8.118
dumb people, 5.19
duty to provide services,
crystallisation of, I.22
education, 5.54–5.56
facilities, 10.13, 10.19–10.47,
12.106
grants, 10.12, 10.19–10.47, 12.106

Disabled people *continued*
guidance, 5.22, 10.21
holidays, 5.70
homelessness, 10.15–10.17
housing, 10.1, 10.12
housing authorities, 10.4, 10.21,
10.23–10.27
Independent Living Fund,
5.144–5.151
information, 2.17–2.39, 5.27
judicial review, 12.106
meals, 5.71
National Health Service,
5.80–5.99
obligatory services, I.18–I.19
Orange Badge Scheme, 5.59
parking, 5.59
priorities, I.13
registration, 2.4–2.9, 11.5, 11.9
residential accommodation, 4.13,
4.90, 4.93–4.94
resources, I.13, 3.71, 3.75
severe or appreciable handicap,
2.9
substantially and permanently
handicapped, 5.22, 5.80, 10.20,
11.4
telephones, 5.72
travel, 5.58–5.59
very severe handicap, 2.9
workshops, 4.93–4.94
Disciplinary procedure, 12.51–12.52
Discretion
assessment of needs, 3.32, 3.52,
3.102
care plans, 3.97
charges, 8.7, 8.13, 8.22, 8.62, 8.67,
8.73–8.77, 8.102, 8.104, 12.57
children, 11.14
direct payments, 5.143
domiciliary services, 5.39
fettering, 1.3, 3.97, 3.102, 4.58,
6.37, 11.14, 12.104–12.105
information, 2.18
judicial review, 12.104–12.105
local authorities complaints
procedure, 12.10–12.11

National Health Service, 6.37
residential accommodation, 4.58
social services authorities, 1.3,
1.11
Discrimination
charges, 8.93–8.95
disabled people, 8.93–8.95, 10.17
European Convention on Human
Rights, 12.130, 12.142
homelessness, 10.17
inhuman or degrading treatment,
12.130
racial, 12.130
sex, 12.130, 12.142
Diseases, 12.134–12.136
Disregard
capital, 4.9, 8.19–8.21
guidance, 4.9
pensions, 8.17
residential accommodation, 4.9,
8.19
Domiciliary care, 5.1–5.151
accommodation, assistance in
finding, 5.27, 5.39
adaptations to the home, 5.39,
5.49–5.50, 5.60–5.69
age, 5.12, 5.87
alcohol dependency, 5.23
assessment of needs, 5.48, 5.53
asylum-seekers, 5.40, 5.91
blind people, 5.15–5.16
car stickers, 5.59
care plans, 3.93, 3.97
carers, 5.49, 7.37, 7.43
charges, 5.77, 11.26–11.28
children, 5.6, 5.46–5.47, 5.58,
5.78–5.79, 11.20, 11.26–11.30
Children Act 1989, 5.78–5.79,
11.20
Chronically Sick and Disabled
Persons 1970, , 5.3–5.4,
5.41–5.79
circulars, 5.34
client groups, 5.13–5.23,
5.35–5.37, 5.44–5.47, 5.76,
5.82–5.90
deaf people, 5.17–5.18

Domiciliary care *continued*
direct payments, 5.28,
5.138–5.151
directions, 5.10–5.11, 5.25–5.27,
5.38, 5.84, 5.93–5.96
disabled people, 5.6, 5.15–5.23,
5.26, 5.41–5.99
adjustment to, 5.26
car stickers, 5.59
information, 5.27
discretion, 5.39
drug dependency, 5.23
dumb people, 5.19
duties, 5.26
target, 5.10
educational facilities, 5.52–5.56
elderly, 5.35–5.37, 5.39, 5.89
exclusions, 5.40, 5.91
expectant or nursing mothers,
5.85, 5.88, 5.94
general practitioners, 6.66
guidance, 5.22, 5.26
holidays, 5.70
homes, 5.27, 5.70
home help and adaptations, 5.39,
5.49–5.50, 5.60–5.69, 5.75, 5.83,
5.98
hostels, 5.26
illness, 5.23, 5.80–5.81, 5.83,
5.86–5.87, 5.95–5.97
information, 5.27, 5.39
laundry services, 5.99
legislation, 5.4–5.40
libraries, 5.51
limitations, 5.38
meals, 5.39, 5.71
mental disabilities, 5.20–5.21,
5.80, 5.86, 5.100–5.137
Mental Health Act 1983,
5.100–5.126
National Assistance Act 1948,
5.9–5.40, 5.73–5.77
National Health Service Act 1977,
5.29–5.34, 5.80–5.99
occupational, social, cultural and
recreational facilities, 5.26
Orange Badge Scheme, 5.59

ordinary residence, 5.12, 5.26,
5.37, 5.43
partially-sighted people, 5.15
powers, 5.27, 5.39
radios, 5.51
recreation, 5.39, 5.51–5.53
registration, 5.14, 5.16, 5.26
rehabilitation, 5.26
residential accommodation, 4.6,
4.12, 5.92
services, 5.24–5.34
social work, 5.26, 5.39
substantially and permanently
handicapped, 5.22, 5.80
telephones and ancillary
equipment, 5.72
televisions, 5.51
travel, 5.39, 5.57–5.59
free or subsidised, 5.27
warden costs, subsidy on, 5.27,
5.39
workshops, 5.26
Dowry payments, 6.149–6.150
Drugs
AIDS/HIV, 9.17, 9.28–9.35
assessment of needs, 9.5
Christian philosophy houses,
9.17
commissioning of services,
9.6–9.11, 9.25, 9.33
community care services,
9.23–9.25
competition, distortion of, 9.8–9.9
consultants, 6.73–6.74
counselling, 9.25
dependency, 4.15, 4.25, 5.23, 5.97,
9.1–9.35
directions, 9.3
domiciliary services, 5.23
emergency action, 9.5
expenditure, 9.26–9.27, 9.32
general houses, 9.17
general practitioners, 6.67–6.70
grants, 9.3, 9.26–9.27, 9.31–9.35
guidance, 6.74, 9.1–9.5, 9.10,
9.15, 9.20–9.21, 9.24, 9.26,
9.30–9.31, 9.35

Drugs *continued*
health authorities, 9.18–9.22, 9.28, 9.35
heavy drinkers' houses, 9.17
hospitals, 6.73–6.74
illness, 5.97
Minnesota method units, 9.17
National Health Service, 9.18–9.22
nursing homes, 9.12–9.22, 9.28
obligation to provide, 6.67–6.70
probation, 9.5
provision of services, 9.6–9.11
purchaser consortia, 9.7–9.9
referrals, 9.5
rehabilitation, 9.17, 9.25
residential accommodation, 4.15, 4.25, 9.10
residential care homes, 9.12–9.22, 9.28
residential units focusing on harm minimisation, 9.17
restricting, 6.74
service user failure, 9.10–9.11
shared care, 9.22
social services authorities, 9.14–9.18, 9.20
therapeutic communities, 9.17
unfair trade practices, 9.8–9.9
Dumb people, 5.19
Duties. *See also* **Assessment of needs**
care plans, 2.3–2.16
damages, 1.6
domiciliary services, 5.10
individuals, to, 1.4
information, 2.17–2.39
inspection, 4.62–4.71
mental disabilities, 5.96
mental hospitals, 5.120–5.125
public law, 1.4–1.9
residential accommodation, 4.21–4.28
social service authorities, 1.2–1.12, 10.40
individuals, to, 1.4
information, 2.17–2.39

planning, 2.3–2.16
public law, 1.4–1.9
staff levels, 1.11
statutory, 1.2–1.12
target, 1.5–1.9, 5.10
Dwelling houses, 8.22–8.26

EC law, 4.85
Education
authorities, 11.24
children, 11.24
disabled people, 5.54–5.56
domiciliary services, 5.53–5.56
learning difficulties, 5.55
Elderly people, I.19
charges, 8.54
closure, 4.76, 4.79–4.82
domiciliary services, 5.35–5.36, 5.89
European Convention on Human Rights, 12.140
guidance, 5.36
homelessness, 10.15, 10.17
information, 5.39
meals, 5.39
residential accommodation, 4.11, 4.76, 4.78–4.82
social security benefits, 8.38
Eligibility
assessment of needs, 3.59–3.84
grants, 10.28, 10.39–10.40, 10.42–10.45
means-testing, 10.43–10.45
resources, 3.59–3.84
unmet need, 3.99
Employment and adaptations to the home, 10.38
Enduring powers of attorney, 2.28–2.29, 7.67, 7.73–7.76, 7.88
Environmental health departments, 4.72–4.74
Equipment, 6.117–6.118
European Convention on Human Rights, I.16, 12.121–12.146
adult abuse, 7.91
closures, 4.82, 12.128, 12.139

European Convention on Human Rights *continued*
correspondence, right to,
12.138–12.141
declarations of incompatibility,
12.124–12.125
discrimination, 12.130, 12.142
elderly people, 12.140
European Court of Human
Rights, 12.145–12.146
ex parte applications, 12.135
exhaustion of domestic remedies,
12.145
fair hearings, 12.137
family life, right to,
12.138–12.141
home, right to, 12.138–12.141
importance of, 12.122
infectious diseases,
12.134–12.136
inhuman or degrading treatment,
12.129–12.130
judicial review, 12.78
legislation, 12.123–12.124
liberty, right to, 12.131
life, right to, 4.82, 12.128
local authorities complaints
procedure, 12.59
main rights, 12.128–12.144
mental disabilities, 7.91, 12.132,
12.143
mental hospitals, 12.132
possessions, right to enjoyment
of, 12.144
privacy, 12.133, 12.138–12.141
racial discrimination, 12.130
registration, 12.140–12.141
remedies, 12.2, 12.145
residential accommodation, 4.82
residential care homes,
12.140–12.141, 12.144
sex discrimination, 12.130,
12.142
European Union, 4.85
Ex parte applications, 12.135
Exhaustion of domestic remedies,
12.145

Expenditure. *See also* **Budget,
Resources**
AIDS/HIV, 9.32
alcohol dependency, 9.32
amount of, I.23
capping, I.24
care plans, 3.92–3.93, 3.97
carers, 7.35, 7.40
charges, 8.51, 8.90
complaints, 6.172
drugs, 9.32
grants, I.24
holidays, 5.70
independent review panels, 6.172
National Health Service, 6.11
residential accommodation,
4.56–4.60
wardens, 5.27, 5.39
Expectant or nursing mothers
age, 4.14
domiciliary services, 5.85, 5.88,
5.94
residential accommodation, 4.14

Fair trials, 12.137
Fairness, 12.108–12.109
Family health services, 6.33–6.34
Family life, right to, 12.138–12.141
Fees
data protection, 2.34
local authorities complaints
procedure, 12.40
local government ombudsman,
12.76
Fixtures and fittings, 10.41
Fundholding, 6.8, 6.12–6.13, 6.17

Gender reassignment, 12.105
General practitioners
appliances, obligation to
prescribe, 6.67–6.70
complaints, 6.160, 6.168
domiciliary care, 6.66
drugs, obligation to provide,
6.67–6.70
fundholding. 6.8, 6.12–6.13, 6.17
abolition of, 6.13

General practitioners *continued*
health authorities, 6.62
independence, 6.62
medical certificates, 6.71
medical services, obligation to
provide, 6.63–6.66
mental disabilities, 6.65
performance, 6.63
prescriptions, 6.67–6.70
primary health care, 6.62–6.71
social security benefits, 6.71
wheelchairs, 6.70
Grants
adaptations to the home, 5.63,
10.13, 10.19–10.47
AIDS/HIV, 9.31–9.35
alcohol dependency, 9.3,
9.26–9.27
care in the community,
5.136–5.137
charges, 8.51
disabled peoples' facilities, 10.13,
10.19–10.47, 12.106
discretionary, 10.38, 10.39
drugs, 9.3, 9.26–9.27
eligibility, 10.28, 10.39–10.40,
10.42–10.45
expenditure, I.24
fixtures and fittings, 10.41
guidance, 10.23, 10.28, 10.38,
10.40–10.41, 10.47
housing, 10.13
authorities, 10.21, 10.23–10.27,
10.46
judicial review, 12.106
loan deferment, 10.46–10.47
local authorities, 10.38
mandatory, 10.29–10.37, 10.39
maximum, 10.19
means-testing, 10.43–10.45
purposes, 10.22
refusal, 10.46
residential accommodation, 4.19,
4.44
resources, 3.66, 10.29
special transitional, I.24, 4.44,
8.51

timescales, 10.46–10.47
Grievance procedure, 12.51–12.52
Griffith Report, I.25–I.26,
8.112–8.115
Guardianship orders, 7.80–7.81
Guidance, 1.20–1.31
adaptations to the home, 5.39,
5.61, 5.66–5.67, 5.69, 10.24,
10.27, 10.31
advice notes, 1.30
advocates, 7.57, 7.59
AIDS/HIV, 9.30–9.31, 9.35
alcohol dependency, 6.74, 9.1–9.5,
9.10, 9.15, 9.20–9.21, 9.24, 9.26,
9.30–9.31, 9.35
assessment of needs, 3.19–3.21,
3.31–3.42, 3.50–3.55, 3.101
capital, 8.31
disregard, 4.9
care in the community, 5.128,
5.136
care plans, 2.13–2.15, 3.84, 3.88,
3.90, 3.95, 3.101
carers, 7.5, 7.8, 7.10, 7.12,
7.16–7.24, 7.29–7.31, 7.49, 7.53
charges, 8.8, 8.31, 8.70–8.78,
8.82–8.92, 8.96–8.100, 8.103,
8.107, 8.110, 8.116
children, 11.8, 11.11, 11.16–11.18,
11.25
circulars, 1.20
closure, 6.52
complaints, 6.161, 6.166–6.169,
6.173, 6.175
continuing care under NHS,
6.81–6.85, 6.93, 6.98–6.104,
6.108–6.118, 6.124–6.131,
6.136–6.137
co-operation, 10.12
copies of, 1.22–1.23
data protection, 2.22, 2.28–2.30,
2.36
departure from, 1.27
direct payments, 5.143
directions and, 1.16, 1.19
disabled people, 5.22, 10.21
domiciliary services, 5.22, 5.26

Guidance *continued*
dowry payments, 6.150
drugs, 6.74, 9.1–9.5, 9.10, 9.15,
  9.20–9.21, 9.24, 9.26, 9.30–9.31,
  9.35
elderly, 5.36
fixtures and fittings, 10.41
grants, 10.23, 10.28, 10.38,
  10.40–10.41, 10.47
health and safety, 4.83, 4.85
homelessness, 4.38, 10.16–10.18,
  11.16–11.18
housing authorities, 10.4, 10.12
information, 2.19
inspection, 4.65
Internet, 1.22–1.23
judicial review, 1.24, 12.114
letters, 1.30
local authorities complaints
  procedure, 12.5–12.12, 12.16,
  12.20–12.21, 12.25–12.30,
  12.40–12.42, 12.51–12.53
local government ombudsman,
  12.42
manual handling, 4.85–4.86
mental disabilities, 7.77
mental hospitals, 5.113,
  5.117–5.119, 8.110
National Health Service, 1.31,
  2.15, 6.39–6.44, 6.54, 6.59
  complaints, 6.161, 6.166–6.169,
  6.173, 6.175
needs, 3.45, 3.49
NHS complaints, 12.53
nursing homes, 4.53, 4.62
ordinary residence, 4.28
registration, 2.6, 2.9, 5.16, 11.9
residential accommodation, 4.57,
  4.62, 4.71, 4.83
resources, 3.60, 3.63
reviews, 3.101
social services authorities, 10.12,
  10.40
substantially and permanently
  handicapped, 5.22
types of, 1.20–1.21
unmet need, 3.99

vulnerable people, 10.17

Health and safety
guidance, 4.83
manual handling, 4.84–4.89
residential accommodation,
  4.83–4.89
Health authorities
alcohol dependency, 9.18–9.22,
  9.35
care in the community, 5.129
care plans, 2.15
complaints, 6.166–6.167
continuing care under NHS,
  6.83–6.84, 6.87, 6.93,
  6.95–6.100, 6.107, 6.113–6.121,
  6.133–6.136
disabled people, 10.4
drugs, 9.18–9.22, 9.35
family health services, 6.33–6.34
general practitioners, 6.62
guidance, 10.4
homelessness, 10.17
illness, 10.4
local authorities, co-operation
  with, 6.46–6.47, 6.59, 6.114
mental hospitals, 5.113, 5.115,
  5.121
National Health Services, 6.8–6.9,
  6.12, 6.14–6.19, 6.23, 6.31–6.36,
  6.41–6.42, 6.47–6.49, 6.59
  complaints, 6.166–6.167,
  12.53–12.54
payments to social services,
  6.138–6.152
nursing homes, 4.53, 4.68
social services authorities,
  4.70–4.71, 5.113, 5.115
payments to, 6.138–6.152
Health improvement programmes,
  6.47–6.50
Health Service Ombudsman,
  6.180–6.181
complaints, 6.173, 6.178–6.181
continuing care under NHS,
  6.78–6.79, 6.117, 6.119, 6.121,
  6.127

Health Service Ombudsman
continued
convenors, 6.173
independent review panels,
6.178–6.179
maladministration, 6.180, 12.62
National Health Service, 6.156
reports, 6.181
HIV. *See* **AIDS/HIV**
Holdsworth, Sir William, I.5
Holidays
disabled people, 5.70
domiciliary services, 5.27, 5.70
expenditure, 5.70
homes, 5.27
illness, 5.97
recuperation, 5.97
Home care. *See* **Adaptations to the
home, Domiciliary care**
Homelessness
AIDS/HIV, 10.17
assessment of needs, 3.13–3.14
children, 10.14, 10.18,
11.15–11.19
disabled people, 10.15–10.17
discrimination against, 10.17
elderly people, 10.15, 10.17
guidance, 4.38, 10.16–10.18,
11.16–11.18
health authorities, 10.17
housing authorities, I.9, 10.16,
10.18, 11.18
illness, 10.15–10.17
learning difficulties, 10.17
mental disabilities, 10.16–10.18
ordinary residence, 4.37–4.38
residential accommodation, 4.42,
10.14
social services authorities, 10.14,
10.16, 10.18, 11.18
temporary accommodation,
10.14
vulnerable people, 3.13–3.14,
10.17, 11.16
Homes, 8.22–8.26, 12.138–12.141
Hospitals. *See also* **Mental hospitals**
appliances, 6.73

closure, I.23, 6.37, 6.51–6.53,
6.137
community health services,
6.26–6.32
consultant services, 6.72–6.74
continuing care under NHS, 6.78,
6.126
drugs, 6.73–6.74
general practitioners, 6.72–6.74
learning difficulties, 6.137
NHS trusts, 6.72
premature discharge, 6.78
Secretary of State, 6.26–6.31
Hostels, 5.26
Housing, 10.1–10.47. *See also*
Housing authorities
assessment of needs, 10.5,
10.8–10.13
care plans, 10.8–10.13
children, 11.12–11.14
collaboration, 10.8–10.13
disabled people, 10.1, 10.13,
10.19–10.47
grants, 10.13, 10.19–10.47
homelessness, 10.14–10.18
housing associations, 10.12
mental disabilities, 10.1, 10.6
possession proceedings,
10.5–10.6
reasonableness, 10.7
refusal of, 10.7
Rowntree Report, 10.2
Housing associations, 10.12
Housing authorities
adaptations to the home,
5.63–5.64, 10.25, 10.27,
10.39–10.40
assessment of needs, 10.8–10.13
care plans, 10.8–10.13
children, 11.18
collaboration, 10.8–10.13
disabled people, 10.21,
10.23–10.27
grants, 10.21, 10.23–10.27, 10.46
guidance, 10.12
homelessness, I.9, 10.16, 10.18,
11.18

Housing authorities *continued*
  maladministration, 10.11
  social services authorities,
    5.63–5.64, 10.8–10.13
Human rights. *See also* **European
  Convention on Human Rights,
  Human Rights Act 1998**
  charges, 8.114
  guardianship orders, 8.114
  National Health Service,
    6.36–6.37
Human Rights Act 1998
  entry into force, 12.121
  local authorities complaints
    procedure, 12.59
  removal, 4.72
  resources, 3.83

Illegality, 12.95–12.106
Illness. *See also* **AIDS/HIV,
  Disabled people, Mental
  disabilities**
  alcohol dependency, 5.97
  carers, 7.38
  day centres, 5.97
  definition, 5.86
  directions, 5.95–5.97
  domiciliary services, 5.23,
    5.80–5.81, 5.83, 5.86–5.87,
    5.95–5.97
  drug dependency, 5.97
  holidays, 5.97
  homelessness, 10.15–10.17
  housing authorities, 10.4
  laundry services, 5.99
  meals, 5.97
  night-sitter services, 5.97
  prevention of, 5.95–5.97
  recreation, 5.97
  residential accommodation, I.10,
    4.12
Income
  assessment of, 8.96–8.98, 10.45
  charges, 8.14–8.17, 8.26, 8.65,
    8.96–8.98
  liable relatives, 8.65
  means-testing, 10.45

  rent, 8.26
Income support, I.8, 8.27–8.28,
    8.32, 8.38, 8.51, 8.86–8.88
Incontinence supplies, 6.119–6.121
Independent Living Fund
  assessment of needs, 5.149
  charges, 8.89
  contacting, 5.151
  contributions, 5.150
  direct payments, 5.139,
    5.144–5.151
  disabled people, 5.144–5.151
  extension, 5.145–5.146
  local authorities, 5.148
  qualifying, 5.148–5.149
Independent review panels, 6.165,
    6.170–6.179
Independent sector
  judicial review, 12.81
  local authorities complaints
    procedure, 12.56
  nursing homes, 4.71
  residential accommodation, 4.44
Infectious diseases, 12.134–12.136
Information
  assessment of needs, 3.24, 3.41
  care plans, 2.19–2.20
  charges, 8.83–8.85, 8.96, 8.101
  circulars, 2.19
  continuing care under NHS,
    6.126–6.128, 6.130
  data protection, 2.21–2.29
  disabled people, 2.17–2.39, 5.27
  domiciliary services, 5.27
  duties, 2.17–2.39
  elderly people, 5.39
  guidance, 2.19
  local authorities complaints
    procedure, 12.32
  National Health Service,
    6.154–6.155
  obligatory services, 2.18
  publicity, 2.19
  social services authorities,
    2.17–2.39
Inhuman or degrading treatment,
    12.129–12.130

In-patient care, 6.87–6.100
Inspection
definition, 4.65
duties, 4.62–4.71
guidance, 4.65
mental disabilities, 4.68–4.71
nursing homes, 4.68–4.71
purpose of, 4.65
registration, 4.66–4.67
residential accommodation,
4.62–4.71
residential care homes, 4.63–4.68
standards, 4.65
units, 4.65–4.67
Intensive services, 6.116–6.121
Internet, 1.23
Interviews, 3.23

Joint beneficial ownership,
8.23–8.25
Judicial review, 12.77–12.115
abuse of power, 12.110–12.111
adaptation of homes, 12.106
alternative remedies, 12.87–12.90
complaints, 12.83–12.84,
12.87–12.90
consultation, 12.112–12.113
decision-making, 12.77–12.83,
12.86, 12.91, 12.94–12.95,
12.99–12.103, 12.106,
12.113–12.115
facts, not in accordance with,
12.101
default procedure, 12.87–12.88
delegation or dictation, unlawful,
12.106
disabled people, 12.106
discretion, fettering of,
12.104–12.105
European Convention on Human
Rights, 12.78
fairly, duty to act, 12.108–12.109
gender reassignment, 12.105
grants, 12.106
grounds for, 12.91–12.115
guidance, 1.24, 12.114
illegality, 12.95–12.106

independent sector, 12.81
legitimate expectations, 12.79,
12.110–12.111
local authorities, 12.82–12.84,
12.89, 12.93
monitoring officers of,
12.82–12.84
local government ombudsman,
12.71–12.73
mandatory or directory
requirements, duty to act in
accordance with, 12.114
misdirection of law, 12.98–12.100
natural justice, 12.107, 12.109
procedural impropriety,
12.107–12.115
reasonableness, 12.78–12.79,
12.93, 12.102
reasons, 12.115
regulations, 1.14
rehabilitation, 12.104
relevant and irrelevant
misdirections, 12.102–12.103
social services authorities, 12.106
staff levels, 1.11
standing, 12.85–12.86
ultra vires, 12.96–12.97
Wednesbury unreasonableness,
12.93, 12.102

Laming letter, 1.30
Laundry services, 5.99
Learning difficulties
continuing care under NHS,
6.85–6.86, 6.137
education, 5.55
homelessness, 10.17
Legitimate expectations, 12.79,
12.110–12.111
Letters, 1.30, 3.11, 6.42
Liable relatives
capital, 8.65
charges, 8.15, 8.63–8.65
income, 8.65
income support, 8.63
payments from, seeking, 8.64
spouses, 8.63–8.65

Liberty, right to, 12.121
Libraries, 5.51
Life, right to, 4.82, 12.128
Local authorities. *See also* Housing
  authorities, Local authorities
  complaints procedure, Social
  services authorities
advocates, 7.59
alcohol dependency, 9.26
carers, 7.33, 7.56
charges, 8.4, 8.6, 8.9, 8.11, 8.15,
  8.21–8.22, 8.25, 8.34
  children, 11.26–11.27, 11.30
  deliberate deprivation of capital,
  8.36–8.50
  residential homes, 8.51–8.55
children, 11.26–11.27, 11.30
continuing care under NHS, 6.77,
  6.93, 6.135
default procedure, 12.116–12.118
deliberate deprivation of capital,
  8.36–8.50
drugs, 9.26
grants, 10.38
health authorities, co-operation
  with, 6.46–6.47, 6.59
Independent Living Fund, 5.148
judicial review, 12.82–12.84,
  12.89, 12.93
local government ombudsman,
  12.63, 12.68–12.70
monitoring officers, 12.83–12.84
National Health Service, 6.2–6.6,
  6.46–6.47, 6.50, 6.59,
  6.142–6.146, 6.149
residential homes, 8.51–8.55
Local authorities complaints
  procedure, 12.5–12.59 ho
advocacy, 12.17
assistance, 12.17
charges, 12.57
children, 12.58–12.59
compensation, 12.38–12.40
criminal offences, 12.52
delay, 12.40
designated officers, 12.9
directions, 12.9–12.10, 12.12,

  12.17–12.19, 12.22–12.26, 12.32
disciplinary procedures,
  12.51–12.52
discretion, 12.10–12.11
European Convention on Human
  Rights, 12.59
fees, 12.40
formal stage, 12.16–12.25
good practice, 12.5, 12.42
grievance procedures,
  12.51–12.52
guidance, 12.5–12.12, 12.16,
  12.20–12.21, 12.25–12.30,
  12.40–12.42, 12.51–12.53
hearings, 12.26–12.37
Human Rights Act 1998, 12.59
independence, 12.26–12.28, 12/59
independent service providers,
  12.56
informal stage, 12.12–12.15
information, 12.32
investigations, 12.20–12.25
leaflets, 12.15
maladministration, 12.15
National Health Service,
  12.53–12.55
natural justice, 12.25, 12.29–12.30
notification of results, 12.23
private sector providers, 12.56
problem-solving stage,
  12.12–12.15
qualifying individual, 12.6, 12.8
reasons, 12.25, 12.45–12.46, 12.49
recommendations, 12.35–12.37,
  12.39–12.49
registration, 12.13, 12.16
reports, 12.23–12.25
representation, 12.29
residential care homes, 12.56
review stage, 12.26–12.45
special cases, 12.50
standing, 12.6–12.8
structure of system, 12.9–12.52
subsequent action, 12.46–12.49
timescale, 12.14, 12.19, 12.22,
  12.26, 12.30, 12.32–12.34, 12.46
writing, complaints in, 12.18

Local Authority Social Services Act 1970, 1.1, 1.10–1.12, 1.15–1.16
Local Government Ombudsman
adaptations to the home, 5.62, 5.63
advantages, 12.72
alternative remedies, 12.64
assessment of needs, 3.37–3.38
charges, 8.76, 8.78, 8.101
compensation, 12.38–12.39, 12.70–12.71
delay, 12.71
designated officers, 12.9
disadvantages, 12.73
fees, 12.76
guidance, 12.42
judicial review, 12.71, 12.73
legal representation, 12.29
local authorities, initial approaches to, 12.63, 12.68–12.70
maladministration, 12.60–12.62, 12.66
mental hospitals, 5.123, 5.125
National Health Service, 6.56
procedure, 12.69–12.76
qualifying individuals, 12.8
powers, 12.60
recommendations, 12.36–12.37
regional offices, 12.75
replies to complaints, 12.63
reports, 12.65, 12.67, 12.73, 12.76
residential accommodation, 4.58
social services authorities, 12.66
time limits, 12.62, 12.72
website, 12.74
Long-term care, 6.76, 6.80, 6.105

Maladministration
adaptations to the home, 5.62
assessment of needs, 3.28
Health Service Ombudsman, 6.180, 12.62
housing authorities, 10.11
local authorities complaints procedure, 12.15

local government ombudsman, 12.60–12.62, 12.66
mental hospitals, 5.125
National Health Service, 6.58
residential accommodation, 4.55
Manual handling, 4.84–4.89
Meals
disabled people, 5.71
domiciliary services, 5.39, 5.71
elderly, 5.39
illness, 5.97
wheels, on, 5.71
Means-testing
capital, 8.19
charges, 8.7–8.8, 8.83, 8.88, 8.96–8.97
eligibility, 10.43–10.45
grants, 10.43–10.45
income, 10.45
Medical certificates, 6.71
Medical equipment, 6.117–6.118
Mental disabilities, 7.1–7.2. *See also*
Care in the community,
Learning difficulties, Mental
hospitals
adult abuse, 7.89–7.91
affairs, 7.67–7.69
alleviation of, 5.96
assessment of needs, 3.37–3.43
best interests of patients, 7.85, 7.87
capacity, 7.66–7.68, 7.80, 7.84, 7.87
carers, 7.5
charges, 5.101
continuing care under NHS, 6.85–6.86
Court of Protection, 7.69
court's inherent jurisdiction, 7.82–7.85
criminal offences, 7.90
data protection, 2.27–2.30
decision-making, 7.63–7.91
declarations, 7.82–7.84
duties, 5.96
domiciliary services, 5.20–5.21, 5.80, 5.86, 5.100–5.137

Mental disabilities *continued*
enduring powers of attorney,
7.67, 7.73–7.76, 7.88
European Convention on Human
Rights, 7.91, 12.132, 12.143
general practitioners, 6.65
guardianship, 7.80–7.81
guidance, 7.77
homelessness, 10.16–10.18
housing, 10.1, 10.6
jurisdiction, 7.82–7.85
Mental Health Act Commission,
12.2
National Health Service, 6.30,
6.60
nursing homes, 4.50, 4.68–4.71
possession proceedings, 10.6
powers of attorney, 7.67,
7.70–7.76, 7.88
prevention of, 5.96
property, 7.67–7.69
receivership, 7.69
reform, 7.63, 7.82, 7.86–7.90
remedies, 12.2
residential accommodation, 4.15,
4.24, 4.68–4.71, 5.100
Secretary of State, 6.30
social security appointees,
7.77–7.79
standard of proof, 7.66
Mental Health Act 1983, 1.7,
5.100–5.126
Mental hospitals
after-care services, 5.109,
5.115–5.116, 5.124–5.125, 8.109
age, 5.103
charges, 5.123–5.124, 8.2,
8.109–8.110
client groups, 5.103–5.114
closure of, I.20
code of practice, 5.111
criminal offences, 5.105–5.108
decision-making, 7.64–7.65
detention, 5.102–5.125
ceasing to be detained,
5.109–5.112
reasons for, 5.104–5.108

domiciliary services, 5.102–5.125
duties, duration of the,
5.120–5.125
European Convention on Human
Rights, 12.132
guidance, 5.113, 5.117–5.119,
8.110
health authorities, 5.113, 5.115,
5.121
leave of absence, 5.111
local government ombudsman,
5.123, 5.125
maladministration, 5.125
ordinary residence, 5.114
residence, district or area of,
5.113–5.114
residential accommodation,
duty to provide, 4.91–4.92,
5.122
social services authorities, 5.113,
5.115
Misdirection in law, 12.98–12.100
Mothers. *See* **Nursing or expectant
mothers**

National assistance, I.8
National Assistance Act 1948,
I.4–I.14, 1.7, 4.1–4.2, 5.9–5.40,
5.73–5.77
National Health Service, 6.1–6.181.
See also **Continuing care under
NHS**, **General practitioners**,
**Health authorities, NHS
complaints**
after-care services, 6.61
alcohol dependency, 9.18–9.22
budget, 6.15, 6.17, 6.138,
6.140–6.142
sharing arrangements,
6.146–6.152
care plans, 2.15
carers, 7.24
charges, 6.45, 6.144
circulars, 6.39–6.42, 6.50, 6.152
access to, 6.44
codes of practice, 6.153–6.156
collaboration, duty of, 6.54–6.61

National Health Service *continued*
commissioning, 6.11–6.13,
6.17–6.20
community health services,
6.26–6.32
comprehensive health service,
duty to provide, 6.35–6.38
co-operation, duty of, 6.46–6.61
creation of, 6.5
decision-making, 6.35
directions, 6.148
disabled people, 5.80–5.99
disclosure, 6.58
discretion, 6.37
domiciliary services, 5.80–5.99
dowry payments, 6.149–6.150
drugs, 9.18–9.22
Executive Letters, 6.42
expenditure, 6.11
extra-contractual referrals, 6.12
family health services, 6.33–6.34
fundholding practices, 6.8,
6.12–6.13, 6.17
guidance, 1.31, 2.15, 6.21,
6.39–6.44, 6.54, 6.59,
6.146–6.147, 6.150
health authorities, 6.8–6.9, 6.12,
6.14–6.19, 6.23, 6.31–6.36,
6.41–6.42, 6.47–6.49, 6.59
payments to social services,
6.138–6.152
health care, 6.4–6.22
health improvement
programmes, 6.47–6.50
health service commissioners,
6.156, 6.18–6.181
historical overview, 6.4–6.22
hospitals, 6.26–6.32
human rights, 6.36–6.37
information, 6.155–6.156
joint finance, 6.148
local authorities, 6.2–6.6,
6.46–6.47, 6.50, 6.59,
6.142–6.146, 6.149
local government ombudsman,
6.56
local health groups, 6.20–6.22

maladministration, 6.58
medical/social divide, 6.45–6.61
mental disabilities, 6.30, 6.60
openness, 6.153–6.156
partnership arrangements, 6.139,
6.143–6.145
poor law, 6.4
primary health groups, 6.11–6.18,
6.62–6.74
reasonableness, 6.28
reform, 6.10–6.11
residential accommodation, 4.90
Secretary of State, 6.26–6.31, 6.41
social services, payments to,
6.138–6.152
transfer of payments, 6.149
trusts, 6.11–6.19, 6.32, 6.72
Wales, 6.19, 6.21–6.22
Wednesbury unreasonableness,
6.42
**National Health Service and
Community Care Act 1990**,
I.10, I.21–I.27, 6.3
National Health Service Act 1977,
1.5, 5.80–5.99, 6.7, 6.23–6.44
Natural justice, 12.25, 12.29–12.30,
12.107, 12.109
Needs. *See also* **Assessment of
needs, Unmet needs**
care and attention, 4.5
carers, 7.30
children, 11.1–11.30
definition, 3.43–3.49
guidance, 3.45, 3.49
hospital discharges, 3.49
psychological, 3.47, 3.89
religion, 3.46
variation, 3.49
Negligence, 6.166
NHS. *See* **National Health Service**
NHS complaints
guidance, 12.53
health authorities, 6.166–6.167,
12.53–12.54
local authorities complaints
procedure, 12.53–12.55
nursing homes, 12.53

NHS complaints *continued*
overlap, 12.53–12.55
social services authorities,
12.53–12.54
Night-sitter services, 5.97, 7.44,
5.97
Nuisance, 10.6
Nursing homes, 4.44, 4.49–4.53
alcohol dependency, 9.12–9.22,
9.28
charges, 8.52
closure, 4.76–4.82
continuing care under NHS,
6.76–6.80, 6.92–6.93, 6.97,
6.116–6.121, 6.129
contracts with, 6.93
definition, 4.49–4.50
drugs, 9.12–9.22, 9.28
guidance, 4.53, 4.62
health authorities, 4.53, 4.68
independent, 4.71, 6.97
inspection, 4.68–4.71
mental disabilities, 4.50,
4.68–4.71
NHS complaints, 12.53
registration, 4.50–4.51, 4.54,
4.68–4.69
services provided by, 4.52
Nursing mothers. *See* **Expectant or
nursing mothers**

Obligatory services, I.17–I.19, 2.18
**Occupational, social, cultural and
recreational facilities**, 5.26
Occupational therapists, 5.62
Old people. *See* **Elderly people**
Ombudsman. *See* **Health Service
Ombudsman, Local
Government Ombudsman**
Openness, 6.153–6.156
Orange Badge Scheme, 5.59
Ordinary residence
assessment of needs, 3.17
children, 4.34
circulars, 4.29
definition, 4.29–4.33
disputed, 4.35–4.36

domiciliary services, 5.12, 5.26,
5.37, 5.43
duration, 4.31
guidance, 4.28, 4.33, 4.38
homelessness, 4.37–4.38
mental hospitals, 5.114
residential accommodation, 4.26,
4.28–4.39
settled residence, lack of,
4.37–4.38
urgent need, 4.39

Palliative health care, 6.112–6.115
Parents, 7.47
Parking, 5.59
Partially-sighted people, 5.15
Patients' Charter, 5.135
Payments. *See* **Direct payments**
Pensions, 8.17
Plans. *See* **Care plans**
Poor law, I.4–I.8, 6.4
Possession proceedings
adjournment, 10.5
housing, 10.5–10.6
mental disabilities, 10.6
nuisance, 10.6
reasonableness, 10.5–10.6
Possessions, right to enjoyment of,
12.144
Powers of attorney, 2.28–2.29, 7.67,
7.70–7.76, 7.88
Priorities
assessment of needs, 3.28–3.29
disabled people, I.13
resources, 3.66
Privacy, 12.133, 12.138–12.141
Private sector. *See* **Independent
sector**
Probation, 9.5
Procedural impropriety,
12.107–12.115
Property
capital, 8.22
cautions, 8.48–8.50
charges, 8.22–8.26, 8.48–8.50
European Convention on Human
Rights, 12.144

Property *continued*
joint beneficial ownership,
8.23–8.25
possessions, right to enjoyment
of, 12.144
protection of, 4.75
residential, 8.22–8.26
Provision of services. *See* **Obligatory
services**
Psychological needs, 3.47, 3.89
Public law
duties, 1.4–1.9
private law, crystallising into, 1.9
social services authorities, 1.4–1.9

Racial discrimination, 12.130
Radios, 5.51
Reasonableness
adaptations to the home, 10.24
charges, 8.62, 8.73, 8.80,
8.82–8.83, 8.87, 8.91
housing, 10.7
judicial review, 12.78–12.79,
12.93, 12.102
National Health Service, 6.28,
6.42
possession proceedings,
10.5–10.6
residential accommodation, 4.23
time limits, 3.27
Wednesbury, 6.42, 12.93, 12.102
Reassessment, 3.84, 3.88, 3.90, 3.95,
3.101
Receivership orders, 7.69
Recreation, 5.26, 5.39, 5.51–5.53,
5.98
Referrals, 6.12, 9.5
Reform
advocates, 7.59
care plans, 3.95
carers, 7.45
charges, 8.51
mental disabilities, 7.63, 7.82,
7.86–7.90
National Health Service, 6.10
need for, I.15, I.28
objectives for, I.26

Registration
care plans, 2.4–2.9
children, 2.9, 11.5, 11.9
compiling, 5.26
disabled people, 2.4–2.9, 11.5,
11.9
domiciliary services, 5.14, 5.16,
5.26
dual, 4.54
enduring powers of attorney,
7.75
European Convention on Human
Rights, 4.64, 12.140–12.141
form of, 2.6
guidance, 2.6, 2.9, 5.16, 11.9
inspection, 4.66–4.67
local authorities complaints
procedure, 12.13, 12.16
maintaining, 5.26
nursing homes, 4.50–4.51, 4.54,
4.68–4.69
purpose, 2.5
residential accommodation, 4.63,
4.66–4.67
residential care homes, 4.46–4.47,
4.54, 4.63–4.64, 9.13,
12.140–12.141
severe or appreciable handicap,
2.9
units, 4.66
very service handicap, 2.9
Regulations, 1.13–1.14, 1.17
Rehabilitation
alcohol dependency, 9.17, 9.25
continuing care under NHS,
6.101–6.105, 6.109
domiciliary services, 5.26
drugs, 9.17, 9.25
judicial review, 12.104
social, 5.26
Relatives, 5.143. *See also* **Liable
relatives**
Religion, 3.46
Remedies, 12.1–12.146. *See also*
**Complaints, Local government
ombudsman**
default procedures, 12.116–12.120

Remedies *continued*
European Convention on Human
Rights, 12.2, 12.121–12.146
exhaustion of domestic, 12.145
judicial review, 12.77–12.115
mental disabilities, 12.2
Removal
environmental health
departments, 4.72–4.74
Human Rights Act 1998, 4.72
property, protection of, 4.74
residential accommodation,
4.72–4.75
vulnerable people, 4.73
Rent, 8.26
Reorganisation, 1.1
Residence. *See* **Ordinary residence**
Residential accommodation, I.9,
I.11, 4.1–4.95. *See also* **Hostels,
Nursing homes, Residential
care homes**
age, 4.11–4.12, 4.14
agreements, 4.61
alcohol dependency, 4.15, 4.24,
9.10
asylum-seekers, 4.16–4.20
bodily functions, assistance with,
4.5
capital, 4.9, 8.19–8.20
care and attention, 4.5–4.26
charges, 8.1–8.66, 8.111
children, 11.30
less dependent residents,
8.56–8.59
temporary residents, 8.60–8.62
children, 4.95, 11.30
choice of, 4.55–4.61
circulars, 4.81
client groups, 4.10–4.21
closure, 4.76–4.82
consultation, 4.78, 4.80, 4.82
criteria, 4.4
destitution, 4.5, 4.16–4.20
directions, 4.3, 4.28, 4.55,
4.60–4.61
disabled people, 4.13, 4.90,
4.93–4.94

discretion, 4.58
disregard, 4.9, 8.19
domiciliary services, 4.6, 4.12,
5.92
drug dependency, 4.15, 4.25,
9.10
duties, 4.21–4.28
inspection, 4.62–4.71
property protection, 4.75
elderly, 4.11, 4.76, 4.79–4.82
environmental health
departments, 4.72
European Convention on Human
Rights, 4.64, 4.82
expectant or nursing mothers,
4.14
expenditure, 4.56–4.60
grants, 4.19, 4.44
guidance, 4.57, 4.62, 4.71, 4.83
health and safety, 4.83–4.89
health authorities, co-operation
with social services authorities,
4.70–4.71
homelessness, 4.42, 10.14
Human Rights Act 1998, 4.72,
4.82
illness, I.10, 4.12
independent sector, 4.44
inspection, 4.62–4.71
less dependent residents,
8.56–8.59
life, right to, 4.82
local government ombudsman,
4.58
maladministration, 4.55
manual handling, 4.84–4.89
mental disabilities, 4.12, 4.15,
4.24, 4.91–4.92, 5.100
mental hospitals, 5.122
National Assistance Act 1948,
4.1–4.2
National Health Service, 4.90
long stay accommodation, 4.77
nature of, 4.40–4.54
'not otherwise available to them',
4.6–4.8
ordinary housing, 4.41–4.43

Residential accommodation
continued
ordinary residence, 4.26,
4.28–4.39
personal care, 4.5
powers, 4.21–4.28
property, duty to protect, 4.75
refusal, 4.23
registration, 4.63–4.64, 4.66–4.67
removal powers, 4.72–4.75
residential care homes, 4.45–4.46,
4.54
safety net, 4.17
self-funders, 4.7–4.8, 8.21
social services authorities, I.10,
4.90, 8.58
health authorities, co-operation
with, 4.70–4.71
temporary residents, 8.60–8.62
top up, 4.56, 8.55
transfers, 4.78
workshops, 4.93–4.94
Residential care homes, 4.45–4.48
alcohol dependency, 9.12–9.22,
9.28
charges, 8.52
children, 11.12–11.14
closure, 6.53
continuing care under NHS,
6.92–6.93, 6.119, 6.129
definition, 4.45
direct payments, 5.143
drugs, 9.12–9.22, 9.28
European Convention on
Human Rights, 12.140–12.141,
12.144
independent, 8.5
inspection, 4.63–4.68
local authorities complaints
procedure, 12.56
possessions, right to enjoyment
of, 12.144
registration, 4.46–4.47, 4.54,
4.63–4.64, 9.13, 12.140–12.141
small homes, 4.46, 12.140–12.141
social security benefits, 7.78–7.79
Residential property, 8.22–8.26

Resources, I.14. *See also*
Expenditure
adaptations to the home, 10.42
allocation panels, 3.76–3.77
assessment of needs, 3.25,
3.59–3.84
care plans, 3.65
charges, 8.21
demand, 3.65
disabled people, I.13, 3.71, 3.75
eligibility, 3.59–3.84
grants, 3.66, 10.29
guidance, 3.60, 3.63
Human Rights Act 1998, 2.83
priorities, 3.66
reassessment, 3.70
risk assessment, 3.61
shortages, 3.78–3.82
waiting lists, 3.78–3.81
Respite care, 6.106–6.111, 7.33, 7.42
Risk assessment, 3.61

Secretary of State, 1.15, 1.17
default procedure, 12.118–12.119
hospitals, 6.26–6.31
mental disabilities, 6.30
National Health Service, 6.41
Seebohm Report, 1.1
Self-funders, 4.7–4.8, 8.21
Sex discrimination, 12.130, 12.142
Shared care, 6.106–6.111, 7.33, 7.42,
9.22
Shortages, 3.78–3.82
Small claims, 8.106
Social security benefits
appointees, 7.77–7.79
attendance allowance, 8.89–8.95
carers, 7.25
continuing care under NHS, 6.76
disability living allowance,
8.89–8.95
elderly people, 8.38
general practitioners, 6.71
income support, I.8, 8.27–8.28,
8.32, 8.38, 8.51, 8.86–8.88
medical certificates, 6.71
mental disabilities, 7.77–7.79

Social security benefits *continued*
  residential allowance, 8.27–8.28
  residential care homes, 7.78–7.79
Social services authorities
  adaptations to the home,
    5.63–5.64, 5.66–5.67, 10.25,
    10.27, 10.39–10.40
  alcohol dependency, 9.14–9.18,
    9.20
  assessment of needs, 10.8–10.13
  care in the community, 5.129
  care plans, 10.8–10.13
  carers, 7.32, 7.37, 7.49–7.50
  charges, 8.1–8.2, 8.4, 8.54, 8.107
  children, 11.14, 11.18,
    11.24–11.25, 11.29
  collaboration, 10.8–10.13
  continuing care under NHS, 6.81,
    6.97
  damages, 1.4
  direct payments, 5.139
  director of social services, 1.10
  discretion, 1.3, 1.11
  drugs, 9.14–9.18, 9.20
  duties, 1.1–1.12, 10.40
    individuals, to, 1.4
    information, 2.17–2.39
    planning, 2.3–2.16
    public law, 1.4–1.9
  functions, 1.1–1.12
  guidance, 10.12, 10.40
  health authorities, 4.70–4.71,
    6.114, 6.138–6.152
  homelessness, 10.14, 10.16, 10.18,
    11.18
  housing authorities, 5.63–5.64,
    5.113, 5.115, 10.8–10.13
  information, 2.17–2.39
  judicial review, 12.106
  Local Authority Social Services
    Act 1970, 1.1
  local government ombudsman,
    12.66
  mental hospitals, 5.113, 5.115
  NHS complaints, 12.53–12.54
  payments, 6.138–6.152
  planning, 2.3–2.16
  powers, 1.1–1.12
  public law, 1.4
  reorganisation, 1.1
  residential accommodation, I.10,
    4.90, 8.58
  services not provided by, 8.107
  staff levels, 1.11
  statutory duties and powers,
    1.2–1.12
Social work, 2.37, 5.26, 5.39
Specialist care, 6.90–6.93,
  6.116–6.121
Spouses
  capital, 8.20–8.22
  charges, 8.20–8.22, 8.63–8.65
  liable relatives, 8.63–8.65
Staff
  criminal offences, 12.52
  disciplinary procedures,
    12.51–12.52
  grievance procedures,
    12.51–12.52
  inadequate, 1.11
  judicial review, 1.11
Statutes, 1.1–1.12
Statutory instruments, 1.13–1.14,
  1.17
Subsidies, 5.27
Supervision
  after-care, 5.126
  care in the community,
    5.126–5.127
  Secretary of State, 1.15

Telephones, 5.72
Television, 5.51
Tenancies, 8.26
Third parties
  assessment of needs, 3.50
  charges, 8.98
  data protection, 2.35–2.36, 2.39
  direct payments, 5.140–5.141
  disclosure, 2.29
Time limits
  assessment of needs, 3.26–3.30
  complaints, 6.161–6.162, 6.170,
    6.172

Time limits *continued*
extension, 6.161
local authorities complaints
procedure, 12.14, 12.19, 12.22,
12.26, 12.30, 12.32–12.34, 12.46
local government ombudsman,
12.62, 12.72
reasonableness, 3.27
variation, 6.162
Time off, 7.46
Transactions at an undervalue,
8.46–8.47
Transfers
capital, 8.43–8.47
charges, 8.43–8.47, 8.53
closure, 4.78
dowry payments, 6.149
NHS trusts, 6.32
residential accommodation, of
capital after entering, 8.43–8.47
Transparency, 6.153–6.156
Transsexuals, 12.105
Travel
children, 5.58
disabled people, 5.58–5.59
domiciliary services, 5.27, 5.39,
5.57–5.59
free, 5.27
subsidised, 5.27
Trusts
budget, 6.17
complaints, 6.166–6.167
consultants, 6.72
funding, 6.32
National Health Service,
6.11–6.19, 6.32, 6.72
complaints, 6.166–6.167
primary care, 6.17
role of, 6.19
transfers, 6.32

Types of community care services,
I.12

Ultra vires, 12.96–12.97
Unfair trade practices, 9.8–9.9
Unmet needs
care plans, 3.99–3.100
eligibility, 3.99
guidance, 3.99
recording of, 3.99–3.100

Voluntary organisations, 7.25
Vouchers, 4.19
Vulnerable people, 2.2. *See also*
**AIDS/HIV, Alcohol
dependency, Children, Disabled
people, Drugs,
Illness, Learning difficulties, Mental
disabilities**
children, 11.16
guidance, 10.17
homelessness, 3.13–3.14, 10.17,
11.16
removal, 4.73
residential accommodation, 4.73

Waiting lists, 3.78–3.81
Wales, 6.19, 6.21–6.22
Wardens, 5.27, 5.39
Wednesbury unreasonableness
judicial review, 12.93, 12.102
National Health Service, 6.42
Wheelchairs, 6.70
Wireless, 5.51
Workshops
disabled people, 4.93–4.94
domiciliary services, 5.26
hostels, 5.26
residential accommodation,
4.93–4.94

 # Legal Action Group

Working with lawyers and advisers to promote equal access to justice

Legal Action magazine
The only monthly magazine published specifically for legal aid practitioners and the advice sector.

2000 annual subscription: £75
Concessionary rates available for students and trainees – call the LAG office for details.

Books
LAG's catalogue includes a range of titles covering:

- community care
- crime
- debt
- education
- family
- housing

- human rights
- immigration
- personal injury
- practice & procedure
- welfare benefits
- LAG policy

Community Care Law Reports
The only law reports devoted entirely to community care issues. Compiled by an expert team and published quarterly, each issue contains:

- editorial review
- community care law update
- law reports

- guidance
- cumulative index
- full tables

Training
Accredited with the Law Society, the Bar Council and the Institute of Legal Executives, LAG provides topical training courses for lawyers, advisers and other professionals.

Conferences
LAG runs major conferences to examine issues at the cutting-edge of legal services policy and to inform practitioners of their implications.

For further information about any of Legal Action Group's activities, please contact:

Legal Action Group, 242 Pentonville Road, London N1 9UN

DX 130400 London (Pentonville Road)
Telephone: 020 7833 2931
Fax: 020 7837 6094
e-mail: lag@lag.org.uk
www.lag.org.uk